dateline

A DAY-BY-DAY GUIDE TO PEOPLE, PLACES, AND EVENTS

dateline

A DAY-BY-DAY GUIDE TO PEOPLE, PLACES, AND EVENTS

MILLENNIUM HOUSE

Produced by Millennium House Pty Ltd
52 Bolwarra Rd, Elanora Heights, NSW, 2101, Australia
Ph: 612 9970 6850
Fax: 612 9970 8136
email rightsmanager@millenniumhouse.com.au

Text © Millennium House Pty Ltd 2006

Reprinted 2009

All rights reserved. No part of this publication may be reproduced, stored in a retrieval system, transmitted in any form or by any means, electronic, mechanical, photocopying, recording or otherwise, without the prior written permission of the Publisher.

The moral rights of all contributors have been asserted.

ISBN 978-1-921209-63-5

ISBN 978-1-921209-56-7 (Cased)

Millennium House would like to hear from photographers interested in supplying photographs.

Printed in China

Colour separation Pica Digital Singapore

Photo credits appear on page 524.

Publisher	Gordon Cheers
Associate publisher	Janet Parker
Project management	Limelight Press Pty Ltd
Project manager	Jayne Denshire
Art director	Jacqueline Richards
Contributors	Sabina Collins
	Serene Conneeley
	Todd Fitzgerald
	Donyale Harrison
	Anita Jankovic
	Elisabeth Knowles
	Klay Lamprell
	Kate McAllan
	Julie Simpkin
Editorial	Roland Arvidssen
	Katri Hilden
Production	Simone Coupland, Bernard Roberts

Opposite A sun dial, one of the oldest forms of telling the time

CONTENTS

Evolution of the calendar   8

JANUARY
Introduction   36
January 1 to 31   40
Days to remember   72

FEBRUARY
Introduction   76
February 1 to 29   80
Days to remember   110

MARCH
Introduction   114
March 1 to 31   118
Days to remember   150

APRIL
Introduction   154
April 1 to 30   158
Days to remember   190

MAY
Introduction   194
May 1 to 31   198
Days to remember   230

JUNE
Introduction   234
June 1 to 30   238
Days to remember   270

JULY
Introduction   274
July 1 to 31   278
Days to remember   310

AUGUST
Introduction 314
August 1 to 31 318
Days to remember 350

SEPTEMBER
Introduction 354
September 1 to 30 358
Days to remember 390

OCTOBER
Introduction 394
October 1 to 31 398
Days to remember 430

NOVEMBER
Introduction 434
November 1 to 30 438
Days to remember 470

DECEMBER
Introduction 474
December 1 to 31 478
Days to remember 510

Index 512

Evolution of the calendar

A calendar is simply a way to mark time, a system we have devised – and changed – over centuries to plan the future, remember the past and coordinate our lives. It is any system for dividing time over extended periods, and lets us know when religious holidays fall, when to celebrate a birthday or anniversary, when bills and taxes are due, when to go to work and how old we are. It gives us a temporal context in which to live and a way to mark the progress of humankind. It shapes us and – to a certain degree – controls us.

This solar calendar from ninth- to tenth-century Byzantine times relied on the sun to cast a shadow from its dial and thus show the time.

CALENDAR DEFINITION
A chart showing the days and months of the year, from the Latin *calendarium*, meaning "moneylender's account book," itself a derivation of the word *calendae* (or *kalendae*), meaning "first day of the month."

THROUGHOUT TIME, different countries, cultures, and civilizations have had their own unique calendars, including the complex Mayan version of the ancient Central Americans; the system of the Roman Empire, which was chiseled into stone; the scientifically precise Persian version, that reflected the Sun; and the Islamic system that follows the cycles of the Moon. But today, in a global world, the common-use calendar is the Gregorian, introduced in 1582 by Pope Gregory XIII.

Several others are still used, especially for the timing of religious festivals, but usually they are used alongside the Gregorian, which is the standard for international Government, politics, science, and history. It didn't matter so much in ages past that different countries had conflicting calendar systems, but now as the world becomes one, as business and science is extended internationally, as one country's politics affects people around the globe, and overseas travel becomes more common, a standard calendar is necessary for civil use around the world.

Seasonal calendars

As long as humans have thought and communicated, they have needed a way to mark the days, record history, and plan future events. Since the beginning of the world, the pattern of the seasons and the movement of the Sun and the Moon have been the basis by which time was measured – and this remains true today. Different cultures and countries have had different ways to mark it, but all are dependent on nature as the basis of their timekeeping. Even in the industrialized modern world, so far removed from the cycles of the Earth, the calendar remains tied to the movement of the planets and the seasons.

Day and night is ruled by the rising and setting of the Sun. In the calculation of time, the Earth's

rotation on its axis marks a day, the moon's orbit around the Earth marks the passing of a month, and the Earth's orbit around the sun determines the passage of a year. These remain constants throughout every calendar of the world, both old and new, and the lengths are now scientifically determined by astronomers who are amazed that the people of centuries past could calculate these cycles so accurately without the technological advancements and precise scientific equipment we now have at our disposal.

Ancient observatories such as Stonehenge were instrumental in helping astronomers calculate the patterns in the movements of the Earth relative to the heavens. More recently, the Jantar Mantar in Jaipur, India, is one of six observatories built by the Maharaja Jai Sing II in the eighteenth century.

Yet these massive structures were by no means the first exponents of astronomy in India. Records date back as far as 2000 B.C.E. relating to the study of the stars, and an undated Sanskrit couplet even refers to the existence of "suns in all directions" – suggesting an understanding that the sun is one of many similar bodies (stars) surrounding the Earth. In the seventh century, an Indian astronomer is said to have estimated the Earth's circumference as 22,370 miles (36,000 km) – remarkably close to the 24,901 (40,075 km) we now believe it to be.

In ancient times, when life revolved around agriculture, and the Sun and Moon were seen as deities to be worshipped, the year was divided by the eight *sabbats*, or festivals, which marked the turning of the seasons and the cycles of the Earth. People in these times had to know when the seasons began and ended and how long they lasted in order to plant and harvest crops, hunt migratory prey, and even move their tribe to warmer climes before the harsh winter approached. They divided their year by seasons, not months, and celebrated each change. The spring and autumn equinoxes (Latin for "equal night"), when the Earth is in balance and the

Astrological symbols and celestial movement across the sky are shown on this eighteenth-century planisphere. A planisphere is a flat map of the sky and is used to locate stars and celestial bodies.

"Dost thou love life? Then do not squander time, for that is the stuff life is made of." — BENJAMIN FRANKLIN

Mexican artist Rufino Tamayo (1899–1991) uses the sun and the moon in his fresco imagery of day and night. The fresco is housed in the National Anthropological Museum in Mexico.

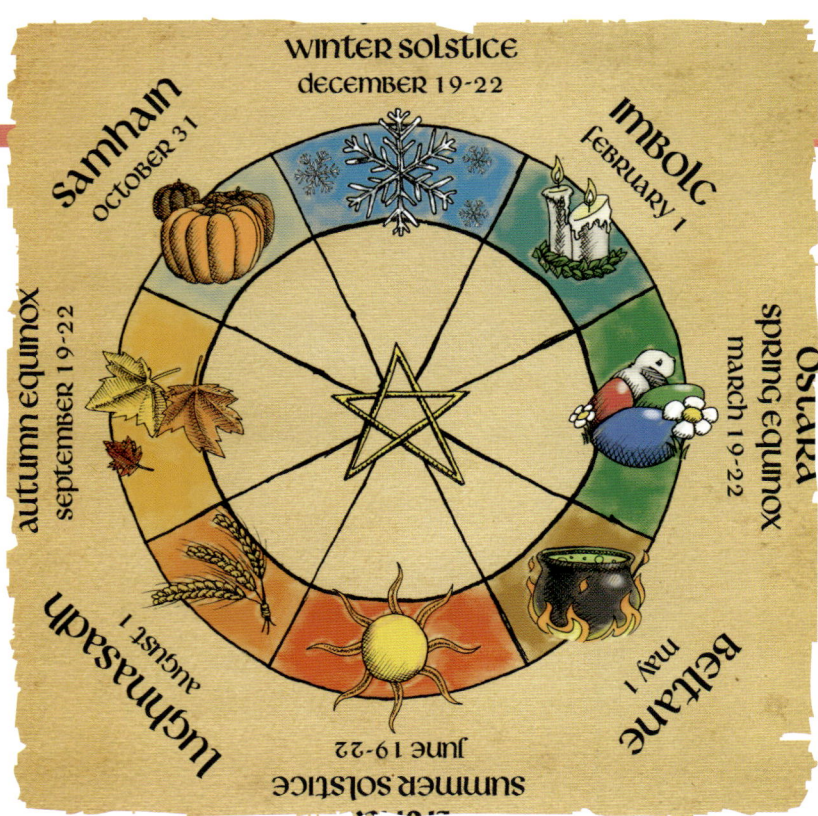

The Wheel of the Year comprised eight special days, or *sabbats,* that fell about six weeks apart and related to the cycle of the seasons.

The annual cycle of growing and harvesting crops has been central to timekeeping throughout history. This fifteenth-century German tapestry depicts outdoor workers of the day.

length of day and night is exactly equal, as well as the summer and winter solstices (Latin for "sun stands still"), where the Sun is at its northern or southernmost extreme, split the year in four and were the acknowledged midpoint of each season – the summer solstice was known as midsummer and the winter solstice as midwinter.

The four cross-quarter days, which took place halfway between the celestial occurrences and were tied to agricultural events such as the harvest, marked the beginning of each season. These people, now referred to as pagan or pre-Christian, were very aware of when these seasonal events occurred and the Sun's position in the sky throughout the year. They watched the skies and observed the behavior of birds and animals and the growth cycle of plants and trees. They built stone circles and ritual cairns that were aligned to sunrise on the morning of the solstices and equinoxes, to alert them to the day on which they occurred. This cycle of days was known as the Wheel of the Year.

The Wheel of the Year

There were eight days, known as sabbats, that made up the Wheel of the Year, and they fell roughly six weeks apart. They were a reliable way to mark and record time – thus their use as the basis of the calendars we still use today.

The spring, or vernal, equinox, known as *Ostara* and celebrated around March 21 in the Northern Hemisphere (September 21 in the south) is one of only two times in the year when the length of day and night is exactly equal. The sun sits directly above the equator on its journey northward, creating equal light and dark on both hemispheres. Ancient peoples – who spent their time outdoors tending to crops and were acutely aware of seasonal shifts – noticed that from this day forward the Sun would rise a little earlier each day and set a little later, that the barren coldness of winter was definitely over, and that summer was approaching. It was a time of growth and fertility, when the crops would be sown, the buds on the trees would open, birds would build

nests and lay eggs, and new life was celebrated. Thanks were given to the fertility goddess Ostara, whose symbols were an egg and a hare – still honored and celebrated around the world today in the form of chocolate eggs and the Easter bunny. The spring equinox is the basis of many calendars, and a year is commonly measured from one spring equinox to the next.

Beltane, on April 30/May 1 in the Northern Hemisphere (October 31/November 1 in the south), is a cross-quarter day marking the midpoint between spring and summer. The evidence of new life is everywhere – in abundant blossoms, the hatching of birds, bees pollinating flowers – proving that time is moving forward and progressing through the year. It was a fertility festival, where lovers would leap over the fires hand in hand and come together in sacred union in the fields, symbolically encouraging the fertility of the crops. Maypole dancing, representing the union of the god and the goddess, was performed on this day, and in some parts of the world this activity is still part of May Day festivities.

The summer solstice, known as *Litha* and celebrated around June 21 in the Northern Hemisphere (December 21 in the south), marks the longest day and the shortest night of the year. The sun reaches its northernmost latitude, and is furthest from the Equator, before it turns back and heads south again. Crops were growing, animals in the field were being born and life was blooming. Fires burned through the night to pay tribute to the power of the sun god on whom they relied for life, light, and warmth – but ancient peoples knew that from this time forward the days would get shorter and winter would once more approach, creating a significant marker of the turning Wheel of the Year.

Lughnasadh, or *Lammas*, on August 1/2 in the Northern Hemisphere (February 1/2 in the south), is a cross-quarter day marking the midpoint between summer and autumn. It was the date of the first harvest festival, a time of feasting and thanksgiving for the life-giving properties of the grain, and an acknowledgment of the cycle of sowing and reaping of the crops. Loaves were baked and symbolic sacrifices were made to ensure successful harvests to come. This festival was also a respite for the farmers and peasants, who had toiled long hours to bring in the harvest, and a celebration of their abundance.

The autumn equinox, known as *Mabon* and celebrated around September 21 in the Northern Hemisphere (March 21 in the south), is characterized, like the spring equinox, by the fact that the length of day and night is exactly equal, as the sun travels back across the Equator toward the south. From this point forth the days become shorter than nights and the weather cooler, as winter approached. It is the moment of balance in nature and within – from this day leaves start to fall, plants begin to wither, birds migrate, and signs of life start to disappear as the year turns.

Samhain, celebrated on October 31/November 1 in the Northern Hemisphere and today as Halloween (Samhain is on April 30/May 1 in the south), is a cross-quarter day marking the midpoint between autumn and winter. In ancient times food had to be stored at this time for the cold barren months ahead when snow would cover the land and fresh food would be scarce. Animals, which could no longer find grass for grazing, were slaughtered and stored

The seasons are symbolized in this third-century mosaic called *Four Seasons*, from the house of Dionysos, in the Roman city of Volubilis in the Province of Mauretania Timgitania, Morocco. Clockwise from top left: Spring, Summer, Autumn, Winter.

Right *Labours of the Months* from the Osterreichisches National Bibliothek in Vienna. In the Middle Ages, the months were defined by the flow of agricultural activity throughout the year.

This early twentieth-century drawing by A. V. Lochkine, *The Tale of Winter Arriving*, depicts the Northern Hemisphere tradition of bringing an evergreen inside at Christmas to symbolize the hope of spring's return.

for eating. The harsh conditions also increased the human death rate. It was also the night when the veil between the worlds was at its thinnest, and people honored their ancestors and tried to commune with the dead.

The winter solstice, also known as *Yule* and falling around December 21 in the Northern Hemisphere (June 21 in the south), marks the shortest day and the longest night of the year. It was a significant day in ancient cultures because it marked the important transition between dark and light. It was the lowest point of the year in terms of daylight and energy – the land was barren and seemed infertile and dead – but it was also the point at which the Wheel of the Year turned again toward summer. From this point on the days would get longer and the sun would get stronger. The Christmas tree decorated around the world today harks back to this time, when an evergreen was brought inside as a symbol of hope of spring's return. It was a time of feasting, celebration, and gift giving in honor of the birth of the sun god – traditions that live on today.

Imbolc, on February 1/2 in the Northern Hemisphere (August 1/2 in the south), is a cross-quarter day marking the midpoint between winter and spring, and celebrates the return of light to the land. Imbolc is thought to mean "in the belly," and is also associated with *oimelc*, or "ewe's milk," as in many countries lambs were born at this time. The first signs of the end of winter appeared – the first tentative flowers began to bloom – symbolizing the return and renewal of the life force of the land and its people.

Even today, when the seasons are not so defined and we no longer live in harmony with the Earth's rhythms or agricultural cycles, modern Pagans celebrate the Wheel of the Year as an honoring of nature and an acknowledgment of the continuing cycle of life, death, and rebirth. It is the turning of the Wheel of the Year, a celebration of the significant points throughout the seasons, and thus reflects the calendar as we know it today.

> *"For everything there is a season,*
> *And a time for every matter under heaven:*
> *A time to be born, and a time to die;*
> *A time to plant, and a time to pluck up what is planted…"*
>
> ECCLESIASTES

This Aztec stone sun calendar is an iconic symbol of Mexico. The Aztec calendar was similar to that of the Maya but used a more primitive numbering system. It had a method of counting the days as well as counting the years.

> *"The finest workers in stone are not copper or steel tools, but the gentle touches of air and water working at their leisure with a liberal allowance of time."* — HENRY DAVID THOREAU

Ancient observatories

Long before there were the calendars we know today, ancient civilizations built incredible monuments to track the movement of the Sun, Moon, and stars, and thus mark the passing of time. Throughout the British Isles, Egypt, and South and Central America are complex astronomical structures that even now mark particular days of the year. Their type of astonomy known as archeoastronomy, these ancient observatories continue to baffle scientists today with their precise measurements.

Stonehenge, on the Salisbury Plain in Wiltshire, England, is the most famous stone circle in the world. This ancient megalithic construction was built between 2800 and 1500 B.C.E., and is thought to have been an astronomical calendar or temple to the Sun. On the morning of the summer solstice, the Sun rises over the Heel Stone and its rays shine directly into the center of the monument, marking that significant day of the year. Other stones have been identified as tracking the phases of the Moon and predicting eclipses.

Newgrange, in County Meath, north of Dublin, Ireland, is a prehistoric passage tomb that is part of the significant Bru na Boinne complex. It comprises a long passage that leads to a chamber in which ancient rituals were carried out, and the remains of people held. Most significantly, as the Sun rises on the morning of the winter solstice each year, it shines directly along the passage into the chamber for about 15 minutes. Dated from 3200 B.C.E., it is the most famous of Ireland's prehistoric sites, yet only one of hundreds there that mark the passage of the year and act as a prehistoric calendar.

The Great Pyramid near Cairo, Egypt, was built with alignment to the four cardinal directions. It functions as an enormous sun dial, and its shadow to the north, and its reflected sunlight to the south, marks the solstices and the equinoxes. Nabta Playa, 500 miles (800 km) south of Cairo, has a stone circle dated to 5000 B.C.E., which aligns with the summer solstice.

Machu Picchu, in the Urubamba Valley of Peru, is one of the world's most beautiful and important ancient ruined cities. Among the temples, plazas, and ceremonial baths is a structure called the *Intihuatana*, meaning "tie the sun" or "hitching post of the sun." It is believed to have been designed as an astronomic clock by the Incas – but it told not the time of the day but the time of the year, precisely indicating the days of the two equinoxes among other significant celestial events.

Many other stone circles, alignments, pyramids, and monuments track the movement of the planets, the passing of time, and the dates of the

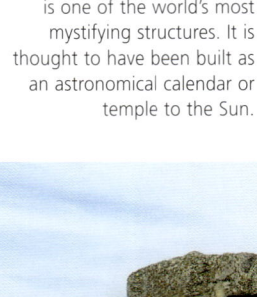

The massive stone circle contruction of Stonehenge is one of the world's most mystifying structures. It is thought to have been built as an astronomical calendar or temple to the Sun.

year. The Callanish Stone Circle in the Outer Hebrides of Scotland is aligned to the summer solstice, and the Palace of the Governor at the Mayan ruins of Uxmal in Yucatan, Mexico, is aligned to the path of the planet Venus.

Lunar and solar calendars

All calendars today and throughout history have been based on the movement of the Sun, the Moon, or both. While the Sun and the cycle of the seasons indicates the length of a year, the cycles of the Moon were also important to ancient civilizations as a way to mark the passing of time, and this is still reflected in some calendars today.

While it takes many years to observe the movement of the Earth in relation to the Sun and to determine the pattern of solar years, the Moon and its phases are easily observed and regular. For this reason the first calendars were lunar calendars, with Cro-Magnon people credited with inventing one around 32,000 B.C.E. Religious days, harvest dates, and events were planned for the new moon, full moon, or its quarter phases, and time was marked by the cycles of the waxing and waning of the golden orb. Today, with precise astronomical calculations able to be made for the Sun and its position and movement, most calendars are solar or lunisolar.

Lunar calendars, such as the Islamic calendar, are based on the cycles of the Moon, or moon phases, rather than the Sun and the seasons. A month that echoes the moon is known as a synodic (from the Greek *sunodos*, meaning "conjunction") or lunar month, and is measured primarily from new moon to new moon, although in some areas such as Tibet and northern India, a month is calculated from full moon to full moon. One of these lunar cycles is 29.5306 days – or just over 29 days, 12 hours, and 44 minutes – long, so the months usually alternate between 29 and 30 days in length to even this out. A lunar calendar is thus composed of 12 months – six of 29 days and six of 30 days – and runs for 354 days. Because there is a difference of around 11 days between a lunar and a solar year, the dates on a lunar calendar will shift from year to year with respect to the seasons. For this reason, today most lunar calendars are also lunisolar, with intercalary months inserted to keep them in sequence with the solar, or seasonal, year.

Solar calendars, such as the Persian and Gregorian calendars, are based on the movement of the Earth around the Sun. In these, a calendar year is kept to the same length as a tropical or solar year, or the time it takes for a complete cycle of the seasons, calculated to 365.24219 days, or just over 365 days, 5 hours, and 48 minutes. There are different ways to "round off" the length of the year to the nearest day: some calendars add an intercalary day to average it out over several years. A good example is the Gregorian leap year, which adds an extra day on every year exactly divisible by four. The 12-minute discrepancy is compensated for by eliminating the leap year on three out of four centennial years.

In other cases, the calendar is evened out by synchronizing the new year with the exact moment of the spring equinox each year. Either way, each year is subdivided into months, but no attempt is made to associate the start of the months or their length to the phases of the moon, thus the classification as a purely solar calendar.

Lunisolar calendars, such as the Jewish calendar, are synchronized to the movement of both the Moon and the Sun. This type of calendar is one where the passing of time is based on the lunar months, but which also takes into account the solar year, resulting in the addition of an intercalary month as required to bring everything back into alignment and compensate for the shift in the seasons and the difference between 12 lunar cycles and one solar cycle.

Intihuatana is from the Inca city of Machu Picchu in Peru. This stone was said to be able to indicate the precise timing of the two equinoxes by the movement of the Sun in relation to it.

This cross calendar, now housed in the National Anthropological Museum in Mexico, dates back to the pre-Columbian Huaztec civilization.

"Rest not. Life is sweeping by; go and dare before you die. Something mighty and sublime, leave behind to conquer time." GOETHE

Origins of the calendar we use today

Today the internationally recognized calendar is the Gregorian. It is used in most countries of the world. In some places it is used alongside another, such as in China, which has its own traditional lunar calendar for planning holy days but uses the Gregorian for civil purposes. The Gregorian calendar is now used throughout almost the entire modern world, the most famous exceptions being the Greek and Russian Orthodox churches, which still observe the old Julian calendar, and Iran, which has its own method of calculating the passing of time.

The Gregorian is very similar to the Julian calendar, with a small modification to increase its accuracy, and has its roots in the Roman method of charting time.

The Roman calendar

Long before the Christian Era, the priesthood of ancient Rome and its empire controlled the calendar and kept track of time. It was much more fluid than it is now, partly because life back then was so different. People worked from sun up to sun down, rather than any specific hour. The longer days of summer and the shorter days of winter were taken into account, with an "hour" varying in length between 45 minutes and almost 90, rather than the standard 60 minutes imposed since those times. In some ways, life was much more relaxed back then – bus timetables, deadlines, and specific meeting times were unheard of. People weren't ruled by time as we are now, rather by the seasons, the period of daylight in each day, and the weather.

Romulus, the first ruler of Rome, is thought to have introduced the Roman calendar in the eighth century B.C.E. Of course people back then didn't calculate time in the way we do now, from the birth of Jesus Christ – the Roman Empire was established before then, and thus we can only apply such dates retrospectively. Rome was founded in what we now refer to as 753 B.C.E, but which the Romans referred to as year 1. The Roman calendar counted the years *ab urbe condita* – "from the founding of the city" of Rome, and so the year we would now call 600 B.C.E. was in fact 154 A.U.C. (although to the people of that time, years were more commonly identified by the name of the two consuls who ruled during that year, and past time was referred to by "the year of the reign of…").

Their year began on the spring equinox, the day they called Martius 1, which occurs around March 21 in the Gregorian calendar. They had 10 months of around 30 days each – Martius, Aprilis, Maius, Junius, Quintilis, Sextilis, September, October, November, and December. The first four were named after gods; the last six were taken from their words for five, six, seven, eight, nine and ten, as they were the fifth, sixth etc. month of their year. The months we now know as January and February didn't exist back then – instead the 10 months were followed by a period of winter that had no name or number and could vary in length depending on the rest of the year. (Most calendars are considered complete calendars as they provide a way of naming each consecutive day. The Roman calendar was an incomplete calendar as the days of the winter months were not named, but merely lumped together.)

According to tradition, during this time the months could vary between 20 and 35 days in

Although it was not discovered until 1897, the Coligny calendar dates back to the late first or early second century. It is thought to be the best known example of a Celtic calendar and uses Roman letters and numerals to represent different times of the year.

Pope Gregory XII presides over the commission for reform of the Julian calendar in this sixteenth-century painting from the Archivio di Stato di Siena in Italy.

length, although the ideal was six months of 30 days, and four months of 31, plus the winter period. Their only rule was that the whole year contained 360 days. This was open to corruption from the high priest in charge of the calendar, who could add or subtract days for political gain as he saw fit. Frustrated by the variations, Numa Pompilius, the second King of Rome, made revisions to the calendar around 700 B.C.E. He added the months of Februarius, named after the purification festival, and Januarius, named after Janus, the god of doors, following December. Around 150 B.C.E. the order of these months was reversed and Januarius became the first month, giving us the order we still use today.

Pompilius and his advisers calculated that the Moon completed 12 of its 29.5 day-cycles in 354 days, while the Earth took around 365 days to go once around the Sun. He declared that there would be 12 months – four of 31 days, seven of 29 days, and one of 28 days – to be in rough alignment with the moon cycles, although some say they were divided like this because the Romans thought that even numbers were unlucky and avoided them at all costs. So his calendar comprised Martius (31 days), Aprilis (29), Maius (31), Junius (29), Quintilis (31), Sextilis (29), September (29), October (31), November (29), December (29), February (28), January (29) – making a total of 355 days. This was 10 days shorter than the solar year so he ordered the addition every other year of a 22- or 23-day month called Mercedinus to even it out. This month was inserted after February 23 or 24 and had the effect of making such years 377 or 378 days long.

In theory this would keep the calendar year fairly close to the solar year, however the high priest was still in charge of adding the intercalary month, and could still lengthen or shorten the year to suit his purposes or those of the king. As a result, the year varied over time with the intercalary month sometimes overlooked, sometimes added twice in a row, and thus the seasons were often out of step with the calendar. Accuracy also perished over the centuries due to slight changes in the Earth's rotation.

By the time of the reign of Julius Caesar, from 63–46 B.C.E. (691–708 A.U.C.), the calendar had descended into chaos. Only five intercalary months were added during his reign, instead of eight, and there were none at all in the last five years. It was clear that some manner of reform was urgently needed.

Christian Orthodox priests celebrate Christmas in Darmstadt, Germany. Orthodox Christians in some parts of Europe including Russia, Serbia, and the Ukraine set the date of Christmas by the Julian calendar – January 7 in the Gregorian calendar.

The Julian calendar

In 46 B.C.E. – or in the calculations of the day, 708 A.U.C. – Rome's leader Julius Caesar ordered reform of the Roman calendar. Advised by the Alexandrian astronomer Sosigenes, he first added 67 days to the current year, to compensate for the overlooked intercalary months (22+23+22) of recent times. This made the current year 445 days long, and brought the days back into alignment with the solar year. Then he decreed that the new calendar – named the Julian after himself – would take effect on the first day of Januarius 709 A.U.C. (or January 1, 45 B.C.E.). It was to be a 12-month solar calendar consisting of 365 days, with an extra day added every four years to compensate for the extra quarter-day of a solar year. The months were redistributed slightly so that there were seven of 31 days in length, four of 30 days, and one of 28, which would have 29 in a leap year. Although it was much simpler, in the first 36 years there were errors as the priests erroneously added a leap year every three years instead of every four. In 8 B.C.E. (746 A.U.C.), new ruler Caesar Augustus compensated for this by skipping several leap years and then restoring the correct frequency.

To honor Julius Caesar for reforming their calendar, the Roman senate named the seventh month after him, as it was the month of his birth. Formerly called Quintilis, as it had been the fifth month in the Roman calendar that started in March, they renamed it Julius, a name that lives on today in the Gregorian calendar as July. Sadly he only lived through one Julius though – he was murdered in March the following year, in 44 B.C.E. But his creation endured, becoming the predominant calendar throughout Europe and the settled world for the next 1,600 years, and still used in some countries until quite recently. The Julian calendar was followed in Russia until 1917 and China until 1949, and the Eastern Orthodox Church still observes it today.

Augustus was also honored for his part in reforming the calendar – in 8 B.C.E. Sextilis, the sixth month in the old Roman calendar, was renamed Augustus, which we know today as August, because this was the month when several significant events in his rise to power occurred. And although it has been reformed a little since its beginnings more than 2,000 years ago, the Julian calendar remains the basis of the calendar we use today.

The Gregorian calendar

By the 1400s the Julian calendar had fallen out of sequence with seasonal time by more than a week, with the spring equinox falling around March 12 rather than March 21. This happens because in assuming a year to be 365.25 days long, and adding one day every four years to compensate for this, rather than its actual 365.24219 days, the calendar year is several minutes longer than the actual year. This seems unimportant from year to year, and even over a person's lifetime, but over centuries it adds up.

"Time is the most valuable thing a man can spend."
THEOPHRASTUS, PHILOSOPHER

The difference grows by three days every four centuries, so that in the twenty-first century the Gregorian calendar is 13 days ahead of the Julian. This is why Orthodox Churches, which still use the latter, celebrate Christmas 13 days later on January 7 in the Gregorian year. According to their calendar, that day is December 25.

The backward drift of the spring equinox concerned church leaders because Easter was becoming hard to calculate. The date of Easter is determined by the spring equinox and the phases of the Moon, so any change in these dates will affect the timing of Easter. In the Christian world, Easter is the celebration of the death and resurrection of Jesus around 30 C.E. At the First Council of Nicaea in 325 C.E., convened by the Roman Emperor Constantine, Easter Sunday was set as the first Sunday following the first full moon that occurs on or after the spring equinox, which they fixed as March 21.

The concern with the Julian calendar was that as the spring equinox fell earlier and earlier each year, Easter would also shift backward, no longer being linked to the event it commemorates, and putting it closer and closer to the set date of Christmas.

In the late 1400s Pope Sixtus IV decided reformation was necessary to halt this shift, but the astronomer he called on, Regiomontanus, died before anything could be done, and the idea was forgotten. Finally in 1582 Pope Gregory XIII demanded change. Modifications were suggested by Aloysius Lilius, a doctor from Naples, to compensate for the extra day every 128 years that the Julian calendar was in error. It was decided that a new way of calculating leap years would make the calendar year 365.2425 days long, rather than 365.25, and a rule-based calendar was created that would take this into account and remain accurate for centuries to come.

To solve the problem of the equinox, Gregory ordered that the day after October 4, 1582, be October 15 – thus losing the extra 10 days and putting the human-imposed calendar's passing of time back in sequence with the movement of actual time, as defined by the Earth's orbit around the sun. To avoid the same problem recurring, he also decreed that leap days would be added every four years as usual – except in centennial years that weren't divisible by 400. The modification was also fairly accurate. The Gregorian calendar year differs from the solar year by only 28 seconds, which adds up to a day's difference every 3,323 years – not enough to concern anyone! This also solved the problem with Easter, which can now never fall before March 22 or after April 25. The changes were decreed by Pope Gregory XIII – hence the calendar's name – on February 24, 1582, in the papal bull *Inter Gravissimas*, and went into effect in October of that year.

The changeover

While the new Gregorian calendar was more accurate than the Julian and it made sense that everyone adopt it, a spanner was thrown in the works by the mood of other nations in those times. Catholic countries such as Italy, Portugal, and Spain made the change on the day suggested, and as a result St. Teresa of Avila died on October 4, 1582, and was buried the next day – on October 15!

The head of Pope Sixtus IV is shown on this coin from c. 1480. In the late 1400s Pope Sixtus IV called for reform of the Julian calendar to halt the backward shift of Easter, but his adviser died before changes were in place and the idea was forgotten.

This section of a twelfth-century Byzantine fresco found in the Dark Church in Goreme, Cappadocia, depicts the Roman Emperor Constantine. He convened the first Council of Nicaea in 325 C.E., where Easter Sunday was set as being the first Sunday after the first full moon on or after the spring equinox.

*"Look to this day for it is life, the very life of life...
For yesterday is already a dream and tomorrow is only a vision. But today, well lived, makes
yesterday a dream of happiness and every tomorrow a dream of hope."* SANSKRIT PROVERB

But many other countries, particularly Protestant ones, resented the church's control and refused or delayed implementing it in defiance of the Pope. Protestant Germany and the Netherlands didn't adopt the change until 1700, and Britain and its colonies didn't switch over until 1752, continuing to use the Julian calendar until that time, which caused confusion throughout Europe, especially as time went on and ties between the countries, and communication and travel from one to the other, increased.

For the uneducated people on the street in England, not privy to the knowledge of the priests and astronomers, there was great fear over the change. Because it required the deduction of 11 days (an extra day had accrued because of the time it took them to change) in order to bring the calendar back into line with the seasons, many thought these days had been deducted from their lifespan. There was rioting in the streets.

Changes in the 1500s and 1600s required 10 days to be dropped. Changes in the 1700s required 11 days to be dropped. Changes in the 1800s required 12 days to be dropped. Changes in the 1900s required 13 days to be dropped. And in the twenty-first century, the Julian is running 13 days behind the Gregorian, caused by the year 2000 being a leap year in both calendars.

All eastern European countries had adopted the Gregorian calendar by 1923 – but their national Eastern Orthodox Churches hadn't, and still haven't; thus they continue to celebrate Easter according to the Julian calendar. And while some, including Constantinople, Alexandria, Greece, Romania, Poland, and Bulgaria, later accepted a revised Julian calendar that has a solar (but not lunar) part identical to the Gregorian, and thus celebrate Christmas on December 25 (but lunar-decided Easter according to their own rules), others, including Russia, Serbia, and the Ukraine, adhere totally to the old Julian calendar, and thus celebrate Christmas on January 7 in Gregorian terms – which in the Julian calendar is December 25, as it is now 13 days behind.

New Year's Day

In the Western world, New Year's Day is celebrated on January 1 of each year. It is the first day of the year in the Gregorian calendar. But this is only the day chosen by those who follow the Gregorian calendar. Every culture that has a yearly calendar celebrates the end of one year and the beginning of the next, and while it appears there is variation between these dates in terms of the Gregorian calendar, they are all celebrated on the first day of the first month of their new year.

Some New Year dates around the world

Chinese New Year is the main holiday of the year for more than one quarter of the world's population, and consists of a 15-day period of celebrations, festivities, gift giving, family gatherings, feasts, and prayers. Their lunar New Year generally falls on the day of the second new moon after the winter solstice, between January 21 and February 21 in Gregorian terms.

In the Eastern Orthodox church, which still uses the Julian calendar, New Year's Day is celebrated on January 14 of the Gregorian calendar, as this is January 1 in the Julian. Many

Chinese New Year firecrackers are set off in honor of the kitchen god in this Chinese watercolor painting.

people in countries where Eastern Orthodoxy predominates celebrate both dates, with the Gregorian day as a civil holiday and their own day as a religious festival.

Rosh Hashanah (Hebrew for "head of the year") is the two-day celebration of the Jewish new year, which commemorates the creation of the world. It begins on the first day of *Tishri*, the first month of the Hebrew calendar, which falls between September 5 and October 5 in Gregorian dates. It is characterized by the blowing of the *shofar* – a trumpet made from a ram's horn – prayers, special foods, and *tashlikh*, the symbolic casting away of sins from the previous year.

In the solar-based Iranian calendar, the first day of the year, Farvardin 1, falls on the spring equinox, which is around March 21 on the Gregorian calendar. *Norouz*, their New Year's Day, marks the beginning of spring, and celebrations acknowledge the symbolic awakening or rebirth of life after the barrenness of winter. It is a holiday marked by ceremonies and rituals involving house cleaning, seed sprouting, fire festivals, and mass picnics.

In Thailand, Cambodia, and Laos, New Year's Day is called *Songkran* and is celebrated from April 13 to April 15. The date of the festival was originally set by astrological calculation, but it is now fixed. Since January 1, 1940, the Gregorian new year has officially begun the year, but the traditional day remains a national holiday on which people throw water, exchange gifts, visit their families, and do community service at the temple.

The Punjabi new year, called *Vaisakhi*, is also celebrated on April 13, and marks the beginning of the spring and the end of the harvest in India.

The Islamic or Muslim new year occurs on the first day of *Muharram*, the first month in the Islamic calendar. Since it is based on 12 lunar months of around 354 days, the date of this in the Gregorian calendar falls around 11 days earlier each year – and two Muslim New Years will occur in 2008. There is no religious significance attached to this day, and many Muslims don't acknowledge it. Some remember the life of the Prophet Muhammad and the *Hijra* he made; for others it is a day of mourning and marks the anniversary of the day Muhammad's grandson was martyred.

In Ethiopia, New Year's Day, or *Enkutatesh*, is celebrated on Meskerem 1 on the Ethiopian calendar (around September 11 in the Gregorian).

This postcard from c. 1900 depicts the ceremonial blowing of the *shofar*, or horn, in celebration of the Jewish new year festival of *Rosh Hashanah*, held on the first day of *Tishri*, the first month of the Hebrew year.

"Time has no divisions to mark its passage, there is never a thunderstorm or blare of trumpets to announce the beginning of a new month or year. Even when a new century begins, it is only we mortals who ring bells and fire off pistols." THOMAS MANN

"In the perception of the smallest is the secret of clear vision; in the guarding of the weakest is the secret of all strength." LAO TZU

Other calendars

Other major calendars that are still used for religious and/or social purposes include the Chinese, Hebrew, Islamic, Iranian, Hindu, and Julian calendars. These are mainly used to set the dates for religious and national holidays, with the Gregorian used alongside the traditional for day-to-day life.

The Chinese calendar

The Chinese calendar is lunisolar, incorporating both lunar and solar aspects, although the emphasis is on the Moon. In China today, the Gregorian calendar is used for most civil activities, but the traditional Chinese calendar is employed to determine holidays such as Chinese New Year and the *Duan Wu* and Mid-Autumn festivals. It is also used for agricultural purposes, astrology, and for choosing events such as the most auspicious date for a wedding, funeral, business event, or the opening of a building.

This traditional calendar is known also as the agricultural, the old, and the *yin* calendar, while the Gregorian is known as the standard, Western, new or *yang* calendar. While the latter was adopted by the Republic of China from January 1, 1912, for official business, the general population continued to use the old calendar. The governing of China was in chaos for several years as competing warlords sought to rule, but in October 1928 the Republic of China was reconstituted and the Gregorian calendar was officially adopted, effective from January 1, 1929.

The beginnings of the Chinese calendar can be traced back to the third millennium B.C.E. It is written that Emperor Huang Di devised it in 2637 B.C.E., while the earliest archeological evidence of it appears on oracle bones from the fourteenth century B.C.E., showing a 12-month year having an occasional thirteenth and even a fourteenth month added. There have been a few reforms over the centuries, the most recent in 104 B.C.E., but the format has remained basically the same.

The Chinese calendar is first and foremost a lunar calendar, which measures its time by the waxing and waning of the Moon. Its form of measurement is a lunar, or synodic, month, which is just over 29.5 days in length – the time it takes for the Moon to go through an entire cycle.

To mimic this, lunar calendars usually alternate months of 29 and 30 days to compensate for the half days. The months in the Chinese calendar are not named but simply numbered.

In China, a lunar month begins on the astronomical new moon, when the Sun and the Moon are astronomically conjunct; in other words, the Moon, in its monthly orbital motion around the Earth, lies directly between the Earth and the sun, so the illuminated half of the moon faces the Sun and the dark half faces the Earth, making the Moon invisible to us. It is sometimes referred to as the dark moon, and is followed soon after by the first sighting of the crescent moon.

The new year begins on the day of the second new moon after the winter solstice, which means it can occur from January 21 to February 21 in Gregorian time. Occasionally it falls on the day of the third new moon after the solstice, depending on when the intercalary month is added, but this is rare and won't occur again until 2033.

A lunar year is made up of 12 lunar months, which gives a period of 354 days. This is just over 11 days less than a solar year, which means that over time the calendar dates drift away from the seasons. To correct for deviations of the calendrical year from the solar year, intercalary months are added. Without this, the New Year and all other lunar-based festivals would occur earlier and earlier, so that the Spring Festival would no longer fall in spring and so forth.

While complex rules have been developed to add intercalary months to most lunar calendars, such as for the Hebrew, the Chinese approach is more arbitrary. They insert an extra month whenever the calendar moves too far from the seasonal year cycle, and the pattern is roughly seven times in every 19 years.

The Chinese calendar also measures time differently to the rest of the world. While it has the longest chronological record in history, dating from about 2600 B.C.E., the Chinese mark the passing of time by periods of 60 years, which is made up of five cycles of their repeating pattern of 12 animal years. After one 60-year cycle, it starts over again and repeats in the same order. Each of the 60 years is differentiated by combining the five elements – metal, water, wood, fire, and earth – with the 12 animal signs that identify each of

This Thai calendar (c. 1850) depicts the 12-animal cycle of the Thai horoscope through images of deities being fanned and other godlike figures. The Thai calendar is similar to the Chinese calendar. Many Thais determine their age from the sequence of the animals.

the years. Rather than speaking of the year 2007, they identify it as the Year of the Pig. These years begin on the first day of their lunar year, and identify each as accurately as the Western number, such as 1996, does. The pattern of years runs Rat, Ox, Tiger, Rabbit, Dragon, Snake, Horse, Goat, Monkey, Rooster, Dog, and Pig.

Each year in a 60-year cycle is identified by pairing one of the elements with one of the animal signs. For example, the Year of the Tiger, which began in 1998, was more specifically an Earth Tiger year, while the one beginning in 2010 will be a Metal Tiger year. The previous Metal Tiger year was in 1950, and the next will be in 2070. This distinguishes each year within the 60 years, which, at the time the method was devised, was usually enough because a human lifespan has only grown longer in recent times.

The 60-year system cycles continuously, and determines the animal sign and element – and thus the year – under which a person is born. The clues this gives about a person's character are taken very seriously in China, and parents try to give birth to children in the Year of the Dragon or Monkey, as people born then are deemed to have a luckier life.

Other traditional Eastern calendars are very similar to the Chinese. The Korean is identical, the Vietnamese is the same except that it uses the Cat instead of the Rabbit in its zodiac, the Tibetan is similar except for the choice of animal names, and the traditional Japanese calendar is basically the same but uses a different method of calculation, which means that some years their calendars coincide, and other years they don't.

Many people have argued to abolish the Chinese calendar altogether, as the Gregorian is more accurate and relevant in a globalized world. However it remains culturally essential, and most of the traditional festivals, such as Chinese New Year and the Mid-Autumn Festival, are determined by the lunar dates of this calendar.

Chinese astrology

Linked closely to this calendar is the Chinese form of astrology, as significant to the Chinese as the Western concept of being born under a sun sign such as Aries or Virgo. Unlike Western astrology however, which has 12 zodiac signs based on the movement of the planets, Chinese horoscopes correspond to the year of birth, and assign an animal and all its qualities to each year in a 12-year cycle. An element is also assigned and gives further clues to a person's character. The

The first six animal signs of the Chinese zodiac are (clockwise from top left): Rat, Ox, Tiger, Rabbit, Dragon, and Snake.

Chinese zodiac signs are recognized throughout the world and embraced by many other cultures. They often appear on Japanese New Year cards, and Australia and the U.S. are just two of several countries which issue stamps each year to commemorate the year of the particular animal.

Chinese astrology is the oldest known horoscope system in the world, with origins tracing back to 2637 B.C.E.. It is based on the ancient Oriental art of divination and character reading, and the philosophy of Confucius, Lao Tse, and the I Ching. It is described as an ancient viewpoint on temperament and personality, and today it is becoming as popular in the West as any other form of astrology.

Western and other astrology

Western astrology – the study of the positions and aspects of the Sun, Moon, and planets at the time of one's birth, and the belief that they influence one's personality, health, the career a person is most suited to, one's choice of partner, and the events in life – was also based on ancient calendars. The first sign of its zodiac, Aries, started on the day of the spring equinox, March 21, which for centuries was the start of the year, and the 12 signs followed a seasonal pattern, with Libra beginning around the time of the autumn equinox, Cancer beginning at the time of the summer solstice, and Capricorn at the winter solstice.

The modern form of astrology is thought to have begun in Babylon in the nineteenth century B.C.E., when it was considered a science closely linked to astronomy. The planets were observed and their movements correlated with events such as famine and war. The Mayans had also developed an astrological system around this time, and there is evidence of its use even earlier, in the stone circles of Great Britain, France, and Egypt.

Around the sixth century B.C.E., the Greeks coined the term "zodiac" for the movement and pathways of the planets, and the Persians developed mathematical astronomy, which led to the ability to create horoscopes and their popularity as a form of divination.

Another form is Celtic tree astrology, which is based on the cycle of the Moon rather than the Sun. The year is divided into 13 lunar months, and each is associated with a tree sacred to the Celtic priests, or druids, such as rowan, oak, and hawthorn. The origins of this method are obscured by time and the fact that druid lore was an oral tradition and was never written down. Some scholars debate its historical accuracy, yet many others have written extensively on this magical form of astrology, and it is used today to give further insight into a person's life, often alongside the more traditional form.

The characteristics of each sign of both Western and Celtic astrology are described throughout this book on the day on which the sign begins.

The Chinese zodiac

The sign for each year begins on Chinese New Year, not January 1, so if you were born in the first few weeks of the year you will have to check when the changeover was. For example:

 1996 Year of the Rat began February 19
 1997 Ox began February 8
 1998 Tiger began January 28
 1999 Rabbit began February 16
 2000 Dragon began February 5
 2001 Snake began January 24
 2002 Horse began February 12
 2003 Goat began February 1
 2004 Monkey began January 22
 2005 Rooster began February 9
 2006 Dog began January 29
 2007 Pig began February 18

The Rat
The cycle begins with the Rat, thus those born in its year like to be first. Rats are funny, charming, adaptable, extroverted, charismatic, and persuasive. They are strong leaders, but can also be indecisive, manipulative, stubborn, selfish, and judgmental.

> *"How do I know where creation comes from? I look inside myself and see it."*
>
> FROM THE TAO TE CHING

The Ox
Ox people are patient, helpful, logical, and down to earth. They are conscientious, reliable, balanced, and responsible, but can also be stubborn, slow, and possessive, and refuse to listen or take a risk.

The Tiger
Tigers are warm-hearted, powerful, sensual, adventurous, determined, regal, and self-assured. They have a humanitarian streak and are romantic, frank, and open, but can be selfish, inflexible, rash, and too proud to ask for help.

The Rabbit
Rabbits are quick, creative, understanding, gentle, loyal, ambitious, and sensitive. They know how to make the best of themselves but can also be superficial, aloof, overly sensitive, and unable to deal with adversity, and may not finish what they start.

The Dragon
Dragons are powerful, artistic, enthusiastic, and mystical. They attract wealth and are intense, bright and successful, but can also be irritable, egotistical, quick-tempered, hypercritical, demanding, and hard to get close to.

The Snake
Snakes are strong, charismatic, determined, sensual, and enigmatic. Shrewd in business, they are good communicators and make the best of things, but can also be fickle, possessive, secretive, double-crossing, lazy, self-indulgent, and hold a grudge.

The Horse
Horses are easygoing, friendly, high-spirited, humorous, and get along with everyone. They are quick-witted, competitive, romantic, and self-possessed, but they get bored quickly and can be impatient, selfish, irresponsible, stubborn, hot-tempered, childish, and tactless.

The Goat
Goats are kind, unassuming, whimsical, artistic, determined, practical, good-natured, and altruistic. They crave security and respect rules, but can be overly sensitive, insecure, undisciplined, stubborn, and suffer depression if they don't like their surroundings.

The Monkey
Monkeys are witty, sociable, playful, passionate, inventive, and fascinated with learning, but have a short attention span. They can succeed in anything, but can also be egotistical, lazy, unscrupulous, manipulative, and need to be noticed.

The Rooster
Roosters are resourceful, organized, dedicated, and self-assured. They work hard, follow the rules and are romantic, vivacious, and amusing, but can also be conceited, overly critical, self-absorbed, pretentious, and too blunt, and see the world in black and white.

The Dog
Dogs have empathy, warmth, integrity, and an interest in others, and are giving, honest, faithful, protective, trustworthy, and courageous. They are high achievers, yet can also be very stubborn, guarded, bossy, introverted, cynical, and defensive.

The Pig
Pigs are generous, supportive, naive, confident, and sincere. They have a thirst for knowledge and will work hard and find success, but can also be lazy, insecure, untrusting, extravagant, indulgent, wary, and helpless, and refuse to compromise.

The remaining six animal signs of the Chinese zodiac are (clockwise from top left): Horse, Goat, Monkey, Rooster, Dog, and Pig.

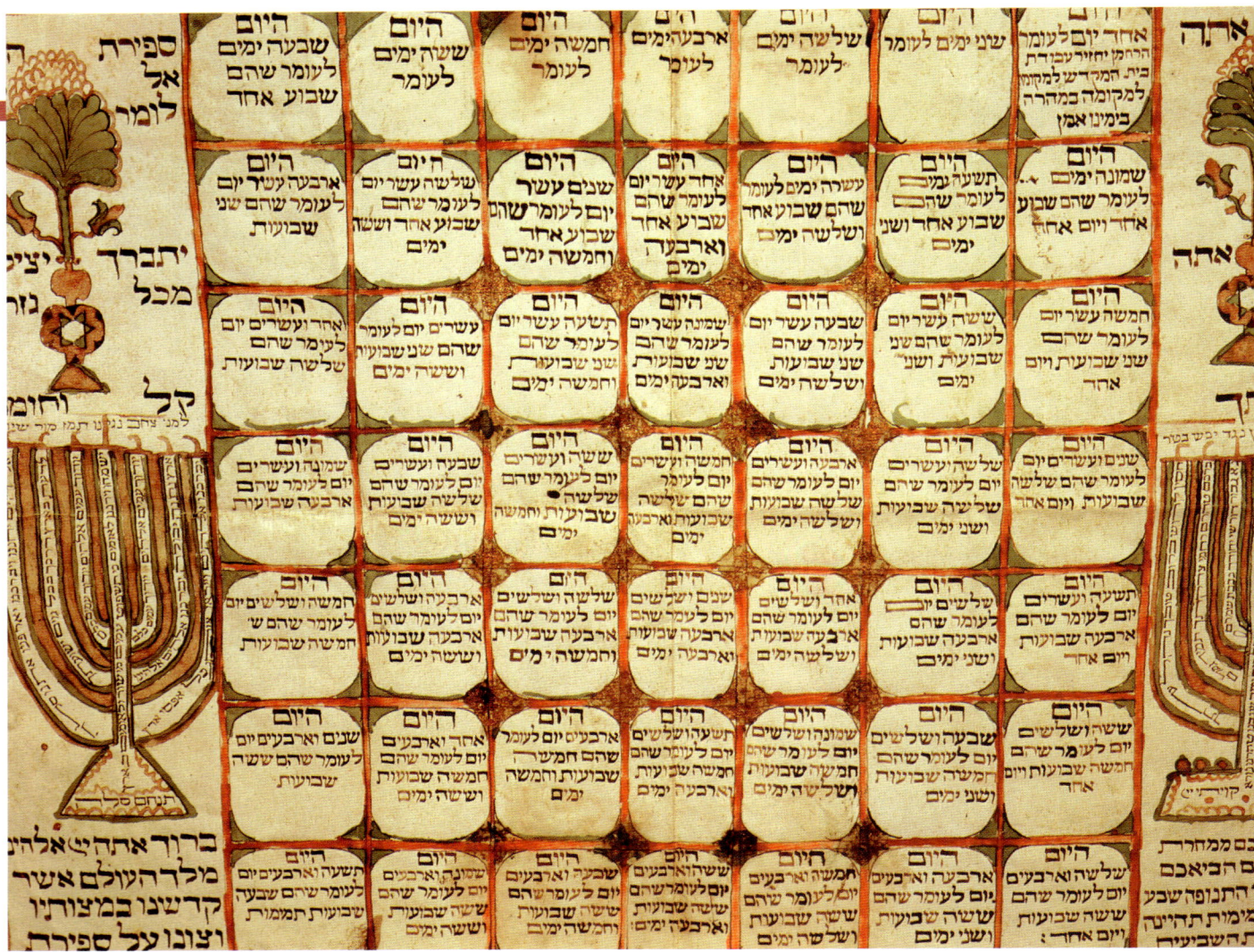

In this nineteenth-century Jewish calendar on parchment from Omer in the Near East, symbols of the Hebrew faith, such as the *menorah* candlestick, decorate the borders.

The Hebrew calendar

The Hebrew, or Jewish, calendar is used for religious purposes by Jews all over the world, alongside the Gregorian, and is the official calendar of Israel. It determines the dates of Jewish holidays, the beginning of the new Jewish year, the date to commemorate the death of a relative, and many other spiritual and religious events.

Although it is hard for people who follow the Gregorian calendar to grasp, Jewish holidays do not change their date every year. *Hanukkah* always begins on the twenty-fifth day of the month of *Kislev*; however, because the Hebrew calendar is not locked to the solar year in the same way, it will start on a different day of the Gregorian calendar from year to year, somewhere from late November to December.

The Hebrew year comprises 12 synodic months of either 29 or 30 days in length, with 13 months in leap years. The lunar month begins when the first sliver of moon becomes visible after the dark of the moon. In ancient times, *rosh chodesh* (the first of the month), was determined by observation. But in the fourth century, a fixed calendar based on mathematical and astronomical calculations was established. The months are numbered from *Nisan*, considered the spring new year and the point from which major religious festivals and holy days are counted, however the civil year begins on the first day of *Tishri*, the autumn new year, when the year number increases by one and the festival of *Rosh Hashanah* (New Year's Day) is celebrated.

The Hebrew calendar is a lunisolar calendar in that it strives to have its months coincide with the synodic months but also have its years coincide with the solar year. This is a complicated goal, however, with their rules for determining the dates changing slightly over the years.

Using a purely lunar calendar of 354 days, the month of Nisan, for example, which is supposed to occur in spring, would fall 11 days earlier each year, eventually occurring in different seasons. To keep it in line with the seasons and the solar year, an intercalary month must be added every few years to compensate for the 11 lost days.

The Greek astronomer Meton is credited with solving this problem in the fifth century B.C.E. He came up with a pattern of adding seven intercalary months during a 19-year cycle, the Metonic cycle. He calculated that every 19 years a solar and lunar calendar will coincide if seven months are added, because 19 solar years equals 6939.602 days and 235 synodic months equals 6939.688 days.

The pattern of additions is n-n-L-n-n-L-n-n-n-L-n-n-L-n-n-L-n-L (where "n" is a normal year and "L" has a leap month added), with a month added in the third, sixth, eighth, eleventh, fourteenth, seventeenth, and nineteenth years of a 19-year cycle. The additional month is known as Adar I, and is inserted before the regular month of Adar, which becomes known as Adar II in a leap year. The current cycle of 19 years began in the year that started on October 2, 1997, in Gregorian time. As there is a difference of about two hours in each 19-year cycle, giving a margin of error of one day every 219 years, there should be an additional day added every 219 years.

With the Metonic compensation, Nisan starts 11 days earlier for two or three years, then jumps forward 29 or 30 days, balancing the seasonal drift.

Years are either *kesidrah*, or common, years of 354 days long (384 days in a leap year), *chaserah* years of 353 or 383 days long, where a day is taken away from the month of Kislev, or *shlemah* years of 355 or 385 days long, where a day is added to the month of *Heshvan*.

Jews have been using a lunisolar calendar since Biblical times, and they date their calendar from what is referred to in Gregorian times as 3761 B.C.E., considered the year of creation. This means that January 1, 2007 is in fact Tevet 11, 5767 in the Hebrew calendar, and September 13, 2007 is the first day of their new year, Tishri 1, 5768.

The Islamic calendar

The Islamic calendar, also known as the Muslim or Hijri calendar, is used by Muslims to determine the day on which to celebrate Islamic holy days. It is the official calendar in countries around the Gulf region, including Saudi Arabia, while other Muslim countries use the Gregorian calendar for civil purposes and the Islamic for religious ones. As with the Hebrew calendar, these holy days are fixed on the same day of their calendar every year, even though they appear to shift in Gregorian terms because the two calendars are not synchronized.

This calendar is a lunar one – the only widely used lunar calendar in the world – and is based purely on the cycles of the Moon. Each month starts on the day of the new moon, but while most lunar calendars use precise astronomical calculations for this, the Islamic one has retained an observational definition of the new moon, starting the new month when the crescent moon is first seen. This makes it impossible to be certain in advance of exactly when a specific month will begin, which means the first day of *Ramadan* is never known ahead of time, although it can be estimated within a day or two because

The Gezer Calendar is from the biblical city of Gezer in Israel. This limestone tablet is the oldest-known Hebrew epitaph, dating back to the tenth century B.C.E., and sets out the year in terms of the agricultural and seasonal tasks of the time.

The holy fasting month of Ramadan is one of the most important months in the Islamic calendar. This young Pakistani girl has decorated her hand with henna to celebrate the Muslim festival of *Eid al-Fitr* which falls at the end of Ramadan.

*"Come out of the circle of time
And into the circle of love."*

RUMI, PERSIAN POET AND MYSTIC

Saudi men perform the *Eid al-Fitr* prayer outside the Imam Turki mosque in Riyadh at sunrise. Muslims around the world celebrate *Eid al-Fitr*.

the astronomical new moon can be calculated. If the weather is cloudy in Saudi Arabia when the new moon is expected, people are sent up in the sky in airplanes to observe the moment the moon appears.

The Islamic year is made up of 12 synodic months. As a synodic month is 29.5306 days – or just over 29 days, 12 hours, 44 minutes – in length, the months usually alternate between 29 and 30 days, although this is not specifically prescribed, as a month's length depends on when the next new moon is sighted.

This makes their year 354 days in length – just over 11 days shorter than a solar year – so the calendar is not fixed to the seasons. This means that the spring equinox, for example, will fall on a different date every year, and the seasons will drift out of sync with the calendar dates. For example, the equinox on March 21, 2005, Gregorian, fell on Safar 10; March 21, 2006, fell on Safar 21; and March 21, 2007, is on Rabi I 2.

In a lunar calendar, the pattern of the lunar months will repeat every 33 years, and holy days will fall in the same season and on the same Gregorian day as they did 33 years ago. Thus while occurring on the same day in the Islamic calendar every year, a holy day that falls in the middle of winter one year will be celebrated approximately 11 days earlier seasonally every year after that, occuring in the middle of summer 16 years later, and not falling at midwinter for a further 16 or 17 years.

As the Islamic year is 11 days shorter than a solar year, it advances more quickly than a Gregorian year, so 33 Islamic years correspond within a few days to 32 Gregorian years. For example, in the Gregorian year 1968, the month of Ramadan began on November 22, just before the start of winter in the Northern Hemisphere. Sixteen years later, in 1984, Ramadan began on June 1, the start of summer. In 2000, Ramadan began on November 27. Thirty-two Gregorian years passed in this cycle, while 33 Islamic years did. (All conversions from the Islamic calendar to the Gregorian are accurate to within a day because the start of a new month is dependent on the new moon being observed, not calculated.)

The passing of time is also marked in a different way in the Islamic calendar. The calendar used today was introduced in 638 C.E. by Umar ibn Al-Khattab, a companion of the Prophet Muhammad, in an attempt to rationalize the various systems used until then. It was retroactively decided that the calendar would start from the year 1, or 622 C.E. in Gregorian time, which is when the Hijra occurred. The Hijra, which chronicles the migration of Muhammad from Mecca to Medina, is the central historical event of early Islam.

Before this a lunisolar calendar was used, with an intercalary month inserted as required to keep in step with the seasons. However Muhammad forbade the intercalary month, releasing the calendar from the seasons. The first day of the Islamic calendar, Muharram 1 in the year 1 A.H., corresponds to July 16, 622 C.E. in Gregorian years. Years are designated either "H" or "A.H." – the latter being an abbreviation of the Latin *Anno Hegirae*, meaning "in the year of the Hijra." In the year 2007 in the Gregorian calendar, 1,385 years will have passed since the advent of the Islamic calendar, but 1,427 years will have passed in the Islamic.

Because of its acknowledgment of the starting date of the new Muslim chronology, the Islamic calendar has a deep religious and historical significance, and is more than just a way to date religious events and the passing of time.

This Chinese Muslim prays in the Niujie Mosque in Beijing, China, to mark the Festival of Fast-Breaking once the month-long fast of Ramadan ends. The Niujie Mosque is the largest mosque in Beijing.

The Iranian calendar

Also known as the Persian or Jalaali calendar, this is used today in Iran and Afghanistan as the official calendar. It is a solar calendar that is observation-based rather than rule-based, as each new year begins on the spring equinox as precisely determined by astronomical observations from Tehran and Kabul. It is the perfect solar calendar, because each calendar year corresponds exactly to the solar year.

The year starts on the spring equinox, which falls on the first day of their first month, called *Farvardin* – around March 21 in the Gregorian calendar. Each year has 12 months, with the first six being 31 days in length, the next five 30 days, and the last month 29 days, or 30 in a leap year.

The first six months are longer because the seasons do not actually have an equal number of days, and spring and summer are in fact slightly longer than autumn and winter. This is because the sun moves slightly slower on its ecliptic path (the apparent path of the sun on the sky) in the Northern Hemisphere spring and summer.

The calendar also uses a sophisticated intercalation system which has a cycle of 2,180 years, making it more accurate than its Gregorian counterpart. In basic terms, it follows a pattern of inserting a leap year every four years for seven cycles, followed by a leap year in the fifth year, although sometimes this fifth year occurs after six cycles, to ensure the exact moment of the spring equinox remains as their New Year's Day. If this falls before noon, then that day is the first day of the year; if it occurs after noon, the following day begins the calendar year. In other words, the year begins at the midnight closest to the instant of equinox. No matter what time the equinox begins, be it 3:00 A.M. or 3:00 P.M., celebrations are timed to that second, in much the same way as the Western world celebrates as the clock strikes midnight on December 31.

The Persians, ancestors of the modern Iranians, have long placed importance on a calendar to mark the passing of time and record their history. They have always used the Sun to calculate their year, as it has significance for them and their culture, rather than the Moon. The history of the Iranian calendar dates back to at least 750 B.C.E., when there is evidence of a lunisolar administrative calendar borrowed from the Babylonians, as well as a solar calendar widely used by the Iranians.

The current form of the calendar was introduced by astronomer and poet Omar

Below A comparative table of various calendars.

The Islamic calendar does not correspond with any other calendar and is not in sync with the Gregorian equivalents in this table. Its lunar year is 11 days shorter than a solar year, so any fixed day on this calendar will change seasonally each year.

Gregorian equivalent	HEBREW	ISLAMIC	IRANIAN	HINDU
March–April	1. Nisan, 30 days	1. Muharram, 30 days	1. Farvardin, 31 days	1. Chaitra, 30/31 days
April–May	2. Iyar, 29 days	2. Safar, 29 days	2. Ordibehesht, 31 days	2. Vaisakha, 31 days
May–June	3. Sivan, 30 days	3. Rabi I, 30 days	3. Khordad, 31 days	3. Jyaistha, 31 days
June–July	4. Tammuz, 29 days	4. Rabi II, 29 days	4. Tir, 31 days	4. Asadha, 31 days
July–August	5. Av, 30 days	5. Jumada I, 30 days	5. Mordad, 31 days	5. Sravana, 31 days
August–September	6. Elul, 29 days	6. Jumada II, 29 days	6. Shahrivar, 31 days	6. Bhadrapada, 31 days
September–October	7. Tishri, 30 days	7. Rajab, 30 days	7. Mehr, 30 days	7. Asvina, 30 days
October–November	8. Heshvan, 29/30 days	8. Sha'ban, 29 days	8. Aban, 30 days	8. Karttika, 30 days
November–December	9. Kislev, 29/30 days	9. Ramadan, 30 days	9. Azar, 30 days	9. Margasirsa, 30 days
December–January	10. Tevet, 29 days	10. Shawwal, 29 days	10. Dey, 30 days	10. Pausa, 30 days
January–February	11. Shevat, 30 days	11. Dhu al-Qa'dah, 30 days	11. Bahman, 30 days	11. Magha, 30 days
February–March	12. Adar I, 30 days (leap years only)	12. Dhu al-Hijjah, 29/30 days	12. Esfand, 29/30 days	12. Phalguna, 29/30 days
February–March	12. Adar, 29 days (13. Adar II in leap years)			

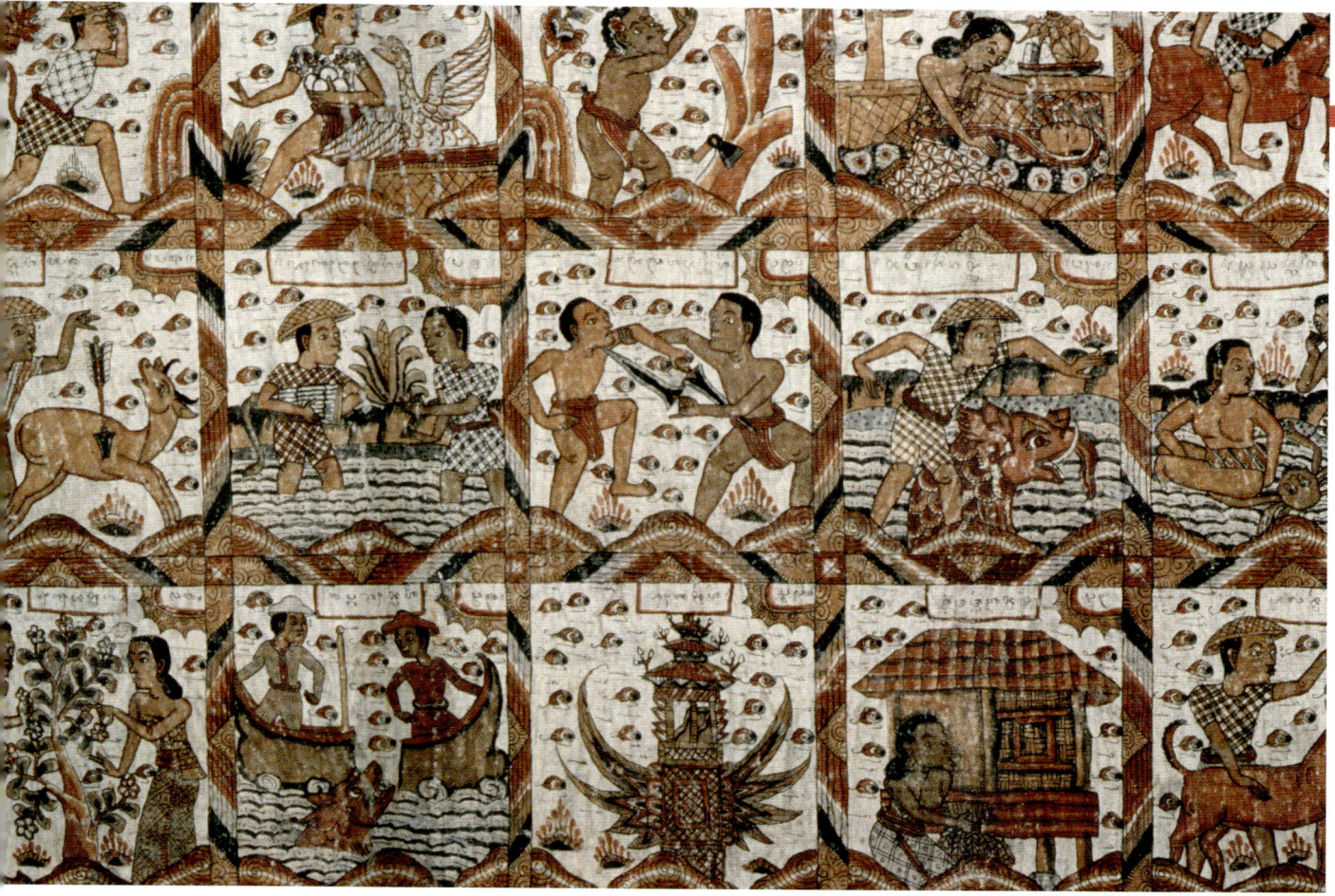

Khayyam, who made reforms to the previous method on the Gregorian date of March 21, 1079 C.E., or New Year's Day of the year 458 in the Iranian calendar. He also set the start of the era to the first day of the month of Farvardin in the year 1, which is the spring equinox of March 22, 622 C.E. in Gregorian time. It was officially adopted by the Iranian Parliament on Farvardin 11, 1304, or March 21, 1925.

The Hindu calendar

There are various Hindu calendars in use at the present time. In India the Indian National calendar is the official civil one, and is used alongside the Gregorian. It is a solar calendar with 12 months that are either 30 or 31 days in length. Like the Iranian calendar, the months in the first half of the year are slightly longer, to take into account the slower movement of the sun across the ecliptic.

The year begins on the first day of the month called *Chaitra*, which is the day of the spring equinox. This is said to fall on March 22 in Gregorian terms, unless it is a leap year, in which case it is on March 21. Chaitra has 30 days in a common year, and 31 in a leap year. This calendar was officially reformed in 1957, and the leap years coincide with those of the Gregorian calendar.

There is also a *panchang*, or religious calendar, which calculates the dates of religious festivals and auspicious times and days for performing rituals. The name is derived from the Sanskrit word *pancha*, meaning five, relating to the five characteristics which each day of the year is assigned. The name of each day within the week is only one of that day's defining factors. Other properties of each day include the position of the Moon at sunrise, and its travel across the sky relative to the constellations.

When the Calendar Reform Committee made its survey in the mid-1950s, there were around 30 calendars used for this purpose, hence the need for an official one to coordinate celebrations around the country and the world.

This religious calendar is a lunisolar one which is based on the movement of the Sun and especially the Moon. Like the Chinese calendar, most religious festivals occur on specified lunar dates. It is an extremely elaborate system, and calculating the dates of the religious holidays is confusing. For this reason the official dates are calculated by the India Meteorological Department every year and published annually to avoid the hassle of people having to work them out for themselves.

This Balinese calendar painted on fabric depicts aspects of life through the Indonesian year. The Balinese use two different calendars – one that aligns with other Hindu calendar traditions, and one that is thought to be indigenous to Bali.

The four cardinal points of the Egyptian zodiac, represented by the women in white, and 36 decans (10-day divisions in the year) are depicted on papyrus in this copy of the ceiling image from the Temple of Hathor in Denera, Egypt. The original work dates back to the Ptolemaic dynasty c. 305–30 B.C.E.

Ancient and alternative calendars

While most of these calendars are no longer in use and have been forgotten, the foundations of some of them are echoed in those still used today.

Alternatives for the Gregorian calendar have been suggested over the years, such as calendars with a 13-month year and an "unattached" additional day whose length is modified as necessary to match the solar cycle. However, despite consideration by the UN in the 1950s, it seems unlikely that any such calendar will make the Gregorian obsolete in the foreseeable future.

The Babylonian calendar

This ancient lunisolar calendar is thought to have been the main influence on the Egyptian, Hebrew and Islamic versions. It came into use sometime before 2000 B.C.E.. The year began on the day of the first new moon after the spring equinox, and each month that followed began at the next new moon, making it lunar based. The year was made up of 12 months of either 29 or 30 days, with an intercalary month added periodically to bring the calendar back into line with the solar year. For centuries it was an observational calendar, each month beginning when the crescent moon was physically sighted, but around 500 B.C.E. the months began to be regulated, and the pattern known as the Metonic cycle was employed.

The Egyptian calendar

Around 6,000 years ago, priests in Egypt studied the night sky and discovered that the appearance of the star Sirius coincided with the beginning of the Nile flood each year. Based on this and other agricultural events, they created a seasonal calendar that gave a rough guide to farming life. But they needed a more specific way to gather taxes and conduct business.

Thus a standard calendar with 12 months of 30 days each was introduced. They soon realised this was five days shorter than a solar year, and that the beginning of the year had been slipping back through the seasons, so they added five days to each year to bring it into line. These days became a festival period rather than being integrated into the rest of the calendar, although later the pattern may have changed. This version is said to have been in use in 2400 B.C.E. and possibly even before.

While it was quite accurate – and was the basis of the Roman calendar which later became the Julian – it was limited by its overlooking of the extra quarter day in each year.

In 238 B.C.E., the Ptolemaic rulers decreed that an extra day should be added every four years to compensate for the difference, but this was not implemented until Caesar declared himself ruler in 30 B.C.E. and enforced the change, renaming it the Coptic calendar. Other sources claim the Egyptians were the first to come up with the idea of adding a leap day every four years to keep the calendar in sync with the solar year, and that the Romans later adopted this solution for their calendar. The Coptic or Alexandrian calendar, based on the ancient Egyptian one, is today used by the Coptic Orthodox church.

The ancient Greek calendar

There were various calendars in use in ancient Greece around the fourth and fifth centuries B.C.E., including the Attic and Hellenic ones. Their year commonly began on the first new moon after the summer solstice – around June 21 in the Gregorian calendar – and comprised a year made up of 12 lunar months of 29 or 30 days in length. To anchor the dates to the seasons and maintain it as a lunisolar calendar, a month was intercalated roughly every three years, in no discernable pattern. The calendar was at the mercy of the rulers of the time, who were known to insert days when it pleased them to give more time for festival preparations, or "freeze time" to allow more days of war. Greek astronomer Meton was credited with developing the Metonic cycle of intercalary months around 450 B.C.E., and it is likely that this pattern of adding seven months every 19 years was adopted then.

The Mayan calendar

The calendar of this ancient civilization is of interest now because it was thought that it prophesied the end of the world in 2012 – instead it marks the end of an age and the start of a new one. On the day of the winter solstice in 2012, which will fall around December 21, their great circle of time calculation, which began in what we refer to as 3114 B.C.E., will end – and the next one will start.

It is the most complex of all calendars, with four separate calendars operating at once, which can be synchronized and interlocked in complex ways, their combinations giving rise to further, more extensive cycles.

The *Tzolkin* is a sacred Mayan religious calendar based on a cycle that repeats every 260 days. It combines with the *Haab*, the common, roughly seasonal calendar that consists of 18 months of 20 days each, followed by a short month of five days. While the latter calendar is 365 days in length, the Mayans never used it on its own to determine the length of the year, instead combining the two. Each cycle of Tzolkin and Haab repeated itself every 52 Haab years – more than the life expectancy of most people – so this was deemed sufficient.

Another form of calendar, known as the Long Count, was used to track longer periods of time, and for identifying when one event occurred in relation to others. A 584-day Venus cycle was also maintained, which reflected the appearance and conjunctions of the planet Venus and was used to decide when to go to war.

The French Revolutionary calendar

This was introduced in France in 1793 during the French Revolution. Each year began at the autumn equinox, which is around September 21 in the Gregorian calendar, and contained 12 months of 30 days each, followed by five (or six in a leap year) days that were not part of any month – much like the Egyptian calendar. The months were Vendemiaire, Brumaire, Frimaire, Nivose, Pluviose, Ventose, Germinal, Floreal, Prairial, Messidor, Thermidor, and Fructidor. In addition, instead of a seven-day week, each month was divided into three portions of 10 days each, with the last day a holiday. This upset workers, who were used to having every seventh day off rather than every tenth.

The calendar began on Vendemiaire 1 of year 1, which was on September 22, around the autumn equinox, of 1793 in Gregorian time. Leap years were added in a pattern to ensure that the autumn equinox always fell on Vendemiaire 1. It was a simple and effective calendar, yet it was discarded 14 years later, at the end of the revolution.

The Baha'i calendar

This solar calendar, used by those of the Baha'i faith, was introduced on March 21, 1844, in Gregorian time, the date on which the Baha'i prophet, the Bab, started his ministry. Their year begins on the spring equinox, which is their New Year's Day, called *Naw Ruz*. It falls on the first day of their first month, called Baha. Each year contains 365 or 366 days, like the Gregorian, and adds leap years in the same pattern. However their year is made up of 19 months that are each 19 days in length, with an extra four days (five in a leap year) added between the last two months, which are not part of the calendar but are given over to festivities, feasting, and gift giving. The names of the months translate as Splendor, Glory, Beauty, Grandeur, Light, Mercy, Words, Perfection, Names, Might, Will, Knowledge, Power, Speech, Questions, Honor, Sovereignty, Dominion, and Loftiness. Days are considered to begin at sunset on the previous day.

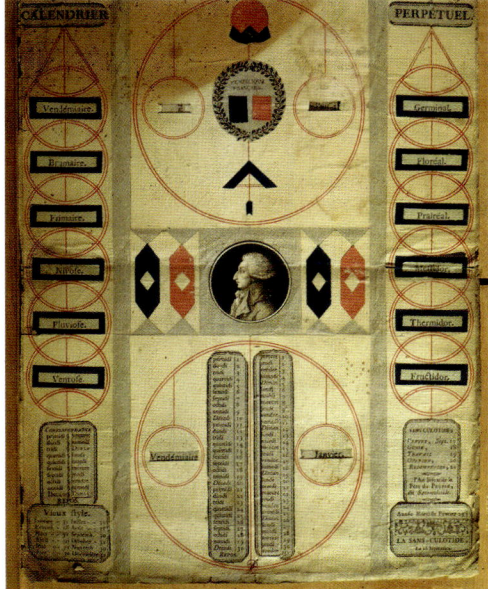

This engraving of a perpetual calendar from eighteenth-century France shows the relation between the years and months of the French Revolutionary calendar. The work is housed in the Musée Carnavalet in Paris.

JANUARY

"For last year's words belong to last year's language
And next year's words await another voice.
And to make an end is to make a beginning."

T.S. ELIOT, "LITTLE GIDDING"

The Leaning Tower of Pisa was closed to the public in January, 1990, the first time in 800 years, due to safety concerns. After more than a decade of restoration work, the tower's lean was marginally corrected, and its future was ensured for at least another two centuries.

January

The first month in the Gregorian calendar, January is the month of beginnings, named after the Roman god Janus, the keeper of gates, doors, and archways, and custodian of transitions from old to new. In January, Earth makes its closest approach to the Sun, an event astronomers call the perihelion. Our closer distance to the Sun gives us more solar energy in January than any other time of the year.

Aquarius star sign and scene of feasting from the *Calendar and Book of Hours*, from fifteenth-century France. January begins in the sign of Capricorn and ends in the sign of Aquarius.

SPECIAL DATES

With leap years exempted, January always begins on the same day of the week as October.

Silver didrachm coin of the god Janus. Janus was worshipped as the god of all doors, gates, and entrances, depicted with two faces looking in opposite directions, back to the past and forward to the future.

THE MONTH OF JANUARY was born with the first reform of the calendar in 713 B.C.E. by Numa Pompilius, the second of the seven traditional kings of Rome. He is said to have reduced the 30-day months to 29 days and to have added January and February to the end of the calendar, and thus brought the length of calendar year up to 355 days. January continued to have 29 days until the rule of Julius, at which time it became 31 days long.

The word "January" probably comes from the Latin *Januarius*, a combination of *Janu(s)* for the ancient sky god Janus, and *-arius* for "pertaining to." Janus may have evolved from the goddess Juno, who was celebrated in January when the god of the Aeon died and was reborn from Mother Time. Juno was thus personified at the gate of her temples with two faces looking in opposite directions, the outward passage looking toward birth and the reverse passage looking at death. She was addressed as Antevorta and *Postvorta* – the goddess who looks forward and backward.

As the Roman religion became increasingly patriarchal, Juno's image underwent a transformation, first to an androgynous Janua–Janus, and then to a masculine form, Janus. Janus was depicted with two faces. Originally one face was bearded while the other was not, which may have symbolized the sun and the moon. Later both faces were bearded. Janus was invoked at times of beginnings, such as planting, harvest, marriage, and birth. Janus also represents the transition between primitive life and civilization, the countryside and the city, peace and war, and youth to maturity.

As with other months, the historic name for January in different cultures often describes the weather, flora and fauna, and activities of the farmers at that time. Among the Angles and Saxons, January was *Wulfmonath*, meaning "wolf month," since it was the time of year when the wolves were unable to find food and their hunger drove them into the villages. Charlemagne, the ninth-century king of the Franks, named January *Wintarmanoth* for "winter month." In Japan, the old lunar/solar calendar named each month according to its number in the year, with January being first *Mutsuki*, also known as the month of good relations. In Finnish, January is called *Tammikuu*, meaning "month of the oak," and in Czech, January is known as *Leden*, which translates to "ice month."

In many cultures, people kept track of the seasons by naming each full moon. Names for the January full moon include Chaste Moon, Cold Moon, Snow Moon, Ice Moon, Moon of Little Winter, Big Winter Moon, Disting Moon, Hardship Moon, Quiet Moon, Wolf Moon, Old Moon, and Moon After Yule.

January birthflower

The carnation is linked to the month of January. Native to the Near East, the name of this flower is derived from the word "coronation" because the flowers were used in ancient Greek ceremonial crowns. While white carnations are said to symbolize pure love and red flowers are said to represent deep love, Christian legend has it that pink carnations symbolize a mother's love because carnations sprung from Mary's tears as she watched her son Jesus carry the cross. The Snowdrop, originally from Europe and Asia, is also sometimes referred to as January's flower. Its name is derived from the Greek word *galanthus* meaning "milkflower," and *nivalis*, which is Latin for "resembling snow."

This fifteenth-century Bohemian fresco, Snowball Fight, from *Cycle of the Months* (in Buonconsiglio Castle, Torre Aquila Trento), reflects the winter activity reminiscent of January in the Northern Hemisphere.

Marking a new year

In some countries and cultures, the start of a new year may be celebrated according to the Julian calendar or to traditional lunar/solar calendars. In the Eastern Orthodox Church, for example, New Year is celebrated on January 14, which is January 1 in the Julian calendar. Many people in countries where Eastern Orthodoxy predominates celebrate both dates, with the Gregorian day as a civil holiday and their own day as a religious festival.

The widespread adoption of the Gregorian calendar, however, has meant that on January 1, most countries will hold some kind of celebration to see in a new year. The day is usually celebrated as a holiday, with symbolic festivities at midnight of the night before, and the making of resolutions to keep throughout the year. Colombians, Cubans, Puerto Ricans, and Ecuadorians may burn Mister Old Year, a male doll dressed up in old clothes from each family member and stuffed with items that represent bad memories or sadness. In Spain, they might eat one grape for each chime of the clock towards midnight. Called *tomar las uvas*, the tradition farewells *Nochevieja*, "The Old Night." In Japan, late on New Year's Eve, people eat buckwheat noodles called *toshikoshisoba*, or year-crossing noodles. The Buddhist temple bells will ring 108 times at midnight to purify the listeners of the 108 sins or evil passions that plague every human being. In Greece,

Young women turning 20 are officially recognized as adults in Japan during the Coming of Age festival. Here, tour guides for the day hang voting tablets, or *ema*, with written wishes on a display board in Tokyo's Meiji Shrine to celebrate the day.

January birthstone

The garnet is the birthstone for January. This stone received its name from the Latin word for pomegranate, *granatum*, because its crystals were likened to the seeds of the pomegranate fruit. Some primitive cultures used garnets to stop bleeding and cure inflammation, while others used garnets as bullets. Garnets occur in all colors of the rainbow except blue, and are the stone of the second wedding anniversary.

New Year's Day is also the Festival of St. Basil. Children will leave their shoes by the fireside so that St. Basil, renowned for his kindness, will fill the shoes with gifts. In Venezuela, Argentina, Bolivia, and Mexico, those with hopes of traveling in the new year will carry a suitcase around the house at midnight.

The first day of the Gregorian year has not always been on January 1. In ancient Roman times, the spring equinox was the start of the year, and named *Martius 1*, falling on what is March 21 in Gregorian dates. When Julius Caesar reformed the calendar in 46 B.C.E., he declared the first day of *Janarius* the beginning of the year – but church leaders disapproved of the wild parties that took place to mark the day, so in 567 C.E. the Council of Tours shifted the date, creating much confusion, with many countries having two New Year's Days – one for civil purposes, the other when the year turns.

Floating celebrations, past and present

Some holidays and observances in January are held in accordance with the lunar calendars and religious traditions of the past, and do not have fixed dates of celebration. In Scotland and northern England, for example, the main midwinter celebration was Handsel Monday, held on the first Monday after the beginning of the new year. *Handsel*, an Old Norse word for "luck" or "good omen," became the name for a gift that it was customary to give at the beginning of the first working week of a new year.

In England, the beginning of the agricultural year was celebrated with Plough Sunday, traditionally held on the Sunday after Epiphany, between January 7 and January 13. On Plough Sunday a ploughshare was brought into a church, with prayers for the blessing of the land. Work in the fields would not begin until the day after the blessing. The celebration is seeing resurgence in some communities.

Coming of Age Day in Japan, known as *Seijinshiki*, is a national holiday held the second Monday of January for those becoming 20 years old in the new calendar year. Started in the seventh century, it was intended to celebrate the rebirth of young people into the society as responsible adults. In 1948, January 15 was designated Coming of Age Day as a symbol of Japan's rebirth after World War II. After 2000 it was changed to the second Monday in January to allow for a three-day weekend.

The traditional Viking fire festival *Up-helly-aa*, from the Norn *helli* for "holy-day" and Old Norse *uppi* for "at an end," is held in Lerwick, Shetland, on the last Tuesday of January. Guizers, a squad of men in costume, complete with horned helmets, axes, and shields, begin a procession through the streets that will eventually be joined by a thousand more, each carrying a torch of fire they will use to burn a full-size replica of a Viking longship.

During the *Up-helly-aa* fire festival, locals dressed as Vikings march through the streets of Lerwick, Shetland. The climax of the day comes with participants in full costume hauling a Viking longship through the streets to the edge of town where up to 1,000 paraders will throw their flaming torches into the galley and watch the ship burn.

January 1

"Every new year is the direct descendant, isn't it, of a long line of proven criminals." OGDEN NASH

HISTORICAL EVENTS

- **404** Last known gladiator competition in Rome.
- **1808** Importation of slaves into the U.S. is banned; the illegal slave trade continues.
- **1818** Mary Shelley's novel *Frankenstein*, subtitled *The Modern Prometheus*, is published.
- **1892** Ellis Island in New York opens to determine the eligibility of immigrants to the U.S., eventually processing some 20 million people.
- **1934** Nazi Germany passes the Law for the Prevention of Genetically Diseased Offspring, which allows for forced sterilization.
- **1959** New cultivars of plants must be named in a modern language, not Latin, to distinguish them from their botanical names.
- **1978** Air India Flight 855 Boeing 747 explodes and crashes into the sea off the coast of Bombay, killing 213 people.
- **1999** A single currency, the Euro, is established for 11 European Union countries (now 12); Euro banknotes and coins enter circulation on January 1, 2002.
- **2000** No major crisis arises from the computer "millennium bug" (see below.)

Births
- **1449** Lorenzo de Medici, statesman
- **1735** Paul Revere, silversmith and American patriot
- **1863** Pierre de Coubertin, initiator of the modern Olympic games
- **1879** E. M. Forster, novelist
- **1895** J. Edgar Hoover, FBI director
- **1909** Dana Andrews, actor
- **1919** J. D. Salinger, novelist

Deaths
- **1716** William Wycherley, dramatist
- **1782** Johann Christian Bach, composer
- **1953** Hank Williams, singer
- **1972** Maurice Chevalier, actor and singer
- **1994** Cesar Romero, actor

Washington D.C. comes alight in the first few moments of the year 2000.

DAY TO REMEMBER

Traditional day New Year's Day From ancient times, and across all cultures and nationalities, the start of a new year has been cause for celebration. The new year was once commemorated with festivities over a few days when spring began and the crops were planted. The Romans observed the new year in late March, but over time their calendar was so interfered with by various emperors that it was no longer in sync with the movement of the Earth around the Sun. In 45 B.C.E., when Julius Caesar reworked the dates and established the Julian calendar, January 1 was defined as the beginning of the new year. The early Christian church condemned revelry on this date as paganism, and continued to do so until the Middle Ages when the adoption of the Gregorian calendar led to widespread acceptance of January 1 as New Year's Day – the day to make resolutions that can be broken throughout the year.

Y2K

Before 2000, computer programmers used the last two numbers of any given year to signify that year. For example, 65 was used for 1965. The rationale was that they needed to conserve memory space and that the software they were writing would in any case be obsolete by the end of the century. In the early 1990s, with the two-number code still in use, programmers became concerned that in the year 2000, computers may interpret the 00 to mean the year 1900 instead of 2000. Programs which performed calculations based on dates would, at the very least, run the risk of producing incorrect data, and at worst cause massive software crashes.

The problem became known as Y2K, combining the letter Y for "year" and K for the Greek prefix "kilo", which means "1000" (2K equaling 2000). The term "millennium bug" was also used, though the year 2000 was not actually the start of the new millennium. Critical government facilities and commercial industries, such as electricity and banking, raced against time to protect data and fortify the hardware, software and operating systems of networked computers and embedded systems.

As Y2K came closer, the computer industry grew richer, with most large companies replacing their affected systems and devices. The insurance industry also profited, selling insurance to cover possible Y2K problems.

On the stroke of the new year, the lack of impact was almost a letdown. Speculation continues as to how much Y2K was hype or whether the unprecedented overhaul of the computerised world saved the day.

January 2

DATEline

"The most exciting phrase to hear in science, the one that heralds new discoveries, is not 'Eureka!' [I found it!] but 'That's funny...'"   ISAAC ASIMOV

HISTORICAL EVENTS

1860   The discovery of a new planet, named Vulcan, is announced at a meeting of the Académie des Sciences in Paris; the claim is never substantiated.
1879   Fred Spofforth claims the first hat-trick in Test cricket, taking three wickets in consecutive deliveries on the Sydney Cricket Ground in Australia, playing against England.
1920   U.S. Attorney General A. Mitchell Palmer unleashes the second stage of his raids on suspected anarchist, communist, unionist, and radical Americans, arresting some 6,000 people without warrants.
1941   The Andrews Sisters – LaVerne, Maxene and Patty – record "Boogie Woogie Bugle Boy" on Decca Records.
1959   Luna 1, launched by the U.S.S.R. in the direction of the Moon, is the first artificial object to reach the escape velocity of the Earth.
1968   Dr. Christiaan Barnard performs the second successful heart transplant into a human (see below).
1969   Australian media magnate Rupert Murdoch becomes owner of the News of the World newspaper group. It is his first Fleet Street newspaper.
1971   At Ibrox football stadium in Glasgow, Scotland, 66 fans are killed and 200 injured when spectator barriers collapse; it is the second such incident at Ibrox.
1987   The publishers of Enid Blyton's *Noddy* books agree to transform Golliwogs into inoffensive gnomes.

Births

1647   Nathaniel Bacon, American colonist and plantation owner
1920   Isaac Asimov, author
1936   Roger Miller, singer
1939   Jim Bakker, televangelist
1968   Cuba Gooding Jr., actor
1969   Christy Turlington, model

DAYS TO REMEMBER

Traditional day   Kakizome Japanese New Year celebrations begin on January 1 and last for two weeks. January 2 is set down for *kakizome*, or "first writing" of *shodou*, the Japanese calligraphy. Traditionally, each member of the family takes a turn dipping a brush into freshly mixed ink and inscribing a favorite poem or proverb onto a long strip of paper.

Religious day   St. Basil's Day As one-time Bishop of Caesarea and one of the most distinguished Doctors of the Church, St. Basil (c. 329–379) was a defender of the church against the heresies of the fourth century. As one of The Three Cappadocians, Basil was instrumental in making the clergy more disciplined and ensuring a greater church presence in maintaining peace and providing charity. He is also known as St. Basil the Great.

In December 1967, Christiaan Barnard, a cardiothoracic surgeon in Cape Town, South Africa, became the first person to perform a heart transplant on a human being. He braved the scrutiny of medical ethics advisers when he turned off the ventilator of a brain-dead woman, harvested her heart and transferred it into the body of heart patient Louis Washkansky. To prevent rejection of the heart, Barnard weakened Washkansky's immune system; 18 days later, he died from a lung infection. Barnard conducted his second transplant operation on January 2, 1968. This patient, dentist Philip Blaiberg, survived for 19 months and heart transplants became standard surgery from that time.

January 3

"Nothing takes the taste out of peanut butter quite like unrequited love."
CHARLIE BROWN IN *PEANUTS*

HISTORICAL EVENTS

1871 Henry W. Bradley claims the U.S. patent for oleomargarine, a butter substitute based on clarified beef fat developed by French chemist Hippolyte Mège-Mouriés in 1869.
1888 Marvin C. Stone, a manufacturer of paper cigarette holders, patents the spiral winding process to manufacture the first paper drinking straws: Previously, rye grass had been used.
1924 English explorer Howard Carter discovers the sarcophagus of Tutankhamen in the Valley of the Kings, near Luxor, Egypt.
1957 Hamilton Watch Company introduces the first battery-powered watch.
1987 Aretha Franklin becomes the first woman to be inducted into the U.S. Rock and Roll Hall of Fame.
1988 Margaret Thatcher, the first female prime minister in European history, becomes the longest-serving British Prime Minister in the twentieth century.
1993 The U.S. and Russia agree to each cut nuclear warheads by up to 3,500 – the largest reduction to date. U.S. President George H. W. Bush says the treaty offers parents and children "a future free from fear."
2000 The last daily *Peanuts* comic strip is published (see below).

DAY TO REMEMBER

Religious day St. Genevieve's Day
St. Genevieve (c. 422–512), who became a nun at the age of 15, prophesied invasions and disasters for Paris. When Paris was besieged by the Franks, she encouraged its defence, organized prayers for protection, and led an expedition for food. In 1129, the procession of her relics through Paris is believed to have ended an epidemic. She is Patroness of Paris.

Births
1892 J. R. R. Tolkien, writer and philologist
1907 Ray Milland, actor
1932 Dabney Coleman, actor
1942 John Thaw, actor
1945 Stephen Stills, singer, songwriter, and guitarist
1946 Victoria Principal, actress
1956 Mel Gibson, actor and director
1960 Joan Chen, actress
1969 Michael Schumacher, race car driver

Deaths
1795 Josiah Wedgwood, potter
1963 Jack Carson, actor
1967 Jack Ruby, killer of Lee Harvey Oswald
1979 Conrad Hilton, hotelier

Peanuts was a highly popular daily comic strip written and drawn by American cartoonist Charles M. Schulz. It ran for 50 years, from October 2, 1950, and was noted for its subtle social commentary on issues such as racial and gender equality. At its peak, *Peanuts* ran in more than 2,600 newspapers, with a readership of 355 million in 75 countries, and was translated into some 40 languages. It was also published in book form and televised as animation. Schulz died the night before the final daily strip was published in newspapers on January 3, 2000.

January 4

DATEline

"Genius is one percent inspiration and ninety-nine percent perspiration." — THOMAS EDISON

HISTORICAL EVENTS

1904 Thomas Edison's movie crew films the electrocution of an elephant in front of a paying audience of 1,500 people at Coney Island, New York.
1958 Sir Edmund Hillary, the first person to reach the top of Mt Everest, is the first explorer to reach the South Pole since Captain Robert Scott in 1912.
1959 The Russian *Luna 1* becomes the first spacecraft to reach the vicinity of the Moon.
1962 New York City introduces a train that operates without a crew on board.
1972 Rose Heilbron becomes the first female judge to sit at the Old Bailey in London.
1981 *Frankenstein*, the most expensive dramatic production in Broadway history, opens and closes, losing U.S. $2 million.
1990 A crowded passenger train collides with a standing freight train in Pakistan's Sindh Province, killing some 300 people.
1991 Fu Mingxia, a 12-year-old from China, becomes the youngest world champion in aquatic event history at the World Swimming Championships.
2000 Catherine Hartley and Fiona Thornewill are the first British women to walk across Antarctica to the South Pole. Thornewill and her husband Mike are also the first married couple to make the journey.
2001 The Gower brothers launch "RuneScape," which becomes one of the most popular online Java-based games in the world (see below.)

Births
1643 Isaac Newton, scientist and philosopher
1785 Jakob Grimm, philologist and folklorist
1809 Louis Braille, teacher of the blind, inventor of Braille
1869 Tommy Corcoran, baseball player
1914 Jane Wyman, actress
1937 Dyan Cannon, actress

Deaths
1877 Cornelius Vanderbilt, entrepreneur
1960 Albert Camus, philosopher and writer, Nobel Prize laureate
1965 T. S. Eliot, writer, poet and Nobel Prize laureate
1969 Violet and Daisy Hilton, English conjoined twin actresses
1986 Christopher Isherwood, writer

DAY TO REMEMBER

International day World Braille Day Louis Braille, blinded as a toddler, developed a system of raised dots for printing to enable the blind or visually impaired to read.

The world of "RuneScape"

"RuneScape" is a web-based, online, role-playing game, set in a medieval fantasy world and played by some two million people internationally. Updated regularly with new storylines, quests and maps, players take on quests and go into combat, killing monsters and fighting other oponents to gain wealth.

With its own jargon and commodities such as armor, "RuneScape" players develop a strong sense of community. The passionate involvement of players has led Jagex, the commercial operation behind "RuneScape," to provide information on epilepsy, repetitive strain injury, and protecting privacy. The Jagex website also reminds players to keep the game in perspective, given both the potential for fanatical involvement and the deep sense of frustration and loss that can be experienced if the game is not going well.

Andrew Gower first created the game in 1998, with a different name, "DeviousMUD." Three versions later, under the name "RuneScape," the game was so popular that an additional service was launched, giving players the opportunity to buy special access to updates. The game was still free to play, but paying members had a wider choice of play options. In the first week after launch, over 5,000 people subscribed, making "RuneScape" instantly one of the largest pay-to-play Java games in the world. At peak times now, some 150,000 players are online across 120 international servers.

January 5

"Radio has no future. Heavier-than-air flying machines are impossible. X-rays will prove to be a hoax." — WILLIAM THOMSON, PHYSICIST

Births
- 1855 King Camp Gillette, inventor
- 1900 Yves Tanguy, painter
- 1910 Jack Lovelock, athlete
- 1931 Robert Duvall, actor and director
- 1932 Umberto Eco, philologist and writer
- 1946 Diane Keaton, actress

Deaths
- 1933 Calvin Coolidge, thirteenth U.S. President
- 1941 Amy Johnson, aviator
- 1943 George Washington Carver, educator, activist, and botanist
- 1998 Sonny Bono, singer, actor, and U.S. Congressman

HISTORICAL EVENTS
- **1896** An Austrian newspaper reports that German physicist Wilhelm Roentgen has discovered a new type of radiation called X-rays, using the mathematical designation for something unknown.
- **1914** Ford Motor Company announces an eight-hour workday and a minimum wage of five U.S. dollars for a day's labor.
- **1919** The Free Committee for a German Workers Peace is founded, which will become the Nazi party.
- **1948** Warner Brothers shows the first color newsreel, screening the Tournament of Roses Parade and the Rose Bowl.
- **1961** Mr Ed, a "talking" horse, makes his debut on U.S. television for what will become a six-year run.
- **1964** Pope Paul VI meets the Greek patriarch Athenagoras I in Jerusalem, the first meeting of Catholic and Orthodox Christianity leaders since 1439.
- **1972** U.S. President Richard Nixon orders the development of a space shuttle program.
- **1993** During hurricane-force winds, the oil tanker MV *Braer* runs aground on the coast of the Shetland Islands north of Scotland, spilling 84,700 tons of oil.
- **1993** Washington State executes Westley Allan Dodd by hanging; it is the first legal hanging in the U.S. since 1965 (see below).

DAYS TO REMEMBER

Religious day Birthday of Guru Gobind Singh (Sikhism) Guru Gobind Singh, the tenth Sikh Guru, formed the order of the Khalsa on Vaisakhi (Baisakhi). Significant dates in the lives of the Gurus are referred to as Gurpurbs, and are marked with an akhand path, an unbroken reading of the Guru Granth Sahib.

Religious day St. John Neumann's day Born in Prachatitz, Bohemia, John Nepomucene Neumann (1811–1860) completed theological studies in Prague before traveling to the U.S. in 1836. There he established a number of educational academies and hospitals, and was canonized in 1977 by Pope Paul VI. He was the first American male saint.

Dodd is hanged

Westley Allan Dodd, from Seattle, Washington, in the U.S., began sexually abusing young children when he was 13 years of age, starting with his young cousins. His victims – over 50 in all – were children below the age of 12, some of whom were as young as two years old. Dodd became increasingly perverse, at one point writing about his desire to eat the genitals of his victim. When he was arrested, the police found with him a homemade, as yet unused, torture rack. Dodd was sentenced to death for molesting and then stabbing the Neer brothers Cole, aged 11, and William, aged 10, in a Washington park in 1989, and for the rape and murder of Lee Iseli, aged four years. He wanted to be punished to the full extent of the law, saying, "I must be executed before I have an opportunity to escape or kill someone within the prison. If I do escape, I promise you I will kill and rape and enjoy every minute of it." Dodd himself chose hanging as the method of his execution "because that's the way Lee Iseli died." The last hanging in Washington had been in January 1963, when Joseph Chester Self was hanged for murder. The U.S. Supreme Court invalidated death penalty laws in 1972 but Washington voters chose to reinvoke the penalty in 1975. Dodd still had to prevail over protests by the anti-capital-punishment lobby to be allowed to die.

January 6

Fat, sponge, and unsterilized silicone have been used at least since 1865 to increase the size of women's breasts, but the modern era of implants was ushered in when plastic surgeons working with the Dow Corning Corporation implanted a silicone breast prosthesis in 1962. Thirty years later, the U.S. Government suspended the general use of breast implants following thousands of reports of serious side effects from leaking silicone, including tissue disease, immunological and neurological disorders and infection, as well as rupture, deflation, scarring, and hardening of the implants. Elsewhere in the world, silicone implants are still widely available.

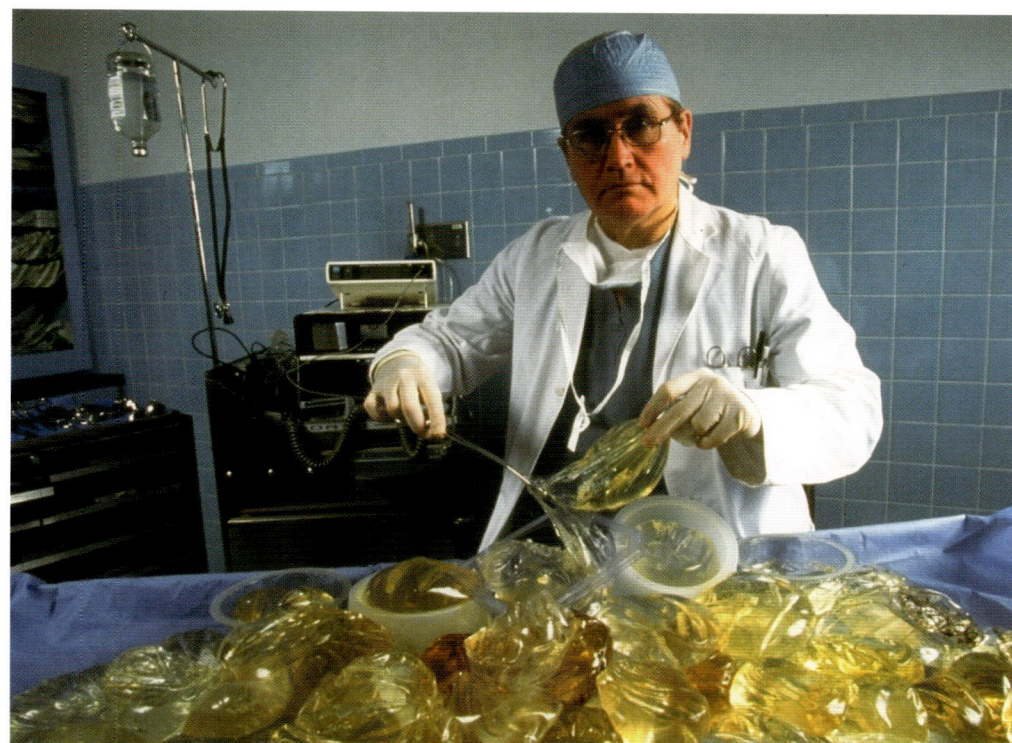

HISTORICAL EVENTS

- 1838 Samuel Morse first successfully tests the electrical telegraph.
- 1907 Maria Montessori, an Italian educator, scientist, doctor, philosopher, feminist, and humanitarian, opens her first school and daycare center for working-class children in Rome.
- 1942 Pan American Airlines, the major U.S. airline from the 1930s, becomes the first commercial airline to have a flight around the world.
- 1950 The U.K. recognizes the rule of the Communist People's Republic of China. The Republic of China retaliates by severing diplomatic relations with Britain.
- 1974 In response to an energy crisis, daylight saving time starts nearly four months early in the U.S., forcing many children to commute to school before sunrise.
- 1992 The U.S. Government recommends doctors suspend the use of silicone breast implants, except in specific, medically justified circumstances (see above).
- 1994 American figure skater Nancy Kerrigan is bashed on the right leg by an assailant under orders from associates of rival Tonya Harding.

DAYS TO REMEMBER

Religious day The Epiphany The twelfth day of Christmas is recognised as the day of the visit of the wise men, or magi, to the baby Jesus.

Religious day Three Kings Day In Latin America, Puerto Rico, the Caribbean, and Spain, children leave hay by their bedsides the night before as a treat for the Three Kings' beasts of burden and await the next morning's presents.

Religious day Christmas Many Eastern Orthodox and Armenian churches still use the Julian calendar, and celebrate Christmas 13 days after Western churches.

Births

- 1706 Benjamin Franklin, statesman
- 1883 Khalil Gibran, writer and painter
- 1910 Loretta Young, actress
- 1914 Danny Thomas, singer, actor, and comedian
- 1920 Sun Myung Moon, evangelist
- 1920 John Maynard Smith, biologist
- 1931 Capucine, actress
- 1944 Bonnie Franklin, actress
- 1954 Anthony Minghella, director
- 1955 Rowan Atkinson, comedian and actor
- 1960 Nigella Lawson, chef and writer

Deaths

- 1852 Louis Braille, teacher of the blind and inventor of Braille
- 1884 Gregor Johann Mendel, geneticist
- 1919 Theodore Roosevelt, twenty-sixth U.S. President
- 1992 Dizzy Gillespie, jazz trumpeter
- 1993 Rudolf Nureyev, ballet dancer
- 2006 Lou Rawls, singer

January 7

"When one door closes another door opens; but we often look so long and so regretfully upon the closed door, that we do not see the ones which open for us." — ALEXANDER GRAHAM BELL

Births
- **1925** Gerald Durrell, naturalist, zookeeper, author and television presenter
- **1948** Kenny Loggins, singer
- **1956** David Caruso, actor
- **1964** Nicolas Cage, actor

Deaths
- **1920** Edmund Barton, first Prime Minister of Australia
- **1988** Trevor Howard, actor
- **1989** Hirohito, Emperor of Japan

HISTORICAL EVENTS

- **1610** Galileo Galilei observes the four largest moons of Jupiter for the first time.
- **1894** Scottish inventor William Kennedy Laurie Dickson receives a patent for motion picture film – a strip of images on a wheel passed in front of an illuminated lens.
- **1904** Marconi International Marine Communication Company introduces a distress signal CQD, building on the general call code CQ; two years later it is replaced by SOS.
- **1927** The first commercial transatlantic telephone call is made from New York city to London, 90 years after Alexander Graham Bell patented his electro-dynamic transmitter/receiver telephone.
- **1953** President Harry Truman announces the U.S. has developed a hydrogen bomb that is a thousand times more powerful than the existing atomic bomb.
- **1980** In a landslide election, the people of India vote Indira Gandhi back into power less than three years after rejecting her. Gandhi had previously ruled India for 11 years.
- **1990** The Leaning Tower of Pisa is closed to the public for the first time in 800 years amid safety fears (see right).
- **1999** The impeachment trial of U.S. President Bill Clinton begins; the charges of perjury and obstruction of justice arise from his relationship with White House intern Monica Lewinsky.

DAYS TO REMEMBER

Religious day Christmas (Ethiopia) Traditionally, young men played a game similar to hockey, called genna, on this day, and now Christmas has also come to be known by that name.

Religious day St. Raymond of Peñafort's Day As a philosophy teacher and lawyer, St. Raymond (1175–1275) joined the Dominicans in 1218. Summoned to Rome in 1230, he was canonized in 1601 by Pope Clement VIII. St. Raymond is the patron saint of lawyers, canonists, and medical-record librarians.

In 1990, engineers anticipated that the closure of the Leaning Tower of Pisa for stabilization efforts would last just a few years. A complex project involving giant steel braces and massive excavation work was designed to take the tower fractionally more upright, and extend its life by a couple more centuries. When work began, the tower leaned more than 13 feet (3 m), the result of its construction with a shallow foundation in unstable subsoil. More than a decade later, the lean was corrected by just over a foot (40 cm). The tower was finally reopened on December 15, 2001.

January 8

DATEline

"I don't know anything about music. In my line you don't have to." — ELVIS PRESLEY

HISTORICAL EVENTS

1889 Herman Hollerith receives a patent for his electric tabulating machine, developed to process data for the 1890 U.S. Census. The 1880 census had taken seven years to tabulate.

1926 Abdul-Aziz ibn Saud becomes the King of Hejaz and renames it Saudi Arabia.

1935 Professor Arthur C. Hardy patents the first spectrophotometer, which he calls a "photometric apparatus." His invention is capable of detecting and recording two million different shades of color.

1958 Fourteen-year-old Bobby Fischer wins the U.S. Chess Championship.

1961 The French people vote to grant Algeria its independence.

1964 President Lyndon B. Johnson declares a war on poverty in the U.S., "to pursue victory over the most ancient of mankind's enemies."

1992 While on a state visit to Japan, U.S. President George H.W. Bush becomes ill and is shown on television vomiting into the lap of the Prime Minister of Japan, Kiichi Miyazawa, during a state dinner.

1994 Russian cosmonaut Valeri Polyakov on *Soyuz TM-18* leaves for Mir. He will stay on the space station until March 22, 1995, for a record 437 days in space.

2001 The High Court in the U.K. rules that the assumed identities and whereabouts of the two boys who murdered toddler James Bulger in 1993 will be kept secret for the rest of their lives (see below).

2006 An earthquake measuring 6.9 on the Richter scale, epicentered just off the Greek island of Kythira, hits much of the country and is felt throughout the entire eastern Mediterranean Sea.

Births
- 1583 Simon Episcopius, theologian
- 1924 Ron Moody, actor
- 1935 Elvis Presley, singer
- 1937 Shirley Bassey, singer
- 1942 Stephen Hawking, physicist and author
- 1947 David Bowie, musician
- 1949 Wolfgang Puck, chef

Deaths
- 1642 Galileo Galilei, astronomer and physicist
- 1941 Lord Robert Baden-Powell, soldier, writer, and founder of Scouting
- 1989 Bruce Chatwin, novelist
- 1990 Terry-Thomas, actor, comedian
- 1996 François Mitterrand, President of France
- 1997 Melvin Calvin, American chemist, Nobel Prize laureate

The Bulger abduction

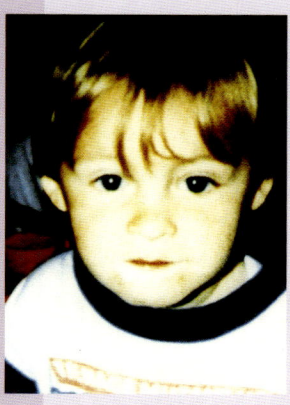

Robert Thompson and Jon Venables were 10 years old when they abducted two-year-old James Bulger from a Liverpool shopping center in the U.K. and battered him to death on a railway in February 1993. They were convicted of murder in November that year and sent to separate secure units.

On January 8, 2001, the High Court ruled that new identities should be given to the boys on their release from prison and their anonymity was to be protected by injunctions forbidding publication of their assumed names, whereabouts, photographs, and descriptions of their appearances. Noting the continuing public outrage at James' death and the serious desire for revenge being expressed by some members of the community, the president of the High Court Family Division, Dame Elizabeth Butler-Sloss, said she made the decision in order to protect the lives of Thompson and Venables. "If any section of the media decided to give information leading to the identification of either young man, such publication would put his life at risk. In the exceptional circumstances of this case, and applying English domestic law and the right of life enshrined in Article 2 of the European Convention, I have come to the conclusion that I am compelled to take steps in the almost unique circumstances of this case to protect their lives and physical well-being."

On January 1, 2006, the British media reported that Robert Thompson, now aged 23, was a father. Reports stated that he was living in the north of England, using a pseudonym, and that the mother of his child had no idea of his real identity.

January 9

> *"All men are frauds. The only difference between them is that some admit it. I myself deny it."* — H. L. MENCKEN

HISTORICAL EVENTS

- **1349** The Jewish population of Basel, Switzerland, believed by the town residents to be the cause the ongoing bubonic plague, is rounded up and incinerated on an island.
- **1431** Judges' investigations for the trial of Joan of Arc begin in Rouen, France, which was then under English-occupation government.
- **1768** Philip Astley stages the first modern circus in London, conducting shows of acrobatic riding; he uses a circular arena for better audience vantage and so riders can utilize centrifugal force for balance.
- **1839** The French Academy of Sciences announces the daguerreotype photography process (named after inventor Louis J. M. Daguerre). It exposes an image directly onto a mirror-polished surface of silver.
- **1894** New England Telephone and Telegraph installs the first battery-operated telephone switchboard in Lexington, Massachusetts.
- **1901** Frank Hornby, a clerk form Liverpool, U.K., submits an application for his invention Mechanics Made Easy, soon to be called Meccano.
- **1964** Conflict erupts over the right to fly the Panamanian flag alongside the U.S. flag in the Panama Canal Zone. Some 22 Panamanians and four U.S. citizens die. The day is commemorated as Martyrs' Day.
- **1986** After losing a patent battle with Polaroid, Kodak leaves the instant camera business.
- **2002** The U.S. Department of Justice announces it will pursue a criminal investigation of Enron (see right).

DAYS TO REMEMBER

Religious day Feast of the Black Nazarene
In Manila, Philippines, a statue of Christ known as the Black Nazarene is carried through town. Thousands come from all over the country, mostly barefoot as a sign of humility, to touch the statue. It was brought to Manila from Mexico in 1606, and has been housed at St. John the Baptist Church in Quiapo since 1787.

Religious day St. Theophan's Day
Also known as Theophan Zatvornik, St. Theophan the Recluse (1815–1894), was ordained in 1841. He played an important role in translating the Philokalia, a classic of Orthodox spirituality, into Russian. From 1872 until his death, he discontinued all contact with people except for the chief priest and his confessor, though he received as many as 40 letters a day, all of which he answered.

Births
- **1898** Gracie Fields, vaudeville performer
- **1908** Simone de Beauvoir, author
- **1913** Richard Nixon, thirty-seventh U.S. President
- **1935** Bob Denver, actor
- **1941** Joan Baez, singer and activist
- **1942** Susannah York, actress
- **1956** Imelda Staunton, actress
- **1958** Mehmet Ali Ağca, attempted assassin of Pope John Paul II
- **1965** Joely Richardson, actress

Deaths
- **1995** Peter Cook, actor, satirist, writer, and comedian

Enron fraud

Prior to its bankruptcy in 2001, Enron Corporation, based in Houston, Texas, was a major distributor of electricity and gas throughout the U.S. and a supplier of power plants, pipelines and other energy infrastructure to the world. Enron was also a significant player in communications and emerging technologies, developing an innovative web-based transaction system that allowed consumers to buy, sell, and trade Enron commodity products globally. The company employed around 21,000 people and claimed revenues of U.S. $101 billion in 2000. *Fortune* magazine named it America's Most Innovative Company for six consecutive years.

Enron's global reputation was, however, dogged by rumors of unethical practices in developing countries and corrupt accounting procedures. In 2001, a series of scandals revealed that Enron was guilty of institutionalized and systematic accounting fraud, and that massive losses suffered by the company had not been reported.

Enron shares – blue-chip stock trading at U.S. $90 – dropped to U.S. 30 cents. Its European operations filed for bankruptcy on November 30, 2001, and the company sought Chapter 11 protection in the U.S. two days later. (Under Chapter 11 of the U.S. Bankruptcy Code, a court can grant complete or partial relief from most of the company's debts and its contracts.) Thousands of Enron employees were left without jobs or their life savings, and investors suffered billions of dollars in losses. On January 9, 2002, the U.S. Department of Justice announced it would pursue a criminal investigation of Enron, and Congressional hearings began on January 24. Lawsuits were also brought against Enron's accountancy firm, Arthur Andersen, for obstruction of justice during investigations.

Enron is still in operation, managing a portfolio of assets and liquidating some remaining businesses.

January 10

DATEline

"My only international rival is Tintin. We are both little people who are not afraid of big ones."

CHARLES DE GAULLE

HISTORICAL EVENTS

- **1832** Thomas Hodgkin presents a paper to the London Medical and Surgical Society entitled "Some Morbid Appearances of the Absorbent Glands and Spleen" documenting a rare lymphatic condition now known as Hodgkin's disease.
- **1863** The first section of the London Underground Railway, the world's first underground passenger railway, opens.
- **1901** In Beaumont, Texas, the Lucas Gusher at Spindletop oil field becomes the first major oil find in the U.S., spilling out 100,000 barrels of oil a day.
- **1927** The futuristic film *Metropolis* by Fritz Lang premiers; it is the most expensive silent film to date, costing approximately 7 million German Marks (equivalent to around U.S. $200 million today).
- **1929** Tintin, a comic book character created by Belgian writer and artist Georges Remi, makes his debut (see below).
- **1946** The first General Assembly of the United Nations opens in London. Fifty-one nations are represented.
- **1969** After 147 years, the last issue of the U.S. magazine, *Saturday Evening Post*, is published.
- **2000** America Online announces an agreement to buy Time Warner for U.S. $162 billion. It is the largest corporate merger in history.

Births
- 1869 Grigori Rasputin, monk
- 1883 Aleksei Nikolaevich Tolstoi, writer
- 1904 Ray Bolger, actor, singer, and dancer
- 1927 Johnnie Ray, singer
- 1944 Frank Sinatra Jr., singer
- 1945 Rod Stewart, singer
- 1949 George Foreman, boxer
- 1949 Linda Lovelace, actress
- 1953 Pat Benatar, singer

Deaths
- 1862 Samuel Colt, inventor
- 1917 Buffalo Bill, American frontiersman and showman
- 1971 Gabrielle "Coco" Chanel, fashion designer
- 1981 Richard Boone, actor

DAYS TO REMEMBER

Religious day Eid al-Adha (Feast of Sacrifice) An important feast of the Muslim calendar, Eid al-Adha concludes the pilgrimage to Mecca. It lasts for three days and commemorates Ibrahim's (Abraham's) willingness to obey God by sacrificing his son.

Religious day Maria Dolores Rodríguez Sopeña's Day Eye surgery at age eight left Spanish-born Maria (1848–1918) with limited sight. At age 17 she began working with the sick and poor. In 1885 she opened a welfare center for former prisoners, eventually expanding her work into a number of poor and crowded Madrid neighborhoods and then throughout Spain.

The Adventures of Tintin, written and illustrated by Georges Remi (pen name Hergé) from 1929 until his death in 1983, was one of the most popular comic strips of the twentieth century. The series portrayed the travels of a young reporter, Tintin, with his dog Snowy, friend Captain Haddock, and other supporting characters. While the early works were characterized by right-wing sentiment and racial stereotyping, a marked shift took place when Hergé met Zhang Chongren (right), a Chinese art student who helped him sensitively depict China under invasion from the Japanese and convinced him of the importance of thorough research. They met again 46 years later, by which time some 200 million copies had been sold, with translations into more than 50 languages.

January 11

"Smoking is one of the leading causes of statistics." — FLETCHER KNEBEL, WRITER

Births
- 1930 Rod Taylor, actor
- 1960 Stanley Tucci, actor
- 1962 Susan Lindauer, peace activist and accused spy
- 1966 Kelley Law, curler
- 1972 Amanda Peet, actress

Deaths
- 1928 Thomas Hardy, writer

HISTORICAL EVENTS

- **1908** A prominent young lawyer, Mohandas (Mahatma) Gandhi, is jailed in Johannesburg, South Africa, for refusing to register as an Asian (see left).
- **1922** Frederick Banting and Charles Best first use insulin to treat diabetes in a human patient.
- **1935** Amelia Earhart is the first woman to fly solo from Hawaii to California.
- **1962** An avalanche of rocks and ice on the extinct Huascaran volcano in Peru results in an estimated 4,000 deaths. In 1970, another massive landslide kills some 20,000 people.
- **1964** U.S. Surgeon General Luther Leonidas Terry reports officially for the first time that smoking may be hazardous to health.
- **1974** The Rosenkowitz sextuplets are born in Cape Town, South Africa, and become the first known set of sextuplets to survive their infancy. They are three boys and three girls.
- **1992** Paul Simon is the first major recordng artist to tour South Africa after the end of the Apartheid era's cultural boycott.
- **1993** For its "dirty tricks" campaign against Virgin Atlantic, British Airways agrees to pay damages of £500,000 to owner Richard Branson, £110,000 to his airline and legal costs of up to £3 million.
- **1994** The Irish Government announces the end of a 15-year broadcasting ban on the IRA and its political arm, Sinn Fein.
- **2005** Black Tuesday bushfires sweep across the southern Eyre Peninsula in South Australia, killing nine people.

DAYS TO REMEMBER

Traditional day Burning of the Clavie In Burghead, Scotland, a traditional ritual to celebrate hogmany – New Year's Eve – is the Burning of the Clavie. Celebrated on January 11 in honor of the pre-Gregorian calendar, a half-barrel known as a Clavie is filled with tar-soaked wood shavings, lit with a piece of burning peat from a local household fire and carried around the streets by the elected Clavie King.

Religious day St. Godfrey of Cappenberg's Day Descendant of Charlemagne and a wealthy count in Westphalia Germany, St. Godfrey (1097–1127) was brought to an active faith by his friend St. Norbert. He turned his castle, his lands, and wealth over to Norbert for use by the Church. Godfrey also built several hospitals. He was studying for the priesthood when he died.

National day Unity Day (Nepal) Focusing on family values and a spirit of community, Unity Day is a celebration of togetherness and peace for people of all cultures.

Working as a young lawyer in South Africa, Mohandas Gandhi became active in opposing institutionalized racial intolerance and educating fellow Indians on their civil rights. In 1906, when the Government imposed compulsory fingerprint registration, Gandhi campaigned for the adoption of Satyagraha, a philosophy of non-violent resistance. Thousands of Indians were jailed or killed for refusing to register or burning their registration cards. On January 11, 1908, Gandhi was jailed for the first time, given a sentence of two months' imprisonment. Public outcry over government brutality in the face of peaceful Indian protest finally forced a compromise with Gandhi, under which Indians would register voluntarily and the highly restrictive Black Act would be repealed. Gandhi became known as Mahatma for "great soul."

DATE*line*

January 12

HISTORICAL EVENTS

1592 *Titus Andronicus*, possibly Shakespeare's earliest tragedy, is first staged at the polygonal Rose Theatre.
1915 The U.S. House of Representatives rejects a proposal to give women the vote.
1945 The Soviets begin a large offensive in Eastern Europe against the Nazis.
1963 Twenty-four days into Zanzibar's independence from the U.K. as a constitutional monarchy, its sultan is overthrown; three months later Zanzibar merges with the mainland state of Tanganyika to form Tanzania.
1965 Scientists conduct what they called a "controlled excursion," burning up a nuclear rocket in Nevada, producing a radioactive cloud over Los Angeles.
1967 James Bedford, a psychology professor, becomes the first person to be cryonically preserved with intent of future resuscitation.
1969 British hard-rock band Led Zeppelin release their first album.
1991 An act of the U.S. Congress authorizes military force to drive Iraq out of Kuwait.
1998 Nineteen European nations agree to forbid human cloning in response to the announcement by Richard Seed that he intends to clone humans using techniques that created Dolly the sheep.
2006 Mehmet Ali Ağca, would-be assassin of Pope John Paul II, is released from Turkish prison and put back in a few days later (see below).
2006 During a Muslim ritual, 362 people are crushed near Mecca in Saudi Arabia.

DAY TO REMEMBER

Religious day St. Sava's Day The son of the Serbian leader Stefan Nemanja, St. Sava (1169–1235) ran off to join a monastery on the holy Mount Athos. His father, on retirement, joined him, and the two devout believers founded the Serbian Monastery Hilandar, which became the fount of Serbian Orthodoxy and Serbian education.

Births
1893 Hermann Göring, Nazi official
1893 Alfred Rosenberg, Nazi official
1896 Rex Ingram, Irish director and actor
1899 Paul Hermann Müller, chemist
1905 Tex Ritter, actor and singer
1916 Pieter Willem Botha, President of South Africa
1917 Maharishi Mahesh Yogi, founder of the Transcendental Meditation movement
1926 Ray Price, singer
1944 Joe Frazier, boxer
1951 Kirstie Alley, actress
1954 Howard Stern, radio host
1960 Oliver Platt, actor
1974 Melanie Chisholm, singer

Deaths
1960 Nevil Shute, writer
1976 Agatha Christie, writer
2003 Maurice Gibb, singer, songwriter, and musician

Assassination attempt a prophecy?

In 1979, Mehmet Ali Ağca, a member of the Turkish Grey Wolves fascist movement, was sentenced to life in prison (36 years under Turkish law) for the murder of newspaper editor-in-chief Abdi Ipekçi. He served less than six months before he escaped, resurfacing in 1981 in Rome where he shot at, and critically wounded, Pope John Paul II in St. Peter's Square. The pontiff underwent emergency surgery for serious wounds to the abdomen and hand.

Ağca's motives have been the subject of conjecture, from Cold War plots involving Russia and Bulgaria to claims that the incident was predicted by the Madonna. Ağca says the shooting was the fulfilment of a prophecy the Virgin Mary told children at Fatima, Portugal, in 1917.

The relationship between victim and attacker furthered the mystery surrounding the shooting. Pope John Paul II asked people to "pray for my brother [Ağca], whom I have sincerely forgiven." He met Ağca and spoke privately with him at the Italian prison where Ağca was being held. Their conversation has never been revealed. Over the years, the Pope also kept in touch with Ağca's family.

Ağca was pardoned after 19 years' imprisonment in Italy, but was extradited to Turkey to carry out the rest of his Turkish life sentence. On January 12, 2006, he was released on parole. He enjoyed a few days of freedom before being detained again to finish serving his life sentence.

January 13

"Nothing is particularly hard, as long as you divide it into small jobs." — HENRY FORD

HISTORICAL EVENTS

- 1854 The accordion is patented by Anthony Faas.
- 1915 An earthquake in Avezzano, Italy kills 29,800 people.
- 1930 The *Mickey Mouse* comic strip makes its first appearance.
- 1938 The Church of England accepts the theory of evolution.
- 1942 Henry Ford patents the Soybean Car, which is 30 percent lighter than a regular car. The car uses soybean fiber in plastic panels attached to a steel frame.
- 1957 The Wham-O Company develops the first plastic Frisbee.
- 1992 Japan apologizes for forcing Korean women into sexual slavery during World War II (see below.)
- 1993 American, British, and French fighter jets carry out a series of bombing raids over southern Iraq as punishment for Iraqi breaches of the "no-fly zone" set up after the Gulf War.
- 2001 An earthquake hits El Salvador, killing more than 800 people.

DAYS TO REMEMBER

Religious day Lohri According to the Hindu calendar, the bonfire festival of Lohri falls in mid-January. In the morning children go from door to door singing and asking for Lohri "loot" in the form of money and sweets. In the evening, huge bonfires are lit and people gather to sing, exchange gifts, and distribute *prasad* (offerings made to God).

Religious day St. Knut's Day In Scandinavian countries, King Knut, or Canute IV of Denmark, who ruled Denmark from 1080–1086, is honored for his virtue and generosity. He declared that Christmas should be celebrated for 20 days, officially ending the season on January 13. The sweets that decorate the Christmas tree are eaten and the trees are taken down.

Births
- 1884 Sophie Tucker, singer, comedienne, and vaudeville performer
- 1919 Robert Stack, actor
- 1931 Charles Nelson Reilly, actor
- 1934 Rip Taylor, actor
- 1961 Julia Louis-Dreyfus, actress
- 1964 Penelope Ann Miller, actress
- 1966 Patrick Dempsey, actor
- 1969 Stephen Hendry, snooker player
- 1977 Orlando Bloom, actor

Deaths
- 1691 George Fox, founder of the Quakers
- 1929 Wyatt Earp, Western lawman
- 1941 James Joyce, writer
- 2002 Ted Demme, film and television director

Japan's "comfort women"

During World War II, up to 200,000 "comfort women," some as young as 11 years old, were forced to deliver sexual services to Japanese soldiers. The majority, such as Moon Pil-Ki (right), came from Korea, which was occupied by the Japanese military. Others were from the Philippines, Thailand, Vietnam, Singapore, China, Taiwan, Dutch East Indies, and other Japanese-occupied regions. Japanese authorities believed that by providing sex on demand, the soldiers' morale, and thereby effectiveness, would be improved.

Many comfort women were tricked or defrauded, while others were kidnapped. "I was playing jump-rope in front of my house when an automobile pulled over. I had never seen a car before in my village. When the driver offered me a ride, I, curious and naive, climbed in with my friend," said Kim Yoon Shim, about her abduction at the age of 13.

In the late 1980s the story of the comfort women began to emerge. In 1991, a South Korean woman, Grandma Kim Hak Soon, became the first person to speak publicly about the existence of comfort women. Other survivors came forward, and the international community became aware of the wartime practices. Documents retrieved by history professor Yoshimi Yoshiaki forced the Japanese Government to admit involvement of the state in the operation of the comfort stations. Prime Minister Miyazawa Kiichi expressed his regret and apologies during his state visit to South Korea in January 1992. The issue of legal responsibility and compensation is still unresolved.

January 14

"Weaseling out of things is important to learn. It's what separates us from the animals ... except the weasel." — HOMER SIMPSON

HISTORICAL EVENTS

1794 Elizabeth Hog Bennett becomes the first woman in the U.S. to successfully give birth to a child by Caesarean section. Her husband, a doctor, performed the operation, without anesthetic.

1907 An earthquake in Kingston, Jamaica, kills more than 800 people and destroys 75 percent of its buildings.

1914 Henry Ford announces the newest advance in assembly line production, a continuous-motion method that reduces assembly time from 12½ hours to 93 minutes.

1943 Franklin D. Roosevelt becomes the first President of the U.S. to travel via airplane while in office, flying from Miami, Florida, to Morocco to meet with British Prime Minister Winston Churchill to discuss World War II.

1954 Marilyn Monroe marries baseball legend Joe DiMaggio. The marriage lasts nine months. After her death, DiMaggio has red roses delivered to her crypt twice a week.

1975 Teenage heiress Lesley Whittle is kidnapped from the bedroom of her home in Shropshire, England, by triple murderer Donald Neilson, nicknamed the Black Panther. He kills her.

1990 *The Simpsons* first airs on television.

1994 U.S. President Bill Clinton and Russian President Boris Yeltsin sign the Kremlin Accords, treaties aimed at stopping the preprogrammed aiming of nuclear missiles.

2002 The U.K. foot-and-mouth crisis is declared officially finished (see right).

On January 14, 2002, the U.K. was declared free of the foot-and-mouth disease that had plagued its agricultural communities for over 11 months. From the time the first signs of the disease were discovered on 19 February, 2001, at an abattoir in Essex, over six million animals were slaughtered. With less than adequate supplies of vaccine, and a slow response to the initial report of outbreak, the disease spread rapidly. Farming industries were devastated, as was tourism, with the closure of many rural sites and hiking paths to prevent the virus being transmitted by shoes and car tyres. The cost to the U.K. was estimated at £8 billion.

Births		Deaths	
1684	Jean-Baptiste van Loo, painter	1898	Lewis Carroll, writer and mathematician
1875	Albert Schweitzer, physician, missionary, and musician	1957	Humphrey Bogart, actor
1892	Hal Roach, film producer	1965	Jeanette MacDonald, actress and singer
1905	Cecil Beaton, photographer	1977	Peter Finch, actor
1925	Yukio Mishima, writer	1977	Anaïs Nin, author
1938	Jack Jones, singer and actor	1986	Donna Reed, actress
1941	Faye Dunaway, actress	2004	Ron O'Neal, actor
1949	Lawrence Kasdan, director and screenwriter	2006	Shelly Winters, actress
1967	Emily Watson, actress		

DAYS TO REMEMBER

Traditional day Pongal An Indian festival giving thanks for the harvest of the crops, *Pongal* in Tamil literally means "boiling over." Pongal is historically a secular festival independent of religion. It is celebrated by all people in the South Indian state of Tamil Nadu. While Pongal is predominantly a Tamil festival, the same period also marks similar festivals celebrated in several other places under different names.

Traditional day New Year In the Eastern Orthodox Church, the new year is on January 14. In countries where Eastern Orthodoxy predominates, the Gregorian day is celebrated as a civic holiday and the Julian date as a religious holiday.

Religious day St. Felix of Nola's Day As a Christian priest, in 250 C.E., St. Felix was chained in a dungeon and tortured, but an angel appeared and led him out to freedom. He resumed his denunciation of pagan gods, and was again arrested and tortured. He hid in a recess between two adjacent walls, and eventually died there in peace. He is the patron saint of eye trouble.

January 15

"A man can't ride your back unless it is bent." — MARTIN LUTHER KING, JR.

Between 1974 and 1984, the television show *Happy Days* portrayed the relationship dynamics, disasters, and joys of the Cunningham family, a middle-class, midwestern American family in the 1950s. A generation of teenage viewers whose cultural life was characterized by shoulder-length hair, women's liberation, and open sexuality identified with the inner turmoil and outer conflicts negotiated by *Happy Days* characters in their idealized, conservative environment. With highly successful spin-off shows including *Mork & Mindy* and *Laverne & Shirley*, *Happy Days* aired for 11 seasons, becoming one of the longest-running primetime programs in television history.

Births
- 1622 Molière, playwright
- 1842 Josef Breuer, psychologist
- 1906 Aristotle Onassis, businessman
- 1913 Lloyd Bridges, actor
- 1926 Maria Schell, actress
- 1929 Martin Luther King, Jr., American civil rights leader
- 1957 Julian Sands, actor

Deaths
- 1955 Yves Tanguy, painter
- 2005 Walter Ernsting, author
- 2005 Dan Lee, animator

HISTORICAL EVENTS

1797 The first top hat is worn in London. Haberdasher James Hetherington is fined £50 for wearing it and causing a breach of the peace.

1846 Angélique Cottin, 14 years old, of La Perriere, France, experiences a frightening phenomenon observed by many: Objects, including furniture, violently retreat at the touch of her hand or clothing. The phenomenon lasts for 10 weeks.

1885 Wilson Bentley takes the first photograph of a snowflake.

1903 The Australian government starts a system of bonus payments to sugar growers to employ white labor.

1919 In Boston, a large molasses tank bursts and a wave of molasses runs through the streets at an estimated 35 miles an hour (60 km/h), killing 21 and injuring 150.

1919 Rosa Luxemburg and Karl Liebknecht, two of the most prominent socialists in Germany, are tortured and murdered by the Freikorps.

1931 A dance marathon closes at the Playland Ballroom on Bitter Lake, north of Seattle, after 1,545 hours (70 days, or more than two months) of continuous dancing.

1951 Ilse Koch, the "Bitch of Buchenwald" – wife of the commandant of the Buchenwald concentration camp – is sentenced to life imprisonment in a court in West Germany.

1974 *Happy Days* premieres on ABC in the U.S. (see left).

1991 The UN deadline for the withdrawal of Iraqi forces from occupied Kuwait expires, preparing the way for the start of Operation Desert Storm.

2001 The multilingual, free-content website Wikipedia goes public. Written collaboratively by volunteers, it now has over a million registered contributors.

DAYS TO REMEMBER

Religious day Pilgrimage of Cristo Negro de Esquipúlas (Guatemala) In the seventeenth century, Esquipúlas, the leader of a Mayan village in the southwest of Guatemala, surrendered to the invading Spaniards rather than have his people suffer brutality. In return, the Spaniards named the town after him, and had a large figure of Christ carved out of a dark wood as a gift to the town. The figure became renowned for miraculous healing powers and developed a cult following.

Religious day St. Ita of Killeedy's Day Born Deirdre of Irish nobility, St. Ita (475–570) founded a popular convent in County Limerick, which came to be known as Killeedy, or "Ita's cell", and a school for boys in Killeedy. St. Ita also founded a school for small boys; among her pupils were a number of future saints including Cummian of Clonfert, and Brendan of Clonfert.

DATEline

January 16

"If I knew I was going to live this long, I'd have taken better care of myself." — MICKEY MANTLE

HISTORICAL EVENTS

1581 English Parliament outlaws Roman Catholicism.
1868 A patent for a refrigerator car called an "ice box on wheels" is granted to William Davis, a fish dealer in Michigan, U.S.
1945 Adolf Hitler moves into his underground bunker, the so-called Führerbunker.
1961 Mickey Mantle becomes the highest-paid baseball player of his time by signing a $75,000 contract.
1969 Czech student Jan Palach sets fire to himself as a protest against the Soviet invasion of his country in 1968. He dies three days later.
1991 The U.S. begins bombing Iraq.
1994 Canadian rock musician Bryan Adams plays before 2,500 people in Ho Chi Minh City. He is the first Western entertainer to perform in Vietnam since the end of the Vietnam War in 1975.
2001 A fuel supply tanker to the Galapagos Islands in the Pacific runs aground off the island of San Cristobal, causing severe damage to the environment.
2003 Space Shuttle *Columbia* takes off for mission STS-107; *Columbia* disintegrates sixteen days later on re-entry.
2005 Adriana Iliescu, at the age of sixty-six, becomes the oldest woman in the world to give birth (see below).

Births
1853 Andre Michelin, industrialist
1908 Ethel Merman, actress, singer
1910 Dizzy Dean, baseball player
1918 Stirling Silliphant, writer and producer
1932 Dian Fossey, zoologist
1948 John Carpenter, film director
1950 Debbie Allen, actress, dancer, and choreographer
1956 Martin Jol, Dutch football manager
1959 Sade, singer
1974 Kate Moss, model

Deaths
1942 Carole Lombard, actress
1957 Arturo Toscanini, conductor
1962 Ivan Meštrovi, sculptor
2002 Ron Taylor, actor

A mother at 66

Thought to be the oldest woman in the world to give birth, Adriana Iliescu, a retired university professor from Bucharest, Romania, became a mother for the first time at age 66. Daughter Eliza Maria, conceived from a donor egg and sperm, was delivered prematurely by Caesarean section after her twin sister died in the womb. Eliza weighed 3 pounds (1.5 kg).

The birth sparked media headlines internationally, and prompted comment from religious, political, and medical groups regarding the risks to the welfare of mother and child, and the morality of using technological resources to assist reproduction after a certain age.

Iliescu said she had always wanted to be a mother but had been unable to conceive. In 2004 she underwent in vitro fertilization and became pregnant with triplets. In the first trimester one of the three fetuses died. The remaining two, both girls, survived for 33 weeks of pregnancy. When the smaller of the two died, doctors decided to deliver the last surviving child. Iliescu was not the only new mother in her age group. In 2003, 65-year-old Satyabhama Mahapatra from Orissa, India gave birth to a boy. She had been impregnated with an egg from her 26-year-old niece that had been fertilized by her husband.

DAYS TO REMEMBER

National day Religious Freedom Day Each year, the U.S. President declares January 16 to be Religious Freedom Day. The day is the anniversary of the passage, in 1786, of the Virginia Statute of Religious Freedom. Drafted by Thomas Jefferson, this historic law provided the inspiration and the framework for the religious freedom clauses in the First Amendment to the U.S. Constitution.

Religious day First Martyrs of the Franciscan Order In 1219, St. Francis of Assisi sent friars Berard, Otto, Peter, Accursio, and Aiuto to preach the gospel to Muslims in western North Africa. They traveled from Italy to Aragon, Spain, then to Coimbra, Portugal, and began their mission with the Moors in Seville, Spain. When they began preaching in the streets and squares, they were imprisoned and then banished to Marrakesh. After continuing to denounce the teachings of the Prophet, they were put to death by the Sultan himself. They died on January 16, 1220.

January 17

"Leadership is a potent combination of strategy and character. But if you must be without one, be without the strategy." — GENERAL NORMAN SCHWARZKOPF

HISTORICAL EVENTS

1773 Captain James Cook becomes the first explorer to cross the Antarctic Circle.
1893 Queen Liliuokalani is deposed and the Kingdom of Hawaii becomes a republic.
1929 Popeye the Sailor Man, a cartoon character created by Elzie Crisler Segar, first appears in the comic strip *Thimble Theatre*.
1945 Soviet forces help liberate the almost completely destroyed Polish city of Warsaw from the Nazis during World War II.
1977 Convicted murderer Gary Gilmore is executed by a firing squad in Utah, ending a 10-year moratorium on the death penalty in the U.S.
1991 Gulf War: Operation Desert Storm begins early in the morning. Iraq fires eight Scud missiles into Israel in an unsuccessful bid to provoke Israeli retaliation.
1994 An earthquake measuring 6.6 on the Richter scale devastates the U.S. city of Los Angeles, killing more than 20 people.
1995 A magnitude 7.2 earthquake hits near Kobe, Japan, causing extensive property damage and killing over 6,000 people (see below.)
2002 Mount Nyiragongo erupts in the Democratic Republic of Congo, displacing an estimated 400,000 people.

DAYS TO REMEMBER

Religious day St. Jenaro's Day Jenaro Sánchez DelGadillo (1886–1927) was ordained a priest in 1911 in Mexico. When anti-religious laws were introduced, he celebrated Mass in private homes. He was arrested on January 17, 1927, and hanged from a mesquite tree. His corpse was then mutilated and left hanging as a warning to other worshippers.

Births
1763 John Jacob Astor, entrepreneur
1820 Anne Brontë, author
1899 Al Capone, gangster
1899 Nevil Shute, author
1922 Betty White, actress
1928 Vidal Sassoon, cosmetologist
1931 James Earl Jones, actor
1942 Muhammad Ali, boxer
1962 Jim Carrey, actor and comedian
1971 Kid Rock, singer

Deaths
395 Theodosius I, Roman Emperor
1861 Lola Montez, Irish-born adventurer
1893 Rutherford B. Hayes, nineteenth President of the U.S.
1961 Patrice Lumumba, Prime Minister of the Democratic Republic of the Congo
1991 King Olav V of Norway

The Great Hanshin Earthquake

The 7.2 magnitude Great Hanshin Earthquake of 1995 hit the Kobe area at 5:46 A.M. on Tuesday, January 17, leaving over 6,000 people dead, 30,000 injured, 300,000 homeless, and 110,000 buildings damaged. It was the worst quake to hit Japan since the Great Kanto Earthquake of 1923 which killed 143,000 people. No city block was spared, with many buildings leaning on their foundations. Many people in smaller wooden dwellings and larger high-rises were left homeless in near-freezing temperatures.

Immediately after the earthquakes in San Francisco (1989) and Los Angeles (1994), Japanese authorities claimed that Japanese construction – unlike that of the U.S. and other countries – was uniquely capable of withstanding quakes of great magnitude. The Kobe quake dramatically proved how misplaced this confidence was.

No-one predicted the Kobe earthquake. Specialists had forecast earthquakes near Shizuoka or Tokyo, but none occurred there. Authorities in the Kobe area admitted they had been caught unprepared by the earthquake.

One of the most puzzling aspects of the disaster was the reluctance of Japanese authorities to accept assistance from foreign countries. Motivated by national pride and self-sufficiency, Japanese bureaucrats resisted allowing medicines and relief personnel into the country without first subjecting them to time-consuming procedures, such as obtaining government licenses. The disaster provoked considerable discussion in Japan and abroad about lessons to be learned for managing similar catastrophes in the future.

January 18

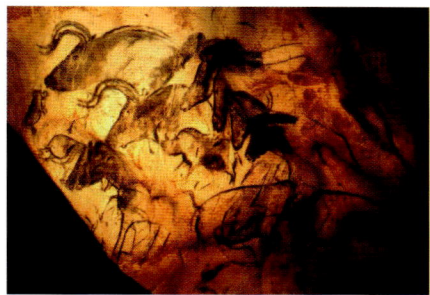

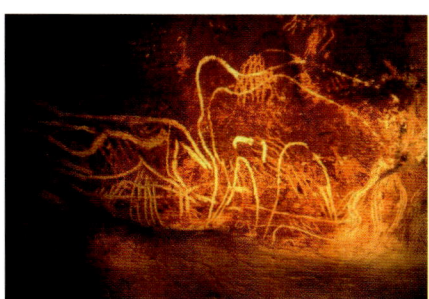

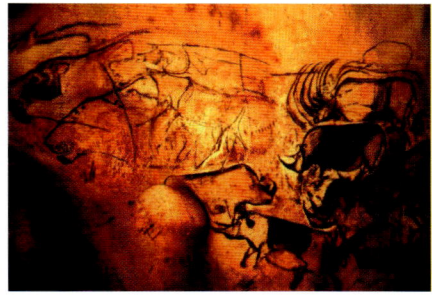

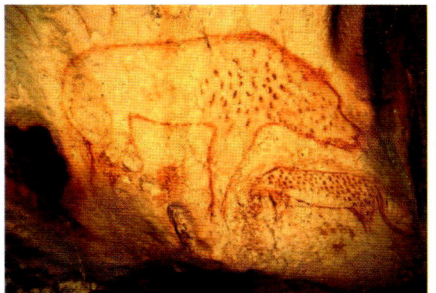

In southern France near Vallon-Pont-d'Arc, a network of caves was discovered in 1995 containing paintings and engravings between 17,000 and 20,000 years old. The entrance to the caves had been closed by a rockslide and was discovered when hikers noticed a cool breeze coming up from the rocky ground. After clearing some rubble, the hikers found a passage into a huge cavern. Inside, they found more than 300 magnificent images, including lions encountering bison, a pair of rhinoceroses clashing horns, and a herd of wild horses following long-horned aurochs, an extinct species of ox.

Births
- 1882 A. A. Milne, author
- 1892 Oliver Hardy, comedian and actor
- 1904 Cary Grant, actor
- 1913 Danny Kaye, actor
- 1934 Raymond Briggs, writer and illustrator
- 1949 Philippe Starck, designer
- 1950 Gilles Villeneuve, race car driver
- 1955 Kevin Costner, actor

Deaths
- 1936 Rudyard Kipling, writer and Nobel Prize laureate
- 1966 Kathleen Norris, writer
- 1980 Sir Cecil Beaton, fashion designer

HISTORICAL EVENTS

- **1788** The first 736 convicts transported from England to Australia land in Botany Bay, creating the first Australian penal colony.
- **1884** An 83-year-old doctor, William Price, attempts to cremate the body of his illegitimate infant son, Jesus Christ Price, setting a legal precedent for cremation in the U.K.
- **1916** A chondrite-type meteorite weighing 21½ ounces (611 g) strikes a house near the village of Baxter in Missouri, U.S.
- **1943** The first uprising of Jews against the Nazis in the Warsaw Ghetto takes place in Poland.
- **1944** The Metropolitan Opera House in New York City for the first time hosts a jazz concert. The performers are Louis Armstrong, Benny Goodman, Lionel Hampton, Artie Shaw, Roy Eldridge, and Jack Teagarden.
- **1977** Scientists identify a previously unknown bacterium as the cause of the mysterious "legionnaire's disease."
- **1977** Australia's worst rail disaster occurs at Granville, Sydney killing 83 passengers and injuring 213.
- **1995** A network of caves featuring ancient paintings and engravings is discovered near Vallon-Pont-d'Arc in southern France (see left).
- **1997** Boerge Ousland of Norway becomes the first person to cross Antarctica alone and unaided.
- **2003** In Canberra, Australia, a firestorm kills four people and destroys 491 homes.

DAY TO REMEMBER

Religious day Jaime Hilario Barbal's Day An exceptional teacher and catechist, Jaime (1898–1937) believed strongly in the value of universal education, especially for the poor. When the Spanish Civil War broke out and religious people were swept from the streets, he was confined on a prison ship, convicted of being a Christian brother, and condemned to death. Two rounds of volley fire from a firing squad did not kill him, possibly because some of soldiers intentionally shot wide; their commander then killed Jaime with five shots at close range. He was one of 97 LaSalle Brothers killed in Catalonia during the Spanish Civil War and the first to be recognized as a martyr.

January 19

HISTORICAL EVENTS

1883 The first electric lighting system employing overhead wires, built by Thomas Edison, begins service at Roselle, New Jersey.
1915 George Claude patents the neon discharge tube for use in advertising.
1915 German zeppelins bomb the cities of Great Yarmouth and King's Lynn in the U.K., killing more than 20 people in the first major aerial bombardment of a civilian target in World War I.
1945 Soviet forces liberate the ghetto of Łód . Out of 230,000 inhabitants in 1940, less than 900 survived Nazi occupation.
1966 Indira Gandhi is elected Prime Minister of India.
1977 President Gerald Ford pardons Iva Toguri D'Aquino A.K.A. "Tokyo Rose."
1981 U.S. and Iranian officials sign an agreement to release 52 American hostages after 14 months of captivity.
1983 Apple Computer, Inc. releases the Apple Lisa, the first commercial personal computer to have a graphical user interface and a computer mouse.
1988 Writer Christopher Nolan, who cannot move or speak because of an accident at birth, wins the Whitbread Book of the Year prize.
1990 Police in Johannesburg, armed with batons and dogs, break up a demonstration against rebel cricketers who are defying a ban on playing cricket in racially segregated South Africa.
2001 The American twin girls at the center of an Internet adoption scandal are seized from a hotel in north Wales and taken into care (see right).

DAYS TO REMEMBER

Religious day Canute IV's Day Canute IV (c. 1040–1086), the illegitimate son of King Sweyn III Estrithson of Denmark and nephew of King Canute, who had ruled England from 1016 to 1035, succeeded his brother Harald the Slothful as King of Denmark. A zealous Christian, he proclaimed Christianity in the territories he conquered and is said to have chastized his body with fasting and discipline. Late in his life he repented for the merciless acts he'd performed when he took over England. He was killed in the Church of St. Alban's in Odense, Denmark during a rebellion headed by his brother Olaf. The monks of Odense saw Canute's death as martyrdom and accepted him as a saint.

Traditional day National Popcorn Day (U.S.) This fun traditional day reportedly has its origins with a one-off Superbowl tie-in. The celebration was such a success that it continues to be informally repeated on this day.

"You cannot shake hands with a clenched fist."   INDIRA GANDHI

Births

1807	Robert E. Lee, American Confederate general
1809	Edgar Allan Poe, writer and poet
1839	Paul Cézanne, painter
1913	Minnesota Fats, American billiards player
1917	John Raitt, singer and actor
1923	Jean Stapleton, actress
1931	Tippi Hedren, actress
1939	Phil Everly, musician
1941	Tony Anholt, actor
1942	Michael Crawford, singer and actor
1943	Janis Joplin, singer
1946	Dolly Parton, singer and actress
1949	Robert Palmer, singer and guitarist
1957	Mickey Virtue, musician

Twins for sale

Ian and Judith Kilshaw from the Welsh village of Buckley became famous worldwide in 2001 when it was revealed that they had not only paid £8,200 to buy twin American girls through an Internet site, but that they had in effect stolen the babies from another adoptive couple. The media went wild with the twist in the story: A Californian couple, Richard and Vickie Allen, had already paid adoption brokers £4,000 for the babies and had been caring for them for two months when the babies' natural mother, Tranda Wecker, asked for a final farewell visit. Reportedly, Wecker then kidnapped her babies and sold them to the Kilshaws (pictured right), using the same adoption brokers. The British couple knew the babies, Belinda and Kymberley, were already adopted, but allegedly Wecker insisted they were the preferred couple, so they took the babies to England, believing their adoption was legal.

Local social services and police officers confronted the Kilshaws in a chaotic three-hour scene which was filmed by a U.S. television network. The babies were removed and put into the care of foster parents. The Kilshaws became the subject of media frenzy. Amid sensational headlines, polls, debates, and commentary on internet sales of children, neighbors came forward with stories of the Kilshaws' private life that included wild parties, a strange menagerie of pets, exorcisms, a stream of tenants, and a caravan park in the garden. Judith's gregarious behavior particularly drew attention, with one headline calling her "the most hated woman in Britain."

British and U.S. judges ruled the babies should be returned to America. Eventually, both the Kilshaws and the Allens dropped their bid for custody of the girls, who are now cared for by foster parents in the U.S.

January 20

"Acting is all about honesty. If you can fake that, you've got it made." — GEORGE BURNS

HISTORICAL EVENTS

- 1885 L. A. Thompson patents the roller-coaster.
- 1929 *In Old Arizona*, the first full-length talking movie filmed outdoors, is released.
- 1942 Nazis at the Wannsee conference in Berlin decide on the "final solution" to the "Jewish problem": Exterminate all Jewish people.
- 1944 The British Royal Air Force drops 2,300 tons of bombs on Berlin.
- 1945 Franklin D. Roosevelt is inaugurated for an unprecedented fourth term as President of the U.S. and dies three months later.
- 1969 The first pulsar ("pulsating star") is visually identified, in the Crab Nebula (see below).
- 1981 Iran releases 52 American hostages minutes after Ronald Reagan is inaugurated as U.S. President.
- 1991 Sudan's Government imposes Islamic law nationwide, worsening the civil war between the country's Muslim north and Christian south.
- 2001 Philippine President Joseph Estrada is ousted in a peaceful people-power revolution, succeeded by Gloria Macapagal-Arroyo.

DAYS TO REMEMBER

National day U.S. Presidential Inauguration Day Prior to 1933, U.S. Presidents were inaugurated on March 4, but when the Twentieth Amendment was passed, January 20 became the official date for inauguration.

Religious day Ennen no Mai (Japan) On January 20 every year, the final day of the annual festival at Jyogyodo in Japan, the Dance of the Ennen is presented as a dedication to the Motsuji Temple in praise of the deity Matarashin. The dance is more than 800 years old.

Saint day St. Sebastian's Day St. Sebastian (c. 260 C.E.) was a Gallic officer in the Roman army. He was martyred in 288 by being shot with arrows and left for dead. He survived, recovered, and returned to preach to Diocletian. The Emperor then had him beaten to death. He is the patron saint of archers.

Births
- 1896 George Burns, actor, comedian
- 1906 Aristotle Onassis, industrialist
- 1910 Joy Adamson, naturalist and writer
- 1920 Federico Fellini, film director
- 1926 Patricia Neal, actress
- 1930 Buzz Aldrin, astronaut
- 1946 David Lynch, film director
- 1965 Sophie, The Countess of Wessex, the wife of Prince Edward, Earl of Wessex
- 1968 Melissa Rivers, reporter and actress
- 1969 Skeet Ulrich, actor

Deaths
- 1984 Johnny Weissmuller, swimmer and actor
- 1990 Barbara Stanwyck, actress
- 1993 Audrey Hepburn, actress
- 1997 Curt Flood, baseball player
- 2003 Al Hirschfeld, caricaturist

In 1969, the first pulsar was optically identified in the Crab Nebula. A pulsar is a rapidly spinning neutron star that has a mechanism to beam light, much like a lighthouse. The Crab Nebula is about 7,000 light years away in the constellation Taurus. The Crab Pulsar rotates about 30 times a second, emitting a double pulse in each rotation. In visible light, the Crab Pulsar appears to be a star near the center of the nebula, but close examination shows it to be pulsing.

January 21

"A lie told often enough becomes the truth." — VLADIMIR LENIN

HISTORICAL EVENTS

- 1189 Phillip II, Henry II, and Richard the Lion-Heart start the third Crusade to recover the Holy Land from the Muslims.
- 1789 The first American novel, *The Power of Sympathy*, is printed in Boston, Massachusetts.
- 1853 Russell L. Hawes patents the envelope-folding machine.
- 1911 The first Monte Carlo motor-car rally takes place.
- 1919 Meeting in the Mansion House, Dublin, the nationalist Sinn Fein movement adopts Ireland's first constitution.
- 1976 The first commercial service of supersonic jetliner Concorde takes off.
- 1977 U.S. President Jimmy Carter pardons nearly all Vietnam War draft evaders.
- 1994 Lorena Bobbitt is found not guilty by reason of temporary insanity of severing the penis of her husband John Bobbitt (see below).
- 2004 China ushers in the Year of the Monkey, a sign of business prosperity in Chinese astrology.

DAY TO REMEMBER

Religious day St. Agnes' Day A common account of St. Agnes of Rome (c. 250 C.E.), one of the virgin martyrs of Rome, is that immediately after the imperial edict against Christians, when Agnes was 12 or 13 years of age, she refused to renounce her faith. After suffering various tortures, she was executed. Eight days later, she appeared in a vision to her parents, dressed in white, attended by a white lamb. On her feast day two lambs are blessed at her church in Rome, and their wool is shorn and woven into the palliums (bands of wool) which the Pope confers on archbishops as a symbol of their jurisdiction. Some claim that the legend of Agnes springs from the cult of the Danish goddess Yngona, who shares the same feast day.

Star sign

AQUARIUS

January 21–February 19

Born under the sign of the water bearer, the typical Aquarian is witty, conceited, and independent. They can also be diplomatic, gentle, kind, and vague. They are "big picture" people, creative, and original thinkers.

Births

- 1885 Umberto Nobile, politician, and airship designer
- 1905 Christian Dior, fashion designer
- 1924 Benny Hill actor, comic, and singer
- 1941 Plácido Domingo, tenor
- 1956 Geena Davis, actress

Deaths

- 1924 Vladimir Lenin, Russian revolutionary
- 1950 George Orwell, writer
- 1959 Cecil B. DeMille, director
- 1993 Charlie Gehringer, baseball player
- 1997 Colonel Tom Parker, manager of Elvis Presley

Celtic tree sign

ROWAN

January 21–February 17

The Rowan tree protected the Celts from evil spells and bad luck. Sprigs of the tree were placed in barns and houses, and worn on the person. The trees were planted around graveyards to protect the dead. Rowan tree people are said to be passionate, although they often hide this beneath a cooler façade. They are highly principled, visionary, and unique, and are prepared to fight for their beliefs. They are pioneering and likely to achieve many things in their life. Their ruling planet is Uranus.

On January 21, 1994, Lorena Bobbitt of Virginia, U.S. was found not guilty of severing the penis of her husband John Bobbitt by reason of temporary insanity. She claimed she attacked him after he raped her, cutting off the penis with a kitchen knife as he lay sleeping. Her defense argued that an irresistible impulse led her to cut off her husband's penis and that she was not responsible for her actions. She was committed to a mental health facility and released 45 days later. Her husband, who had his penis surgically reattached, subsequently divorced her and starred in two porn movies.

January 22

> *"If one morning I walked on top of the water across the Potomac River, the headline that afternoon would read 'President Can't Swim.'"* — LYNDON B. JOHNSON

Births

- 1654 Richard Blackmore, physician and writer
- 1729 Gotthold Ephraim Lessing, author and philosopher
- 1732 George Washington, the first U.S. President
- 1788 George Gordon (Lord) Byron, poet
- 1931 Sam Cooke, singer
- 1934 Bill Bixby, actor
- 1940 John Hurt, actor
- 1959 Linda Blair, actress
- 1960 Michael Hutchence, musician
- 1965 Diane Lane, actress

Deaths

- 1901 Queen Victoria of Great Britain, aged 82, after a reign of 64 years
- 1973 Lyndon B. Johnson, thirty-sixth U.S. President
- 1994 Telly Savalas, actor
- 1995 Rose Fitzgerald Kennedy, John F. and Robert F. Kennedy's mother
- 2004 Billy May, composer and musician
- 2004 Ann Miller, actress and dancer

HISTORICAL EVENTS

- **1840** The first British colonists reach New Zealand.
- **1905** When Russian workers march in peaceful protest on the Winter Palace, a hundred are massacred by Czarist troops. Known as Bloody Sunday, the incident ignites the Russian Revolution.
- **1957** The New York City "Mad Bomber," George P. Metesky, is arrested in Waterbury, Connecticut and is charged with planting more than 30 bombs.
- **1966** The U.S.S.R. launches *Kosmos 110*, carrying the two-dog crew of Ugolyok and Veterok into Earth's orbit. It returns after a 22-day flight, a canine space record not surpassed by humans until 1974, when Skylab 2 keeps three men in space for 28 days.
- **1968** The TV sketch comedy *Rowan & Martin's Laugh-In* debuts on NBC in the U.S.
- **1973** The U.S. Supreme Court delivers its decision in the case of Roe v. Wade, striking down State laws restricting abortion during the first six months of pregnancy (see below).
- **1987** Pennsylvania politician R. Budd Dwyer commits suicide by shooting himself in the mouth on national television after being convicted of bribery and corruption charges.
- **1992** Roberta Bondar becomes the first Canadian woman in space. During her space flight, Dr. Bondar serves as prime payload specialist for the first International Microgravity Laboratory Mission. Also the first neurologist in space, she spends eight days in orbit, circling the Earth 129 times.
- **1998** Suspected Unabomber Theodore Kaczynski pleads guilty and accepts a sentence of life without the possibility of parole.
- **2002** K-mart becomes the largest retail chain in American history to file for bankruptcy protection.

Abortion on trial

Roe v. Wade, a famous case decided in 1973 by the U.S. Supreme Court, legalized abortion in the first trimester of pregnancy. In one of the Supreme Court's most controversial decisions, the Court declared by a vote of seven to two that laws against abortion violate the constitutional right to privacy.

The decision was based on two cases: That of an unmarried woman ("Jane Roe," whose real name was Norma McCorvey) from Texas, where abortion was illegal unless the mother's life was at risk. Roe had allegedly become pregnant as a result of being raped. The other case was that of a poor, married mother of three from Georgia, where State law required permission for an abortion from a panel of doctors and hospital officials. Henry Wade was the Texas Attorney General who defended the anti-abortion law.

While establishing the right to an abortion, the decision gave individual States the right to intervene in the second

Pro-life and pro-choice activists hold signs side by side during the 2005 "March for Life" in Washington D.C.

and third trimesters of pregnancy to protect the woman and the "potential" life of the unborn child. Denounced by the National Council of Bishops, the decision gave rise to a vocal anti-abortion movement, and sparked a great deal of controversy worldwide.

January 23

DATE*line*

"I do not take drugs. I am drugs."
SALVADOR DALI (PICTURED RIGHT)

Missionary and sons burned to death

Australian missionary Graham Stewart Stains and his two sons were burned alive by radical Hindus in eastern India. Staines, aged 58, and his two sons, Timothy and Phillip, aged eight and 10, were sleeping in their car in Manoharpur village of Orissa's Keonjhar district of India early in the morning of January 23, 1999, when a mob blocked the doors of their station wagon, poured gasoline on the vehicle and shouted political slogans as the father and two sons burned alive.

Graham Staines went to India from Australia in 1965 to treat lepers in Daripada, Orissa. He married his wife Gladys in the 1980s and together they became involved in ministry to the poor and helpless. He had gone to Manoharpur village for an evangelism campaign. The murders were attributed to a radical Hindu activist group, the Bajrang Dal, opposed to religious conversions of Hindus to Christianity or Islam. They have called repeatedly for the expulsion of Christian missionaries from India.

Gladys Staines and her daughter Esther remain in India, continuing their work. Gladys announced her forgiveness of those who had murdered her family. "*Forgive* was the shortest, most eloquent, most powerful sermon India has ever heard," said one leader of the Government. "Our sister, through her pain, through her tears, did what Jesus would do. I don't think it is an accident that after that event, we have seen unprecedented numbers of people turning to Christ."

India is a country populated by more than one billion people. Two percent are Christian.

Births
1737	John Hancock, American Revolutionist
1832	Edouard Manet, artist
1899	Humphrey Bogart, actor
1928	Jeanne Moreau, actress
1944	Rutger Hauer, actor
1948	Anita Pointer, singer
1950	Richard Dean Anderson, actor
1957	Princess Caroline of Monaco
1964	Mariska Hargitay, actress

Deaths
1803	Arthur Guinness, Irish brewer
1931	Anna Pavlova, ballerina
1944	Edvard Munch, painter
1989	Salvador Dalí, artist
2004	Helmut Newton, photographer
2005	Johnny Carson, television host

HISTORICAL EVENTS

1510 Henry VIII of England, then 18 years old, takes part *incognito* in a tournament at Richmond and is applauded for his jousting before revealing his identity.
1556 The deadliest earthquake in history, the Shaanxi earthquake, hits Shaanxi Province, China. The death toll is as high as 830,000.
1849 Elizabeth Blackwell becomes the first U.S. female doctor.
1907 Charles Curtis from Kansas becomes the first Native American U.S. senator.
1911 Nobel Prize winner Marie Curie is refused acceptance to the all-male membership of the French Academy of Sciences. She goes on to win a second Nobel Prize.
1964 Dr. James Hardy, at the University of Mississippi, U.S., transplants the heart of a chimpanzee named Bino into the chest of Boyd Rush, aged 68. It is the first animal-to-human heart transplant. Rush dies 90 minutes later.
1973 U.S. President Richard Nixon announces that a peace accord has been reached in Vietnam.
1978 Sweden becomes the first nation in the world to ban aerosol sprays, believed to be damaging to Earth's protective ozone layer.
1999 Australian missionary Graham Stewart Stains and his two sons are burned alive by radical Hindus while sleeping in their car in eastern India (see above).
2002 Reporter Daniel Pearl is kidnapped – and subsequently murdered – in Karachi, Pakistan.

DAY TO REMEMBER

Religious day St. Ildephonsus' Day
St. Ildephonsus (c. 607–667) came from a noble family and was probably a pupil of St. Isidore of Seville. While still quite young, he entered the Benedictine monastery of Agalia near Toledo, and went on to become its Abbot. In 657 he was elected to succeed his uncle, St. Eugenius, as Archbishop of Toledo. His devotion to the Blessed Virgin was a favorite subject for medieval artists. St. Ildephonsus was a prolific writer, producing among other works a history of the Spanish Church during the first two thirds of the seventh century, entitled *Concerning Famous Men*.

January 24

"History will be kind to me for I intend to write it." — WINSTON CHURCHILL

HISTORICAL EVENTS

41 C.E. Roman Emperor Gaius Caesar (Caligula), known for his eccentricity and cruel despotism, is assassinated by his disgruntled Praetorian Guards. He is succeeded by his uncle Claudius.

1848 The California gold rush begins when James W. Marshall finds gold at Sutter's Mill near Sacramento. At the time California has 14,000 inhabitants; by the end of the following year there are 80,000.

1888 Jacob L. Wortman patents the typewriter ribbon.

1902 Denmark sells the Virgin Islands in the West Indies to the U.S.

1908 The world's first Boy Scout organization is formed in England by Sir Robert Baden Powell.

1924 St. Petersburg, Russia, is renamed Leningrad in the wake of the Russian Revolution.

1972 Japanese soldier Shoichi Yokoi is found in a Guam jungle where he has been in hiding since 1944, when U.S. forces liberated the island during World War II (see below).

1989 Serial killer Ted Bundy, convicted of the murder of three women, is executed by electric chair in Florida, U.S. Just before he dies he confesses to killing a further 19 women.

DAYS TO REMEMBER

Religious day Sugamo Togenuki Jizoson (Japan) At the Soto Buddhist Koganji Temple, a grand festival is held three times a year, each on January, May, and September 24. The festival's highlight is *tenkyo*, or a special chant of Mahaprajnaparamitasutra (the Great Wisdom Sutra), which is performed by nearly 20 monks of the temple at breakneck speed. The chant is believed to be effective for good health.

Religious day St. Francis de Sales' Day Known as the gentleman saint, St. Francis (1567–1622) was born into a wealthy family and became a Doctor of Law at the University of Padua, Italy. However, he entered the priesthood and pursued a life of prayer. His simple, clear explanations of Catholic doctrine and his gentle manner saw him appointed Bishop of Geneva at the age of 35. A great traveler and prolific correspondent, he helped found the Order of the Visitation with St. Jeanne de Chantal. He is the patron saint of journalists, writers, and editors.

Births
- **76 C.E.** Hadrian, Roman Emperor
- **1540** Edmund Campion, Jesuit
- **1670** William Congreve, playwright
- **1679** Christian Wolff, philosopher
- **1862** Edith Wharton, writer
- **1917** Ernest Borgnine, actor
- **1941** Neil Diamond, singer
- **1941** Aaron Neville, singer
- **1943** Sharon Tate, actress
- **1949** John Belushi, actor
- **1966** Jimeoin, comedian and actor
- **1986** Mischa Barton, actress

Deaths
- **1595** Archduke Ferdinand II of Austria
- **1920** Amedeo Modigliani, painter and sculptor
- **1965** Winston Churchill, U.K. Prime Minister
- **1971** Bill W., American co-founder of Alcoholics Anonymous
- **1986** L. Ron Hubbard, writer and founder of Scientology
- **1986** Vincente Minnelli, film director
- **1989** Ted Bundy, American serial killer
- **2005** June Bronhill, opera singer

In 1972, Japanese soldier Shoichi Yokoi was found in a Guam jungle where he had been hiding for 28 years in adherence to the Imperial Army's non-surrender code. Japan occupied Guam during the war and most of its 22,000 troops were killed when U.S. troops recaptured the island in 1944. Left behind by the retreating Japanese forces, Yokoi waited for the return of the Japanese authorities, surviving on a diet of nuts, berries, frogs, snails, and rats, and by weaving materials from tree bark. Upon his discovery, he went home to Japan where he was hailed as a hero. Yokoi subsequently married, became a regular commentator on television programs and wrote a best-selling book on his experiences. In 1997, aged 82, he died of a heart attack.

January 25

"For most of history, Anonymous was a woman." — VIRGINIA WOOLF

The Manson Family murders

On a hot August night in 1969, young movie actress Sharon Tate was eight months pregnant and living in a secluded Los Angeles mansion. Her husband, film director Roman Polanski, was away shooting a film, and Tate invited three friends for an impromptu gathering. When the Polanski's housekeeper arrived at the house the next morning she discovered the gruesome murders of Tate and friends.

In November that year, while in prison in connection with a car theft, a woman named Susan Atkins boasted to an inmate that she was responsible for the murder of Sharon Tate. Under police questioning, she named her accomplices as Charles "Tex" Watson, Patricia Krenwinkel and Linda Kasabian – all members of a cult known as The Family, led by self-styled guru Charles Manson. Atkins led police to other murders committed by Family members.

Manson never killed any of his victims himself. He persuaded his followers to embark on the murder sprees of wealthy people in their homes and cast suspicion on black militant groups such as the Black Panthers. Seven months after the trial began, the jury took nine days to find Manson and his followers guilty. The jury fixed the sentence as death, but in 1972 the California Supreme Court abolished the death penalty and all sentences were automatically commuted to life terms.

HISTORICAL EVENTS

1858 "The Wedding March" by Felix Mendelssohn becomes a popular wedding recessional after it is played on this day at the marriage of Queen Victoria's daughter, Victoria, to Friedrich of Prussia.
1949 In the first Israeli election, David Ben-Gurion becomes Prime Minister.
1959 The Second Vatican Council starts work on reforming and modernizing the Catholic Church.
1960 The U.S. National Association of Broadcasters responds to the Payola scandal by fining disc jockeys who accepted money for playing particular records.
1971 Charles Manson and three female "Family members" are found guilty of murder and sentenced to death (see above).
1971 Idi Amin leads a coup deposing Milton Obote and becomes Uganda's president.
1980 Ex-Beatles singer Paul McCartney is deported from Japan for possession of marijuana after spending nine days in jail.
1999 An earthquake measuring 6.0 on the Richter scale hits western Colombia, killing at least 1,000 people.
2005 A stampede during a Hindu pilgrimage in India kills at least 250.

Births
1759 Robert Burns, poet
1858 Kokichi Mikimoto, pearl-farm pioneer
1874 William Somerset Maugham, writer
1882 Virginia Woolf, writer
1900 Yojiro Ishizaka, writer
1944 Leigh Taylor-Young, actress
1981 Alicia Keys, singer and musician

Deaths
1947 Al Capone, American gangster
1990 Ava Gardner, actress

DAYS TO REMEMBER

National day Burns Day (Scotland) All over the world, Scots gather to honor the life and work of national poet, Robert Burns, born on this day in 1759. While they vary in form, most Burns Suppers include a traditional Scottish meal, Scotch whisky, and recitations of works by and about Burns.

Religious day St. Dwynwen's Day Also known as Dwyn, Donwen, Donwenna, Dunwen, St. Dwynwen was one of 24 daughters of a fifth-century Welsh saint and king, Brychan Brycheiniog of Brechon. She founded a convent on what is now Llanddwyn Island and her holy well, a fresh-water spring called Ffynnon Dwynwen, became a place of pilgrimage. She is credited with the saying: "Nothing wins hearts like cheerfulness."

National day Tatiana Day (Russia) Celebrated since 1755, this day honors Russian students and marks the day that Moscow University was founded.

January 26

"There is no security on this earth, there is only opportunity."
GENERAL DOUGLAS MACARTHUR

HISTORICAL EVENTS

- **1340** English monarch King Edward III is proclaimed king of France.
- **1531** An estimated 30,000 people die in an earthquake in Lisbon, Portugal.
- **1871** British Rugby Union football is formed.
- **1905** The world's largest diamond, the 3,106-carat Cullinan, is found in South Africa.
- **1911** Glenn H. Curtiss flies the first successful seaplane.
- **1926** Television is first demonstrated in London by John Logie Baird.
- **1992** Boris Yeltsin announces that Russia will stop targeting U.S. cities with nuclear weapons.
- **1994** A man fires two blank shots at Prince Charles in Sydney, Australia (see below).
- **1998** On American television, U.S. President Bill Clinton denies he had "sexual relations" with former White House intern Monica Lewinsky.
- **2001** An earthquake hits Gujarat, India, causing more than 20,000 deaths.
- **2005** Dr. Condoleezza Rice is sworn in as U.S. Secretary of State, becoming the first African American woman to hold the post.
- **2005** A helicopter crash in eastern Iraq kills 31 U.S. soldiers.

DAYS TO REMEMBER

National day Australia Day A public holiday commemorates January 26, 1788, when Captain Arthur Phillip founded the colony of Australia. Citizenship ceremonies and the presentation of community awards combine with local events and celebrations.

Religious day Michael Kozal's Day Born to a peasant family and ordained a priest in 1918, Michael Kozal (1893–1943) became a bishop and was arrested by the Gestapo in 1939 as part of the Nazi persecution of the Catholic Church. He was imprisoned and tortured at Wloclawek, Lod, Szczeglin, Berlin, and Dachau. Michael spent 21 months in Dachau, ministering to other prisoners before being executed on January 26, 1943. He was beatified by John Paul II with canonization pending.

Births

- **1880** Douglas MacArthur, American general
- **1905** Maria von Trapp, singer
- **1915** William Hopper, actor
- **1918** Nicolae Ceausescu, Romanian dictator
- **1925** Paul Newman, actor
- **1928** Roger Vadim, film director and actor
- **1941** Scott Glenn, actor
- **1955** Eddie Van Halen, musician
- **1958** Ellen DeGeneres, American actress, comedian, and talk-show host

Deaths

- **1567** Nicholas Wotton, English diplomat
- **1823** Edward Jenner, physician
- **1962** Lucky Luciano, mobster
- **1973** Edward G. Robinson, actor
- **1979** Nelson Rockefeller, Governor of New York and U.S. Vice-President
- **1998** Shinichi Suzuki, Japanese music teacher

In 1994 David Kang fired two blank shots from a starting pistol and rushed onto the stage as Prince Charles, the heir to the British throne, was about to hand out Australia Day awards in Sydney. Kang was wrestled to the ground by then New South Wales State Premier John Fahey and Australian of the Year Ian Kiernan. In court Kang said he was attempting to highlight the plight of Cambodian boat people. He was sentenced to 500 hours community service. Ten years later he became a barrister and now specialises in criminal and medical law.

DATE*line*

January 27

"When anyone asks me how I can best describe my experience in nearly forty years at sea, I merely say uneventful."   E. J. SMITH, CAPTAIN RMS *TITANIC*

HISTORICAL EVENTS

1606 Opening day of the trial of Guy Fawkes and other English Catholics accused of attempting to assassinate the Protestant King. Four days later they are found guilty, and hung, drawn, and quartered.

1654 Some 150 Sephardic families (Jews of Spanish-Portuguese extraction) flee Brazil for New Netherland (now known as New York), a colony run by the Dutch West India Company. Colony manager Peter Stuyvesant motions to eject the families, but the company refuses.

1945 Auschwitz – the largest killing camp established by the Nazis, responsible for the deaths of well over a million Jewish people – is liberated by the Soviets.

1967 Astronauts Gus Grissom, Edward White, and Roger Chaffee are killed in a fire during a test of the *Apollo 1* spacecraft at the Kennedy Space Center.

1967 More than 60 nations sign the Outer Space Treaty, banning nuclear weapons to be used in space.

1983 The world's longest subaqueous tunnel (33.5 miles [53.90 km]) opens in Japan, connecting the islands of Honshu and Hokkaido.

1984 Michael Jackson's hair catches on fire during the filming of a Pepsi commercial in Los Angeles. Jackson is hospitalized for a few days.

1995 Manchester United's Eric Cantona is fined £20,000 and banned from playing football over his kung fu-style attack on a fan.

1997 It is revealed that French museums contain nearly 2,000 pieces of art stolen by Nazis (see below).

2002 Several explosions at a military dump in Lagos, Nigeria, cause the deaths of more than 1,000 people.

Births

1720 Samuel Foote, dramatist, and actor
1756 Wolfgang Amadeus Mozart, composer
1805 Samuel Palmer, artist
1832 Lewis Carroll, author
1850 Edward J. Smith, captain of the *Titanic*
1903 John Carew Eccles, neuropsychologist
1921 Donna Reed, actress
1936 Troy Donahue, actor
1948 Mikhail Baryshnikov, dancer
1956 Mimi Rogers, actress
1964 Bridget Fonda, actress
1965 Alan Cumming, actor
1979 Daniel Vettori, cricketer
1979 Rosamund Pike, actress
1980 Marat Safin, tennis player

Deaths

1901 Giuseppe Verdi, composer
1910 Thomas Crapper, inventor
1967 Crew of *Apollo 1*:
    Roger Chaffee
    Virgil "Gus" Grissom
    Edward White
1986 Lilli Palmer, actress

Stolen art discovered

In 1997, an official report by an independent government agency revealed that nearly 2,000 works of art seized from Jews during the Nazi invasion of France were still in the care of French museums. The report was released to the public some 16 months after its publication, and was produced in the wake of a 1995 book *The Lost Museum: The Nazi Conspiracy to Steal the World's Greatest Works of Art*, by journalist Hector Feliciano.

Thousands of French Jews were deported by the Germans during World War II. For his book, Feliciano sourced material from German looting inventories, declassified documents, and more than 200 interviews with art dealers, art historians, military officers, and Jewish collectors who survived the holocaust.

According to the book, more than 20,000 pieces were sent to Germany, many bearing the mark "Property of the Third Reich." Some were destined for a museum of European art that Hitler planned to create; others entered the private collections of top Nazi dignitaries, or were sold in France and Switzerland.

The French collections were part of an estimated 1.5 million pieces of art the Nazis are thought to have stolen from private and public collections. As museums and claimants come forth, a central registry has been set up, and organizations in individual countries are providing information and services to assist people trying to locate, or receive compensation for, artworks and other cultural property.

DAY TO REMEMBER

International day Holocaust Memorial Day The United Nations observes this day in memory of over six million Jewish people slaughtered by Nazis during World War II. Many countries observe this day.

January 28

"He who is dying of hunger must be fed rather than taught." — ST. THOMAS AQUINAS

HISTORICAL EVENTS

1547 King Henry VIII of England dies and is succeeded by his nine-year-old son, Edward.
1916 Louis D. Brandeis becomes the first Jewish judge appointed to the U.S. Supreme Court.
1921 A symbolic Tomb of the Unknown Soldier is installed beneath the Arc de Triomphe in Paris to honor the unknown dead of World War I.
1935 Iceland becomes the first country to legalize abortion.
1961 The Republic of Rwanda is proclaimed.
1986 Space Shuttle *Challenger* explodes 73 seconds after lift-off, killing all seven astronauts onboard (see left).
1998 Gunmen hold at least 400 children and teachers hostage for several hours at an elementary school in Manila, Philippines.
1999 Car company Ford announces it is buying the Volvo company for U.S. $6.45 billion.
2002 An Ecuadorian Airlines Boeing 727-100 crashes in the Andes in southern Colombia, killing 92 people.

The space shuttle *Challenger* flew nine successful missions before its fateful final lift-off in 1986. It was the first flight of the Teacher In Space Program, carrying teacher Christa McAuliffe as one of the astronauts. Selected from more than 11,000 applicants, McAuliffe said, "I watched the Space Age being born and I would like to participate." From the beginning, the mission was plagued by problems. Lift-off was delayed six times before *Challenger* finally took off at 11:38 A.M. Just 73 seconds into the mission, the shuttle exploded, killing the entire crew.

DAYS TO REMEMBER

Religious day Freya's Day On the ancient Runic calendar, this day is a Norse-derived celebration giving thanks to Freya, the sun goddess, for light, fire, sunlight, and the return of spring.

Religious day St. Thomas Aquinas' Day Regarded as the greatest theologian of the Catholic Church, St. Thomas (1225–1274) was the son of a count. He joined the Dominican Friars in 1244, despite his family's efforts to keep him from the order by force.

Births

- **1706** John Baskerville, printer
- **1912** Jackson Pollock, painter
- **1933** Susan Sontag, writer and activist
- **1936** Alan Alda, actor, writer, and director
- **1950** Barbi Benton, actress
- **1968** Sarah McLachlan, singer, and songwriter
- **1980** Nick Carter, singer
- **1981** Elijah Wood, actor
- **1984** Andre Iguodala, basketball player

Deaths

- **1939** William Butler Yeats, writer
- **1949** Jean-Pierre Wimille, race-car driver
- **1986** Crew of space shuttle *Challenger*:
  Greg Jarvis
  Christa McAuliffe
  Ronald McNair
  Ellison Onizuka
  Judith Resnik
  Francis R. Scobee
  Michael J. Smith

January 29

DATEline

"Security is when everything is settled, when nothing can happen to you; security is the denial of life." — GERMAINE GREER

Births

- 1737 Thomas Paine, American patriot
- 1860 Anton Chekhov, writer
- 1874 John D. Rockefeller Jr., American entrepreneur
- 1880 W. C. Fields, actor
- 1915 Victor Mature, actor
- 1918 John Forsythe, actor
- 1939 Germaine Greer, feminist writer
- 1940 Katharine Ross, actress
- 1942 Claudine Longet, singer and dancer
- 1945 Tom Selleck, actor
- 1947 Linda B. Buck, scientist
- 1952 Tommy Ramone, musician and record producer
- 1954 Oprah Winfrey, talk-show host, producer, actress, and publisher
- 1968 Edward Burns, actor
- 1970 Heather Graham, actress
- 1970 Rajyavardhan Singh Rathore, shooter
- 1979 Sui Feifei, basketball player

Deaths

- 1963 Robert Frost, poet
- 1964 Alan Ladd, actor
- 1977 Freddie Prinze, actor and comedian
- 1980 Jimmy Durante, actor, singer, and comedian
- 1986 Leif Erickson, actor

HISTORICAL EVENTS

- 1886 The first successful gasoline-driven automobile is patented by Karl Benz, in Karlsruhe, Germany.
- 1933 The President of Germany, Paul von Hindenburg, appoints Adolf Hitler as Chancellor of Germany.
- 1944 A total of about 300 men, women, and children are massacred indiscriminately in Koniuchy, Poland. The same day, 285 German bombers attack London and the Battle of Cisterna takes place in central Italy.
- 1996 After widespread criticism, French President Jacques Chirac announces a "definitive end" to French nuclear testing.
- 1996 La Fenice, Venice's opera house, is destroyed by fire.
- 1998 In Birmingham, Alabama, a bomb explodes at an abortion clinic, killing one person and severely wounding another.
- 2001 Thousands of student protesters in Indonesia storm Parliament and demand that President Abdurrahman Wahid resign due to alleged involvement in corruption scandals.
- 2002 In his State of the Union Address, U.S. President George W. Bush describes "regimes that sponsor terror" as an Axis of Evil.
- 2004 A dead whale explodes in Tainan, Taiwan. A build-up of gas in the decomposing sperm whale is suspected of causing the explosion (see below).

DAY TO REMEMBER

Religious day St. Aquilinus' Day Aquilinus was born in Bavaria. Leaving his native land to avoid being made a bishop, he went to Italy and settled in Milan. He was a vigorous opponent of Arianism, a view held by followers of Arius, a Christian priest who lived and taught in Alexandria, Egypt, in the early fourth century. Arianism contests the notion of the trinity — that God exists, simultaneously and eternally as a communion of the Father, the Son, and the Holy Spirit. In 650 C.E., St. Aquilinus was murdered by a group of Arians.

In 2004 in Tainan, Taiwan, a 56-foot (17 m) sperm whale had died after becoming beached. It took more than 13 hours, three large cranes and 50 workers to shift the bull whale onto the back of a truck. The decomposing carcass was being transported through the center of Tainan when it blasted open, reportedly splattering blood and entrails over surrounding shop-fronts, bystanders, and cars. A build-up of gas in the whale's body was suspected of causing the explosion.

January 30

"We cannot always build the future for our youth, but we can build our youth for the future."
FRANKLIN D. ROOSEVELT

Births
- 1882 Franklin D. Roosevelt, thirty-second U.S. President
- 1930 Gene Hackman, actor
- 1931 Allan W. Eckert, historian, naturalist, and author
- 1931 Shirley Hazzard, author
- 1932 Knock Yokoyama, comedian and politician
- 1937 Vanessa Redgrave, actress
- 1941 Dick Cheney, U.S. Vice-President
- 1951 Phil Collins, musician
- 1951 Charles S. Dutton, actor
- 1974 Christian Bale, actor

Deaths
- 1948 Mohandas Karamchand Gandhi (Mahatma Gandhi), politician
- 1948 Orville Wright, American aviation pioneer
- 1951 Ferdinand Porsche, automotive engineer
- 1995 Gerald Durrell, naturalist, zookeeper, author, and television presenter

HISTORICAL EVENTS

- 1595 Shakespeare's *Romeo and Juliet* is first performed.
- 1835 Mentally ill Richard Lawrence attempts to assassinate President Andrew Jackson in the U.S. capitol – the first assassination attempt against a U.S. President. Both of his pistols misfire and Jackson beats his would-be assassin with his cane.
- 1847 Yerba Buena, California, is renamed San Francisco.
- 1945 The *Wilhelm Gustloff* sinks in the Baltic Sea in the deadliest maritime disaster in recorded history, killing approximately 8,000 people.
- 1948 Indian pacifist and leader Mahatma Gandhi is assassinated by Nathuram Godse, a Hindu extremist.
- 1968 The Tet Offensive begins when Viet Cong forces launch a series of surprise attacks in South Vietnam.
- 1969 The Beatles hold their last public performance, on the roof of Apple Records in London. The impromptu concert is broken up by the police.
- 1972 British paratroopers kill 14 Roman Catholic civil rights marchers in Northern Ireland. The day becomes known as Bloody Sunday (see below).
- 2003 Belgium legally recognizes same-sex marriage, voting in legislation that comes into effect June 1.
- 2005 Amid violence and threats to boycott the results, Iraq holds an election for its National Assembly, the country's first free election since 1953.

DAYS TO REMEMBER

Religious day Feast of the Three Hierarchs Celebrations are held for St. Basil, St. Gregory, and St. John Chrysostom – the Three Hierarchs of the Greek Orthodox church.

Religious day St. Bathild's Day Kidnapped in her youth from her native England and taken to France, St. Bathild (c. 620–680) eventually married the King in 649. She used her royal position to help the poor and ultimately forbade the enslavement of Christians.

Bloody Sunday

In 1972, 14 unarmed men and boys were shot dead and 13 others were wounded after British paratroopers opened fire on Roman Catholic civil rights marchers in the Bogside area of the city of Derry, in Northern Ireland. The march was called to protest against internment without trial.

Most of the marchers followed the organizers' instructions and turned right into Rossville Street to hold a meeting at Free Derry Corner. However, a section of the crowd continued along William Street to the British Army barricade, where a riot developed.

Confrontations between the Catholic youth of Derry and the British Army had become a common feature of life in the city, and many observers reported that the rioting was not particularly intense. An order was given for the 1st Battalion Parachute Regiment to move into William Street to arrest rioters. As aggression towards the troops mounted, and despite a cease-fire order from British headquarters, soldiers fired more than a hundred rounds into the crowd.

Bloody Sunday overshadows most other violent instances in the history of troubles in Northern Ireland, because it was carried out by the forces of the British Government and not paramilitaries. When it arrived in Northern Ireland, the British Army had been welcomed as a neutral force, there to protect Catholics from Protestants and vise-versa.

In Ireland, for many decades the term Bloody Sunday evoked a memory of November 21, 1920, when 14 British secret service men were simultaneously killed by the Irish Volunteers in their Dublin homes. In retaliation, auxiliary police killed 12 spectators and players, and injured 60 others at a Dublin football match.

January 31

"One of the advantages of being disorderly is that one is constantly making exciting discoveries." — A. A. MILNE

HISTORICAL EVENTS

- **1747** The first venereal-diseases clinic opens at London Dock Hospital.
- **1876** The U.S. orders all Native Americans to move onto reservations.
- **1915** World War I: Germany uses poison gas against Russians. Some 18,000 artillery shells containing liquid xylyl bromide tear gas (known as T-Stoff) are fired during the Battle of Bolimov. Instead of vaporizing, the chemical freezes, and fails to have an impact.
- **1929** The Soviet Union exiles revolutionary leader and writer Leon Trotsky.
- **1953** A fierce storm and high spring tide force a surge of water to burst through the dikes and over the banks of low-lying coastal areas of northern Belgium and southern Netherlands. More than 1,800 people die.
- **1961** Ham the Chimp travels into outer space aboard *Mercury Redstone 2*.
- **1968** The Viet Cong attack the U.S. embassy in Saigon, Vietnam.
- **1990** The first McDonald's opens in Moscow, Russia, breaking the fast-food company's opening-day records for the number of customers served.
- **2005** The child molestation trial of superstar Michael Jackson begins in California (see below.)

DAY TO REMEMBER

Religious day St. John Bosco's Day Born in Piedmont in Italy, John Bosco's father died when he was young. Ordained in 1841, John (1815–1888) worked with poor and orphaned children, giving them a place to socialize and pray, and explaining the faith in short, simple treatises they could learn to write out. To further his work, he founded Orders whose mission was to work with and educate youth. He is patron saint of Christian apprentices, editors, and publishers.

Births
- **1797** Franz Schubert, composer
- **1872** Zane Grey, American Western writer
- **1902** Tallulah Bankhead, actress
- **1919** Jackie Robinson, baseball player
- **1921** Carol Channing, actress
- **1923** Norman Mailer, writer and journalist
- **1937** Philip Glass, composer
- **1937** Suzanne Pleshette, actress
- **1938** Queen Beatrix of the Netherlands
- **1956** Johnny Rotten, singer
- **1959** Anthony LaPaglia, actor
- **1959** Kelly Lynch, actress
- **1970** Minnie Driver, actress
- **1973** Portia de Rossi, actress

Deaths
- **1606** Gunpowder Plot conspirators executed: Guy Fawkes, Ambrose Rokewood, and Thomas Wintour
- **1956** A. A. Milne, author
- **1974** Samuel Goldwyn, film studio executive

Superstar on trial

In February 2003, a documentary by Martin Bashir raised new suspicions about Michael Jackson's behavior with the children who visited his Neverland ranch. A year later, a grand jury indicted Jackson on charges of molesting the boy shown in the documentary, giving him alcohol, and conspiring to hold him and his family captive.

During the trial, which lasted almost 14 weeks, Jackson steadfastly proclaimed his innocence, although he did not testify on his own behalf. A number of prosecution witnesses painted a picture of a seedy Neverland environment where Jackson plied young boys with alcohol and pornography and then persuaded them to engage in sexual acts. The defense, however, was able to construct a portrait of a conniving mother who coerced her family into concocting lies to extort money from celebrities. In the absence of a believable accuser, the prosecution was unable to prove to the jury that Jackson had committed any crimes against the boy and his family.

The jury deliberated for about 32 hours before returning their verdict. Shouts and cheers of celebration erupted from a huge throng of fans outside the courthouse in Santa Maria, California, when the "not guilty" verdict was read. Had he been found guilty, Michael Jackson would have faced a possible sentence of more than 18 years in prison. The case continues to dog the superstar's reputation.

DAYS TO REMEMBER *January*

1
New Year's Day
The adoption of the Gregorian calendar led to widespread acceptance of January 1 as New Year's Day in most parts of the world

2
Kakizome Part of Japanese New year. Set down for the first writing of *shodou*, the Japanese calligraphy

3
St. Genevieve Day Genevieve is Patroness of Paris

4
World Braille Day To honor Louis Braille, who developed a system of raised dots so that blind or visually impaired people could read

5
Birthday of Guru Gobind Singh, the tenth Sikh Guru

8
The Hajj The first day of the pilgrimage to Mecca which every adult Muslim must attempt to undertake at least once in their life

9
Feast of the Black Nazarene In the Quiapo district of Manila, Philippines, a statue of Christ known as the Black Nazarene is carried through town

10
Eid al-Adha or Feast of Sacrifice The final stage of the pilgrimage to Mecca, which lasts three days

11
Burning of the Clavie A traditional ritual to celebrate *hogmanay* – New Year's Eve – in Burghead, Morayshire

12
St. Sava Day Sava founded the Serbian Monastery Hilandar in Mount Athos

15
A celebration for the pilgrimage of Cristo Negro de Esquipúlas, Guatemala

16
Religious Freedom Day (U.S.) The U.S. President calls upon Americans to "observe this day through appropriate events and activities in homes, schools, and places of worship"

17
St. Jenaro Day Jenaro Sánchez DelGadillo was noted for his pastoral work and care for the sick

18
Jaime Hilario Barbal Day Jaime was one of 97 LaSalle Brothers killed in Catalunia during the Spanish Civil War and the first to be recognized as a martyr

19
Paul Cézanne, painter, was born in 1839

22
George Washington, first U.S. President, was born in 1732

23
St. Ildephonsus Day Ildephonsus' devotion to the Blessed Virgin was a favorite subject for medieval artists

24
Sugamo Togenuki Jizoson Grand Festival Held three times a year at the Soto Buddhist Koganji Temple

25
All over the world, Scots gather to honor the life and work of national poet, Robert Burns, born on this day in 1759

26
Australia Day Commemorates the day in 1788 when Captain Arthur Phillip founded the Australian colony

29
St. Aquilinus Day Aquilinus was a vigorous opponent of Arianism. In 650, a group of Arians murdered him

30
Feast Day of The Three Hierarchs Celebrations are held for St. Basil the Great, St. Gregory the Theologian, and St. John Chrysostom – the Three Hierarchs of the Greek Orthodox Church

31
John Bosco Day St. John is the patron saint of Christian apprentices, editors, and publishers

6

Three Kings Day The most festive day of the Nativity season in Latin America, Puerto Rico, the Caribbean, and Spain

7

Ethiopian Christmas called *Lidet*, falls on this day as Ethiopia retains the Julian calendar

13

Lohri According to the Hindu calendar, the bonfire festival of Lohri celebrates the harvesting of the Rabi (winter) crops

14

Pongal An Indian festival giving thanks for the harvest of the crops

20

U.S. Presidential Inauguration Day The official date for Inauguration

21

The first day of the star sign of Aquarius

27

International Holocaust Memorial Day In memory of over six million Jewish people slaughtered by Nazis during World War II

28

Sun Goddess Freya On the ancient Runic calendar, the half-month of Elhaz begins today with a sacrifice to the Sun goddess Freya

Top Right Ferry Boat race, Australia Day, January 26
Right Pongal Indian festival, January 14

FEBRUARY

"Why, what's the matter that you have such a February face, so full of frost, of storm and cloudiness?"

WILLIAM SHAKESPEARE, *MUCH ADO ABOUT NOTHING*

Visitors to the Aichi World Exposition in Japan are delighted by sophisticated 3D dioramas of animals as part of the "Ubiquitous Entertainment Ride." It is a major evolution since the first 3D film, *Bwana Devil*, was screened in February, 1953.

February

Pisces star sign and scene of a man warming his feet by the fire from *Calendar and Book of Hours*, from fifteenth-century France. February begins in the sign of Aquarius and ends in the sign of Pisces.

SPECIAL DATES
February begins on the same day of the week as March and November in a common year, and on the same day of the week as August in a leap year.

This third-century painting depicts St. Valentine. According to one legend, St. Valentine was a kind Roman priest who married young couples against the wishes of Emperor Claudius II, and was beheaded for his deeds on February 14. In reality, the origins and identity of St. Valentine are unclear. St. Valentine was recognized as a martyr and is patron saint of butchers and lovers.

February is the second month in the Gregorian calendar. Added to the Roman calendar along with January in the sixth century B.C.E., *February was named after a Roman festival of purification and cleansing called* Februa, *held by the Romans as a rite of spring and a tribute to oncoming fertility.*

THERE IS CONTENTION between historians regarding the number of days in *Februarius*, as it was once known. Some believe that February originally had 29 days, with 30 in a leap year, until the Roman Senate gave one of the days to the month of August (named after Augustus Caesar) to make it the same length as July. Other historians believe there is little evidence for this – that February always had 28 days, with 29 in a leap year, in order to even out the calendar.

Defining and naming periods of time is a complicated business. Most calendars periodically add in an extra day or month in order to keep the calendar year in sync with an astronomical or seasonal year. The Gregorian calendar, used by most modern countries, adds a twenty-ninth day to February approximately every fourth year in order to align with the seasons. It takes 365.2422 days for Earth to make one revolution around the Sun. This is called a "tropical" year, incorporating the four seasons. If we based every calendar year on 365 days, we would be out of kilter with the tropical year by six hours. After 100 years, this calendar would be more than 24 days ahead of the seasons. By adding leap years, the calendar will follow the seasons more closely. The Gregorian calendar rule with regard to leap years adds a twenty-ninth day to February in all years evenly divisible by four, except for century years, which receive the extra day only if they are evenly divisible by 400.

In 1700, Sweden dropped the leap year so that February 28 was always followed by March 1. This Swedish calendar was one day ahead of the Julian calendar and 10 days behind the Gregorian calendar. Twelve years later, this idea was abandoned and Sweden had a double leap year: two days were added to February, so that in 1712, the day of February 30 actually existed. After adding this extra day, Sweden eventually ended up being back in sync with the Julian calendar.

A month by any other name
Linguists debate the correct pronunciation of the word "February." Because it can be awkward to pronounce two syllables with an "r" in succession, and because February's predecessor on the calendar – January – is similar-sounding and easy

February birthflower

The iris is February's birthflower and shares the same purple color as this month's birthstone, amethyst. Purple is said to represent devotion, virtue, and tranquility. This sculptural flower is named after the messenger of the gods, and the rainbow linking Earth with other worlds. It comes in a wide variety of flower colors across the many species. Violets and primrose, also purple, are recognized as February's flowers as well.

to say, many people drop the first "r" in February. Some linguists proclaim it one of the most mispronounced words in the English language, while others accept the common usage with a single "r" pronunciation.

For the Anglo-Saxons, the pronunciation of February was not an issue – they called the month *Solmoneth* (mud month), or sometimes *Kale-monath* and *Sprout-kale* in relation to the time of the year that kale and cabbage were in season. In the old Japanese calendar, the month is called *Kisaragi*, meaning "the month changing clothes." In Finnish, the month is called *Helmikuu*, meaning "month of the pearl." The full moon of February has been called Trapper's Moon, Budding Moon, Bony Moon, Little Famine Moon, Ice Moon, Full Snow Moon and Moon of the Dark Red Calf.

Floating celebrations

National public holidays commemorating historical and political events are often given an arbitrary date to suit the economic smooth-running of the country. This is the case with several special dates in February. Mexico, for example, used to celebrate *Dia de la Constitucion* – the official holiday which commemorates the Mexican Constitution of 1917 – on February 5. This was the date the constitution was ratified, and schools were given extended holidays if the day fell on a Tuesday or Thursday. It is now held on the first Monday of February in order to create a long weekend.

The exact date in mid-February of Japan's biggest snow festival, *Yuki Matsuri* held in Sapporo, Hokkaido, is decided immediately after each festival finishes. From simple beginnings – in 1950 some teenagers built ice figures in Odori Park, providing much-needed entertainment for a locality demoralized by post-war unemployment – the festival now attracts more than two million visitors each year, and features over 200 astonishing and elaborate snow and ice sculptures of differing sizes and complexity, built by individuals and teams.

Each February, Sapporo City is transformed into an open-air fantasy land of snow statues and ice sculptures, as varied as replicas of famous architectural monuments to scenes from current movies.

A Jewish settler and his family plant a tree in the southern Gaza Strip settlement of Morag during the Jewish festival of *Tu B'shevat* – the New Year for trees.

Members of the congregation, carrying marks of the cross in ash on their foreheads, pray during an Ash Wednesday mass. Ash Wednesday is the first day of Lent in the Christian calendar.

Religious festivities are commonly held in accordance with regional, spiritual, and ethnic traditions, using lunar and lunisolar calendars. In India, the fairs and festivals of February include celebrations of the shifting seasons, as well as tributes to gods and goddesses, saints and gurus, teachers and prophets. A vibrant festival in Mizoram celebrates the arrival of spring. In West Bengal, Saraswati – the goddess of learning and the wife of Brahma – is worshipped in the festival of Vasant Panchami. In the Rajasthan Desert, the Festival of Jaisalmer is a jamboree of snake charmers, puppeteers, acrobats, and folk performers, held to coincide with the full moon. The Baneshwar Fair, in which tribes from neighboring states join together to offer prayers to Lord Shiva, is held on the full moon day.

In the Jewish calendar, *Tu B'Shevat* – the New Year for Trees – is celebrated on the fifteenth day of *Shevat* (the eleventh month), which generally falls on a date in late January through to mid-February. Historically, this was the date used to calculate the age of trees for tithing – taxing annual produce as a contribution to the Temple. Tu B'Shevat was also used to assess whether a tree was mature enough for its fruit to be harvested, in accordance with the belief that fruit from trees was not to be eaten during the first three years of a tree's life and the fourth year's fruit was for God.

In the Christian calendar, February is often the month of holidays and celebrations held in the lead-up to Easter. The period of Lent, a time of spiritual discipline manifested in abstinence and prayer, occurs 46 days before Easter. The first day of Lent is Ash Wednesday, a day of repentance signified by a cross marked in ash on the forehead. Depending on the date of Easter, Ash Wednesday can be held as early as February 4 or as late as March 10. Shrove Tuesday – the last day to feast before Lent begins – is held on

Black History Month in the U.S. commemorates writer Langston Hughes (above left), protester Rosa Parks (below left) and activist Malcolm X (far left), among others, for their contribution to the struggle for African American civil rights.

the Tuesday before Ash Wednesday. Also called Pancake Day because of the fried batter that is traditionally eaten on this day, or *Mardi Gras* which is French for "Fat Tuesday," the date of Shrove Tuesday can vary from February 3 to March 9.

In tribute to St. Ia, an Irish Christian missionary whose feast is celebrated on the first Monday after Candlemas (February 2), the village of St. Ives in Cornwall, England hurls a silver ball from person to person. The proceedings start at 10:30 A.M. and whoever is holding the ball at 12.00 P.M. receives a traditional reward of five shillings.

In another unusual February tribute, a church service for clowns is held at Holy Trinity Church in Dalston, East London, on the first Sunday in February. A tradition since 1946, clowns from all over the world and from all religions attend in full "slap" to honor Joseph Grimaldi, known as the "father" of modern-day clowns, and to give thanks for the gift of laughter.

Common causes

In the U.S., February is Black History Month, celebrating African Americans and commemorating the struggle for civil rights. Prominent people and important events featured during Black History Month include: Freedom Day, when President Abraham Lincoln approved the thirteenth Amendment to the Constitution abolishing slavery; the birthday of Langston Hughes, a writer and member of the 1920s' artistic movement, the Harlem Renaissance; the birthday of Rosa Parks, famous for her refusal in 1955 to obey a bus driver's command to give up her seat to a white passenger; the birthday and death of Frederick Douglass, an adviser to Abraham Lincoln during the Civil War and an outspoken campaigner for black rights; and the death of Malcolm X, a militant advocate of black sociopolitical independence.

February birthstone

Amethyst is the birthstone for February. This precious stone is a quartz that ranges in color from pale lilac to deep purple. The name comes from the Greek word *amethystos*, meaning "not drunk" – it was believed amethyst could prevent its wearers from intoxication. Throughout history and across cultures, amethysts have been used to promote sobriety, quicken the intelligence, enhance physical and spiritual health, encourage celibacy, and to symbolize piety and power. It is said that St. Valentine, who is celebrated in February, wore an amethyst engraved with the figure of his assistant, Cupid.

February 1

"If this thing doesn't come out right, don't worry about me, I'm just going on higher."
MICHAEL P. ANDERSON, SPACE SHUTTLE *CHALLENGER* CREW

HISTORICAL EVENTS

1788 Isaac Briggs and William Longstreet patent the steamboat.
1814 Mayon Volcano in the Philippines erupts, killing around 1,200 people; it is the most devastating eruption of this still active volcano.
1884 The first edition of the *Oxford English Dictionary* is published.
1893 Thomas A. Edison finishes construction of the first motion picture studio, the Black Maria in West Orange, New Jersey.
1896 The opera *La Bohème* premieres in Turin, Italy.
1920 The Royal Canadian Mounted Police begins operations.
1968 Viet Cong officer Nguyen Van Lem is executed by Nguyen Ngoc Loan, a South Vietnamese National Police chief. The execution is videotaped and photographed by Eddie Adams and helps sway public opinion against the Vietnam war.
1979 Ayatollah Khomeini is welcomed back into Tehran, Iran, after spending nearly 15 years in exile.
1989 The Western Australian towns of Kalgoorlie and Boulder amalgamate to form the City of Kalgoorlie–Boulder.
2003 Space shuttle *Columbia* disintegrates over Texas upon re-entry, killing all seven astronauts on board (see below).

Births

1859 Victor Herbert, cellist and conductor
1895 John Ford, film director
1901 Clark Gable, actor
1922 Renata (Ersilia Clotilde) Tebaldi, operatic diva
1931 Boris Yeltsin, Russian President
1937 Don Everly, singer
1938 Jacky Cupit, golfer
1942 Terry Jones, actor
1954 Bill Mumy, actor
1968 Lisa Marie Presley, daughter of Elvis

Deaths

1851 Mary Shelley, English author
1966 Hedda Hopper, gossip columnist
1966 Buster Keaton, American actor
2003 The crew of the space shuttle *Columbia*: Astronauts Michael P. Anderson, David Brown, Kalpana Chawla, Laurel Clark, Rick D. Husband, Willie McCool, Ilan Ramon

DAY TO REMEMBER

Religious festival Imbolc The festival of Imbolc, one of the cornerstones of the Celtic calendar, was held in association with the new farming season, with rituals performed to increase the power of the sun over the coming months. Imbolc is still a special time for Pagans.

In 2003, space shuttle *Columbia* disintegrated over Texas upon re-entry into the Earth's atmosphere, killing all seven astronauts on board. Debris from the shuttle scattered across Texas and Louisiana, crashing into car parks, forests, backyards, a reservoir, a rooftop, and a dentist's office. It was the first accident during landing in 42 years of space flight. The world's first reusable space vehicle, *Columbia* was the oldest of a fleet of four. Her sister ship *Challenger* exploded soon after lift-off 17 years previously, also killing all seven astronauts on board.

February 2

"Mistakes are the portals of discovery." JAMES JOYCE

Amin's reign of terror

Idi Amin was an army officer and President of Uganda (1971 to 1979) whose regime was notorious for its brutality. Hundreds of thousands of Ugandans were tortured and murdered during his presidency. Up to 6,000 of the army's 9,000 soldiers were executed because Amin believed they were loyal to his rivals.

Determined to make Uganda "a black man's country," Amin expelled 40,000–80,000 Indians and Pakistanis. Most of those expelled were third-generation descendants of workers brought to Uganda by the British colonial administration. Amin then launched a campaign of persecution against rival tribes, murdering between 100,000 and 500,000 people. Among those to die were politicians, diplomats, academics, clergy, doctors, bankers, journalists, and foreigners. So many corpses were thrown into the Nile River that workers had to continuously remove them to stop the intake ducts at a nearby dam from clogging up.

A combination of falling coffee prices (Uganda's main export), as well as the murder and expulsion of so many essential personnel, saw Uganda's economy spiral downward. In an attempt to divert attention from the country's internal problems, Amin attacked Tanzania in 1978. Tanzanian troops, assisted by armed Ugandan exiles, quickly beat Amin's army. Amin fled to Libya, leaving Uganda with an annual inflation rate of 200 percent, a national debt of U.S. $320 million, and a physically, mentally, culturally, and spiritually devastated population.

HISTORICAL EVENTS

- **1887** In Punxsutawney, Pennsylvania, U.S., the first Groundhog Day is observed.
- **1899** The Australian Premiers' Conference held in Melbourne decides to locate Australia's capital (Canberra) between Sydney and Melbourne.
- **1933** Just two days after becoming Chancellor of Germany, Adolf Hitler dissolves the German Parliament.
- **1943** The last German forces surrender to the Soviets after the Battle of Stalingrad.
- **1971** After a coup in Uganda, Idi Amin replaces President Milton Obote as leader (see above).
- **1972** The British Embassy in Dublin is destroyed in protest over Bloody Sunday.
- **1989** The last Soviet armored column departs from Kabul, ending nine years of military occupation of Afghanistan.
- **1990** In South Africa, President F.W. de Klerk allows the African National Congress to legally function again and promises to set human rights activist Nelson Mandela free.
- **2006** An ageing Egyptian passenger ferry carrying more than 1,400 people sinks in the Red Sea off the Saudi coast.

Births
- 1882 James Joyce, poet, author
- 1942 Graham Nash, singer, musician
- 1947 Farrah Fawcett, actress
- 1954 Christie Brinkley, model

Deaths
- 1969 Boris Karloff, actor
- 1970 Bertrand Russell, mathematician and philosopher, recipient of the Nobel Prize in Literature
- 1979 Sid Vicious, musician (Sex Pistols)
- 1987 Alistair MacLean, novelist
- 1995 Donald Pleasence, actor
- 1996 Gene Kelly, dancer and actor

DAYS TO REMEMBER

Religious day Candlemas This Christian festival marks the ritual purification of the Virgin Mary 40 days after the birth of Jesus, and the presentation of Jesus in the temple.

Religious day Catherine del Ricci's Day At the age of 20, Catherine (1522-1590) began a 12-year cycle of weekly ecstasies from noon Thursday until 4:00 P.M. Friday. Her sisters could follow the course of Christ's Passion, as wounds appeared on her body corresponding in order from the scourging and crowning with thorns.

February 3

"Life is what happens to you while you're busy making other plans." — JOHN LENNON

HISTORICAL EVENTS

- 1690 The colony of Massachusetts issues the first paper currency in America.
- 1916 Parliament buildings in Ottawa, Canada, burn down.
- 1931 The Napier earthquake, New Zealand's worst natural disaster, kills 258 people.
- 1947 Percival Prattis becomes the first African American news correspondent allowed in the U.S. House and Senate press gallery.
- 1959 It is discovered that a plane crash has killed rock-and-roll performers Buddy Holly, Ritchie Valens, and The Big Bopper (see below).
- 1964 The Beatles receive their first gold album award for *Meet the Beatles*.
- 1967 Ronald Ryan, the last person to be executed in Australia, is hanged in Pentridge Prison, Melbourne.
- 1972 The first Winter Olympics to be held in Asia open in Sapporo, Japan.
- 1984 The birth of the world's first baby conceived by embryo transplant is announced in Long Beach, California.
- 1995 Air Force Lt. Col. Eileen Collins becomes the first female space-shuttle pilot as *Discovery* blasts off from Cape Kennedy, Florida.

Births
- 1809 Felix Mendelssohn, composer
- 1894 Norman Rockwell, artist
- 1907 James A. Michener, novelist
- 1927 Val Doonican, Irish singer and entertainer
- 1947 Melanie (Safka), singer
- 1950 Morgan Fairchild, actress

Deaths
- 1468 Johannes Gutenberg, publisher
- 1924 Woodrow Wilson, twenty-eighth U.S. President
- 1956 Émile Borel, French mathematician, politician and resistance fighter

DAYS TO REMEMBER

Traditional day Setsubun (Japan) Meaning "seasonal division," this festival is held one day before the start of spring according to the Japanese lunar calendar.

Religious day St. Stephen's Day An Italian monk, St. Stephen (1774–1840) devoted himself to preaching and religious education for children, organizing a free school for poor children called La Scola per Gnent (the School for Nothing), with nearly 500 students and several lay teachers. During a cholera epidemic in 1840, St. Stephen worked tirelessly to assist his community until he too succumbed to the disease.

In the early hours of February 3, 1959, famous rock-and-rollers The Big Bopper (Jiles P. Richardson), Buddy Holly (Charles Holley), and Ritchie Valens (Richard Valenzuela) were killed when their chartered plane fell into a snow-covered field within minutes of takeoff from the Mason City Airport in the U.S. state of Iowa. The pilot, Roger A. Peterson, also died in the crash. The plane was discovered when daylight broke, a few miles north of Clear Lake, Iowa, where the musicians had appeared as part of a Winter Dance Party Tour. The coroner's investigation reported "disturbing wreckage and debris from the crash." The deaths have become known as "The Day The Music Died."

February 4

"Few men have virtue to withstand the highest bidder." — GEORGE WASHINGTON

HISTORICAL EVENTS

1789 George Washington is elected the first U.S. President, and three years later on this day is elected to a second term.
1862 Bacardi is founded as a small rum distillery in Santiago de Cuba in eastern Cuba.
1913 A patent for a "demountable tire-carrying rim" was issued to Louis Henry Perlman of New York City. This is the first automobile tire rim designed to be removed and remounted.
1948 Ceylon (later renamed Sri Lanka) becomes independent within the British Commonwealth.
1966 A Nippon Airways Boeing 727 jet plunges into Tokyo Bay, killing 133.
1974 The Symbionese Liberation Army kidnaps newspaper heiress Patty Hearst in Berkeley, California (see below).
1976 In Guatemala and Honduras, an earthquake kills more than 22,000 people.
1997 O. J. Simpson is found to be civilly liable for the deaths of his wife Nicole Brown Simpson and Ronald Goldman.
2003 The Federal Republic of Yugoslavia officially becomes two republics called Serbia and Montenegro, and adopts a new constitution.

Births
1677 Johann Ludwig Bach, composer
1902 Charles Lindbergh, pilot
1918 Ida Lupino, film actress and director
1921 Betty Friedan, feminist
1941 John Steel, musician (The Animals)
1947 Dan Quayle, U.S. Vice-President
1948 Alice Cooper, musician
1975 Natalie Imbruglia, musician and actress

Deaths
1983 Karen Carpenter, singer and musician
1987 Liberace, musician
2006 Betty Friedan, feminist

DAYS TO REMEMBER

Religious day St. John de Brito's Day This young Jesuit (1637–1693) studied the complex Indian caste system and established himself as an Indian ascetic. As a Pandara Swami, he converted as many as 10,000 people to Christianity. This angered the Brahmins, the highest Indian caste, who had him beheaded.

Religious day St. Veronica's Day While Jesus was carrying his cross, St. Veronica is believed to have offered him a cloth to wipe the sweat from his face. When he returned the cloth, an image of his face had miraculously appeared on the cloth. She is the patron saint of photographers.

The Patty Hearst abduction

On February 4, 1974, Patty Hearst, heiress to the Hearst newspaper fortune, was abducted by members of the Symbionese Liberation Army (SLA). They claimed they were starting a revolution of the underprivileged by declaring war on people with status and money. Patty's father, Randolph, initially responded to the groups' demands, distributing millions of dollars worth of food to the poor. In the ensuing weeks, several tapes of Patty's voice were released, increasingly toeing the SLA party line.

On April 15, police reviewing video tape of a bank robbery in San Francisco were amazed to see the face of 20-year-old Patty brandishing a gun in the hold-up. In September 1975, Patty was found in an apartment with two other SLA members. Patty claimed that prior to the robbery, her abductors had used mental, physical, and sexual abuse to brainwash her.

Patty was found guilty and sentenced to 25 years for the robbery, with an additional 10 years for a firearms charge. A judicial review shortened the sentence to seven years. Patty served 21 months before U.S. President Carter commuted her sentence in 1979.

February 5

"I not only use all the brains that I have, but all that I can borrow."

U.S. PRESIDENT WOODROW WILSON

HISTORICAL EVENTS

- **1885** King Léopold II of Belgium establishes the Congo as a personal possession.
- **1917** The U.S. Congress passes a law, over President Woodrow Wilson's veto, banning most Asian immigration to the U.S.
- **1936** Charlie Chaplin releases the last ever silent movie, *Modern Times*.
- **1958** A hydrogen bomb is lost by the U.S. Air Force off the coast of Savannah, Georgia, never to be recovered (see below).
- **1972** Bob Douglas becomes the first African American elected to the Basketball Hall of Fame.
- **1988** The charity organization Comic Relief in the U.K. holds the first Red Nose Day, raising £15 million.
- **1997** The "Big Three" banks in Switzerland announce the creation of a $71 million fund to aid Holocaust survivors and their families.
- **2001** Tom Cruise and Nicole Kidman announce that they have separated.
- **2004** Twenty-three Chinese people drown when a group of 35 cockle-pickers are trapped by rising tides in Morecambe Bay, England. Twenty-one of the bodies are recovered.
- **2004** Rebels from the Revolutionary Artibonite Resistance Front capture the city of Gonaïves, starting the 2004 Haiti rebellion.

DAYS TO REMEMBER

Religious day St. Agatha's Day After rejecting the advances of a Roman official, St. Agatha of Sicily (c. 230 C.E.) was imprisoned, tortured, had her breasts cut off, and eventually died in prison. She is venerated as patron saint of breast cancer patients.

National day Kashmir Day A minute's silence is observed in Pakistan to demonstrate solidarity with the Kashmiris in protesting India's occupation of the Kashmir valley.

Births
- **1878** André Citroën, French automobile pioneer
- **1906** John Carradine, actor
- **1908** Daisy and Violet Hilton, conjoined twin actresses
- **1919** Red Buttons, actor
- **1929** Al Worthington, baseball player
- **1945** Charlotte Rampling, actress
- **1948** Christopher Guest, actor, writer, director, and composer
- **1948** Barbara Hershey, actress
- **1962** Jennifer Jason Leigh, actress
- **1964** Laura Linney, actress
- **1969** Bobby Brown, singer

Deaths
- **1937** Lou Andreas-Salome, writer
- **1962** Jacques Ibert, composer
- **1977** Oscar Klein, physicist
- **1991** Dean Jagger, actor
- **1999** Wassily Leontief, economist, Bank of Sweden Prize winner
- **2006** Norma Candal, actress and comedienne

Has anybody seen our nuclear bomb?

On the night of February 5, 1958, a B-47 bomber carrying a hydrogen bomb on a training flight off the U.S. coast of Georgia collided with an F-86 fighter. The bomber was severely damaged, so before attempting to land, the pilot jettisoned the bomb into the tidal sands of Wassaw Sound off Tybee Island.

The Air Force looked for the bomb for two months before calling the search off and requesting a new H-bomb to replace the one it had lost. This was a major embarrassment for all concerned; since 1945, the U.S. had lost more than 10 nuclear weapons. In a joint statement to the press, the Defense Department and the Atomic Energy Commission, admitted that radioactivity could be "scattered" by the detonation of the H-bombs, but down-played the possibility of that ever happening.

Remarkably, though the "Tybee Bomb" had long been a subject of local lore, the incident drew little attention until some four decades later when a deep-sea salvage company, run by former Air Force personnel and a CIA agent, believed it had found the location of the 7,600-pound (3,500 kg) bomb. The media got hold of the story, and the case of the "Tybee Bomb" came under national scrutiny.

There remains controversy over whether to undertake the long and costly process of once more attempting to recover the bomb. While there is no official acknowledgment – apart from the pilot's testimony – that the bomb has its plutonium capsule attached, it does contain a store of uranium, which presents the possibility of an environmental disaster. The bomb also holds some 400 pounds (180 kg) of conventional explosives. Some experts, however, believe that given the presence of unstable chemicals and deteriorating explosives, it is safer to leave the bomb intact – wherever it might be.

February 6

"I know nothing about sex because I was always married." — ZSA ZSA GABOR

HISTORICAL EVENTS

- **1819** Sir Thomas Stamford Raffles founds Singapore.
- **1840** The British and the Maoris sign the Treaty of Waitangi, founding New Zealand.
- **1904** The Russian–Japanese war begins.
- **1952** Elizabeth II becomes Queen upon the death of her father George VI. At the exact moment of succession, she is in a tree house at the Treetops Hotel in Kenya.
- **1959** Jack Kilby of Texas Instruments files the first patent for an integrated circuit which initiates the digital revolution and eventually wins a Nobel Prize (see right).
- **1996** A Dominican Alas Nacionales Boeing 757-225 crashes after take-off into the Atlantic Ocean on the coast of the Dominican Republic, killing 189 passengers.
- **2004** In Russia, a suicide attack in the Moscow metro kills 40 commuters, and injures 129 others. The blast is blamed on Chechen separatist groups.
- **2005** Jerrick De Leon, born 13 weeks premature, becomes the world's smallest infant to survive an open-heart procedure, called an arterial switch.

DAYS TO REMEMBER

Religious day The Nagasaki Martyrs Twenty-six Franciscan and Jesuit missionaries and Japanese converts, accused of preaching and supporting the outlawed faith of Christianity, were crucified in 1597 at Nagasaki, Japan.

Traditional day Bob Marley Day Born on February 6, 1945, in Jamaica, Robert Nesta Marley is celebrated for popularizing reggae music throughout the world. The themes of his songs often represented issues faced by the poor and oppressed. He died in 1981 from cancer and was buried with his Gibson guitar and Bible. In 1991 his birthday was proclaimed Bob Marley Day.

Births
- 1564 Christopher Marlowe, playwright
- 1895 Babe Ruth, baseball player
- 1911 Ronald Reagan, fortieth U.S. President
- 1912 Eva Braun, mistress of Adolf Hitler
- 1917 Zsa Zsa Gabor, actress
- 1932 François Truffaut, film director
- 1950 Natalie Cole, singer
- 1962 Axl Rose, singer (Guns N' Roses)
- 1966 Rick Astley, singer

Deaths
- 1993 Joseph Mankiewicz, director, producer, and writer
- 1994 Joseph Cotten, actor
- 1994 Jack Kirby, comic book writer
- 1998 Carl Wilson, musician (The Beach Boys)

In the 1950s, after the breakthrough in electronics created by transistor technology, new ways to further miniaturize electronics were being sought. Jack Kilby of Texas Instruments filed a patent for an integrated circuit, with all components formed on the one small piece of semiconducting material, on February 6, 1959. Within 20 years, the technology had advanced to the point where chips were as small as the one pictured above. Today, by chemically altering tiny areas on a sliver of silicon, we can create the resistors, capacitors, diodes, transistors, and other electronic components that work together to form a circuit. The integrated circuit is used in most modern technologies, controlling everything from laptops to cars to satellite transmissions, and continues to enable increasingly complex, more reliable, and cost-effective electronics.

February 7

"No one is useless in this world who lightens the burdens of another." — CHARLES DICKENS

HISTORICAL EVENTS

1856 The colonial Tasmanian Parliament in Australia passes the first piece of legislation (the Electoral Act 1856) anywhere in the world providing for elections by way of a secret ballot.

1942 In Banja Luka, Croatian Nazis kill 2,300 Serbian civilians, among them 551 children.

1964 The legendary Beatles arrive on their first visit to the U.S.

1971 Women gain the right to vote in Switzerland.

1979 Pluto moves inside Neptune's orbit for the first time since either planet was known to science.

1984 Astronauts Bruce McCandless II and Robert L. Stewart from space shuttle *Challenger* make the first untethered spacewalk.

1990 The Central Committee of the Soviet Communist Party agrees to give up its monopoly of power.

1991 The IRA launches a mortar attack on 10 Downing Street during a Cabinet meeting (see below).

1992 The European Union is formed.

DAY TO REMEMBER

Religious day Giles Mary-of-Saint-Joseph's Day
A rope maker by trade, Giles (1729–1812) applied to become a priest but lacked the education and so became a lay brother. He worked with the sick, especially lepers, traveling outside the city to help people who had become shunned and isolated. Even in life he was considered a saint. Huge crowds turned out for his funeral.

Births
- **1478** Sir Thomas More, statesman, humanist, and author
- **1812** Charles Dickens, novelist
- **1908** Buster Crabbe, swimmer and actor
- **1920** An Wang, computer pioneer
- **1945** Pete Postlethwaite, actor
- **1960** James Spader, actor
- **1962** Garth Brooks, singer
- **1967** Chris Rock, comedian and actor

Deaths
- **1652** Gregorio Allegri, composer
- **1736** Stephen Gray, astronomer and scientist
- **1938** Harvey Firestone, manufacturer
- **1993** Lillian Gish, actress
- **1999** King Hussein of Jordan
- **1999** José Silva, founder of the Silva Method

On the morning of February 7, 1991, senior figures in the British Government gathered at 10 Downing Street, the official residence of the British Prime Minister, to discuss their strategy in the Gulf War. Just after 10:00 A.M., a mortar shell exploded in the back garden, shattering windows in the Cabinet room. The mortar had been launched from a white van parked in the area. Two other mortars launched seconds later caused damage to numbers 11 and 12 Downing Street, the offices of the Treasury and Foreign Ministry. The mortars were claimed by the Provisional IRA. Each of the missiles had missed their target, the intention being a direct hit on the Cabinet room. An IRA car bomb (right) exploded in the same vicinity in 1973.

February 8

"A single death is a tragedy; a million deaths is a statistic." — JOSEPH STALIN

Champion racehorse abducted

Born in 1978 and bred in Ireland at stables owned by the Aga Khan, Shergar was a beloved racehorse whose greatest success was winning the 1981 Epsom Derby by 10 lengths – the biggest margin in the race's history. When he was retired to stud, 34 syndication shares were sold for £250,000 each.

On February 8, 1983, a week before the start of Shergar's second breeding season, two armed and masked men burst into the home of head groom James Fitzgerald, locking his family in a downstairs room before forcing him at gunpoint to release Shergar from his security stable. Ransom demands came through, though it has never been clarified how much was demanded and who was claiming responsibility for the kidnap. The syndicate refused to pay, and Shergar's disappearance continues to remain a mystery.

Of the theories that abound regarding the kidnapping, most point to the involvement of the IRA as a fund-raiser to buy weapons. Years later, a documentary claimed that Gardai, the Irish police service, had uncovered a bullet magazine for a specialist firearm at the scene of the kidnapping. It was linked to a gun used in attacks on the British Army in the north. Sean O'Callaghan, a former IRA member, turned informer, claimed that the IRA had demanded a £5 million ransom that was never met, and that the horse had been killed by his abductors soon after he was taken because they were unable to handle him.

To this day Shergar's fate has still not been confirmed.

HISTORICAL EVENTS

- **1587** Mary, Queen of Scots, is beheaded, accused of plotting against her cousin, Queen Elizabeth of England.
- **1855** Across a large area of Devon, England, people awake to find strange hoof-shaped tracks in the snow, even passing over rooftops. Clergymen say it is the devil looking for sinners, and the tracks become known as The Devil's Footprints.
- **1924** The first state execution in the U.S. using gas takes place in Nevada State Prison.
- **1969** Just after midnight, a large meteorite scatters several tons of material over a massive area of Chihuahua, Mexico. Named after the closest village, Allende, the meteorite is dated at 4.5 billion years old.
- **1983** Racehorse Shergar is kidnapped in Ireland, and never recovered. Lloyds of London pays $10.6 million in insurance (see above).
- **1989** An Independent Air Boeing 707 crashes into Santa Maria Mountain in the Azores Islands off the coast of Portugal, killing 144 passengers.
- **1998** Female ice hockey is played in the Olympics for the first time.

Births
- **1828** Jules Verne, author
- **1920** Lana Turner, actress
- **1925** Jack Lemmon, actor and film director
- **1931** James Dean, actor
- **1932** John Williams, composer and conductor
- **1940** Ted Koppel, journalist
- **1941** Nick Nolte, actor
- **1950** Dan Seals, singer
- **1953** Mary Steenburgen, actress
- **1955** John Grisham, novelist

Deaths
- **1587** Mary, Queen of Scots
- **1999** Iris Murdoch, author

DAYS TO REMEMBER

Religious day Nirvana Day Also known as Parinirvana, this is the celebration of Buddha's death when he reached total Nirvana, at the age of 80.

Religious day St. John of Matha's Day At the first Mass St. John (1160–1223) celebrated, he had a vision which inspired him to found the Order of the Most Holy Trinity and of Captives. Today the Order has about 600 members working in prison ministries.

February 9

Births
- 1883 Garnet Carter, inventor of miniature golf
- 1854 Aletta Henriette Jacobs, physician and family planning pioneer
- 1923 Norman E. Shumway, surgeon and pioneer in heart transplant surgery
- 1942 Carole King, singer and composer
- 1943 Joe Pesci, actor
- 1945 Mia Farrow, actress
- 1955 Charles Shaughnessy, actor
- 1979 Zhang Ziyi, actress

Deaths
- 1881 Fyodor Dostoyevsky, novelist
- 1976 Percy Faith, musician and composer
- 1981 Bill Haley, musician
- 2002 Princess Margaret, U.K. royal
- 2006 Freddie Laker, entrepreneur

HISTORICAL EVENTS
- 1885 The first Japanese people arrive in Hawaii.
- 1895 William G. Morgan invents volleyball.
- 1900 The Davis Cup tennis competition is established.
- 1950 Senator Joseph McCarthy accuses the U.S. State Department of being filled with communists (see below).
- 1960 Joanne Woodward receives the first star on the Hollywood Walk of Fame.
- 1962 Jamaica becomes an independent nation within the Commonwealth of Nations.
- 1969 The Boeing 747 undergoes its first test flight.
- 1965 The first U.S. combat troops are sent to South Vietnam.
- 1996 The IRA declares the end of its 18-month ceasefire, shortly followed by a large bomb in London's Canary Wharf.
- 2001 The American submarine USS *Greeneville* accidentally strikes and sinks the *Ehime-Maru*, a Japanese training vessel operated by the Uwajima Fishery High School.

DAY TO REMEMBER

Saint's day St. Apollonia's Day A holy virgin in Egypt, St. Apollonia (c. 249 C.E.) suffered martyrdom during an uprising against Christians. Her teeth were broken with pincers and she was given the choice of renouncing Christ or being burned alive. She leapt onto the fire herself. She is the patron saint of dentists and toothaches.

> *"McCarthyism is Americanism with its sleeves rolled."*
> JOSEPH R. MCCARTHY

The McCarthyist regime

Joseph McCarthy became a Republican senator in 1947. His early years in the Senate were unimpressive. In 1949, however, McCarthy found a cause amid the anti-communist political atmosphere of the Cold War era. He claimed he knew the names of 205 Communist party members holding high positions in the State Department. A committee looked into the accusations and reprimanded McCarthy for making false claims, but despite these sanctions, McCarthy intensified his attacks.

Re-elected in 1952, McCarthy was appointed chairman of the Permanent Investigations Subcommittee of the Senate Government Operations Committee. By 1953, McCarthy was accusing people from all walks of life of being Soviet spies or Communist sympathizers and bringing them before Congressional inquiries. The subsequent innuendo and rumor-mongering cost many people their jobs.

It was his investigation of the activities of an Army dentist that eventually led to his downfall. In 1954, the Army launched a counterattack, and McCarthy's own subcommittee decided to hold hearings on the matter. The televised hearings exposed McCarthy's actions as irresponsible and dishonest. On December 2, 1954, the Senate voted overwhelmingly to censure McCarthy.

McCarthy responded with a bitter attack on the administration and apologized to the American people for urging them to vote for Eisenhower. Over the next three years, his health deteriorated and he began to drink heavily. He died in 1957, officially of acute hepatitis, but unofficially of cirrhosis of the liver.

February 10

"Do not fear death so much, but rather the inadequate life." — BERTOLT BRECHT, *THE MOTHER*

In the late 1950s, U-2 pilots carried out espionage missions for the U.S. Central Intelligence Agency and Airforce over hostile countries, gathering photographic evidence of military and political installations. On May 1, 1960, the U-2 flown by Francis Powers (right) was shot down by a surface-to-air missile over Sverdlovsk in the Soviet Union. He was convicted of espionage and sentenced to seven years of hard labor. Initially the U.S. denied the purpose of the mission; however, the Soviets had recovered the surveillance camera and Powers' survival pack. On February 10, 1962, the U.S. agreed to exchange Powers for captured Soviet Colonel Vilyam Fisher (alias Rudolf Abel). The incident worsened East–West relations, and the exchange of spies was considered a face-saving political act rather than a humanitarian one.

Births
- 1893 Jimmy Durante, actor, singer, and comedian
- 1898 Bertolt Brecht, author
- 1901 Stella Adler, actress
- 1930 Robert Wagner, actor
- 1939 Roberta Flack, singer
- 1941 Michael Apted, director
- 1944 Peter Allen, singer and actor
- 1950 Mark Spitz, swimmer
- 1955 Greg Norman, golfer
- 1963 Lenny Dykstra, baseball player

Deaths
- 1837 Aleksandr Pushkin, poet and novelist
- 1912 Joseph Lister, surgeon
- 1917 John William Waterhouse, artist
- 1932 Edgar Wallace, novelist and screenwriter
- 1957 Laura Ingalls Wilder, author
- 1993 Fred Hollows, ophthalmologist
- 2005 Arthur Miller, playwright

HISTORICAL EVENTS

- 1355 The St. Scholastica's Day riot between locals and students in Oxford, England, leaves 63 students and 30 locals dead. For the next 500 years as compensation, the mayor and 62 citizens attend St Mary's church every February 10 and pay one penny each.
- 1763 The 1763 Treaty of Paris ends the Seven Years War and France cedes Canada to Great Britain.
- 1863 Alanson Crane patents the fire extinguisher.
- 1870 The YWCA (Young Women's Christian Association) is founded.
- 1931 New Delhi becomes the capital of India.
- 1962 Captured American U2 spy plane pilot Francis Gary Powers is exchanged for captured Soviet spy Rudolf Abel (see above).
- 1964 The aircraft carrier HMAS *Melbourne* collides with the HMAS *Voyager* off the south coast of New South Wales, Australia. The *Voyager* sinks with a loss of 82 lives.
- 1999 Avalanches in the French Alps kill at least 10 people.
- 2005 North Korea suspends multi-nation talks and officially admits to developing nuclear weapons.

DAYS TO REMEMBER

Religious day Feast Day of St. Paul's Shipwreck Celebrated on this day in Malta, the feast commemorates the shipwreck of St. Paul in Malta in 60 C.E. St. Paul stayed in Malta for three months, performing miracles and converting the local people.

Religious day St. Scholastica's Day The twin sister of St. Benedict of Nursia, St. Scholastica (440–543) was a nun in the area around St. Benedict's Abbey of Monte Cassino in Italy. On Scholastica's last annual visit with her brother, who was a monk, she begged him to stay for the evening. When he refused, Scholastica closed her hands in prayer and a wild storm started outside so that Benedict was unable to return to his monastery. Three days later, he saw his sister's soul leaving the earth and ascending to heaven in the form of a shining white dove. Benedict later discovered that Scholastica had indeed died that day.

February 11

"To be free is not merely to cast off one's chains, but to live in a way that respects and enhances the freedom of others." — NELSON MANDELA

HISTORICAL EVENTS

- 660 B.C.E. Traditional founding date of Japan by Emperor Jimmu.
- 1809 Robert Fulton patents the steamboat.
- 1916 Emma Goldman, a Lithuanian-born anarcho-communist, is arrested for lecturing on birth control.
- 1971 The U.S., U.K., U.S.S.R., and other nations sign the Seabed Treaty, outlawing nuclear weapons in international waters.
- 1978 China lifts a ban on works by Aristotle, Shakespeare, and Dickens.
- 1979 Ayatollah Ruhollah Khomeini seizes power in Iran.
- 1990 Nelson Mandela, a political prisoner for 27 years, is freed from Victor Verster prison outside Cape Town, South Africa (see below).

DAYS TO REMEMBER

Religious day Feast Day of Our Lady of Lourdes It is claimed that the Virgin Mary appeared to 14-year-old Bernadette Soubirous (now St. Bernadette) in a Lourdes grotto in 1858. Thousands of pilgrims come to the site from all over the world. The Catholic Church has officially recognised more than 60 miracle healings from the spring's water.

National day Inventors' Day The U.S. Congress has appointed this day in recognition of the great advancements in technology and quality of life thanks to the inventions of innovative – and in many cases courageous – people.

Births
- 1847 Thomas Alva Edison, inventor and businessman
- 1909 Joseph Mankiewicz, film director
- 1917 Sidney Sheldon, author
- 1919 Eva Gabor, actress
- 1934 Mary Quant, fashion designer
- 1936 Burt Reynolds, actor
- 1937 Bill Lawry, cricketer
- 1938 Manuel Noriega, dictator
- 1962 Sheryl Crow, singer/songwriter, musician
- 1969 Jennifer Aniston, actress

Deaths
- 1650 René Descartes, philosopher
- 1963 Sylvia Plath, writer
- 2000 Roger Vadim, film director

In June 1964, Nelson Rolihlahla Mandela was sentenced to life imprisonment for his role in the armed resistance against apartheid in South Africa. He spent the first years of his sentence on Robben Island, off Cape Town, doing hard labor. The weight of international opinion and the relaxation of apartheid laws led to his eventual release from Victor Verster prison near Cape Town 27 years later. People celebrated throughout the world and thousands filled the streets in Cape Town. On May 10, 1994, Mandela was inaugurated President of South Africa.

DATEline

February 12

"Study the past if you would define the future." CONFUCIUS

HISTORICAL EVENTS

1541 Santiago, Chile is founded by Spanish conquistador, Pedro de Valdivia.
1879 The first artificial ice rink in North America opens at New York City's Madison Square Garden.
1909 The National Association for the Advancement of Colored People (NAACP) is founded in the U.S.
1912 China adopts the Gregorian calendar.
1973 The first American POWs are released by the Viet Cong during the Vietnam War.
1999 President Bill Clinton is acquitted by the U.S. Senate in his impeachment trial (see right).
2001 The first spacecraft lands on an asteroid. NEAR (Near Earth Asteroid Rendezvous) *Shoemaker* spacecraft touches down in the "saddle" region of asteroid 433 Eros.
2002 The trial of former President of the Federal Republic of Yugoslavia, Slobodan Milosevic, begins at the United Nations war crimes tribunal in The Hague.
2004 Mattel Inc. announces the split of Barbara Millicent Roberts and Ken Carson (A.K.A. Barbie and Ken) after 43 years of dating.

DAY TO REMEMBER

Saint day Julian the Hospitaller's Day While on a hunting trip, a stag spoke to Julian (c. 7 C.E.) and predicted he would kill his own parents. Tragically the prophecy was fulfilled; grief-struck, Julian built a hospice beside a river where he cared for the poor and sick, and rowed travelers across the river for free. One night, Julian gave his bed to a pilgrim leper who revealed himself to be an angel and announced that Christ had accepted Julian's penance.

Births
1567 Thomas Campion, composer and poet
1809 Charles Darwin, naturalist
1809 Abraham Lincoln, sixteenth U.S. President
1818 Otto Ludwig, writer
1828 George Meredith, writer
1857 Bobby Peel, cricketer
1881 Anna Pavlova, ballerina
1884 Max Beckmann, painter
1915 Lorne Greene, actor
1923 Franco Zeffirelli, film and opera director

Deaths
1538 Albrecht Altdorfer, painter
1804 Immanuel Kant, philosopher
1929 Lillie Langtry, singer and actress
1971 James C. Penney, department store founder
1993 James Bulger, toddler, murder victim

Sex scandal in the White House

Bill Clinton became the second president in U.S. history to be impeached for perjury and obstruction of justice. These charges stemmed from an accusation of sexual harassment by Paula Jones, a former Arkansas state employee. According to her story, in 1991 she was escorted to the hotel room of Clinton, then Governor of Arkansas, where he propositioned her. She sued him but the lawsuit was eventually dismissed without proceeding to trial because Jones was unable to demonstrate any damages. Clinton paid Jones an out-of-court settlement of U.S. $850,000 to stop her from making an appeal. He was also fined U.S. $91,000 for a contempt-of-court citation for evasive and misleading answers.

Investigations of the Jones case led to further accusations of sexual misconduct, in particular with White House intern Monica Lewinsky. While working as a paid staffer at the Pentagon, Lewinsky had a short-term sexual relationship with the President. Clinton and Lewinsky both agreed that the relationship involved oral sex but not sexual intercourse. The news of this affair, and the resulting investigation and impeachment, became known as the Lewinsky scandal or Monicagate. The House Judiciary Committee presented four articles of impeachment against President Clinton to the House, two of which, perjury and obstruction of justice, were passed. The other two charges consisted of improperly influencing witnesses and obstruction of justice. On this day in 1999, the President was acquitted by the Senate of both charges.

February 13

"I do not feel obliged to believe that the same God who has endowed us with sense, reason, and intellect has intended us to forgo their use." — GALILEO GALILEI

Births
- 1743 Joseph Banks, botanist and naturalist
- 1933 Kim Novak, actress
- 1934 George Segal, actor
- 1938 Oliver Reed, actor
- 1942 Peter Tork, musician and actor
- 1944 Stockard Channing, actress
- 1944 Jerry Springer, television host
- 1950 Peter Gabriel, musician
- 1974 Robbie Williams, singer

Deaths
- 1883 Richard Wagner, composer
- 2002 Waylon Jennings, musician

HISTORICAL EVENTS
- 1633 Galileo Galilei arrives in Rome to be tried by the Inquisition for his belief that the Earth revolves around the Sun.
- 1668 Spain recognizes Portugal as an independent nation.
- 1692 Thirty-eight Scots from Clan Macdonald are killed at Glen Coe for not pledging allegiance to the new King of Great Britain, William of Orange.
- 1894 Auguste and Louis Lumière patent the Cinematographe, a combination movie camera and projector.
- 1955 Israel obtains four of the seven Dead Sea scrolls.
- 1960 France tests its first atomic bomb.
- 1974 Aleksandr Solzhenitsyn, winner of the Nobel Prize in Literature in 1970, is exiled from the Soviet Union (see below).
- 1990 An agreement is reached for a two-stage plan to reunite Germany.
- 1996 The Nepalese People's War begins.
- 2001 An earthquake measuring 6.6 on the Richter scale hits El Salvador, killing at least 400 people.

DAY TO REMEMBER
Religious day St. Fulcran's Day
In 949, St. Fulcran (c. 920–1006) was consecrated Bishop of Lodeve, France. Bishop for 57 years, he rebuilt many churches and convents, founded the monastery of St. Sauveur and built several hospitals for the poor. Buried in the cathedral of Lodeve, his body was disinterred and burned by the Huguenots in 1572.

On this day in 1974, Aleksandr Solzhenitsyn, winner of the Nobel Prize in Literature, was exiled from the Soviet Union. Arrested for privately criticizing Stalin, he was sentenced to eight years in a labor camp. This gave him fuel for his novel, *One Day in the Life of Ivan Denisovich*, but it was his monumental history of Soviet prisons, *The Gulag Archipelago*, that brought international awareness of the horrors of the system. He was deported and stripped of his Soviet citizenship. He lived in the U.S. until 1994, then returned to Russia with his wife.

February 14

"One word frees us of all the weight and pain of life: That word is love." — SOPHOCLES

HISTORICAL EVENTS

- 1779 Navigator and explorer Captain James Cook is killed by the natives of the Sandwich Islands.
- 1876 Alexander Graham Bell and Elisha Gray separately apply for a patent for the telephone. The U.S. Supreme Court rules in favor of Bell.
- 1900 In South Africa, 20,000 British troops invade the Orange Free State.
- 1918 The Soviet Union adopts the Gregorian calendar.
- 1924 The International Business Machines Corporation (IBM) is founded.
- 1929 St. Valentine's Day Massacre: Seven gangster rivals of Al Capone are murdered in Chicago, Illinois.
- 1945 Chile, Ecuador, Paraguay, and Peru join the United Nations.
- 1989 Iranian leader Ayatollah Khomeini issues a *fatwa* encouraging Muslims to kill the author of *The Satanic Verses*, Salman Rushdie (see right).
- 1989 The first of 24 satellites of the Global Positioning System is placed into orbit.
- 2005 Lebanon's former Prime Minister, Rafik Hariri, is assassinated, prompting the Cedar Revolution.

DAYS TO REMEMBER

Traditional day St. Valentine's Day Lovers all over the world exchange cards and gifts on this day. There were at least three different St. Valentines, all martyrs, and all mentioned in the early martyrologies under the date of February 14. Two were Italian, one African. Since so little is known or can be confirmed about them, in 1969 the Catholic Church officially dropped February 14 as the Feast of St. Valentine.

Religious day St. Trifon's Day On February 14, people in Bulgaria may be celebrating both St. Valentine's Day and St. Trifon's Day. St. Trifon Zarezan, who had the divine power to cure any sickness, cut off his nose on this day while pruning the vines in his vineyard. Every year, a ceremonial pruning of the vines is part of a celebration held to honor St. Trifon, guardian of vine-growers, tavern-keepers and gardeners.

Florence Henderson (second from top left) is best known for her role as Carol Brady in the legendary American television series *The Brady Bunch*.

Births

- 1404 Leone Battista Alberti, painter, poet, and philosopher
- 1894 Jack Benny, actor and comedian
- 1913 Jimmy Hoffa, U.S. labor union leader
- 1929 Vic Morrow, actor
- 1934 Florence Henderson, actress
- 1944 Carl Bernstein, journalist
- 1944 Alan Parker, film director and writer

Deaths

- 1744 John Hadley, inventor
- 1975 P. G. Wodehouse, writer
- 2003 Dolly the sheep, first cloned mammal

Writer's death sentence

In 1989, Iranian leader Ayatollah Khomeini issued a *fatwa* calling on Muslims to kill the author of *The Satanic Verses*, Salman Rushdie.

"I inform the proud Muslim people of the world that the author of *The Satanic Verses* book – which is against Islam, the Prophet, and the Koran – and all involved in its publication, who were aware of its content, are sentenced to death."

He then added, "Anyone who dies in the cause of ridding the world of Rushdie will be regarded as a martyr and go directly to heaven." Khomeini also offered a U.S. $3 million bounty. India, Pakistan, South Africa, Saudi Arabia, and Egypt all banned the book. The Indian-born British author went into hiding, making only rare public appearances.

After the death of Khomeini in 1989, Rushdie made an apology and a statement of adherence to Islam, but this was deemed inadequate. Ayatollah Khomeini had declared, "Even if Salman Rushdie repents and becomes the most pious man of [our] time, it is incumbent on every Muslim to employ everything he has, his life and his wealth, to send him to hell…" Bookstores were firebombed for selling the book, book-burning rallies were held, and personal attacks were carried out on Rushdie's publishers and translators, one of whom died.

In 1998, the Iranian Government declared that it would not carry out the death sentence against Rushdie, and the writer came out of hiding. Iranian clerics, however, have not declared the *fatwa* lifted.

February 15

In 2003 over the weekend of February 15 and 16, protests against the Iraq War occurred in over 700 locations worldwide. In a display of global defiance, millions of people took to the streets to protest against the American invasion of Iraq. Protesters called for U.S. President George W. Bush not to break ranks with the United Nations Security Council and to find a peaceful way to disarm Iraq. Banners declaring everything from "Quakers for Peace," the "Socialist Alliance", and "Free Palestine" waved side by side. Estimates of protest action suggest the involvement of up to 30 million people, making this the largest day of protest in history.

HISTORICAL EVENTS

- 399 B.C.E. The Athenian philosopher Socrates is tried and sentenced to death.
- 1852 Great Ormond Street Hospital for Sick Children, London, admits its first patient.
- 1879 U.S. President Rutherford B. Hayes signs a bill allowing female attorneys to argue cases before the Supreme Court.
- 1903 Morris Michtom and his wife Rose introduce the first teddy bear in America.
- 1936 Adolf Hitler announces the building of Volkswagens for the German people.
- 1961 Sabena Flight 548 crashes in Belgium, killing 73, including the entire U.S. figure skating team and several coaches.
- 1965 A new red-and-white maple leaf design is adopted as the flag of Canada, replacing the old Canadian Red Ensign banner.
- 1989 The Soviet Union officially announces that all its troops have left Afghanistan, ending nine years of military conflict.
- 2003 Protests against the Iraq War take place worldwide (see above).

DAYS TO REMEMBER

Historical day Lupercalia (Ancient Rome) This festival was held near the cave where the founders of Rome, Romulus and Remus, were suckled by a she-wolf. The Lupercalia was held in honor of Lupercus, who protected the Roman flocks from wolves.

Religious day Candlemas (Eastern Orthodox) Although Candlemas is observed on February 2 in the West, for churches that have kept the Julian calendar, it is celebrated on February 15. The date of Candlemas is set 40 days after the birth of Jesus.

Religious day Jon Frum Day Although most of Vanuatu is Christian, some locals from Tanna Island follow Jon Frum, a cargo cult worshipping a white North American named Jon Frum. Members believe that when Frum returns, the mountains North will crumble, filling the rivers with fertile land, and the villages will become prosperous.

Births

- 1571 Michael Praetorius, composer and organist
- 1564 Galileo Galilei, astronomer and physicist
- 1856 Emil Kraepelin, psychiatrist who differentiated schizophrenia and manic–depressive illness
- 1861 Alfred North Whitehead, mathematician and philosopher
- 1882 John Barrymore, actor
- 1907 Cesar Romero, actor
- 1931 Claire Bloom, actress
- 1946 Marisa Berenson, actress
- 1947 John Coolidge Adams, composer
- 1951 Jane Seymour, actress
- 1954 Matt Groening, cartoonist

Deaths

- 1621 Michael Praetorius composer and organist
- 1965 Nat King Cole, singer and musician
- 1984 Ethel Merman, singer and actress
- 1988 Richard P. Feynman, theoretical physicist

February 16

DATE*line*

"The woman who is known only through a man is known wrong."

HENRY B. ADAMS

HISTORICAL EVENTS

- 600 Pope Gregory I decrees that "God bless you" is the correct response to a sneeze.
- 1568 The entire population of the Netherlands – three million people – is sentenced to death by the Roman Catholic church for heresy.
- 1923 Howard Carter unseals the burial chamber of Pharaoh Tutankhamen.
- 1937 Wallace H. Carothers receives a patent for nylon.
- 1959 Fidel Castro becomes President of Cuba.
- 1983 The Ash Wednesday bushfires in Victoria and South Australia claim the lives of over 70 people in Australia's worst recorded fires (see below).
- 1987 The trial of John Demjanjuk, accused of being a Nazi guard and dubbed "Ivan the Terrible" in the Treblinka extermination camp, starts in Jerusalem.
- 1991 U.S. and U.K. war planes bomb the suburbs of Baghdad during the Gulf War, injuring at least 11 civilians and killing three others.
- 1998 China Airlines Flight 676 crashes into a residential area nearby Chiang Kai-shek International Airport, killing all 196 on board and six people on the ground.
- 2005 The Kyoto Protocol on climate change comes into force, following its ratification by Russia.

Births
- 1838 Henry Adams, historian and novelist
- 1935 Sonny Bono, entertainer and U.S. congressman
- 1958 Ice-T, rapper, songwriter, and actor
- 1959 John McEnroe, tennis player
- 1973 Cathy Freeman, athlete

Deaths
- 2001 William Masters, gynecologist and sexologist
- 2004 Shirley Strickland, athlete

DAYS TO REMEMBER

Religious day St. Daniel's Day An Egyptian who ministered to Christians, St. Daniel (c. 280) was condemned during the persecutions of the Roman Emperor Maximus to work the mines of Cilicia. When his continuing faith was exposed, he was arrested, tortured, and beheaded in 309, by order of the governor Firmilian.

Ash Wednesday

At the beginning of each summer, Australians await with cynicism the media pronouncement that the bushland is a "tinderbox." Bored with the cliché, Australians are nonetheless alert to the truth behind it: Every few years severe bushfires cause widespread devastation. Almost a quarter of the fires are deliberately lit; the rest are accidental or occur naturally. Fuelled by hot, windy conditions, the flames suck up dry, discarded bark, branches, and leaves, and feed off flammable oils in the eucalypt trees.

In the summer of 1983, most of southeastern Australia was in drought. Fire-fighters had been working hard in the months before, clearing away forest fuel, putting in firebreaks, training additional staff, and organizing extra fire-fighting equipment. A total fire ban was in place.

On February 16 – Ash Wednesday for Christians, the first day of Lent when a smudge of ash is dabbed on their foreheads – the temperature climbed quickly to more than 105°F (40°C). Winds from the desert region of central Australia were picking up speeds of over 60 miles per hour (100 km/h). Branches were crashing into power lines, showering dry grasses and bush with sparks. It was an arsonist's playground. Of 100 separate fires spotted that day throughout the states of South Australia and Victoria, many appeared to be deliberately lit. As the afternoon grew hotter, the fires grew worse. Hundreds of police officers and soldiers joined the paid fire-fighters and volunteers. Altogether 17,000 men and women joined forces to battle the fires.

With the help of rain in South Australia, the fires were brought under control on Wednesday night. In Victoria, smaller fires burned until Sunday. When the ashes had settled, the tragic outcome became clear: Amid the heartbreaking loss of vegetation, agriculture, homes, and animals, over 70 people were dead.

February 17

> "My Grandmother is over 80 and still doesn't need glasses. Drinks right out of the bottle."
> — HENNY YOUNGMAN

HISTORICAL EVENTS

- **1867** The first ship passes through the Suez Canal.
- **1895** *Swan Lake*, with music by Peter Ilyich Tchaikovsky, is first performed at full length in St. Petersburg, Russia.
- **1933** The U.S. magazine *Newsweek* is published for the first time.
- **1933** The Blaine Act ends Prohibition, allowing the sale of alcohol in the U.S.
- **1938** The first public experimental demonstration of Baird color television is transmitted from Crystal Palace to the Dominion Theatre, London.
- **1947** *The Voice of America* begins to transmit radio broadcasts into the Soviet Union.
- **1949** Chaim Weizmann is elected first President of Israel.
- **1959** The first weather satellite, Vanguard 2, is launched to measure cloud-cover distribution.
- **1995** The Cenepa War between Peru and Ecuador ends on a cease-fire brokered by the United Nations.
- **1996** In Philadelphia, Pennsylvania, world champion Garry Kasparov beats the Deep Blue supercomputer in a chess match (see below).

DAY TO REMEMBER

Saint's day St. Fintan's Day According to legend, an angel visited St. Fintan's mother to explain that she would have a holy son. Fintan of Clonenagh (c. 550) was reputed to have the gifts of prophecy and witnesses say that when he prayed, he was surrounded by light.

Births

- 1864 Banjo Paterson, poet
- 1929 Patricia Routledge, actress
- 1930 Ruth Rendell, writer
- 1934 Alan Bates, actor
- 1934 Barry Humphries, actor and comedian
- 1941 Gene Pitney, singer
- 1945 Brenda Fricker, actress
- 1953 Norman Pace, actor and comic
- 1954 Rene Russo, actress
- 1962 Lou Diamond Phillips, actor
- 1963 Michael Jordan, basketball player
- 1981 Paris Hilton, heiress and actress

Deaths

- 1673 Jean Baptiste Molière, playwright
- 1982 Lee Strasberg, actor

In February 1996, Garry Kasparov played a six-game chess match against Deep Blue, a computer developed by IBM. Kasparov was the highest-rated chess player in the world. He beat the computer and declared his 4–2 victory a "win for mankind," claiming the match was one of the most difficult of his career. With the benefit of studying the weaknesses and strengths in Kasparov's play against Deep Blue, the IBM team created an improved IBM computer program, unofficially nicknamed Deeper Blue, which Kasparov played against in 1997. He was defeated – the first time the grand master ever lost a six-game match in championship play.

DATE*line*

February 18

"Don't part with your illusions. When they are gone you may still exist, but you have ceased to live." — MARK TWAIN

Births

- 1896 André Breton, writer
- 1898 Enzo Ferrari, race car driver and manufacturer
- 1906 Hans Asperger, pediatrician
- 1919 Jack Palance, actor
- 1922 Helen Gurley Brown, editor and publisher
- 1931 Toni Morrison, writer, Nobel Prize laureate
- 1948 Sinéad Cusack, actress
- 1950 John Hughes, director, producer, and writer
- 1950 Cybill Shepherd, actress
- 1954 John Travolta, actor
- 1957 Vanna White, game show presenter
- 1960 Greta Scacchi, actress
- 1964 Matt Dillon, actor
- 1965 Dr. Dre, rapper and record producer
- 1968 Molly Ringwald, actress

Deaths

- 1455 Fra Angelico, artist
- 1546 Martin Luther, religious reformer

HISTORICAL EVENTS

- 1885 Mark Twain's *Adventures of Huckleberry Finn* is published.
- 1911 The first official flight with airmail takes place in Allahabad, British India. Henri Pequet delivers 6,500 letters to Naini, just over six miles (10 km) away.
- 1929 The first Academy Awards are announced.
- 1930 While studying photographs of the night sky, Clyde Tombaugh discovers the ninth planet in our solar system, Pluto.
- 1930 Elm Farm Ollie becomes the first cow to fly in an airplane, and also the first cow to be milked in an airplane.
- 1943 Nazi Joseph Goebbels delivers the Sportpalast speech, asking a Facist audience if they want total war. They do.
- 1953 The first 3D film, *Bwana Devil*, opens in New York City (see below).
- 1991 The IRA explodes bombs in the early morning at both Paddington Station and Victoria Station in London.

DAY TO REMEMBER

Religious day St. William's Day William Harrington (c. 1560–1594), ordained in 1592, tried to convert English Protestants to Catholicism. He was arrested and hanged, drawn, and quartered in 1594 for being a priest.

Celtic tree sign

ASH
February 18–March 17

In the Celtic tradition, ash tree people are reliable and trustworthy, staying ever faithful to their family and friends. They are also vivacious, ambitious, and compassionate towards others. They are quite down to earth yet are still open to exploring spirituality and destiny.

3D movies take the 1950s by storm

Arch Oboler's movie *Bwana Devil* started the 3D craze of the 1950s. It starred Robert Stack, Barbara Britton, and Nigel Bruce. Audience members were issued with disposable two-color cardboard glasses to enable them to see the 3D effect. Producer Sidney Pink, considered the father of the genre, used a camera with two lenses to create the effect. He went on to produce more than 50 3D movies.

The first publicly screened 3D movie was presented at the World Fair of 1903 in Paris. Barely a minute long, it could only be viewed by one person at a time on a modified stereoscope, as no other projection process dividing the left and right pictures for viewing had been invented. The first screening of a 3D film for a paying audience was on June 10, 1915, when the short film *Jim the Penman* was shown in New York, along with scenes from rural America and the Niagara Falls. This was the first time audiences wore the special glasses with one green lens and one red lens.

At first industry experts predicted that 3D would do for movies what the "talkies" had done earlier. Titles such as *Hondo*, *Kiss Me Kate* and *Dial M for Murder* were filmed in 3D, but eventually their 2D versions attracted more audiences.

February 19

"Many of life's failures are people who did not realize how close they were to success when they gave up." — THOMAS EDISON

Births
- 1873 John Reed Swanton, anthropologist and ethnology expert
- 1906 Eugene Eisenmann, ornithologist
- 1924 Lee Marvin, actor
- 1940 Smokey Robinson, musician
- 1946 Karen Silkwood, activist
- 1952 Amy Tan, novelist
- 1955 Jeff Daniels, actor
- 1960 Andrew, Duke of York
- 1963 Seal, singer

Deaths
- 1951 André Gide, writer, Nobel Prize laureate
- 2001 Stanley Kramer, director
- 2003 James Hardy, surgeon

HISTORICAL EVENTS

- **1878** The phonograph is patented by Thomas Edison.
- **1906** Wheat flakes made by Dr. John Kellogg and his brother Will go on sale in the U.S.
- **1915** The Battle of Gallipoli officially begins, with French and British ships shelling Turkish fortifications along the Dardanelles Strait in a bid to reopen the important Black Sea supply route to Russia.
- **1942** Nearly 250 Japanese warplanes attack the northern Australian city of Darwin, killing some 1,100 people.
- **1985** William J. Schroeder becomes the first artificial heart recipient to leave hospital (see right).
- **1985** *EastEnders* first airs on televisions across Great Britain.
- **1986** The Soviet Union launches the Mir space station.
- **2002** NASA's Mars Odyssey space probe begins to map the surface of Mars using its thermal-emission imaging system.
- **2004** Nazi-hunter Simon Wiesenthal is awarded an honorary knighthood for a "lifetime of service to humanity."
- **2006** The Rolling Stones hold the world's largest concert in Copacabana beach, Rio de Janeiro, Brazil. More than one million people attend.

DAY TO REMEMBER

Religious day St. Odran's day St. Odran (c. 452) was St. Patrick's chariot driver. Legend has it that one day on the road he spotted an ambush ahead. He traded places with Patrick without telling him why and died from the attack meant for his passenger.

Building an artificial heart

As early as the 1950s, scientists began to develop devices to keep patients alive until donors became available. The history of the artificial heart goes back to the kidney dialysis machine invented in 1943 by Dr Willem Kolff. Known today as the father of artificial organs, he developed an artificial heart in the mid-1950s, and in the 1960s formed an artificial-organ research program.

The most famous artificial heart is the Jarvik heart, developed in the late 1970s and named after Robert K. Jarvik, who based his original design on the work of Kolff's students. Designed to function like the natural heart, the Jarvik-7 had two pumps, like ventricles, each with a disc-shaped mechanism that pushed the blood from the inlet valve to the outlet valve. Because they required an outside power source that entered the heart through the chest, the system was open to infection and the artificial hearts were not always successful.

Today, artificial organs no longer need a connection through the skin. In 1991, researchers at the University of Ottawa Heart Institute developed a system that "broadcasts" electrical power through the skin, to power devices such as the AbioCor heart (pictured above).

While these pumps are still only temporary devices to sustain a patient until a human heart is available for transplant, researchers predict they will eventually become permanent replacements.

February 20

HISTORICAL EVENTS

1472 Christian I, the King of Denmark, Norway, and Sweden, pawns the isles of Orkney and Shetland to James III of Scotland in lieu of a royal dowry for his daughter Princess Margaret.

1725 The first reported case of white men scalping Native Americans takes place in New Hampshire colony. Ten sleeping Indians are scalped for a £100/scalp bounty.

1816 Gioachino Rossini's *The Barber of Seville* debuts at Teatro Argentina in Rome.

1835 Concepción, Chile, is destroyed by an earthquake.

1944 "Big Week" of World War II begins with American bomber raids on Nazi aircraft-manufacturing centers.

1962 Aboard *Friendship 7*, John Glenn orbits the Earth three times in 4 hours, 55 minutes, becoming the first American to orbit the Earth.

1987 In Salt Lake City in the U.S. a bomb explodes in a computer store. The "Unabomber" becomes the target of the FBI's most expensive manhunt in history.

1991 A gigantic statue of Albania's long-time dictator, Enver Hoxha, is brought down in the Albanian capital, Tirana, by mobs of angry protesters (see below).

2002 In Reqa Al-Gharbiya, Egypt, a fire on a train injures more than 65 and kills at least 370 people.

DAY TO REMEMBER

Religious day St. Wulfric's day St. Wulfric (c. 1110–1154), born in Bristol, England, was ordained a priest though he never joined an order, and was a counselor to King Henry I and King Stephen. In the early 1120s he was touched by divine grace and, after a period in solitude, emerged austere and devoted. He became known for his gift of prophecy. In his later years, he copied and bound books and crafted items for use in Mass.

Star sign

PISCES
February 20–March 20

Born under the sign of the fish, the typical Piscean can be tranquil one moment and tempestuous the next. Their acute sensitivity can make them very kind or very anxious, needing to escape when life gets too much.

Births
- **1924** Gloria Vanderbilt, clothing designer and entrepreneur
- **1925** Robert Altman, film director
- **1927** Sidney Poitier, actor
- **1937** Nancy Wilson, singer
- **1949** Ivana Trump, skier, model, and socialite
- **1966** Cindy Crawford, model
- **1967** Kurt Cobain, musician

Deaths
- **1993** Ferruccio Lamborghini, automobile manufacturer
- **1996** Solomon Asch, psychologist
- **2005** Sandra Dee, actress

A network of over 600,000 concrete bunkers built across Albania is the bizarre legacy of dictator Enver Hoxha. When the Hoxha regime (1944–1985) finally crumbled after the collapse of Communism, the world discovered a backward country, not only by Western capitalist standards, but also by those of other Eastern Bloc countries. With little industry and barely any telecommunications technology, Albanians were using farming techniques from the previous century. It appeared that Hoxha's main legacy was this complex of bunkers built to repel attack from enemies – one bunker for every five people.

February 21

DATEline

"I told you I was sick." — ERMA BOMBECK, ON HER TOMBSTONE

Malcolm Little was a prominent African American civil rights leader. After a difficult childhood led him to a life of crime, he spent time in prison where he gave up his old identity and became Malcolm X, fiery spokesman for the Nation of Islam. He advocated black pride and economic independence, urging African Amercian people to give up Christianity, reject integration and refuse to follow the values and practices of decadent white society. He was both loved and despised, revered and feared. An assassin's bullet cut him down on this day in 1965 at the age of 39.

Births

- 1621 Rebecca Nurse, American accused witch
- 1903 Anaïs Nin, writer
- 1907 W. H. Auden, poet
- 1924 Robert Mugabe, first President of Zimbabwe
- 1927 Erma Bombeck, humorist
- 1927 Hubert de Givenchy, fashion designer
- 1933 Nina Simone, singer
- 1946 Alan Rickman, actor
- 1961 Christopher Atkins, actor
- 1979 Jennifer Love Hewitt, actress and singer

Deaths

- 1938 George Ellery Hale, astronomer
- 1941 Sir Frederick Grant Banting, first to extract insulin from the pancreas

HISTORICAL EVENTS

- 1431 The trial of Joan of Arc begins.
- 1804 A self-propelled steam locomotive runs for the first time in Wales.
- 1842 John J. Greenough patents the sewing machine.
- 1848 Karl Marx, aged 29, publishes *The Communist Manifesto* in England.
- 1875 Jeanne Calment is born, going on to live for 122 years 164 days, the longest confirmed lifespan for any human being in history.
- 1947 In New York City, Edwin Land demonstrates the first "instant camera" – the Polaroid Land Camera – to a meeting of the Optical Society of America.
- 1953 Francis Crick and James D. Watson discover the structure of the DNA molecule.
- 1965 Malcolm X is assassinated at the Audubon Ballroom in New York City (see above).
- 1973 Over the Sinai Desert, Israeli fighter aircraft shoot down a Libyan Airlines jet, killing 108 people.

DAYS TO REMEMBER

Religious day St. Eleanora's day The daughter of Count Raymond IV of Provence, St. Eleanora (1226–1296) married King Henry III of England. She was widowed in 1273 after 37 years of marriage and became a Benedictine nun.

International day International Mother Language Day Over the past 300 years, almost half of the world's 6,000 languages have died out, disappearing at a dramatic and steadily increasing pace. International Mother Language Day was proclaimed by UNESCO in 1999 to promote linguistic and cultural diversity and multilingualism.

February 22

"In the future everyone will be famous for 15 minutes." — ANDY WARHOL

HISTORICAL EVENTS

- **1879** In Utica, New York, Frank Woolworth opens the first of many five-and-ten-cent Woolworth stores.
- **1907** Cabs with taxi meters begin operating in London.
- **1940** Five-year-old Tenzin Gyatso is enthroned in Tibet as His Holiness, the fourteenth Dalai Lama.
- **1956** Elvis Presley enters the music charts for the first time, with *Heartbreak Hotel*.
- **1958** Egypt and Syria join to form the United Arab Republic.
- **1983** Hindus kill 3,000 Muslims in Assam, India.
- **1984** A Houston boy, David Vetter, who has spent his life in a plastic bubble because he has no immunity to disease, dies 15 days after being removed from the bubble for a bone-marrow transplant. He is 12 years old.
- **1997** In Roslin, Scotland, scientists announce that an adult sheep named Dolly has been successfully cloned (see below).
- **2006** At least six men steal £53 million from a bank in Tonbridge, Kent. It is the U.K.'s biggest robbery.

DAYS TO REMEMBER

Religious day The Feast of the Chair of St. Peter Revered by Catholics around the world, St. Peter was a fisherman and brother of St. Andrew the Apostle, who led him to Christ. A miracle worker and the first Pope, he was martyred c. 64 B.C.E., crucified head downward because he claimed he was not worthy to die in the same manner as Christ.

International day Founder's Day/Thinking Day Around the world, Boy Scouts and Girl Guides celebrate the shared birthday of Robert Baden-Powell and his wife Olave, the founder of Scouting and the World Chief Guide respectively.

Births
- **1732** George Washington, first U.S. President
- **1857** Robert Baden-Powell, founder of the Scouting movement
- **1908** Sir John Mills, actor
- **1918** Robert Pershing Wadlow, the world's tallest human
- **1932** Ted Kennedy, U.S. senator
- **1950** Julie Walters, actress
- **1962** Steve Irwin, herpetologist and television personality
- **1975** Drew Barrymore, actress

Deaths
- **1987** Andy Warhol, artist, director, and writer
- **1995** Ed Flanders, actor
- **2002** Sir Raymond (William) Firth, social anthropologist
- **2005** Simone Simon, actress

Dolly the sheep cloned from adult cell

In 1997, scientists in Roslin, Scotland, announced that a sheep named Dolly had been successfully cloned from adult cellular material. The cloning aroused both interest and concern, particularly because it raised the possibility of human cloning with all the attendant scientific and ethical implications.

The feat was cited by *Science* magazine as the breakthrough of 1997. In previous cloning experiments with cattle and mice, the "donor" chromosomes came from very early embryos or, in the case of cloned frogs, from young tadpoles. Dolly was different. She was generated from a specialized adult cell. To create Dolly, scientists used a cell derived from the udder of a six-year-old sheep in the final stage of pregnancy. The researchers fused the adult udder cell with a donor cell from a different sheep. Then they made the nucleus of the donor cell "quiet" so that it stopped behaving like an udder cell and could be reprogrammed to become an embryo. The resulting embryo, Dolly, carried all of the chromosomes from the donor udder cell and none of the nuclear chromosomes from the host egg cell, making her an exact copy of her donor-cell "mother."

Although most Finn Dorset sheep live to be 11 to 12 years of age, Dolly, suffering from lung cancer and crippling arthritis, was put down at the age of six by lethal injection. Dolly was a mother to six lambs, bred the old-fashioned way.

February 23

"I am certain of nothing but the holiness of the heart's affections and the truth of imagination. What the imagination seizes as beauty must be truth – whether it existed before or not." JOHN KEATS

Up until the 1950s, summer was an anxious time for many parents because it was then that children became infected with the crippling disease poliomyelitis, or polio. That anxiety was banished when Dr. Jonas Salk developed a vaccine against the disease. Dr. Salk never patented his polio vaccine and distributed the formula freely so the world could benefit from his discovery. As a result, he saved millions from death or lives spent in wheelchairs. Today the Jonas Salk Institute for Biological Studies in La Jolla, California, continues his work with research into diseases such as cancer and HIV/AIDS.

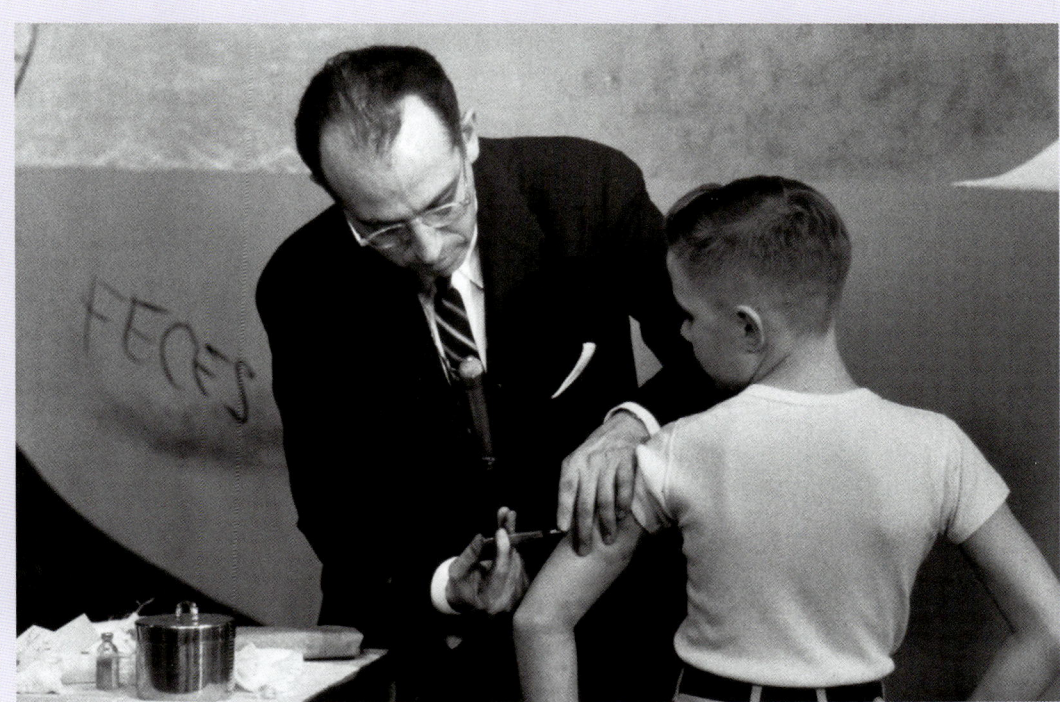

HISTORICAL EVENTS

- 1455 Traditional date for the publication of the Gutenberg *Bible*, the first Western book printed from movable type.
- 1689 Dutch prince William III is proclaimed King of England.
- 1874 Walter Winfield patents a game called "sphairistike," now more commonly known as lawn tennis.
- 1893 Rudolf Diesel receives a patent for the diesel engine.
- 1905 Chicago, Illinois attorney Paul Harris and three other businessmen meet for lunch to form the Rotary Club, the world's first service club.
- 1919 Benito Mussolini forms the Fascist Party in Italy.
- 1954 The first mass vaccination of children against polio begins in Pittsburgh, Pennsylvania (see above).
- 1987 Supernova 1987A in LMC is first sighted. It is the first supernova visible to the naked eye since 1604 and is the brightest of the twentieth century, .
- 1991 Ground troops cross the Saudi Arabia border and enter Iraq, starting the ground phase of the Gulf War.
- 1999 An avalanche destroys the Austrian village of Galtür, killing 31.

Births
- 1633 Samuel Pepys, diarist
- 1685 Georg Friedrich Händel, composer
- 1743 Mayer Amschel Rothschild, banker
- 1863 Charles Joseph Chamberlain, botanist
- 1928 Vasili Lazarev, cosmonaut
- 1940 Peter Fonda, actor
- 1951 Shigefumi Mori, mathematician
- 1965 Kristin Davis, actress
- 1973 André Tanneberger, disc jockey,
- 1983 Mido, footballer
- 1994 Dakota Fanning, actress

Deaths
- 1792 Joshua Reynolds, painter
- 1821 John Keats, poet
- 1965 Stan Laurel, American actor and comedian
- 1995 James Herriot, writer

DAY TO REMEMBER

Religious day St. Polycarp's Day A revered Christian leader, at the age of 86, St. Polycarp (c. 69–155) was sentenced to be burned to death. When the flames did not harm him, he was killed with a dagger and his body burned. The story of Polycarp's martyrdom is considered the earliest preserved reliable account of a Christian martyr's death.

February 24

"Be like a postage stamp. Stick to one thing until you get there." — JOSH BILLINGS

Plane peels open during flight

On February 24, 1989, United Airlines Flight 811 took off from Honolulu International Airport bound for Sydney, Australia, via Auckland, New Zealand. As the plane was climbing between 22,000 and 23,000 feet, vibrations and grinding sounds were felt and heard for about 30 seconds. No-one knew it at the time but faulty wiring in the cargo door latch was allowing it to open.

As the door opened, an explosive decompression occurred. The cargo door and five rows of business-class seats were blown out of the aircraft, along with nine passengers. A huge hole in the aircraft's fuselage left the passenger cabin exposed to the elements at 22,000 feet.

The explosion had knocked out the aircraft's oxygen supply so the pilots plunged the Boeing 747 into a nosedive in an attempt to reach an altitude where passengers and crew could breathe again. The explosion also destroyed the number-three engine, and the number-four engine was on fire. At this point the aircraft was approximately 20 miles (32 km) from Honolulu.

Despite having limited control of the aircraft and doubts about the plane's landing gear and structural integrity, the pilot made a perfect landing. All 10 evacuation slides on the aircraft were deployed and passengers and crew safely disembarked. The cargo door was later recovered by U.S. Navy divers.

HISTORICAL EVENTS

1804 London's Drury Lane Theatre burns to the ground, leaving owner Richard Brinsley Sheridan destitute.
1839 William Otis receives a patent for the steam shovel.
1857 The first shipment of perforated postage stamps is received by the U.S. Government.
1938 The first toothbrushes made with nylon bristles instead of animal hair go on sale.
1945 American forces liberate the Philippine capital, Manila, from the Japanese empire.
1946 In a coup, Juan Perón becomes President of Argentina.
1981 Buckingham Palace announces the engagement of Prince Charles and Lady Diana.
1989 United Airlines Flight 811 rips open during flight, sucking nine passengers out of the business-class section (see above).
1998 English pop singer Elton John is knighted.

DAYS TO REMEMBER

National day Flag Day (Mexico) On this day in 1821, the Plan de Iguala treaty proclaimed Mexico an independent country.

National day Independence Day (Estonia) The Republic of Estonia was founded on this day in 1918, which was celebrated as Independence Day until the Soviet occupation in 1940. On February 24, 1989, the red flag of Soviet Estonia was replaced by the blue, black, and white Estonian flag, and the day was celebrated once again as a public holiday.

Traditional day Dragobete (Romania) This holiday is known as "the day when the birds get engaged." It is very similar to St. Valentine's Day.

Births

1743 Edmund Cartwright, inventor
1786 Wilhelm Grimm, author
1815 Anthony Trollope, author
1877 Ettie Rout, activist
1890 Marjorie Main, actress
1914 Ralph Erskine, architect
1934 Renata Scotto, soprano
1938 James Farentino, actor
1943 George Harrison, musician (The Beatles)
1947 Edward James Olmos, actor
1948 Dennis Waterman, actor
1966 Billy Zane, actor
1982 Klára Koukalová, tennis player
1987 Mayuko Iwasa, entertainer and model

Deaths

1990 Johnnie Ray, singer
1993 Bobby Moore, footballer
2002 Leo Ornstein, composer and pianist
2006 John Martin, broadcaster
2006 Dennis Weaver, actor

Elton John performed with Stevie Wonder in 1998 – the year Elton was knighted – at an official dinner with Bill Clinton at the White House in Washington D.C. to honor British Prime Minister Tony Blair.

February 25

"What luck for rulers that men do not think." — ADOLF HITLER

Births
- 1841 Pierre-Auguste Renoir, painter and sculptor
- 1873 Enrico Caruso, tenor
- 1901 Zeppo Marx, actor
- 1910 Millicent Fenwick, human rights activist
- 1922 "Texas Rose" Bascom, trick roper
- 1935 Sally Jessy Raphaël, talk-show host

Deaths
- 1723 Sir Christopher Wren, architect
- 1850 Daoguang, Emperor of China
- 1983 Tennessee Williams, playwright
- 2001 Sir Donald Bradman, cricketer

HISTORICAL EVENTS

- **1570** Pope Pius V excommunicates English Queen Elizabeth I from the Catholic Church and absolves her subjects from having to pledge allegiance to her.
- **1836** Samuel Colt receives a patent for a pistol that uses a revolving cylinder containing powder and bullets in six individual tubes.
- **1837** The first U.S. electric printing press is patented by Thomas Davenport.
- **1932** Austrian immigrant Adolf Hitler receives German citizenship.
- **1964** Cassius Clay (who later becomes Muhammad Ali) beats Sonny Liston in Miami Beach, Florida, and is crowned the Heavyweight Champion of the World.
- **1968** In a single ceremony, 430 Unification Church couples wed in Korea.
- **1986** President Ferdinand Marcos of the Philippines flees the nation after 20 years of rule; Corazon Aquino becomes the first Filipino woman president.
- **1991** During the Gulf War, an Iraqi Scud missile hits American military barracks in Dhahran, Saudi Arabia, killing 28 U.S. marines.
- **1994** Inside the Tomb of Abraham, Dr. Baruch Kappel Goldstein kills 29 Palestinian worshippers and injures 125 more before being beaten to death by survivors. Subsequent rioting kills 26 more Palestinians and nine Israelis.
- **2006** The world's estimated population reaches the 6.5 billion mark (see right).

DAY TO REMEMBER

Religious day St. Adela's Day St. Adela (c. 1060–1137) was a princess, the daughter of William the Conqueror, King of England. She married Stephen of Blois in 1080 and was active in English politics throughout her life. She endowed several churches and monasteries and was famous for her generous spirit.

World population

An extra 500 million people appeared on the face of the Earth between 2000 and 2006. In 1987, the world's population was 5 million. Thirteen years later it tipped 6 million. What will our population be in another six, 10, or 50 years time?

The growth of any population – trees or monkeys or people – is limited by the availability of resources like food, water, and space. Once populations use up their resources, they cannot continue to grow. They will plateau or may even decline. Because birth and death rates aren't constant across countries and through time, estimating population growth can be extremely complex. Disease or disaster can cause death rates to increase for certain periods. A booming economy, or even a blackout across a big city like New York, might mean higher birth rates for a given year.

Currently, the rate of Earth's population growth is slowing down. Throughout the 1960s, the world's population was growing at about two percent per year. By 1990, growth was down to one and a half percent, and by 2015 it is expected to drop to one percent. Family planning initiatives, an ageing population, the effects of diseases such as AIDS, natural disasters including earthquakes and the devastating tsunami of 2005—as well as wars—are some of the factors which are responsible for this rate decrease.

Still, the numbers are breathtaking. By 2015, estimates suggest there will be seven billion people on the planet. By 2050, there may be as many as ten billion people. Can Earth support this population? When will we reach the limit of our resources? If humans wish to expand their population beyond the limits of the Earth's resources, where will they go?

Year	Population
1700	600,000,000
1800	900,000,000
1900	1,500,000,000
1987	5,000,000,000
2000	6,000,000,000
2006	6,500,000,000

February 26

"An invasion of armies can be resisted, but not an idea whose time has come." — VICTOR HUGO

Eight years before it was totally destroyed, the World Trade Center in New York City was badly damaged when a car bomb planted by Islamic terrorists exploded in an underground garage. The bomb left six people dead and 1,000 injured. The men carrying out the attack were followers of Umar Abd al-Rahman, an Egyptian cleric who preached in the New York City area. When Ramzi Youssef was eventually convicted of the bombing, it emerged he had direct contact with Osama bin Laden and received funds from al-Qaeda.

Births
- 1361 Wenceslaus, Holy Roman Emperor, King of Bohemia
- 1564 Christopher Marlowe, dramatist
- 1802 Victor Hugo, writer
- 1808 Honoré Daumier, painter, illustrator, and sculptor
- 1829 Levi Strauss, clothing designer
- 1846 Buffalo Bill, pioneer, officer, and hunter
- 1914 Robert Alda, actor
- 1916 Jackie Gleason, actor, writer, composer, and comedian
- 1950 Helen Clark, Prime Minister of New Zealand
- 1953 Michael Bolton, singer
- 1956 Keisuke Kuwata, singer
- 1973 Ole Gunnar Solskjaer, football player
- 1974 Sébastien Loeb, race car driver

Deaths
- 1921 Carl Menger, economist
- 1966 Vinayak Damodar Savarkar, freedom fighter and writer
- 1971 Fernandel, actor
- 1994 Bill Hicks, comedian

HISTORICAL EVENTS
- 1797 The Bank of England issues the first £1 note.
- 1952 Winston Churchill announces that Britain has developed its own atomic bomb, making it the third nuclear power after the U.S. and U.S.S.R.
- 1991 Tim Berners-Lee introduces WorldWideWeb, the first internet browser.
- 1991 On Baghdad Radio, Iraqi leader Saddam Hussein announces the withdrawal of Iraqi troops from Kuwait.
- 1993 In New York City, a truck bomb parked below the North Tower of the World Trade Center goes off, killing six and injuring more than 1,000 (see above).
- 1995 The oldest investment banking firm in the U.K., Barings Bank, collapses after a securities broker, Nick Leeson, loses $1.4 billion by speculating on the Singapore International Monetary Exchange using futures contracts.
- 1998 A jury rejects a lawsuit by Texas cattlemen who claim Oprah Winfrey's televised comments about mad-cow disease have caused the beef market to plummet and cost them millions of dollars.

DAYS TO REMEMBER

Religious day Start of Ayyám-i-Há (Baha'i faith) The period of the Intercalary Days, which begin February 26 and end March 1, is devoted to service, gift giving and preparing for the Bahai fast.

Religious day St. Nestor's Day St. Nestor (c. 251) was arrested during the rule of Roman Emperor Trajanus Decius and sentenced to death for refusing to make Pagan sacrifices.

DATEline

February 27

"Ideas are like rabbits. You get a couple and learn how to handle them, and pretty soon you have a dozen." — JOHN STEINBECK

HISTORICAL EVENTS

- **1879** Constantine Fahlberg discovers the artificial sweetener saccharin by accident.
- **1883** Oscar Hammerstein patents the first practical cigar-rolling machine.
- **1900** The British Labour Party is formed.
- **1942** French Jews are transported to Nazi Germany for the first time.
- **1955** *Billboard* annouces that seven-inch, 45-rpm singles are outselling 78-rpm singles for the frist time in the U.S.
- **1990** The Exxon Corporation and Exxon Shipping are indicted on five criminal counts after the 1989 *Exxon Valdez* oil spill.
- **1991** U.S. President George Bush declares on live television, "Kuwait is liberated. Iraq's army is defeated. I am pleased to announce that at midnight tonight, exactly 100 hours since ground operations began and six weeks since the start of Operation Desert Storm, all United States and coalition forces will suspend offensive combat operations."
- **1997** Divorce is legalized in Ireland (see right).
- **1999** Colin Prescot and Andy Elson set a world endurance record by spending 233 hours and 55 minutes in a hot air balloon while trying to circumnavigate the world.
- **2002** A train catches fire a few minutes after it leaves the Godhra railway station in India, killing more than 50 Hindu pilgrims and triggering riots that lead to the death of thousands of people, mostly Muslims.
- **2004** A large ferry carrying 900 people is bombed by terrorists in the Philippines killing 116 passengers.

DAYS TO REMEMBER

Religious day St. Auguste's Day Auguste Chapadelaine (1814–1856) was a French priest who traveled to China to do missionary work. He was eventually arrested and tortured for trying to convert Chinese people to Christianity. He was beheaded in Kwang-Si Province, China.

International day Polar Bear Day This day celebrates the world's largest land-based carnivore. Polar bears are native to the U.S. (Alaska), Canada, Russia, Greenland, and Norway. Their existence is threatened by pollution, poaching, and industrial accidents.

Divorce becomes legal in Ireland in 1997

Up until the ninth century, divorce was legal by mutual consent in Ireland. This was written into Irish law, along with a range of circumstances under which divorce was acceptable. The Roman Catholic Church supported the idea of divorce until they began to define marriage as an "indissoluble bond" from the twelfth century onward.

After Henry VIII created the Anglican Church, English law became more lenient about divorce, but Irish law remained unchanged. It was not until 1980 that a group of Irish women formed the Divorce Action Group. They campaigned to remove the constitutional ban on divorce. A referendum in 1986 rejected the change, but nine years later there was another vote. On November 24, 1995, over a million Irish voters decided in favor of lifting the ban on divorce. This vote was the smallest margin in Irish history, with just 50.28 percent voting "yes." The Family Law Act now states that the court will grant a decree of divorce if it feels confident that the applicants are aware of the alternatives to divorce and that there is no possibility of reconciliation.

Births
- **1807** Henry Wadsworth Longfellow, poet
- **1861** Rudolf Steiner, philosopher
- **1902** John Steinbeck, writer, Nobel Prize laureate
- **1912** Lawrence Durrell, writer
- **1926** David H. Hubel, neuroscientist
- **1930** Joanne Woodward, actress
- **1932** Elizabeth Taylor, actress
- **1934** Ralph Nader, consumer activist
- **1935** Mirella Freni, soprano
- **1980** Chelsea Clinton, daughter of former U.S. President Bill Clinton

Deaths
- **1892** Louis Vuitton, luggage maker
- **1936** Ivan Pavlov, physiologist
- **1993** Lillian Gish, actress
- **2002** Spike Milligan, comedian

February 28

"I've always been interested in people but I've never liked them." — HENRY JAMES

On February 28, 1993, U.S. law enforcers raided a compound in Waco, Texas, occupied by members of an apocalyptic religious group called the Branch Davidians, led by David Koresh. It was rumored that the cult illegally earned money from arms sales and that an arsenal of explosives and weapons were stockpiled inside. During the raid, four agents and six Davidians were killed, triggering a 51-day siege that ended when the complex was consumed by fire, killing a further 76 men, women, and children, as well as sect leader, David Koresh. Defectors from the sect alleged that Koresh practiced polygamy with underage brides, physically abused children, and stockpiled illegal weapons. Some survivors of the massacre were tried and acquitted of conspiring to murder federal agents; others were convicted of voluntary manslaughter.

HISTORICAL EVENTS

- **364** Valentinian I is appointed Roman Emperor.
- **1790** John Irving becomes the first convict to be freed in Australia.
- **1883** The first vaudeville theater is opened, in Boston, U.S.
- **1940** Basketball is televised for the first time.
- **1947** In Taiwan, a civil protest is put down with a loss of 30,000 civilian lives.
- **1975** A major underground train crash at Moorgate Station, London, kills 43 people.
- **1983** The final episode of *M*A*S*H* is broadcast in the U.S. It is the most watched television episode in history.
- **1986** Olof Palme, Prime Minister of Sweden, is shot dead walking home from a Stockholm cinema.
- **1993** U.S. law enforcement agents raid the Branch Davidian compound in Waco, Texas, in an effort to arrest cult leader David Koresh (see above).
- **2004** Over one million Taiwanese participating in the 228 Hand-in-Hand Rally form a 300 mile (500 km) human chain to commemorate the 1947 massacre of 30,000 civilians.

Births

- **1820** Sir John Tenniel, cartoonist and illustrator
- **1824** Charles Blondin, acrobat and aerialist
- **1903** Vincente Minnelli, film director
- **1911** Denis Parsons Burkitt, surgeon and medical researcher
- **1923** Charles Durning, actor
- **1945** Bubba Smith, football player and actor
- **1948** Bernadette Peters, actress and singer
- **1948** Mercedes Ruehl, actress
- **1970** Lemony Snicket, writer
- **1973** Eric Lindros, hockey player
- **1974** Lee Carsley, footballer
- **1985** Jelena Jankovic, tennis player

Deaths

- **1875** Sir Goldsworthy Gurney, steam carriage inventor
- **1916** Henry James, writer
- **1956** Frigyes Riesz, mathematician
- **1985** Ray Ellington, singer
- **1998** Dermot Morgan, actor and comedian

DAYS TO REMEMBER

Religious day St. Hedwig's Day St. Hedwig (1371–1399) became Queen of Poland at the age of 11, upon her father's death. She reluctantly married Jagiello, non-Christian Prince of Lithuania, at age 13 for political reasons. She eventually converted her husband to Christianity and revised the laws of Poland to provide help for the poor. She died, aged 28, during childbirth.

Religious day St. Oswald's Day Valued for his encouragement of learning in the clergy and his efforts to revive monastic discipline, Oswald, Archbishop of York, died in the act of washing the feet of the poor.

February 29

"Isn't it sad, that in a time when we face so many devastating problems — poverty, HIV/AIDS, war, and conflict — that in our Communion we should be investing so much time and energy on disagreement about sexual orientation?" — ARCHBISHOP DESMOND MPILO TUTU

HISTORICAL EVENTS

- **45 B.C.E.** Julius Caesar adjusts 46 B.C.E., known as the Year of Confusion, with 445 days, by fixing 365 days and six hours as the length of a year, with an extra day added every four years.
- **1288** It becomes legal in Scotland for women to propose marriage to men only on this day (every leap year).
- **1504** Christopher Columbus uses his knowledge of a lunar eclipse to frighten Native Americans so they will provide him with supplies.
- **1960** An earthquake in Morocco kills one third of the population of Agadir (12,000 people) in just 15 seconds.
- **1964** In Sydney, Australian swimmer Dawn Fraser sets a new world record in the 100-meter freestyle swimming competition (58.9 seconds).
- **1988** South African archbishop Desmond Tutu is arrested during a five-day anti-apartheid demonstration in Cape Town (see below).
- **2000** A six-year-old student shoots and kills a six-year-old classmate, Kayla Rolland, at Theo J. Buell Elementary School in Mount Morris Township, Michigan, U.S.
- **2004** New Zealand director Peter Jackson's film *Lord of the Rings: Return of the King* wins 11 Oscars. Only two films before have achieved this record: *Ben Hur* and *Titanic*.

Births
- **1692** John Byrom, poet
- **1792** Gioacchino Rossini, composer
- **1840** John Philip Holland, inventor of the modern submarine
- **1896** Morarji Desai, Indian Prime Minister
- **1904** Jimmy Dorsey, band leader
- **1916** Dinah Shore, singer
- **1960** Tony Robbins, motivational speaker
- **1980** Simon Gagné, hockey player
- **1984** Darren Ambrose, footballer

Deaths
- **1592** Alessandro Striggio, composer
- **1744** John Theophilus Desaguliers, philosopher
- **1820** Johann Joachim Eschenburg, literary critic
- **1980** Gil Elvgren, artist
- **1992** Ruth Pitter, poet
- **2004** Jerome Lawrence, playwright

Nobel laureate arrested

On February 29, 1988, Archbishop Desmond Tutu, Secretary-General of the South African Council of Churches and a prominent anti-apartheid campaigner, was arrested alongside other clergy for protesting against the banning of anti-apartheid political organizations.

In 1984, Tutu had been awarded a Nobel Peace Prize for his "role as a unifying leader figure in the campaign to resolve the problem of apartheid in South Africa." In 1986, when Tutu was elected the first black Anglican Archbishop of Cape Town, he used his position to intensify his criticism of apartheid. He spoke poignantly of having returned to South Africa from study in England: "Our youngest, who was born in England, said, 'Daddy, I want to go on the swings,' and I said with a hollow voice…'No, darling, you can't go.' What do you say, how do you feel, when your baby says, 'But Daddy, there are other children playing there?' How do you tell your little darling that she cannot go because though she is a child, she is not that kind of child. And you

died many times and were not able to look your child in the eyes because you felt so dehumanized, so humiliated."

Six months after Tutu's arrest, the headquarters of the South African Council of Churches was bombed; it later transpired that the bombing had been ordered by South African President P.W. Botha. Still, Archbishop Tutu refused to be silenced.

Finally, in 1994, a new constitution guaranteed all South Africans "equality before the law and equal protection of the law" as well as full political rights.

DAYS TO REMEMBER *February*

1
Imbolc One of the cornerstone festivals of the Celtic calendar

2
Candlemas This Christian festival marks the ritual purification of the Virgin Mary 40 days after the birth of Christ

3
Setsuban A Japanese day of observance held one day before the start of spring according to the Japanese lunar calendar

4
Charles Lindbergh, pilot, was born in 1902

5
Kashmir Day A minute's silence is observed in Pakistan in protest of India's occupation of the Kashmir Valley

8
Nirvana Day Also known as Parinirvana, this is the celebration of Buddha's death when he reached total Nirvana

9
St. Apollonia's Day St. Apollonia was a holy virgin in Egypt and is the patron saint of dentists and sufferers from toothaches

10
Feast Day of St. Paul's Shipwreck Celebrated in Malta, the feast commemorates the shipwreck of St. Paul in Malta in 60 C.E.

11
Inventors Day This day in the U.S. recognizes the great advancements in technology

12
Charles Darwin, naturalist, was born in 1809

15
Lupercalia This ancient Roman festival was held near the cave where the founders of Rome were suckled by a she-wolf

16
St. Daniel's Day An Egyptian from the third century who ministered to Christians and was beheaded for his faith

17
St. Fintan's Day Fintan of Clonenagh was reputed to be a holy son, surrounded by light when he prayed

18
St. William's Day William Harrington was hanged, drawn, and quartered in 1594 for being a priest

19
St. Odran's Day Odran was St. Patrick's chariot driver and was said to have died from an attack meant for his passenger

22
Founder's Day/ Thinking Day Boy Scouts and Girl Guides celebrate the birthday of scout movement founder Robert Baden-Powell and his wife, Olaf

23
St. Polycarp's Day The story of St. Polycarp's martyrdom is the earliest reliable account of a Christian martyr's death

24
Dragobete This Romanian holiday is known as "the day the birds get engaged"

25
St. Adela's Day St. Adela endowed several churches and monasteries and was known for her generous spirit

26
Start of Ayyam-i-Ha In the Baha'i faith, the period between February 26 and March 1 is devoted to service, gift giving, and preparing a feast

29
The last day of February in a Leap Year

6

Bob Marley Day
Proclaimed on the birthday of reggae musician Bob Marley

7

Giles Mary-of-Saint-Joseph's Day Giles worked for the sick, especially lepers, and was considered a saint, even in life

13

St. Fulcran's Day A bishop for 57 years who founded the monastery of St. Sauveur

14

St Valentine's Day
Lovers all over the world exchange cards and gifts on this day

20

Sidney Poitier, actor, was born in 1927

21

International Mother Language Day
Proclaimed in 1999 to promote linguistic and cultural diversity

27

Polar Bear Day Celebrates the threatened existence of the world's largest land-based carnivore

28

St. Oswald's Day
Oswald, Archbishop of York, died in the act of washing the feet of the poor

Top Right Inventors Day, U.S., February 11
Right Valentine's Day, February 14

MARCH

"March comes in like a lion and goes out like a lamb." PROVERB

In March, 1989, the worst oil spill in history, the *Exxon Valdez* disaster, took place in the virgin waters of Prince William Sound, Alaska. Now, almost two decades later, the repercussions are still being felt after the greatest ecological sea catastrophe of our time.

March

Aries star sign and scene of men chopping and pruning fruit trees from *Calendar and Book of Hours*, from fifteenth-century France. March begins in the sign of Pisces and ends in the sign of Aries.

SPECIAL DATES

Mother's Day, or Mothering Sunday, is a Christian festival held on the fourth Sunday in Lent, which often falls in March. In medieval times, people would go to their Mother, or main, church to take part in such services.

Mars, Greek God of War by Diego Velasquez (c. 1599–1660), at the Museo del Prado, Madrid. The month of March, from the Roman month *Martius*, was named for the god Mars. Initially Mars is thought to have been a god of fertility and agriculture. He later took on aspects of the Greek god of war, Ares.

March, the third month in the Gregorian calendar, heralds spring in the Northern Hemisphere and autumn in the Southern. The first equinox of the year falls in March. Both spring and the equinox are the focus of festivals in many cultures. In the Northern Hemisphere, it is a time of celebration for the return of warmer days, and for renewal. In traditional cultures in the Southern Hemisphere it is the time to celebrate the harvest.

THE NAME OF THE MONTH of March derives from the Roman month *Martius*. According to the Roman calendar, the calends, or first day of Martius was New Year's Day. This changed with the introduction of the Julian calendar, when the calends of *Januaris*, or January, became the first day of the year.

The Roman month of Martius was named for the god Mars, one of the three most important Roman gods. In legend, Mars was the father of Romulus, the founder of Rome, and so was considered the protector of the city.

Mars' connection with agriculture makes the naming of the first month of spring after him obvious, but his associations with war also make him a suitable candidate. The Romans considered spring a fortuitous time to go to war. March was the first month of the season of war, which ran right through summer and into autumn.

While ceremonies and festivals associated with Mars also took place at other times of the year, they were especially prevalent in March. On March 1, 12 young patrician men who had been elected as *Salii* ("leapers" or "dancers") put on the armor sacred to Mars and danced along a set route through the streets of Rome, beating their shields with their spears. The procession paused periodically to perform a war dance and chant an ancient hymn.

The great age of this ritual is indicated by the old-fashioned armor, including bronze figure-eight shaped shields reminiscent of Mycenaean shields, and the archaic form of the words of the hymn, which by the time of the late Republic were virtually impossible for Romans to understand. This ritual was repeated each day until March 24, with the Salii stopping each

> ### March birthflower
> In the Northern Hemisphere, March is in early spring, so not surprisingly the flowers associated with it are the daffodil and the jonquil. Arriving immediately after winter, these flowers represent new beginnings, desire, affection, and cheerfulness.

night in a different house for a feast. On March 14 a horse race was held in honor of Mars on the sacred *Campus Martius* (Field of Mars), where the Roman army trained. On March 19 the sacred spears of Mars were taken from their holding place in his sanctuary in the Forum and blessed, and on March 23, the sacred trumpets were treated in the same way.

Ceremonies in honor of Mars were not the only ones undertaken in this month. One of the other significant rituals took place on March 1 in the Temple of Vesta. There the Vestal Virgins marked the beginning of the ancient New Year by rubbing sticks together to rekindle the sacred fire.

The equinox and the changing seasons

The first of the two annual equinoxes takes place on or around March 21. On this day there are 12 hours of sunlight and 12 of darkness, and after it the days become longer in the Northern Hemisphere and shorter in the Southern Hemisphere. There are ceremonies and celebrations concerned with this event in many cultures, no matter what calendar system is in use.

In the Northern Hemisphere the coming of longer, warmer days means the beginning of the growing season and of hard work tilling and sowing the soil. Many cultures held, and still do hold, festivals and ceremonies to welcome spring and please the spirits and gods to ensure a good crop. Just as Roman festivals did, they often incorporated themes of rebirth and renewal.

Norooz is a New Year celebration held on or around the equinox, marked by festivals in Iran, Iraq, and Afghanistan, and in parts of other nations in the region. It has its roots in the Zoroastrian religion. Iranians prepare for Norooz by spring-cleaning their homes. On the day, they wear new clothes, light bonfires to bring warmth to the New Year, and hold family parties.

Easter, the Christian festival commemorating the death and resurrection of Jesus Christ, is timed by Western churches so the Resurrection falls on the first Sunday after the Paschal full moon, as the first full moon on or after the northern vernal equinox is known. This means that the earliest date on which Easter Sunday can occur is March 22 and the latest is April 25.

There are many forms of church services held around the world to celebrate Easter, but they all have at their core Christ's death and rebirth. Many different local pagan spring traditions have also merged with the Easter story. The name Easter is itself thought to have come from the name of a pagan goddess, Ostara, who was celebrated at this time in Germanic cultures. The merging of these traditions means there are

La Primavera (Spring), by Giuseppe Arcimboldo (c. 1527–1593), depicts spring's symbolic welcoming of the growing season. The sixteenth-century painting resides at the Academia San Fernando in Madrid, Spain.

The Indian festival of *Holi* includes celebrations of sacred Hindu stories; here a performer in the streets of Jaipur plays the god Krishna.

March birthstone

Aquamarine is the birthstone for March. This stone is said to be the treasure of mermaids and it brings luck to sailors. It is also said to relieve grief. Bloodstone is another gemstone associated with the month of March. It is green jasper with flecks of iron oxide and represents courage. It is said to aid circulatory problems.

varied celebrations held around this religious event, from the elaborate parades and feasts that are held before Lent begins, to the painting of eggs and the eating of chocolate eggs brought by the Easter bunny on Easter Sunday.

Holi, a Hindu festival held in India, also merges a number of traditions. It begins on the day after the full moon in the Hindu lunar month of *Phalguna*, which means it falls in late February or early March. In northern India the days are becoming longer and warmer, while further south, the wheat harvest has just been gathered in.

On the night of the full moon, bonfires are lit. They commemorate the story of the child Prahlad, a faithful worshiper of Lord Vishnu, who was taken into a huge fire by his evil aunt Holika. She was believed to be immune to flames and held him on her lap, sure that he would burn, but Prahlad was saved by Vishnu and Holika burned to death instead. A large stick representing Prahlad is placed in the center of the bonfire and is removed and "saved" once the fire is burning fiercely.

On the following morning, Hindus hold riotous, joyous celebrations. They chase each other, throwing and squirting colored paint called *gulal*. This tradition is based on the story that the god Krishna loved to squirt his companion Radha and her friends with colored paint as a prank.

The Jewish *Pesach*, or Passover, is an eight-day religious festival that also centers on the idea of being saved. It begins on the fifteenth day of the Jewish month of *Nissan*, which means it falls in late March or early April. The festival commemorates the Jews' escape from two centuries of slavery in Egypt.

The name "Passover" comes from the last of the 10 plagues that God brought on Egypt when the Pharaoh refused to set Moses and his people free: When the Holy Spirit passed through Egypt at midnight on the fifteenth of Nissan, all the first-born children in the land died, including those of the Pharaoh. Only Jewish children survived, as God had instructed families to make a special mark above their doors so that their households would be "passed over."

After this event, the terrified Pharaoh finally told the Jewish people they could leave. The Jews quickly ate, even though their bread had not yet risen, and left as the sun rose. After three days the

Left Jewish families pray and read the story of the Exodus from Egypt before they eat their Seder meal at Passover.

Below This fifteenth-century text *Agada Pascatis* shows a Jewish family celebrating the Passover as it is celebrated today, by eating symbolic food and reading the story of the Exodus.

Pharaoh changed his mind and pursued the Jews. They only escaped when God parted the waters of the Red Sea for them to cross, then let them close back over the Pharaoh's pursuing army.

During the Passover festival, the story of the Exodus is retold and special unleavened breads are eaten to remind Jews that Moses and his people had to flee before their bread had time to rise.

In the Southern Hemisphere the seasons are reversed. There, March and the equinox mark the beginning of autumn and the harvest. An early Spanish observer in 1535 reported what was probably one of the last of the Inca harvest festivals – an elaborate eight-day affair that celebrated the maize crop. The Incas were conquered by Europeans, as were many other southern peoples. Northern immigrants brought their traditional festivals with them and in many cases their festivals have overridden the traditions of indigenous cultures. Therefore celebrations such as Easter, with its symbolism of rebirth and spring, occur in March in the Southern Hemisphere as well.

Even so, harvest festivals still do take place in the Southern Hemisphere in March. For instance, in the Andes in Bolivia, farmers gather at festivals that center on the potato. They dress in traditional ceremonial costume and hold dances and feasts to celebrate a successful harvest. In southern nations such as Australia, where European religious festivals are largely followed, celebrations are held for the harvest of the southern grape crop and to commercially promote the wines they are turned into.

March 1

The first day of spring in the Northern Hemisphere, and the first day of autumn in the Southern Hemisphere

"It looked to me like what you might imagine a diseased brain, or a brain of some madman would look like..." PHYSICIST MARSHALL ROSENBLUTH, WITNESS OF THE "BRAVO" EXPLOSION

HISTORICAL EVENTS

1562 Religious wars in France are sparked when François, Duc de Guise, massacres Huguenots holding a service in a barn in Vassy. The wars rage for 35 years.
1692 The Salem witch trials begin in Salem Village, Massachusetts Bay Colony.
1872 The U.S. Congress authorizes the creation of the world's first national park, Yellowstone National Park.
1912 Suffragettes smash store front windows in London demonstrations.
1932 Charles Lindbergh III, the 22-month-old son of Charles and Anne Lindbergh, is kidnapped and held for ransom. He is found dead in May.
1954 The U.S. detonates its second H-bomb on the Bikini Atoll (see below).
1966 U.S.S.R.'s probe *Venera 3* crashes on Venus, making it the first unmanned spacecraft to land on another planet.
1983 Swatch watches go on sale in an attempt by the Swiss watch industry to recapture some of the market lost to Japanese watchmakers. "Swatch" is a contraction of the words "Second Watch" – they are marketed as fun accessories instead of prestige timepieces.
1994 Israel releases around 500 Arab prisoners in an effort to placate Palestinians over the Hebron massacre.

Births
1810 Frédéric Chopin, composer
1917 Robert Lowell, poet
1922 Yitzhak Rabin, Israeli Prime Minister
1927 Harry Belafonte, singer
1944 Roger Daltry, rock singer
1954 Ron Howard, actor, director, and producer

Deaths
1984 Jackie Coogan, actor
2006 Peter Osgood, footballer

DAYS TO REMEMBER

Religious day St. David's Day St. David (c. 250–601) founded 12 monasteries in Wales. At the last monastery he established, the monks lived extremely austere lives. He is the patron saint of Wales and of poets.

Traditional day Baba Marta (Bulgaria) Baba Marta, or Grandmother Marta, is an old lady who becomes cross when the seasons change. To welcome spring and to please her so she will not keep them cold, Bulgarians traditionally wear red and white tokens around their wrists.

Historical day Roman New Year Until Julius Caesar changed the Roman calendar in 45 B.C.E., the New Year fell on March 1.

On this day in 1954, the U.S. tested its second H-bomb, codenamed "Bravo," on Bikini Atoll. The explosion was the equivalent of 15 megatons of TNT. The explosion was about three times larger than expected, making it more than 1,000 times greater than the bomb dropped on Hiroshima.

Bravo created a fireball nearly 3 miles (5 km) across and blasted a crater about 1 mile (1.5 km) wide in the coral reef. Radioactive ash and powdered coral rained down over a wide area, falling on military personnel, evacuated Bikini Islanders, and the crew of a Japanese fishing vessel. Many received severe radiation poisoning. More than 50 years later the islanders were still unable to return to their contaminated home.

March 2

DATE*line*

"It's a very beautiful work, but there are already too many walls between people."
MIKHAIL GORBACHEV, ON THE GREAT WALL OF CHINA

HISTORICAL EVENTS

1807 U.S. Congress abolishes the slave trade, effective from January 1, 1808.
1933 The film *King Kong* premiers in New York. The story of the gigantic gorilla from Skull Island becomes a classic. It stars Fay Wray as the girl whom the gorilla becomes fascinated with.
1943 As a German bombing of London begins, a crowd stampedes to reach shelter in Bethnal Green Railway Station and 173 people are trampled to death.
1946 Ho Chi Minh is elected the President of North Vietnam.
1965 Australian swimmer Dawn Fraser is banned from competition for 10 years for allegedly stealing a flag from the palace of the Japanese Emperor during the 1964 Olympic Games in Tokyo.
1969 The supersonic airliner Concorde takes its maiden flight in Toulouse, France (see below).
1970 Prime Minister Ian Smith declares Rhodesia a republic, independent from Britain.
1972 The stunt motorcyclist Evel Knievel breaks his back during a stunt at the Cow Palace in San Francisco.
1989 Representatives of the 12 nations of the European Community agree to ban the production of all chloroflurocarbons by the end of the twentieth century.
2002 The U.S. invasion of Afghanistan, Operation Anaconda, begins.

Births
1900 Kurt Weill, German composer
1904 Dr. Seuss, (Theodor Seuss Geisel), children's writer and publisher
1931 Tom Wolf, writer
1931 Mikhail Gorbachev, last President of the U.S.S.R.
1950 Karen Carpenter, singer
1961 Simone Young, conductor
1962 Jon Bon Jovi, singer, and actor

Deaths
1791 John Wesley, founder of the Methodist Church
1835 Emperor Franz II, last Holy Roman Emperor
1930 D. H. Lawrence, writer
1939 Howard Carter, archaeologist
1999 Dusty Springfield, singer

Concorde's first flight

The Concorde had been planned since the end of 1956, and in November, 1962, the U.K. and France signed a treaty of collaboration for a project to realize their dream. The aircraft's name was chosen to reflect this spirit of cooperation. A prototype was built at the Aerospatiale plant in Toulouse, France, and the first working plane was finished in early 1969.

On March 2, 1969, a crowd gathered to watch the first Concorde supersonic jet take its test flight in Toulouse. Two previous tests had been cancelled due to high winds. This time, pilot André Turcat took the plane up to 10,000 feet (3,000 m), but he only flew it at a speed of 300 miles per hour (480 km/h). This was far below the jet's supersonic speed. It was later to reach speeds of 1,300 miles per hour (2,080 km/h). The test flight took 27 minutes, and as the pilot returned to the airport he said, "Finally the big bird flies, and I can say now that it flies pretty well."

A Concorde being constructed in Bristol, England, was completed soon after and took its first test flight on April 9, flown by Brian Trubshaw. Concordes flew at supersonic speeds for the first time on October 1.

The first commercial flight took place in 1973. The Concorde could travel from Paris to New York in three hours and 45 minutes, a journey which takes a 747 jet almost eight hours. However, the Concorde used a great deal more fuel and could carry only 100 passengers compared to the 500-plus passengers a 747 can carry. This made traveling by Concorde very expensive.

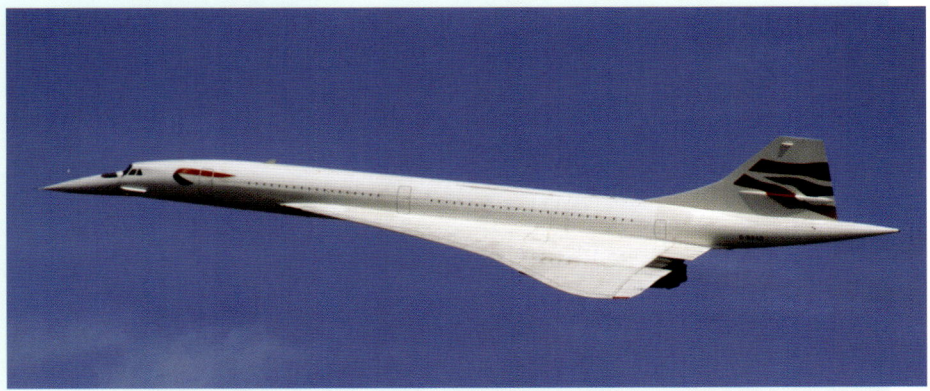

March 3

"Can we get along here? Can we all get along?" RODNEY KING DURING THE LOS ANGELES RIOTS

HISTORICAL EVENTS

1861 Tsar Alexander II frees Russia's serfs from being tied to landowners and gives them allotments of land, which they must pay for over the following 49 years.
1875 George Bizet's opera, *Carmen*, is performed for the first time, in Paris.
1931 "The Star Spangled Banner" becomes the national anthem of the USA.
1974 Turkish Airlines DC-10 crashes near Paris just after take-off from Orly airport on its way to London. All 345 people on board are killed.
1985 A waxwork model of Michael Jackson goes on display at Madame Tussauds, London.
1991 Police in Los Angeles beat Rodney King and the event is caught on videotape (see right).
2005 Abu Bakar Bashir, alleged spiritual leader of Jemaah Islamiah, is convicted of playing a role in the conspiracy that led to the Bali bombing in Oct 2002. He receives a 30-month sentence.

DAYS TO REMEMBER

Religious day Hina Matusuri (Japan) Hina Matusuri is a day for girls in Japan. Their special doll collections are put on display and ceremonies are held. The dolls represent cherished values, such as calmness and dignity.

National holiday Bulgaria celebrates the day it became independent from the Ottoman Empire in 1878.

Births
1847 Alexander Graham Bell, inventor
1887 Rupert Brooke, poet
1911 Jean Harlow, actress
1962 Jackie Joyner-Kersee, athlete

Deaths
1959 Lou Costello, comedian
1983 Hergé, creator of Tintin
1987 Danny Kaye, actor and singer

Police beating caught on video

Early on March 3, 1991, Rodney King was caught speeding and led Los Angeles police officers on an 8-mile (12 km) car chase. At 12:45 a.m. he finally stopped. Officers ordered King to get out of the vehicle and lie on the ground. Accounts of the events that followed vary, but according to the police officers he remained on his hands and knees, refusing to lie down. They tried to force him down, then attempted to subdue him using high-voltage Taser guns, but he rose up and ran towards Officer Laurence Powell.

At this point, George Holliday, standing on a nearby apartment balcony, noticed what was happening and turned on his video camera. He videotaped Powell striking King in the side of the head with a baton. Once King was down, Powell and three other officers continued to beat and kick him, watched by other officers. King was handcuffed and an ambulance was called.

Upon receiving medical attention, King was found to have a broken leg, numerous facial fractures, and cuts and bruises. The incident reports filed by Officer Powell and Sergeant Stacey Koon stated that King had cuts and bruises "of a minor nature."

Holliday sold his videotape and it was shown on television stations around the world, sparking a heated debate about police brutality.

King was released without charge. The four officers were arrested on March 15 and charged with assault and using excessive force. Powell and Koon were also charged with filing false reports.

On April 29, 1992, a jury that didn't include any African Americans acquitted the officers. As news of the verdict spread, racial tensions erupted in Los Angeles. In three days of violent rioting, 55 people were killed and around 2,000 were injured.

A year later, Koon and Powell were convicted under federal U.S. law of violating Rodney King's constitutional rights.

March 4

DATEline

"We're more popular than Jesus Christ now. I don't know which will go first. Rock and roll or Christianity." — JOHN LENNON

Births
- 1678 Antonio Vivaldi, composer
- 1932 Miriam Makeba, singer
- 1939 Paula Prentiss, actress
- 1951 Chris Rea, rock musician

Deaths
- 1193 Saladin, Saracen leader who repelled Richard the Lion-Heart and the Crusaders
- 1994 John Candy, comedian

DAYS TO REMEMBER

Religious day St. Casimir's Day When he refused to lead an army against Hungary, St. Casimir was locked up in Dobzki castle by his father. He later ruled Poland justly in his father's four-year absence. St. Casimir (1458–1484) is the patron saint of Poland.

National day Inauguration Day (U.S.) Every four years from 1789 to 1933, the President of the U.S.A. was sworn in to office on March 4. From 1937 onward, Inauguration Day was held on January 20.

HISTORICAL EVENTS

- 1461 Yorkist King Edward IV usurps his cousin, Lancastrian King Henry VI, from the English throne in the War of the Roses.
- 1787 The U.S. Congress meets for the first time and the Constitution comes into effect.
- 1861 Abraham Lincoln is sworn in as sixteenth U.S. President.
- 1877 Tchaikovsky's ballet *Swan Lake* premiers at the Bolshoi Theatre in Moscow.
- 1945 In Britain, Princess Elizabeth joins the British Army as a driver.
- 1954 The first successful kidney transplant takes place in the Peter Bent Brigham Hospital, Boston.
- 1966 John Lennon sparks controversy when he declares that the Beatles are "more popular than Jesus."
- 1977 An earthquake measuring 7.5 on the Richter scale strikes Bucharest in Romania, killing some 15,000 people.
- 1980 Robert Mugabe gains an overwhelming victory in national elections in Zimbabwe (formerly Rhodesia), becoming the first black president of the nation.
- 2005 Italian journalist Giuliana Sgrena is released by kidnappers in Baghdad, but is then shot at by U.S. troops (see below).

Italian journalist Giuliana Sgrena was taken hostage in Baghdad in February 2005. On March 4 she could hardly believe it when her captors said she was going home. She was bundled into a car, where secret agent Nicola Calipari told her, "Now you are free, don't be afraid."

Close to Baghdad airport, the car approached a U.S. checkpoint. Troops opened fire: Calipari was killed; Sgrena was wounded.

Outraged Italian authorities said U.S. forces were advised the car would be driving through. However, U.S. spokesmen claimed the unidentified, fast-moving car didn't heed their warnings, so troops fired to stop it. In this photo Sgrena is being helped from the plane in Rome the day after.

March 5

"From Stettin in the Baltic to Trieste in the Adriatic, an 'iron curtain' has descended across the Continent." — WINSTON CHURCHILL

HISTORICAL EVENTS

1867 A Fenian uprising against English rule takes place in Ireland, and fails.
1902 In France, the National Congress of miners calls for a general strike for the eight-hour day.
1912 The Italian Army is the first to use aircraft in warfare when they fly dirigibles behind Turkish lines to carry out surveillance.
1940 Members of the Soviet Politburo, including Joseph Stalin, sign the order to kill 25,700 Polish "nationalists and counter-revolutionaries." Nazis later discover the first of the mass graves at Katyn. They are blamed for the massacres at the end of World War II, but the U.S.S.R. finally admits to the murders in 1990.
1946 British Prime Minister Winston Churchill delivers a speech that warns of the threat the Soviet Union poses to the West. His speech popularizes the term "iron curtain" and marks the beginning of the Cold War.
1956 The U.S. Supreme Court upholds the ban on segregation between black and white students in schools, colleges, and universities.
1990 Jennifer Capriati becomes the youngest tennis player to reach a professional tournament final. She is 13 years and 347 days old and is beaten by Gabriela Sabatini: 6–4, 7–5.
1993 Ben Johnson is banned from athletics competition for life after testing positive for performance-enhancing drugs (see right).
1997 North and South Korea meet for peace talks for the first time in 25 years.

DAYS TO REMEMBER

National day Learn from Lei Feng Day Chairman Mao established this commemorative day to encourage people to serve China and the Communist Party. Young soldier Lei Feng was known for serving others with selfless, cheerful devotion. On August 15, 1962, he was on duty when a power pole fell and killed him.

Religious day St. Piran A Pagan Irishman tied a millstone around St. Piran's neck and threw him into the sea. The millstone bobbed to the surface and St. Piran floated to Cornwall, where he made converts to Christianity. St. Piran, patron saint of Cornwall, died on March 5, 480.

Sprinter banned for life

Athletics is one of many sports plagued by the use of performance-enhancing drugs. Although many athletes have tested positive for banned substances before and since, the case of Canadian sprinter Ben Johnson made the world focus on drugs in sport and appreciate just how widespread the problem really was.

The high point of Johnson's career came on September 24, 1988, when he won the gold medal for the men's 100-meter race at the Olympics in Seoul. He ran it in 9.79 seconds, a new world record. But two days later he was stripped of his medal and the record when both his urine samples tested positive for the anabolic steroid stanozolol. As punishment he was banned from competition for two years.

At a Canadian Royal Commission into drugs in sport held after the Seoul Olympics, Johnson claimed he was set up because he had never used stanozolol, although he admitted to having used other steroids. It emerged that at least 40 percent and possibly as much as 80 percent of athletes were using performance-enhancing drugs of one form or another. As Johnson wasn't the only runner using banned substances, he felt unfairly targeted.

Returning to competition in 1991, Johnson couldn't regain his previous strong form. He failed to qualify for the 100-meter final at the Barcelona Olympics in 1992.

At a meet in Canada in February 1993, he tested positive for another banned drug. On March 5, 1993, the International Amateur Athletics Federation announced that in the light of his second positive test Johnson would be banned for life.

Johnson's disallowed record was finally matched by Maurice Greene in 1999, and beaten by Tim Montgomery in 2002 with a time of 9.78 seconds, and again by Asafa Powell in 2005, who ran it in 9.77 seconds.

Births
- 1817 Austin Henry Layard, archaeologist
- 1871 Rosa Luxemburg, socialist writer
- 1908 Sir Rex Harrison, actor
- 1970 John Frusciante, rock musician

Deaths
- 1815 Franz Mesmer, developer of hypnotism
- 1827 Alessandro Volta, physicist
- 1953 Joseph Stalin, dictator
- 1953 Serge Prokofiev, composer
- 1963 Patsy Cline, singer
- 1982 John Belushi, actor

March 6

DATEline

"The more the marble wastes, the more the statue grows." MICHELANGELO BUONARROTI

In 1991 a new computer virus was discovered. It was dubbed "Michelangelo" because it would erase IBM PC hard disks annually on March 6, the Renaissance artist's birthday. In January 1992, two computer companies revealed they had accidentally sent out PCs and floppy disks carrying Michelangelo. Computer software engineers (right) worked on decryption codes. By early March anti-virus programs and books sold out. When the dreaded day arrived, an estimated 10,000 to 20,000 computers were reported to be affected – not the predicted 5 million. Some believed the publicity had prevented a major outbreak by preparing PC users. More cynical observers thought the panic had been fuelled to sell anti-virus products.

HISTORICAL EVENTS

1429 Joan of Arc arrives at the Castle of Chinon in the Loire, and announces to Charles VII's court that she will raise the siege of Orléans and escort him to Reims to be crowned.
1566 David Riccio, adviser to Mary Queen of Scots, is murdered under orders of her husband, Lord Darnley. She states, "Enough of grief. I will study revenge." Less than a year later she has her husband killed.
1836 The 12-day siege of Alamo ends, leaving only six of 155 men alive.
1869 Dmitri Mendeleev, Russian chemist, presents the first periodic table of elements to the Russian Chemical Society.
1899 German researchers Felix Hoffmann and Herman Dreser patent aspirin.
1944 U.S. bombers begin their first air raid on Berlin, dropping some 2,000 tons (2,000 t) of bombs.
1967 U.S. President Lyndon B. Johnson announces his plan to establish a draft lottery to send troops to Vietnam.
1987 The car ferry the *Herald of Free Enterprise* capsizes near the Belgian port of Zeebrugge when a car-loading port is left open. About 200 people are trapped and drown.
1990 Russian Parliament passes a law that allows the ownership of private property.
1992 The Michelangelo computer virus is set to be triggered (see above).

Births
1475 Michelangelo Buonarroti, sculptor and painter
1619 Cyrano de Bergerac, poet and soldier
1806 Elizabeth Barrett Browning, poet
1928 Gabriel Garcia-Márquez, writer
1944 Dame Kiri Te Kanawa, opera singer
1947 Dick Fosbury, high jumper, inventor of the "Fosbury flop"
1972 Shaquille O'Neill, basketball player

Deaths
1836 Davy Crockett, frontiersman
1888 Louisa May Alcott, writer

DAY TO REMEMBER

National holiday Ghana Independence Day Each year Ghana celebrates the fact that it gained its independence from the U.K. on this day in 1957. It was the first sub-Saharan nation to become independent.

March 7

"Nature does nothing without purpose or uselessly." — ARISTOTLE, IN *POLITICS*, BOOK 1

HISTORICAL EVENTS

1530 Pope Clement VII rejects Henry VIII's request to divorce Catherine of Aragon, which leads to Henry separating from the Catholic Church and declaring himself the leader of the Church of England.

1936 Hitler sends German troops into the Rhineland in violation of the Locarno Pact and the Treaty of Versailles.

1942 Japanese troops land in New Guinea.

1965 U.S. state troopers attack demonstrators demanding better voting rights for African Americans as they march from Selma to Montgomery in Alabama.

1977 Prime Minister Ali Bhutto wins national elections in Pakistan and is accused of election rigging. This sparks violent demonstrations between rival political groups that only end in July when the Army takes over and imprisons Mr Bhutto. He is executed in 1979.

1985 The first blood test for HIV/AIDS is released to blood banks (see below).

1997 A teacher at a school in Cheddar, Wessex, is found through genetic testing to be directly descended from a 9,000-year-old skeleton found in the Cheddar Caves.

2005 The city council of Pretoria, capital of South Africa, votes to change the name of the city to *Tshwane*, meaning "We are the same."

Births
- **1792** John Herschel, astronomer
- **1872** Piet Mondrian, painter
- **1952** Sir Vivian Richards, cricketer
- **1960** Ivan Lendl, tennis player

Deaths
- **322 B.C.E.** Aristotle, philosopher
- **1988** Divine, actor
- **1999** Stanley Kubrick, film director

DAY TO REMEMBER

Religious day St. Perpetua and Felicity's Day These two women (c. 203) were arrested in North Africa during the Christian persecutions by Emperor Severus. Perpetua and Felicity refused to renounce their faith and were sent to the arena. A wild cow gored the women and gladiators finished them off with swords.

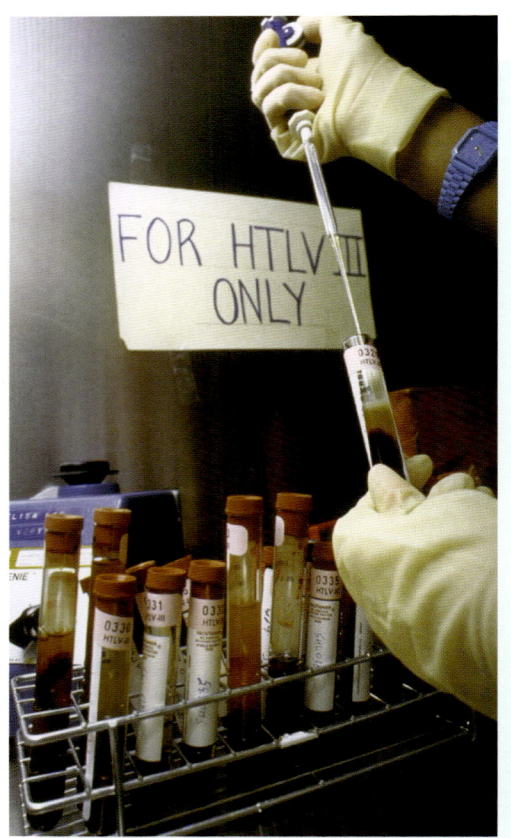

A test for HIV/AIDS

HIV (human immunodeficiency virus) attacks and damages white blood cells, multiplying until the immune system is severely compromised. When this happens, illnesses that would normally be warded off become life-threatening.

The virus is thought to have originated in Africa as early as the 1930s, but it only began to make world headlines in 1981 when an unusual and deadly suite of illnesses appeared in Western nations, notably among homosexual men and intravenous drug users in the U.S.

By early 1982, this phenomenon had been given a name: acquired immune deficiency syndrome. Researchers realized that AIDS could be an infection, and the first cases of transmission via blood products were documented. However, without a clear understanding of the disease, blood bank operators were reluctant to reject donors from identified high-risk groups.

By early 1984, French researchers had discovered the virus that caused AIDS. The knowledge that AIDS was caused by a virus caused a dramatic turnaround in blood-product management strategies. By March 1984, funds were being channeled into developing blood tests for HIV. A breakthrough came with the development of an ELISA (enzyme-linked immunosorbent assay) test that identifies antibodies the body produces in its attempt to fight the virus. Testing positive can indicate the presence of a number of infectious diseases, so further more specific testing is required to confirm HIV status. The advantage of an ELISA test is that it is a quick and cheap initial testing method.

The U.S. Federal Drug Administration passed the first ELISA AIDS test in early March 1985. It was first used in a blood bank in San Francisco on March 7, 1985.

DATEline

March 8

"It's just a job. Grass grows, birds fly, waves pound the sand. I beat people up."

MUHAMMAD ALI, ON BOXING

HISTORICAL EVENTS

1265 The first English "parliament" meets: Simon de Montfort, after defeating Prince Edward, calls a meeting of bishops, knights, and ordinary men from each city and borough in England at Westminster Hall to discuss how the country should be governed.

1702 Queen Anne inherits the throne of Britain when William III dies in a riding accident.

1910 In France, Baroness de Laroche becomes the first woman to gain a pilot's license.

1917 The February Revolution (so-called because this is the month of the Russian calendar that it falls in) begins with riots for food in Petrograd.

1942 The Dutch surrender to Japanese forces on Java after two months of fighting.

1946 The French naval fleet arrives at Haiphong, Vietnam.

1954 France and Vietnam open talks in Paris on a treaty to form the state of Indochina.

1957 Egypt reopens the Suez Canal to international traffic.

1962 The Beatles perform on BBC television for the first time on the show *Teenager Turn*.

1965 The first 3,500 U.S. combat troops land in South Vietnam at Da Nang.

1971 Joe Frazier defeats Muhammad Ali in the boxing match dubbed "The Fight of the Century" (see below).

1978 *The Hitchhiker's Guide to the Galaxy*, by Douglas Adams, is first broadcast on BBC Radio 4.

DAY TO REMEMBER

International day Women's Day This day, marking the achievements and struggles of women, is celebrated in different ways around the world. Parades and marches are held in many countries, and in some nations women are given small gifts. It is a public holiday in Russia.

Births
- 1714 Carl Philipp Emanuel Bach, composer
- 1856 Tom Roberts, painter
- 1859 Kenneth Grahame, children's writer
- 1943 Lynn Redgrave, actress
- 1947 Carol Bayer Sager, singer/songwriter

Deaths
- 1869 Hector Berlioz, composer
- 1999 Joe DiMaggio, baseballer

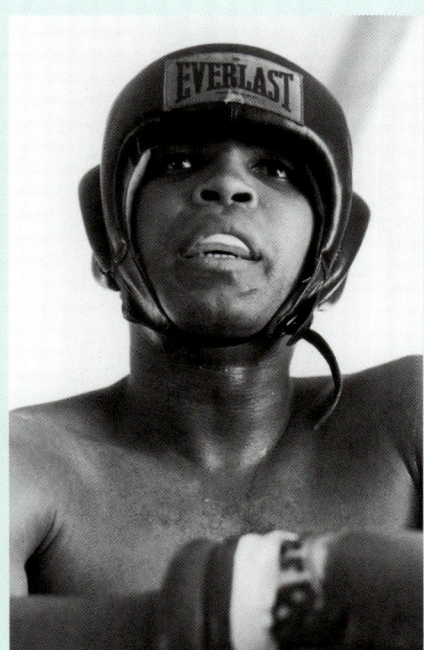

On March 8, 1971, the World Heavyweight Champion, Joe Frazier, met former champion Muhammad Ali at Madison Square Garden in New York in a match that was billed as "The Fight of the Century." The bout was broadcast worldwide and proved to be as exciting as predicted. It lasted 45 minutes, with only one knockdown: Frazier dropped Ali with a left hook in the fifteenth round. Frazier was awarded the match and retained his title. This was Ali's first professional defeat. There were two more matches in the series; Ali (right) won them both.

March 9

> "I am very happy to be here." — SVETLANA ALLILUYEVA, ON DEFECTING FROM THE U.S.S.R.

The first Barbie® doll went on display at a toy fair in New York in 1959. Barbie® was the idea of Ruth Handler, a founder of the Mattel toy company. Ruth noticed her daughter liked to play with adult dolls, but the only ones available were made of paper. In Switzerland, Ruth saw a doll called Lilli that was modeled on a blonde, man-chasing German comic character. Ruth developed her own doll and named her Barbie® after her daughter. Little girls loved Barbie® and soon Mattel was taking back orders. In 1961, they introduced Barbie®'s boyfriend, Ken, named after Ruth's son. In 1965, seven-year-old Becky Ray (right) became the 400,000th member of the Barbie® Fan Club.

HISTORICAL EVENTS

- **1074** Pope Gregory VII excommunicates married priests from the Catholic Church.
- **1796** Napoleon Bonaparte marries Joséphine de Beauharnais in a civil ceremony.
- **1862** The first battle between iron ships: the Union *Monitor* and Confederate *Merrimac*. Neither ship is able to cause significant damage to the other.
- **1932** Eamon De Valera is elected President of the Irish Free State, declaring he will sever ties with the British Crown.
- **1945** U.S. B-29 bombers launch incendiary attacks against Japan. As Japanese houses were tightly packed and made of wood and paper, they burned easily. More than 80,000 people died and 250,000 buildings were destroyed in the resulting firestorm.
- **1959** Barbie® goes on display for the first time at a toy fair in New York (see above).
- **1967** Svetlana Alliluyeva, daughter of Joseph Stalin, defects to the West, seeking asylum in the U.S. Embassy in India.
- **2006** The U.S. military announces that it will close the notorious Abu Ghraib prison in Iraq, the center of controversy over mistreatment of Iraqi prisoners.

DAY TO REMEMBER

Religious day St. Frances of Rome's Day The patron saint of housewives and widows, St. Frances (1384–1440) was born into a wealthy family. She wanted to be a nun but followed her family's wishes and married. She founded the Oblates of Mary, women who devoted themselves to the needy.

Births
- 1892 Vita Sackville-West, writer
- 1934 Yuri Gagarin, cosmonaut
- 1940 Raúl Juliá, actor
- 1943 Bobby Fischer, chess player
- 1964 Juliette Binoche, actress

Deaths
- 1989 Robert Mapplethorpe, photographer
- 1994 Charles Bukowski, writer
- 1996 George Burns, actor
- 2006 Harry Seidler, architect

March 10

"War is never cheap or easy." — PRESIDENT GEORGE W. BUSH

HISTORICAL EVENTS

- **49 B.C.E.** Julius Caesar and his army cross the Rubicon and invade Italy.
- **1629** Charles I of England dissolves Parliament and doesn't recall it for 11 years.
- **1831** The French Foreign Legion is formed, initially to suppress rebellion in Algeria.
- **1876** Alexander Graham Bell speaks on the telephone for the first time, summoning his amazed assistant with the words, "Mr. Watson, come here. I want you."
- **1902** General Koos de la Rey releases British General Lord Methuen, who was captured at the Battle of Tweebosch, the last Boer victory of the Boer War, on March 7.
- **1906** Gas is ignited in a coal mine in Courrieres, France. Around 1,200 coalminers die because of the explosion.
- **1991** The U.S. begins Phase Echo – the withdrawal of its 540,000 troops from the Persian Gulf at the end of the Gulf War.
- **1997** Jean-Dominique Bauby, editor-in-chief of French *Elle* magazine, dies a few days after his book *The Diving Bell and the Butterfly* is published. He dictated the entire book by blinking his left eyelid when the correct letter of the alphabet was recited to him. This was the only muscle he could move after suffering a massive stroke.
- **2001** Taliban officials announce that they have destroyed two colossal ancient statues of Buddha at Bamiyan (see below).

Births
- **1772** Friedrich von Schlegel, writer, philosopher
- **1847** Kate Sheppard, suffragist
- **1928** James Earl Ray, assassin
- **1940** Chuck Norris, actor
- **1957** Osama bin Laden, Islamic extremist
- **1958** Sharon Stone, actress

Deaths
- **1872** Giuseppe Mazzini, social reformer who fought for unification of Italy
- **1988** Andy Gibb, singer
- **1998** Lloyd Bridges, actor
- **2003** Barry Sheene, motorcycle racer
- **2005** Dave Allen, comedian
- **2006** John Profumo, British politician

DAY TO REMEMBER

Religious day St. John Ogilvie St. John (1579–1615) was raised a Calvinist in Scotland but converted to Catholicism. After refusing to recognize the King as head of the Church, he was hanged on March 10, 1615, in Glasgow.

The fall of the Buddhas of Bamiyan

The two giant Buddhas of Bamiyan were built in around the fifth or sixth centuries C.E. They were carved into cliffs of the Bamiyan Valley in central Afghanistan and were part of a Buddhist monastery complex. The statues stood 180 feet (55 m) and 121 feet (37 m) tall. Their bodies were carved out of sandstone, with details such as faces and hands made from mud coated with stucco. A seventh-century traveler described them as being decorated with gold and jewels.

The Buddhist settlement was abandoned when Islam came to the region. Over the years the statues' gold and jewels disappeared. As orthodox Islam considers idols sinful, there were numerous attempts to deface and destroy the statues, primarily by hacking at limbs and cutting away facial features.

In early March, 2001, the Taliban Government in Kabul issued a decree that all statues in Afghanistan should be destroyed, including the Buddhas of Bamiyan, pictured right before and after destruction. Buddhists across Southeast Asia conducted sit-down demonstrations and angry protest marches. Leaders from other Muslim nations, including Pakistan and Iran, called for the destruction to cease. Even the United Nations, which had listed Bamiyan as a World Heritage site, joined the protests.

Ignoring all protests, the Taliban proceeded with the demolition of the statues using explosives and tank barrages. On March 10 they officially announced that the statues had fallen.

March 11

"There will be more if God wills it. You love life, and we love death."
FROM A VIDEOTAPE LEFT BY TERRORISTS IN A BIN NEAR A MOSQUE IN MADRID

HISTORICAL EVENTS

- **1811** The Luddite riots begin in Nottingham, England. Poor workers destroy stocking and lace-making machines that they fear will replace them in factories.
- **1888** The Great White Hurricane hits New York and rages until March 14. With wind speeds up to 60 miles an hour (100 km/h) and snowdrifts reaching 19 feet (6 m) deep, the city comes to a standstill. Throughout the northern U.S.A., 400 people freeze to death.
- **1911** Professor Ernest Rutherford describes the structure of the atom for the first time at the Manchester Literary and Philosophical Society.
- **1942** General Douglas MacArthur states, "I shall return," as he pulls American forces out of the Philippines, realizing that defense against the Japanese Army is futile. He goes to Australia and takes command of the Allied forces in the Pacific and leads them to victory.
- **1966** General Suharto comes to power in Indonesia.
- **1985** Mikhail Gorbachev becomes leader of the Soviet Union after the death of Konstantin Chernenko.
- **1997** Sir Paul McCartney is knighted by Queen Elizabeth II.
- **2004** Ten bombs explode in Madrid in a devastating terrorist attack (see below).
- **2006** Slobodan Milosovic, the former Yugoslav President, is found dead in prison in The Hague before his trial for genocide is concluded.

Births
- **1931** Rupert Murdoch, media baron
- **1952** Douglas Adams, humorous writer

Deaths
- **1950** Sir Ralph Freeman, engineer, designer of Sydney Harbour Bridge
- **1955** Sir Alexander Fleming, the discoverer of penicillin
- **2006** Slobodan Milosevic, imprisoned former Yugoslav President

DAY TO REMEMBER

National day Johnny Appleseed Day
Johnny Appleseed (John Chapman, September 26, 1774–c. March 11, 1847) planted apple orchards in large parts of Ohio, Indiana, and Illinois, preaching as he went. He is thought to have died on or around this date in a snowstorm.

On March 11, 2004, 10 bombs exploded on commuter trains in Madrid during the busy morning rush hour, causing devastation and chaos. Police later found three more unexploded bombs. More than 1,400 people were injured and 191 were killed. At first it was thought that the Basque separatist group ETA was responsible, but it became more certain that an Islamic extremist group carried out the attacks. In national elections three days later, the Spanish Socialist Party won an overwhelming victory and promised to withdraw Spanish troops from Iraq if United Nations forces didn't take over operations there by June.

March 12

"India is a geographical term. It is no more a united nation than the Equator."
WINSTON CHURCHILL, IN A SPEECH AT THE ROYAL ALBERT HALL, 1931

Births
- 1881 Kemal Atatürk, first leader of Turkey
- 1888 Vaslav Nijinski, ballet dancer, and choreographer
- 1912 Edward Albee, playwright
- 1922 Jack Kerouac, poet and writer
- 1946 Liza Minnelli, actress and singer

Deaths
- 1925 Sun Yat-sen, Chinese revolutionary
- 1999 Yehudi Menuhin, violinist

HISTORICAL EVENTS

- **1894** Bottled Coca-Cola is sold for the first time. Dr. John Pemberton created the drink in 1886 and patented it in 1893.
- **1923** Dr. Lee De Forest demonstrates the Phonofilm – the first film with a soundtrack.
- **1930** Mahatma Gandhi begins a civil disobedience march from his ashram to the coastal village of Dandi, 240 miles (380 km) away. There on April 4 he makes salt by boiling dirt and salt in sea water in defiance of British law. He is arrested on May 4.
- **1933** President Paul von Hindenburg orders the flag of the German Republic to be replaced with the empire banner and the swastika.
- **1938** The Anschluss takes place. At 5:30 A.M. German troops enter Austria "to restore order." Adolf Hitler crosses the Austrian border at the town of Braunau, where he was born, and declares that it is now part of Germany. As he drives by, the crowd in Braunau call out *"Ein volk. Ein reich. Ein führer."* (One people. One state. One leader.)
- **1969** Paul McCartney and Linda Eastman marry at Marylebone Registry Office in London.
- **1994** Thirty-three women are the first women ordained as priests in the Church of England (see right).
- **2003** The Chinese Government orders the Rolling Stones to cut four songs from their concerts in Shanghai and Beijing. The songs are "Brown Sugar," "Honky Tonk Woman," "Beast of Burden," and "Let's Spend the Night Together."

The Church of England gains its first female priests

On March 12, 1994, 33 women were ordained as priests in Bristol Cathedral. They were the first women to be ordained in the Church of England.

The Church of England is part of the Anglican Communion of Churches, which encompasses 38 national or multinational churches. The Episcopal Church of the U.S.A. was the first within this group to ordain women in 1974 and others soon followed. In 1989 the Anglican Church of New Zealand ordained the first female bishop.

In the Church of England, however, things moved more slowly. The debate about women's roles as preachers and priests began in 1920 when Maude Royden, a popular London preacher, was banned from the pulpit in 1919. Women were finally permitted to become deacons in 1987. Now they could perform baptisms, marriages, and burials, but they couldn't give communion or administer any other sacraments.

Fierce debate within the church continued, with some more traditional elements saying they would leave the Church of England rather than be ministered to by women. On November 11, 1992, the General Synod passed legislation to allow the ordination of women by two votes. The first women were ordained in 1994, and by the end of the year about 1,500 women had been ordained. Over the next 10 years the number of women priests continued to increase. By 2003 there were more than 2,100. In 2005, almost equal numbers of men and women celebrated their ordination ceremonies.

However, ordination was only the first hurdle. Opposition to women as priests in the Church of England remained. Numerous parishes turned down women as their priests, and female priests faced open hostility, as gently depicted in *The Vicar of Dibley,* a television comedy starring Dawn French, that began filming in 1994.

DAYS TO REMEMBER

National day Flag Day (Venezuela) Flag day commemorates the day in 1806 that Francisco de Miranda attempted to start a revolution and raised a yellow, blue, and red striped flag on his ship.

National day Arbor Day (China) This public holiday is for the planting of trees and to commemorate the death of Sun Yat-sen.

March 13

As classes began on March 13, 1996, at Dunblane Primary School in Scotland, Thomas Hamilton, armed with four guns, walked in the gate. When he reached the gym he opened fire on the Primary 1 class. Sixteen five- and six-year-olds and their teacher, Gwen Mayor, died. Thirteen other children and three teachers were injured. The gunman then shot himself in the head.

Hamilton probably carried out the attack as revenge for allegations made about his suspect behavior around boys.

Queen Elizabeth II and Princess Anne (above) visited the school a few days later to pay their respects. After the massacre, Britain introduced some of the toughest laws on gun ownership in the world.

Births
- 1733 Joseph Priestley, scientist
- 1884 Hugh Walpole, writer
- 1911 L. Ron Hubbard, religious leader

Deaths
- 1842 Henry Shrapnel, soldier, inventor
- 1990 Bruno Bettelheim, psychologist

HISTORICAL EVENTS

- **1781** The astronomer William Herschel discovers the planet Uranus.
- **1865** In the American Civil War, the Confederates pass a law allowing African Americans to enlist in their army. The bill didn't state that they would be freed, but by arming them they were in effect being given their freedom.
- **1868** The first impeachment trial of a U.S. president begins. President Andrew Johnson is accused of illegally removing a federal office holder. He is found not guilty and stays in office until the end of his term.
- **1881** Tsar Alexander II is assassinated in St. Petersburg, Russia, by a bomb thrown by members of The people's Will, a revolutionary group.
- **1928** The poorly constructed St. Francis Dam near Los Angeles, California, bursts, killing more than 400 people.
- **1930** Clyde W. Tombaugh announces the discovery of the ninth planet in the solar system. It is named Pluto on May 24, 1930.
- **1944** London suspends travel between Ireland and Britain due to the Irish Government's refusal to expel Axis-power diplomats within its borders.
- **1985** The first episode of *Neighbours* appears on Australian television. After rating poorly for four months, the show switches channels and actors Kylie Minogue and Jason Donovan join the cast.
- **1996** Sixteen children and a teacher are killed and many others injured when a gunman opens fire at Dunblane Primary School in Scotland (see above).
- **2000** Gridiron's Miami Dolphins quarterback, Dan Marino, retires after a 17-year career. He had played 242 games for Miami and scored 420 touchdowns.

March 14

"It's good to see you all." RICHARD MCILKENNY, ONE OF THE BIRMINGHAM SIX, ON HIS RELEASE

HISTORICAL EVENTS

1489 Queen Isabella of Castile decrees that the 150,000 Jews within Spain's borders must convert to Christianity or be expelled.

1757 British Admiral John Byng is tried and executed by firing squad on board his ship the *Monarch* for losing Menorca to French forces through neglect of duty.

1945 Britain's Royal Air Force 617 Squadron drops the first Grand Slam "dam buster" bombs. The shockwaves destroy the Bielefeld Viaduct in Germany and are felt hundreds of miles away.

1964 Jack Ruby is found guilty of the murder of Lee Harvey Oswald, the accused assassin of President John F. Kennedy.

1984 Gerry Adams, the leader of Sinn Fein, is shot and injured in an assassination attempt in Belfast.

1991 The Birmingham Six are freed after being wrongfully imprisoned for terrorism (see below).

DAYS TO REMEMBER

National day White Day Similar to Valentine's Day, this is a day when men in Japan and Taiwan give women they care about a gift such as chocolate or jewelry to show them appreciation.

Religious festival (Ancient Rome) Horse races were held on this day in honor of Mars, god of war, and rites were held to purify the Roman army.

Births
- 1681 Georg Philipp Telemann, composer
- 1804 Johann Strauss the Elder, composer
- 1854 Paul Erhlich, scientist
- 1879 Albert Einstein, theoretical physicist
- 1923 Diane Arbus, photographer
- 1933 Sir Michael Caine, actor
- 1933 Quincy Jones, musician, composer, and producer
- 1947 Billy Crystal, actor and comedian

Deaths
- 1471 Thomas Malory, writer
- 1757 John Byng, British Admiral
- 1883 Karl Marx, philosopher and political scientist
- 1976 Busby Berkeley, film director
- 2003 Jack Goldstein, artist

Freedom for the Birmingham Six

In 1974 the IRA carried out an extensive bombing campaign in England. On November 21, explosions went off in two central Birmingham pubs, killing 21 and injuring around 180 people.

Earlier that evening Patrick Hill, Gerard Hunter, Richard McIlkenny, William Power, and John Walker had left Birmingham to attend the funeral of an IRA member who had accidentally blown himself up while setting a bomb. As they were being searched while boarding the ferry for Ireland, police received news of the bombing. The men were deemed suspicious and were taken into custody. Hugh Callaghan, who had seen them off at the station, was taken into custody the next day.

On August 15 the following year, the six men were found guilty of murder and were sentenced to life in prison. They appealed the conviction, claiming they had only confessed after being beaten by police. Despite bruises having been visible on their early court appearances, this appeal was dismissed. Fourteen police officers accused of assault were cleared of the allegations against them.

In 1985, journalist Chris Mullins raised doubts about the conviction. Pressure to have the case reexamined continued to grow. In 1991 another appeal was heard. This time it was shown that police had fabricated evidence. This new evidence led to the men's convictions being overturned 16 years after they were sentenced. A jubilant crowd met them as they were released on March 14, 1991. Ten years later they were all awarded compensation for their ordeal.

This monument was built in honor of Karl Marx (left) and fellow philosopher Friedrich Engels in Berlin in 1986.

March 15

HISTORICAL EVENTS

- 44 B.C.E. Julius Caesar is murdered on the steps of the Roman Senate by a group of senators who feared he was planning to make himself King of Rome.
- 1877 Australia and England begin their first Test cricket match at the Melbourne Cricket Ground. Australia wins the match.
- 1906 The Rolls-Royce Company is formed; the Silver Ghost is their first successful car.
- 1909 Selfridges department store opens in London on Oxford Street.
- 1939 Hitler's forces invade Czechoslovakia, breaking the Munich Pact, which was signed on September 30, 1938.
- 1964 Actors Richard Burton and Elizabeth Taylor marry after their romance develops during the filming of *Cleopatra* (see right).
- 1978 Israel invades Lebanon in retaliation for Palestinian guerrilla attacks staged from Lebanese territory. Thousands of Palestinians living in refugee settlements flee. Israel withdraws in June.
- 1981 The passengers and crew of a Pakistani Airways jet held hostage by terrorists are released in Syria after being held for 13 days. One passenger, a Pakistani diplomat, had been killed.
- 2003 The World Health Organization declares SARS – believed to have originated in Guangdong Province, China, in November 2002 – a public health emergency.

DAYS TO REMEMBER

Historical day The Ides of March The middle of each month of the Roman calendar is known as the "Ides" of the month. The Ides of March took on special significance in 44 B.C.E. when Julius Caesar was murdered after being warned by a soothsayer to beware the ides of March.

National day Independence Day (Hungary) This public holiday day marks the failed 1848 revolution of Hungarians against the Austro–Hungarian Empire. They mark their independence in October.

> *"I go the way that Providence dictates with the assurance of a sleepwalker."* ADOLF HITLER, SPEECH IN MUNICH, 1936

Births
- 1835 Eduard Strauss, composer
- 1947 Ry Cooder, musician
- 1961 Fabio Lanzoni, male model

Deaths
- 44 B.C.E. Julius Caesar, Emperor of Rome
- 1975 Aristotle Onassis, shipping magnate
- 1998 Dr. Benjamin Spock, pediatrician

Elizabeth Taylor played Cleopatra and Richard Burton played Mark Antony in the film *Cleopatra*. During filming in 1963 their passionate on-screen romance soon spilled over into real life. The couple married on March 15, 1964, after Taylor had divorced her fourth husband, Eddie Fisher. It was Burton's second marriage. They went on to make many movies together, including *Who's Afraid of Virginia Woolf?* (1966), in which they played a bitterly arguing couple and for which Taylor earned her second Oscar. Burton and Taylor divorced in 1974, reconciled and remarried in 1975, then divorced again in 1976.

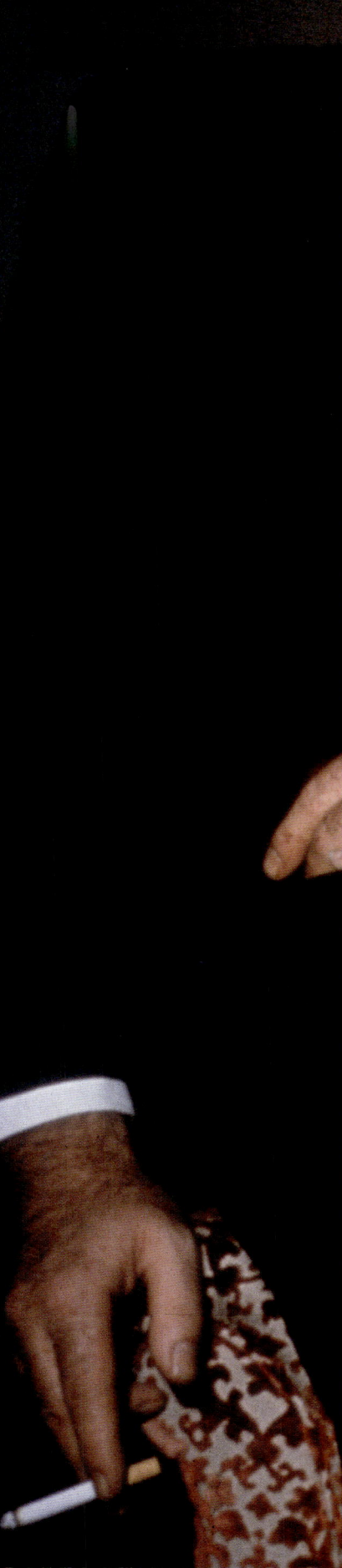

March 16

"Politics begin where the masses are, not where there are thousands, but where there are millions, that is where serious politics begin."
VLADIMIR LENIN, SPEAKING TO THE CONGRESS OF THE RUSSIAN COMMUNIST PARTY, 1918

HISTORICAL EVENTS

1521 Ferdinand Magellan, Spanish explorer, reaches islands in the Pacific Ocean, which he named the Philippines in honor of the Spanish king.
1872 The Wanderers defeat the Royal Engineers in the first FA Cup, the world's oldest football competition.
1917 Tsar Nicholas II of Russia abdicates from the throne after the "February Revolution."
1968 U.S. troops go on a rampage and kill as many as 500 defenseless civilians in the village of My Lai in South Vietnam. On March 29, 1971, Lt. William Calley is found guilty of murder at a U.S. court martial.
1971 Paul Simon and Art Garfunkel win the Grammy Award for Best Album for *Bridge Over Troubled Water*, and the Grammy for Best Single for the title song.
1976 Labour Prime Minister of Britain, Harold Wilson, resigns during his eighth year in the job.
1978 Gunmen from the Red Brigade kidnap the former Prime Minister of Italy, Aldo Moro, in Rome. His bullet-riddled body is found in the trunk of a car in Rome on May 10.
1988 During the Iran–Iraq war, up to 10,000 people are killed in a poison gas attack on the Kurdish town of Halabja by Iraqi forces.
2005 The newly elected Iraqi National Assembly meets for the first time (see below).

Births
1774 Matthew Flinders, explorer
1787 Georg Simon Ohm, physicist
1920 Leo McKern, actor
1926 Jerry Lewis, comedian
1940 Bernardo Bertolucci, film director
1947 Robin Williams, comedian and actor
1953 Isabelle Huppert, actress

Deaths
37 C.E. Tiberius, Roman Emperor
1898 Aubrey Beardsley, artist
1936 Marguerite Durand, journalist and feminist

DAY TO REMEMBER

Historical day Bacchanalia (Ancient Rome) Celebrations began on this day in honor of the god Bacchus. The festival ran for three days and was attended mainly by women. It was banned by the Senate from 186 B.C.E. but endured in southern Italy.

Iraq's elected National Assembly met for the first time on March 16, 2005. Elections had taken place on January 30, 2005. Of the 275 seats, the Shi'ite Islamist alliance had won 140 seats, with a Kurdish coalition winning 75. Women held about one third of all seats.

Minutes before the Assembly took their seats, mortar fire could be heard outside. Even with the violence continuing, many Iraqis felt positive about the inauguration of their National Assembly.

The interim Prime Minister, Ayad Allawi, addressed the new Assembly, stressing the importance of the tasks facing the elected members. Though they were aware of the tensions between the groups involved, many Iraqis felt that it was a first step in rebuilding their nation. Three weeks later Jalal Talabani, a Kurd, became the President of Iraq.

March 17

DATE*line*

HISTORICAL EVENTS

1776 British forces evacuate Boston by sea when they realize that American forces surround the city, bringing their eight-year occupation to an end.
1845 Stephen Perry patents the first rubber band in England.
1861 The Kingdom of Italy is proclaimed; King Victor Emmanuel is the first regent.
1891 The British battleship *Anson* collides with the passenger ship *Utopia* in the Bay of Gibraltar during a storm. The *Utopia* is taking Italian immigrants to America and 576 passengers and crew drown.
1899 A man watching the St. Patrick's Day parade from New York's Windsor Hotel lights his cigar then throws the match out of a window. The match blows into a window below and the hotel burns to the ground, killing 92.
1912 On the return of Robert Scott's expedition from the South Pole, exhausted Captain Lawrence Oates walks into a blizzard to die, sacrificing himself so that the rest of the party will not be slowed down and might survive.
1969 Golda Meir, one of the founders of Israel, becomes Prime Minister and serves until 1974.
2000 More than 500 members of a doomsday cult in Uganda die when their church is gutted by fire (see right).
2002 Robert Mugabe is sworn in as the President of Zimbabwe after being re-elected in elections alleged to be neither free nor fair on March 13. On March 19, Zimbabwe is suspended from the Commonwealth for one year due to election rigging.

DAYS TO REMEMBER

Religious day St. Patrick's Day This patron saint of Ireland (c. 389–461) was captured and taken there as a youth. He escaped back to Britain and studied at a monastery. After becoming a bishop, he returned and converted most of the Irish to Christianity, often through miraculous acts.

Births		Deaths	
1473	James I of Scotland and England	461	St. Patrick, bishop
1834	Gottlieb Daimler, inventor	1741	Jean-Baptiste Rousseau, poet
1846	Kate Greenaway, children's writer	1853	Christian Doppler, mathematician
1919	Nat King Cole, singer	1912	Captain Lawrence Oates, explorer
1938	Rudolf Nureyev, ballet dancer	2005	Andre Norton, writer
1954	Lesley-Anne Down, actress		

In Uganda, near a burned-out church, officials erect a sign near a mass grave to keep people out of the area (see below).

Mass suicide by fire in Uganda

On March 17, 2000, a church burned to the ground in the village of Kanungu, Uganda. This was no ordinary fire: the windows and doors had been nailed shut and the congregation members inside were doused in petrol before the church was set alight.

The church belonged to a cult named the Movement for the Restoration of the Ten Commandments of God. Joseph Kibweteere, an excommunicated Catholic priest, and Credonia Mwerinde, a former prostitute who claimed the Virgin Mary spoke to her, were its leaders. Part of their central teaching was that the world would end on December 31, 1999.

Peter Ahimbisibwe, one of the cult's few survivors, gave clues as to what had happened. He reported that members sold their property and gave everything to their leaders. After January 1, 2000, came and went, followers began to ask how they were going to live. They were told that the world would now end on December 31, 2000. Not everyone was satisfied by this announcement. Those who complained started disappearing.

A week before March 17, cult members were told to prepare for the end. People in Kanungu noticed them buying large amounts of supplies, including soft drinks. There was a feast the night before the fire. On the morning of March 17, the congregation spent several hours chanting and singing in the church before it was engulfed by fire.

The blaze fused bodies together, so it was difficult to tell how many people had died; a figure of 530 was finally arrived at. In the following weeks more bodies were found in mass burials on land belonging to the cult. The victims had been stabbed or strangled. The final number of deaths linked to the cult was nearly 1,000. Its leaders were unaccounted for. They have never been found.

March 18

"I cannot build the best interests of my people on the basis of injustice towards a majority of the other people who share the same country." — F. W. DE KLERK

Births
- 1844 Nikolay Rimsky-Korsakov, composer
- 1869 Neville Chamberlain, British Prime Minister
- 1893 Wilfred Owen, soldier and poet
- 1932 John Updike, writer
- 1936 Frederik Willem de Klerk, South African President
- 1964 Bonnie Blair, speed skater

Deaths
- 1584 Ivan the Terrible, Tsar of Russia
- 1745 Robert Walpole, first British Prime Minister
- 1913 King George I of Greece

Celtic tree sign
ALDER
March 18–April 14

In the Celtic tradition, people born between March 18 and April 14 are associated with the alder tree. They are independent, courageous, and protective, all good qualities in a leader, though they can also act rashly.

HISTORICAL EVENTS

- **1850** Henry Wells and William Fargo found American Express. Initially it is a shipping company, but later it becomes a financial institution as well.
- **1871** The Paris Commune begins when the citizens of Paris rebel against the rulers of the Third Republic and shoot several French generals. The Third Republic's forces besiege the city for two months, ending on May 28.
- **1902** The tenor Enrico Caruso records 10 arias in Milan for the Gramophone Company. He is the first well-known singer to make a record.
- **1921** Fighting breaks out between passengers from two different towns in China on the steamer *Hong Koh*. The rioting distracts the crew and the ship runs aground. More than 1,000 die during the fighting or by drowning.
- **1925** The Tri State Tornado leaves a path of destruction 220 miles (350 km) long across Missouri, Illinois, and Indiana, leaving 689 people dead.
- **1950** The Belgian Government collapses as the people vote for the return of King Leopold III from exile in Switzerland. He had been accused of cooperating with the Nazis. He abdicates in favor of his son, Badouin, in 1951.
- **1962** The French sign a peace treaty with Algerian rebels to end seven years of war and 130 years of French rule in Algeria.
- **1965** Cosmonaut Alexei Leonov is the first man to walk in space, when he leaves the *Voskhod 2* for 12 minutes. His spacesuit balloons and he has to let some air out in order to re-enter the spacecraft.
- **1992** White South Africans vote in a referendum to end apartheid and to give all South Africans the vote (see below).
- **2002** About 24,000 out of 27,000 residents of Gibraltar protest against British plans to share sovereignty of the colony with Spain.

Apartheid was a system of laws introduced in 1948 that segregated South Africans according to race. It controlled the black majority and made them foreigners in their own country. In 1989 F. W. de Klerk (center front) became State President. He believed that apartheid was doomed to failure – it was the cause of violence at home and political isolation from the rest of the world. In 1992 he called a referendum asking if the white voters agreed to end apartheid and to create a government in which all South Africans had an equal say. In the largest turnout of voters ever, 68 percent voted yes.

DATE*line*

March 19

"The struggle for peace and the struggle for human rights are inseparable."
WILLY BRANDT, AFTER ACCEPTING THE NOBEL PEACE PRIZE, 1971

After taking eight years to build, the Sydney Harbour Bridge opened on March 19, 1932. At the time, it was the world's largest single-span bridge. For the first time people could cross the harbor without having to travel by boat. As the Premier of New South Wales, Jack Lang, was about to cut the ribbon, Captain De Groot of the political group the New Guard rode past and slashed it with a sword, declaring the bridge open on behalf of "decent and loyal citizens of New South Wales." He was arrested and taken to a psychiatric hospital.

Births
- 1813 David Livingstone, missionary and explorer
- 1905 Albert Speer, architect and Nazi official
- 1933 Philip Roth, writer
- 1936 Ursula Andress, actress
- 1947 Glenn Close, actress
- 1955 Bruce Willis, actor

Deaths
- 1702 William of Orange, King of England
- 1950 Edgar Rice Burroughs, writer

DAYS TO REMEMBER

Religious day St. Joseph's Day Already betrothed to Mary when he found out she was pregnant, St. Joseph was convinced to marry her by an angel in a dream who said she had conceived her child by the Holy Spirit, and that the baby's name would be Jesus.

Traditional day Father's Day In Spain, Portugal, and Belgium, the day to honor and celebrate fathers is held to coincide with St. Joseph's Day.

Religious day Las Fallas (Valencia, Spain) Las Fallas is a festival in honor of St. Joseph where people hold parades of cardboard and papier-mâché figures filled with firecrackers that they then light.

HISTORICAL EVENTS

- **1900** Sir Arthur Evans announces the discovery of the palace of Knossos on Crete and begins excavations.
- **1932** The Sydney Harbour Bridge is opened. Construction had started eight years earlier (see above).
- **1967** The oil tanker *Torrey Canyon* runs aground and is bombed by the British Government in an attempt to burn the oil and minimize the environmental impact. Despite this, 75 miles (125 km) of the French coast is badly contaminated.
- **1970** Prime Minister Willi Stoph and Chancellor Willy Brandt, the leaders of East and West Germany, meet in East Germany for the first time for talks on improving relations between the two countries.
- **1971** An avalanche triggered by an earthquake kills about 700 people in a mining camp at Chungar, Peru, 10,000 ft (3,000 m) up in the Andes Mountains.
- **1976** It is announced that Princess Margaret and Lord Snowdon are separating after 16 years of marriage. They divorce in 1978.
- **1982** The Argentine flag is raised on South Georgia, leading to the Falklands War.
- **1992** Prince Andrew and his wife Sarah Ferguson, Duke and Duchess of York, separate after six years of marriage, and divorce four years later.

March 20

"Power is my mistress. I have worked too hard in conquering her to allow anyone to take her, or even to covet her." — NAPOLEON BONAPARTE

In 1966 Britain was to host football's World Cup. The Jules Rimet trophy (above) was already on display at Central Hall in Westminster, London. To the horror of football fans everywhere, it was stolen on March 20.

On March 27 the trophy was found when a dog out for a walk, Pickles (above), sniffed at a bundle of newspaper on the ground. His owner, David Corbett (above), investigated and found the cup inside. The original cup was kept permanently in Rio de Janeiro and a copy was awarded to the winners of the tournament. The original was stolen again in 1983, and has yet to be recovered.

HISTORICAL EVENTS

1792 The Legislative Assembly in Paris approves the use of the guillotine.
1815 Napoleon re-enters Paris after escaping from exile in Elba three weeks before, beginning the Hundred Days Rule.
1815 Switzerland, effectively neutral since 1515, has its neutrality recognized and guaranteed in the Vienna Congress of 1815.
1916 Einstein's "Theory of Relativity" is published in German. This paper accounted for the slow rotation of the elliptical orbit of Mercury, and revolutionized physics, and astronomy.
1966 The football World Cup is stolen while on exhibition in London (see above).
1976 Patty Hearst, American newspaper heiress, is convicted of bank robbery. A terrorist group kidnapped her on February 4, 1974, and she joined them in their activities.
1995 The Aum Shinrikyo religious cult releases sarin gas in the Tokyo subway, killing 12 people. Some 5,500 people are treated in hospital.
2003 American missiles are fired on Baghdad, beginning the U.S.-led campaign to oust Saddam Hussein from power.

DAY TO REMEMBER

Religious day St. Alexandra Tsarina Alexandra (1872–1918), born in Germany, renounced Lutheranism when she married Tsar Nicholas II, becoming a devout Russian Orthodox convert. In 2000 the Russian Orthodox Church canonized her, along with her husband and children.

Births
- **43 B.C.E.** Ovid, poet
- **1546** Shaykh Baha'i, theologian and scientist
- **1828** Henrik Ibsen, playwright
- **1904** B. F. Skinner, psychologist
- **1908** Sir Michael Redgrave, actor
- **1917** Dame Vera Lynn, actress and singer
- **1950** William Hurt, actor
- **1957** Spike Lee, filmmaker
- **1958** Holly Hunter, actress

Deaths
- **1413** Henry IV, King of England
- **1727** Sir Isaac Newton, scientist
- **2004** Princess Juliana, formerly Queen Juliana of the Netherlands

March 21

Vernal equinox: The Sun crosses the plane of the Earth's equator, making day and night of equal length all over the world.

HISTORICAL EVENTS

1556 The Archbishop of Canterbury, Thomas Cranmer, is burned at the stake as a heretic. Hundreds more Protestants were executed during the reign of "Bloody Mary," the Catholic daughter of Henry VIII.
1851 The Yosemite Valley is discovered in California, U.S.
1857 An earthquake hits Tokyo; about 107,000 die.
1918 During World War I, Germany launches the Somme offensive in France.
1960 In the black township of Sharpeville in Transvaal, South Africa, Afrikaner police open fire on a group of peaceful black demonstrators, killing more than 50 and wounding 169.
1963 The notorious U.S. Federal Penitentiary, Alcatraz, closes after 29 years in operation (see below).
1980 In a famous cliff-hanger episode of the TV show *Dallas*, JR (played by Larry Hagman) is shot.

DAYS TO REMEMBER

National day Norooz (Iran) The New Day, the most important day of the year in Iran, celebrates the New Year of the Zoroastrian religion on the day of the spring equinox.

Religious day St. Benedict's Day As a boy of 14, St. Benedict (c. 480–547) lived alone in a cave, and his piety attracted many disciples. The name Benedictine was applied to those who followed his rule.

Births

1685 J. S. Bach, composer
1816 Charlotte Bronte, writer
1839 Modest Mussorgsky, composer
1906 John D. Rockefeller III, billionaire philanthropist
1916 Harold Robbins, writer
1958 Gary Oldman, actor

Deaths

1974 Candy Darling, female impersonator
1985 Sir Michael Redgrave, actor
1994 Ayrton Senna, racing-car driver
1999 Ernie Wise, comedian

Star sign

ARIES

March 21–April 20

Born under the sign of the ram, the typical Arian is ambitious and headstrong, bossy, temperamental, and self-centered. These attributes, coupled with energy and persistence, can make an Arian a great leader or organiser. An Arian wants to act, not waste time thinking about it.

From 1850 to 1933 Alcatraz was a fortress that defended San Francisco Bay. In 1934 it became a prison for men other prisons found difficult to manage. One of its most infamous inmates was Al Capone, who arrived in 1934 and left due to ill health in 1939. Alvin Karpis, a member of Ma Baker's notorious gang, spent 26 years there. In the early 1960s, the expense of keeping men on the island and changing notions of prisoner rehabilitation led to the decision to close the prison. The last 27 prisoners were removed on March 21, 1963. The island is now open to visitors.

March 22

> *"I wasn't kissing her, I was just whispering in her mouth."*
> CHICO MARX, ON HIS WIFE DISCOVERING HIM WITH A SHOWGIRL

Births
- 1599 Sir Anthony Van Dyck, painter
- 1887 Chico Marx, comedian
- 1923 Marcel Marceau, mime artist
- 1930 Stephen Sondheim, composer
- 1931 William Shatner, actor
- 1943 George Benson, musician
- 1946 Harry Vanda, composer
- 1948 Andrew Lloyd Webber, composer
- 1949 Fanny Ardant, actress
- 1956 Lena Olin, actress
- 1976 Reece Witherspoon, actress

Deaths
- 1639 Thomas Carew, poet
- 1832 J. W. Goethe, writer
- 1958 Michael Todd, producer

HISTORICAL EVENTS
- **1457** The Gutenberg *Bible*, the first printed book, is published. It is named after the inventor of the printing press, Johannes Gutenberg.
- **1895** Louis Lumière, a French industrial chemist, and his brother Auguste show their first motion picture to an invited audience.
- **1956** American civil rights leader Martin Luther King is convicted of organizing a boycott of buses in Alabama after a black woman was arrested for refusing to give up her seat for a white woman.
- **1963** In Britain, Secretary of State for War, John Profumo, denies having had a sexual relationship with Christine Keeler (see right).
- **1965** The U.S. Government confirms its troops used chemical warfare against the Vietcong in the Vietnam War.
- **1968** Students riot in Nanterre, near Paris. Calling themselves anarchists, 150 students occupy an administrative tower in Nanterre University.
- **1977** Indira Gandhi resigns as Prime Minister of India after her defeat in the elections two days earlier. She is succeeded by Moraji Desai, the leader of the Janata Party.
- **1979** British Ambassador to the Netherlands, Sir Richard Sykes, is assassinated. Police later find the IRA responsible.
- **1979** Israeli Parliament approves a peace treaty with Egypt.
- **1993** Intel introduces the Pentium processor (80586).

DAY TO REMEMBER
International day World Water Day UNESCO has designated this day World Water Day to highlight issues surrounding water conservation and hygiene.

Comedian Chico Marx (center) with brothers Groucho (right) and Harpo (left).

The Profumo affair

In July 1961, John Profumo, the British Secretary of State for War, indulged in a brief affair with showgirl Christine Keeler. (He was married to Valerie Hobson at the time.) It emerged that Keeler had simultaneously been having an affair with a Russian Embassy naval attaché, Yevgeny Ivanov, who was later accused of espionage. This led to fears that pillow talk may have endangered national security.

On March 22, 1963, when questioned in the House of Commons, Profumo claimed there was "no impropriety whatever" in his relations with Keeler. When subsequent evidence proved this claim false, he confessed to misleading the House. He resigned from Parliament on June 5.

The fallout from the ensuing furore included the resignation a month later (through "ill health") of Prime Minister Harold Macmillan, his replacement by stand-in Prime Minister Sir Alec Douglas-Home, and a landslide election win to the opposition Labour Party in 1964.

After Profumo's resignation, Stephen Ward – osteopath, artist, and pimp to the upper classes – was charged with living off the immoral earnings of Keeler and others. Before the jury could return its verdict, Ward committed suicide. The shockwaves from these events were so far-reaching that Profumo's name has become permanently associated with the words "scandal" and/or "affair."

March 23

"I never go outside unless I look like Joan Crawford the movie star. If you want to see the girl next door, go next door." — JOAN CRAWFORD

NATO announces its intention to bomb Kosovo

The North Atlantic Treaty Organization (NATO) made its first attack against a sovereign European nation in 1999 out of fear that another Holocaust was occurring.

Yugoslavia encompassed several ethnic groups within its borders. Tensions between these groups escalated in the political vacuum created by President Tito's death in 1980. By 1991, part of the nation had declared itself a separate republic. From then until 1995 there was a civil war that was marked by violent "ethnic cleansing."

Serbian leader Slobodan Milosevic (see March 11) became President of Yugoslavia in 1997. He wanted to make the province of Kosovo part of a Greater Serbia, even though 90 percent of the population were ethnic Albanian. In 1998 he sent troops to crush Kosovo Albanians' protests and fight Kosovo Liberation Army guerillas. Ethnic cleansing resumed.

International diplomats tried to convince the Serbs to withdraw their troops and for Kosovo Albanians to abandon their secessionist plans. It was obvious the negotiations weren't working after an horrific massacre carried out by Serb forces took place on January 1999 in the ethnic Albanian village of Racak.

On March 23, a NATO negotiator went to Milosevic's White Palace to make it clear that if Milosevic didn't agree to a ceasefire, bombing would begin within 24 hours. Milosevic refused.

The bombing began on March 24. Hundreds of NATO aircraft were involved, and cruise missiles were fired from ships in the Adriatic Sea. It was hoped that this show of force would coerce Milosevic into a ceasefire.

Serb forces continued to attack Albanians. By April, an estimated 850,000 were fleeing for their lives. While Serb authorities claimed they were running from NATO bombs, eyewitnesses, both Serb and Albanian, told of Serbian troops driving people from their homes or executing them.

On June 3, Milosevic finally accepted a peace agreement. United Nations and NATO forces entered Kosovo. On June 10, all air strikes and bombardment ceased.

HISTORICAL EVENTS

1839 The first recorded use of the expression "OK," short for "oll korrect," a slang term in Boston and New York, appears in the *Boston Morning Post*.
1919 Benito Mussolini and several other World War I veterans found the Fasci Italiani di Combattimento, or the Italian Combat Fascists, in Milan. They believe in restoring order to post-war Italy by force.
1956 Pakistan declares itself an Islamic Republic with an Islamic Constitution, the first in the world.
1994 Wayne Gretzky becomes the National Hockey League's all-time leading goal scorer when he scores his 802nd goal in Los Angeles.
1999 NATO gives an ultimatum to Yugoslavia's President Slobodan Milosevic, warning that Serbian military positions will be adopted if he does not withdraw Serbian troops from Kosovo (see left).
2001 The Russian Mir space station is brought down and breaks up over the ocean between Chile and New Zealand. It was launched in February 1986, and had traveled 20.9 billion miles (33.6 billion km) in 86,331 orbits of the Earth.

DAY TO REMEMBER

National day Pakistan National Day This celebration commemorates the day Pakistan became an Islamic republic.

Births
1887 Juan Gris, painter
1900 Erich Fromm, psychoanalyst
1908 Joan Crawford, actress
1910 Akira Kurosawa, film director
1912 Wernher von Braun, space engineer
1929 Sir Roger Bannister, runner

Deaths
1983 Barney Clark, first recipient of an artificial heart, after 112 days
1964 Peter Lorre, actor

March 24

The *Exxon Valdez* oil spill

The oil tanker *Exxon Valdez* left the Alaskan port terminal Valdez on March 23, 1989, bound for California with a near-full load on board. A pilot guided the ship through the dangerous Valdez Narrows and then left. Soon after, Captain Joseph Hazelwood radioed that he was going to move out of the normal shipping lane to avoid some small icebergs. He instructed third mate Gregory Cousins to redirect the ship back into the correct lane once they had passed a certain point, then he retired to his cabin.

Cousins did order the helmsman to turn the ship, but it didn't make the turn correctly and went off-course. It is thought that either he made the call too late, or the helmsman misunderstood and made an error. Whatever the case, the ship struck Bligh Reef at 12:04 A.M.

Eight of the ship's 11 tanks were pierced and some 30 million gallons (42 million l) of crude oil spilled into the pristine environment of Prince William Sound off the south coast of Alaska.

Relatively little help with the clean-up was available until 24 hours after the accident occurred. When booms and skimmers did arrive, the kelp and thick oil clogged the equipment and caused frequent breakdowns. The oil remaining in the tanker was pumped off into smaller ships. The oil slick affected some 1,250 miles (2,900 km) of coastline. It has been estimated that around 250,000 sea birds, 2,800 sea otters, 300 harbor seals, 22 orcas, and untold numbers of fish were killed in the immediate aftermath. Fifteen years after the accident, the region was found to be still suffering, despite ongoing clean-up efforts. In the photo above, another tanker offloads crude oil from the crippled *Exxon Valdez* tanker (right) a few days after the spill.

In 1990 the *Exxon Valdez* was repaired, renamed the *SeaRiver Mediterranean*, and returned to service. In February 1994, Exxon was ordered to pay more than U.S. $5 billion in punitive damages.

HISTORICAL EVENTS

1603 On the death of Queen Elizabeth I, King James VI of Scotland succeeds to the English throne, uniting the two countries, and becoming James I.

1882 In Berlin, Dr. Robert Koch announces that he has isolated the bacterium responsible for tuberculosis. He receives the Nobel Prize for Medicine in 1905.

1900 The construction of the first section of New York's subway system begins. The decision to build a subway came about because the elevated rail system had ceased to function during the Blizzard of 1888.

1958 Elvis Presley becomes a private in the U.S. Army, where he serves for two years, spending much of his time in Germany.

1980 Archbishop Oscar Romero is celebrating Mass in a hospital chapel when he is shot and killed. Despite death threats, the archbishop had continued to speak up against the repressive military rulers of El Salvador.

1989 The *Exxon Valdez* runs aground in Prince William Sound, Alaska, creating one of the most damaging oil spills in history (see left).

1992 It is announced that British satirist magazine *Punch* will cease publication after more than 150 years. Four years later, it is reopened, but folds again in 2002.

1997 The Australian Federal Government overturns the Rights of the Terminally Ill Act that allowed voluntary euthanasia, which had been passed by the Northern Territory two years earlier.

DAY TO REMEMBER

International day World Tuberculosis Day This day is held each year by the World Health Organization to promote the fight against tuberculosis. In 2003, it was estimated that 1.75 million people died from tuberculosis.

Births

- **1693** John Harrison, clockmaker
- **1874** Harry Houdini, magician
- **1903** Malcolm Muggeridge, journalist and critic
- **1936** David Suzuki, environmentalist
- **1943** George Harrison, musician
- **1986** Kyle Maynard, champion wrestler born without arms or legs

Deaths

- **1603** Queen Elizabeth I of England
- **1776** John Harrison, clockmaker
- **1882** Henry Wadsworth Longfellow, poet
- **1905** Jules Verne, author
- **1980** Archbishop Oscar Romero, Archbishop of San Salvador

March 25

DATE*line*

"One day an army of gray-haired women may quietly take over the Earth." — GLORIA STEINEM

HISTORICAL EVENTS

1807 The British Parliament passes the Abolition of the Slave Trade Act, banning the trade of human beings throughout the empire.

1821 Bishop Germanos of Patras raises the Greek flag at the Monastery of Agia Lavra on the Peloponnese. This act of defiance against the Ottoman empire sparks the Greek War of Independence, which the Greeks won in 1829.

1911 A fire starts in a rag bin in the Triangle Shirtwaist factory in New York City. About 250 young female workers die when they are unable to escape through the locked exits.

1957 France, West Germany, the Netherlands, Belgium, Italy, and Luxembourg sign the Treaty of Rome to form the European Economic Community.

1969 John Lennon and Yoko Ono begin their first "bed-in for peace" in Amsterdam (see below).

1975 King Faisal of Saudi Arabia dies. When King Faisal bent forward on the previous day to greet his nephew, Prince Musaed, the mentally unstable prince drew a pistol and shot the King in the head.

1996 On March 20, the British Government admits there is a link between bovine spongiform encephalopathy (BSE), or mad cow disease, and Creutzfeldt-Jakob disease (CJD), a similar disease in humans. Five days later the European Union bans the import of British beef products.

Births
- **1133** Henry II of England, first Plantagenet king
- **1867** Arturo Toscanini, conductor
- **1906** A. J. P. Taylor, historian
- **1934** Gloria Steinem, feminist
- **1942** Aretha Franklin, singer
- **1947** Elton John, singer and songwriter

Deaths
- **1918** Claude Debussy, composer
- **1975** King Faisal of Saudi Arabia

DAYS TO REMEMBER

Religious day The Feast of the Annunciation of Mary This day celebrates the conception of Jesus. The angel Gabriel appeared to Mary and told her she would bear a son conceived by the Holy Spirit, that he would be called Jesus, and would be the Son of God.

National day Independence Day Greeks celebrate their independence from the Ottoman empire on this day.

Married on March 20, 1969, John Lennon and Yoko Ono, a performance artist, spent their honeymoon from March 25 to March 31 in bed to protest against "war and violence in the world." Here they receive the press in the Presidential Suite at the Hilton Hotel, Amsterdam. The track "Amsterdam" from *Wedding Album* was recorded to cassette during this "bed-in." John plays guitar and sings and Yoko sings while friends and the media drop in, making it a document of the event. Lennon was shot dead outside his New York home by Mark Chapman on December 8, 1980.

March 26

"The brain is a wonderful organ. It starts working the moment you wake up and does not stop until you get to the office." ROBERT FROST

HISTORICAL EVENTS

1953 Jonas Salk announces that he has developed a vaccine for poliomyelitis, otherwise known as infantile paralysis. In 1952 there had been 58,000 cases of polio in the U.S. alone. By 1957 the number of cases had fallen to 6,000.

1964 *Funny Girl* starring 21-year-old Barbra Streisand, opens on Broadway. According to *The New York Times*, Streisand "knocked New York on its ear."

1973 The London Stock Exchange admits women for the first time in its 200-year history. Ten women were admitted on this day, and 28 years later Clara Furse gains one of the most senior roles, that of chief executive.

1979 Egyptian President Anwar Sadat and Israeli Prime Minister Manachim Begin sign a peace treaty at the White House in Washington D.C., ending 30 years of conflict. They were jointly awarded the Nobel Peace Prize in 1978.

1997 In San Diego, 39 members of the Heaven's Gate cult are found dead in a mansion. They died believing they would leave their bodies and be taken aboard an alien spacecraft that their leader said was hiding behind the Hale-Bopp comet.

1999 The Melissa computer virus strikes, infecting around one million personal computers and causing around U.S. $80 million worth of damage.

2000 Vladimir Putin, acting President of Russia since the resignation of Boris Yeltsin on December 31, 1999, is elected President. Yeltsin had resigned due to embarrassment over economic mismanagement and health problems.

2000 Pope John Paul II ends his five-day official visit to Israel (see below).

DAY TO REMEMBER

Religious day Birthday of Zarathustra
The prophet of the Zoroastrian religion is believed to have been born on this day some time in the twelfth century B.C.E.

Births
- **1859** Alfred Edward Housman, poet
- **1874** Robert Frost, poet
- **1911** Tennessee Williams, playwright
- **1942** Erica Jong, writer
- **1944** Diana Ross, singer
- **1949** Patrick Süskind, writer

Deaths
- **1827** Ludwig van Beethoven, composer
- **1892** Walt Whitman, poet
- **1902** Cecil Rhodes, British Government administrator
- **1923** Sarah Bernhardt, actress
- **1945** David Lloyd George, U.K. Prime Minister
- **1959** Raymond Chandler, writer
- **1973** Noel Coward, playwright and composer
- **1983** Anthony Blunt, British spy

Pope John Paul II visits Jerusalem

From March 21 to March 26, 2000, Pope John Paul II visited Israel. It was the first visit of a pope since 1964, when Pope Paul VI stayed for 11 hours, visiting only Christian sites.

Pope John Paul II's visit was entirely different. He visited the holy places of Christians, Jews, and Muslims, treating all of them with great respect, and met with political and religious leaders. He also met with Holocaust survivors, blessed Israel, and gave his support to the creation of a Palestinian homeland.

One of the most symbolic moments of the Pope's pilgrimage was his prayer at the Western Wall. This wall forms part of the remains of the retaining wall that Herod the Great built in the first century B.C.E. Jewish people come to touch the Western Wall and pray; special prayers and vows are written on pieces of paper and pushed into cracks in the Wall. In accordance with this tradition, Pope John Paul II spent a few moments in private prayer at the Wall and placed his own prayer into a crevice. The prayer was later taken from the crevice in the Western Wall and placed in the archives of Yad Vashem, the Holocaust memorial.

The text of the prayer is: "God of our fathers, you chose Abraham and his descendants to bring Your name to the nations.

"We are deeply saddened by the behavior of those who in the course of history have caused these children of Yours to suffer and asking Your forgiveness we wish to commit ourselves to genuine brotherhood with the people of the Covenant."

March 27

DATEline

"It's a bum's life. Quitting acting, that's a sign of maturity." — MARLON BRANDO

Two passenger jets preparing for take-off from Los Rodeos Airport in Tenerife were involved in an horrific accident on March 27, 1977. Pan Am Flight 1736 taxied up the runway in thick fog. The KLM Flight 4805 began its take-off run in the opposite direction, despite communication difficulties with the control tower. When the pilots spotted each other, they took evasive action, but the Dutch plane scraped over the top of the American one, ripping it open and setting it on fire. About 60 people leapt from the Pan Am jet; 335 couldn't escape. The KLM plane skidded along the runway and burst into flames, killing all 248 people on board.

Births

- 1863 Sir Henry Royce, founder of Rolls-Royce
- 1901 Kenneth Slessor, poet
- 1924 Sarah Vaughan, jazz singer
- 1942 Michael York, actor
- 1952 Maria Schneider, actress
- 1963 Quentin Tarantino, film director
- 1970 Mariah Carey, singer

Deaths

- 1204 Eleanor of Aquitaine, wife of Henry II and founder of the Plantagenet dynasty
- 1625 James I, King of Britain
- 1968 Yuri Gagarin, cosmonaut
- 1998 Ferry Porsche, car manufacturer
- 2003 Paul Zindel, writer

HISTORICAL EVENTS

1306 Robert the Bruce is crowned King of Scotland and begins to fight for Scottish independence. England recognizes Scotland as a separate nation in 1328, one year before his death.

1625 James I, King of England and Scotland, dies and Charles I becomes King. His reign is fraught with religious and political conflict, resulting in civil war.

1905 Fingerprint evidence is used for the first time in Britain to solve a murder case, that of Ann and Thomas Farrow who had been killed when their shop was robbed. Alfred Stratton's thumbprint was found on their cashbox.

1958 Nikita Khrushchev, already the Soviet First Secretary, becomes the Premier of the U.S.S.R., and so now holds the two top offices.

1973 Sacheen Littlefeather, a young Native American woman, goes on stage at the 1973 Academy Awards to reject the award for Best Actor in *The Godfather* on behalf of Marlon Brando in protest at Hollywood's treatment of her people.

1977 In the worst aircraft accident ever, two planes collide on a foggy runway in Tenerife, killing 583 people (see above).

1980 A North Sea platform, housing men who work on a nearby oil rig, collapses and capsizes in a gale, drowning 123 workers.

1989 Elections are held in Russia for the new Congress of People's Deputies. This is the first election in which there are non-Communist candidates.

DAY TO REMEMBER

National day Armed Forces Day In Myanmar (Burma), this day was formerly known as Resistance Day. It commemorates the uprising of guerilla forces against the Japanese occupation in 1945. The Government marks the day with military parades, while opposition groups hold separate ceremonies.

March 28

"Parents are the bones on which children sharpen their teeth."
SIR PETER USTINOV (PICTURED RIGHT), IN HIS 1977 AUTOBIOGRAPHY

HISTORICAL EVENTS

1854 The Crimean War begins when France and Britain declare war on Russia to stop the Russians from controlling sections of the crumbling Ottoman empire.

1930 The Turkish Post Office officially changes Constantinople's name to Istanbul, a name used by Arabs since the thirteenth century that derives from the Greek phrase *eis ten polin*, "in the city."

1938 Ugo Cerletti and Lucio Bini, Italian psychiatrists, use electric shock treatment for the first time. They used a man found mumbling to himself as he wandered in a railway station as their first patient.

1939 Madrid surrenders to General Francisco Franco, ending the Spanish Civil War. More than one million people had died in the three-year conflict.

1941 Admiral Andrew Browne Cunningham leads the British Royal Navy in destruction of Italian ships at Cape Matapan, the last engagement between the two navies in World War II.

1979 A nuclear accident occurs at the Three Mile Island reactor in Pennsylvania, U.S.A. A partial meltdown of the reactor's core leads to a leak of radioactive steam into the atmosphere, putting workers and surrounding residents at risk.

1986 More than 6,000 U.S. radio stations play "We Are the World" at the same time – 10:15 A.M. U.S. EST.

2001 U.S. President George W. Bush announces the withdrawal of his nation's signature from the Kyoto Protocol (see right).

Births
1438 Santi Raphael, painter
1902 Dame Flora Robson, actress
1868 Maxim Gorky, novelist and playwright
1921 Sir Dirk Bogarde, actor and writer

Deaths
1941 Virginia Woolf, novelist
1943 Sergei Rachmaninoff, composer
1969 Dwight D. Eisenhower, U.S. President
1985 Marc Chargall, painter
1987 Maria von Trapp, singer
2004 Sir Peter Ustinov, actor

DAY TO REMEMBER

National day Teacher's Day Many nations mark special days to show their appreciation of schoolteachers. In the Czech Republic, children bring their teachers flowers on this day, and public officials make public statements praising the work teachers do.

U.S. withdraws from the Kyoto Protocol

The Kyoto Protocol was an international agreement drawn up in response to growing evidence that the global temperature was heating up. This rise in temperature is attributed to the "greenhouse effect," caused by larger amounts of carbon dioxide and other gas emissions entering the atmosphere through human activities, especially the burning of fossil fuels. Global warming has potentially dire consequences for the world's environment and for human societies, including a significant rise in sea levels.

The first convention discussing the agreement was held in 1992; in 1997, the terms of the protocol were finally agreed on and signed. The aims of the treaty were to reduce greenhouse emissions by 5.2 percent below 1990 levels by 2012. Each signatory nation agreed to a specific target; developing countries had comparatively low targets or were asked to comply voluntarily.

President Bill Clinton had signed the Kyoto Protocol, but the U.S. was technically not a party to it as it was never presented to the Senate to be ratified. On March 28, 2001, President George W. Bush announced that the U.S. would withdraw from the agreement, arguing that developing nations did not have to commit to reducing their emissions and as a result the U.S. economy could be weakened.

Many nations responded to this move with dismay, stating that the effectiveness of the treaty would be compromised given that the world's greatest producer of "greenhouse gases" would not participate.

March 29

DATEline

"We have missed getting through by a narrow margin which was justifiably within the risk of such a journey." CAPTAIN ROBERT SCOTT, ON THE EXPEDITION TO THE SOUTH POLE

HISTORICAL EVENTS

1461 The Yorkists defeat the Lancastrians at the Battle of Towton in the War of the Roses. The battle, fought during a snowstorm, is said to be one of the bloodiest to take place on English soil. At least 28,000 men die.

1871 Queen Victoria opens the Royal Albert Hall in London, named for her husband, who had conceived the idea of building the concert hall. She was too overcome to speak, so the Prince of Wales stepped forward and declared the Hall open.

1901 The first federal elections are held in Australia. The interim Prime Minister Edmund Barton is returned to the position.

1912 Antarctic explorer Captain Robert Scott makes the last entry in his journal. He and his starving party perish only a few miles from a food depot.

1951 In New York, Julius and Ethel Rosenberg are found guilty of giving secrets about the atomic bomb to the U.S.S.R.

1973 U.S. prisoners of war are released in Vietnam, and the last troops are withdrawn (see right).

1974 NASA's *Mariner 10* lands on Mercury and takes the first close-up photos of the planet.

1986 Beatles records officially go on sale in Russia, 17 years after the band's last performance.

2004 The Republic of Ireland is the first nation to ban smoking in all closed public places.

DAY TO REMEMBER

National day Youth Day The Republic of China (Taiwan) holds ceremonies to remind its youth of the sacrifice of revolutionaries and soldiers. It commemorates the death of 72 Chinese revolutionaries in the rebellion against the Qing Dynasty in 1911 that is known as the Canton Uprising.

Births
1916 Eugene McCarthy, U.S. senator
1943 Eric Idle, comedian
1963 M. C. Hammer, rap artist
1964 Elle MacPherson, model

Deaths
1891 Georges-Pierre Seurat, painter

U.S. troops leave Vietnam

After many stalled attempts at peace talks between North Vietnam, South Vietnam, and the U.S.A., the Paris Peace Accord was finally signed on January 27, 1973. Under the terms of this agreement, prisoners of war (POWs) were to be released, North Vietnamese forces in the south were not to advance their positions, and South and North Vietnam were to become one nation only by peaceful means. The U.S.A. agreed to withdraw all of its troops. South Vietnamese President Nguyen Van Thieu only accepted the treaty under pressure from the U.S., which threatened to withdraw all support if he did not.

By early 1973 the U.S.A. was eager to pull out. They had sent combat troops to Vietnam in March 1965 before lending considerable indirect support to the South Vietnamese Government. As the war dragged on, large numbers of Americans withdrew their support because of mounting U.S. casualties and reports of U.S. involvement in war crimes. Mass protests increased pressure on the U.S. Government to end their involvement in the war. Other supporters of South Vietnam, such as Australia, had already withdrawn their troops.

Not long after the peace agreement was signed in Paris, North Vietnamese troops violated the ceasefire, but on March 29 the last of the U.S. POWs (pictured above) were released and U.S. troops were withdrawn from South Vietnam anyway. Other U.S. personnel remained behind to assist the government of the South.

By the beginning of the following year, North and South Vietnam were at war again, and without U.S. support the South Vietnamese were driven back. North Vietnamese troops captured Saigon on April 30, 1975, and the last Americans in the country were airlifted out. It has been estimated that more than 2,120,000 people died during the conflict.

March 30

"Honey, I forgot to duck." U.S. PRESIDENT RONALD REAGAN, JOKING TO HIS WIFE NANCY ABOUT BEING SHOT

HISTORICAL EVENTS

1842 Dr. Crawford W. Long uses ether as an anesthetic for the first time when he removes a tumor from a patient's neck.
1856 The Paris Treaty is signed, bringing the Crimean War to an end.
1867 U.S. Secretary of State, William H. Seward, signs a deal buying Alaska from Russia for $7,200,000. The deal is dubbed "Seward's Folly" by the press, as Alaska is seen as an "icebox" separated from the rest of the U.S.A.
1870 The Fifteenth Amendment to the U.S. Constitution is passed, granting African American men the right to vote.
1956 Remote Mt. Bezymianny in Kamchatka, U.S.S.R., erupts, blasting 600 feet (180 m) off the top of the mountain and sending a volcanic column 25 miles (40 km) into the air. There is no recorded loss of life.
1981 U.S. President Ronald Reagan is shot in the chest by John Hinckley, Jr. outside the Washington Hilton Hotel. He survives.
1987 One of Vincent van Gogh's "Sunflowers" paintings sells at Christie's auction rooms for a record U.S. $39,921,759 (see below).

Births
1746 Francisco de Goya, painter
1820 Anna Sewell, children's writer
1853 Vincent van Gogh, painter
1937 Warren Beatty, actor
1968 Celine Dion, singer

Deaths
1840 Beau Brummell, dandy
1986 James Cagney, actor
2002 Elizabeth Bowes-Lyon, the Queen Mother
2004 Alistair Cooke, journalist

DAYS TO REMEMBER

Religious day Spiritual Baptist People in Trinidad and Tobago have a public holiday and celebrate the withdrawal on this day in 1951 of laws that banned their religion.

National day Land Day Arab Israelis commemorate the day in 1976 when six Arabs were killed in Galilee during protests against the Jewish confiscation of Arab-owned land. The day has become a general day of protest at the loss of Arab land to Israel since 1948.

One of Vincent van Gogh's "Sunflowers" paintings went on sale at Christie's auction rooms on March 30, 1987. The Yasuda and Marine Insurance Company bought it for the record price of U.S.$39,921,75. A few months later speculation arose that it was a fake painted by Claude-Emile Schuffenecker, a friend of van Gogh's. In 2002 it was declared genuine once and for all. Art experts believed the confusion came about because the painting was done on cheap canvas that had caused the paint to flake. It had been touched up after van Gogh's death, probably by Schuffenecker, who at one time owned the painting.

DATE*line*

March 31

"It is my dream that the entire Tibetan plateau should become a free refuge where humanity and nature can live in peace and harmonious balance."

THE DALAI LAMA, THE DAY AFTER RECEIVING THE NOBEL PEACE PRIZE

HISTORICAL EVENTS

1814 Paris surrenders to Russian and Prussian forces, the first time the city had been taken by foreign forces in four centuries. Deserted by most of his generals, Napoleon Bonaparte is forced to abdicate on April 6 and is taken into exile on Elba on April 20.

1889 The Eiffel Tower is officially opened. Gustave Eiffel, its designer, climbs the 1710 stairs to unfurl the French flag from the third level.

1901 The Daimler automobile company unveils the first Mercedes. It was made for Emile Jellinek, Consul-General for the Austro–Hungarian Empire, who names it after his daughter.

1959 The fourteenth Dalai Lama, the spiritual and political leader of Tibet, escapes to India after a 15-day journey on foot over the Himalayan Mountains (see right).

1967 Jimi Hendrix burns his guitar on stage for the first time at London's Astoria Theatre and is treated in hospital for burns on his hands.

1991 The Warsaw Pact ends after 36 years. The Soviet Bloc alliance had begun to crumble after peaceful anti-Communist revolutions in 1989.

2005 Brain damaged patient Terri Schiavo dies in the U.S. after having her feeding tube removed on March 19. The dispute between her parents and her husband about whether to remove her feeding tube became a national right-to-die debate.

DAY TO REMEMBER

National day Freedom Day (Malta) The day on which British troops departed from Malta after a defense agreement between the nations expired is commemorated as Freedom Day.

The Dalai Lama flees to India

Following the formation of the Communist Chinese Government in 1950, Chinese repression of Tibetan culture increased steadily, as did Tibetan resistance. Matters came to a head on March 9, 1959, when Chinese officers ordered the fourteenth Dalai Lama, the leader of Tibet, to go alone to their military quarters the next day. This suspicious order prompted 30,000 Tibetans to create a human shield for him by camping around his Norbulinka palace on March 10. While the Chinese army and Tibetan resistance fighters strengthened their positions, a secret escape route was planned for the Dalai Lama.

The Chinese fired two shells at Norbulinka on March 17, and at 10:00 P.M. the Dalai Lama left the palace disguised as a soldier. Over the next two weeks he and an escort of resistance fighters made their way on foot over the Himalayas. At 2:00 A.M. on March 19, the Chinese began to shell the palace in earnest. Thousands of men, women and children who had camped around Norbulinka were killed.

On March 31, the Dalai Lama's party crossed the border into India. Three days later Indian Prime Minister Jawarhalal Nehru announced that they had been granted asylum. The Dalai Lama established a government-in-exile in Dharamsala. Thousands of Tibetans fled their homeland to join him in "Little Lhasa." From this base, the Dalai Lama has led a non-violent campaign to free Tibet ever since.

Births		Deaths	
1596	René Descartes, philosopher	1631	John Donne, clergyman and poet
1732	Franz Joseph Hayden, composer	1837	Charlotte Brontë, novelist
1943	Christopher Walken, actor	1837	John Constable, painter
1971	Ewan McGregor, actor	1980	Jesse Owens, athlete

DAYS TO REMEMBER *March*

1
Roman New Year New Year's Day until 45 B.C.E. when Julius Caesar changed the Roman calendar

2
Mikhail Gorbachev, last President of the U.S.S.R., was born in 1931

3
Hina Matsuri (Japan) A day for girls and their special dolls

4
Inauguration Day Every four years from 1789 to 1933 the U.S. President was sworn into office

5
Learn from Lei Feng Day Chairman Mao established this commemorative day to encourage people to serve China and the Communist Party

8
International Women's Day Marks the achievements and struggles of women, celebrated around the world

9
St. Frances of Rome Day The patron saint of housewives and widows

10
St. John Ogilvie's Day After refusing to recognize the King as head of the Church, John Ogilvie was hanged in 1615

11
Slobodan Milosevic, imprisoned former Yugoslav President, died in 2006

12
Arbor Day (China) This holiday celebrates the planting of trees and commemorates the death of Sun Yat-sen

15
The Ides of March Julius Caesar was forewarned to be wary of this day by a soothsayer, and was subsequently murdered on it in 44 B.C.E.

16
The Bacchanalia festival began in ancient Rome in honor of the god Bacchus

17
St. Patrick's Day The patron saint of Ireland. The day is celebrated with parades, especially in the U.S. and Ireland

18
Ivan the Terrible, Tsar of Russia, died in 1584

19
Las Fallas (Vallencia, Spain) A festival where people hold parades of cardboard figures filled with firecrackers that they then light

22
World Water Day Designated to highlight issues surrounding water conservation and hygiene

23
Pakistan National Day Commemorates the day Pakistan became an Islamic republic

24
World Tuberculosis Day Held each year by the World Health Organization to promote the fight against tuberculosis

25
The Feast of the Annunciation of Mary In the Christian faith, celebrates the conception of Jesus

26
The traditional birthday of Zarathustra, prophet of the Zoroastrian religion

29
Youth Day The Republic of China (Taiwan) holds ceremonies to remind its youth of the sacrifice of revolutionaries and soldiers

30
Spiritual Baptist (Trinidad and Tobago) A public holiday to celebrate the withdrawal on this day in 1951 of laws that banned the local religion

31
Freedom Day (Malta) The day on which British troops departed after a defense agreement between the nations expired

6

Ghana Independence Day Ghana celebrates its independence from the U.K. on this day in 1957

7

St. Perpetua's and St. Felicity's Day They refused to renounce their faith and were sent to their death in the arena c. 203

13

Bruno Bettelheim, psychologist, died in 1990

14

White Day (Japan, Taiwan) A day when men give women they care about a gift to show their appreciation

20

Dame Vera Lynn, actor and singer, was born in 1917

21

The star sign of Aries begins

27

Sir Henry Royce, founder of Rolls-Royce was born in 1863

28

Marc Chargall, painter died in 1985

Top Right Hina Matsuri, Japan, March 3
Right World Water Day, March 22

APRIL

"April, April,
Laugh thy girlish laughter,
Then, in the moment after,
Weep thy girlish tears!"

SIR WILLIAM WATSON

Arguably the most popular rock band in history – The Beatles – broke up in April, 1970, not long after releasing their instantly recognizable album, *Abbey Road*.

April

April, the fourth month of the Gregorian calendar, was described by poet T. S. Eliot in his epic poem The Waste Land *as: "the cruellest month, breeding lilacs out of the dead land, mixing memory and desire, stirring dull roots with spring rain." April is the month during which the season of spring really takes hold in the Northern Hemisphere, as nature blossoms and blooms out of the seeming desolation wrought by winter. Meanwhile, in the Southern Hemisphere April is often the harbinger of the winter to come — it is the equivalent of October in the northern antipodes — and the air adopts a crisp chill.*

Taurus star sign and man with tree branch from *Calendar and Book of Hours*, from fifteenth-century France. April begins in the sign of Aries and ends in the sign of Taurus.

SPECIAL DATES

Sizdah bedar is the thirteenth day of the Persian calendar, which often falls in April. The number thirteen is believed to bring bad luck. It is on this day, rather than April 1, that Iranians play practical jokes on each other. It is also traditional to picnic outdoors and to pray for rain, which is believed to wash away ill fortune.

ORIGINALLY THE SECOND MONTH of the Roman calendar, April was the month that honored the goddess Venus. When Julius Caesar reformed the calendar in 46 B.C.E., April stretched to 30 days and became the fourth month. While the origins of the name "April" remain uncertain, scholars believe it is derived from Venus' Greek counterpart, Aphrodite, whose sacred month was *Aphrilis*.

Both Venus and Aphrodite were the goddesses of love and beauty in their respective cultures, as well as being the patronesses of gardens, vineyards, and vegetation. As statues of these goddesses look strikingly similar in both Roman and Greek archeology, they are thought to be the same deity, and have equivalents in other religions — such as the Egyptian goddess Isis, the Etruscan goddess Apru, and the Babylonian goddess Ishtar. Their parallel mythologies tell tales of fertility and erotic pleasure — both goddesses took many lovers, with Venus having an affair with Mars (god of springtime and war), and Aphrodite with Adonis (who is associated with life, death, and rebirth, and who young women in ancient Greece revered for his godly good looks). Venus was thought to be Mother of the Earth and the Sea, and as such is analogous with April's awakening of Mother Nature, while Aphrodite's many ties with spring make her the perfect inspiration for the month of April. However, an

Venus and Mars are depicted together, no doubt with erotic thoughts in mind, in this sixteenth-century painting by Sandro Botticelli (1445–1510), which hangs in London's National Gallery.

April birthflower

The flowers associated with the month of April are the daisy and the sweetpea. Both blooms are said to symbolize innocence and lasting love, which is why April is often associated with romance. The playfulness of the daisy and the curiousness of the sweetpea are characteristics of blossoming love.

alternative etymology sees the Latin word *aperire* ("to open") as April's root word, in accordance with nature's tendency to "open up" in spring.

Meanwhile, the Anglo-Saxons had another name for April: *Eostur-monath* or *Oster-monath*, which was the month during which feasts are believed to have been held in honor of the Germanic goddess Eostre. Eostur-monath was the lunar month that occurred around April on the Julian calendar. As Christianity took hold in Germanic countries, they named the Christian festival that fell during this period Easter (*Ostern* in German). There is little written about the goddess Eostre. In fact, the only documented mention of her in historical texts is by the English monk and historian Bede, who refers to her as the Anglo-Saxon goddess of spring, or "Paschal season," in his book *De Tempore Ratione* (*On the Reckoning of Time*, 725 C.E.). Modern scholars have begun to doubt Eostre's existence due to lack of correlating evidence from before Bede's time. However, fairytale writer Jacob Grimm postulated in his 1835 work *Deutsche Mythologie* that the old German festival *Ostara* could be linked to a goddess of that name. Regardless of her validity, neo-pagans have included Eostre, a dawn goddess, in their mythology and celebrate her festival day on the vernal equinox, which takes place toward the end of March.

From ancient festivals to modern times

Easter Sunday – or Pascha, the Feast of the Resurrection (of Jesus Christ) in Christian tradition – takes place in April more than any other month. In the western world, Easter Sunday falls between March 22 and April 25, while eastern Christians see it land on any Sunday between April 4 and May 8. As the Easter holidays are part of a movable feast, they adhere to the lunar, rather than Gregorian or Julian, calendar. For a more comprehensive explanation of Easter

The Feast of the Resurrection celebrates Christ rising from the dead. El Greco captured this momentous event in the Christian calendar in his *Resurrection of Christ* (1605–1610), which is housed in Museo del Pardo, Madrid.

and the Jewish festival Passover, or *Pesach*, see the introduction to March on pages 112–117.

Rama Navami occurs on the ninth day of the Hindu New Year, which often falls in the month of April according to the Gregorian calendar. It is a celebration of the birth of Sri Rama, Lord Vishnu's seventh earthly incarnation. Sri Rama was the hero of the Sanskrit epic poem *Ramayana*, and excerpts from this verse are read out in temples on this day as part of a celebration that also includes a ritual in which followers thoroughly clean and decorate their homes. "Spring cleaning" also takes place in many other cultures, but does not always hold religious significance and can take place at any time of year. The symbology of rebirth and starting afresh remains synchronous with spring, however.

The festival *Hanuman Jayanti*, the birthday of Hindu monkey god Hanuman Ji, also often falls in April, during the month of *Chaitra* in the Hindu calendar. This god is venerated for his strength and he is believed to have magical powers that can ward off evil spirits. Throughout India, the faithful visit Hindu temples on this day to decorate their foreheads with red powder, or *sindhoor*. According to Hindu tradition, brides apply this to their foreheads to ensure their husbands' longevity. Legend has it that

Above This artist is creating a bamboo sculpture of the Hindu monkey god, Hanuman, as part of *Hanuman Jayanti*, which falls in April to honor the god's birthday.

Right A Hindu priest decorates idols of Hindu god Rama with flowers on the occasion of *Rama Navami*, which often falls in April.

The Burmese New Year tradition of throwing perfumed water at each other during the Water Festival is depicted in this French engraving from 1881.

Hanuman Ji smeared sindhoor all over his body so that Lord Rama could achieve immortality.

The *Thingyan* Festival sees in the Burmese New Year, which is celebrated in the second week of April with a three-day Water Festival. During this time it is thought that Thagyarmin, or King of the Celestials (the Burmese Buddha), pays a visit to people's homes. The Burmese celebrate by spraying each other playfully with perfumed water, fasting, and performing acts of charity. An important part of the festival sees the sons from a family have their heads shaved, and sent to a monastery for a week or so. Families without sons will often donate money. In big cities such as Rangoon, young people will take to the streets in open-topped jeeps, to drive under water sprayed at them from high-pressure hoses.

In Iceland, *Sumardagurinn Fyrsti*, or the First Day of Summer, is a special celebration that goes back to ancient times. Now celebrated on a Thursday between April 19 and 25 each year, people traditionally swap gifts. Legend has it that summer will be wonderful if the preceding winter's night and the first day of summer "freeze together."

Sechselauten, or the Six Ringing Festival, is a celebration that has been held in Zurich, Switzerland, for more than 600 years. Held on a Sunday and Monday in early April, the festival is a symbolic ringing of bells to indicate that winter has ended and spring is welcomed. The festival began in the Middle Ages, when bells would ring at the end of each day to let the town's guild members know that their working day had come to an end. In winter, this would happen at 7:00 P.M., but at the beginning of spring it would change to 6:00 P.M. Now, all the townsfolk share in the celebrations, which start on the Sunday with a children's pageant. On the Monday, there is a procession of floats bearing the guilds and people dressed in traditional garb. They are followed by Boogg, a snowman effigy stuffed with explosives that the crowd boos until it is set on a pyre. At six o'clock, bells are rung and a band plays while the pyre is lit.

Patriot's Day is held in the northeastern states of the U.S. on the third Monday in April. The three-day long weekend sees re-enactments of Paul Revere's midnight ride, which marked the beginning of the American Revolution in April 1775. The Boston Marathon and various baseball events are also held in honor of this anniversary.

In modern times, April has become the month during which to boost public awareness of a host of social causes. Internationally, it is Child Abuse Prevention Month and Alcohol Awareness Month; in the U.S. it is National Poetry Month.

April birthstone

April's birthstone is the diamond, a gem renowned for its purity, decadence, splendor, and strength. Historically, diamonds were only possessed by royalty and they are still one of the most desired gemstones today. The ancient Greeks believed the "fire" or light inside a diamond reflected the "flame" of love, which is why diamonds remain the preferred stone for engagement rings.

The Boston Marathon is one of the sporting highlights of Patriot's Day, celebrated across the northeastern states of the U.S. in late April each year.

April 1

"Tell me what you eat and I will tell you what you are." — ANTHELME BRILLAT-SAVARIN

HISTORICAL EVENTS

1826 The internal combustion engine is patented by U.S. inventor Samuel Morey. It meets with disinterest during Morey's lifetime and is not used in automobiles until the 1890s.

1867 Singapore becomes a Crown colony, with its administration overseen by London, England.

1918 The Royal Air Force is founded in Britain. Along with the Royal Navy and British Army it forms the British Armed Services.

1924 Adolf Hitler is sentenced to five years in prison for staging the coup d'état known as the Beer Hall Putsch. He serves just nine months, spending his time behind bars writing the Nazi manifesto, *Mein Kampf*.

1976 Steve Wozniak and Steve Jobs form the Apple Computer company. They start out building computers by hand in a garage. By 2005 they employ 14,800 people.

1979 In an overwhelming 98 percent vote, Iran is made an Islamic Republic.

1997 The Hale-Bopp comet reaches its perihelion – the point of its orbit where it comes nearest the Sun.

2001 Yugoslavia's former president, Slobodan Milosevic, is arrested on charges of corruption and stealing state funds after a siege at his Belgrade home.

DAYS TO REMEMBER

Traditional day April Fool's Day (see below).

Religious day St. Hugh's Day This is the feast day for St. Hugh, Bishop of Grenoble (1052–1132), who tried to expose and put an end to abuses in the Catholic Church. He is also known for his great charity, having sold his Episcopal ring to help the poor.

Births
- 1755 Anthelme Brillat-Savarin, lawyer, politician, and writer
- 1815 Otto Von Bismarck, German Chancellor
- 1883 Lon Chaney, actor, *Phantom of the Opera*
- 1908 Abraham Maslow, psychologist
- 1929 Milan Kundera, writer
- 1940 Wangari Maathai, first African woman to win the Nobel Peace Prize (in 2004)
- 1942 Samuel R. Delaney, science fiction writer
- 1949 Gil Scott-Heron, musician
- 1971 Method Man, rap artist

Deaths
- 1947 King George II of Greece
- 1950 Charles Drew, physician
- 1976 Max Ernst, artist
- 1984 Marvin Gaye, singer
- 2003 Leslie Cheung, actor and singer

April Fool's Day

Also known as All Fools Day, April Fool's is the most facetious festival of the year. Less a "holiday" than a celebration of good humor, April 1 is renowned – and sometimes feared – for the proliferation of practical jokes that people play on one another.

Its historical origins are not known for certain, but it is believed to date back to the confusion caused when the Catholic Church changed the calendar from a Julian to Gregorian time line in 1582. Before the change, New Year was celebrated by many cultures at the end of March or early April, to coincide with the start of spring in the Northern Hemisphere.

Some believe the festival began in France. When the country adopted the new calendar, many of its citizens refused to abide by it and still chose to celebrate the new year in early April. More progressive types made fun of those who kept to the ways of old, and would try to fool them with untruths to expose them as simpletons. This evolved into a game called *Poisson d'Avril*, or April Fish, where French schoolchildren surreptitiously tape a picture of a fish onto their classmates' backs.

Even the news media gets in on the act: In 1957, a British current affairs program announced a problem with that year's spaghetti harvest, with accompanying footage of peasants harvesting their crops. Many fell for the gag, and ever since then, normally serious news shows have been subject to elaborate hoaxes worldwide.

April 2

DATE*line*

"A day without laughter is a day wasted."   CHARLIE CHAPLIN

Pope John Paul II passes away

Future Supreme Pontiff of the Catholic Church, Karol Jozef Wojtyla was born on May 18, 1920, in Wadowice, Poland. His childhood was marred by tragedy when his mother and brother died of illnesses. In 1939, Nazi forces occupied Poland and shut down the university where Wojtyla was studying. In 1942 he began studying in a secret Catholic seminary under the Archbishop of Krakow. After the war, he went back to university and continued studying for the priesthood.

In January 1964 he was made Archbishop of Krakow and in 1967 he became a cardinal. He was elected Pope by his peers at the Conclave of October 16, 1978, and was given the name Ioannes Paulus II, or Pope John Paul II.

He proved himself to be a true survivor, weathering two assassination attempts during his papacy. In 1992, he was diagnosed with Parkinson's disease, yet even failing health did not make him resign his post. During his time as Pope, John Paul II became known for his humanitarian charity and openness to all Churches.

At 9:37 P.M. on April 2, 2005, Pope John Paul II died. His funeral was held on April 8, and for the six days between his death and laying to rest, more than 3 million pilgrims visited St. Peters Basilica to pay their respects.

HISTORICAL EVENTS

1513 Spanish explorer Juan Ponce de Leon discovers Florida.
1917 Jeannette Pickering Rankin becomes the first female member of the U.S. Congress.
1930 Haile Selassie becomes Emperor of Ethiopia.
1972 Performer Charlie Chaplin returns to the U.S. for the first time in 20 years, to accept an Academy Award, which will be presented on April 10. He vowed never to return to his country of birth after being labeled a Communist.
1978 The first episode of *Dallas* screens on U.S. television. It runs for 13 years.
1982 Argentina invades the Falkland Islands.
1989 Russian leader Mikhail Gorbachev goes to Cuba to meet Fidel Castro, in an attempt to mend the rift that is forming between the Communist nations.
1998 Maurice Papon, former French Cabinet Minister, is found guilty of committing war crimes against the Jews during World War II.
2002 A siege takes place inside Bethlehem's Church of the Nativity. Up to 200 armed Palistinians force their way inside and hold over 200 nuns and priests captive for 38 days before negotiating a release plan with the Israeli military.
2005 The head of the Catholic Church, Pope John Paul II, dies after almost 27 years of papacy (see above).

DAYS TO REMEMBER

International day International Children's Book Day Held on this day – the date of Hans Christian Andersen's birth – Children's Book Day sees teachers worldwide encourage their students to read.

National day Sizdah be-dar (Iran) This is the last day of New Year's celebrations – the thirteenth day on the Persian calendar. People participate in public events such as picnics, during which they may throw *sazbeh* (seeds) into rivers to symbolize the cycle of life.

Births

1725 Casanova, adventurer and philanderer
1805 Hans Christian Andersen, writer
1891 Max Ernst, artist
1927 Kenneth Tynan, critic and writer
1939 Marvin Gaye, singer
1940 Penelope Keith, actress
1947 Camille Paglia, feminist
1953 Jim Allister, Irish politician
1971 Todd Woodbridge, tennis player

Deaths

1742 James Douglas, physicist
1922 Hermann Rorschach, psychologist
1966 C. S. Forester, writer
1996 Minnie Pearl, hillbilly comedienne
2005 Pope John Paul II

April 3

"The only thing new in this world is the history that you do not know." — HARRY S. TRUMAN

HISTORICAL EVENTS

- **33 C.E.** The traditional date associated with the crucifixion of Jesus Christ.
- **1885** Gottlieb Daimler patents the first water-cooled engine.
- **1922** Joseph Stalin takes over from Vladimir Lenin as leader of the Soviet Union.
- **1941** Hungarian and German troops invade Yugoslavia during World War II.
- **1948** Harry S. Truman signs the Marshall Plan, which gave over U.S. $13 billion to European countries to assist in fiscal reparations necessary after World War II.
- **1956** Elvis Presley sings "Heartbreak Hotel" live on national television (see right).
- **1968** Martin Luther King, Jr. gives a speech in support of striking sanitation workers in Tennessee. "I've been to the mountain top," he says, "And I've seen the promised land."
- **1972** The first mobile phone call is made in New York.
- **1986** IBM launches its first laptop computer, the PC Convertible.
- **1996** The suspected "Unabomber" is arrested. Recluse Theodore Kaczynski, a former mathematics professor, sent mail bombs to various universities and airlines over a period of almost 18 years, killing three people and injuring up to 29.

DAY TO REMEMBER

Religious day St. Mary's day Mary (c. 344 C.E.) was a prostitute for 17 years before repenting before a statue of the Blessed Virgin in Jerusalem. She then gave her life to God, living alone and existing on a diet of wild herbs in the Jordanian desert for almost 50 years.

Births
- 1715 William Watson, physician
- 1783 Washington Irving, writer
- 1880 Otto Weininger, philosopher
- 1924 Marlon Brando, actor
- 1924 Doris Day, actress
- 1930 Helmut Kohl, German Chancellor
- 1934 Jane Goodall, zoologist
- 1954 Elisabetta Brusa, composer
- 1958 Alec Baldwin, actor
- 1961 Eddie Murphy, actor and comedian

Deaths
- 1882 Jesse James, outlaw
- 1965 Ernst Kirchweger, Communist revolutionary
- 1991 Graham Greene, writer
- 2000 Terence McKenna, philosopher

Almost one quarter of the U.S. population tuned in to the *Milton Berle Show* on this day to watch Elvis Presley's live performance of "Heartbreak Hotel." Within the week it became his first hit single. Elvis (above) performed the song around the country and it remained number one on the mainstream charts for the next eight weeks.

April 4

"Growing old is a case of mind over matter. If you don't mind, it doesn't matter." — JACK BENNY

Births
- 1802 Dorothea Dix, social activist
- 1846 Comte de Lautréamont, writer
- 1911 Max Dupain, photographer
- 1915 Muddy Waters, musician
- 1932 Andrei Tarkovsky, film director
- 1951 Hun Sen, Cambodian Prime Minister
- 1960 Hugo Weaving, actor
- 1973 David Blaine, magician

Deaths
- 1609 Charles de L'Écluse, botanist
- 1841 William Henry Harrison, ninth U.S. President
- 1932 Wilhelm Ostwalt, chemist and Nobel laureate
- 1979 Ali Bhutto, Pakistani president

HISTORICAL EVENTS
- **1581** Sir Francis Drake becomes the first seafaring captain to circumnavigate the globe.
- **1818** U.S. Congress introduces the American flag – it has 13 red and white stripes and 20 stars, which symbolize each state of the Union. More stars are added with each new member state.
- **1905** An earthquake in India kills 20,000 people.
- **1918** The Second Battle of the Somme, Germany's offensive against the Allies in World War I, concludes with massive casualties on both sides.
- **1939** U.S. comedian Jack Benny is fined $10,000 upon pleading guilty to charges of buying smuggled gems.
- **1949** The Western military alliance NATO (North Atlantic Treaty Organization) is formed.
- **1968** Black civil rights campaigner Martin Luther King, Jr. is shot dead (see below).
- **1979** Zulfikar Ali Bhutto, deposed Prime Minister of Pakistan, is executed by hanging for the alleged murder of a political opponent.
- **1983** Space shuttle *Challenger* makes its first voyage into space.

Martin Luther King, Jr. is assassinated

On this day in 1968, Martin Luther King was assassinated in Memphis, Tennessee. The civil rights campaigner was standing on a hotel balcony when he sustained a single shot to the head. King was rushed to hospital but died shortly afterward. He was 39 years old.

It was a violent end to the career of a man who had dedicated himself to black rights in the U.S., which earned him a Nobel Peace Prize in 1964. It was not the first time attempts had been made on the controversial crusader's life – previous attacks included the bombing of his home in 1956.

After the tragic shooting, friends and colleagues paid their respects to King as his body lay in state in Memphis.

Martin Luther King, Jr. was born in Atlanta, Georgia, on January 15, 1929. His father was a Baptist minister and his mother was a schoolteacher. From an early age, he was aware of racial prejudice and the need for equality. At 19, he followed in his father's footsteps by becoming ordained into the Baptist ministry. In 1955 he became the spokesperson for his people when he joined the boycott of buses after an African American woman named Rosa Parks refused to give up her seat to a white man. The next year, the U.S. Congress ruled bus segregation was illegal and for the rest of his life King fought to overthrow segregation and racial discrimination in all public life.

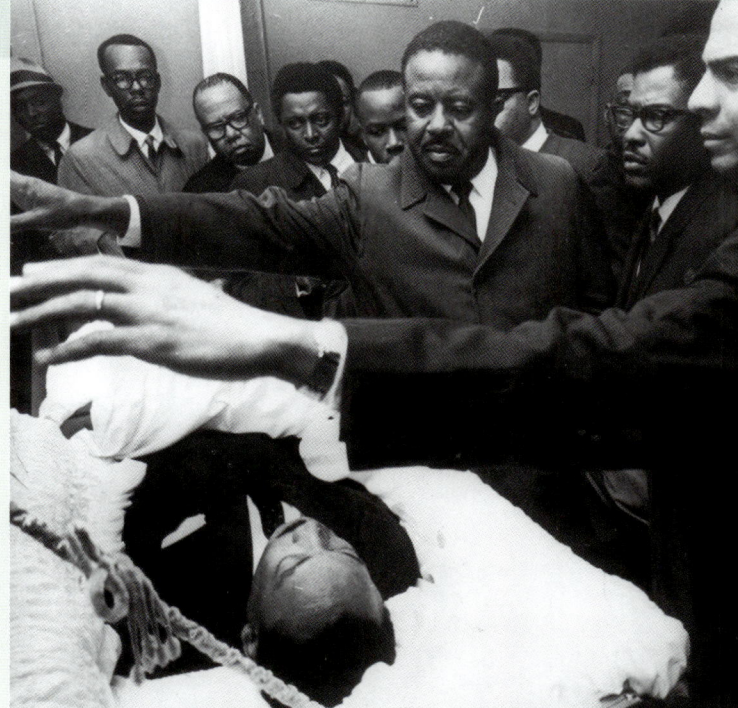

King's assassination led to rioting in more than 100 cities across the U.S., with many believing his death was part of a government conspiracy. It was not until June 8, 1968, that King's killer, James Earl Ray, was taken in for questioning. He was convicted and sentenced to 99 years imprisonment. In 1998, he died in jail.

April 5

"It is up to us to give ourselves recognition. If we wait for it to come from others, we feel resentful when it doesn't, and when it does, we may well reject it." — SPENCER TRACY

HISTORICAL EVENTS

- **33 C.E.** The Resurrection of Jesus (as estimated by scientist Sir Isaac Newton).
- **1614** Powhatan Indian chief's daughter Pocahontas marries British tobacco farmer John Rolfe.
- **1804** The High Possil meteorite hits Earth near Glasgow in Scotland. This is the first recorded meteorite strike to be both witnessed and fully investigated.
- **1951** Julius and Ethel Rosenberg are sentenced to death for conspiring to pass classified information to the U.S.S.R.
- **1955** Winston Churchill resigns as U.K. Prime Minister.
- **1986** The La Belle discothèque is bombed in a terrorist attack in West Berlin, Germany. Two people are killed and more than 100 injured.
- **1988** Arab terrorists hijack a Kuwait Airlines jumbo jet and free 25 of 111 hostages in Iran. Two hostages are killed before the 16-day stand-off ends in surrender.
- **1992** Peace protestor Suada Dilberovic is murdered by Serb paramilitaries. Thus begins the Siege of Sarajevo, the longest siege in modern warfare, lasting until February 29, 1996.
- **1994** Grunge icon Kurt Cobain shoots himself in the head (see right).
- **1998** The largest suspension bridge in the world is opened in Japan, linking the islands of Honshu and Shikoku. The main span is 1.25 miles (1.1 km) long. Construction took 10 years at a cost of U.S. $3.6 billion.

DAY TO REMEMBER

Traditional day Ch'ing Ming (China) This Chinese festival, whose name translates to the Festival of Pure Brightness, is a celebration of spring and the rebirth of nature.

Births
- **1588** Thomas Hobbes, philosopher
- **1784** Louis Spohr, violinist and composer
- **1900** Spencer Tracy, actor
- **1908** Bette Davis, actress
- **1934** Roman Herzog, politician
- **1937** Colin Powell, U.S. Secretary of State
- **1942** Peter Greenaway, film director
- **1973** Pharrell Williams, record producer and musician

Deaths
- **1967** Hermann Joseph Muller, geneticist
- **1976** Howard Hughes, aviator and film producer
- **1994** Kurt Cobain, singer
- **1997** Allen Ginsberg, poet

Kurt Cobain commits suicide

The singer, guitarist, and songwriter for three-piece rock group Nirvana, Kurt Cobain was widely held to be the forefather of the grunge movement in Seattle, Washington. His tortured vocals and distorted guitar sounds became synonymous with the genre, as did his penchant for dressing in torn jeans and checked flannel shirts.

Kurt Cobain was born on February 20, 1967, in Aberdeen, Washington. A happy early life was punctured by his parents' divorce in 1975. He was diagnosed with behavioral problems when he was seven, in particular ADHD (attention-deficit hyperactivity disorder).

Cobain eventually found a surrogate family in the Seattle underground punk rock scene. It was here he met bassist Krist Novoselic, and Nirvana was formed in 1986. Along with drummer Chad Channing, they released their debut album *Bleach*, on seminal grunge label Sub Pop, in 1989. It wasn't until drummer Dave Grohl joined the band, however, that Nirvana hit their peak. Their first major-label venture, *Nevermind*, sold more than 10 million copies in the U.S. alone.

In December 1991, Cobain's girlfriend, Courtney Love, singer of punk band Hole, became pregnant. The couple married in February the next year and their daughter, Frances Bean, was born on August 18, 1992. In March 1994, Cobain suffered a drug overdose, which resulted in him being taken to a detoxification facility. On April 1, he escaped from the center. He was not seen again until April 8, when he was found dead in his Seattle home. The autopsy report revealed that Cobain had died of a "self-inflicted shotgun wound to the head." The date of death was established to be April 5, 1994.

April 6

"Always forgive your enemies; nothing annoys them as much." — OSCAR WILDE

HISTORICAL EVENTS

- **648** B.C.E. First solar eclipse recorded by the ancient Greeks.
- **1832** Indian Sauk warrior Black Hawk declares war on the United States after being tricked into signing away ownership of his territory. Five hundred Sauk Indians fought in the ensuing battle but only 150 survived.
- **1895** Oscar Wilde is arrested for the crime of homosexuality after losing a libel case to the Marquess of Queensbury. He is sentenced to two years hard labor.
- **1896** The first modern Olympic Games is opened in Athens, after a 1,500 year ban (see below).
- **1906** The first animated cartoon is copyrighted.
- **1917** The U.S. enters World War I by declaring war on Germany.
- **1968** Race riots break out across the U.S. in the aftermath of the assassination of Martin Luther King on April 4.
- **1974** Swedish band ABBA wins the Eurovision song contest with their song "Waterloo."
- **1994** The Presidents of two African states – Rwanda and Barundi – are killed when Tutsi extremists shoot down the plane they are traveling in.

Births
- **1483** Raphael, architect and painter
- **1671** Jean Baptiste-Rousseau, poet
- **1820** Felix Nadar, photographer
- **1866** Butch Cassidy, outlaw
- **1890** Anthony Fokker, aircraft designer
- **1928** James Watson, geneticist
- **1929** André Previn, composer
- **1942** Barry Levinson, film director
- **1965** Frank Black, musician

Deaths
- **1528** Albrecht Dürer, artist
- **1971** Igor Stravinsky, composer
- **1992** Isaac Asimov, science fiction writer
- **1998** Wendy O. Williams, singer
- **2005** Rainier III, Prince of Monaco

DAY TO REMEMBER

Religious day St. Sixtus I's Day Ruling the Roman Catholic Church from about 114 to 126 C.E., St. Sixtus was the Pope who succeeded St. Alexander.

The birth of the modern Olympiad

The opening ceremony of the first Olympic Games in 1,500 years took place on this day in 1896, in the Panathinaiko Stadium, Athens. The event attracted an estimated 80,000 spectators and was the largest international sports event up to that point in history.

The ancient Olympic Games were a regular sporting event held every four years from as early as 776 C.E. The athletic competitions which comprised the Games were staged in Olympia, Greece, which was regarded as a sanctuary to the Gods. Sports included wrestling, long jump, javelin, discus, and chariot racing. Athletes competed naked as a celebration of the beauty and capabilities of the human body, and winners received olive branches.

In 393 C.E. Roman Emperor Theodosius I banned the Games as part of the Christian backlash against paganism. The last traces of the Olympiad were erased when Olympia was destroyed by an earthquake in the 600s.

An international committee proposed a rebirth of the event, but the Games of the First Olympiad nearly stalled due to a lack of finances. Seeing the value of

the Games, Crown Prince Constantine of Greece stepped in with a personal contribution, and his generosity stirred the public to donate to the cause as well. The new Games boasted 43 events over nine sports: fencing, cycling, wrestling, athletics, shooting, gymnastics, swimming, tennis, and weight lifting. As with the ancient Olympic Games, women were not allowed to compete. As a protest, female athlete Stamata Revithi ran the marathon course one day after the men had competed in their race on the track.

The closing ceremony was held on April 12, and it was during his congratulatory closing speech that Greece's King George expressed his wish that the Olympic Games remain in Athens in perpetuity. However, the International Olympic Committee disagreed and the next Games took place as planned in Paris in 1900.

April 7

"A kiss that is never tasted is forever and ever wasted." — BILLIE HOLIDAY

Births
- 1652 Pope Clement XII
- 1770 William Wordsworth, poet
- 1860 Will Keith Kellogg, cereal maker
- 1870 Gustav Landauer, German anarchist
- 1897 Walter Winchell, journalist
- 1915 Billie Holiday, singer
- 1939 Francis Ford Coppola, film director
- 1951 Janis Ian, singer
- 1954 Jackie Chan, actor
- 1964 Russell Crowe, actor

Deaths
- 858 Pope Benedict III
- 1614 El Greco, painter
- 1947 Henry Ford, car manufacturer
- 1978 Jim Clark, motor racing world champion

HISTORICAL EVENTS

- **1795** France adopts the metric system of measurement.
- **1805** Ludwig van Beethoven conducts the first public performance of his *Symphony No.3 in E Flat Major* (otherwise known as the *Eroica* symphony) in Vienna.
- **1906** Italy's Mount Vesuvius erupts, killing more than 100 people and losing 352 feet (107 m) in height.
- **1926** Revolutionary Irishwoman Violet Gibson wounds Benito Mussolini when she shoots him in the face during an assassination attempt.
- **1943** Swiss chemist Dr. Albert Hoffman creates LSD (lysergic acid diethylamide).
- **1963** Josip Broz Tito becomes "President for life" of Yugoslavia.
- **1978** U.S. President Jimmy Carter postpones production of the neutron bomb.
- **1983** Don Peterson and Story Musgrave perform the first space shuttle spacewalk, or extravehicular activity (EVA).
- **1989** Forty-two Soviet sailors die when their submarine *Kosmolets* sinks off the coast of Norway.
- **1994** The Rwandan genocide begins in Kigali as already tense relations between Tutsi rebels and Hutu militia erupts into violence. In the ensuing civil war, 900,000 Tutsi civilians are killed.
- **2001** NASA launches an unmanned spacecraft to orbit Mars (see below).

DAY TO REMEMBER

International day World Health Day Celebrated by 191 countries worldwide, this day is an attempt to highlight global health issues. It has been celebrated annually since the World Health Organization was formed by the UN on this day in 1948.

2001 Mars Odyssey is launched

The *2001 Mars Odyssey* spacecraft was launched from Kennedy Space Center on April 7, 2001, as part of NASA's Mars Exploration program. *Odyssey* arrived in the planet's orbit on October 24, 2001. The orbiter carried three pieces of scientific equipment that were designed to gather as much information about the Red Planet as possible, mapping the chemical and geological properties of the surface of Mars.

The Thermal Emission Imaging System (THEMIS) is a camera-like machine that uses wavelength and infrared imaging to photograph Mars so scientists can take note of geographic features. Each week, THEMIS takes hundreds of photographs of the Martian surface, which are uploaded to the University of Arizona website.

The Gamma Ray Spectrometer (GRS) detects water deposits on Mars, and notes any seasonal changes by monitoring the polar ice caps. Finally, the Mars Radiation Environment Experiment (MARIE) was designed to measure space radiation inside the craft to determine the hazards of potential future human exploration of the area. Unfortunately, on October 28, 2003, a solar event damaged the device and no data have been gathered from MARIE since.

Odyssey also relays back to Earth any information from the robotic rovers on the Red Planet's surface. Originally intended to end in August 2004, the Mars Odyssey Mission was extended and, at the time of printing, it is expected to stay in orbit until 2008, when the rover *Phoenix* will be sent to Mars to drill for soil samples.

April 8

DATE*line*

"Only put off till tomorrow what you are willing to die having left undone." — PABLO PICASSO

An ancient Greek statue dating back to c. 130 B.C.E., the *Venus de Milo* was discovered by a peasant on the Aegean island of Melos on April 8, 1820. Made of marble, the sculpture was lying in two pieces with part of an arm nearby. The larger-than-lifesize sculpture (80 inches or 203 cm tall) depicts the goddess of love and beauty and is thought to have been crafted by sculptor Alexandros of Antioch. The famously armless sculpture was given to King Louis XVIII, who later donated it to Paris' Louvre Museum, where it remains to this day.

HISTORICAL EVENTS

1820 The *Venus de Milo* is discovered on Melos, an Aegean island (see above).

1945 Lutheran pastor Dietrich Bonhoeffer is hanged for plotting against the Nazi dictatorship in Germany.

1953 Jomo Kenyatta is sentenced to seven years hard labor for his alleged involvement with the rebel Mau Mau movement in Kenya, a nationalist society who wanted to get European settlers out of Africa. In 1963 he became the first Prime Minister of Kenya.

1986 Actor Clint Eastwood becomes mayor of Carmel, California.

1990 Director David Lynch's surreal serial *Twin Peaks* premieres on U.S. television, sparking the question "Who killed Laura Palmer?"

1994 Grunge singer Kurt Cobain's body is found in his Seattle, Washington home after an apparent suicide.

2004 The Humanitarian Ceasefire Agreement is signed by the Sudanese Government and two rebel groups – the Justice and Equality Movement and the Sudanese Liberation Army. This attempt to put an end to the Darfur Conflict failed, as rebel attacks continued despite the ceasefire agreement.

2005 Pope John Paul II's funeral takes place at St. Peter's Basilica.

DAYS TO REMEMBER

Religious day Hana-matsuri (Japan) Also known as Flower Festival, this day commemorates the birthday in 563 B.C.E. of Prince Siddhartha, the Gautama Buddha and founder of Buddhism. Japanese Buddhists celebrate on this day each year, but most other Buddhists follow the precept that Buddha was born on the eighth day of the fourth month of the Chinese calendar, so for them this holiday often falls in May.

Traditional day Roma Nation Day This observed day is an international celebration for the living culture of the nomadic Roma people of Europe, sometimes referred to as gypsies.

Births
- 1605 King Philip IV of Spain
- 1859 Edmund Husserl, philosopher
- 1911 Melvin Calvin, chemist and Nobel laureate
- 1918 Betty Ford, U.S. President's wife
- 1941 Vivienne Westwood, fashion designer
- 1949 John Madden, theater and film director
- 1955 Barbara Kingsolver, writer
- 1963 Julian Lennon, musician
- 1968 Patricia Arquette, actress

Deaths
- 1950 Vaslav Nijinsky, ballet dancer
- 1973 Pablo Picasso, artist
- 2003 Anita Borg, computer scientist

April 9

HISTORICAL EVENTS

1667 The world's first public art exhibition opens in Paris at the Palais Royale.
1865 The American Civil War ends when Robert E. Lee surrenders his Confederate troops to the General of the Union forces, Ulysses S. Grant, in Virginia.
1867 The U.S. signs a treaty with Russia to purchase Alaska.
1940 Germany surprises the Allies by invading Norway, a neutral country during World War II. By June, the nation has fallen to the Nazis.
1959 America's first astronauts are introduced to the world. The "Mercury Seven," as they became known, are all military test pilots, chosen to be at the forefront of America's attempt to be the first country to put a man in space. The U.S.S.R. beats them to it on April 12, 1961.
1999 Nigerian President Ibrahim Bare Mainassar is killed in an ambush during an attempted coup. Within days, a military junta headed by Major Daouda Wanke takes control of the country, promising a public election process within the year.
2002 The Queen Mother's funeral is held in Westminster Abbey.
2003 As U.S. forces take control of Baghdad, Iraqis turn on a statue of their former leader, Saddam Hussein (see below).
2005 Prince Charles and Camilla Parker Bowles marry in a civil ceremony.

DAYS TO REMEMBER

Religious day Feast of Glory The Feast of *Jalal*, or Glory, is celebrated by people of the Baha'i faith, a church set up by a Persian exile in the nineteenth century.

Religious day St. Acacius' Day This is the feast day of St. Acacius, bishop of Amida in Mesopotamia. In a bid to stop Persian persecution of Christians, he is said to have sold the sacred vessels of his church.

Births
- 1794 Theobald Boehm, inventor of the flute
- 1821 Charles Baudelaire, poet
- 1830 Eadweard Muybridge, motion-picture pioneer
- 1872 Leon Blum, French Prime Minister
- 1908 Victor Vasarely, painter
- 1918 Jorn Utzon, architect
- 1919 J. Presper Eckert, computer pioneer
- 1926 Hugh Hefner, editor and publisher
- 1932 Carl Perkins, musician
- 1954 Dennis Quaid, actor

Deaths
- 1626 Sir Francis Bacon, philosopher
- 1959 Frank Lloyd Wright, architect
- 1961 King Zog of Albania
- 2005 Andrea Dworkin, feminist

Hundreds of Iraqis milled in Paradise Square, Baghdad, to celebrate the overthrow of Saddam Hussein's 25-year rule and the liberation of the city on this day in 2003. Emotional locals attempted to tear down a huge statue of the dictator by pulling a rope tied around its neck. When this didn't work, U.S. forces helped by using a military vehicle to topple the effigy. An American soldier caused an uproar when he scaled the statue and tied a U.S. flag over the bronze Hussein's face. Many in the crowd misunderstood this act and jeered at the Americans until it was replaced with the flag that had been Iraq's emblem before Hussein came to power. When the statue hit the ground, locals attacked it, breaking off its head, which they dragged around the city streets to inform others that the war had ended.

April 10

> *"Working gets in the way of living."*
> — OMAR SHARIF

Births
- 1389 Cosimo de Medici, Italian ruler
- 1829 William Booth, founder of the Salvation Army
- 1847 Joseph Pulitzer, journalist
- 1917 Robert Burns Woodward, chemist and Nobel laureate
- 1929 Max von Sydow, actor
- 1932 Omar Sharif, actor
- 1941 Paul Theroux, writer
- 1960 Afrika Bambaata, musician and activist
- 1988 Haley Joel Osment, actor

Deaths
- 1512 King James V of Scotland
- 1919 Emiliano Zapata, Mexican revolutionary
- 1931 Khalil Gibran, poet
- 1954 Auguste Lumière, film pioneer
- 1966 Evelyn Waugh, writer

HISTORICAL EVENTS

- **1866** Activist Henry Bergh establishes the ASPCA (American Society for the Prevention of Cruelty to Animals).
- **1912** The RMS *Titanic*, the largest passenger steamship in the world, leaves Southampton, England, on her maiden voyage, headed for New York.
- **1919** Emiliano Zapata, a Mexican revolutionary, is shot dead by government forces.
- **1941** Croatia declares independence during World War II.
- **1942** The Bataan Death March begins, upon the fall of Luzon to the Japanese. About 75,000 Filipino and American troops are captured and forced to walk 85 miles (137 km) in six days. Many hundreds die during the march.
- **1953** The first 3D color feature film from a major studio, *The House of Wax*, premieres at New York City's Paramount Theater.
- **1970** Paul McCartney announces the end of The Beatles (see right).
- **1972** An earthquake in southern Iran kills about 4,000 people and obliterates the farming town of Ghir.
- **1998** After 30 years of conflict, Northern Ireland signs a peace treaty known as The Good Friday Agreement. In October 2002 the agreement is suspended after each side accuses the other of not acting in accordance with the deal.

DAY TO REMEMBER

Religious day St. Michael de Sanctis' Day Born in Catalonia, Spain, St. Michael de Sanctis (1591–1625) led a life of exemplary devotion. He died on April 10 at just 35 years of age; many miracles have been attributed to him.

The Beatles break up

With the release of his debut solo album *McCartney* on April 10, 1970, Paul McCartney shocked fans by announcing the split of the most popular band in the world.

Things had not been going well with The Beatles since their manager Brian Epstein's death in 1967. McCartney tried to manage the group for a short while, but the other members did not take to his leadership. When new manager Allan Klein was appointed, McCartney had had enough. After announcing the demise of The Beatles in his album's sleeve note, McCartney filed a lawsuit against his three band mates and manager, asking for the immediate legal dissolution of The Beatles on December 31, 1970.

It was a sad and acrimonious end to a partnership that had produced 13 well-received albums in a little less than a decade (1962–1970) and melded seemingly disparate musical styles. When their album *Sgt. Pepper's Lonely Hearts Club Band* was released in 1967, it quickly became the biggest-selling album of all time. To date, record label EMI states that The Beatles have sold more than one billion records worldwide.

The Beatles, pictured below in 1966 – four years before the break-up – evolved from a number of bands that John Lennon had formed in Liverpool from 1957. McCartney joined him shortly after, as did George Harrison in 1958. Ringo Starr was brought in when the band signed its first recording contract, and EMI label Parlophone did not approve of original drummer Pete Best.

The Beatles were one of the first mainstream acts to incorporate experimental and Eastern sounds into their albums in the late 1960s. Upon their break-up, George Harrison, Paul McCartney, and John Lennon all pursued solo careers. Ringo Starr also attempted a solo career, but was never touted as more than a "likable curiosity."

April 11

"I suffer fools gladly because I am one of them." HARRY SECOMBE

Witch trials end in Germany

On this day in 1775, the last recorded execution of a convicted witch took place in Bavaria, Germany. Her name was Anna Maria Schwiigel, and her crime was to believe in a faith that was not Christianity.

The first recorded execution for being a witch occurred in 383, when Spanish bishop Priscillian of Avila was burned to death for practicing magic. In 906, the Canon Episcopi was put into effect, essentially giving the Church reason to believe that anyone who did not follow the Christian faith was a devil worshipper.

In 1022, a group of mystics were charged with commiting devil worship, participating in sexual orgies and performing child sacrifice. They were all burned at the stake, kicking off a series of persecutions across Europe and the Americas that did not really slow down until the mid-1700s.

In 1231, Conrad of Marburg became Germany's first Inquisitor. He is quoted as saying, "We would gladly burn 100 if just one of them was guilty." Pope Gregory IX aided his cause by naming him a "champion of Christendom" in 1233.

Often people who disagreed with the State, rather than the Church, were accused of witchcraft. In 1431, the trial of Joan of Arc included accusations of witchcraft. In 1440, French nobleman Gilles de Rais was accused of murdering young boys as part of a Satanic ritual. In 1486, *Malleus Maleficarum (Hammer of Witches)* was published, a manual for witch hunters which blamed "carnal lust" for people becoming witches.

Mass witch trials and executions continued throughout Europe and gained even more impetus throughout the seventeenth century, with torture often becoming "necessary" to gain a confession. In 1682, a royal edict in France declared that sorcery and witchcraft did not exist, but it took a few more years for the phenomenon of witch hunting to die out completely.

HISTORICAL EVENTS

- **1775** The last recorded execution for witchcraft takes place (see above).
- **1814** Napoleon abdicates the French throne and is exiled to the Isle of Elba.
- **1868** Japan abolishes the Shogunate, a style of feudal government based around its shogun leaders.
- **1951** In a move that shocks both the public and military personnel, president Harry S. Truman relieves General Douglas MacArthur of command of the U.S. forces in Korea on the grounds of insubordination.
- **1957** Britain agrees to Singapore becoming a self-governed nation, to take effect the following year.
- **1961** The Nazi War Crimes Trial begins in Israel, with Adolf Eichmann facing 15 charges of crimes against humanity. His lawyer says his client is "free of guilt," but in December 1961 Eichmann is found guilty on all counts and sentenced to death. He is hanged in May 1962.
- **1970** Apollo 13 is launched for America's third lunar landing mission. Two days later, an oxygen tank explodes and the mission is aborted.
- **1979** Ugandan dictator Idi Amin is overthrown.
- **1981** Brixton race riots see the streets of South London ablaze after a young black man is arrested. About 400 people are injured in three days of rioting.

DAY TO REMEMBER

Religious day Martyr Antipas' Day Martyr Antipas was the Bishop of Pergamos, one of the "seven churches of the Apocalypse" in the Greek Orthodox faith. The faithful pray to Antipas when they have ailments concerning the teeth.

Births
- **146** Septimus Severis, Roman emperor
- **1721** David Zeisberger, missionary
- **1722** Christopher Smart, poet
- **1794** Edward Everett, professor who admitted the first black student to Harvard University
- **1819** Charles Halle, pianist
- **1908** Leo Rosten, humorist
- **1930** Anton LaVey, founder of the Church of Satan
- **1962** Vincent Gallo, actor and director

Deaths
- **1926** Luther Burbank, botanist
- **1987** Primo Levi, chemist
- **2001** Harry Secombe, actor and comedian

April 12

"As through the calendar I delve
I pause to rejoice in April twelve.
Yea, be I in sickness or be I in health
My favorite date is April twealth." —OGDEN NASH

HISTORICAL EVENTS

1606 Great Britain unveils the Union Jack as its flag.
1633 Galileo is convicted of heresy for believing the Earth revolves around the Sun, and spends the rest of his life under house arrest. It is not until 300 years later that the Church concedes he was right and clears his name.
1861 The American Civil War begins when Confederate forces open fire on Fort Sumter, South Carolina.
1945 Harry S. Truman becomes thirty-third President of the United States.
1961 Soviets win the "Space Race" when Russian Cosmonaut Yuri Gagarin orbits Earth in the first manned space mission.
1975 The Khmer Rouge takes over Phnom Penh, Cambodia. The U.S. admits defeat and pulls its Embassy staff out of the capital.
1981 The first space shuttle mission is launched, with *Columbia* taking its maiden flight (see below).
1997 A terrorist attack is thwarted at the last minute during Pope John Paul II's visit to Sarajevo. It is believed Bosnian Serbs planted at least 20 anti-tank mines under a bridge on the Pope's route, but police were tipped off shortly before the Pope arrived in the country.

Births
- **1748** William Kent, architect
- **1884** Otto Meyerhof, biochemist
- **1903** Sally Rand, dancer
- **1940** Herbie Hancock, composer
- **1947** David Letterman, U.S. talk-show host
- **1949** Scott Turow, writer
- **1979** Claire Danes, actress

Deaths
- **1945** Franklin D. Roosevelt, twenty-sixth U.S. President
- **1975** Josephine Baker, actress
- **1989** Abbie Hoffman, political activist

DAY TO REMEMBER

International day Yuri's Night This is an international commemorative celebration of the first human being in space, Yuri Gagarin. The night was first celebrated in 2001, with the hope that it will increase public interest in space exploration.

The first space shuttle mission began on this day in 1981 with the launch of *Columbia* at Cape Canaveral, Florida. The space shuttle was the first manned spacecraft to be able to return through the atmosphere in one piece, with the aim of reusing it for future space missions. *Columbia* spent two days in space on its first mission, and orbited the Earth 36 times. It flew 28 missions all up, and a total of more than 125 million miles (201 million km) before tragically breaking up after it re-entered the Earth's atmosphere in February 2003, killing all seven astronauts on board.

April 13

DATE*line*

"I never had an occasion to question color, therefore I only saw myself as what I was – a human being." SIDNEY POITIER

HISTORICAL EVENTS

1829 Roman Catholics are granted freedom to practice their religion in Britain.
1873 More than 300 armed white men clash with militant African Americans over the outcome of a local election in Louisiana. More than 100 African Americans are killed in what became known as the Colefax Massacre.
1919 British soldiers open fire on a crowd of innocent Indians at Jallianwala Bagh in what becomes known as the Amritsar Massacre. The official death toll is 379, but witness accounts suggest it to be closer to 1,000.
1921 The Spanish Communist Workers' Party is founded by the *terceristas* in an attempt to enlist labor forces to the Communist party.
1943 The 200th anniversary of third U.S. President Thomas Jefferson's birth is commemorated with a dedication ceremony for the Jefferson Memorial in Washington D.C.
1945 German SS and Luftwaffe troops kill more than 1,000 prisoners of war near the town of Gardlegen in Germany.
1964 Sidney Poitier becomes the first African American actor to receive an Academy Award for his role in *Lilies of the Field*. It was his second nomination.
1989 Israeli soldiers attack Arab villagers on the West Bank, killing six Palestinians. The Israelis respond by saying the soldiers were attacked by rioting youths. In May it is found that the Israeli Army violated regulations.
1997 Tiger Woods becomes the youngest golfer to win the Masters Tournament (see below).

DAYS TO REMEMBER

Religious day Baisakhi (birth of the Sikh nation) On this day in 1699, Gobind Singh – the tenth guru of the faith – asked for followers to give up their lives for their religion. Five volunteers came forward, who became the five leaders of the *Khalsa Panth*.

Traditional day New Year's Day April 13 is the first day of the Thai calendar. It is also Cambodia's New Year.

Births
1570 Guy Fawkes, conspirator
1743 Thomas Jefferson, third U.S. President
1866 Butch Cassidy, outlaw
1906 Samuel Beckett, writer
1922 Julius Nyerere, Tanzanian politician
1923 Don Adams, actor
1939 Seamus Heaney, writer and Nobel laureate
1941 Michael Stuart Brown, geneticist
1963 Garry Kasparov, chess player

Deaths
1641 Richard Montagu, clergyman
1925 Elwood Haynes, automotive engineer
1938 Grey Owl, conservation pioneer

Eldrick "Tiger" Woods, 21, became the youngest golfer to win the U.S. Masters Tournament on this day in 1997. Not only was he the youngest player to win, but he did so with a record margin of 12 strokes, three more than the previous record holder. By the end of the 1997 PGA season, he had also broken the record for earnings made in a single season – more than U.S. $2 million. In June 2000, he beat his own record by winning the U.S. Open by a 15-stroke margin, and by that stage he was earning approximately U.S. $10 million a season. He was the world's number-one golfer for a record 264 weeks, finally losing the mantle to Fijian-born Vijay Singh in 2004.

April 14

"Whenever I hear anyone arguing for slavery I feel a strong impulse to see it tried on him personally." — ABRAHAM LINCOLN

HISTORICAL EVENTS

- **1828** The first edition of Noah Webster's *Dictionary of the English Language* is copyrighted.
- **1865** Abraham Lincoln is shot by John Wilkes Booth, and dies in hospital the next day.
- **1895** Thomas Edison's "kinetoscope" is launched in a New York arcade. A viewer is shown "peep show" slides of sequential photographs. It is a precursor to motion pictures.
- **1912** Just before midnight, the "unsinkable" RMS *Titanic* hits an iceberg in the North Atlantic Ocean.
- **1927** The first Volvo, nicknamed "Jakob," is completed in Gothenburg, Sweden.
- **1944** Freighter SS *Fort Stikine* catches fire in Bombay (now Mumbai) harbor, setting off 1,400 tons of explosives that were on board the vessel. The Bombay Docks Explosion sank nearby ships and killed about 800 people.
- **1965** Richard Hickock and Perry Smith are executed by hanging for the 1959 murders of the Cutter family in Kansas. The crime was the subject for Truman Capote's "non-fiction novel" *In Cold Blood*.
- **1986** Ronald Reagan orders bombing raids on Tripoli and Benghazi in Libya as retaliation for the April 5 bombing of a discothèque in West Berlin in which two U.S. Army officers were killed. Sixty people die in the raids.
- **1988** The Soviet Union agrees to withdraw from Afghanistan after a decade of fighting Muslim guerillas for occupation.
- **2003** Scientists finish identifying all the genes that make up human DNA (see below).

Births
- **1578** King Phillip III of Spain
- **1872** Abdullah Yusuf Ali, Islamic scholar
- **1904** Sir John Gielgud, actor
- **1925** Abel Muzorewa, Zimbabwean Prime Minister
- **1935** Erich von Däniken, writer
- **1936** Frank Serpico, first policeman to testify against corruption within the U.S. police force
- **1940** Loretta Lynn, singer
- **1942** Valentin Lebedev, Russian cosmonaut
- **1973** Adrien Brody, actor

Deaths
- **1792** Maximilian Hell, astronomer
- **1917** Ludovich Lazarus Zamenhof, creator of the "international language" Esperanto
- **1986** Simone de Beauvoir, writer

DAYS TO REMEMBER

Traditional day New Year's Day Sri Lanka and certain parts of India regard this day as the beginning of the new year.

Traditional day Black Day In South Korea, single people get together to eat noodles with black bean sauce in an informal celebration.

Human Genome Project is completed

On April 14, 2003, the Human Genome Project came to an end after 13 years of research conducted by geneticists from around the world. The goal was to identify all the genes that make up human DNA – approximately 30,000 in all – and map the sequences of the three billion chemical base pairs. Because everyone has a different genetic sequence, the data were gleaned from an amalgamation of genes, from cell samples given by anonymous donors of both sexes.

The project was an American initiative, but soon partnerships were made with the U.K., Germany, China, France, and Japan. The project cost U.S. $3 billion. The project had been pitched in 1986 but formally began in 1990. The main program was concluded in 2003 – two years ahead of schedule – but much important and useful information emerged as the project was being conducted. It was especially beneficial to cancer research as it opened up new avenues of genetic research. As well as promising potential health breakthroughs, understanding our genetic makeup can provide insight into behavioral traits.

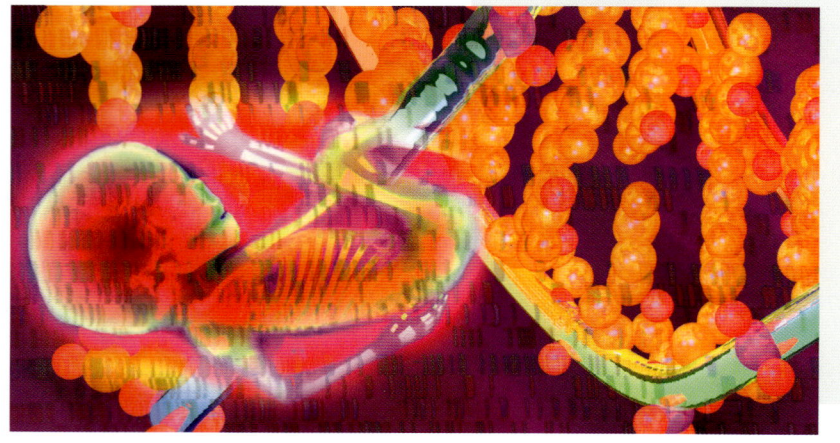

April 15

HISTORICAL EVENTS

1755 *A Dictionary of the English Language* by Samuel Johnson is published in London.
1865 Andrew Johnson becomes seventeenth President of the United States after Abraham Lincoln dies of a gunshot wound.
1912 The *Titanic* sinks after hitting an iceberg (see below).
1945 British troops liberate the concentration camp at Bergen-Belsen. Inside, up to 30,000 dead bodies are found, along with thousands of diseased inmates.
1959 Fidel Castro visits the U.S. just months after staging a revolution in Cuba, invited there by the American Society of Newspaper Editors. President Eisenhower refuses to meet him.
1983 Disneyland opens in Tokyo.
1989 During a football match, a stampede takes place in the grandstands at Hillsborough in Sheffield, England. The resulting crush of people leaves 96 fans dead and many injured.
1989 Former Secretary General Hu Yaobang dies, sparking the Tiananmen Square protests in the People's Republic of China.

The sinking of the *Titanic*

"Unsinkable" luxury cruise liner RMS *Titanic* sank at 2:20 A.M. on April 15, 1912, drowning all but 706 of the 2,223 passengers and crew on board after hitting an iceberg off the coast of Canada.

The *Titanic* was one of three "superliners" intended to cater to international business travel. It took five years to build, using over 3,000 specialized tradespeople to fit out the interior, which included Turkish baths, a library, gymnasium, and swimming pool. The ship was 88.2 feet (270 m) long.

The *Titanic* was the largest and most luxurious vessel of its time. Its passengers included some of the richest industrialists of the era, whose combined wealth is thought to have been close to U.S. $600 million.

After leaving Southampton, England, on its maiden voyage to New York, the *Titanic* was doing close to its top speed of 23 knots at the time of the collision, 11:40 P.M. on April 14.

The ship began sinking and lifeboats were dispatched shortly after midnight. There were only enough lifeboats for half the passengers and crew, but even so, many boats were launched before reaching their capacity. At 2:10 A.M. the *Titanic*'s stern lifted out of the water, breaking the ship in two pieces. The bow sank straight away, as did the stern, to the depths at 2:20 A.M.

The *Titanic*'s resting place was discovered in 1985 by oceanographer Dr. Robert Ballard. He kept the location secret for many years fearing looters would strip the ship of its valuables. He finally revealed its location and many expeditions have since been made, with salvaged objects showing up in maritime museums.

Births

1452 Leonardo da Vinci, artist
1684 Catherine I of Russia
1809 Hermann Grassmann, mathematician
1843 Henry James, writer
1933 Elizabeth Montgomery, actress
1940 Jeffrey Archer, writer
1955 Dodi Al-Fayed, businessman
1959 Emma Thompson, actress

Deaths

1865 Abraham Lincoln, sixteenth U.S. President
1898 Kepa Te Rangihiwinui, Maori leader
1998 Pol Pot, Cambodian dictator
1990 Greta Garbo, actress

DAYS TO REMEMBER

Religious day St. Paternus' Day A hermit bishop in France, St. Paternus (482–565) was renowned for his charity work and preaching abilities. He and his "companion monk," St. Scubilion, died of illness in separate towns on the same day.

Historical day Tipsa Diena In ancient Latvian mythology, this was a minor festival to signify the time of year fields should start being ploughed.

Celtic tree sign

WILLOW
April 15–May 12

In the Celtic tradition, people born under the willow tree are influenced by the Moon. They show empathy toward others and are honest and intuitive, trusting their gut rather than their intellectual response to situations. They have a curiosity for the way of the world and love to travel and dream. Although moody and restless at times, willow people appreciate beauty around them and are tenacious.

April 16

"All I ask is the chance to prove that money won't make me happy." — SPIKE MILLIGAN

Great train robbers get 307 years

On this day in 1964, the 12 main players involved in Britain's biggest heist received a combined sentence of 307 years imprisonment. Known as the Great Train Robbery, the heist saw a mail train held up en route between Glasgow and London. The thieves bagged £12 million ($21 million) in used bank notes.

Antiques dealer Bruce Reynolds was the brains behind the operation, organizing a disparate gang of would-be criminals with special skills – including a bookie, a retired train driver and a solicitor – to carry out the "perfect crime."

The robbery took place at 3:30 A.M. on August 8, 1963. The mail train was stopped when the gang sent false light signals to the driver, indicating that he should stop. When the driver got out to see what was wrong, a group of men dressed as train workers attacked him, hitting him violently over the head before forcing him to drive the train a little further down the track near the getaway vehicle. About 120 sacks of money were then stolen.

After the robbery, the gang hid out in a safehouse in Oxfordshire, playing Monopoly with the money they had stolen. Ironically, it was this pastime that led to the thieves' capture. As police closed in, the gang fled, leaving fingerprints behind on cups and the Monopoly set.

Most of the robbers fled overseas, but were eventually rounded up and put on trial. They were each given a jail term of between 20 and 30 years.

The crime bore all the hallmarks of a Hollywood movie, and not surprisingly, the perpetrators and anyone associated with the operation attained celebrity status.

HISTORICAL EVENTS

- **1917** Vladimir Lenin, leader of the Bolshevik party, returns to Petrograd from exile in Finland in the wake of Nicholas II's abdication. The city was in the grip of strikes due to food shortages, and Lenin called for "Peace, land and bread."
- **1943** Just nine days after synthesizing LSD-25, Swiss chemist Albert Hoffman accidentally consumes some of the formula, experiencing its hallucinogenic qualities. The drug did not gain wide appeal until the 1960s.
- **1945** Soviet forces begin their final assault on the Nazis in Berlin during World War II.
- **1947** At Galveston Bay, Texas, a fire on a French freighter causes chemicals in the ship's hold to ignite. The resulting explosion kills about 600 people and almost destroys the city.
- **1964** The 12 thieves involved in Britain's Great Train Robbery are sentenced to a total of 307 years in prison (see above).
- **1972** Apollo 16 launches from Cape Canaveral, Florida, on the sixth lunar landing mission. The astronauts explore the moon's surface using the lunar rover vehicle to collect rock samples before returning safely to Earth.

DAY TO REMEMBER

Religious day St. Bernadette's Day Born in Lourdes, Southern France, in 1844, St. Bernadette was a peasant girl who reported many visions of "a lady." The Catholic Church confirmed that these were visions of the Virgin Mary.

Births
- 1728 Joseph Black, chemist
- 1823 Ferdinand Eisenstein, mathematician
- 1867 Wilbur Wright, aviator
- 1889 Charlie Chaplin, actor and writer
- 1918 Spike Milligan, comedian
- 1921 Peter Ustinov, actor and writer
- 1922 Kingsley Amis, writer
- 1924 Henry Mancini, composer
- 1927 Pope Benedict XVI
- 1939 Dusty Springfield, singer
- 1962 Ian MacKaye, musician

Deaths
- 1783 Christian Mayer, astronomer
- 1828 Francisco de Goya, painter
- 1946 Arthur Chevrolet, car designer
- 1991 David Lean, film director

April 17

"A slip of the foot you may soon recover, but a slip of the tongue you may never get over."
BENJAMIN FRANKLIN

Births
1734 Taksin, King of Thailand
1882 Artur Schnabel, pianist
1885 Isak Dinesen, writer
1894 Nikita Khrushchev, leader of the Soviet Union
1929 James Last, composer
1948 Jan Hammer, composer
1952 Zeljko Raznatovic, Serbian nationalist
1957 Nick Hornby, writer
1967 Liz Phair, musician

Deaths
1790 Benjamin Franklin, U.S. statesman and inventor
1942 Jean Perrin, physicist
1998 Linda McCartney, photographer, activist
2003 Paul Getty, philanthropist

HISTORICAL EVENTS

1397 Geoffrey Chaucer tells his *Canterbury Tales* in the court of King Richard II.
1865 Mary Surratt is arrested for her part in conspiring to assassinate Abraham Lincoln. In July, she becomes the first woman executed by the U.S. Government.
1924 MGM Studios is born from a merger of Metro Pictures, Goldwyn Pictures, and Louis B. Mayer Pictures (see right).
1961 CIA-trained Cuban refugees land in Cuba from the U.S., intent on ousting Fidel Castro. The Bay of Pigs invasion, as it becomes known, is a huge failure.
1964 The first Ford Mustang is unveiled at New York's World's Fair. It was the most successful automotive launch in history and the vehicle is still one of the most popular muscle cars of all time.
1969 Palestinian militant Sirhan Sirhan is convicted of assassinating U.S. Senator Robert F. Kennedy.
1970 The aborted Apollo 13 lunar module returns to Earth safely, touching down in the Pacific Ocean.
1975 Cambodia falls to the Khmer Rouge during the Vietnam War.
1999 A nail bomb explodes in Brixton, London, injuring 45 people. Before the end of the month, right-wing extremist David Copeland sets off two more bombs in London, wounding a further 72 people.

DAY TO REMEMBER

Religious day St. Anicetus' Day A Pope of the Catholic Church, Anicetus (c. 154–167 C.E.) forbade Catholic clergymen from growing long hair so they are not confused with Gnostics of the era. It is believed he died a martyr's death.

MGM Studios is born

America's Metro-Goldwyn-Mayer film company was formed on this day in 1924, a merger between three major movie players – Metro Pictures Corporation, Goldwyn Pictures Corporation and Louis B. Mayer Pictures.

The silent partner in the merger was Loews Inc., run by vaudeville theater owner Marcus Loew. Louis B. Mayer was made head of the studio and the company adopted Goldwyn's motto *Ars Gratia Artis* or "art for art's sake," as well as its roaring lion mascot, Leo (pictured below).

The first major hit for the company was period epic *Ben-Hur*, the most expensive movie ever made at that time. Big names from MGM include Greta Garbo, Clark Gable, Joan Crawford, Jean Harlow, and Robert Montgomery. The public's perception of MGM as a sophisticated, glitzy production house was sealed. Even during the Depression, the studio never lost money.

In the early 1940s, MGM opened an animation unit, which introduced the world to Hanna-Barbera's Oscar-winning *Tom and Jerry* cartoon.

In the late 1950s, MGM started losing money for the first time and despite trying its hand at television, by the 1960s the studio was struggling to survive. From producing 50 films a year in its prime, the studio made only five big movies per annum by the 1970s. After acquiring United Artists in a failed attempt to expand the company, MGM was bought out by a succession of entrepreneurs, including a short-lived deal with Ted Turner, and a messy period with Italian fraudster Giancarlo Parretti. Nevada businessman Kirk Kerkorian bought the studio three times. On April 8, 2005, Sony and Comcast Corporation bought the ailing company for U.S. $4.8 million.

April 18

"I never think of the future. It comes soon enough." — ALBERT EINSTEIN

HISTORICAL EVENTS

1906 San Francisco is hit by an earthquake measuring 7.8 on the Richter scale. More than 3,000 people die and almost 300,000 are left homeless due to the quake itself and resulting fires.

1923 Yankee Stadium is opened in the Bronx, New York. It is the first arena of its kind, with the term "stadium" harkening to ancient Greek athletic arenas.

1958 Poet Ezra Pound is released from an insane asylum upon orders from the U.S. Federal Court. The American expatriate had been brought back to the U.S. from Italy to face charges of treason, but was imprisoned on the basis of insanity due to "a grandiosity of beliefs."

1980 Rhodesia formally becomes the Republic of Zimbabwe, with Rev. Dr. Canaan Banana as its first President. Bob Marley plays at the ceremony (see below).

1983 A delivery van driven by a suicide bomber explodes at the U.S. Embassy in Beirut, killing 63 people.

1988 John Demjanjuk, a retired Ukrainian-born U.S. car factory worker, is found guilty of war crimes in Israel. It is believed he is "Ivan the Terrible," a guard at the Treblinka death camp in Poland, but upon appeal of his death sentence it becomes apparent that this was a case of mistaken identity.

2002 A new order of carnivorous insects called *Mantophasmatodea* (common name Gladiators) is classified, becoming the first new order of insects since 1914.

DAYS TO REMEMBER

Religious day St. Perfecto's Day After refusing to acknowledge Muhammad, St. Perfecto – a Spanish Catholic – was executed on this day in 850 C.E.

National day Patriot's Day (U.S.) This day commemorates the start of the American War of Independence in 1775 on the night Paul Revere warned the militia forces in Massachusetts that British troops were advancing from Boston.

Births
- 1580 Thomas Middleton, dramatist
- 1590 Ahmed I, Emperor of the Ottoman empire
- 1857 Clarence Darrow, attorney
- 1897 Ardito Desio, mountaineer
- 1947 Kathy Acker, writer
- 1954 Rick Moranis, comedian
- 1969 Princess Sayako of Japan
- 1971 David Tennant, actor

Deaths
- 1796 Johan Wilcke, physicist
- 1898 Gustave Moreau, painter
- 1955 Albert Einstein, scientist
- 2002 Thor Heyerdahl, explorer and anthropologist

Bob Marley played a concert to a group of select dignitaries, including Prince Charles of Britain and Indira Ghandi of India, on Zimbabwe Independence Day, April 18, 1980. In an official ceremony moments beforehand, the African nation Rhodesia became independent from Britain and was renamed Zimbabwe. As the new flag was hoisted, Bob Marley and the Wailers were welcomed to the stage, but as they began to play the public tried to break into the stadium, angry at being excluded from the performance and desperate to see their hero play – Marley's song "Zimbabwe" had been something of an anthem for the Zimbabwe National Liberation Army. Riot police fired tear gas into the surging crowd before the Wailers were urged to continue their set. The next day, a public performance was allowed to go ahead at Marley's request, with an audience of 100,000 people.

April 19

"You only live once, but if you live it right once is enough." — MAE WEST

HISTORICAL EVENTS

1775 The American War of Independence begins with a "shot heard around the world." When British soldiers try to confiscate colonists' firearms, a gun battle breaks out and the locals force the English out of town.

1861 Sixteen people in Baltimore become the first casualties of the American Civil War when an angry secessionist mob attacks troops headed for the U.S. capital.

1927 Mae West is charged with obscenity and sentenced to 10 days in jail for the play she wrote and starred in, called *Sex*. It had already been showing for a year, and 325,000 people had seen it before the New York Police Department shut it down.

1951 Douglas MacArthur, one of the most controversial generals in U.S. military history, retires from the military.

1956 Prince Rainier III of Monaco marries Hollywood starlet Grace Kelly (see below).

1971 Charles Manson, leader of the commune cult The Family, is sentenced to death for masterminding murders including that of actress Sharon Tate and her unborn baby. He has always maintained his innocence.

1993 A 51-day siege at Waco, Texas, ends with a fire breaking out in the Branch Davidian headquarters. About 80 cult members die, including their leader, David Koresh.

1995 A car bomb explodes in Oklahoma City, killing 168 people and wounding 500 more. Gulf-war veteran Timothy McVeigh is later sentenced to death for the attack, and is executed on June 11, 2001.

2005 German Joseph Ratzinger is elected Pope Benedict XVI.

Births
- **1452** King Ferdinand II of Aragon
- **1832** José Echegaray y Eizaguirre, writer and Nobel laureate
- **1892** Germaine Tailleferre, composer
- **1903** Eliot Ness, law enforcer
- **1919** Merce Cunningham, choreographer
- **1933** Jayne Mansfield, actress
- **1935** Dudley Moore, actor
- **1953** Ruby Wax, comedienne
- **1965** Suge Knight, record producer
- **1987** Maria Sharapova, tennis player

Deaths
- **1054** Pope Leo IX
- **1882** Charles Darwin, biologist
- **1993** David Koresh, Branch Davidian cult leader
- **1998** Octavio Paz, writer

DAYS TO REMEMBER

National day Primrose Day To mark the anniversary of the death of former U.K. Prime Minister Benjamin Disraeli, many people decorate his statue in Parliament Square, London with primroses.

Religious day St. George of Antioch's Day A monk and bishop, St. George of Antioch was banished by Byzantine Emperor Leo V and died in exile on this day in 814.

Religious day Easter Sunday According to the Gregorian calendar, Easter Sunday falls on this date more often than any other date throughout history.

Hollywood actress Grace Kelly married Prince Rainier III of Monaco on April 19, 1956, the climax to a real-life fairytale romance. A civil ceremony had already been held in the throne room of the palace the day before, with the religious Nuptial Mass held in the Cathedral of Monaco. A message of blessing from the Pope was read out at the end of proceedings. Kelly gave up her acting career to become Her Serene Highness Princess Grace of Monaco. The couple had three children – Caroline, Albert, and Stephanie – before Princess Grace was tragically killed in a car accident on September 14, 1982.

April 20

> "We learn from failure, not from success!" — BRAM STOKER, AUTHOR OF *DRACULA*

Apollo 16 team lands on the moon

In the early hours of April 20, 1972, the Apollo 16 crew land on the surface of the Moon after problems with the propulsion system of command module *Casper* nearly saw the mission aborted.

Apollo 16 had been launched from Kennedy Space Center on April 16, the tenth manned lunar mission of NASA. The goal of the expedition was to explore the lunar highlands. The crew included Commander John W. Young, Command Module Pilot Thomas K. Mattingly Jr. and Lunar Module Pilot Charles Duke Jr. Young stayed orbiting the moon in *Casper* while the other two astronauts explored the surface in lunar module *Orion*.

The Apollo 16 mission was the fifth time humans had been on the moon, and the first time anyone had landed on the moon's highlands, near the Descartes Crater. Until that time, the area had been thought to be volcanic, but subsequent tests proved the surface was made of breccias, or impact-formed rock.

Performance tests on the lunar module included testing the landspeed of the lunar rover vehicle, which reached a top speed of 11 miles per hour (18 km/h). The astronauts were on the surface for a total of 71 hours and collected 109 pounds (95 kg) of lunar samples.

The mission ended successfully when the crew returned to Earth on April 27, 1972.

HISTORICAL EVENTS

1657 Jewish people in New Amsterdam (New York, U.S.) are granted the freedom to practice their religion.

1792 France declares war on Austria.

1861 During the American Civil War, Colonel Robert E. Lee resigns from the U.S. Army when his home state of Virginia leaves the Union. He is made Major General of Virginia's Confederate forces.

1862 Louis Pasteur and Claude Bernard complete their first pasteurization test.

1902 Pierre and Marie Curie isolate radium from the mineral pitchblende. A year later, the married couple are awarded a Nobel Prize for their research into radioactivity.

1972 Lunar module *Orion* touches down on the Moon's surface (see left).

1974 The conflicts in Northern Ireland claim their 1,000th victim, a Roman Catholic gas station owner.

1999 In Littleton, Colorado, two students open fire on schoolmates and teachers in what becomes known as the Columbine High School Massacre.

2004 Insurgents fire mortars on Abu Ghraib prison, just outside Baghdad. Twenty-two detainees are killed and almost 100 are injured.

DAYS TO REMEMBER

Traditional day Cannabis Celebration Many pro–marijuana rallies are organized on this day. *High Times* magazine cites the date as relating to "four-twenty," the time in the afternoon when teenagers would meet after school to smoke cannabis.

Religious day St. Theodore's Day St. Theodore The Hairy died on this day in 330 C.E. The hermit was so named because he wore a shirt made out of coarse hair.

Births
- **570 C.E.** Muhammad, founder of Islam
- **1818** Heinrich Gobel, inventor
- **1889** Adolf Hitler, leader of the Nazi Party
- **1893** Joan Miró, painter
- **1896** Wop May, aviator
- **1915** Joseph Wolpe, psychotherapist
- **1941** Ryan O'Neill, actor
- **1943** Edie Sedgwick, actress
- **1951** Luther Vandross, singer
- **1964** Crispin Glover, actor

Deaths
- **1769** Pontiac, Native American chief
- **1912** Bram Stoker, author
- **1992** Benny Hill, comedian
- **2003** Bernard Katz, biophysicist

DATE*line*

April 21

"In every walk with nature, one receives far more than he seeks." — JOHN MUIR, ENVIRONMENTALIST

Brazilian Ayrton Senna da Silva won his first Formula One championship – the Portuguese Grand Prix in Estoril – on this day in 1985. It was the start to an illustrious nine-year motor racing career that saw him win 41 F1 championships. He was such a fast driver during qualifying trials that he won pole position in 65 races. He died aged 34, on May 1, 1994, when the car he was driving in the San Marino Grand Prix crashed into an unprotected wall. He is considered one of the best drivers in motor racing history.

Births
- 1816 Charlotte Bronte, writer
- 1838 John Muir, environmentalist
- 1864 Max Weber, economist
- 1912 Marcel Camus, film director
- 1915 Anthony Quinn, actor
- 1923 John Mortimer, barrister
- 1926 Queen Elizabeth II, United Kingdom
- 1927 Gerald Flood, actor
- 1936 James Dobson, evangelist
- 1947 Iggy Pop, musician

Deaths
- 1073 Pope Alexander II
- 1910 Mark Twain, writer
- 1918 Manfred von Richthofen, German pilot
- 1938 Allama Iqbal, philosopher
- 1977 Gummo Marx, comedian

HISTORICAL EVENTS

- **1918** During World War I, Manfred von Richthofen (A.K.A. The Red Baron) is shot down over the Somme in France. He flew 80 victorious missions during his career in the German Imperial Air Service.
- **1944** French women are granted the right to vote.
- **1960** Brasilia takes over from Rio de Janeiro as the capital of Brazil.
- **1960** The Orthodox Baha'i faith, an "independent world religion," founds a church in Washington D.C.
- **1965** The second, and last, New York World's Fair opens in New York. It was touted to be an international showcase for emergent consumerism and technological advancements, but ended in controversy over financial mismanagement.
- **1967** A coup d'état, led by Colonel George Papadopoulos, takes place in Greece. The country remains under the control of a military regime for the next seven years.
- **1985** Ayrton Senna wins his first Formula One championship (see above).
- **1989** Protests in Tiananmen Square in Beijing escalate. More than 100,000 Chinese students assemble, concerned that the death of deposed politician Hu Yaobang will stall reform. By mid-May over a million protesters fill the square.
- **1994** Polish astronomer Aleksander Wolszczan publishes his findings that there is another planetary system outside our solar system. It is the first extra-solar planetary system whose existence has been proved.

DAYS TO REMEMBER

Religious day Grounation Day This festival is celebrated on this day each year by Rastafarians in Jamaica to coincide with the anniversary of Haile Selassi's visit to the country in 1966.

Historical day Rome's Birthday According to ancient mythology, Rome was founded on this day in 753 B.C.E. After arguing with his twin Remus over where the city should be located, Romulus killed his brother and became Rome's first king.

Star sign

TAURUS

April 21–May 21

Born under the sign of the bull, the typical Taurean is reliable, faithful, conservative, and grounded. He or she can also be a bit "bull headed" when it comes to getting their own way. An earth sign, Taurus is a hard worker and thinks long-term so loyalty in matters of love and business are assured. Taurean people are creative and original thinkers.

April 22

"Before you try to keep up with the Joneses, make sure they're not trying to keep up with you."
ERMA BOMBECK

HISTORICAL EVENTS

- **1509** Henry VIII becomes King of England upon the death of his father.
- **1886** Seduction becomes illegal in the U.S. state of Ohio. The law specifies that it is unlawful for male teachers to have sex with female students no matter how old they are.
- **1889** President Benjamin Harrison allows white American settlers to claim "unassigned lands" in Oklahoma, kicking off a land rush.
- **1913** The first issue of the Soviet Communist Party newspaper *Pravda* (meaning "The Truth") rolls off the presses in St. Petersburg.
- **1915** During World War I, German forces fire chlorine gas on French soldiers during the Second Battle of Ypres. It is widely held that this marked the beginning of the use of chemical weapons in war.
- **1954** At the height of America's fear of Communism, scaremonger Republican Senator Joseph McCarthy and the U.S. Army go head-to-head in the Army–McCarthy hearings, starting on this day.
- **1959** Dame Margot Fonteyn lands in New York after a stint in a Panama jail (see below).
- **1971** Haitian dictator François "Papa Doc" Duvalier dies of prostate cancer in Port-au-Prince. During his 14-year rule he survived six assassination attempts.
- **1997** Troops storm the Japanese Embassy in Peru, ending a four-month siege in which Tupac Amaru rebels held 72 hostages.
- **2000** Armed U.S. forces raid a Miami home and seize six-year-old Elian Gonzalez, an illegal immigrant who lost his mother in a shipwreck off the coast of Florida. A custody battle ensues between his Cuban father and American in-laws before Elian is returned to Cuba. Fidel Castro attends his seventh birthday party.

Births
- **1610** Pope Alexander VIII
- **1692** James Stirling, mathematician
- **1724** Immanuel Kant, philosopher
- **1870** Vladimir Lenin, leader of the Soviet Union
- **1899** Vladimir Nabakov, writer
- **1904** Robert Oppenheimer, physicist
- **1922** Charles Mingus, musician
- **1923** Bettie Page, pin-up model
- **1937** Jack Nicholson, actor
- **1946** John Waters, film director

Deaths
- **1778** James Hargreaves, inventor
- **1984** Ansel Adams, photographer
- **1994** Richard Nixon, thirty-seventh U.S. President
- **1996** Erma Bombeck, humorist and writer

Dame Margot Fonteyn is released

British prima ballerina Dame Margot Fonteyn arrived in New York on April 22, 1959, after being released from a jail in Panama. She was taken into custody for 24 hours following the disappearance of her husband, Roberto Arias, former Panamanian Ambassador to London. Fonteyn denied any knowledge of his whereabouts, even though he had "disappeared" during a fishing trip he had taken with her in the Gulf of Panama. Arias was suspected of planning a coup to overthrow Panamanian President Ernesto de la Guarda. On April 26, a small band of rebels thought to have been led by him attempted to invade Panama but failed.

A few years later, Arias returned to Panama and won a seat in the National Assembly, but in 1964 he was shot by a rival and rendered quadriplegic. Dame Margot Fonteyn remained faithful to her husband despite his failed revolution, disability, and numerous infidelities. She returned to Panama in 1967 so he could resume his political career.

Fonteyn had been knighted in 1956 at just 35 years of age for her contribution to ballet. In the 1960s, she made a comeback partnered by Russian Rudolf Nureyev, an arrangement that lasted throughout the 1970s. In 1979, the Royal Ballet awarded her the ultimate honor in ballet circles – the title *prima ballerina assoluta*. Despite arthritis, she continued to dance well into her sixties, before dying of cancer in 1991.

April 23

DATE*line*

"In order to attain the impossible, one must attempt the absurd." — MIGUEL DE CERVANTES

Births

- 1676 King Frederick I of Sweden
- 1775 William Turner, ornithologist
- 1895 Ngaio Marsh, writer
- 1928 Shirley Temple, actress and singer
- 1936 Roy Orbison, singer
- 1939 Lee Majors, actor
- 1941 Paavo Lipponen, Finnish Prime Minister
- 1954 Michael Moore, film director and author
- 1955 Judy Davis, actress
- 1968 Timothy McVeigh, terrorist

Deaths

- 1616 Miguel de Cervantes, writer
- 1986 Otto Preminger, film director
- 1998 James Earl Ray, the assassin of Martin Luther King
- 2002 Linda Lovelace, actress

HISTORICAL EVENTS

- 1014 King Brian of Ireland is killed by a group of retreating Norsemen after a failed Viking raid.
- 1533 The Archbishop of Canterbury annuls the marriage of Catherine of Aragon and King Henry VIII. To do this, he had to first pass a law repudiating jurisdiction of the Roman Catholic Church over England.
- 1564 Shakespeare is believed to have been born (see below).
- 1942 Germans begin the Baedeker Raids on England during World War II, beginning with a bomb strike over Exeter in retaliation for the British raid on Lubeck.
- 1968 Britain starts using decimal currency, with the introduction of the 5p and 10p coin.
- 1975 U.S. President Gerald Ford announces that the Vietnam War is over. By the end of April, North Vietnamese troops have overthrown Saigon and the South Vietnamese surrender, officially ending the war.
- 1981 Sicilian Mafia Boss Stefano Bontade is murdered in Palermo, triggering a Mob war.
- 1984 Scientists discover the HTLV-3 virus, which is thought to cause AIDS. In 1987, its name is changed to HIV.
- 2003 Beijing closes all schools for two weeks due to a SARS (severe acute respiratory syndrome) virus scare.

DAYS TO REMEMBER

National day St. George's Day Being the patron saint of England, St. George's Day is in effect England's national day. St. George was a cavalryman who died in 303 C.E., and his flag was a red cross on a white background. While St. George is often portrayed as a dragon slayer, this is essentially a metaphor for Christianity's triumph over paganism.

Traditional day Biertag (Germany) Beer Day, or *Biertag* as it is known in Germany, is the anniversary of this day in 1516 when Duke Wilhelm IV passed an edict stating that beer should contain nothing but the following ingredients: malt, yeast, hops, and water.

Facts about one of history's greatest playwrights are difficult to verify, but it is believed that on this day in 1564, William Shakespeare was born. Raised in Stratford-Upon-Avon, he moved to London at about the age of 20. There, he became an actor and playwright. When theaters were closed during the Plague, he took to writing sonnets and narrative poetry instead. In 1599 he became a partner in the successful Globe Theatre. He is believed to have died in Stratford in 1616 (also on April 23), having written 37 plays and 154 sonnets. In the centuries that have passed since his death many theories began to emerge about his true identity. In 2006, the British Portrait Gallery displayed this group of paintings by various artists who claimed to represent Shakespeare. Research on these pictures could cast new light on the Bard's authentic appearance.

April 24

> *"The pessimist sees difficulty in every opportunity. The optimist sees the opportunity in every difficulty."* — WINSTON CHURCHILL

HISTORICAL EVENTS

- **1184 B.C.E.** Greeks storm the city of Troy by hiding inside the Trojan Horse.
- **1916** The Easter Rebellion begins in Dublin when the Irish Republican Brotherhood stages an uprising against British rule.
- **1953** U.K. Prime Minister Winston Churchill receives his knighthood from Queen Elizabeth II.
- **1967** A Russian space mission ends in tragedy when *Soyuz 1* crashes to Earth upon re-entry. Cosmonaut Vladimir Komarov dies in the crash.
- **1980** U.S. President Jimmy Carter orders military intervention in a bid to end the six-month Iran Hostage Crisis, in which 52 American hostages are being held in Tehran. The mission is aborted but during withdrawal a helicopter crashes, killing eight U.S. soldiers. The hostages were finally released after 444 days.
- **1981** The first IBM personal computer enters the marketplace.
- **1990** The space shuttle *Discovery* takes off, putting the Hubble telescope into orbit (see below).
- **1993** An IRA bomb explodes in Bishopsgate, London. The medieval church of St. Ethelburga is destroyed, one person is killed and 40 injured in the blast.
- **2005** An inauguration ceremony takes place for Cardinal Joseph Ratzinger, in which he assumes the name Pope Benedict XVI, thus becoming the 265th Pope of the Roman Catholic Church.

Births
- 1580 Vincent de Paul, saint
- 1815 Anthony Trollope, writer
- 1904 Willem de Kooning, painter
- 1905 Robert Penn Warren, poet
- 1906 William Joyce, fascist
- 1934 Shirley MacLaine, actress
- 1942 Barbra Streisand, singer
- 1952 Jean-Paul Gaultier, fashion designer
- 1960 Paula Yates, TV presenter

Deaths
- 1731 Daniel Defoe, writer
- 1960 Max Von Laue, physicist
- 1980 Alejo Carpentier, writer
- 2004 Estée Lauder, cosmetics manufacturer

The launch of the Hubble telescope

Named for Edwin Hubble, the cosmologist who first observed that the universe was expanding, the Hubble space telescope was launched on this day in 1990 aboard the space shuttle *Discovery*. It was deployed into orbit 375 miles (604 km) above Earth on April 25, 1990, and has circled the planet once every 95 minutes ever since. The telescope cost more than U.S. $2.5 billion to construct.

Just weeks into the mission, scientists became disappointed with the images being collected, as they seemed only marginally better than those captured by land-based telescopes. It soon became apparent that the Hubble's optical system was failing due to a distortion in the main mirror.

In December 1993, seven astronauts took 10 days to service the telescope and install the COSTAR, or Corrective Optics Space Telescope Axial Replacement. The resolution of images improved dramatically, instantly transforming the public perception of Hubble from an expensive joke to one of the most important pieces of astronomical equipment ever built. Among more than 400,000 observations made by Hubble are images of black holes, the birth and death of stars, and the most detailed picture of Mars ever taken.

Since its deployment, the Hubble space telescope was serviced by shuttle astronauts who updated or replaced equipment, ensuring the telescope remained on the cutting edge of technology. The last manned servicing mission was in March 2002 – future servicing missions were cancelled after the *Columbia* tragedy due to the high risk involved in carrying them out, but in 2005 NASA administrator Michael Griffin revised this decision, and plans are underway to service Hubble again before its mission ends around 2010.

April 25

DATE*line*

"It isn't where you came from, it's where you're going that counts." — ELLA FITZGERALD, SINGER

The Battle of Gallipoli began on this day in 1915 on what is now known as Anzac Cove, Turkey. While British troops landed at Cape Helles, the Australian and New Zealand Army Corps (ANZACs) were to alight at "Z Beach," a site north of Gaba Tepe on the Aegean coast, as a back-up to the main offensive. Unfortunately, bungled planning saw the ANZACs land 1.5 miles (2.4 km) north of their objective, before dawn on April 25. The pitch darkness concealed the fact that they were heading into unfamiliar territory – a narrow cove fronted by sheer ravines and rough terrain. Many battalions ran straight into a hail of bullets. Among those that died at Gallipoli, 8,709 were Australian, and 4,852 were New Zealanders – over one third of the total ANZAC forces sent to battle.

HISTORICAL EVENTS

1792 The first execution by guillotine occurs in France.
1859 Work begins on construction of the Suez Canal in Egypt. The 101-mile-long (162.5 km) artificial canal allows ships access from the Mediterranean Sea to the Indian Ocean via the Red Sea, rather than having to sail around the Cape of Good Hope, Africa.
1898 The United States declares war on Spain with the goal of ousting Spanish leadership in Cuba.
1915 ANZAC troops land in Gallipoli, Turkey (see above).
1953 Cambridge University scientists James Watson and Francis Crick announce the "secret of life," DNA. The "double helix" structure of DNA is the basis of all genetic information.
1983 Soviet leader Yuri Andropov invites an American schoolgirl to visit the U.S.S.R. after he reads her letter outlining her fear of nuclear war. She accepts and becomes America's youngest Ambassador.
2005 The final piece of the Obelisk of Axum, an ancient Ethiopian granite column, is returned to its homeland after being looted by the Italian Army in 1937.

DAY TO REMEMBER

National day Freedom Day (Portugal) Today is the anniversary of the Carnation Revolution of 1974, where many military insurgents put carnations in their gun barrels, to signify the peaceful overthrow of the Fascist Government in Portugal.

Births

1599 Oliver Cromwell, English lord
1710 James Ferguson, astronomer
1908 Edward R. Murrow, journalist
1911 Jack Ruby, killer of Lee Harvey Oswald
1917 Ella Fitzgerald, singer
1921 Karel Appel, painter
1940 Al Pacino, actor
1945 Björn Ulvaeus, singer
1969 Renée Zellweger, actress

Deaths

1644 Chongzhen, Emperor of China
1800 William Cowper, poet
1995 Ginger Rogers, dancer
2002 Lisa "Left Eye" Lopes, rap artist

April 26

"The secret of staying young is to live honestly, eat slowly, and lie about your age."
LUCILLE BALL

Births
- 121 C.E. Marcus Aurelius, Roman Emperor
- 1711 David Hume, philosopher
- 1812 Alfred Krupp, industrialist
- 1888 Anita Loos, writer
- 1889 Ludwig Wittgenstein, philosopher
- 1900 Charles Richter, geophysicist
- 1914 Bernard Malamud, writer
- 1938 Duane Eddy, musician
- 1961 Joan Chen, actress
- 1963 Jet Li, martial artist

Deaths
- 1970 Gypsy Rose Lee, actress
- 1976 Sid James, comedian
- 1989 Lucille Ball, actress and comedienne
- 2004 Hubert Selby Jr., writer

HISTORICAL EVENTS

- 1865 U.S. President Abraham Lincoln's assassin, John Wilkes Booth, is found hiding in a barn. He is shot dead by the cavalry.
- 1933 Nazi Germany's secret police force, the *Geheime Staatspolizei* (Gestapo), is formed.
- 1937 During the Spanish Civil War, a small town in the north of Spain, Guernica, is bombed by the Germans. Generalissimo Francisco Franco had agreed to the Luftwaffe testing their efficacy on the township.
- 1942 An explosion kills 1,549 miners at the Honkeiko Colliery in Manchuria.
- 1954 The Geneva Conference begins. Representatives from the U.S., Soviet Union, Great Britain, China, and France try to resolve problems in Asia – in particular French Indochina and Korea.
- 1962 The U.S. rocket *Ranger* lands on the far side of the Moon. It was intended that the craft send pictures back to Earth, but it suffered equipment failure.
- 1986 The world's worst nuclear disaster occurs at Chernobyl in the Ukraine (see right).
- 2005 Syria withdraws the last of its troops from Lebanon, after a 29-year occupation.

DAY TO REMEMBER

Religious day St. Trudpert's Day St. Trudpert (c. 644) was a seventh-century Irish missionary in Germany who was killed by a serf. The peasant had resented the hard work involved in clearing land for Trudpert's hermitage.

The Chernobyl nuclear disaster

On April 26, 1986, the worst nuclear accident in history took place at the Chernobyl nuclear plant in Pripyat in the Ukraine, a station housing four nuclear reactors.

At approximately 1:24 A.M. an explosion caused by steam build-up occurred in reactor number four. The blast tore off the reactor lid, and as superheated nuclear fuel met with oxygen from the atmosphere, a fire broke out.

Plant staff had been conducting an experiment on the reactor at the time of the incident, and there is evidence that proper safety procedures were not followed. Another contributing factor to the magnitude of damage caused was that the reactor was only partially contained – meaning that

if an accident were to occur, radioactive material could easily escape into the atmosphere. The fact that the reactor's control rods – which contributed to maintaining safe power levels – were not constructed of the appropriate materials also played a part in causing the accident.

The scale of the disaster was not immediately obvious to staff, with many engaging in a clean-up operation without protective clothing, which would eventually see many die of acute radiation poisoning in the coming weeks. Emergency fire crews who came to extinguish the flames met a similar fate – with 203 people being hospitalised due to exposure to radioactive materials, and 47 deaths.

It was not until two days after the accident that a committee sent to review the scene admitted the possible dangers and evacuated 50,000 people from Pripyat, with a total of around 300,000 people subsequently being permanently relocated. A radioactive exclusion zone exists in the Ukraine even today.

About 60 percent of the nuclear fallout from the leak fell on neighboring country Belarus, while a nuclear "plume" drifted as far afield as the parts of the eastern U.S. To halt further leakage of nuclear materials, the reactor was contained within a concrete sarcophagus, which is slowly deteriorating. Plans are underway to embed it in a second tomb.

The Chernobyl Forum, comprising the World Health Organization, the United Nations, and the International Atomic Energy Agency, believe the number of deaths related to the accident will be around 4,000 – including those who died immediately and those who will later die of cancer. Other sources believe the numbers are much higher – with Greenpeace estimating 67,000 deaths in Russia alone.

April 27

"Write it on your heart that every day is the best day in the year." — RALPH WALDO EMERSON

Democratic elections in South Africa

The first post-apartheid elections were held in South Africa on April 27, 1994, seeing black activist Nelson Mandela sworn in as President on May 10. His inauguration was a stark contrast to the 27 years he had spent jailed as a political prisoner for advocating the abolition of racial segregation.

During his imprisonment, Mandela urged his fellow revolutionaries to fight on, which ensured he would not be freed from Robben Island until 1990, at which time President F. W. de Klerk bowed to international pressure. From 1990 to 1993, South Africa was in turmoil as apartheid was legally abolished after a referendum. Far from being a peaceful transition, massacres took place across the nation, and the leader of the Communist Party, Chris Hine, was assassinated.

In 1994, the first democratic election in South Africa was conducted under the guidance of the Independent Election Commission. Nineteen political parties were represented. Almost 20 million votes were collected in more than 9,000 ballot stations over three days, starting on April 27 – of these, about 16 million participants had never voted before. Mandela's African National Congress party won 252 seats in the National Assembly, with 62.6 percent of the popular vote.

Mandela's election put an end to more than 300 years of white supremacy in South Africa. As the first black President of South Africa, he aided the transition from a minority rule to an open democracy. During his five years in office, he served to change international perceptions of his country. In 1999, he stepped down, succeeding his post to his former deputy Thabo Mbeki.

HISTORICAL EVENTS

1667 Blind and destitute poet John Milton sells the publishing rights to his epic *Paradise Lost* for £10.
1775 British Parliament passes the Tea Act, lowering tea tax and allowing the East India Company to monopolize the tea trade in America.
1865 A boiler malfunction causes the American steamboat *Sultana* to explode on the Mississippi River, killing 1,700 people. Most were recently emancipated Union soldiers on their way home after the end of the Civil War.
1941 German forces invade Athens during World War II.
1950 Racial groups are officially segregated in South Africa with the passing of the Group Areas Act.
1961 After 150 years of British rule, West Africa's Sierra Leone wins independence.
1992 Serbia and Montenegro become the Federal Republic of Yugoslavia.
1994 With the abolition of apartheid, the first fully democratic multi-racial elections are held in South Africa (see above).
2005 The Airbus A380 makes its maiden flight from Toulouse, France. It replaces the 747 jumbo jet as the world's largest passenger plane.

DAY TO REMEMBER

International day World Day of Design This day is observed by many countries in recognition of "the vital role of design in the public arena."

Births
1737 Edward Gibbon, historian
1759 Mary Wollstonecraft Shelley, writer
1791 Samuel Morse, inventor
1822 Ulysses S. Grant, eighteenth U.S. President
1840 Edward Whymper, mountain climber
1920 Edwin Morgan, poet
1927 Coretta Scott King, activist
1931 Igor Oistrakh, violinist
1951 Ace Frehley, musician (KISS)

Deaths
1656 Jan van Goyen, painter
1882 Ralph Waldo Emerson, essayist
1921 Arthur Mold, cricketer
1998 Carlos Casteneda, writer

April 28

"Progress is man's ability to complicate simplicity." THOR HEYERDAHL

HISTORICAL EVENTS

1789 There is mutiny on the HMS *Bounty* when Captain William Bligh's crew, led by Master's Mate Fletcher Christian, rebels. Bligh is cast off into the sea in a small boat and manages to navigate the Torres Strait to Timor using a pocket watch.

1920 Azerbaijan, a country in the Caucasus, joins the Soviet Union.

1945 Italian Communist partisans assassinate Fascist dictator Benito Mussolini, his mistress, and a group of loyal followers. They were caught as they were trying to flee to Switzerland.

1947 Norwegian marine biologist Thor Heyerdahl sets out from Peru on the raft *Kon-Tiki* to prove that Peruvians could have settled Polynesia. The journey to the Tuamotu Islands takes 101 days.

1969 Charles de Gaulle resigns as President of France after his proposals for constitutional reform are rejected by a majority of voters in a referendum.

1994 CIA double agent Aldrich Ames is jailed for life after pleading guilty to selling U.S. secrets to the Soviet Union, and later Russia.

1996 Gunman Martin Bryant opens fire at Port Arthur, a small tourist area in Tasmania, Australia, killing 35 people and wounding 37 more. His motive remains unknown, but he is currently serving a never-to-be-released life sentence.

2001 Billionaire Dennis Tito lifts off for the International Space Station (see below).

2003 Apple's iTunes music store opens, with customers downloading one million songs in the first week of business.

Births
- **1715** Franz Sparry, composer
- **1900** Jan Oort, astronomer
- **1908** Oskar Schindler, Austrian industrialist
- **1916** Ferruccio Lamborghini, car maker
- **1926** Harper Lee, writer
- **1928** Yves Klein, painter
- **1937** Saddam Hussein, Iraqi leader
- **1941** Ann-Margret, actress
- **1948** Terry Pratchett, author
- **1953** Kim Gordon, musician

Deaths
- **1192** Conrad of Montferrat, King of Jerusalem
- **1945** Benito Mussolini, Italian dictator
- **1992** Iceberg Slim, writer
- **1992** Francis Bacon, painter

DAY TO REMEMBER

Historical day Florifertum In ancient Rome, this day marked the beginning of *Florifertum*, or the Festival of Flowers, a celebration from late April to early May dedicated to the goddess Flora. The populace would dress in colorful garb to celebrate the beginning of the cycle of life.

Dennis Tito becomes the first "space tourist"

Billionaire businessman Dennis Tito became the first "space tourist" on April 28, 2001. Initially rejected by NASA, the Californian financier joined a Russian supply mission to the International Space Station, paying $20 million for the opportunity.

Initially, Tito was set to visit the Mir space station, but when this destination was decommissioned (and fell to Earth) he was offered a seat on board a *Soyuz* supply mission. That the 60-year-old would now be allowed to visit an international space station sparked a feud between Russian and American space agencies, as NASA had denied Tito's request because he was not a trained astronaut.

However, Tito was not completely unfamiliar with outer space. He earned a Bachelor of Science degree in Astronautics and Aeronautics from New York University, and in the 1960s he had been an engineer at the NASA/Caltech Jet Propulsion Laboratory.

After 900 hours of cosmonaut training, Tito's trip took just eight days. He described experiencing his "life's dream" as "a crossing point in my life."

April 29

"When we are no longer able to change a situation, we are challenged to change ourselves."
VIKTOR FRANKL, AUSTRIAN PSYCHOTHERAPIST INCARCERATED AT DACHAU

HISTORICAL EVENTS

1429 Seventeen-year-old French peasant Joan of Arc leads troops into the city of Orléans, which has been under siege by the English. By May 8, the English have retreated.
1770 Captain James Cook lands in Australia, in a cove he names Botany Bay.
1916 Irish nationalists surrender to the British in Dublin, ending the Easter Rebellion.
1945 Dachau is liberated by U.S. forces. It was the first concentration camp in Nazi Germany, having opened in 1933.
1967 Muhammad Ali is stripped of his boxing title after refusing to join the U.S. Army (see below).
1969 Jazz great Duke Ellington is awarded the Presidential Medal of Freedom, the highest civilian award in America.
1992 The Los Angeles race riots break out after a mainly white jury acquit police officers of beating African American Rodney King. The ensuing chaos results in up to 60 dead, 2,000 wounded, and U.S. $1 billion worth of damage.
1993 Queen Elizabeth II announces that she will open the doors to Buckingham Palace to the public for the first time. The £8 entrance fee is hoped to earn enough money to restore Windsor Castle, damaged by fire the previous year.
2002 The U.S. is voted back in to the United Nations Commission for Human Rights, after one year's expulsion for refusing to recognize the International Criminal Court.

Births

1863 William Randolph Hearst, newspaper publisher
1876 Empress Zauditu of Ethiopia
1893 Harold Urey, chemist and Nobel laureate
1899 Duke Ellington, musician
1901 Hirohito, Emperor of Japan
1931 Frank Auerbach, painter
1934 Otis Rush, musician
1954 Jerry Seinfeld, comedian
1958 Michelle Pfeiffer, actress
1970 Andre Agassi, tennis player

Deaths

1380 Catherine of Siena, saint
1768 Georg Brandt, chemist
1966 William Eccles, physicist
1980 Alfred Hitchcock, film director

DAY TO REMEMBER

National day Emperor's Birthday (Japan)
In 1948, a law was passed to create consecutive public holidays extending from this day into the beginning of May, incorporating Greenery Day, Boys' Day and Constitution Memorial Day. Many businesses shut down over this period.

On April 29, 1967, boxer Muhammad Ali was relieved of his boxing title after refusing induction into the U.S. Army, stating that it was "against the teachings of the Holy Koran." The Heavyweight Champion of the World was one of the most controversial conscientious objectors in the Vietnam War. Born Cassius Clay on January 17, 1942, Ali converted to Islam shortly after winning his first boxing title and maintained that he would not fight in any wars other than those "declared by Allah." Stripped of his title, Ali fought international opponents and non-title matches. He was not granted another boxing license in the United States until 1970, when he was granted the right to box in Georgia. The New York Supreme Court also ruled that he had been unjustly denied a license, by which time he was well on the way to a comeback.

April 30

DATE*line*

"Ninety-nine percent of the world's lovers are not with their first choice. That's what makes the jukebox play." — WILLIE NELSON, COUNTRY SINGER

HISTORICAL EVENTS

1483 Pluto moves inside Neptune's orbit, making it the planet furthest from the sun until mid-1503.

1803 France sells Louisiana to the United States for U.S. $15 million.

1938 Bugs Bunny makes his debut in the animated short film series *Porky's Hare Hunt*.

1945 Adolf Hitler kills himself in an underground bunker in Berlin (see right).

1973 U.S. President Richard Nixon appears on television admitting his administration is at fault for the Watergate scandal, but not accepting personal responsibility. He also announces the resignation of his key advisers.

1975 Communist forces gain control of Saigon and the Vietnam War officially ends.

1993 The World Wide Web is born. It is launched by CERN, the European Organization for Nuclear Research, who announce that it will be free for anyone to use.

1993 The world number-one women's tennis star Monica Seles is stabbed during a quarterfinal match in Hamburg. The perpetrator was a mentally unstable man who wanted her opponent, Steffi Graf, to regain her top ranking.

2003 Libya accepts responsibility for a 1998 terrorist attack in which a Pan Am flight was bombed over Lockerbie, Scotland, causing 270 deaths.

DAY TO REMEMBER

Traditional day Walpurgis Night Signaling the beginning of spring, this Viking festival used to be celebrated with night-time bonfires. It took on the name Walpurgis Night when Catholic St. Walburga became associated with the occasion.

Births
- 1602 William Lilly, astrologer
- 1662 Queen Mary II of England
- 1777 Carl Friedrich Gauss, physicist
- 1877 Alice B. Toklas, writer and lover of Gertrude Stein
- 1909 Queen Juliana of the Netherlands
- 1933 Willie Nelson, singer
- 1943 Bobby Vee, singer
- 1954 Jane Campion, film director
- 1956 Lars von Trier, film director
- 1982 Kirsten Dunst, actress

Deaths
- 1696 Robert Plot, naturalist
- 1883 Edouard Manet, painter
- 1982 Lester Bangs, journalist
- 1989 Sergio Leone, film director

Hitler commits suicide

Nazi Führer Adolf Hitler and his new wife Eva Braun committed suicide in his Berlin bunker on this day in 1945. At around midnight the day before, he married Braun in an underground ceremony, after which he wrote out a will declaring Martin Bormann his deputy. He also took the opportunity to expel former right-hand men Hermann Goering and Heinrich Himmler for perceived disloyalty – they had become concerned for their leader's mental state and had begun to doubt his ability to head the party in recent weeks.

Such measures were taken as Hitler conceded that the Third Reich was about to fall. The Führer and his closest aides had moved into the bunker – a series of subterranean rooms situated 56 feet(17 m) below the Reich Chancellory garden – on January 16, as Allied forces closed in. As well as having room for medical staff, aides, and a telephonist, the bunker housed exquisite furnishings and artworks salvaged from the Chancellory.

April 22–23 saw an exodus of most bunker staff, but Hitler chose to stay to the end. On April 30, Allied and Soviet troops raised their flags in the Reichstag and simultaneously moved into Berlin, prompting Hitler and Braun to swallow cyanide capsules. Fifteen minutes later, Hitler shot himself in the head. Afterwards, Bormann doused their bodies with gasoline and set fire to them. At some point that day propaganda minister Joseph Goebbels, his wife, and six children also committed suicide. One week later, Germany surrendered unconditionally, ending World War II.

DAYS TO REMEMBER *April*

1
April Fool's Day A day renowned – and sometimes feared – for the proliferation of practical jokes that people play on one another

2
International Children's Book Day Held on Hans Christian Andersen's birthday, teachers worldwide encourage their students to read

3
Feast Day for St. Mary of Egypt Mary existed on a diet of wild herbs in the Jordanian desert for almost fifty years

4
William Henry Harrison, ninth U.S. President, was born in 1841

5
Ch'ing Ming (Festival of Pure Brightness) This Chinese festival is celebrated 106 days after the winter solstice as a celebration of spring

8
Japanese Budchists celebrate this day as the birthday of Prince Siddhartha, the Guatama Buddha and founder of Buddhism

9
Feast of Glory Celebrated by people of the Baha'i faith

10
Feast Day of St. Michael de Sanctis Born in Catalonia, Spain, and died at just 35 years of age, having led a life of exemplary devotion

11
Feast Day of Martyr Antipas Bishop of Pergamos, one of the "seven churches of the Apocalypse" in the Greek Orthodox faith

12
Yuri's Night Commemorates the first human being in space, Yuri Gagarin

15
Tipsa Diena A minor festival in ancient Latvian mythology to signify when fields should start being ploughed

16
Feast Day for St. Bernadette A peasant girl who reported many visions of "a lady," whom the Catholic Church confirmed to be the Virgin Mary

17
Benjamin Franklin, U.S. statesman and inventor, died in 1790

18
Patriot's Day (U.S.) The anniversary of the start of the American War of Independence in 1775

19
Easter Sunday According to the Gregorian calendar, Easter Sunday falls on this date more than any other throughout history.

22
International Earth Day Designed to raise awareness about pollution and its effects on the environment

23
National Beer Day (Germany) Duke Wilhelm IV passed an edict in 1516 stating that beer should contain nothing but malt, yeast, hops, and water

24
Republic Day (Gambia) In 1965, The Gambia, the smallest country in Africa, became independent of British rule

25
Freedom Day (Portugal) Anniversary of the Carnation Revolution of 1974

26
Feast Day of St. Trudpert A missionary in Germany, killed by a serf who resented the hard work involved in clearing land for Trudpert's hermitage

29
Public Holiday in Japan to mark the anniversary of Emperor Showa in 1901

30
Walpurgis Night (Scandanavia) Viking festival to signal the start of spring

7
World Health Day Celebrated by 191 countries worldwide to highlight global health issues

14
New Year's Day in Sri Lanka and parts of India

21
The star sign of Taurus begins

28
Florifertum or Festival of Flowers The first day of a celebration from late April to early May dedicated to the goddess Flora

Top Right Yuri's Night, April 12
Right International Children's Book Day, April 2

MAY

"What potent blood hath modest May." RALPH W. EMERSON

Mt. Everest, the world's highest mountain, was famously conquered for the first time by New Zealander Sir Edmund Hillary and sherpa Tenzing Norgay in May, 1953.

May

May, the fifth month in the Gregorian calendar, has 31 days along with six of the other Gregorian months. During May in the Northern Hemisphere, spring is in full bloom and is making way for summer; in the Southern Hemisphere, mild autumn days are being overtaken by the winter cold. This month starts with Beltane, one of the cross-quarter days of the calendar, which falls halfway between the Northern Hemisphere's summer solstice and spring equinox.

Gemini star sign and scene of falconry from *Calendar and Book of Hours,* from fifteenth-century France. May begins in the sign of Taurus and ends in the sign of Gemini.

SPECIAL DATES

May 1 is May Day – a day for workers to unite as well as a day to welcome summer in the Northern Hemisphere.

Mother's Day in the U.S., Australia, and New Zealand is on the second Sunday on May.

This fifteenth-century Bohemian fresco depicts the month of May from one of the Cycle of Months. Throughout history, May in the Northern Hemisphere has signaled the return to warmer months and an abundance of spring growth and rebirth.

IT IS GENERALLY ACKNOWLEDGED that the month of May is named in honor of the Roman goddess Maia. In Roman mythology, Maia was an earth goddess. As with her Greek counterpart, the Roman Maia symbolized youth, life, rebirth, love, and sexuality. She was also held as the goddess of plants and of the spring, and was worshiped as a "good mother." To honor her, the Romans held the celebration of *Floralia*. Floralia was a time of great merriment and rejoicing in ancient Rome. During the festival, Romans would cast off their habitual white robes for more colorful garments, especially green ones. They would also deck themselves and everything around them in flowers, then engage in revelrous activities.

In medieval poetry and romance, the month of May is associated with love and nature. May celebrations were an invitation for all of humanity to join in. The English poet Geoffrey Chaucer writes in his poem "Court of Love" that early on May Day "goeth forth all the court, both most and least, to fetch the flowers fresh, and branch and bloom." In northern parts, May Day signaled the end of the winter months and the delight of ensuing warmth and nature's renewal.

Seasonal festivities

The festival of the Beltane is a significant part of celebrations in Europe, beginning on April 30 and ending on the eve of May 1. As summer begins, the weather becomes warmer, the plant world blossoms, and an exuberant mood prevails. This time has also been associated with unabashed sexuality and promiscuity, with young people spending the night in the woods "a-maying" and dancing around the maypole until the morning. The lyrics of the lighthearted tune by legendary Lerner and Lowe capture this side of May's mood: "It's May, it's May, the lusty month of May…those dreary vows that ev'ryone

People raise the maypole on May 1 as part of summer celebrations in several countries, notably those with Germanic heritage such as the Stamberg District in Bavaria, Germany.

May birthflower

The sweetly perfumed lily of the valley is the birthflower for May. Said to represent new happiness, humility, and a completeness in life, this pretty plant with dainty white bell-shaped flowers has been the national flower of Finland since the early 1980s. It is traditonally associated with May 1, especially in France where the flower is sold in the streets on that day.

takes, ev'ryone breaks. Ev'ryone makes divine mistakes! The lusty month of May!"

Despite the congeniality of the month, it is also an old belief that May is an unlucky month in which to be married. This superstition, current even today, is Roman in origin and was mentioned by the poet Ovid who noted that lovers should wait until the auspicious month of June before getting married.

The maypole is a tall wooden pole that is traditionally erected in May to celebrate the arrival of summer in the Northern Hemisphere. In Germanic and Scandinavian countries, several long, colored ribbons are suspended from the top, festooned with flowers, draped in greenery, and strapped with large circular wreaths. The British version is a comparatively recent development and is less decorative and smaller. Usually placed in the village green, children perform dances around the maypole, weaving among one another while holding the ribbons to create striking patterns.

The first day of May is celebrated around the world as a day of solidarity among workers. May Day, which established itself after the Haymarket riots of 1886 in Chicago, acknowledges the social and economic successes of the labor movement throughout the world. Workers take to the streets in peaceful marches to stand up for workers' rights, such as the eight-hour day, and to mark what has become the traditional socialist holiday.

Beltane is not just related to celebrations. In pre-Christian times it also marked the beginning of the pastoral summer season when the herds of livestock were driven out to summer pastures and mountain grazing lands. The lighting of bonfires on the evening of Beltane on mountains and hills was one of the main activities of the festival.

Japanese workers carrying red cards and placards during a May Day procession in 1948 at the Emperor's Palace, Tokyo, to protest against low wages and inflation.

Customs and culture

The Filipino festival called *Santacruzan*, a beauty pageant held during the *Flores de Mayo* festival each May, is celebrated by Filipino communities in other countries as well. This procession took place in Taiwan.

May celebrations that revolve around the harvest are not limited to Europe and North America. The Buddhist Plowing Festival is celebrated in May, usually in Asia. When the moon is half-full, two white oxen pull a gold-painted plow, followed by four girls dressed in white, who scatter rice seeds from gold and silver baskets. The Plowing Festival celebrates the Buddha's first moment of enlightenment, which is said to have happened when the Buddha was seven years old, when he had gone with his father to watch the plowing. In present-day Thailand this celebration is known as *Raek Na* and is carried out each year to bring good fortune to all plants, and to boost morale.

In northeastern Thailand, locals hold a festival in May called *Bun Bang Fai*, or the Rocket Festival, which is an unusual blend of the sacred and the profane. Celebrated with dance, song, music, and revelry – and, of course, skyrockets – it serves to assure abundant rainfall, which guarantees a good harvest and the welfare of the villagers. The celebration involves launching huge homemade rockets across an empty farm field for the delight of local spectators. The rocket launching itself is competitive, with prizes given for the best explosion and the greatest distance – sometimes close to a mile.

In the Philippines, flowers are in full bloom in May, and among the many festivals held during the month is the *Flores de Mayo* or Flowers of May. In this predominantly Catholic country, the festival is dedicated to the Virgin Mary, and each of the 31 days of the month is a floral tribute to the virtues of the Virgin. During the festival children carry baskets of flowers in the church aisles every day, and church altars are festooned with flower arrangements. The fragrance of many flowers floats in the air, including the scent of kalachuchi, rose, and the sampaguita – the Philippines' national flower.

The highlight of the month-long festival is the *Santacruzan*, the "Queen of Filipino Festivals." While the Flores is by itself a Catholic festival, the Santacruzan is a beauty pageant where the young women or *sagalas* walk in procession with escorts beneath hand-carried arches made of bamboo and adorned with flowers. The sagalas each play a role that showcases the accolades of the Lady and as the procession progresses, devotees follow along the streets. The procession finally ends at the local church where a celebratory Mass is held.

While the Virgin Mary is celebrated in the Philippines, mothers across the world are also celebrated on Mother's Day, which is usually the second Sunday in May. In 1907 the idea

Prague in the Czech Republic is the place to dance and make merry in May during the World Roma Festival, which brings together Romany culture and traditions from Roma gypsies around the world.

of a day set apart every year to honor mothers was initiated by Anna Jarvis of Philadelphia, who suggested the wearing of carnations on the second Sunday in May to celebrate motherhood. Her enthusiastic campaign for a nationwide observance attracted so much public support that American President Woodrow Wilson issued a proclamation designating the second Sunday in May 1914 the first national Mother's Day. However, in Mexico, Mother's Day is always celebrated on May 10.

May has not always been associated with the good things in life. In Japan there is an expression called "May sickness" or rather "May depression" (*gogatsubyo*). This encompasses a diverse set of symptoms, caused by entering the month of May. The beginning of April marks the start of the school year, the university semester, and the fiscal year in Japan, and at that time, most graduates enter companies and start working.

The cherry blossom season also starts around this time in Japan and gets huge publicity because it symbolizes the "new beginning of life" after the long season of winter. Many younger people enter new surroundings – be it school, university, or workplace – however after a month, they still haven't become accustomed to their new environment and in May, start longing for the places they know. This feeling of being lost and lonely, combined with the hot and rainy weather, makes for a proper depression, called the May sickness.

On a happier note, in the Czech Republic the World Roma Festival or *Khamoro* is held every May in the nation's capital, Prague. Khamoro is an international gypsy Roma festival that draws international Roma musicians from across the world to the streets and clubs of Prague.

Similarly in Denmark, an annual carnival takes place in the northern city of Aalborg in the last weekend in May. Attracting over 100,000 people, it has become northern Europe's largest carnival parade. On the Friday before the weekend, the Battle of Carnival Bands takes place, with colorful processions through the city when bands compete to be the leading carnival group. During the carnival the streets are filled with brightly dressed people reveling in the spring mood. Concerts take place day and night and the carnival ends with a grand finale fireworks display on the harbor.

May birthstone

Emerald is considered the birthstone for May and is the green variety of beryl. Thought by many people to instil wisdom and patience, this precious stone has also symbolized love and fidelity throughout time. Its rich green color reflects the new growth of springtime. Ancient civilizations depicted emerald as a symbol of spring and rebirth in their art.

May 1

"The art of leadership is saying no, not yes. It is very easy to say yes." — TONY BLAIR

HISTORICAL EVENTS

1707 Scotland and England are united by an Act of Parliament. England, Wales, and Scotland are united to form Great Britain.

1786 Mozart's opera *The Marriage of Figaro* premieres in Vienna, Austria.

1851 The Great Council Exhibition, the first-ever World's Fair, opens in the grand Crystal Palace in London, England.

1931 The 102-story Empire State Building opens in New York City.

1941 Orson Welles' film *Citizen Kane* debuts at the RKO Palace in New York.

1964 The first BASIC program runs on a computer at Dartmouth College. BASIC was the first multi-purpose programming language that anyone could use, at a time when computers relied on customized programs written by scientists.

1967 Elvis Presley marries Priscilla Beaulieu in Las Vegas (see below).

1997 Britain's Labour Party led by Tony Blair wins a landslide victory in a national election.

1997 On the TV show *Ellen*, 42 million viewers see the main character, played by Ellen DeGeneres, announce that she is a lesbian. It is one of the highest-rating episodes in the duration of the show.

Births
- **1852** Calamity Jane, Wild West performer
- **1913** Walter Susskind, conductor
- **1944** Rita Coolidge, singer
- **1946** Joanna Lumley, actress
- **1946** John Woo, director, producer, writer, and actor
- **1954** Ray Parker Jr., singer and songwriter

Deaths
- **1873** David Livingstone, physician and explorer
- **1945** Paul Joseph Goebbels, Nazi Minister of Propaganda
- **1994** Ayrton Senna, grand prix driver

DAYS TO REMEMBER

Religious day Bealtaine In the Pagan wheel of the year, May begins with the summer festival of Bealtaine in the Northern Hemisphere.

Religious day St. Philip's Day and St. James' Day Philip and James were two of the disciples of Jesus. St. James' mother, Mary, was one of those at the cross and tomb.

International day May Day A holiday celebrating workers, this date is often synonymous with socialism and communism, although May Day is an official Government labor holiday in many countries across the world.

On May 1, 1967, Elvis Presley (32) married Priscilla Anne Beaulieu (21) at the Aladdin Hotel in Las Vegas. Their daughter, Lisa Marie Presley, was born nine months later to the day, on February 1, 1968. The couple had met eight-and-a-half years prior when Elvis was on his tour of duty to Germany and Priscilla, 14 years old, was living in Wiesbaden while her stepfather, Paul Beaulieu, was serving in the U.S. Air Force. Their marriage lasted six years. They separated in February of 1972 and divorced "amicably" in October, 1973.

DATE*line*

May 2

"Justice is incidental to law and order." J. EDGAR HOOVER

A winning play

On this day in 1949, Arthur Miller's *Death of a Salesman* won him the Pulitzer Prize. In the same year, the play won the Tony Award and was acknowledged not only as a work which brought the playwright international fame, but also as a foremost accomplishment of modern American theater.

The story centers on the tragic tale of a 60-year-old salesman named Willy Loman who, when fired from his job, loses his grip on reality and his will to live. It comments on the American Dream; the individual's investment, and belief in it, and ultimate disappointment when the outcome is unattained. In the end, Willy commits suicide in his car, believing the insurance money will give his family a more financially secure, and therefore better existence. In Willy's mind, he is worth more to his family dead than alive.

Many have commented that the context of the play mirrors some of Miller's own experiences as a boy growing up in New York City during the 1930s. The Miller family fortune was lost in the Depression and the experience of sudden poverty strongly influenced his views of the modern "insecure" American existence. Among his other famous works is the politically charged *The Crucible*, which was first produced in 1953 and adapted twice for film. Arthur Miller (pictured on the right, with director Elia Kazan) died on February 10, 2005, and is remembered as one of the most significant American writers of the twentieth century.

HISTORICAL EVENTS

1887 Reverend Hannibal W. Goodwin applies for the patent on his invention of celluloid photographic film.
1945 As World War II draws to a close in Europe, German forces in the capital surrender to the Soviet Army, ending the Battle of Berlin.
1949 Arthur Miller wins the Pulitzer Prize for *Death of a Salesman* (see above).
1969 The *Queen Elizabeth 2* ocean liner takes its maiden voyage. The *QE2* remained the Cunard Lines' flagship vessel until 2004.
1994 At the conclusion of Souths Africa's first democratic election, Nelson Mandela claims victory over President F.W. de Klerk.
1998 Cambodian refugees enter Thailand as Government troops declare that they have nearly destroyed the Khmer Rouge.

DAYS TO REMEMBER

Religious day St. Augustin Schoeffer's Day A French saint in the Catholic Church, St. Augustin was a missionary to IndoChina and was martyred in 1851.

Religious day Yashodhara's Day In India, this day honors Prince Siddhartha's wife. She became a Buddhist nun when Siddhartha (Buddha) attained enlightenment.

Births
1729 Catherine the Great of Russia
1860 Theodor Herzl, Zionist
1892 Manfred von Richthofen, the Red Baron
1903 Benjamin Spock, pediatrician
1921 Satyajit Ray, filmmaker
1969 Brian Lara, cricketer

Deaths
1519 Leonardo da Vinci, artist and scientist
1957 Joseph R. McCarthy, Republican politican
1972 J. Edgar Hoover, head of the FBI
1999 Oliver Reed, actor

May 3

"Moses dragged us for forty years through the desert to bring us to the one place in the Middle East where there was no oil." — GOLDA MEIR

HISTORICAL EVENTS

- **1923** After almost 27 hours in the air, John McCready and Oakley Kelly land in California, completing the first nonstop flight across the U.S.
- **1937** Margaret Mitchell wins a Pulitzer Prize for her novel *Gone with the Wind*.
- **1960** The musical *The Fantastics* opens in New York. It closes on January 13, 2002, after 17,162 shows.
- **1973** The Sears Tower in Chicago is completed, making it the world's tallest building at a total of 1,707 feet (520 m) high.
- **1988** The Reagan administration acknowledges the use of astrological advice in scheduling the President's diary (see below).
- **1999** Bill Gates, owner of Microsoft, pledges $25 million over five years to help develop a vaccine against AIDS.
- **2000** The trial opens in the Netherlands of two alleged Libyan intelligence agents accused of blowing up Pan Am Flight 103 over Lockerbie, Scotland, in 1988.
- **2001** The UN War Crimes Tribunal issues an arrest warrant for Serbian Nationalist leader Slobodan Milosevic.

Births
- **1469** Niccolò Machiavelli, philosopher
- **1898** Golda Meir, Israeli Prime Minister
- **1904** Bing Crosby, singer and actor
- **1906** Mary Astor, actress
- **1920** "Sugar" Ray Robinson, middleweight boxer
- **1928** James Brown, singer
- **1936** Engelbert Humperdinck, singer

Deaths
- **1926** Napoleon V. Bonaparte, pretender to the French throne
- **1965** Howard Spring, author
- **1989** Christine Jorgensen, first transsexual

DAY TO REMEMBER

Religious day St. Theodosius of Kiev's Day St. Theodosius was an eleventh-century saint and is considered today to have been the first to introduce monasticism in the Russian Orthodox Church.

Presidency by the stars

On this day in 1988 the White House, the office of President Ronald Reagan, acknowledged that the First Lady, Nancy Reagan, had used astrological advice in scheduling the President's diary. In his memoir, *For the Record*, former White House Chief of Staff Donald Regan revealed the extent of the First Lady's reliance on a San Francisco astrologer, later identified as Joan Quigley.

Regan claimed that the First Lady's faith in the astrologer's pronouncements led to the "random factor in the Reagan presidency" and claimed that at times, the President was a virtual prisoner in the White House. Both Reagans (pictured right) had always been superstitious and in his 1965 autobiography, *Where's the Rest of Me?*, Reagan described their obsession with syndicated horoscopes.

In 1981 Quigley showed the First Lady how astrological readings could have foretold that on or around March 30, 1981, would be extremely dangerous for the President. On that day John Hinckley Jr. made an assassination attempt on, and wounded, the President. From then on, the First Lady, obsessed with her husband's safety, was convinced of Quigley's power to protect him. It was reported that the President's diary was color-coded according to the astrologer's advice. Quigley was later to write a book entitled *What Does Joan Say? My Seven Years as White House Astrologer to Nancy and Ronald Reagan*.

DATE*line*

May 4

"I never thought I'd land in pictures with a face like mine." AUDREY HEPBURN

On May 4, 1979, Margaret Thatcher, leader of the Conservative Party, made history by becoming Britain's first ever female prime minister. On the steps of the Prime Minister's office, Number 10 Downing Street, she quoted from St. Francis of Assisi: "Where there is discord, may we bring harmony. Where there is error, may we bring truth. Where there is doubt, may we bring faith. And where there is despair, may we bring hope."

HISTORICAL EVENTS

1626 Dutch explorer Peter Minuit lands on what is now Manhattan Island.
1715 A French manufacturer debuts the first folding umbrella.
1932 Mobster Al Capone, convicted of income tax evasion, goes to jail in Atlanta. Still capable of running his business dealings from inside prison, he is moved to Alcatraz.
1970 Four students are killed by guardsmen at a Kent State University student rally against the Vietnam War.
1979 Margaret Thatcher becomes Britain's first female prime minister (see above).
1994 Israeli Prime Minister Yitzhak Rabin and PLO leader Yasser Arafat sign a historic accord on Palestinian autonomy which grants self-rule in the Gaza Strip and Jericho.
1997 After losing to world chess champion Garry Kasparov the year before, and undergoing major upgrades, IBM's Deep Blue computer defeats Kasparov.
2000 The "I LOVE YOU" e-mail virus hits millions of computers around the world, causing more than $2 billion in damage.

DAY TO REMEMBER

Religious day St. Florian's Day The patron saint of fire fighting, St. Florian was a Roman soldier who converted to Christianity and was burned alive rather than renounce his faith.

Births
1826 Frederick Church, artist
1882 Sylvia Pankhurst, historian and feminist
1928 Hosni Mubarak, Egyptian President
1929 Audrey Hepburn, actress
1939 Amos Oz, author
1958 Keith Haring, artist

Deaths
1969 F. Osbert S. Sitwell, poet
1980 Josip Broz Tito, leader of Yugoslavia
1984 Diana Dors, actress
1995 Louis Krasner, violinist
1997 Alvy Moore, actor and producer

May 5

"From each according to his ability, to each, according to his need." — KARL MARX

HISTORICAL EVENTS

1891 Carnegie Hall (then named Music Hall) has its opening night in New York with Tchaikovsky as the guest conductor.
1893 Panic hits the New York Stock Exchange, causing many European investors to withdraw from their U.S. interests, and a severe depression ensues. About 500 banks and 15,000 companies go bankrupt as a result of the crash.
1961 Alan Shepard, flying the *Freedom 7* capsule as part of the Mercury space exploration program, becomes the first American to travel in space.
1962 The *West Side Story* soundtrack goes to number one in the U.S. and stays there for 54 weeks.
1979 *Voyager 1* passes Jupiter, 19 months after being launched from Earth. At the time of printing, it is the fastest-moving artificial object from Earth, traveling at more than 10 miles per second (16 km/s) relative to the Sun.
1980 A siege at the Iranian Embassy in London ends as British commandos and police storm the building.
1987 The U.S. Congress opens hearings into the Iran–Contra affair (see below).
1996 The body of former CIA Director William E. Colby is found on a riverbank eight days after he had disappeared.

Births
1813 Soren Kierkegaard, philosopher and theologian
1818 Karl Marx, philosopher
1908 Rex Harrison, actor
1942 Tammy Wynette, singer
1943 Michael Palin, actor and screenwriter

Deaths
1821 Napoleon Bonaparte, Emperor of France
1981 Bobby Sands, IRA hunger-striker
1983 John Williams, actor
1992 Jean-Claude Pascal, actor

DAYS TO REMEMBER

Religious day St. Jutta's Day Born in 1200, this patron saint of Prussia is venerated for donating her property to the poor and caring for the sick.

National day El Cinco de Mayo (The Fifth of May) (Mexico) This national celebration is also widely celebrated in the U.S. It commemorates the Mexican victory at the Battle of Puebla on May 5, 1862, over the French Expeditionary Forces.

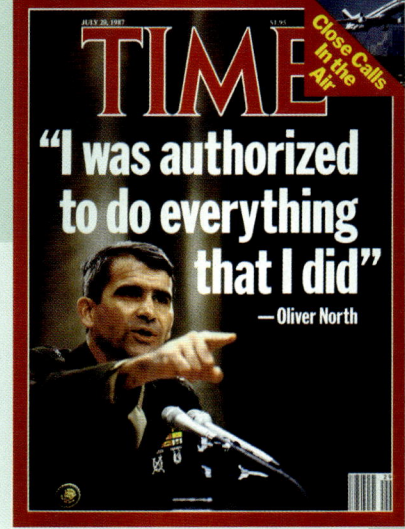

The Iran-Contra scandal

On May 5, 1987, congressional hearings opened into the Iran-Contra affair – a secret arrangement to provide funds to the Nicaraguan Contra rebels from profits gained by selling arms to Iran. President Ronald Reagan's Republican administration wanted to aid the Contras, who were conducting a guerrilla war against the Sandinista Government of Nicaragua. The administration also wanted to pacify "moderates" within the Iranian Government in order to secure the release of American hostages held by pro-Iranian groups in Lebanon.

However, the Democratic-controlled Congress enacted legislation that prohibited any Government agency from providing military aid to the contras from December 1983 to September 1985. The Reagan administration circumvented these limitations by using the National Security Council (NSC), which was not explicitly covered by the law, to arrange secret military aid to the Contras. Under Robert McFarlane and later John Poindexter the NSC raised funds for the Contras; the operation was directed by NSC staffer Marine Lt. Col. Oliver North.

McFarlane and North were also involved in the shipment of arms to Iran despite a U.S. trade and arms embargo. When the scandal broke in November 1986, Poindexter resigned and North was fired. A subsequent presidential commission was critical of the NSC, while the congressional hearings uncovered a web of official deception, mismanagement, and illegality.

Criminal convictions resulted for McFarlane, North, and Poindexter. However, North's and Poindexter's were vacated because of immunity agreements. Reagan and Vice-President George Bush both claimed to have been unaware of the affair and no evidence was found to link them to any crime.

May 6

DATEline

"Law is born from despair of human nature." — JOSE ORTEGA Y GASSET

On May 6, 1937, the German zeppelin airship LZ 129, known as the *Hindenburg*, burst into flames on arrival at Lakehurst, New Jersey, U.S. Of the 97 passengers and crew, 35 perished, as well as a member of the ground crew. It and sister airship LZ 130 were the largest aircraft built in history, at more than three times the length of a 747. The radio witness report by Hebert Morrison – which included his famous quotation "Oh, the humanity!" – is one of the most emotional and compelling reports of a disaster ever broadcast, and the dramatic newsreel and photographs effectively spelled the end of the airship as a form of transport.

HISTORICAL EVENTS

1682 King Louis XIV, after extensive renovations, moves his court and the Government from Paris to his chateau at Versailles, France.
1889 The Eiffel Tower is officially opened, marking the start of the *Exposition Universelle*. The tower had originally been intended to stand for only 20 years, but its rise to iconic status ensured its future.
1914 The British House of Lords rejects women's suffrage.
1937 The *Hindenburg* crashes on arrival at Lakehurst, New Jersey (see above).
1954 Roger Bannister becomes the first person to run a mile in less than four minutes. His 3:59.4 record is broken by Australian John Landy just 46 days later.
1981 Maya Ying Lin's design for the Vietnam Veterans' Memorial, popularly known as The Wall of D.C., is chosen from a total of 1,421 entries. Lin, then 21, had originally designed the memorial as a student project.
1994 Britain's Queen Elizabeth II and French President François Mitterand formally open the Channel Tunnel between their countries. The 31-mile (50-km) long tunnel is exceeded in length only by Japan's Seikan Tunnel.
2001 In Syria, Pope John Paul II prays in the Great Umayyad Mosque, the first time a pontiff ever visits and prays in a Muslim mosque.

Births
1856 Sigmund Freud, psychoanalyst
1883 Jose Ortega y Gasset, philosopher and author
1895 Rudolph Valentino, actor
1915 Orson Welles, actor, director, and writer
1953 Tony Blair, U.K. Prime Minister
1961 George Clooney, actor

Deaths
1862 Henry David Thoreau, writer
1987 William J. Casey, CIA Director
1992 Marlene Dietrich, actress and singer
1994 Fred Sadoff, actor

DAY TO REMEMBER

Religious day Inghean Bhuidhe's Day In Celtic mythology, Inghean Bhuidhe was originally the "yellow-haired girl" associated with the harvest and summer. She was the goddess of ripening and fertility, but after Christianization in Ireland she was turned into a saint and her feast day is celebrated on this day.

May 7

"Take away love and our Earth is a tomb." — ROBERT BROWNING

HISTORICAL EVENTS

- **1663** The Theatre Royal in Drury Lane, London, opens.
- **1915** The British Cunard ocean liner *Lusitania*, on a voyage from New York to Liverpool, sinks off the cost of Ireland after being struck by a German U-boat.
- **1941** Glenn Miller and His Orchestra record "Chattanooga Choo Choo," which is to become the first gold record in history.
- **1945** Germany formally surrenders to the Allied forces, marking the end of World War II in Europe (see below).
- **1954** The French lose the Battle of Dien Bien Phu in Vietnam after 55 days, effectively bringing the First Indochina War to a close. Three years later, the Second Indochina War – better known as the Vietnam War – begins.
- **1995** Jacques Chirac, the conservative mayor of Paris, wins France's presidency.
- **1998** The $34.7 billion merger of Daimler-Benz and Chrysler Corporation is confirmed. At the time of the event, it is the largest industrial merger in history.

Births
- **1812** Robert Browning, poet
- **1901** Gary Cooper, actor
- **1909** Edwin H. Land, inventor
- **1919** Eva "Evita" Peron, First Lady of Argentina
- **1943** Peter Carey, writer

Deaths
- **1825** Antonio Salieri, composer
- **1970** Carlos Estrada, composer
- **1994** Clement Greenberg, art critic
- **2000** Douglas Fairbanks Jr., actor
- **2006** Richard Carleton, journalist

DAY TO REMEMBER

Religious day St. Nil Sorsky's Day This Russian Orthodox saint was a leader of the Russian medieval movement that opposed ecclesiastic land ownership in the fifteenth century.

The war in Europe ends

This day in 1945 marked the end of World War II in Europe, when Germany formally surrendered to the Allied forces. The global military conflict took more than 40 million lives between 1939 and 1945 and was the largest and deadliest war in history. The following day, May 8, was declared Victory in Europe Day, or VE Day, and has become renowned for the spontaneous bursts of public jubilation that occurred.

Massive celebrations took place across the world. In London more than a million people massed at landmarks including Trafalgar Square and Buckingham Palace. King George VI, Queen Elizabeth, and the Prime Minister, Winston Churchill, appeared on the balcony of the Palace to cheering crowds. Similar celebrations took place in the U.S., notably in Times Square, New York. President Harry Truman dedicated the victory to the memory of his predecessor, Franklin D. Roosevelt, who had died less than a month earlier.

The Allies had agreed to mark May 9, 1945, as VE Day, but western journalists broke the news of Germany's surrender prematurely, precipitating the earlier celebration. The Soviet Union kept to the agreed date, and Russia and other former Soviet states still commemorate the end of World War II in Europe on May 9. Also known as the Great Patriotic War in Russia, the day is celebrated in Moscow each year with a traditional military parade in Red Square.

May 8

DATE*line*

"There was no difference between the behavior of a god and the operations of pure chance."

THOMAS PYNCHON

Births
- 1899 Friedrich August von Hayek, economist
- 1906 Roberto Rossellini, film director
- 1937 Thomas Pynchon, novelist
- 1970 Michael Bevan, cricketer

Deaths
- 1880 Gustave Flaubert, novelist
- 1976 Ulrike Meinhof, leader of the Red Army Faction
- 1987 Pam Ewing, character on *Dallas* played by Victoria Principal
- 1988 Robert A. Heinlein, writer
- 1994 George Peppard, actor

HISTORICAL EVENTS

- **1660** The son of the late Charles I is proclaimed King of England, ending 11 years of civil war.
- **1947** The House Un-American Activities Committee (HUAC) convenes in Hollywood to investigate communists in the film industry.
- **1958** Unrest breaks out among segregationalists in Little Rock when Ernest Green becomes the first African American to graduate from an Arkansas public school. President Eisenhower orders the 101st Airborne Division of the National Guard to take charge of the situation.
- **1963** Sean Connery appears as James Bond in *Dr. No*, the first instalment in the Bond film franchise (see below).
- **1967** Champion boxer Muhammad Ali is indicted for refusing induction into the U.S. Army.
- **1980** Almost two hundred years after Edward Jenner discovered the vaccination for smallpox, the World Health Organization (WHO) declares that the disease has been eradicated.
- **1984** The Soviet Union announces it will not participate in the Summer Olympics planned for Los Angeles.
- **1996** South Africa approves a National Constitution that guarantees equal rights for all races.

The first time "Bond. James Bond" was heard by U.S. audiences was on May 8, 1963. Sean Connery, a relative unknown, debuted as the British secret agent in the original screen adaptation of author Ian Fleming's series of novels. In what would become classic "James Bond 007" behavior, he managed to kill the villain and get the girl, Honey Ryder, played by the defining Bond Girl, Swiss actress Ursula Andress.

May 9

"The darkest places in hell are reserved for those who maintain their neutrality in times of moral crisis." — DANTE ALIGHIERI

HISTORICAL EVENTS

1754 The first American newspaper cartoon is published in Benjamin Franklin's *Pennsylvania Gazette*.

1960 The U.S. Food and Drug Administration (FDA) approves a pill for birth control use. It goes on sale two days later (see below).

1962 A ruby laser beam is successfully bounced off the Moon for the first time by Louis Smullin and Giorgio Foccio from the Massachusetts Institute of Technology.

1978 The body of former Italian Prime Minister Aldo Moro, who had been abducted by the Red Brigades, is found in a car in the center of Rome.

1980 The SS *Summit Venture* collides with the Sunshine Skyway bridge in Florida during a storm. A large section of the bridge collapses and 35 people are killed.

1997 An Australian study reports that some mice, after prolonged exposure to cellular phone radiation, showed an increase in lymphoma cancer.

2006 Two miners, Todd Russell and Brant Webb, are freed after being trapped underground for 14 days in a goldmine at Beaconsfield, Australia.

Births
- **1265** Dante Alighieri, poet
- **1934** Alan Bennett, playwright and actor
- **1936** Albert Finney, actor
- **1936** Glenda Jackson, actress
- **1949** Billy Joel, singer and pianist

Deaths
- **1903** Paul Gauguin, artist
- **1966** Alfred Mendelsohn, composer
- **1986** Tensing Norgay, mountain climber
- **1993** Freya Stark, author

DAY TO REMEMBER

International day Europe Day This day is celebrated in Europe to mark the Schuman Declaration of 1950, which first proposed the creation of what is now known as the European Union.

Sex and drugs rolled into one

The psychedelic 1960s are synonymous with sex and drugs. In May 1960, America mass marketed its first oral contraceptive, Enovid. Some say that when the FDA approved the birth control pill on May 9, 1960, it helped prompt the sexual revolution.

Suddenly, sex and drugs were combined in a single pill. Enovid's pharmaceutical creator, G. D. Searle and Company, was initially unconvinced that healthy women would take a drug on a daily basis solely to prevent pregnancy and originally applied for U.S. Government approval of the drug as a treatment for gynecological complaints. Yet, after only a year, a reported one million women were using "The Pill" in the U.S. alone. By 1965 more than five million women were taking the drug despite its very high doses of estrogen and progesterone which caused an array of side effects.

The net result meant women were in control of their own bodies chemically, which in turn ensured the next stage of female independence. Until the 1960s, women's lives had been obstructed from further development in the workplace due to the demands of pregnancy and child rearing. Feminist historians have often referred to the contraceptive pill as the single most important technological achievement in the twentieth century. It transformed the structure of society by redefining the social and economic roles of women.

May 10

DATE*line*

"Making peace, I have found, is much harder than making war." — GERRY ADAMS

HISTORICAL EVENTS

1534 Jacques Cartier, often described as one of the first Europeans to discover Canada, begins exploring Newfoundland.
1901 The flag of Australia is chosen from entries in a nationwide design competition.
1908 The first Mother's Day observance takes place during church services in West Virginia and Philadelphia.
1924 J. Edgar Hoover is appointed head of the FBI.
1954 "Rock Around the Clock" is recorded by Bill Haley and His Comets. The song had been written about two years earlier but Haley's producer at the time had refused to let him record it.
1981 François Mitterrand defeats Valery Giscard d'Estaing to become President of France in the second round of presidential elections.
1988 An eight-day shipyard strike in Gdansk, Poland, ends after intervention by the Polish Government and without an agreement being made. However, on August 26, the Ministry for Internal Affairs declares its willingness to meet with union leader Lech Wałesa and negotiate.
1995 Britain lifts its 23-year ban on talks with Sinn Fein, the political wing of the IRA (see below).

Births
- 1884 Harry S. Truman, U.S. President
- 1899 Fred Astaire, singer and actor
- 1933 Barbara Taylor Bradford, author
- 1957 Sid Vicious, musician (Sex Pistols)
- 1960 Paul Hewson A.K.A. "Bono", singer (U2)
- 1965 Linda Evangelista, model

Deaths
- 1774 Louis XV, King of France
- 1818 Paul Revere, patriot
- 1925 William Massey, Prime Minister of New Zealand
- 1977 Joan Crawford, actress

DAY TO REMEMBER

Religious day St. Comgall's Day This saint was the founder and abbot of the great Irish monastery at Bangor, now in Northern Ireland.

On May 10, 1995, Britain lifted its 23-year ban on talks with Sinn Fein, the political wing of the IRA. Pictured is Sinn Fein leader Gerry Adams, who had moved the organization from being little more than a political mouthpiece of the IRA to becoming a professionally organized political party in both Northern Ireland and the Republic of Ireland.

May 11

"Life is ten percent what you make it, and ninety percent how you take it." — IRVING BERLIN

HISTORICAL EVENTS

1860 Giuseppe Garibaldi, Italian patriot and military leader, lands at Marsala, Sicily, at the start of his campaign to reunify Italy.

1949 Siam changes its name to Thailand. The word Thai represents the country's largest ethnic group (the Tai people) and also translates as "freedom."

1949 Israel is admitted to the United Nations as the world body's fifty-ninth member by a vote of 37 to 12.

1961 President Kennedy authorizes American advisers to aid South Vietnam against the forces of North Vietnam.

1969 The Monty Python comedy troupe forms (see right).

1981 The Andrew Lloyd Webber musical *CATS* premieres in London. It goes on to run for exactly 20 years and becomes one of the best-loved musicals of all time.

1998 The first Euro coin is struck at France's official mint, making France the first EU country to produce the new currency.

DAYS TO REMEMBER

Religious day St. Mocius' Day This priest in Macedonia, who lived in the third century, is also known as "the Holy Hieromartyr." He was beheaded after he destroyed a Pagan statue.

Religious day St. Mamertus' Day The Archbishop of Vienne in Gaul in the fifth century, this saint is remembered for his introduction of litanies prior to Ascension Day as an intercession against earthquakes and other disasters.

Births
- **1888** Irving Berlin, songwriter
- **1894** Martha Graham, choreographer
- **1904** Salvador Dali, artist
- **1933** Louis Farrakhan, Muslim religious leader
- **1942** Ian Drury, singer
- **1950** Jeremy Paxman, broadcaster

Deaths
- **1988** Harold "Kim" Philby, spy
- **1992** Carlos Herrera, inventor of the Margarita
- **2001** Douglas Adams, author

Monty Python's flying start

Most of the members of the Monty Python group met while at university. (John Cleese, Graham Chapman, and Eric Idle were at Cambridge together, while Michael Palin and Terry Jones were at Oxford. Terry Gilliam, the only American in the six, met them later.) Even though some had worked with each other before, it was not until this day in 1969 that their particular comedic chemistry came to revolutionize contemporary comedy.

From 1969 to 1974, the BBC broadcast the TV series, *Monty Python's Flying Circus*, conceived, written, and performed equally by all six members. It was a loosely structured sketch show that pushed the boundaries of what was then considered acceptable. Whether it was John Cleese's "Ministry of Silly Walks" or the "Dead Parrot Sketch," English audiences couldn't get enough, both in terms of the surrealistic and absurdist style, for example when Palin performed the "Fish Slapping Dance," or the more "realistic" Eric Idle's cheeky, innuendo-driven mode of comedy and his "nudge, nudge, wink, wink" sketch. Terry Gilliam, the team's animator and co-writer, has remarked on the interplay of the group as "this amazing chemical balance…I don't think you could invent a group that would work better."

The *Monty Python's Flying Circus* TV show eventually comprised 45 episodes over four series. However, the Python phenomenon was much greater, generating stage tours, four films, several albums, and a number of books and computer games. It also ensured the members' individual success and stardom away from the Python realm. In this photograph, standing from left to right, are the six members of the troupe — Terry Jones, John Cleese, Terry Gilliam, Graham Chapman, Eric Idle, and Michael Palin — elaborately costumed in readiness for another hilarious sketch.

DATE*line*

May 12

"The very first requirement in a hospital is that it should do the sick no harm."
FLORENCE NIGHTINGALE

Births
- 1765 Lady Emma Hamilton, mistress of Lord Nelson
- 1820 Florence Nightingale, nurse
- 1828 Gabriel Dante Rosetti, poet and painter
- 1907 Katherine Hepburn, actress
- 1936 Frank Stella, painter
- 1946 Daniel Libeskind, architect
- 1975 Jonah Lomu, rugby player

Deaths
- 1985 Jean Dubuffet, artist
- 1994 John Smith, British Labour Party leader
- 1995 Giorgio Belladonna, bridge champion
- 2001 Perry Como, singer

HISTORICAL EVENTS

- 1792 A toilet that flushes itself at regular intervals is patented.
- 1871 After a tense protest by three African Americans, the Louisville district court rules that streetcars in Kentucky can no longer be segregated by race.
- 1908 Wireless Radio Broadcasting is patented by Nathan B. Stubblefield.
- 1926 Dmitri Shostakovitch's First Symphony premieres in Leningrad (now St. Petersburg). Shostakovich wrote the piece at age 19, as his conservatory graduation project.
- 1932 The body of the kidnapped infant son of Charles and Anne Lindbergh is found less than 5 miles (8 km) from their home in New Jersey, U.S.
- 1978 The U.S. Commerce Department states that hurricanes will no longer be named only after women.
- 1997 Australian Susie Maroney becomes the first person to swim from Florida to Cuba (see below).

DAY TO REMEMBER

Religious day St. Pancras' Day This Roman citizen converted to Christianity, and was beheaded in 304 C.E. at the age of 14 for his faith. He is a patron saint of children and is also invoked against headaches and perjury.

On May 12, 1997, Australian swimmer Susie Maroney became the first person to swim from Cuba to Florida. She was 22 years old and accomplished the feat in 24½ hours. Susie's career produced a long list of world records and endurance achievements, which subsequently saw her inducted into the International Hall of Swimming Fame twice. When questioned why she does it, she replied, "You get going in a swim and it just [gets] addictive."

May 13

"I don't like money, actually, but it quiets my nerves." — JOE LOUIS

Churchill addresses Cabinet

On May 13, 1940, Winston Churchill met his Cabinet for the first time since becoming Prime Minister of Britain three days earlier. He stated, "I have nothing to offer but blood, toil, tears, and sweat." He repeated that phrase later in the day when he asked the House of Commons for a vote of confidence in his new multiparty Government. As early as 1933 Churchill had warned of the danger that Adolf Hitler's fascist dictatorship in Germany represented to the civilized world. However, despite increasingly disturbing trends such as Hitler's 1936 anti-Jewish laws, Churchill was ridiculed by members of his own party, who labeled him a warmonger, and kept on the Government's backbenches.

Under Prime Minister Chamberlain, Britain declared war on Nazi Germany when it invaded Poland in September 1939. Chamberlain was finally forced by public opinion to admit Churchill into the Cabinet, and he succeeded Chamberlain as Prime Minister on May 10, 1940. By the middle of 1940, Hitler was at the pinnacle of his power. He controlled much of Europe and North Africa with the most technologically advanced and powerful armed forces in history.

Churchill understood the great danger the Nazis posed to Britain and the world and he employed powerful rhetoric to convince the Cabinet and the people of Britain to fight. The philosopher Isaiah Berlin said he "imposed his will and imagination on his countrymen." In time, they "approached his ideals and began to see themselves as he saw them."

Celtic tree sign

HAWTHORN
May 13–June 9

According to Celtic tradition, people born between May 13 and June 9 have qualities connected to the hawthorn tree. Hawthorn tree people are able to sense the weakness of others and act on it without being ruthless. They are good innovators, appreciating the need for change and the processes for creating it. They love to perform, are creative and expressive, and are good communicators.

HISTORICAL EVENTS

- **1568** Mary, Queen of Scots, is defeated by the English at the Battle of Langside.
- **1637** Cardinal Richelieu of France creates the table knife.
- **1940** The newly elected British Prime Minister Winston Churchill, at a perilous time in the nation's history, states, "I have nothing to offer but blood, toil, tears, and sweat" (see left).
- **1965** The *Luna 5* spacecraft, launched by the U.S.S.R. to explore the possibility of landing safely on the Moon, malfunctions and crashes on the lunar surface.
- **1981** John Paul II is shot and seriously wounded in St. Peter's Square by Turkish assailant Mehmet Ali Ağca.
- **1991** South African black activist Winnie Mandela is convicted of abducting four young black activists. One of them, James Seipei (A.K.A. Stompie Moeketsi), is found stabbed to death later.
- **1999** In response to President Boris Yeltsin's dismissal of Prime Minister Yevgeny Primakov, Russia's lower parliament begins debate on Yeltsin's impeachment.

DAY TO REMEMBER

Religious day St. Abban's Day Known as St. Abban the Hermit, this saint was an Irish Roman Catholic who lived in Abingdon, England.

Births
- 1907 Daphne du Maurier, author
- 1914 Joe Louis, world heavyweight boxing champion
- 1929 Burt Bacharach, singer and composer
- 1939 Harvey Keitel, actor
- 1940 Bruce Chatwin, author
- 1961 Dennis Rodman, NBA forward (Chicago Bulls)

Deaths
- 1835 John Nash, architect
- 1961 Gary Cooper, actor
- 1962 Franz Kline, artist
- 1993 Joaquin Garcia, comic actor

May 14

> "Cruel leaders are replaced only to have new leaders turn cruel." — "CHE" GUEVARA

When the all-volunteer military replaced the draft in 1973, the U.S. Armed Forces accelerated its recruitment of women soldiers. However, until the mid-1960s, about 70 percent of enlisted women worked in office jobs. Then on May 14, 1973, the U.S. Commission on Civil Rights endorsed the proposed Federal Equal Rights Amendment. In the amendment, it stated that women were to receive equal treatment in the military when it came to educational and employment opportunities. This development opened up military jobs for women, ultimately leading to combat-related roles.

Births
- 1727 Thomas Gainsborough, artist
- 1771 Thomas Wedgwood, inventor
- 1928 Ernesto "Che" Guevara, communist revolutionary
- 1944 George Lucas, writer and director
- 1944 Francesca Annis, actress
- 1969 Cate Blanchett, actress

Deaths
- 1978 Sir Robert Menzies, twelfth Prime Minister of Australia
- 1987 Rita Hayworth, actress
- 1991 Jiang Qing, widow of Chinese leader Mao Zedong
- 1998 Frank Sinatra, singer and actor
- 2000 Keizo Obuchi, Japanese Prime Minister

HISTORICAL EVENTS

- **1643** Louis XIV becomes King of France at the age of four upon the death of his father, Louis XIII.
- **1796** English physician Edward Jenner administers the first vaccination against smallpox to his gardener's son.
- **1870** The first game of rugby union in New Zealand is played in Nelson between Nelson College and the Nelson Rugby Football Club.
- **1878** Vaseline, a registered trademark for petroleum jelly, is first sold.
- **1955** The Warsaw Pact is formed. It includes eight communist bloc countries: The Soviet Union, Albania, Bulgaria, Czechoslovakia, East Germany, Hungary, Poland, and Romania.
- **1969** Abortion and contraception are legalized in Canada.
- **1973** The U.S. Supreme Court approves equal rights for women in the military (see above).
- **1984** Jeane Sauve is appointed as the first woman Governor-General of Canada.
- **1986** Anne Frank's complete diary is published
- **2000** In Washington D.C., about 750,000 people take part in the Million Mom March for tougher gun laws. The March is a response to white supremacist Buford Furrow shooting at children at a Jewish community center in 1999.

DATEline

May 15

"If you could say it in words there would be no reason to paint." — EDWARD HOPPER

HISTORICAL EVENTS

1829 Joseph Smith, founder of the Mormon Church, is "ordained," according to himself, by John the Baptist.
1940 Nylon stockings go on general sale for the first time in the U.S. Nylon is the first commercially successful polymer, made entirely from the basic ingredients of coal, water, and air.
1941 The legendary Yankee baseball player Joe DiMaggio begins his 56-game hitting streak (see below).
1944 Generals Eisenhower and Montgomery, Prime Minister Churchill, and King George VI discuss Britain's D-Day plan.
1948 Britain's 28-year Mandate over Palestine ends.
1957 The U.K. tests its first thermonuclear weapon, the "Green Granite" bomb. The bomb yields about 300 kilotons, well short of the expected capacity of 1 megaton.
1958 *Sputnik III*, a Soviet research station, is launched to explore the upper atmosphere and near space.
1972 Okinawa, a Japanese island under U.S. control since 1945, is returned to the Japanese Government.
1988 The U.S.S.R. starts to withdraw its 115,000 troops from Afghanistan, more than eight years after Soviet forces enter the country.

Births
1567 Claudio Giovanni Antonio Monteverdi, musician and composer
1905 Henry Fonda, actor
1909 James Mason, actor
1923 Richard Avedon, photographer
1930 Jasper Johns Jr., artist
1948 Brian Eno, electronic musician and music producer

Deaths
1967 Edward Hopper, artist
1980 Len Lye, artist and sculptor
1986 Theodore H. White, journalist
2003 June Carter Cash, singer and actress

DAY TO REMEMBER

Religious day St. Dymphna's Day After her mother's death, St. Dymphna's father went mad with grief and ultimately killed his daughter in fury. St. Dymphna is the patron saint of insanity and those suffering from mental illness.

On May 15, 1941, Joe DiMaggio began his 56-game hitting streak, which many commentators rate as the top baseball feat of all time. DiMaggio was a Major League baseball center fielder who played his entire career (1936–1951) for the New York Yankees. In its obituary after his death in 1999, the *Washington Post* newspaper stated that his "superlative play on the baseball field enshrined him in the hearts of sports fans everywhere and made him a universal symbol of athletic grace and excellence."

213

May 16

"I left the ending ambiguous, because that is the way life is." — BERNARDO BERTOLUCCI

HISTORICAL EVENTS

- **1770** Marie Antoinette (14) marries the future King Louis XVI of France (15).
- **1929** Hollywood stages an experimental publicity stunt for the movie industry at the Hollywood Roosevelt Hotel. This later evolves into the Academy Awards extravaganza.
- **1969** The Soviet-launched *Venera 5* reaches Venus and successfully parachutes into the dense, hostile atmosphere. It sends information about the planet back to Earth for 53 minutes before dropping to the surface.
- **1985** Michael Jordan is named NBA Rookie of the Year.
- **1988** The U.S. Surgeon General declares that nicotine's "pharmacological and behavioral processes" are addictive in ways similar to heroin and cocaine.
- **1989** Soviet President Mikhail S. Gorbachev meets with Chinese leader Deng Xiaoping, formally ending a 30-year rift (see below).
- **1999** The Cabinet in Kuwait votes to give women the right to vote in the 2003 elections.
- **2000** Lady Hillary Rodham Clinton is nominated for the U.S. Senate by the New York Democratric Party, with her husband at her side.

Births
- **1801** William H. Seward, who bought Alaska for 2 cents per acre
- **1905** Henry Fonda, actor
- **1919** Liberace, performer and pianist
- **1940** Bernardo Bertolucci, filmmaker
- **1955** Olga Korbutt, gymnast

Deaths
- **1703** Charles Perrault, fairytale author
- **1990** Sammy Davis Jr., entertainer
- **1990** Jim Henson, "Muppets" creator
- **2003** Robert Stack, actor

DAY TO REMEMBER

Religious day St. Brendan's Day Celtic saint and hero of legendary Atlantic voyages, St. Brendan established many monasteries in Ireland, including the legendary Clonfert in County Gallway in 560.

China meets the U.S.S.R.

On May 16 1989, Soviet leader Mikhail Gorbachev met the leader of the People's Republic of China, Deng Xiaoping, in Beijing. It was the first Sino-Soviet summit since 1959 and the Chinese leader hoped that the visit would cement his role as a world statesman. However, Gorbachev's visit only gave momentum to the emerging democracy movement in China as international attention focused on the historic meeting.

When he arrived the previous day, his escort had been blocked by protestors on nearly every street in Beijing, which gave Gorbachev and his wife, Raisa, an opportunity to talk to the local people. Two days before Gorbachev arrived, 200 students began a hunger strike in Tiananmen Square to demand political freedom. By May 16 the number of hunger strikers had increased to 3,000 and 500 had lost consciousness. Hundreds of thousands of demonstrators came to Tiananmen Square to support the strikers, forcing the Government to cancel plans to welcome Gorbachev in the square. After meeting Deng, Gorbachev once again stopped to talk to the locals.

The embarrassing protests during Gorbachev's visit further polarized an already divided Politburo. On May 16 one of its members, Zhao Ziyang, proposed that the Politburo Standing Committee accept some of the students' demands but he was outvoted four to one. The Soviet leader returned to Moscow later that day and the protest movement was violently suppressed on June 4.

May 17

"I shall be an autocrat, that's my trade; and the good Lord will forgive me, that's his."
CATHERINE THE GREAT

HISTORICAL EVENTS

- **1809** The Papal States are annexed by France. Pope Pius VII responds by excommunicating Napoleon, who, in return, holds the pontiff prisoner.
- **1845** The rubber band is patented.
- **1846** The saxophone is patented by Adolphe Sax. The instrument comes to be associated with immorality, which leads to the Vatican officially condemning its use.
- **1961** Cuban leader Fidel Castro offers to exchange prisoners captured in the abortive Bay of Pigs invasion for 500 bulldozers.
- **1989** More than one million people swarm into central Beijing to support Chinese students who are undergoing a hunger strike for democracy.
- **1992** Pro-democracy protests begin in Thailand (see right).
- **2004** Same-sex marriage becomes legal in Massachusetts, U.S.

DAYS TO REMEMBER

National day Norway National Day This is the anniversary of the day in 1814 when the Constitution of Norway was signed and the Danish Crown Prince Christian Frederik was elected King of Norway by the Constitutional Assembly.

Religious day Bruno, Bishop of Würzburg's Day Prince-Bishop of Würzburg from 1034 until his death (c. 1045), Bruno was the son of Conrad I, Duke of Carinthia. He was not officially canonized but is revered as a saint.

Births		Deaths	
1900	Ayatollah Ruhollah Khomeini, Iran's spiritual and revolutionary leader	1510	Sandro Boticelli, painter
1911	Maureen O'Sullivan, actress	1727	Catherine I, Empress of Russia
1918	Birgit Nilsson, operatic soprano	1888	Giacomo Zanella, poet
1935	Dennis Potter, writer	1996	Kevin Gilbert, singer, composer, and instrumentalist
1936	Dennis Hopper, actor	2000	Donald Coggan, 101st Archbishop of Canterbury
1956	"Sugar" Ray Leonard, boxer		
1961	Enya, singer		

Black May

On this day in 1992, pro-democracy protests began in Thailand with hundreds of thousands taking to the streets of Bangkok, the nation's capital, to demand an end to authoritarian rule. Since 1945, Thailand had been ruled by autocratic Governments and military coups were the usual means of regime change. However, 1992 proved to be a turning point, as an organised political alliance between military factions opposed to the previous year's coup leaders, small to medium businesspeople, intellectuals, students, and members of political parties, combined to thwart a new dictatorial alliance between the military and big business.

The demonstrations soon degenerated into chaos as the military violently quelled dissent. Over the next few days the world watched in horror as ordinary people were indiscriminately killed or injured, including medics treating the wounded, in what was to become known as the Black May upheaval. There were also scenes of incredible bravery as protestors faced fully armed troops.

In the midst of the threat of anarchy and the breakdown of social order, pictures were broadcast of Prime Minister Suchinda and one of the leaders of the demonstrators, Major-General Chamlong Srimuang, prostrate before King Bhumibol Adulyadej as he admonished them and demanded an end to the disorder. The promise of a revived constitution and elections in September 1992 helped to re-establish order in the capital. However, political commentators have argued that many of the issues that provoked the Thais to protest are still to be resolved.

May 18

"Minor things can become moments of great revelation when encountered for the first time."
DAME MARGOT FONTEYN

HISTORICAL EVENTS

1802 Great Britain declares war on Napoleon's France.
1804 The French Senate proclaims Napoleon Bonaparte Emperor of France.
1896 In the Plessy v. Ferguson case, the U.S. Supreme Court rules to give states the authority to segregate people according to race as long as facilities for both races are of equal quality.
1897 Bram Stoker's novel *Dracula*, inspired partly by Transylvanian legend and partly by historical events, is published.
1965 *Star Trek* creator Gene Roddenberry suggests 16 names, including Kirk, for the captain of *Star Trek's* flagship spacecraft, the USS *Enterprise*.
1980 Mt. St. Helens in Washington state erupts, killing 57 people (see below).
1982 Reverend Sun Myung Moon, founder and self-professed Messiah of the Unification Church, is convicted of tax evasion. Supporters rally around him as he serves 13 months of his 18-month sentence.
1990 A French TGV train hits a record speed of 320 miles per hour (515.3 km/h).
1991 After answering an advertisement on the radio for an "astronaut wanted, no experience necessary," Helen Sharman is selected from 13,000 applicants and blasts off on a Soviet scientific mission, becoming the first British person in space.

Births
1868 Nicholas II, the last Russian Tsar
1872 Bertrand Russell, mathematician, philosopher, and social reformer
1883 Walter Gropius, founder of the Bauhaus school of design
1919 Dame Margot Fonteyn, ballet dancer
1920 Pope John Paul II

Deaths
1911 Gustav Mahler, composer
1973 Jeanette Rankin, first U.S. congresswoman
1988 Daws Butler, cartoon voice (Yogi Bear and Huckleberry Hound)
1995 Elizabeth Montgomery, actress

DAY TO REMEMBER

Religious day St. Felix of Cantalica's Day Born to peasant parents in Cantalice, Italy, St. Felix spent 38 years aiding the sick and the poor in Rome. St. Felix was canonized in 1709.

This photograph was taken in Washington during Mt. St. Helens' catastrophic eruption on May 18, 1980. The entire north face of the mountain slipped away, suddenly exposing the partly molten rock, shot through with gas and steam. The volcanic ash column rose so high into the atmosphere that it deposited ash in 11 states. The May 18 eruption is documented as the most deadly and economically destructive volcanic eruption in U.S. history. Fifty-seven people and hundreds of animals died from its devastating effects.

DATE*line*

May 19

"The one thing I do not want to be called is 'First Lady.' It sounds like a saddle horse."

JACQUELINE KENNEDY

HISTORICAL EVENTS

1922 The Young Pioneer movement is established in the U.S.S.R. as a Communist equivalent to the Scouting movement. Many Scout masters had fought with the Bolsheviks during the Russian Civil War, leading to the eradication of Scouting as such.

1943 U.K. Prime Minister Winston Churchill pledges British support in the war against Japan to the U.S. Congress.

1962 Marilyn Monroe sings "Happy Birthday" to President Kennedy at Madison Square Garden (see right).

1982 Sophia Loren starts her prison term at Caserta, Naples, for tax evasion. She spends 18 days of her 30-day sentence behind bars.

1994 After a five-year development by biotechnology company Calgene Inc., the U.S. Food and Drug Administration approves the first genetically engineered tomato.

DAYS TO REMEMBER

Religious day St. Pudentiana's Day A lady of Rome, the daughter of Senator St. Pudens and sister of St. Praxedes, St. Pudentiana is said to have given her wealth to the poor and helped bury martyred Christians.

National day Commemoration of Pontian Greeks' Genocide (Greece) Between 1916 and 1919, the Turkish state was allegedly responsible for the slaughter of about 300,000 Greeks living in the Province of Pontos. This day was established by the Greek Government to honor those who died.

Births
- 1861 Dame Nellie Melba, opera singer
- 1890 Ho Chi Minh, revolutionist and leader of North Vietnam
- 1925 Malcolm X (Malcolm Little), African American Muslim leader
- 1925 Pol Pot, Cambodian dictator and mass murderer
- 1934 James Lehrer, broadcast journalist
- 1939 Nancy Kwan, actress
- 1941 Nora Ephron, screenwriter and director
- 1945 Pete Townshend, musician (The Who)

Deaths
- 1786 John Stanley, composer
- 1965 Tui Malila, world's oldest tortoise (born 1773)
- 1994 Jacqueline Lee Bouvier Kennedy Onassis, U.S. First Lady
- 1998 Uno Sosuke, Japanese Prime Minister

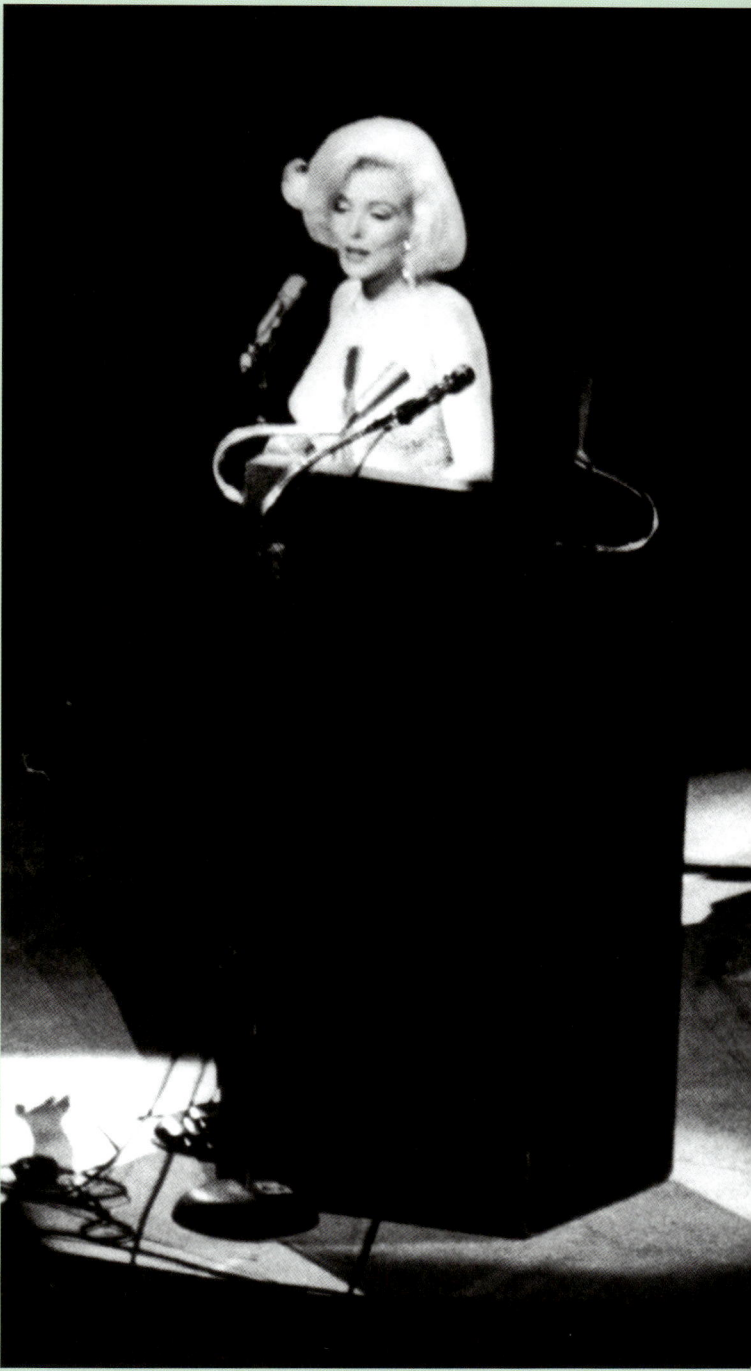

On May 19, 1962, actress Marilyn Monroe sang "Happy Birthday" to President John F. Kennedy. JFK thanked Marilyn, saying, "I can now retire from politics after having had 'Happy Birthday' sung to me in such a sweet, wholesome way."

May 20

"The most difficult thing is the decision to act, the rest is merely tenacity. The fears are paper tigers. You can do anything you decide to do." — AMELIA EARHART

Births
- 1799 Honore de Balzac, novelist
- 1806 John Stuart Mill, philosopher and economist
- 1908 James Stuart, actor
- 1915 Moshe Dayan, Israeli general and Minister of Defense
- 1972 Busta Rhymes, singer and rapper

Deaths
- 1506 Christopher Columbus, explorer
- 1996 John Pertwee, actor
- 2001 Renato Carosone, musical maestro

HISTORICAL EVENTS

- **1773** The explorer Captain James Cook releases the first sheep in New Zealand.
- **1873** Levi Strauss of San Francisco and Jacob Davis of Nevada receive a patent for miners' work pants (see right).
- **1902** Cuba gains independence from the United States.
- **1932** Amelia Earhart takes off from Newfoundland to begin the world's first solo nonstop flight across the Atlantic Ocean by a female pilot, landing in Ireland the next day.
- **1959** Ford wins a battle with Chrysler to call its new car "Falcon." The Falcon goes on to become one of the biggest-selling names in world automotive history.
- **1993** An estimated 93 million people tune in for the final episode of *Cheers* on the NBC TV network in the U.S.
- **1996** Iraq and the UN sign a memorandum for the revenue from oil sales to be exchanged for humanitarian aid, otherwise known as the Oil For Food Program.
- **1999** In Canada the Supreme Court strikes down a heterosexual definition of "spouse" as unconstitutional.

DAY TO REMEMBER

Religious day St. Stephen of Piperi's Day A saint of the Serbian Orthodox Church, St. Stephen of Piperi lived a life of asceticism in the seventeenth century. His venerated relics are believed to produce miracles and remain in the Moraca monastery in Montenegro, where he was abbot.

Blue jeans are patented

On May 20, 1873, Levi Strauss and Jacob Davis received patent number 139,121 from the U.S. Patent and Trademark Office. This day would become the birthday of arguably the quintessentially American garment – blue jeans. Levi Strauss, an emigrant from Germany, decided to settle in San Francisco and opened a successful dry-goods store, "Levi Strauss & Co." One of Levi's many customers was a tailor named Jacob Davis from Nevada.

Davis had been experimenting with metal rivets in his denim work trousers in response to his clientele's complaints about the poor durability of work clothes. Davis' rivet-strengthened trousers were such a success that he became nervous someone might steal his idea. However, the cost of the patent was too much for Davis and he approached Strauss for the $68 in return for equal rights to the patent. Strauss saw the potential and agreed to pay the amount.

The blue jeans created by Levi Strauss and Jacob Davis have becamed an international phenomenon, an icon of American culture. Holding a patent on this process meant that for nearly 20 years, Levi Strauss & Co. was the only company allowed to make riveted clothing until the patent entered the public domain in 1891. On the expiration of the patent, dozens of garment manufacturers began to imitate the original riveted clothing made by Levi Strauss & Co. Although denim pants had been around as work wear for many years, it was two visionaries, Levi Strauss and Jacob Davis, who turned denim, metal, and thread into the most popular clothing product in the world today.

May 21

DATEline

"As long as the plots keep arriving from outer space, I'll go on with my virgins."

DAME BARBARA CARTLAND

HISTORICAL EVENTS

1471 Henry VI, King of England and France, is killed in the Tower of London. Edward IV takes the throne.

1536 Genevea, Switzerland, officially adopts the Reformation.

1819 The first bicycles in the U.S., otherwise known as "swift walkers," are introduced in New York City.

1840 The Treaty of Waitangi is signed by Maori chiefs of New Zealand and representatives of Queen Victoria. It becomes the cause of much controversy and disagreement with regards to land ownership.

1968 The nuclear-powered U.S. submarine *Scorpion* is last heard from by the U.S. Navy. There are 99 men aboard. The sub's remains are later found on the ocean floor 400 miles (640 km) southwest of the Azores Islands, Portugal.

1980 The Star Wars sequel *The Empire Strikes Back* premieres. Building on 1977's *Star Wars*, it sets George Lucas well on the way to iconic status as a filmmaker, despite being directed by Irvin Kershner, an associate.

1991 A Tamil suicide bomber assassinates Indian Prime Minister Rajiv Gandhi at a campaign rally near Madras (see below). About 14 other people are also killed; Gandhi's mother, Indira, had been assassinated in 1984.

DAY TO REMEMBER

Religious day St. Elena's Day Near Cagliari in Sardinia, people dress in traditional costumes and make an offering of eight large loaves of bread sweetened with jam to St. Elena. Her feast day as a saint of the Orthodox Christian Church is celebrated with that of her son on this day.

Births
- **1471** Albrecht Durer, painter, printmaker, and art theorist
- **1527** Philip II, King of Spain and Portugal
- **1844** Henri Rousseau, painter
- **1904** Fats Waller (Thomas Wright), jazz singer and composer
- **1944** Mary Bourke Robinson, first woman President of Ireland

Deaths
- **1995** Les Aspin, U.S. Secretary of Defense
- **2000** Dame Barbara Cartland, novelist
- **2000** Sir John Gielgud, actor

On this day in 1991, Rajiv Gandhi, the 46-year-old former Indian Prime Minister, was assassinated by a female suicide bomber at a campaign rally for the national elections. His death marked the end of the Gandhi dynasty, which had ruled India for all but five years since independence from Britain in 1949.

May 22

"Share our similarities, celebrate our differences." — M. SCOTT PECK

HISTORICAL EVENTS

1843 The first wagon train, with more than 1,000 people, departs Missouri for Oregon. The pioneers are tempted by reputedly paradisical climatic conditions in the West. About 700 people safely reached their destination.

1892 Dr. Washington Sheffield invents the toothpaste tube.

1939 Adolf Hitler and Benito Mussolini sign a "Pact of Steel," committing Germany and Italy to a military alliance which forms the Axis powers.

1961 The revolving restaurant Eye of the Needle (now called SkyCity Restaurant) opens in Seattle at the top of the city's Space Needle.

1964 President Lyndon Johnson presents his "Great Society" (see right).

1992 Bosnia, Croatia, and Slovenia join the UN.

1992 Johnny Carson hosts NBC TV's *Tonight Show* for the last time after nearly 30 years.

2003 In Fort Worth, Texas, Annika Sorenstam becomes the first woman to play the PGA Tour in 58 years.

DAY TO REMEMBER

Religious day St. Fulk's Day A pilgrim who aided plague victims and who died of the plague himself, St. Fulk was officially recognized as a saint in 1572.

Births
- 1813 Richard Wagner, composer
- 1844 Mary Cassatt, impressionist painter
- 1907 Lord Laurence Olivier, actor
- 1936 M. Scott Peck, psychiatrist and author

Deaths
- 1885 Victor-Marie Hugo, novelist and poet
- 1967 J. Langston Hughes, Poet Laureate
- 1970 Joseph W. Krutch, writer

Star sign

GEMINI
May 22–June 20

Gemini's symbol is the twins; it is ruled by the quick and lively planet Mercury, named after the messenger of the gods. Those born under the sign of the twins are intelligent and quick-witted, but can be prone to restlessness if others do not keep up with them. Gemini is a changeable sign, which governs communication and the intellect.

Johnson's "Great Society"

On 22 May, 1964, American President Lyndon Johnson announced a massive social and economic reform campaign – the "Great Society." At its essence was Johnson's belief that "the demands of morality, and the needs of spirit, can be realized in the life of the nation." The Great Society espoused the grand vision of the just distribution of resources to all Americans and the rejection of the notion of national wealth and personal income as ends in themselves.

In a period of rising economic growth, he stated that, "The challenge of the next half century is whether we have the wisdom to use that wealth to enrich and elevate our national life." His beliefs were formulated in the context of an environment where the country had suffered the trauma of President Kennedy's assassination, was seeing the rise of the civil rights movement as led by Martin Luther King Jr. (pictured on right) and other social movements, and was beginning to acknowledge the extent of poverty throughout the United States.

The wide range of social programs Johnson proposed covered a broad sweep of American life, including Medicare for the elderly, education assistance for the young, a higher minimum wage, poverty-alleviation grants, and legal protection for African Americans. He also suggested higher unemployment benefits, housing for the homeless, improved education for Native Americans, pensions for the retired, tax rebates for business, and subsidies for farmers, to name just a few.

May 23

DATEline

> *"Tell them I don't smoke cigars."*
> OUTLAW BONNIE PARKER, WHEN ASKED BY PERCY BOYD WHAT SHE WANTED HIM TO TELL THE PRESS

The "Great Leap Forward"

On May 23, 1958, Mao Zedong, leader of the People's Republic of China, instituted the "Great Leap Forward." Running from 1958 to early 1960, it was a campaign aimed at using the communist state's cheap labor supply to rapidly industrialize the economy. Mao believed that through collectivization and mass labor, China's steel production would surpass that of the U.S. within 15 years.

Tens of millions of peasants were mobilized to produce steel, the ultimate symbol of industrialization. About 25,000 communes were set up, each with backyard steel furnaces where peasants produced small pieces of cast iron made out of scrap metal. Across the country people left their usual work in order to smelt iron, often abandoning the production of food.

The Chinese economy initially grew, and iron production increased 45 percent in 1958, but the disastrous scheme faltered, ultimately proving the misguided premise of the campaign itself. The country was reduced to mass famine, with more than 30 million dying of starvation. After the death of Mao and the start of Chinese economic reform under Deng Xiaoping, the Government admitted that the Great Leap Forward had been a major economic disaster.

HISTORICAL EVENTS

1785 Benjamin Franklin writes to a friend announcing his invention of bifocals.

1949 The Federal Republic of [West] Germany officially comes into existence with Bonn as the capital.

1958 Mao Zedong starts his ironically titled "Great Leap Forward" movement in China (see above).

1969 The Who release their rock opera *Tommy*. It includes an elaborate plot about a psychologically damaged boy, and sets a precedent for works as diverse as Pink Floyd's *The Wall*, W.A.S.P.'s *The Crimson Idol*, and Green Day's *American Idiot*.

1990 Neil Bush, son of one U.S. President and brother of another, testifies about the collapse of the Silverado Savings and Loan. The main reason for the company's demise is believed to be the fact that two of Bush's associates failed to repay loans totaling more than $130 million.

1996 South Korean officials confirm that a North Korean pilot flew his unarmed MIG-19 jet to South Korea, becoming the first North Korean pilot to defect since 1983.

2004 Part of Charles De Gaulle International Airport Terminal 2E collapses, killing five people and injuring three.

DAYS TO REMEMBER

Religious day Declaration of the Báb The Baha'i faith celebrates this day when the Báb, a descendant of the Prophet Muhammad, declared himself "Messenger of God" and "Herald of one greater to come," later known to be Baha'u'llah.

Historical day Flora's Day In Roman mythology, Flora was the goddess of flowers, gardens, and Spring. This was a feast of the rose, a flower loved by the Romans, and especially sacred to the love goddess Venus, who was also honored on this festival day.

Births
- **1734** Franz Anton Mesmer, physician and hypnotist
- **1883** Douglas Fairbanks, actor
- **1951** Anatoli Karpov, world chess champion
- **1974** Jewel, singer

Deaths
- **1906** Henrik Ibsen, writer
- **1934** Bonnie Parker, outlaw
- **1934** Clyde Parker, outlaw
- **1937** John D. Rockefeller, entrepreneur

May 24

> *"A week is a long time in politics."* — HAROLD WILSON

HISTORICAL EVENTS

1844 Samuel F. B. Morse, before a crowd of dignitaries in the chambers of the U.S. Supreme Court, taps out the message, "What hath God wrought?" to his associate in Baltimore, Alfred Vail, demonstrating the electrical telegraph.

1862 Westminster Bridge, designed by Thomas Page and Charles Berry, opens across the Thames.

1915 Thomas Edison invents the telescribe to record telephone conversations.

1971 Senator Neville Bonner becomes the first Australian Aboriginal parliamentarian.

1976 Britain and France open the trans-Atlantic Concorde service to Washington. The Concorde is the first commercial supersonic transport.

1991 Israel begins airlifting almost 15,000 Ethiopian Jews to safety as Ethiopian rebels continue to advance on Addis Ababa.

1994 Four men convicted of bombing New York's World Trade Center are each sentenced to 240 years in prison.

1995 Heidi Fleiss is sentenced to three years in prison and fined $1,500 for running a call-girl ring that catered to the rich and famous (see below).

1997 The Ukraine opens its first McDonald's restaurant in the city of Kyiv.

2000 The Government of Israel completes withdrawal of its troops from south Lebanon, ending about two decades of occupation.

Births
- **1686** Gabriel Daniel Fahrenheit, physicist
- **1819** Victoria, Queen of England
- **1928** William Trevor, novelist
- **1940** Joseph Brodsky, author
- **1960** Kristin Scott Thomas, actress

Deaths
- **1974** Duke Ellington, jazz musician
- **1995** Harold Wilson, U.K. Prime Minister

DAYS TO REMEMBER

Religious day St. Sarah's Day Each year in late May, Gypsies from all over Europe gather to venerate St. Sarah. In a grand procession culminating in days of praying and feasting, they dress a statue of the saint in layers of clothes and jewels and take her down to the sea.

National day Eritrea National Day This day marks Eritrea's independence from Ethiopia in 1993. Eritrea is one of the youngest nations in the world.

On May 24, 1995, heavy media coverage ensued when Heidi Fleiss, "Hollywood Madam," was convicted on three counts of pandering. Pandering is established when "evidence shows that the accused succeeded in inducing a victim to become an inmate of a house of prostitution." Fleiss was sentenced to three years in prison and fined $1,500.

May 25

DATE*line*

"I have never given adoration to anybody except myself."
OSCAR WILDE, WHEN QUESTIONED WHETHER HE HAD EVER ADORED A MAN

On this day in 1986, more than five million Americans held hands for 15 minutes across the U.S. with the aim of helping the homeless. The path stretched for more than 4,000 miles (6,400 km) from New York City's Battery Park to a pier in Long Beach, California. Many high-profile celebrities and politicians participated in the national fundraising effort, including President Reagan's nemesis, Speaker of the House of Representatives, Tip O'Neill (pictured, second from left).

Births
- 1803 Ralph Waldo Emerson, essayist and philosopher
- 1878 Bill "Bojangles" Robinson, tap dancer
- 1926 Miles Davis, jazz trumpeter
- 1927 Robert Ludlum, spy novelist
- 1932 John Gregory Dunne, author and poet
- 1938 Raymond Carver, writer
- 1939 Ian McKellen, actor
- 1963 Mike Myers, actor and comedian

Deaths
- 1543 Nicolaus Copernicus, astronomer
- 1946 Patty Smith Hill, songwriter
- 2005 Graham Kennedy, television personality

HISTORICAL EVENTS

- 1895 Convicted of "committing acts of gross indecency with other male persons," playwright Oscar Wilde is sentenced to two years' hard labor in Reading Gaol.
- 1937 The first airmail letter to circle the globe returns to New York.
- 1953 Exploring the possibilities of atomic bombs as tactical weapons, the U.S. tests its only nuclear artillery shell in Nevada. Further developments included the MK-54 "Davy Crockett," which could be launched from a bazooka-like device.
- 1955 Kanchenjunga, the third-highest mountain in the world (after Mt. Everest and K2), is successfully climbed by U.K. mountaineers George Band and Joe Brown. Respecting the beliefs of the local people, who consider the summit to be holy, they stop several feet from the actual peak of the mountain.
- 1961 President Kennedy asks the nation to work toward putting a man on the Moon by the end of the decade.
- 1986 An estimated seven million people participate in Hands Across America (see above).
- 1994 The UN Security Council lifts a 10-year-old ban on weapons exports from South Africa, scrapping the last of its apartheid-era embargoes.

DAYS TO REMEMBER

National day Tap Dance Day (U.S.) This observed day celebrates the birthday of Bill "Bojangles" Robinson, the "king" of tap dancers.

National day Día de la Revolución de Mayo (Argentina) This holiday, whose name translates to May Revolution Day, celebrates the First Junta created in Buenos Aires in 1810. The junta removed Spanish Viceroy Baltasar Hidalgo de Cisneros from power; the day also celebrates Argentina's official independence from the Spanish crown in 1816.

May 26

"Civility costs nothing, and buys everything." — MARY WORTLEY MONTAGU

HISTORICAL EVENTS

1521 Martin Luther is banned by the Edict of Worms because of his religious beliefs and is formally declared an outlaw.

1896 The Dow Jones Industrial Average (DJIA) is first published. It is the oldest stock market index still used today in the U.S.

1960 UN Ambassador Henry Cabot Lodge accuses the Soviets of hiding a microphone inside a wood carving of the Great Seal of the United States that they presented to the U.S. embassy in Moscow.

1966 A Buddhist nun sets herself on fire at the U.S. Consulate in Hue, South Vietnam. It is one of many acts of self-immolation by Buddhists in protest at the Vietnam War.

1989 The Danish Parliament allows legal marriage between homosexuals.

1993 In a speech on health reform, First Lady Hillary Rodham Clinton denounces price gougers and profiteers in medicine (see below).

DAYS TO REMEMBER

Religious day St. Philip Neri's Day This Italian reformer gave his life to the sick of Rome. In 1548 he founded the "Confraternity of the Most Holy Trinity to care for pilgrims and convalescents."

National day National Sorry Day (Australia) As the result of an inquiry in 1998 into the forced removal of Aboriginal children from their families earlier that century, a National Sorry Day was instituted to acknowledge the wrong that had been done to indigenous families, and so that a process of reconciliation could begin.

Births
- 1689 Mary Wortley Montagu, essayist
- 1799 Alexander Pushkin, poet
- 1907 John Wayne (Marion Michael Morrison), actor
- 1920 Peggy Lee, jazz singer
- 1927 Jacques Bergerac, actor
- 1966 Helena Bonham Carter, actress

Deaths
- 1703 Samuel Pepys, diarist
- 1939 Charles H. Mayo, surgeon, co-founder of the Mayo Clinic
- 1976 Martin Heidegger, philosopher
- 2005 Chico Carrasquel, Major League baseball player

Hillary speaks out

In 1993, the newly elected President Bill Clinton named his wife, Hillary Rodham Clinton, to chair the Task Force on National Health Care Reform. Her work, later dubbed "Hillary Care," has been highly publicized, and equally scrutinized.

In her May 26 speech on health reform, she spoke out against "proponents of the status quo" who opposed a Government-regulated system of providing health care for all by means of subsidies derived from taxation – "socialized medicine" in other words. She went on to condemn what she regarded as "price gouging, cost shifting, and unconscionable profiteering" practices by doctors. She offered a clear-cut appeal to class envy, declaring that, "Too many people have made too much money" in the health care field.

Hillary raised public awareness of health issues such as expanding health insurance coverage and ensuring that children receive proper immunization. Then in September 1993, her husband, President Clinton, echoed these themes in his address to Congress. In dynamic tones, he urged officials "to fix a health care system that is badly broken… giving every American health security – health care that is always there."

However, most of these efforts failed, due to the enormous power of health care lobbies. Of her efforts, Hillary has said in more recent times, "When people ask me about health care reform, I tell them that I am disappointed we were not able to make more progress." She has also said, "Now I'm from the school of smaller steps, but I believe we must continue to make progress. It's still important that we increase access to quality health care for working families."

May 27

"*Power is the ultimate aphrodisiac.*"   HENRY KISSINGER

Births
- 1907 Rachel Carson, biologist and writer
- 1923 Henry Kissinger, U.S. Secretary of State
- 1957 Siouxsie Sioux, musician
- 1958 Neil Finn, musician
- 1975 Jamie Oliver, chef and television personality

Deaths
- 1964 Jawaharlal Nehru, independent India's first Prime Minister
- 1987 John Howard Northrop, chemist and Nobel Prize laureate
- 1993 Werner Stocker, actor

HISTORICAL EVENTS
- 1703 Peter the Great founds St. Petersburg (later known as Leningrad) as the capital of Russia.
- 1905 The Japanese fleet destroys the Russian East Sea fleet in the Straits of Tsushima.
- 1937 The newly completed Golden Gate Bridge connecting San Francisco and Marin County, California, is opened to pedestrians. The bridge quickly becomes the symbol of San Fransisco.
- 1967 In the largest majority of any Australian referendum, voters overwhelmingly supported a proposal to count indigenous people in the national census.
- 1993 Five people are killed in a bombing at the Uffizi museum of art in Florence, Italy, and more than 30 paintings are ruined or damaged.
- 1994 Nobel Prize-winning author Alexandr Solzhenitsyn returns to Russia after two decades in exile (see right).
- 1995 Actor Christopher Reeve is paralyzed from the neck down after falling from his horse in a riding competition.
- 1999 Exxon and Mobil shareholders approve a $81.2 billion merger to create the world's largest oil company.
- 2000 Australian Prime Minister John Howard presents the "Declaration of Reconciliation" in an effort to heal the history of racism toward indigenous Australians.

DAY TO REMEMBER

Religious day Bede the Venerable's Day An Anglo-Saxon Benedictine monk, Bede was a prolific historian of his time. What we know of England before the eighth century is mainly the result of this man's writing, especially from his best-known work, *Historia ecclesiastica gentis Anglorum*, which begins "Britannia is an island in the ocean and once was called Albion."

The return of Solzhenitsyn

On this day in 1994, Alexandr Solzhenitsyn, the Nobel Prize-winning dissident author, flew back to his native Russia after 20 years of exile in the U.S. Imprisoned for 10 years for political dissent under Stalin, Solzhenitsyn was stripped of his citizenship and expelled from the Soviet Union in 1974. In 1990 Mikhail Gorbachev restored his citizenship and the following year dropped treason charges.

When he returned to the far eastern Russian port of Magadan, he was greeted by 2,000 people and given flowers and the traditional welcome gift of bread and salt. He reminded the Russians and the world not to forget the millions of victims of Soviet repression. "Today, in the heat of political change," he said, "those millions of victims are too lightly forgotten, both by those who were touched by that annihilation and even more so by those who were responsible for it." He arrived with his wife, Natalya, and the youngest of his three sons, Stephan, and then traveled across Russia by train, arriving in Moscow on July 23.

Solzhenitsyn expressed his shock at what he had seen on his journey, and attacked the leaders of the new Russia for betraying its people. In December 1998, he refused to accept a state medal from President Boris Yeltsin to mark his eightieth birthday, saying that he could not accept the Order of St Andrew from a leader who had reduced Russia to a state of ruin.

May 28

"A medium Vodka dry Martini – with a slice of lemon peel. Shaken and not stirred."

IAN FLEMING, CREATOR OF JAMES BOND

The candle is lit

On this day in 1981, Peter Benenson celebrated the twentieth anniversary of Amnesty International by relighting the original candle, which he first lit when he founded the humanitarian organization in 1961, on the steps of St. Martin-in-the-Fields, London.

The birth of the organization which would ultimately evolve into Amnesty International took place in 1960, when Benenson, a British lawyer, was reading the newspaper on his way to work. The story told of the imprisonment of two Portuguese students who were sentenced to seven years for raising a toast to freedom in a Lisbon restaurant.

This incident motivated Benenson to launch a one-year campaign called "Appeal for Amnesty 1961" in the London *Observer* newspaper. The campaign began with a potent article written by Benenson entitled "The Forgotten Prisoners." In it he wrote, "Open your newspaper – any day of the week – and you will find a report from somewhere in the world of someone being imprisoned, tortured, or executed because his opinions or religion are unacceptable to his Government. The newspaper reader feels a sickening sense of impotence. Yet if these feelings of disgust all over the world could be united into common action, something effective could be done."

Benenson's article asked readers to write letters expressing support for the students. The response was so great that within a year, groups of supporters had formed in more than a dozen countries, all of them writing to defend victims of injustice. The campaign grew enormously, and by the end of 1961 the organization Amnesty International (AI) had been formed. Today Amnesty International remains true to its origins, "independent of any Government, political ideology, economic interest, or religion. It does not support or oppose any Government or political system, nor does it support or oppose the views of the victims whose rights it seeks to protect. It is concerned solely with the impartial protection of human rights."

There are upward of 7,500 AI groups with almost two million members operating in 162 countries and territories. Since AI was formed it has worked to defend more than 44,600 prisoners in hundreds of countries.

Births
- **1738** Dr. Joseph Guillotine, inventor of the guillotine
- **1759** William Pitt the Younger, U.K. Prime Minister
- **1908** Ian Fleming, author
- **1912** Patrick White, writer and Nobel Prize laureate
- **1940** Maeve Binchy, writer
- **1968** Kylie Minogue, singer

Deaths
- **1843** Noah Webster, lexicographer
- **1972** Edward VIII, Duke of Windsor
- **2003** Martha Scott, actress

HISTORICAL EVENTS

- **1915** John B. Gruelle patents the Raggedy Ann doll. It is one of the earliest examples of merchandise tying in with fiction, in this case, an illustrated children's book.
- **1961** Amnesty International is founded by Peter Benenson (see left).
- **1971** U.S. President Nixon orders John Haldeman to do more wiretapping and political espionage against the Democrats. The orders are recorded on tape.
- **1987** Mathias Rust, aged 19, lands a small private plane on a bridge near Red Square, Moscow, without having been intercepted by any Soviet air defenses. He spends 432 days in prison.
- **1999** In Milan, Italy, after 22 years of restoration work, Leonardo da Vinci's masterpiece "The Last Supper" is put back on display.

DAY TO REMEMBER

National Day Ethiopia National Day This observed day celebrates the defeat of the Mengistu regime in Ethiopia on this day in 1991.

May 29

"You know you are getting old when the candles cost more than the cake." — BOB HOPE

New Zealander Edmund Hillary and Nepalese Sherpa Tenzing Norgay became the first people to reach the summit of Mt. Everest. On Hillary's return to England, the BBC asked how the men reacted when they reached the top of the world. "We shook hands and gave each other the odd thump on the back," he responded. Their stay would last a mere 15 minutes since their oxygen reserves were low.

HISTORICAL EVENTS

1453 Constantinople falls to Muhammad II, ending the Byzantine Empire.
1919 Charles Strite patents a pop-up toaster.
1942 The movie *Yankee Doodle Dandy*, starring James Cagney, premieres at a war-bonds benefit in New York.
1953 Edmund Hillary of New Zealand and Tensing Norgay of Nepal become the first people to conquer Mt. Everest (see above).
1957 At 89 years old, Frank Lloyd Wright travels to Iraq to design an opera house for Baghdad which is never built.
1963 Timothy Leary and Richard Alpert, both psychology professors, are fired from Harvard for experimenting with psychedelic drugs.
1972 Twenty-six people are killed when three Japanese gunmen massacre passengers and staff at Tel Aviv's Lod Airport. The shootings are a reprisal attack for the killing of two Arab hijackers three weeks earlier.
1985 At Heysel Stadium in Brussels, Belgium, 35 people are killed in rioting which erupts between British and Italian spectators at the European Cup soccer final.
1990 Boris N. Yeltsin is elected President of the Russian Republic in the third round of balloting by the Russian Parliament.

Births
- 1903 Bob Hope, comedian
- 1946 Fernando Buesa, politician
- 1958 Annette Bening, actress
- 1961 Melissa Etheridge, singer and songwriter

Deaths
- 1814 Empress Josephine, first wife of Napoleon Bonaparte
- 1970 Eva Hesse, artist
- 1971 Max Trapp, composer
- 1979 Mary Pickford, actress
- 1982 Romy Schneider, actress
- 1994 Erich Honecker, East German leader

DAY TO REMEMBER

National day Oak Apple Day (U.K.) This designated day commemorates the restoration of the monarchy in England, in May 1660. In some parts of the country, the day is also known as Shick-Shack Day or Arbor Day. In 1664 it was commanded by an Act of Parliament to be observed as a day of thanksgiving. English people wore sprigs of oak with gilded oak-apples.

May 30

"I do not agree with what you have to say, but I'll defend to the death your right to say it."
— VOLTAIRE

HISTORICAL EVENTS

- **1431** Joan of Arc is burned at the stake in Rouen, France (see below).
- **1896** The first car accident occurs in New York City when Henry Wells hits cyclist Eveylin Thomas.
- **1962** A CIA memo briefing for Attorney General Robert Kennedy reveals $150,000 was offered to the U.S. mob for the assassination of Fidel Castro. The mob insisted on attempting the job free of charge.
- **1967** Evel Knievel successfully jumps over a line of 16 cars on his motorcycle at the Ascot Speedway in California.
- **1968** After surviving World War II, the University of Leipzig's gothic church Paulinerkirche, is blown up by East German dictator Walter Ulbricht.
- **2000** It is reported that physicists have conducted experiments in which light beams appear to travel faster than the speed of light.

DAYS TO REMEMBER

Religious day St. Isaac of Dalmatia's Day A Byzantine monk who was imprisoned for denouncing the Roman Emperor Valens for the heresy of Arianism, St. Isaac later founded a monastery in Constantinople, where he died on May 30, 383. St. Isaac's Cathedral in the city of St. Petersburg commemorates him on this day.

Religious Day St. Joan of Arc's Day Joan of Arc was beatified in 1909 and canonized in 1920.

Births
- **1846** Peter Carl Fabergé, master jeweler and goldsmith
- **1926** Christine Jorgensen, activist
- **1947** Vashti Murphy McKenzie, one of the first female bishops
- **1951** Zdravko Čolić, singer
- **1981** Devendra Banhart, singer and songwriter

Deaths
- **1593** Christopher Marlowe, dramatist and poet
- **1640** Peter Paul Rubens, painter
- **1778** Voltaire, writer
- **1960** Boris Pasternak, poet and novelist

The death of Joan of Arc

From 1330, France was at war against England for the duration of what is called the Hundred Years War. By 1429, the English, with help from their allies the Burgundians, had occupied Paris and much of France. The French lacked leadership and a deep sense of hopelessness was felt in France as Henry V of England was claiming the French throne.

After Joan, a simple and pious girl, persuaded the Dauphin of her calling to save France, she passed an examination by a board of theologians. She was given troops to command and the rank of captain. She led the troops to a miraculous victory over the English at the Battle of Orleans.

The fighting continued in other locations along the Loire and in 10 days she defeated the English to the east of the city, freeing the bridge over the Loire in the course one day. The chief of the English company was killed in this battle, bringing about victory and the lifting of the siege. Later, Joan persuaded the Dauphin that he should be crowned Charles VII. At the coronation she was given the seat of honor beside the King.

Then, in 1430, the Burgundians captured Joan while she was defending Compiegne, and she was sold to the English.

The English, in turn, handed her over to the ecclesiastical court at Rouen to be tried for witchcraft and heresy, and for wearing male clothing, which was considered an offense against the church.

Reports as to whether Charles VII attempted to rescue her vary, but what is known is that on May 30, 1431, she was burned at the stake at the age of nineteen. Then, in 1456, her mother insisted that a second trial be held and she was pronounced innocent of the charges against her. Joan was beatified in 1909 and then canonized in 1920. Her public activity lasted only two years, from February 1429 to 30 May, 1431 – one year at war and one year in captivity.

DATEline

May 31

"I am as bad as the worst, but thank God I am as good as the best." — WALT WHITMAN

Births
- 1819 Walt Whitman, poet
- 1838 Henry Sidgwick, philosopher
- 1915 Judith Wright, poet
- 1930 Clint Eastwood, actor and director
- 1945 Rainer Werner Fassbinder, filmmaker

Deaths
- 1594 Tintoretto, painter
- 1809 Franz Joseph Haydn, composer
- 1986 James Rainwater, physicist and Nobel Prize laureate
- 1996 Timothy Leary, professor and philosopher

HISTORICAL EVENTS

1879 The first electric railway opens at the Berlin Trades Exposition.

1902 The Second Boer War ends between Great Britain and the two Boer republics of South Africa.

1907 Taxicabs begin running in New York. The word *taxi* is derived from the invention of the taximeter in 1891, so called because it calculates how much passengers are to be taxed for their journey.

1927 After a production run of more than 15 million vehicles, the last Model T Ford is assembled.

1942 A Japanese midget submarine strikes the HMAS *Kuttabul* in Sydney Harbour, Australia, killing 19 sailors. It is the most damaging of several midget submarine attacks against Sydney on this day.

1955 A decree rendered by the U.S. Supreme Court orders that schools in all states must end racial segregation "with all deliberate speed."

1961 South Africa becomes an independent republic.

1990 *Seinfeld*, starring Jerry Seinfeld, first airs on NBC TV in the U.S. (see right).

DAY TO REMEMBER

International day World "No Tobacco" Day The Member States of the World Health Organization created World No Tobacco Day in 1987 to draw global attention to the problems of smoking and the preventable death and disease it causes.

Jerry Seinfeld (Jerry Seinfeld), Elaine Marie Benes (Julia Louis-Dreyfus), George Costanza (Jason Alexander), and Cosmo Kramer (Michael Richards) appeared in *Seinfeld*, the "show about nothing," which aired for the first time on this day on NBC TV in the U.S. The show is known for its take on the minutiae of life. Despite its success, *Seinfeld* did not crack the ratings' top 30 until its fourth season. However, by its sixth, it was number one.

DAYS TO REMEMBER *May*

1
In the Pagan Wheel of the Year, Beltane in the Northern Hemisphere and Samhain in the Southern Hemisphere

2
Ysahodhara, the consort of Buddha, is honored in India

3
Feast Day for St. Theodosius of Kiev Considered today to be the first person to introduce monasticism in the Russian Orthodox Church

4
Feast Day for St. Florian The patron saint of fire fighting and Poland. St. Florian was burned alive rather than renounce his faith

5
El Cinco de Mayo (Mexico, U.S.) Commemorates Mexican victory at the Battle of Puebla

8
George Peppard, actor, died in 1994

9
Europe Day Marks the Schuman Declaration of 1950 that first proposed the creation of what is now known as the European Union

10
Feast Day for St. Comgall This saint was the founder and abbot of the great Irish monastery at Bangor, now in Northern Ireland

11
Feast Day for St. Mocius This priest in Macedonia was beheaded after he destroyed a Pagan statue

12
Feast Day for St. Pancras A patron saint of children and is also invoked against headaches and perjury

15
Feast Day for St. Dymphna Patron saint of insanity and those suffering from mental illness

16
St. Brendan's Day Celtic saint who established many monasteries in Ireland including the legendary Clonfert in County Gallway in 560

17
Norway National Day In 1814 the Constitution of Norway was signed and the Danish Crown Prince Christian Frederik was elected King of Norway

18
Feast Day for St. Felix of Cantalica Born to peasant parents in Cantalice, Italy, St. Felix was canonized in 1709

19
Feast Day for St. Pudentiana Traditional Christian saint of unknown dates

22
The first day of the star sign of Gemini

23
Feast Day for the Roman Goddess of Spring, Flora In Roman mythology, Flora was the goddess of flowers, gardens, and the season of Spring

24
St. Sarah's Day Celebrated in Carmague, France. Each year in late May, Gypsies from all over Europe gather here to venerate St. Sara

25
National Tap Dance Day (U.S.) Celebrates the birthday of Bill "Bojangles" Robinson, the "king" of tap dancers

26
National Sorry Day (Australia) Instituted to acknowledge the wrong that had been done to indigenous Australian families

29
Oak Apple Day (U.K.) Commemorates the restoration of the monarchy in England, in May 1660

30
Feast Day for St. Joan of Arc Joan of Arc was beatified in 1909 and canonized in 1920

31
World No Tobacco Day Created in 1987 to draw global attention to the tobacco epidemic and the preventable death and disease it causes

6
Feast Day of Inghean Bhuidhe After Christianisation in Ireland, Inghean Bhuidhe was turned into a saint

7
Feast Day for St. Nil Sorsky This Russian Orthodox saint was a leader of the Russian medieval movement

13
Feast Day for St. Abban the Hermit An Irish Roman Catholic saint who lived in Abingdon, England

14
Ernesto "Che" Guevara, communist revolutionary, was born in 1928

20
Feast Day for St. Stephen of Piperi St. Stephen's venerated relics are believed to produce miracles and remain in the Moraca monastery in Montenegro where he was abbot

21
Feast Day for St. Elena Near Cagliari in Sardinia, people make an offering of bread sweetened with jam to St. Elena

27
Feast Day for Bede the Venerable An Anglo-Saxon Benedictine monk

28
Dr. Joseph Guillotine, inventor of the guillotine, was born in 1738

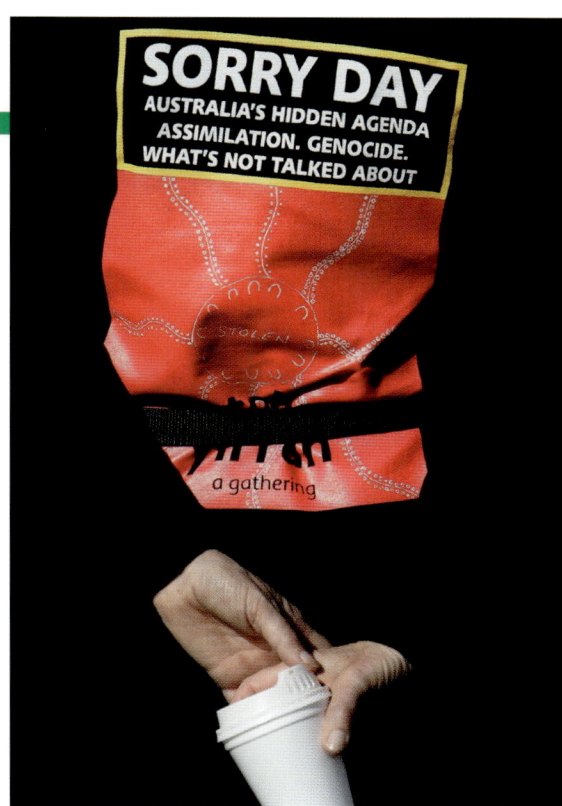

Right National Sorry Day, Australia, May 26

Below National Tap Dance Day, May 25

JUNE

"*No price is set on the lavish summer; June may be had by the poorest comer.*"
JAMES RUSSELL LOWELL, *THE VISION OF SIR LAUNFAL* (PART I, PRELUDE)

The colorful, Government-sanctioned celebrations pictured above in Tiananmen Square, China, are a far cry from the massacre of peaceful protesters which took place there in June, 1989, and was televised live worldwide by Western reporters.

June

The sixth month in the Gregorian calendar, June is an important month in all ancient cultures, marking the summer solstice in the north and winter solstice in the south. In the Northern Hemisphere it is a time of repleteness, when harvests begin and days are long and warm. It has long been associated with weddings and fertility. In the Southern Hemisphere it marks the shortest days of winter and the start of the wait for spring.

Cancer star sign and scene of hoeing from *Calendar and Book of Hours*, from fifteenth-century France. June starts in the sign of Gemini and ends in the sign of Cancer.

SPECIAL DATES
The Queen's Birthday is celebrated in Australia (except WA) and Bermuda on the second Monday in June.

Father's Day in the U.S., U.K., the Netherlands, Ireland, France, India, Canada, and others is on the third Sunday in June.

THE NAME OF THE MONTH OF JUNE comes from the Roman month *Junius*. It is usually thought to be derived from *Junonius* – sacred to Juno – but Ovid wrote that it was derived from *juniores*, meaning "youths," for a month dedicated to the young, though he also wrote that it had been named in honor of Juno and so may have just been punning.

Juno was the wife of Jupiter, ruler of the gods, and was seen particularly as a guardian for women. Incorporating elements of the Greek goddesses Hera and Pallas Athena, Juno was a complex goddess, with many warrior aspects, and was often depicted wearing an animal skin. Different incarnations of Juno were evoked at different times in a woman's life, from marriage, to childbirth, to protection in times of danger. She took on many aspects including Juno Fortuna, goddess of fate; Juno Sospita,

This relief stone work from the first century C.E. shows Vestia, the virgin goddess, seated with four vestal virgins. In Roman times, the festival of *Vestalia* in June was dedicated to Vesta.

goddess of fertility; Juno Moneta, adviser and admonisher; Juno Caprotina, goddess of erotic love; Juno Populonia, goddess of conception; and Juno Pronuba, arranger of appropriate matches. She was worshipped by Roman women on the Kalends, the first of each lunar month, in commemoration of the lunar cycles of her devotees. But Junius was her special month, devoted to marriage and the family.

In Rome, Junius was seen as a particularly propitious time to marry. More than superstition, this was a logical ancient belief. A pregnancy that began in June or soon after would have the fruitful harvest months to see it through the dangerous first trimester, and be well established before any winter hardships came along. Then a spring birth would be gentle for the newborn baby. Eight days of the month were, however, not available for Roman weddings. Those eight days marked the festival of *Vestalia* – from June 7 to 14 – which were dedicated to Vesta, goddess of the hearth and Juno's sister. All secular activities were kept to a minimum at this time, and married women were allowed to enter the shrine of Vesta, where normally only vestal virgins were permitted. The festival concluded with the cleansing of the temple storehouse in hopes of a bountiful forthcoming harvest. This also served to placate the Penates, the gods of the household who would protect the food of the city.

June festivities

The two-day Jewish festival of *Shavu'ot*, also known as the Festival of Weeks, occurs 49 days after Passover, often in the first half of June. It is a harvest festival, but also celebrates the giving of the Torah. Traditionally, the faithful would stay up reading the Torah through the first night and then pray as soon as possible in the morning. The book of Ruth is also traditionally read during the festival.

Christianity adopted many of the traditions for these festivals into its June celebrations. The most notable is Pentecost. Held on the fiftieth day after Easter, Pentecost marks the coming of the Holy Spirit in the early Christian church and has become conflated with many of the traditions that were attached to Shavu'ot, especially the celebratory aspects.

In the U.K., Pentecost is known as Whit Sunday and churches were once dressed in green wreaths and boughs to celebrate it. Whit Walks would follow services in later years with many of the congregation walking about town dressed in their best, preferably white. It was seen as a good time to match-make the young. Weddings were popular at this time, too.

A peculiar British folk myth holds that any child born on Whit Sunday would either kill or be killed – a fate that could only be overcome by a mock funeral for the child, or by squashing an insect in the child's hand.

Three other great Christian festivals are associated with June. The first is Ascension Day, the Thursday 40 days after Easter, which marks the Ascension of Christ into the heavens. The second is St. John's Day, and the third is the feast day of Saints Peter and Paul on June 29. This day commemorates the martyrdom of the two leading members of the early church and is a solemnity, the highest degree for a liturgical feast. Even there, traces of the old myths crept into celebrations. In the U.K., girls who wished to dream of their future husbands would take nine keys – symbols of St. Peter the gatekeeper to heaven – to bed with them, tied into their hair, and recite a poem asking the saint to grant them a favor.

New priests lie in front of Pope Benedict XVI during a Pentecost mass at St. Peter's Basilica at the Vatican, Rome. In the Roman Catholic faith, the Pentecost mass celebrates the descent of the Holy Spirit upon the apostles, 50 days after the resurrection of Christ at Easter. Pentecost is observed in May or June, depending on when Easter falls.

June birthflower

June's birthflower is the rose, which blooms at its best in the Northern Hemisphere at this time of year. In the Southern Hemisphere, warm areas will even see the last of autumn spot blooms. The rose is associated with beauty and love, and is still sought after for its health-giving and cosmetic properties. June is National Rose Month in the U.S.

Crowds gather each year at the ancient stone circle of Stonehenge on Salisbury Plain, England, to celebrate the summer solstice, which shifts between June 21 and June 24. At dawn, people watch the midsummer sun as it rises over the megalithic monument.

Midsummer

Before Christianity, and before Rome, June was already a significant month due to the timing of the summer solstice (the winter solstice in the Southern Hemisphere). The date shifts between June 20 and 23, though many countries have chosen to mark it officially on June 24. Structures dedicated to marking or calculating the exact date of the solstice stretch back to prehistoric times and include Anasazi buildings in North America, the temple of Karnak in Egypt, and many megalithic structures across northern Europe, the most famous of which is Stonehenge, on the Salisbury Plain in the U.K.

Stonehenge's stones weigh up to 50 tons each and the construction methods used are still a mystery, although we do know that it was built in three stages between about 3,000 and 1,500 B.C.E. Its main axis is aligned along the midsummer sunrise. Speculation as to what role the solstice played in the religious rituals of the builders continues among academics; currently the structure is thought to have been linked to funereal rites. In more recent times, Stonehenge has attracted large crowds of neo-Pagans searching for religious meaning. Crowds of up to 30,000 people damaged several of the stones until unrestricted access was banned in 1985.

Common Midsummer festivities across northern Europe include bonfires in Finland, Norway, Latvia, Estonia, and Denmark. These date back to Pagan celebrations, and the early Christian church in these countries tried to stop the practice. St. Eligius wrote to the inhabitants of Flanders in the seventh century, "No Christian on the feast of St. John or the solemnity of any other saint performs *solestitia* [summer solstice rites] or dancing or leaping or diabolical chants." And in much of southern Europe and in the U.K., the practice did die out, albeit slowly.

In the north, though, it is considered one of the great festivals of the year and is most often celebrated on its eve. Traditional elements still accompany the bonfires. In Norway, mock marriages are held to symbolize new life; in Denmark, a straw witch is often burnt; in Estonia,

June birthstone

Pearl is the birthstone of June. Chinese myth holds that these gems came from the brains of dragons. Pearls are associated with love and purity, and were once used in shimmering make-up, partly for their beauty and partly for their supposed aphrodisiac effect. June has two alternate gemstones, the moonstone and alexandrite.

people jump over the bonfires and girls pick flowers in hopes of dreaming of their future husbands; in Latvia, girls wear wreaths of flowers and men wreaths of oak as they also leap over bonfires; in Sweden a maypole replaces the fire and holds a similar role as a symbol of fertility.

It wasn't just in the East that this solstice was associated so strongly with women. In China it saw the astrological movement into the Yin part of the year, which celebrated the earth and feminine forces.

The Christian church did succeed in putting its stamp over Midsummer, though. June 24 became the feast of St. John the Baptist. Unlike other saints' days, this one is marked on the anniversary of his birth, not his death. It is celebrated even when it falls on a Sunday, which is not usual, and holds the status of a solemnity. Despite St. Eligius and others who frowned on the practice, the traditional bonfires were made over as St. John's Fires in many parts of Europe and were lit on the eve of the feast and at the end of the day's religious ceremonies. The connection with marriage and fertility was not lost – in many parts of Europe it was thought a boy and girl who successfully leapt together over the embers of the bonfire would be married within the year. The Baptist's reputation also attracted some folk practices. In much of northern and eastern Europe, people would bathe in the sea on the morning of St. John's day in a bid to cure illness and to seek divine rebirth.

In the modern world, the most famous celebration of Midsummer is Shakespeare's anarchic comedy, *A Midsummer Night's Dream*. The whole play is set within the wedding celebrations for Duke Theseus and Hippolyta. Two couples, Hermia and Lysander, and Helena and Demetrius, are brought to a happy ending by the machinations of the fairies of the woods, acting under King Oberon and Queen Titania. The whole play celebrates the trials, the difficulties, and ultimately the triumph of marriage, with Shakespeare playing freely with many Midsummer traditions, including the underlying Paganism of the celebrations – even referencing the warrior wife Juno in the character of Hippolyta. Above all, it is a play that focuses on joy, and joy is the whole point of Midsummer – one last warm riot of feasting before the hard work of harvest would begin.

Left In the Ukraine, the summer solstice is considered one of the great festivals of the year. Young people leap over the flames of bonfires to clean themselves of ill and bad luck, and the girls wear wreaths of flowers.

Below This nineteenth-century painting depicts a sleeping Titania, Sheakspeare's good-spirited queen from *A Midsummer Night's Dream*. The wistful painting is housed in the Bibliothòque des Arts Décoratifs, Paris.

June 1

The first day of summer in the Northern Hemisphere, and the first day of winter in the Southern Hemisphere

> *"I do not want the peace which passeth understanding, I want the understanding which bringeth peace."* — HELEN KELLER

HISTORICAL EVENTS

1494 Eight bolls (nearly 320 gallons [1,200 l]) of malt are recorded as being delivered to Friar John Cor for the first known batch of scotch whisky in Scotland.

1660 Mary Dyer is hanged in Boston, Massachusetts, a martyr for her Quaker beliefs.

1831 The position of the North Magnetic Pole, on the Boothia Peninsula, is discovered by James Clark Ross.

1942 Warsaw underground newspaper *Liberty Brigade* publishes the first news of the gassing of tens of thousands of Jews at Chelmno death camp in Poland.

1943 Actor Leslie Howard (*Gone with the Wind*, *Brief Encounter*) is killed when a civilian flight from Lisbon to London is shot down by the Germans during World War II. It had been rumored Churchill was on board.

1958 Charles de Gaulle is brought out of retirement to lead France by decree for six months in a time of national crisis. He holds office for 10 years.

1967 The Beatles release their most famous album, *Sgt. Pepper's Lonely Hearts Club Band*.

1968 Deaf and blind disabled activist Helen Keller dies in Westport, Connecticut, at the age of 87.

1979 Ninety years of white rule in Rhodesia come to an end as the Government of Bishop Muzorewa takes power, ousting Prime Minister Ian Smith and changing the country's name to Zimbabwe.

2001 Crown Prince Dipendra Bir Bikram Shah Dev of Nepal massacres his family during a royal dinner (see below).

Births

- **1801** Brigham Young, religious leader
- **1878** John Masefield, poet
- **1926** Marilyn Monroe (born Norma Jeane Mortenson), actress
- **1926** Andy Griffith, actor
- **1930** Edward Woodard, actor
- **1936** Gerald Scarfe, British cartoonist and illustrator
- **1937** Morgan Freeman, actor
- **1937** Colleen McCullough, writer
- **1947** Ron Wood, guitarist (Rolling Stones)
- **1968** Jason Donovan, actor and singer
- **1974** Alanis Morissette, singer

Deaths

- **1660** Mary Dyer, English Quaker
- **1769** Edward Holyoke, clergyman and president of Harvard University
- **1943** Leslie Howard, actor
- **1968** Helen Keller, humanitarian
- **2001** Queen Aishwarya of Nepal
- **2001** King Birendra of Nepal
- **2002** Hansie Cronje, cricketer

Nepal mourns the deaths of King Birendra and Queen Aishwarya along with seven others. All were slain on this day by Crown Prince Dipendra, who had argued with his family over his choice of bride. After shooting the royals, the Crown Prince turned the gun on himself and died 30 hours later. The King's middle brother, Prince Gyanendra, succeeded him to the throne. The succession precipitated a steady worsening in Nepal's political problems and Maoist rebellion, and the horror of the massacre led to a series of conspiracy claims that further undermined political stability in the troubled nation.

June 2

"The British Constitution has always been puzzling and always will be." — QUEEN ELIZABETH II

HISTORICAL EVENTS

1793 Jean-Paul Marat leads the expulsion of 31 Girondists from the French National Convention. It precipitates the Reign of Terror that sees 17,000 to 40,000 "counter revolutionaries" guillotined over the next year.

1865 The surrender of forces under Confederate General Edmund Kirby Smith at Galveston, Texas, marks the end of the American Civil War.

1896 Guglielmo Marconi receives a patent for the radio.

1924 Native Americans born within the territorial limits of the U.S. are granted citizenship by the Indian Citizenship Act.

1946 Italians vote in a referendum to turn Italy from a monarchy into a Republic. King Umberto II is exiled.

1953 The coronation of Queen Elizabeth II is held in London; it is the first to be televised (see below).

1965 The first contingent of Australian combat troops arrives in South Vietnam.

1966 *Surveyor 1* touches down on the surface of the Moon – the first U.S. spacecraft to soft-land outside Earth.

1979 Pope John Paul II visits his native Poland, becoming the first Pope to visit a Communist country.

1999 Television begins broadcasting in Bhutan.

Births
- **1740** Donatien Alphonse François (the Marquis de Sade), French author
- **1840** Thomas Hardy, writer
- **1904** Johnny Weissmuller, swimmer and actor (star of *Tarzan*)
- **1941** Stacy Keach, actor
- **1941** Charlie Watts, musician (Rolling Stones)
- **1965** Mark Waugh, cricketer
- **1965** Steve Waugh, cricketer

Deaths
- **1882** Giuseppe Garibaldi, Italian revolutionary
- **1941** Lou Gehrig, American baseball player
- **1962** Vita Sackville-West, writer and gardener
- **1970** Bruce McLaren, car racer, designer, and manufacturer

DAYS TO REMEMBER

Religious day St. Nicephorus' Day
The death of this saint is celebrated by the Greek Orthodox Church. He was Patriarch of Constantinople from 806 to 815 and wrote many treatises which outlined the faith, as well as a chronology of the world from Adam and Eve to his own time.

National day Festa della Repubblica (Italy) This day, whose name translates to Republic Day, commemorates the birth of the *Repubblica Italiana* and the end of the monarchy in 1948.

London came to a standstill on this day in 1953 for the coronation of Queen Elizabeth II. The Princess Elizabeth was in Kenya when her father, King George VI, died on February 6, 1952. She flew home immediately and was proclaimed Queen shortly afterward. The long planning period for the actual coronation allowed for detailed preparations, especially since most of the nobility were still emerging from wartime rationing. Her dress was woven from silk grown in Britain and embroidered with motifs from around the Commonwealth. The ceremony was televised and watched by more than 20 million Britons, then relayed quickly to more than 100 million international viewers.

June 3

"These are the voyages of the starship Enterprise. *Its five-year mission … to boldly go where no man has gone before."* — GENE RODDENBERRY, 1967

HISTORICAL EVENTS

- **1140** French scholar, poet, and eunuch Peter Abelard is found guilty of heresy.
- **1916** The U.S. Congress establishes the Reserve Officers Training Corps for officer training in colleges.
- **1923** Italian women are granted the right to vote by dictator Benito Mussolini.
- **1928** A Japanese bomb blast kills Manchurian warlord Zhang Zuolin and destabilises northern China.
- **1938** "Degenerate art" is removed from galleries by the Third Reich. It is defined as any kind of modern art (such as abstract art) which does not conform to classical standards of purity and beauty, conversely described as "heroic art."
- **1969** The last episode of the original *Star Trek* series, produced by Gene Roddenberry, airs for the first time in the U.S.
- **1969** HMAS *Melbourne* collides with U.S. Navy destroyer USS *Frank E. Evans* off South Vietman (see right).
- **1973** Reggae band Bob Marley and The Wailers releases the album *Exodus*.
- **1991** Mount Unzen erupts in Japan in Kyushu; 43 scientists and journalists are killed.
- **1992** The Mabo decision is handed down in the Australian High Court recognizing the falsity of "terra nullius" in relation to indigenous land rights.

Births
- **1808** Jefferson Davis, first and only President of the Confederate States of America
- **1904** Charles R. Drew, physician
- **1906** Josephine Baker, dancer, singer, and actress
- **1911** Paulette Goddard, actress
- **1926** Allen Ginsberg, American poet
- **1936** Larry McMurtry, author
- **1950** Suzi Quatro, musician and singer

Deaths
- **1875** Georges Bizet, French composer
- **1899** Johann Strauss II, Austrian composer
- **1924** Franz Kafka, novelist
- **1963** Pope John XXIII
- **1977** Roberto Rossellini, film director
- **1989** Ayatollah Ruhollah Khomeini, Iranian Shi'ite leader
- **1991** Katia and Maurice Krafft, vulcanologists
- **2001** Anthony Quinn, actor

The USS *Frank E. Evans* disaster

Most of the 272 men on board the USS *Frank E. Evans* were asleep at 3:15 A.M. on June 3, 1969. A short while before, the Australian aircraft carrier HMAS *Melbourne* had signaled the smaller American destroyer to take up position behind the carrier. Despite having well-rehearsed procedures for such a manoeuvre, the *Frank E. Evans* moved across the path of the carrier. It was later found that an inexperienced officer had been left in charge.

Unable to avoid the collision, the *Melbourne* ploughed into the smaller vessel, slicing it in half. On board the carrier, emergency stations had been sounded. Aircrew on the deck rushed to help, and used fire hoses as makeshift ladders. The front section of the *Frank E. Evans* sank in less than nine minutes. Of the 111 men on the front section of the ship, 38 made it off alive and were picked up by the Australians. The stern was secured to the carrier with cables, and cargo nets were used to help men escape onto the carrier. Only one drowned in the stern.

Despite the full moon, the *Frank E. Evans* was in the carrier's shadow, and it was all but impossible to see men in the water. The *Melbourne* used its signal lights to search, while the Westland Wessex helicopters that were based on the carrier used their spotlights and winches to assist in the rescue.

A court-martial and the inquiry that followed found Captain Stevenson not at fault and a series of commendations were given to the crew. Yet the U.S. Government promoted the belief that it was an Australian-caused accident, well away from the combat zone, to avoid political fallout. While the crew of the *Evans* had served in the Vietnam conflict, the disaster took place during Operation Sea Spirit exercises, so the names of the dead were not added to the Vietnam Veterans Memorial in Washington, a decision that is still being challenged.

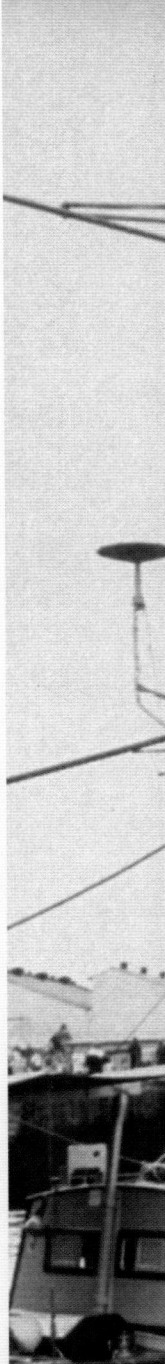

DATE*line*

241

June 4

> "Men their rights and nothing more; women their rights and nothing less."
> SUSAN B. ANTHONY, AMERICAN SUFFRAGETTE

A New King for Nepal

On June 4, 2001, Gyanendra became King of Nepal, following the massacre of members of the Nepalese royal family three days earlier. On June 1, in the Nepalese capital of Kathmandu, Crown Prince Dipendra killed nine members of the Nepalese royal family, including his parents—King Birendra and Queen Aishwarya—before turning the gun on himself. The massacre occurred following a heated argument over Dipendra's choice of bride, Devyani Rana, which had reportedly been opposed by the Queen.

Apparently intoxicated, Dipendra went back to his room, later returning dressed in army fatigues and armed with an automatic weapon.

Others killed in the attack included the King's sisters, Princess Sharda and Princess Shanti; his brother-in-law, Kumar Khadga; and Dipendra's brother Niranjan and his sister Shruti.

Dipendra was taken to a Kathmandu hospital suffering self-inflicted gunshot wounds. After lapsing into a coma, he was pronounced dead some 30 hours later. There has been much speculation as to whether or not Dipendra acted alone in the elimination of his family.

King Birendra had ruled the country for almost 30 years. Dipendra was heir to the throne, and became king of the country while in hospital following the massacre.

On Dipendra's death, Gyanendra, Birendra's brother, became king on June 4. He is the only king of the country to have been crowned twice, with his first brief reign of several months (November 1950 to February 1951) occurring when he was a young child, aged 4. Gyanendra's second ascendancy to the throne was made official today, though it was a low-key affair, with an official coronation ceremony planned for a later date.

Births

- **470 B.C.E.** Socrates, Greek philosopher
- **1738** King George III of Great Britain
- **1867** Carl Gustav Mannerheim, President of Finland
- **1907** Rosalind Russell, actress
- **1924** Dennis Weaver, actor
- **1928** Dr. Ruth Westheimer, sex therapist and author
- **1932** Maurice Shadbolt, writer
- **1966** Cecilia Bartoli, mezzo-soprano
- **1971** Noah Wyle, actor
- **1975** Angelina Jolie, actress

Deaths

- **1798** Giacomo Casanova, philanderer and writer
- **1830** Antonio José de Sucre, South American independence hero
- **1941** Kaiser Wilhelm II, last German emperor
- **1968** Dorothy Gish, actress

HISTORICAL EVENTS

- **1783** The Montgolfier brothers launch their paper-lined silk balloon at Anonay in France – the first hot-air balloon.
- **1919** The U.S. Congress approves the Nineteenth Amendment to the United States Constitution, guaranteeing suffrage to women.
- **1939** The SS *St. Louis*, carrying 963 Jewish refugees, is denied permission to land in Florida, U.S. Forced to return to Europe, most of its passengers later die in Nazi concentration camps.
- **1940** The Battle of Dunkirk ends; more than 300,000 Allied troops had been evacuated, many by civilian ships.
- **1944** Rome surrenders to the Allies – the first Axis capital to fall in World War II.
- **1989** Solidarity wins the first partly free parliamentary elections in post-war Poland. This begins a series of peaceful anti-communist revolutions in eastern Europe and the eventual end of the Soviet Union.
- **1989** Around 575 people are killed at Ufa in Russia when two trains pass near a leaking gas pipeline, sparking an explosion that derailed both.
- **2001** Three days after the massacre of nine members of the Nepalese royal family—including the King and Queen—at the hand of Prince Dipendra, who also died later—Prince Gyanendra becomes king of the tiny landlocked nation.

DAY TO REMEMBER

Religious day St. Francis Caracciolo's Day One of the founders of the Order of the Minor Clerks Regular, this saint was noted for his fasting and is patron saint of Italian cooks.

DATE*line*

June 5

"Politics is supposed to be the second oldest profession. I have come to realize that it bears a very close resemblance to the first." RONALD REAGAN

HISTORICAL EVENTS

1851 *Uncle Tom's Cabin, or Life Among the Lowly*, Harriet Beecher Stowe's anti-slavery epic, begins its serialisation in the *National Era* abolitionist newspaper.

1947 United States Secretary of State George Marshall calls for economic aid to war-torn Europe – the beginning of the Marshall Plan.

1963 John Profumo, the British Secretary of State for War, resigns in a sex scandal.

1967 Israel begins the Six-Day War with simultaneous attacks on the air forces of Egypt, Jordan, and Syria.

1968 U.S. presidential candidate Robert F. Kennedy is shot at the Ambassador Hotel in Los Angeles, California, by Sirhan Sirhan. He dies the next day (see below).

1981 The first five cases of what would come to be known as AIDS are reported by the Centers for Disease Control and Prevention in the U.S.

1984 The Prime Minister of India, Indira Gandhi, orders an attack on the Golden Temple, the holiest site of the Sikh religion. Official casualties are 576 combatants killed and 335 wounded; independent observers estimate that thousands of unarmed Sikh civilians are also killed in the crossfire.

1989 The Unknown Rebel halts the progress of a column of advancing tanks for more than half an hour after the Tiananmen Square protests of 1989.

DAYS TO REMEMBER

International day World Environment Day This United Nations holiday is dedicated to improving the environment around the world.

National day Constitution Day (Denmark) Celebrates the founding of Denmark's constitution and constitutional monarchy in 1848.

Religious day St. Boniface's Day An English missionary, this saint is credited with converting the Germans to Christianity in 732.

Births
- 1718 Thomas Chippendale, furniture maker
- 1883 John Maynard Keynes, economist
- 1919 Richard Scarry, children's author
- 1939 Margaret Drabble, novelist
- 1941 Spalding Gray, actor and screenwriter
- 1949 Ken Follett, Welsh author
- 1954 Nicko McBrain, musician (Iron Maiden)
- 1971 Mark Wahlberg, singer and actor

Deaths
- 1910 O. Henry, author
- 1916 Lord Horatio Kitchener, British field marshal
- 1921 Georges Feydeau, playwright
- 1999 Mel Tormé, singer, composer, and actor
- 2004 Ronald Reagan, fortieth U.S. President

Minutes after giving a rousing speech to his supporters at the Ambassador Hotel on this day in 1968, Robert F. Kennedy was shot three times by Sirhan Sirhan, allegedly over Kennedy's support for Israel in the Six-Day War. Kennedy, Attorney General in his brother's administration, had been well on the way to securing the Democratic nomination for the 1968 presidential race. He had a strong record in civil rights and had served three-and-a-half successful years as Senator for New York. His last words were, reportedly, "Is everyone all right?" Kennedy died early the next day. Sirhan was convicted of the assassination and is still in jail.

June 6

> "*The free men of the world are marching together to victory.*"
> GENERAL DWIGHT D. EISENHOWER GIVING THE D-DAY ORDER ON JUNE 6, 1944

When pretty, young David Jones of Brixton, London, decided that his stage presence, David Bowie, needed a bit more life, he invented Ziggy Stardust with the release of his album *The Rise and Fall of Ziggy Stardust and the Spiders from Mars*. This spiky-haired, sexually indiscriminate, hard-living, peace-loving alien from Mars became the focus of what many critics hail as the greatest concept album of the 1970s. In addition to unleashing a wave of lipstick-wearing young men on the world, Ziggy Stardust saw the blossoming of Glam Rock, which would send its influences out across the music sphere: Bodysuits to disco, make-up and album story arcs to heavy metal, art-school inspirations to Goth and, eventually, the British dance music movement.

Births
- **1599** Diego Velázquez, painter
- **1799** Alexander Pushkin, poet
- **1868** Robert Falcon Scott, explorer
- **1875** Thomas Mann, writer, Nobel Prize laureate
- **1901** Sukarno, first President of Indonesia
- **1954** Harvey Fierstein, actor
- **1955** Sandra Bernhard, actress and comedienne
- **1956** Björn Borg, tennis player

Deaths
- **1891** Sir John A. Macdonald, first Prime Minister of Canada
- **1941** Louis Chevrolet, automotive pioneer and race car driver
- **1961** Carl Jung, psychiatrist
- **1968** Robert F. Kennedy, United States Attorney General and Senator for New York
- **1976** J. Paul Getty, industrialist
- **2005** Anne Bancroft, actress

HISTORICAL EVENTS

1844 The Young Men's Christian Association (YMCA) is founded in St. Paul's churchyard, London.

1925 Walter Percy Chrysler founds the Chrysler Corporation, which will become one of the most famous automobile manufacturers in the U.S.

1944 D-Day arrives. What would be known as the Battle of Normandy begins. Operation Overlord sees 155,000 Allied troops land on the beaches of Normandy in France. It is the largest amphibious mission in military history and begins a change in fortunes for the Allied nations.

1972 David Bowie's album *The Rise and Fall of Ziggy Stardust and the Spiders from Mars* is released, and the era of Glam Rock begins (see above).

1982 The 1982 Lebanon War begins. Israeli Defense Minister Ariel Sharon is a prime instigator of this invasion of Southern Lebanon to quash the Palestine Liberation Organization's activities and stop Syria's intrusion into the Lebanese civil war. Troops eventually reach as far north as the capital, Beirut.

1985 The Brazilian grave of "Wolfgang Gerhard," who drowned while swimming in 1979, is exhumed in Embu. As had long been rumored, the remains found are proven to be those of Josef Mengele, Auschwitz's Angel of Death.

2002 A small Earth-bound asteroid explodes with near-nuclear force in the atmosphere over the Mediterranean Sea. The fireball causes a riot of UFO reports.

DAYS TO REMEMBER

National day Swedish National Day This is a holiday originally established to commemorate the coronation of King Gustav Vasa in 1523.

Historical day D-Day Anniversary This day celebrates the D-Day landings in 1944. Celebrations are held in the U.K., France, and much of Europe.

June 7

DATE*line*

"Nobody, but nobody, is going to stop breathing on me." — VIRGINIA APGAR

HISTORICAL EVENTS

1099 Starving Crusaders begin the Siege of Jerusalem which would end with their bloody conquest of the city and massacre of its inhabitants on July 15.

1832 Irish immigrants from the ship *Carrick* die of Asiatic cholera in lower Canada. It is the beginning of an epidemic that ultimately kills some 9,000 people.

1862 The ratified treaty between the U.S. and U.K. agreeing to suppress the slave trade comes into action.

1900 The Boxer rebels cut the rail links between Peking and Tientsin in China. It is a prelude to the open war which would break out on June 20.

1909 Virginia Apgar, creator of the Apgar score, is born (see right).

1929 Vatican City is given the status of a sovereign state by the Lateran Treaty. It separates the papal lands from Rome and gives them self-government.

1942 The Battle of Midway ends with severe losses for the Japanese fleet. Midway is retained as a vital landing ground for the Pacific Allies.

1965 The U.S. Supreme Court, in Griswold v. Connecticut, upholds the right of married couples to use contraception.

DAYS TO REMEMBER

National day Union Dissolution Day (Norway) This day celebrates the 1905 dissolution of the Union between Sweden and Norway.

National day Sette Giugno (Malta) Commemoration of the 1919 riot against the British that began the road to self-Government in Malta.

The creator of the Apgar score

Born on this day in 1909, Virginia Apgar was a hard-working and intelligent student, and one of the few women of her generation to enrol in medical school. Despite great skill, Apgar met resistance from senior surgeons but was encouraged by the chair of surgery, Dr. Alan Whipple, to focus on the then poorly regarded field of anesthesia. He saw it as an area where her drive and intelligence could bring about real change. Apgar spent the next nine years working to have anesthesiology recognized as a specialty. In 1949 she was appointed the first woman professor at the Columbia University College of Physicians and Surgeons.

Apgar noted that one of the most difficult areas in her field was obstetrical anesthesia, and saw that all too often newborn children suffered from the effects of drugs given to the mother, and that often treatment was too slow in coming. She devised the Apgar score in 1952 — a test to be given at one minute of age that would observe heart rate, respiratory effort, muscle tone, reflex response, and color, and give each indicator a mark of 0, 1, or 2 points. The points are then totalled to arrive at the baby's score. Soon it became common practice to repeat the test at five minutes to see how the newborn was responding to treatment.

The score became an important tool in spotting early difficulties for newborns. It also led to changes in maternal care, as low scores were associated with some types of anesthesia. It marked a revolution in neonatal care that is still underway. Apgar went on to take a master's degree in public health in 1959 and devoted the rest of her working life to the prevention of birth defects.

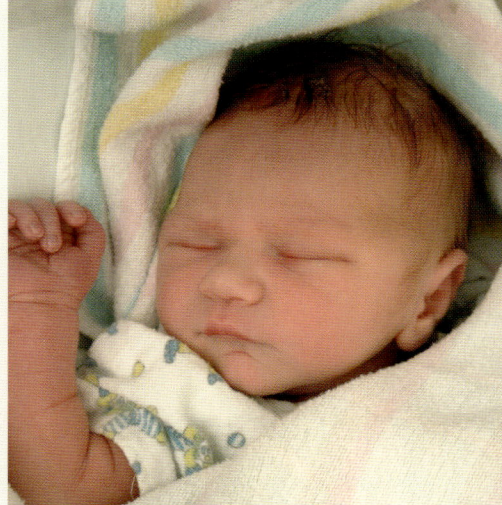

A baby will be given the Apgar score when it is one minute old

Births

1778	Beau Brummell, fashion leader
1848	Paul Gauguin, French painter
1868	Charles Rennie Mackintosh, Scottish architect, designer, and illustrator
1909	Jessica Tandy, actress
1917	Dean Martin, actor
1940	Tom Jones, singer
1952	Liam Neeson, actor
1958	Prince, musician

Deaths

1329	Robert the Bruce, King of Scotland
1866	Chief Seattle, Native American leader
1937	Jean Harlow, actress
1954	Alan Turing, mathematician and computer scientist
1965	Judy Holliday, actress
1967	Dorothy Parker, writer
1970	E. M. Forster, author
1980	Henry Miller, writer

June 8

"War is peace. Freedom is slavery. Ignorance is strength." — GEORGE ORWELL, *NINETEEN EIGHTY-FOUR*

Nineteen Eighty-Four is published

After a stint in the Spanish Civil War and a wartime job writing propaganda for the British Government, George Orwell (born Eric Blair) found himself in a world that was even more disturbing than that which he had posited in his 1944 masterpiece *Animal Farm*. Far from reining in Stalin, the post-World War II carve-up of Europe had given the communist dictator even more power, which deeply alarmed the democratic socialist Orwell. Disturbed by the fact that even in a democratic country such as Britain the Government could enact restrictions and censorship with little public comment, Orwell wrote *Nineteen Eighty-Four*.

The novel tells of Winston Smith, a man in a world of three superpowers — Oceania, Eurasia, and Eastasia — where war is a constant. Political structures are run by the Ministry of Truth, the Ministry of Peace, the Ministry of Love, and the Ministry of Plenty — all overseen in Oceania by Big Brother, the leader of the Party.

The state controls all individuals, televisions are used as a means of communication and control, and anti-government intent is stamped out as "thought crime." Orwell critiqued his own history as a propagandist: Posters promote "doublethink," where two contradictory statements are held at the same time and held as true — war is peace; freedom is slavery; ignorance is strength.

An incisive stab at totalitarianism, *Nineteen Eighty-Four* was a best-seller from the time of publication and remains a favorite on university reading lists. While it was influential in promoting anti-Stalinist feeling in the Britain of the 1950s, even among leftists, Orwell's lasting influences may not have been to his liking. In the twenty-first century, Big Brother is more famous as a reality TV franchise, and political spin doctors appear to be using his appendix "The Principles of Newspeak" as a guide for press releases.

Edmond O'Brien and Jan Sterling star as Winston and Julia in Michael Anderson's film adaptation of George Orwell's novel, *Nineteen Eighty-Four*.

HISTORICAL EVENTS

1783 Laki volcano, in Iceland, begins an eight-month eruption which kills more than 9,000 people through lava, poisonous gas, and famine. Suphurous clouds kill an estimated tens of thousands in the coming months across Europe. In winter, the haze from the eruption brings unseasonably cool temperatures to much of the Northern Hemisphere.
1866 The Canadian Parliament meets for the first time in Ottawa.
1942 Two Japanese imperial submarines shell Sydney and Newcastle, Australia.
1949 *Nineteen Eighty-Four* by George Orwell is published (see above).
1949 Celebrities including Helen Keller, Dorothy Parker, Danny Kaye, Fredric March, John Garfield, Paul Muni, and Edward G. Robinson are named in an FBI report as Communist Party members.
1953 The U.S. Supreme Court rules that Washington D.C. restaurants may not refuse to serve black patrons.
1968 James Earl Ray is arrested for the murder of Dr. Martin Luther King Jr.
1984 The Australian state of New South Wales decriminalizes homosexuality after six years of public protest.

Births
- **1671** Tomaso Albinoni, Italian composer
- **1743** Alessandro Cagliostro, adventurer
- **1810** Robert Schumann, German composer
- **1867** Frank Lloyd Wright, architect
- **1921** Suharto, President of Indonesia
- **1925** Barbara Bush, First Lady of the U.S.
- **1955** Sir Tim Berners-Lee, English inventor of the World Wide Web
- **1957** Scott Adams, cartoonist

Deaths
- **632** Muhammad, Prophet of Islam
- **1376** Edward, the Black Prince, son of Edward III of England
- **1809** Thomas Paine, American revolutionary and writer
- **1876** George Sand, author
- **1924** Andrew Irvine, mountain climber
- **1924** George Leigh Mallory, English mountain climber

June 9

"Have you no sense of decency?" — JOSEPH WELCH TO SENATOR JOSEPH MCCARTHY

HISTORICAL EVENTS

- **68** C.E. Dissolute Roman Emperor Nero commits suicide before he can be executed by the Roman Senate.
- **1311** Duccio's Renaissance masterpiece *Maestà Altarpiece* is installed in the Siena Cathedral in Siena, Italy.
- **1790** *Philadelphia Spelling Book* by John Barry becomes the first book to be copyrighted in the U.S.
- **1856** Some 500 Mormon handcart pioneers leave Iowa City, Iowa, and head west for Salt Lake City, Utah, wheeling all their possessions with them.
- **1931** Robert H. Goddard, the father of U.S. rocket design, patents a rocket-fuelled aircraft design. He is ultimately responsible for the rocket motor on the Bell X-2, the successor to the famous X-1 which broke the sound barrier.
- **1934** Disney's Donald Duck character debuts in the animated short film, *The Wise Little Hen* (see below).
- **1954** Joseph Welch, special counsel for the United States Army, accuses Senator Joseph McCarthy of bad faith and zeolatry during hearings as to whether Communism has infiltrated the U.S Army. It marks the beginning of McCarthy's end.
- **1957** The first ascent of Himalayan Broad Peak, the world's twelfth-highest mountain, is made by Fritz Wintersteller, Marcus Schmuck, Kurt Diemberger, and Hermann Buhl of an Austrian expedition led by Marcus Schmuck.
- **1999** The Kosovo War reaches the beginning of its drawn-out conclusion when the Federal Republic of Yugoslavia and NATO sign a peace treaty.

Births
- **1781** George Stephenson, engineer, inventor of the steam locomotive
- **1865** Carl Nielsen, composer
- **1891** Cole Porter, composer and lyricist
- **1956** Patricia Cornwell, author
- **1961** Michael J. Fox, actor
- **1961** Aaron Sorkin, director, producer, and writer
- **1963** Johnny Depp, actor

Deaths
- **68** Nero, Roman Emperor
- **597** St. Columba, Christian missionary, patron saint of Ireland
- **1870** Charles Dickens, author
- **1958** Robert Donat, actor
- **1964** Max Aitken (Lord Beaverbrook) business tycoon and politician

DAY TO REMEMBER

Religious day St. Columba's Day (St. Columcille in Ireland) This saint (521–597) is honored as one of Scotland's three patron saints. He played a major part in bringing Christianity back to Scotland.

In 1934, a short film called *The Wise Little Hen* featured the first appearance of Donald Duck. In his debut, Donald was appealed to by the hen of the title to help her with her corn farming. He avoided any work and found himself on the outer while she and her family enjoyed the harvest. This began a long, somewhat typecast career of being frustrated by circumstances largely of his own making, bringing on the famously unintelligible Duck tantrums. A bachelor, Donald lives with his nephews Huey, Dewey, and Louie, and is often seen in the company of his Uncle Scrooge and girlfriend Daisy.

June 10

"In the wake of my spiritual experience there came a vision of a society of alcoholics, each identifying with and transmitting his experience to the next – chain style." — BILL WILSON

Births
- 1819 Gustave Courbet, French painter
- 1901 Frederick Loewe, Austrian-born composer
- 1911 Terence Rattigan, playwright
- 1915 Saul Bellow, Canadian-born writer, Nobel Prize laureate
- 1921 Prince Philip, Duke of Edinburgh
- 1922 Judy Garland, actress and singer
- 1923 Robert Maxwell, Slovakian-born newspaperman
- 1928 Maurice Sendak, writer, producer, and illustrator

Deaths
- 323 B.C.E. Alexander the Great
- 1926 Antoni Gaudí, architect
- 1934 Frederick Delius, composer
- 1967 Spencer Tracy, actor
- 1982 Rainer Werner Fassbinder, author and film director
- 2002 John Gotti, American gangster

HISTORICAL EVENTS

- **1776** The Continental Congress appoints a committee to write a Declaration of Independence for what will become the U.S.
- **1886** Mount Tarawera volcano erupts in New Zealand, killing 153 people and destroying the famous Pink and White Terraces – a geological marvel that had been a popular tourist attraction.
- **1909** The SS *Slavonia* transmits an emergency SOS signal – the first ever – when it is wrecked off the Azores, an island group in Portugal.
- **1935** Alcoholics Anonymous is founded in Akron, Ohio, U.S., by Bill Wilson and Dr. Robert Smith (see right).
- **1940** Italy declares war on France and Great Britain, joining Germany.
- **1967** Israel ends the Six-Day War, acceding to a UN ceasefire. It holds the territory gained, setting the stage for over 30 years of territorial disputes.
- **1980** The African National Congress in South Africa publishes Nelson Mandela's call to fight, smuggled from his cell at Robben Island.
- **1996** Peace talks begin in Northern Ireland without Sinn Fein, who cannot guarantee IRA disarmament.
- **1999** Serb forces begin to withdraw from Kosovo after signing an agreement with the NATO powers. As a result, NATO halts its bombing campaign.
- **2003** The Mars Spirit Rover is launched; after six months it is the first Rover to land on Mars and collects invaluable geological data, including suggestions of water.

DAY TO REMEMBER

National day Camões Day (Portugal) This day commemorates the death in 1580 of revered national poet Luis de Camões. His literary skills are considered to have been comparable to the likes of Homer and Shakespeare.

Celtic tree sign

OAK
June 10–July 7

People born under the Celtic tree sign of the oak are known for their generosity of spirit and inner strength. They are able to follow things through to the bitter end because of their unrelenting nature. Although oak tree people don't like change, their ability to cope with difficulty makes them stronger.

AA is formed

When Bill W. found himself in Akron, Ohio, at the end of a miserable day, he wanted nothing more than a good drink. The problem was that Bill was an alcoholic who had recently undergone a religious epiphany about his sobriety. But that moment of clarity seemed a long way away. He knew that the only person who would understand what he was going through was another alcoholic.

Bill explained his experiences to Dr. Bob, a local surgeon who had struggled with alcohol for years. Dr. Bob found himself identifying with the story. He put down his bottle and never took it up again. Together, the two men began telling their story to others in the hope that it would help more as it had helped them. Alcoholics Anonymous was born.

The group relied on peer support and the acceptance that giving up was too hard for an individual alone. The Oxford Group (a religious organisation), and Dr. William Duncan Silkworth, a New York physician, were strongly influential. It rapidly grew in popularity and soon had all the recognisable features of today's AA: The Big Book, former alcoholic sponsors who would work with new members, and the 12-step program.

DATEline

June 11

"If a man hasn't discovered something he will die for, he isn't fit to live." — MARTIN LUTHER KING, 1963

HISTORICAL EVENTS

1509 King Henry VIII of England marries Katherine of Aragon, his first wife.

1892 The Limelight Department, one of the world's first film studios, is officially established in Melbourne, Australia.

1901 New Zealand annexes the Cook Islands, later returning them to self-government.

1937 Stalin begins his purge of the Soviet Army by executing eight generals. Hundreds more ranking military personnel will follow.

1955 At least 83 are killed and 100 are injured when an Austin-Healey explodes after colliding with a Mercedes-Benz at the Le Mans Grand Prix d'Endurance (see right).

1962 Frank Morris, John Anglin, and Clarence Anglin become the only prisoners to successfully escape from the prison on Alcatraz Island in San fransisco Bay. They are never seen again, and it is thought they drowned or were eaten by sharks between the island and the mainland.

1963 Dr. Martin Luther King Jr. is arrested in Florida for trying to end segregation in restaurants. *Time* magazine later names him 1963 Man of the Year.

1963 Alabama Governor George Wallace stands at the door of Foster Auditorium at the University of Alabama in an attempt to stop black students Vivian Malone and James Hood from enrolling. He is ultimately moved by the U.S. Attorney General and the National Guard.

1970 Anna Mae Hays and Elizabeth P. Hoisington officially receive their ranks as U.S. Army Generals, becoming the first females to do so.

1987 Margaret Thatcher wins her third consecutive term as British Prime Minister.

2004 The *Cassini-Huygens* spacecraft makes its closest fly-by of Saturn's moon Phoebe, finding probable evidence of water ice.

DAY TO REMEMBER

National day Kamehameha Day (Hawaii, U.S.) This official state holiday is in honor of King Kamehameha, the unifier and first monarch of Hawaii. The day is celebrated with floral parades, hula competitions, and festivals.

Wreckage, bodies, and belongings were strewn along a section of concourse surrounding the spectators' stand at Le Mans in north-west France on this day in 1955. Two hours into the Le Mans 24-hour race, the Mercedes-Benz driven by Frenchman Pierre Levegh had clipped the Austin-Healey in front of it, then flipped over before crashing against the bank by the spectator enclosure and exploding. At least 83 people were killed, and many more injured. The organizers allowed the race to continue to the end, and no official announcement was made, allegedly to ensure that spectators did not panic.

Births

- **1572** Ben Jonson, dramatist
- **1776** John Constable, painter
- **1864** Richard Strauss, German composer and conductor
- **1879** Max Schreck, actor
- **1910** Jacques-Yves Cousteau, explorer and inventor
- **1932** Athol Fugard, playwright
- **1933** Gene Wilder, actor
- **1939** Jackie Stewart, race-car driver
- **1959** Hugh Laurie, actor and comedian

Deaths

- **1796** Samuel Whitbread, brewer and politician
- **1979** John Wayne (born Marion Morrison), actor
- **1999** DeForest Kelley, actor
- **2001** Timothy McVeigh, terrorist

June 12

"My fellow Americans, I am pleased to tell you I just signed legislation which outlaws Russia forever. The bombing begins in five minutes." RONALD REAGAN, DURING A RADIO TEST, 1984

HISTORICAL EVENTS

- **1942** Anne Frank receives a diary for her thirteenth birthday. She begins writing in it and continues as her Jewish family hide in an Amsterdam attic until their discovery by the Gestapo in 1944.
- **1963** *Cleopatra* premieres at the Rivoli Theater in New York City. A lavish, if melodramatic, production, it sees the blossoming of romance between co-stars Elizabeth Taylor and Richard Burton.
- **1963** African American veteran and civil rights leader Medgar Evers is shot dead in Jackson, Mississippi, by Ku Klux Klan member Byron de la Beckwith. Beckwith is not convicted by the first two all-white juries to try the case, but is eventually jailed in 1994.
- **1964** ANC leader Nelson Mandela is one of eight activists sentenced to life imprisonment for sabotage, in Pretoria, South Africa. Mandela is sent to the notorious Robben Island where he is held until February 11, 1990.
- **1967** The U.S. Supreme Court hands down its judgement on Loving v. Virginia, declaring that interracial marriage in all states is protected by the Constitution.
- **1982** As part of a massed rally, 750,000 people converge on New York City's Central Park to protest against nuclear weapons (see below).
- **1987** In a speech at the Brandenburg Gate, U.S. President Ronald Reagan publicly challenges Mikhail Gorbachev to tear down the Berlin Wall. Two-and-a-half years later, the wall was opened, and then torn down by Berliners.
- **1990** The Parliament of the Russian Federation formally declares its sovereignty in the aftermath of the collapse of the Soviet Union.
- **1991** Boris Yeltsin becomes the first democratically elected President of Russia.
- **1994** Nicole Brown Simpson and Ronald Goldman are murdered outside her home in Los Angeles, California. O. J. Simpson is later acquitted of the killings, but is held liable in a civil suit.

Births
- **1519** Cosimo I dé Medici, Grand Duke of Tuscany
- **1827** Johanna Spyri, author
- **1890** Egon Schiele, painter and graphic artist
- **1924** George H. W. Bush, forty-first U.S. President
- **1929** Anne Frank, diarist
- **1930** Jim Nabors, actor and musician
- **1957** Javed Miandad, Pakistani cricketer and coach

Deaths
- **1957** Jimmy Dorsey, musician
- **1983** Norma Shearer, actress
- **1994** Ronald Goldman, actor and model
- **1994** Nicole Brown Simpson, ex-wife of O. J. Simpson
- **2003** Gregory Peck, actor

DAYS TO REMEMBER

National day Independence Day (Russia) This day marks independence from the Soviet Union in 1990.

National day Dia dos Namorados (Brazil) This is Brazil's version of St. Valentine's Day and comes a day before the Feast Day of St. Anthony, known locally as the marriage saint.

International day World Day Against Child Labor This day is sponsored by the UN's International Labor Organization. Each year it focuses on a different aspect of the illegal child labor trade.

On this day in 1982, New York was filled with the sounds of antinuclear slogans as 750,000 people rallied in Central Park against the aggressive nuclear policies of President Ronald Reagan. The first two years of the Reagan administration had seen increasingly agitated relations between the U.S. and the Soviet administration, then under Leonid Brezhnev, and wide-scale escalation of nuclear arsenals were underway for both superpowers. It was the last antinuclear rally of such magnitude; less than three years later Mikhail Gorbachev would be in power and the Cold War would be coming to an end.

June 13

"Somewhere, something incredible is waiting to be known." — CARL SAGAN

HISTORICAL EVENTS

1774 Rhode Island bans the importation of slaves. It is the first British colony in North America to do so.

1920 The U.S. Postal Service rules that children may not be sent via parcel post.

1934 Adolf Hitler and Mussolini meet for the first time in Venice, Italy. Hitler frequently quoted from his book *Mein Kampf* and a bored Mussolini later referred to him as "a silly little monkey."

1944 Germany launches the first V1 flying bomb attack on England. Only four of the 11 bombs actually hit their targets, but the buzz of their engines and the sudden silence as they fell would strike fear into London.

1967 Solicitor General Thurgood Marshall is nominated as the first African American justice of the U.S. Supreme Court. He serves until 1991.

1971 The *New York Times* begins publishing the Pentagon Papers, exposing the flawed policy decisions that led to the Vietnam War.

1981 Queen Elizabeth II is riding at the Trooping the Colour ceremony in London when a teenager fires six blank shots at her. She steadies her horse and carries on.

1983 *Pioneer 10* becomes the first artificial object to leave the solar system (see right).

2004 A 3.8-pound (1.3 kg) meteorite hits the house of Phil and Brenda Archer in Ellerslie, New Zealand, destroying the roof and a sofa but causing no injuries.

DAY TO REMEMBER

Religious day St. Anthony of Padua's Day Also known as St. Anthony of Lisbon, this saint (1195–1231) is invoked by the faithful to help them find items that have been lost.

Births
- 1752 Fanny Burney, novelist and diarist
- 1865 William Butler Yeats, poet, Nobel Prize laureate
- 1892 Basil Rathbone, actor
- 1893 Dorothy L. Sayers, author
- 1910 Mary Whitehouse, British campaigner
- 1953 Tim Allen, comedian and actor
- 1986 Mary-Kate and Ashley Olsen, actresses

Deaths
- 1231 Anthony of Padua, saint
- 1645 Miyamoto Musashi, swordsman
- 1951 Ben Chifley, Prime Minister of Australia
- 1986 Benny Goodman, musician
- 1987 Geraldine Page, actress

Pioneer 10 leaves the solar system

Launched on March 2, 1972, *Pioneer 10* was sent out to gather electronic data on the solar system in preparation for what was then thought to be decades of burgeoning space travel. In a touch of whimsy, a plaque which attempted to graphically explain where the craft came from and with images of humans was added, for the benefit of any aliens the spacecraft might run into. *Pioneer 10* was the first spacecraft to travel through the asteroid belt, and the first to make direct observations and take close-up shots of Jupiter. *Pioneer 10*'s data was used in the subsequent *Voyager*, *Ulysses*, *Galileo*, and *Cassini* projects, helping to design better spacecraft as well as providing information about the environment of the solar system.

Pioneer 10 itself was a small box of instruments tucked behind a parabolic dish antenna, attached to additional antennae and instruments and a specialized generator. Its mission was originally focused on the Jupiter fly-by, less than three years after it left Earth. Yet valuable data were still being received in early 2002, despite the cutting of tracking in 1997 due to budget constraints. By then, most of its instruments had failed or been turned off, but the Geiger Tube Telescope transmitted data to the end.

The total cost of the mission was about $350 million, with $200 million of that amount being spent on the pre-launch design and development.

On this day in 1983, *Pioneer 10* became the first artificial object to leave the solar system and is now more than 8.1 billion miles (13 billion km) away from Earth. Its last signal was received on January 23, 2003; since then, contact has been lost. It was last headed for the giant red star, Aldebraran, some 2 million years' travel away.

June 14

HISTORICAL EVENTS

1777 The Stars and Stripes is adopted by Congress as the flag of the U.S.
1789 The 19 survivors of the mutiny on HMAV *Bounty*, including Captain William Bligh, reach Timor after a nearly 4,000-mile (6,400 km) journey in an open boat. Bligh's remarkable seamanship is given as the reason for their survival.
1822 Mathematician Charles Babbage proposes the "difference engine" to perform mathematical calculations. It is the first computer design in science.
1839 The first Henley Royal Regatta is held on the River Thames in the U.K.
1905 Sailors on the battleship *Potemkin* revolt, at first over rancid meat, then over the autocracy of their officers and the Tsarist Russian state. The revolt and its suppression form the basis of Eisenstein's 1925 film.
1919 English pilot John Alcock and Scottish navigator Arthur Whitten Brown leave St. John's, Newfoundland, on the first non-stop trans-Atlantic flight, landing in Clifden, Connemara, in Ireland a little over 16 hours later.
1940 A group of 728 Polish political prisoners from Tarnów are the first inmates of the Auschwitz concentration camp.
1982 The Falklands War ends with Argentina's surrender to the U.K.
1985 TWA Flight 847 is hijacked by Shi'ite Hezbollah terrorists. One U.S. Navy diver is killed, but the remaining passengers are released in stages, including Greek singer Demis Roussos.
1986 Alan Jay Lerner, librettist for *Camelot* and *My Fair Lady*, dies (see below).

DAYS TO REMEMBER

Historical day Liberation Day (Falkland Islands) This day marks the end of the Argentinian invasion and Falklands War in 1982.

International day World Blood Donor Day Celebrates voluntary blood donors, held on the birth date of Karl Landsteiner, who discovered ABO blood groups.

> "Don't let it be forgot
> That once there was a spot
> For one brief shining moment
> That was known as Camelot!"
> ALAN JAY LERNER, *CAMELOT*

Births
1811 Harriet Beecher Stowe, author
1909 Burl Ives, musician
1910 Rudolf Kempe, conductor
1928 "Che" Guevara (born Ernesto Rafael Guevara de la Serna), revolutionary
1946 Donald Trump, businessman
1961 Boy George, singer (Culture Club)

Deaths
1926 Mary Cassatt, artist
1927 Jerome K. Jerome, author
1928 Emmeline Pankhurst, feminist
1936 Maxim Gorky, author
1946 John Logie Baird, television pioneer
1986 Alan Jay Lerner, librettist
1991 Dame Peggy Ashcroft, actress

One of Broadway's most successful lyricist/librettists, Alan Jay Lerner's name is rarely heard without that of his writing partner, Frederick Loewe (pictured on Lerner's left). Together they penned blockbusters including *Brigadoon*, *Paint Your Wagon*, *Camelot*, *GIGI*, and *My Fair Lady*. The son of wealthy New York parents, Lerner had a comfortable upbringing, attending school with John F. Kennedy. He met Australian composer Loewe in 1942 and by 1947, they had their first big hit musical with *Brigadoon*. While he wrote with other partners, it was only with Loewe that he had great success. Many of his best tunes are remembered for their sweet, if passing, romance – something that he strongly believed in, marrying eight times.

June 15

"Every time we've moved ahead in IBM, it was because someone was willing to take a chance, put his head on the block, and try something new." — THOMAS J. WATSON, FOUNDER OF IBM

HISTORICAL EVENTS

1215 The Magna Carta is sealed by King John of England; it guarantees that the will of the King can be bound by law.

1381 Wat Tyler's English Peasants' Revolt is bloodily crushed in London, despite promises that the rebels would be safe.

1667 Dr. Jean Baptiste Denis transfuses 12 fluid ounces (350 ml) of sheep blood to a 15-year-old boy, the first recorded transfusion. Denis has some success with his new technique, but is sued for malpractice by the wife of a patient who dies the following year. It emerges that the wife had poisoned the deceased, but transfusions are banned across Europe.

1752 Benjamin Franklin flies a kite with a key attached to it in a thunderstorm to prove that lightning is electricity.

1877 Henry Ossian Flipper becomes the first African American cadet to graduate from the U.S. Military Academy. Four years later the Lieutenant is court martialed on his commanding officer's charges of embezzlement – charges that are later found to be false and unjust.

1911 The Computing-Tabulating-Recording Company, later known as IBM, is incorporated (see right).

1920 Three African American youths, falsely accused of rape, are dragged from their jail cells and lynched in Duluth, Minnesota, by a white mob of around 5,000.

1996 In Manchester, U.K., an IRA-planted bomb injures more than 200 people and devastates a large part of the city center. It had been reported by the terrorists but exploded before it could be defused.

DAY TO REMEMBER

Religious day St. Vitus' Day The patron saint of dancers, young people, and dogs, it is said that believers can obtain a year's good health by dancing before this saint's statue on this day.

Births
- **1330** Edward the Black Prince, Prince of Wales
- **1843** Edvard Grieg, composer
- **1911** W.V. Awdry, children's writer
- **1914** Saul Steinberg, cartoonist
- **1937** Waylon Jennings, singer
- **1949** Simon Callow, actor
- **1954** James Belushi, actor
- **1963** Helen Hunt, actress
- **1964** Courteney Cox, actress

Deaths
- **1381** Wat Tyler, English rebel
- **1984** Meredith Willson, composer
- **1985** Andy Stanfield, athlete
- **1989** Victor French, actor
- **1996** Ella Fitzgerald, singer
- **2003** Hume Cronyn, actor

The birth of IBM

On this day in 1911, three businesses that were concerned with providing machines to business were merged to form the Computing-Tabulating-Recording Company (C-T-R). The firm manufactured and sold machinery ranging from industrial time recorders to meat and cheese slicers. Thomas J. Watson was appointed general manager.

Watson soon began to construct a business focused on customer service, and narrowed the field of production down to large-scale, custom-built tabulating solutions. On February 14, 1924, C-T-R's name was changed to International Business Machines Corporation, reflecting its area of specialty. In 1935, the Social Security Act brought the company a contract to maintain employment records for 26 million people. IBM's success at this monster task set its identity as a trusted brand for decades.

IBM began to expand its research and development sections. The most influential project was 1944's Automatic Sequence Controlled Calculator, also called the Mark I, which was developed with Harvard University and weighed more than 45 tons.

The next models were smaller, faster, and more reliable. Vacuum tubes replaced switches, then transistors moved in. Computers became the central focus of the whole company. IBM invented the computer disk storage system, FORTRAN computer language, interchangeable software, and computer peripherals. It was also one of the pioneers of personal computers (PCs) and networks.

IBM remains one of the most successful computer companies and brands in the world. While many computer users buy their equipment from Apple, IBM's grip on the business sector has never really weakened, and the company is still largely synonymous with PCs.

June 16

> *"'I fear those big words,' Stephen said, 'which make us so unhappy.'"* — JAMES JOYCE, *ULYSSES*

HISTORICAL EVENTS

1487 Nearly two years after Richard II's defeat at Bosworth, England, a Yorkist attempt at overthrowing Henry Tudor is lost at the Battle of Stoke Field, the last of the Wars of the Roses.

1903 Roald Amundsen and his six-man team leave Oslo, Norway, on the first east–west navigation of the Northwest Passage. After two years of Arctic exploration he would complete the trip in August 1905.

1904 James Joyce meets future wife Nora. His fictional character Leopold Bloom spends this day wandering around Dublin in *Ulysses*.

1956 English poet Ted Hughes marries American poet Sylvia Plath.

1960 Alfred Hitchcock's terrifying film *Psycho* opens in New York.

1963 Cosmonaut Valentina Tereshkova becomes the first woman in space (see below).

1972 Five White House operatives break into Democratic headquarters at the Watergate hotel. They are arrested early the next morning and a systematic plot to discredit the Democratic Party is revealed. On August 9, 1974, U.S. President Richard Nixon resigns as a result of the fallout.

1976 Thousands of black schoolchildren protest against poor education in Soweto, South Africa. When they are fired on by police, the protest turns into a riot. The official death toll is 23; locals suggest 200, with others claiming up to 500 children were killed.

1977 Leonid Brezhnev becomes President of the U.S.S.R., a role he will hold until his death in 1982. He oversees an increased political will to engage with the West.

1999 Thabo Mbeki is elected President of South Africa, the second black President after Nelson Mandela.

Births
- **1313** Giovanni Boccaccio, writer
- **1792** Sir Thomas Mitchell, explorer
- **1829** Geronimo, Apache leader
- **1890** Stan Laurel, actor and comedian
- **1912** Enoch Powell, politician
- **1917** Katharine Graham, publisher
- **1934** Dame Eileen Atkins, actress
- **1934** William Forsyth Sharpe, economist, Nobel Prize laureate
- **1937** Erich Segal, author
- **1938** Joyce Carol Oates, writer and university professor
- **1955** Laurie Metcalf, actress

Deaths
- **1464** Roger van der Weyden, painter
- **1869** Charles Sturt, explorer
- **1929** Bramwell Booth, second General of the Salvation Army
- **1959** George Reeves, actor
- **1977** Wernher von Braun, rocket scientist

DAYS TO REMEMBER

National day Youth Day (South Africa) This day remembers the gunning down of black children in the Soweto Uprising, and their fight for decent education.

Religious day Martyrdom Day of Guru Arjan Dev The first Sikh martyr, Arjan Dev was tortured to death for refusing to remove Hindu and Muslim references from his Sikh holy book.

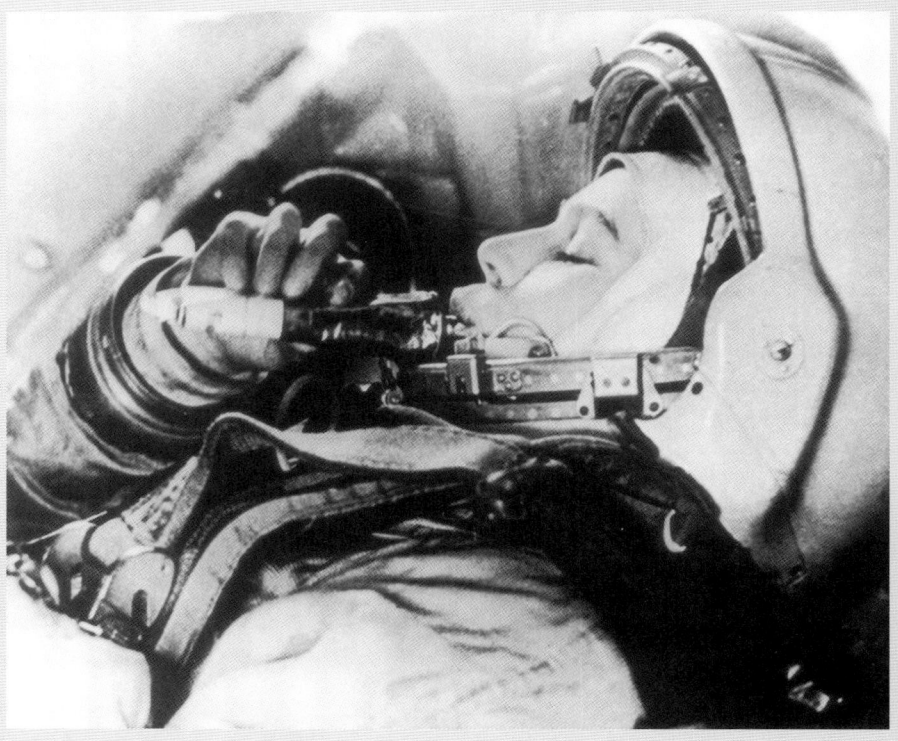

In the late 1950s and early 1960s, both the U.S. and the U.S.S.R. began looking at including women in their space programs. The U.S. abandoned the scheme in 1960, but in 1963, the U.S.S.R. shot Valentina Tereshkova into space on *Vostok 6*. Tereshkova was a keen parachutist, but not trained as an engineer. She was not allowed to take manual control of her spacecraft during its 71 hours in orbit, but she did manage an excellent landing for her re-entry after ejecting at 20,000 feet (6,100 m). Later Tereshkova married fellow cosmonaut Andrian Nikolayev in a propaganda coup; they had a daughter before divorcing.

June 17

"I don't use drugs, my dreams are frightening enough." — M. C. ESCHER

Births
- 1703 John Wesley, founder of Methodism
- 1882 Igor Stravinsky, composer
- 1888 Heinz Guderian, General
- 1898 M. C. Escher, artist
- 1943 Newt Gingrich, U.S. politician
- 1943 Barry Manilow, musician
- 1980 Venus Williams, tennis player

Deaths
- 1898 Edward Burne-Jones, artist
- 1952 Jack Parsons, rocket-fuel pioneer
- 1999 Screaming Lord Sutch, musician and leader of the British Monster Raving Loony Party
- 2005 Billy Bauer, jazz guitarist

HISTORICAL EVENTS

- **1631** Mumtaz Mahal dies in childbirth. Her tomb is lovingly built by her husband, Mughal Emperor Shah Jahan I. It is better known as the Taj Mahal.
- **1923** Enrico Ferrari wins his first race, at Circuito del Savio in Ravenna, Italy. After the race, he meets Countess Paolina Baracca who suggests he adopt her late son's emblem of the prancing horse.
- **1950** Surgeon Richard Lawler performs the first kidney transplant operation at the Little Company of Mary Hospital in Chicago. The recipient, Ruth Tucker, lives for five years.
- **1961** Russian dance prodigy Rudolf Nureyev defects at Le Bourget airport in Paris. The star of the Kirov, he would go on to form a memorable partnership with Dame Margot Fonteyn.
- **1987** The last known dusky seaside sparrow dies in captivity, and the species becomes extinct (see right).
- **1991** The South African Parliament repeals the Population Registration Act, which had, since 1950, required that all South Africans have their race classified and registered at birth.
- **1994** Television helicopters follow a white Ford Bronco weaving through Los Angeles highways pursued by police. Inside is O. J. Simpson, former footballer. After the chase and a failed suicide bid, he is arrested for the murder of his wife, Nicole Brown Simpson, and her friend Ronald Goldman.

The last of the dusky seaside sparrows

Few animals undergo such a public extinction as the dusky seaside sparrow. A small black and white bird that nested mainly in the marshes of Merritt Island, Florida, U.S., the sparrow attracted little attention until its population began to irretrievably crash. Its biggest problem was the nearby Kennedy Space Center. With time-sensitive missions and many staff, the Space Center went to great lengths to reduce the likelihood of disease transmission and to keep its employees comfortable. In the Florida swamps, this meant eradicating mosquitoes.

First Merritt Island was flooded to destroy the shallow pools where mosquitoes bred. Most of the sparrow's population was lost, but a second group was found in other marshes between the Space Center and Disney World. The area was declared a nature reserve, which had very little practical effect: Those marshes were drained to build a highway that linked the Space Center and Disney World. The sparrow's cordgrass habitat was all but wiped out. In addition, DDT was widely sprayed throughout the area in a bid to kill pest insects. It became bound up in the sparrow's food chain, thinning some of their eggshells to a point where they were not viable. On top of every other difficulty, Kennedy seeped pollution in the form of chlorine and other gases from take-offs, sewage, petrochemicals, and other industrial run-off. This also contaminated their food chain.

In 1979–1980, a captive breeding program was begun at Disney World. But only five birds were recovered, all male. Attempts were made to cross-breed them with similar species to preserve some of the dusky seaside sparrow's genetic diversity, but with no success. By March 1986, only one, known as Orange Band, remained.

When the little bird – unusually old, blind in one eye, and not very exciting to look at – died, it was headline news across the U.S., and is still considered the last known extinction of a vertebrate in that country.

June 18

"God will not forgive us if we fail." — LEONID BREZHNEV TO JIMMY CARTER AT THE SALT TALKS

Births
- 1903 Jeanette MacDonald, actress and singer
- 1915 Red Adair, firefighter
- 1942 Sir Paul McCartney, singer and songwriter
- 1942 Thabo Mbeki, President of South Africa
- 1952 Isabella Rossellini, actress
- 1952 Carol Kane, actress
- 1961 Alison Moyet, pop singer

Deaths
- 1928 Roald Amundsen, explorer

HISTORICAL EVENTS

- **1429** French religious military leader Joan of Arc leads troops to a crushing victory of the English at the Battle of Patay, turning the tide of the Hundred Years' War.
- **1812** The United States declares war against Great Britain, and invades the British North American Territories. The war of 1812 ended effectively in a stalemate, but led to the formation of Canada as a nation.
- **1815** At Waterloo, on a field on which he had strategic advantage, Napoleon is defeated by an international army under the command of the Duke of Wellington.
- **1858** Charles Darwin reads Alfred Russel Wallace's unpublished paper that promotes a nearly identical theory of evolution to Darwin's own, which has been unpublished for many years. Darwin promptly rushes to publication, crediting Wallace and remaining on good terms with him.
- **1928** Aviator Amelia Earhart flies across the Atlantic Ocean as a passenger, the first woman to make the trip in an aircraft.
- **1940** Fresh from the miracle retreat at Dunkirk, Winston Churchill rallies Britain against the Nazis with his "Finest Hour" speech.
- **1967** In a display that will be emulated by aspiring rock legends for decades, Jimi Hendrix burns his guitar on stage at the Monterey Pop Festival.
- **1979** Presidents Jimmy Carter and Leonid Brezhnev sign the SALT II pact, which limits nuclear arms (see right).
- **1984** The Battle of Orgreave sees 5,000 police and a similar number of miners clash in South Yorkshire, during the 1984–1985 Miners Strike; 93 arrests are made, with 51 picketers and 72 policemen injured.

Carter and Brezhnev sign SALT II

Between the nuclear crises of 1961's Bay of Pigs and the 1980s' Mutually Assured Destruction philosophy, successive U.S. and U.S.S.R. leaders tried to find some means of limiting the expense of nuclear armament (and the likelihood of conflict). From November 1969 to May 1972, representatives of the two Governments worked on the Strategic Arms Limitation Talks Agreement (SALT I), which would freeze the number of strategic ballistic missile launchers at current levels and allow for new launchers only after the same number of old ones had been dismantled. The agreement was signed on May 26, 1972, by U.S. President Richard Nixon and U.S.S.R. General Secretary Leonid Brezhnev. A new round of negotiations began, now seeking to curtail the manufacture of strategic nuclear weapons and replace the agreement with a more comprehensive treaty.

SALT II sought to limit the number of strategic nuclear delivery vehicles, and the development of new technologies. The basic parts of the treaty were agreed to by Gerald Ford and Brezhnev (right) in 1974, but it wasn't until 1979 that a third U.S. President, Jimmy Carter (left), signed the treaty. The kiss of diplomacy exchanged between the two leaders translated into the kiss of death for Carter. Already under domestic attack for his economic management and his diplomatic failures on the Iranian hostages, he was portrayed as weak and sympathetic to Communism.

Worse was to come. Early in 1980, before the treaty could be ratified by the U.S., the U.S.S.R. invaded Afghanistan, and Carter asked the Senate to delay consideration of the treaty in view of the invasion. Carter lost the 1980 election.

For the next six years, both sides continued to abide by the terms of the unsigned treaty, but in May 1986, U.S. President Ronald Reagan declared that future U.S. nuclear tactical decisions must be based on "the nature and magnitude of the threat posed by Soviet strategic forces and not on standards contained in the SALT structure."

June 19

"I've had about ten operations. I'm a bit like a battered old Escort. You might find one panel left that's original." — IAN BOTHAM, CRICKETER

English Test cricketer Ian Botham was one of the game's great all-rounders. On this day in 1978, he cemented his growing reputation by becoming the first man in the history of the game to score a century and take eight wickets in the one innings in a Test match (against Pakistan, who lost the match). He hit 108 runs and had bowling figures of 8/34. Having made his Test debut only the year before, Botham went on to captain the English side and play in 102 Tests before retiring in 1992. In addition to careers as a commentator and coach, he is a committed charity fundraiser. He never bettered this inning's bowling figures.

HISTORICAL EVENTS

1536 Anne Boleyn, Henry VIII's second wife, is beheaded after accusations of adultery, which were almost certainly false. Shortly thereafter Henry marries Jane Seymour.

1846 The first baseball game under recognizable modern rules is played in Hoboken, New Jersey, U.S. The New York Knickerbocker Club plays the New York Club at Elysian Field.

1865 Slaves in Galveston, Texas, U.S., are finally informed that the Emancipation Proclamation of January 1, 1863, grants them their freedom.

1870 The rebel Southern States are readmitted to the U.S., marking the end of the Confederate States of America.

1912 After being established in New Zealand and Australia in the 1840s and 1850s, the eight-hour workday is established in the U.S. Previously the workday was commonly 10 hours long, and up to 16.

1953 Julius and Ethel Rosenberg are executed in the U.S. for treason. Their accusers declare that they are at the head of a spy ring passing U.S. atomic bomb secrets to the U.S.S.R. Their defenders declare they are the victims of an anti-Communist witch hunt.

1978 Ian Botham becomes the first cricketer in history to score a century and take eight wickets in the one innings in a Test match (see above).

1997 McDonald's wins its "McLibel" case against two activists who had accused it of providing unhealthy food at a damaging cost to the environment. Nevertheless, the suit costs the company £10 million and years of bad publicity.

1999 Author Stephen King is run down by a van. The driver is distracted by a poorly behaved Rottweiler in the back.

DAY TO REMEMBER

National day Juneteenth (U.S.) An unofficial holiday, Juneteenth marks the freeing of the last American slaves held after the U.S. Civil War.

Births
- 1861 Douglas Haig, soldier
- 1896 Wallis Simpson, Duchess of Windsor
- 1897 Moe Howard, comic actor, one of the Three Stooges
- 1903 Lou Gehrig, baseball player
- 1919 Pauline Kael, film critic and author
- 1945 Aung San Suu Kyi, human rights activist
- 1947 Salman Rushdie, author
- 1954 Kathleen Turner, actress
- 1957 Anna Lindh, politician

Deaths
- 1820 Joseph Banks, naturalist and botanist
- 1937 J. M. Barrie, author
- 1953 Julius Rosenberg, spy
- 1953 Ethel Rosenberg, spy
- 1977 Lady Olave Baden-Powell, Chief Girl Guide
- 1993 William Golding, writer, Nobel Prize laureate

June 20

"It's not bragging if you can back it up." — MUHAMMAD ALI

HISTORICAL EVENTS

- **1214** The University of Oxford in the U.K. is granted its charter by papal legate Nicholas de Romanis.
- **1756** A storeroom becomes the Black Hold of Calcutta when 146 British and Anglo-Indian soldiers are imprisoned there. Historians suggest at most 43 die, but one survivor claims the number was 123.
- **1837** Victoria is crowned Queen of England. She will hold the title until her death at age 81 in 1902. She is England's longest-reigning monarch.
- **1942** A Japanese submarine shells Vancouver Island. It is the only time Canadian land territory comes under fire in World War II. Little damage is done.
- **1963** The "hot line," which really *was* a red telephone, is established between the U.S.S.R. and the U.S. as a direct emergency communication device between the leaders following the Cuban Missile Crisis.
- **1967** Boxing champion Muhammad Ali is convicted of draft evasion. He refuses to be involved with the Vietnam conflict, declaring that he has no argument with the Viet Cong. In 1971, his conviction is overturned and he is reclassified as a conscientious objector.
- **1977** Oil begins to flow through the Trans-Alaska Pipeline System (TAPS), despite opposition from environmental groups. All goes well until March 1989 when the *Exxon Valdez* runs aground at Prince William Sound after filling up at Valdez.
- **1991** The German Parliament votes to move the nation's capital from Bonn back to Berlin. The move is completed in September 1999 (see below).
- **1999** NATO declares an official end to its bombing campaign of Yugoslavia, which had been suspended 10 days earlier.
- **2001** General Pervez Musharraf becomes President of Pakistan after a coup d'état the previous year.

Births
- **1860** Jack Worrall, cricketer, footballer, and coach
- **1906** Catherine Cookson, novelist
- **1909** Errol Flynn, actor
- **1924** Chet Atkins, guitar player
- **1924** Audie Murphy, soldier, author, and actor
- **1928** Jean-Marie Le Pen, leader of the National Front party in France
- **1931** Martin Landau, actor
- **1949** Lionel Richie, musician
- **1967** Nicole Kidman, actress

Deaths
- **1947** Bugsy Siegel, gangster
- **1958** Kurt Alder, chemist, Nobel Prize laureate
- **1993** Vince Foster, Deputy White House Counsel

DAYS TO REMEMBER

International day UNHCR World Refugee Day The plight of refugees from trouble zones around the world is highlighted on this day, and Governments are called on to provide support.

The German Parliament, known as the Bundestag, sat in the Reichstag building in Berlin in April 1999, nearly eight years after voting to move back to the pre-War capital on this day in 1991. It was the first time parliament had sat there since the Reichstag Fire in 1933. In between, the Nazis had subverted German democracy and dragged the nation into a disastrous war that saw Berlin finally carved up between the two superpowers. During the post-War period, Bonn served as the capital of West Germany, but, after reunification, public opinion saw Berlin returned to its former importance.

June 21

The summer solstice in the Northern Hemisphere marks the longest day and the shortest night of the year. In the Southern Hemisphere, the winter solstice marks the shortest day and the longest night of the year

"Freedom is what you do with what's been done to you."
JEAN-PAUL SARTRE

HISTORICAL EVENTS

1675 Christopher Wren begins work on rebuilding St. Paul's Cathedral in London after it was destroyed in the Great Fire of 1666.

1854 The first Victoria Cross is won by 20-year-old Irish midshipman Charles Lucas of the Royal Navy. At the start of the Crimean War he flung a live shell from his ship before it could explode.

1864 The Tauranga Campaign of the Maori–British Wars in New Zealand ends after sizable losses on both sides. The British offer to help the Maori replant their food crops.

1939 Baseball legend Lou Gehrig retires from baseball, unable to continue playing due to amyotrophic lateral sclerosis, a wasting disease which would later bear his name.

1945 The Battle of Okinawa ends in a U.S. victory after 82 days of fighting and an estimated 90,000 Japanese deaths.

1964 The "Mississippi Burning" murders occur (see right).

1982 Accused of the attempted assassination of U.S. President Ronald Reagan, John Hinckley Jr. is found not guilty by reason of insanity. He is committed to an institution.

1989 The U.S. Supreme Court rules that flag burning is protected under the U.S. Constitution.

DAYS TO REMEMBER

International day Solstice The solstice falls within one day either side of June 21, marking the longest or shortest day of the year. In the Northern Hemisphere this makes it the summer solstice, in the Southern Hemisphere it is the winter solstice.

Traditional day Fête de la Musique This day of celebration began in France and now takes place in many European countries. It celebrates world music with amateur and professional performances.

Births			
1905	Jean-Paul Sartre, philosopher and writer	1973	Juliette Lewis, actress
1921	Jane Russell, actress	1982	William, Prince of Wales
1948	Ian McEwan, writer	**Deaths**	
1948	Lionel Rose, boxer	1527	Niccolò Machiavelli, historian and political author
1950	Anne Carson, poet		
1953	Benazir Bhutto, Prime Minister of Pakistan	1652	Inigo Jones, architect
		1908	Nikolai Rimsky-Korsakov, composer
1965	Larry Wachowski, film director	1970	Sukarno, President of Indonesia

Star sign

CANCER
June 21–July 23

People born under the sign of the crab are said to be contradictory characters – hard and spiky on the outside, but soft beneath their shell. They are creative and romantic, with a strong sense of tradition. Security and love are the basis of their happiness.

"Mississippi Burning"

Two New York civil rights workers, Michael Schwerner and Andrew Goodman, had been working in African American communities in Meridian, Mississippi, with James Chaney, a young black activist who was working as a liaison officer. As they were driving into town, the local deputy sheriff, who was a member of the Ku Klux Klan, pulled them over, then held them in the county jail for several hours. During this time, other KKK members planned their murders.

The three activists were released from custody, but before they had crossed the county limits, the deputy sheriff reappeared and forced them into his car. The three civil rights workers were driven to a secluded area and gunned down, then buried in graves that the KKK had pre-dug.

The FBI launched an investigation which they code-named MIBURN – Mississippi Burning. The victims' burnt-out car was found two days later, and the investigation intensified. Even after the bodies were found and 19 culprits identified, the State of Mississippi made no arrests. Eventually the Federal Government had to try the case, and brought a charge of violating the civil rights of Schwerner, Goodman, and Chaney, the only charge available at a federal level. Seven of the men were found guilty and sentenced to terms from three to 10 years. None served more than six.

On the forty-first anniversary of the murders, Edgar Ray Killen (pictured) was found guilty of manslaughter and sentenced to 60 years in prison. He was 80 at the time.

June 22

"Probably the one and only time in my whole career I felt like applauding the opposition scoring a goal." ENGLISH STRIKER GARY LINEKER ON THE "GOAL OF THE CENTURY"

HISTORICAL EVENTS

- **1633** The Holy Office in Rome forces Galileo Galilei to recant his view that the Earth rotates around the Sun, on pain of torture.
- **1772** Slavery is outlawed in England as a result of James Somerset's legal case against his "master." British slave traders continue to make profits in the industry for many more decades.
- **1910** German bacteriologist Paul Ehrlich announces his cure for syphilis; it is the first in the new family of drugs that will lead to modern antibiotics.
- **1941** Nazi Germany invades the U.S.S.R. in Operation Barbarossa. Despite early success the Nazis would become bogged down, most notably at Leningrad; under-resourced and unable to withstand the limitless will of Soviet resistance, they complete their retreat in 1944. Meanwhile, the Allies join forces with the U.S.S.R.
- **1970** U.S. President Richard Nixon signs the Twenty-Sixth Amendment, lowering the voting age to 18.
- **1973** Three *Skylab 2* astronauts splash down safely in the Pacific after a then-record 28 days in space.
- **1978** Astronomer James Christy spots a recurring bulge on images of Pluto. He has discovered Charon, Pluto's largest moon (see below).
- **1981** Mark David Chapman pleads guilty to the December 1980 killing of John Lennon, after earlier maintaining his innocence.
- **1986** Legendary Argentine footballer Diego Maradona knocks England out of the World Cup with the controversial "Hand of God" goal and the "Goal of the Century," in Mexico City.
- **1996** The "Quake" computer game is released. It marks a new era of games with realistic textures and advanced modeling. A generation of young men spend many hours shooting sophisticated virtual bad guys.

Births
- **1856** H. Rider Haggard, author
- **1903** John Dillinger, bank robber
- **1906** Billy Wilder, film director
- **1949** Meryl Streep, actress
- **1953** Cyndi Lauper, singer
- **1964** Dan Brown, author
- **1973** Carson Daly, television personality

Deaths
- **1965** David O. Selznick, film producer
- **1969** Judy Garland, singer and actress
- **1987** Fred Astaire, dancer and actor
- **1997** Gérard Pelletier, journalist, politician, and diplomat
- **2002** Ann Landers, columnist

Astronomer James Christy had been poring over highly magnified images of Pluto for some time. There was something odd – an anomaly appeared at regular intervals. As he looked harder, he realized that he had found Pluto's first known moon. Further investigation revealed Charon (named after the ferryman on the River Styx and pronounced in honor of Christy's wife, Charlene), to be about half the diameter of Pluto, making the two more like twin planets. Studies suggest the surface is covered in water ice.

June 23

"Don't carry a gun. It's nice to have them close by, but don't carry them. You might get arrested." — JOHN GOTTI

HISTORICAL EVENTS

- **1919** German forces are defeated at Cesis in northern Latvia during the Estonian Liberation War against the Germans, who were attempting to regain control of the Baltic.
- **1934** William Bayly is convicted of murder in New Zealand, based on traces of bone and ash. It is the first murder to be proved by modern forensics (see right).
- **1956** Gamal Abdel Nasser, who deposed the monarchy four years earlier, is elected President of Egypt. He is the only candidate on the ballot.
- **1960** Japan signs the Treaty of Mutual Co-operation and Security with the U.S.
- **1973** A six-year-old boy is killed in a house fire in Hull, U.K. He is later found to be the first of 26 deaths by fire caused by arsonist Peter Dinsdale, also known as Bruce George Peter Lee.
- **1983** Pope John Paul II meets with Lech Wałesa in Poland. The pontiff and the Solidarity leader work together toward the end of Communism in Poland.
- **1991** "Sonic the Hedgehog" debuts as a video game and character. It becomes one of the most popular games ever and sparks numerous spin-offs.
- **1992** John Gotti, the "Teflon Don," is jailed for life when charges of racketeering and five counts of murder are substantiated.

DAYS TO REMEMBER

Traditional/religious day Midsummer's Eve/Eve of St. John the Baptist This Christianized pagan festival is celebrated across much of Europe on this day, most often with bonfires and rites involving water. It is considered an auspicious time to marry or find a partner.

National day Victory Day (Estonia) This day celebrates the victory of Estonia and Allies over the invading Germans.

Births
- **1894** Alfred Kinsey, entomologist and sexologist
- **1910** Jean Anouilh, dramatist
- **1912** Alan Turing, mathematician
- **1929** June Carter Cash, singer
- **1972** Zinedine Zidane, footballer

Deaths
- **1707** John Mill, theologian
- **1885** Ulysses S. Grant, U.S. General and eighteenth President
- **1995** Jonas Salk, medical researcher

Modern forensics is born

After being alerted to the disappearance of farmers Sam and Christabel Lakey from Ruawaro in New Zealand, police discovered Christabel's body in one of the farm duckponds. Blood stains were also found on the property, leading police to believe Sam must have been shot and his body removed. Suspicion fell on neighbor William Bayly, who had a history of arguments with the couple. He protested his innocence, but police searched his farm thoroughly.

Police found the Lakeys' rifles on his property, and a drum containing charred remains, now reduced to ash, fragments of bone and hair, and lead pellets from a shotgun. Bayly was arrested, and the police believed that he had attempted to dispose of Sam Lakey's body by burning it.

In the subsequent trial, Bayly contended that the remains were those of animals and that Lakey could have buried the guns himself after murdering his wife and absconding. However, forensic scientists went to great lengths to establish the body as Sam Lakey's. They cremated a calf in a similar drum, then they conducted exhaustive tests on the original hair and bone fragments which proved that they were human in origin. Ballistics tests were also used, as was photography of the crime scene, which proved that Lakey had been murdered on his own property. In all, hundreds of pieces of evidence were assembled. On this day in 1934, Bayly was convicted and sentenced to hang. He went to the gallows still protesting his innocence and the circumstantial evidence that had convicted him.

The police forensics involved set new standards and the verdict reached on forensic evidence alone set a precedent in the English-speaking world.

June 24

Births
- 1842 Ambrose Bierce, writer and satirist
- 1850 Lord Horatio Kitchener, field marshal
- 1895 Jack Dempsey, boxer and world heavyweight champion
- 1915 Fred Hoyle, mathematician and astronomer
- 1930 Claude Chabrol, film director
- 1944 Jeff Beck, guitarist

Deaths
- 1519 Lucrezia Borgia, Duchess of Ferrara
- 1968 Tony Hancock, comedian
- 1987 Jackie Gleason, actor and musician

HISTORICAL EVENTS

- **1314** The Battle of Bannockburn ends. Robert I of Scotland, better known as Robert the Bruce, defeats Edward II of England, and the English withdraw from Scotland.
- **1441** Eton College is founded by Henry VI of England. Although it begins as a charitable teaching institution, it becomes one of the U.K.'s most prestigious schools.
- **1509** Henry VIII is crowned King of England after the death of his father, some years after the death of his older brother, Arthur. He would become most famous for his matrimonial problems.
- **1901** Pablo Picasso's first exhibition opens in Paris (see right).
- **1916** America's sweetheart, silent-movie star Mary Pickford, becomes the first film star to be awarded a million-dollar contract. She and husband Douglas Fairbanks epitomize the new Hollywood elite.
- **1948** The U.S.S.R. blocks all road and rail traffic to and from West Berlin. The U.S. responds to the Berlin Blockade with the Berlin Airlift, two days later. After failing to make political mileage and being embarrassed by the airlift, the Soviets re-opened the links on May 12, 1949.
- **1953** John F. Kennedy and Jacqueline Bouvier announce their engagement. They will later be married and have two children before JFK is assassinated in 1963.
- **1978** The first Gay and Lesbian Mardi Gras is held in Sydney, Australia. A peaceful protest ends in a near-riot and the arrest of 53 marchers.
- **1983** Yasser Arafat's PLO is expelled from Damascus, being seen as a threat to the Syrian military.

DAYS TO REMEMBER

Religious day St. John the Baptist's Day This day is celebrated across Europe as a Christian replacement for the pagan Midsummer Day. It is considered the ideal time for weddings.

National day Bannockburn Day (Scotland) Celebrates Robert the Bruce's victory against the English forces of Edward II in 1314.

> *"Good art bristles with razor blades."*
> PABLO PICASSO

Picasso's first professional exhibition

Young Pablo Picasso knew his paintings were good, but at 19, and having recently arrived in Paris from Barcelona, he was still a touch nervous. French critics were notoriously acerbic and he needed a positive response to both establish his reputation and to increase the worth of his works.

Picasso was a precocious talent, first showing his work at age 13. He had already produced hundreds of paintings; this show held 75, which were still representational but had the Modernist focus on "real life," depicting everything from prostitutes to Spanish noblewomen, streetscapes to rural scenes. He had shown them to Ambroise Vollard, Paul Cézanne's dealer, who had agreed to mount the exhibition, which opened on this day in 1901. From the critics who ventured to see the show, he received favorable reviews that went toward establishing his reputation but did not shake the art world.

From there, Picasso went on to greater artistic impacts. He settled in Paris and became a key part of the art scene. He is most often identified by his Cubist works, which shocked the establishment with their revolutionary method of depicting the human form. Picasso always denied being influenced by a previous exhibition of "primitive" art, but then he denied most outside influence, often styling himself as a lone genius.

Despite being primarily concerned with art and women, Picasso was not unaffected by the political turmoil that devastated his beloved Spain and France through the first half of the twentieth century. His best-known painting is *Guernica*, a massive work that was painted in response to the German bombings of the Basque town during the Spanish Civil War.

In later years his work turned more towards design and ceramics. He died in 1973 at the age of 91.

This self-portrait, painted in 1912, now resides at the Art Institute of Chicago, U.S.A.

June 25

> *"In the simplest terms, what we are doing in Korea is this: We are trying to prevent a third world war."* — HARRY S. TRUMAN

Births
- 1852 Antoni Gaudí, architect
- 1900 Louis Mountbatten, Viceroy of India
- 1903 George Orwell (Eric Arthur Blair), writer
- 1924 Sidney Lumet, actor and director
- 1933 James Meredith, American civil rights activist
- 1945 Carly Simon, singer
- 1963 George Michael, singer
- 1963 Yann Martel, author

Deaths
- 1218 Simon de Montfort, fifth Earl of Leicester, French crusader
- 1876 George Armstrong Custer, U.S. Army officer
- 1995 Ernest Walton, physicist, Nobel Prize laureate
- 1997 Jacques-Yves Cousteau, explorer, scientist, and inventor

HISTORICAL EVENTS

1857 Gustave Flaubert goes on trial for public immorality. His tragic novel, *Madame Bovary*, is described as obscene for depicting a woman who embarks on a series of affairs in a search for meaning.

1876 General George A. Custer and over 260 men of the Seventh Cavalry and their Native American interpreters are killed by a force of Sioux and Cheyenne Indians at Little Big Horn in Montana, U.S.

1903 Marie Curie announces that she and her husband Pierre have discovered radium. Marie later dies of radiation sickness.

1938 Founder of the Gaelic League, Dr. Douglas Hyde, takes up the office of first President of Ireland. He is selected for the post unanimously by all parties.

1950 North Korea invades South Korea in a surprise attack. U.S. President Harry Truman sends forces to help South Korea in what will become the "police action" known as the Korean War (see below).

1975 Mozambique achieves independence from Portugal and begins self-government under former guerrilla organization Frelimo.

1986 The U.S. Congress approves $100 million in aid to the Nicaraguan Contras – later accused of drug running – for their fight against the nationalist Sandinista Government.

1993 Kim Campbell becomes the first female Prime Minister of Canada after the retirement of Brian Mulroney.

1997 The remote-controlled *Progress* resupply spacecraft collides with the Russian space station, Mir, creating a leak and subsequent vacuum in part of the space station.

DAYS TO REMEMBER

Religious day Santa Orosia's Day This day honors St. Orosia, the patron saint of bad weather in the Aragon regions of Spain.

National day Independence Day (Mozambique) This day commemorates the departure of the colonial Portuguese from Mozambique in 1975.

After World War II, Korea had been left a state divided, with Soviet support in North Korea and the U.S. backing the south. Early on June 25, 1950, North Korean forces began a push toward the capital, Seoul. U.S. President Harry S. Truman pushed a resolution calling for military assistance through the UN Security Commission, and shortly thereafter U.S. forces were able to turn the tide. Soviet forces were sent in turn, and over the next three years some two-and-a-half million would die in order to establish borders practically identical to those before the action.

June 26

"Every time I think that I'm getting old, and gradually going to the grave, something else happens." ELVIS PRESLEY

The Great Lakes of North America are home to a massive water trade, but were landlocked from the Atlantic. For more than 250 years Canadian and U.S. plans to create a seaway were floated and then dashed. The joint project that finally succeeded was begun in 1954, costing Canada £336.2 million, and the U.S. $133.8 million. The St. Lawrence Seaway was opened on this day in 1959 by Queen Elizabeth II and President Dwight D. Eisenhower and now sees more than 50 million tons of cargo pass through every year.

HISTORICAL EVENTS

1857 Queen Victoria invests the first 62 recipients of the Victoria Cross in Hyde Park, London. They are all Crimean War veterans, some having performed their act of bravery more than three years earlier.

1906 France stages the first Grand Prix for car manufacturers, a 746-mile (1,200 km) course held over two days at Le Mans. Renault wins.

1934 The Focke-Wulf Fw 61 flies for the first time. It is the first helicopter to sustain flight, with twin rotors controlled from a single engine.

1945 The UN Charter is signed by 50 founding nations in San Francisco, California. The organization aims to uphold international law, and promote peace and a better standard of life for all.

1959 Queen Elizabeth II and U.S. President Dwight Eisenhower open the St. Lawrence Seaway, linking North America's Great Lakes with the Atlantic (see above).

1963 John F. Kennedy declares *"Ich bin ein Berliner"* ("I am a citizen of Berlin") on a visit to West Berlin to celebrate the twenty-fifth anniversary of the Berlin Airlift.

1974 A 10-pack of chewing gum in Ohio, U.S., becomes the first product to be sold using a barcode scanner. The gum is currently on display in the Smithsonian.

1977 Elvis Presley gives his last concert, in Indianapolis, U.S. He dies on the morning of August 16, while resting before a performance scheduled for that afternoon.

1979 Muhammad Ali retires as boxing heavyweight World Champion. He makes two comebacks in 1980 and 1981, but loses both.

1993 U.S. President Bill Clinton authorizes a missile attack on Baghdad intelligence headquarters in retaliation for an assassination attempt against former President George H.W. Bush in April in Kuwait. Eight civilians are killed.

1997 *Harry Potter and the Philosopher's Stone* is published. Word-of-mouth advertising sees it gain immense popularity and set the stage for J. K. Rowling's series to break publishing records.

Births

1689 Edward Holyoke, President of Harvard University
1898 Willy Messerschmitt, aircraft designer
1902 William P. Lear, engineer and industrialist
1904 Peter Lorre, actor
1909 Colonel Tom Parker, Elvis Presley's manager
1956 Chris Isaak, singer

Deaths

1939 Ford Maddox Ford, writer
1968 Tony Hancock, comedian
1984 Michel Foucault, literary theorist
1996 Veronica Guerin, journalist
2003 Strom Thurmond, U.S. Senator
2003 Dennis Thatcher MBE, husband of Margaret Thatcher

June 27

> *"We are the Stonewall girls, we wear our hair in curls …"*
> THE CHANT BY A CHORUS LINE OF DRAG QUEENS TAUNTING NEW YORK POLICE, 1969

Births
- 1846 Charles Stewart Parnell, Irish independence fighter
- 1880 Helen Keller, educator and activist
- 1930 Ross Perot, billionaire and politician
- 1949 Vera Wang, fashion designer
- 1955 Isabelle Adjani, actress
- 1963 Meera Syal, writer, comedienne, singer, journalist, and actress
- 1966 J.J. Abrams, television writer and producer
- 1975 Tobey Maguire, actor

Deaths
- 1844 Joseph Smith Jr., founder of The Church of Jesus Christ of Latter-Day Saints
- 2001 Jack Lemmon, actor and film director

The start of Gay Rights in the U.S.

The Stonewall inn, in New York's Greenwich Village, was a typical 1969 gay bar, with drag performances, semi-legal licensing and a mixed clientele of gays, lesbians, and heterosexual visitors. It had been raided several times in the past, so when a bevy of undercover police burst in on a warm summer night, it didn't seem that unusual.

The exact incident that saw the evening turn from standard raid to extensive riot has never been established. Whatever the cause, the usually submissive crowd turned on the police and fought back. Patrons of nearby bars ran onto the streets and joined in. Soon there were some 2,000 rioters and 400 police arrayed against each other. Slogans were chanted and the rioters began by throwing coins at the police in token of the years of bribes paid to police by the gay community, then progressed to violence.

The Tactical Patrol Force, with anti-Vietnam protest training, were brought in to break up the mob. Instead, they were flummoxed by locals who would simply run around the block to outflank the police squads.

The riots were repeated with varying intensity for the next five nights. In their wake, the local gay community forged a political awareness that would see gay rights move into the mainstream. Police, too, reassessed their relationship with the gay community and focused on establishing good interactions with the sizable district. On the thirtieth anniversary, the Stonewall Veterans (pictured) rode in honor during the city's Gay Pride Parade.

HISTORICAL EVENTS

- **1829** English scientist James Smithson dies, leaving behind the bequest which will found the Smithsonian Museum, the foremost science and technology museum in the U.S. – a country with which Smithson had no ties.
- **1898** Joshua Slocum lands his 36-foot (11 m) boat *Spray* at Newport, Rhode Island, completing the first solo circumnavigation of the world.
- **1929** The first public demonstration of color television is given at Bell Laboratories in New York. An American flag and bunch of roses are broadcast.
- **1954** The world's first nuclear power station opens in Obninsk, near Moscow. It produces electricity for about 2,000 homes until 1959 and is then used for the production of isotopes and research until the year 2000.
- **1967** The world's first ATM, designed by John Shepherd-Barron, is installed in a branch of Barclay's Bank in Enfield, North London, U.K.
- **1969** Police raid a gay bar in New York, starting the Stonewall riots (see right).
- **1991** Yugoslav forces sweep into Slovenia after its declaration of independence. It is the start of the Yugoslav Wars, which will claim about 120,000 lives as the Balkan states separate.

DAYS TO REMEMBER

National day National Veterans' Day (U.K.) This day is held in celebration and memory of all who have served in armed conflicts for the U.K.

Traditional day Stonewall Day This is the date of many gay pride celebrations and commemorations for the victims of anti-gay violence in the U.S. and Europe.

June 28

"What is the good of your speeches? I come to Sarajevo on a visit, and I get bombs thrown at me. It is outrageous." — ARCHDUKE FRANZ FERDINAND TO THE MAYOR OF SARAJEVO, 1914

World War I begins in Sarajevo

Austrian Archduke Franz Ferdinand was relatively unpopular in Bosnia Herzegovina, which had been annexed by Austria–Hungary in 1908 – to the displeasure of the large Serbian community who wanted to be unified with Serbia. When Franz Ferdinand visited in 1914, a plan was hatched to assassinate him.

When the seven cars of the Archduke's motorcade passed by Nedeljko Cabrinoviç, one of seven conspirators, he tossed an explosive device which missed the car carrying Franz Ferdinand and his wife Sophie, and destroyed the car behind them, injuring several people. The would-be assassin swallowed a cyanide pill and leapt into the River Miljacka. Unfortunately for him, the pill was not effective and the river contained only about 4 inches (10 cm) of water. He was swiftly arrested.

Meanwhile the motorcade rushed toward the town hall with a huge crowd of onlookers in tow. The Archduke was welcomed by the Mayor of Sarajevo, who greeted him effusively. Ferdinand expressed a desire to visit the wounded from the attack, who were in a nearby hospital. Most of the assassins had by then disbanded, but Gavrilo Princip spotted

the Archduke's car en route. He ran up to the car and fired twice, injuring both Sophie and Ferdinand. They were driven to the Governor's residence, but died of their wounds.

Princip was stopped by a mob of onlookers and handed over to the police. His co-conspirators were also arrested and one claimed the guns were supplied by the Serb Government. This led to Austria–Hungary declaring war on Serbia on July 28, despite Serbia's best attempts to avert it. Many claim that the pro-war factions in Austria–Hungary used the assassination as a mere pretext; others have accused them of engineering it.

Births

- 1491 Henry VIII, King of England
- 1577 Peter Paul Rubens, painter
- 1703 John Wesley, founder of Methodism
- 1712 Jean Jacques Rousseau, social philosopher
- 1902 Richard Rodgers, composer
- 1926 Mel Brooks, comedian, actor, and director
- 1946 Gilda Radner, actress
- 1948 Kathy Bates, actress
- 1954 Alice Krige, actress
- 1966 John Cusack, actor

Deaths

- 1914 Franz Ferdinand, Archduke of Austria
- 1981 Terry Fox, athlete and cancer activist
- 2001 Joan Sims, actress

HISTORICAL EVENTS

- 1880 Ned Kelly, the Australian bushranger, is captured at Glenrowan after a day-long siege. The rest of his gang is killed, but Ned survives to be tried and hanged.
- 1914 Franz Ferdinand, Archduke of Austria, and his wife Sophia are killed in Sarajevo by Serbian nationalist Gavrilo Princip (see above).
- 1919 The Treaty of Versailles is signed; it ends World War I with Germany, but imposes harsh sanctions. Germany's economy is effectively destroyed, setting the ground for the rise of Nationalism which will see the Nazis sweep to power in 1933.
- 1938 Scores of witnesses report a huge fireball breaking up in the sky over Chicora, Pennsylvania, U.S. It is thought to be a 450-ton meteorite, the remains of which land in an empty field near the town, possibly injuring a nearby cow.
- 1967 Following the Six Day War, Israel passes legislation that annexes east Jerusalem, which had previously been governed by Jordan.
- 2004 Sovereign power of Iraq is handed to the Iraqi Interim Government by the U.S.-led Coalition Provisional Authority.

DAYS TO REMEMBER

Religious day St. Irenaeus of Lyons's Day Irenaeus was the first Christian to define the canonical gospels of Matthew, Mark, Luke, and John.

Religious day St. Vitus' Day This Orthodox religious holiday is celebrated as Vidovdan in Serbia and considered a day of great national significance.

June 29

"Pray for the peace of Jerusalem." PSALMS 122:6

In 1967, after the Six Day War, Israel was determined to reunify Jerusalem, which had been split into East and West Jerusalem since 1948. In addition to reclaiming the 2.5 square miles (6 sq km) of Jerusalem that was under the control of Jordan, Israel took an additional 25 square miles (64 sq km) of the West Bank. June 29 was a day of great joy for the Israelis to have their holy city again. However, many Palestinians lost land and rights in the annexation, which has so far led to more than 40 years of conflict and violence. Each year, Israeli nationalists (pictured) take to the streets to mark the reunification of Jerusalem.

HISTORICAL EVENTS

1613 Shakespeare's Globe Theatre in London burns to the ground after a stage cannon ignites the thatch. The Globe 2 is rebuilt the following year.

1960 The BBC's £12 million Television Centre is opened. It signals the beginning of decades of BBC domination of the British screens with classics including *Coronation Street*, *Dr. Who* and *Fawlty Towers*.

1967 Israel removes the barricades between Israeli-controlled West Jerusalem and formerly Jordanian-controlled East Jerusalem, reunifying the city (see above).

1974 Isabel Péron, widow of Juan Péron, is sworn in as Argentina's first female President. She is deposed in a bloodless coup in 1976 and exiled to Spain in 1981.

1976 After choosing to become a colony of the U.K. in 1903, the Seychelles become independent.

1995 The NASA space shuttle *Atlantis* docks with the Russian Mir space station for the first time. Relief crew, supplies, and scientific experiments were delivered in the first hook-up between U.S. and Russian spacecraft in 20 years.

1995 The Sampoong Department Store collapses in Seoul's Seocho-gu district, killing 501 and injuring 937. It is South Korea's worst peacetime disaster, and the building's chairman Lee Joon is sentenced to ten-and-a-half years in jail for his negligence in the poor design and upkeep of the building.

Births
- **1900** Antoine de Saint-Exupéry, pilot and writer
- **1919** Slim Pickens, actor
- **1920** Ray Harryhausen, filmmaker
- **1941** Kwame Ture (Stokely Carmichael), Black Panther
- **1944** Gary Busey, actor
- **1946** Egon von Furstenberg, fashion designer
- **1963** Anne-Sophie Mutter, violinist

Deaths
- **1861** Elizabeth Barrett Browning, poet
- **1933** Fatty Arbuckle, actor
- **1967** Jayne Mansfield, actress
- **1995** Lana Turner, actress
- **2002** Rosemary Clooney, singer and actress
- **2003** Katharine Hepburn, actress

DAYS TO REMEMBER

National day Independence Day (Seychelles) This celebration marks the anniversary of the colony's independence from Britain.

Religious day St. Peter's and St. Paul's Day This day is a local holiday in Rome, where Peter and Paul are patron saints. Peter is also the patron saint of popes, fishermen, potters, and virgins, among others. Paul is the patron saint of hospital administrators. Fair weather on this day is said to betide a year of good fortune.

June 30

"The usual masculine disillusionment is discovering that a woman has a brain."

MARGARET MITCHELL

HISTORICAL EVENTS

1905 Albert Einstein publishes the article "On the Electrodynamics of Moving Bodies"; it is the first paper to mention special relativity, the theory that will change modern physics.

1908 A massive explosion occurs at Tunguska in Siberia. Some 60 million trees are felled across about 800 square miles (2,000 sq km). The cause is thought to be the atmospheric explosion of a meteoroid with the force of 10 to 15 megatons.

1934 Adolf Hitler orders the murder of hundreds of senior Nazis in the Night of the Long Knives. The leadership of the Storm Troopers is particularly targeted as Hitler seeks to remove any potential rivals.

1936 *Gone with the Wind*, by Margaret Mitchell, is published (see below).

1948 Inventors John Bardeen, Walter Brattain, and Bell Labs project manager William Shockley publicly demonstrate the transistor for the first time. All three would share the Nobel Prize for Physics in 1956.

1950 President Truman orders U.S. forces to Korea in accordance with the UN Security Council resolution passed in response to the outbreak of war.

1971 Three cosmonauts on board the Soviet *Soyuz 11* spacecraft die when their ship develops a leak on re-entry and rapidly depressurizes. They had just spent a record 24 days in space.

1977 Englishwoman Virginia Wade wins the Ladies Singles title at Wimbledon, in the centenary year of the Championships and Queen Elizabeth II's Silver Jubilee Year. The Queen is in attendance on the day. Wade is the most recent British champion at the All England Club.

1997 Britain ends 156 years of sovereignty over the city-state of Hong Kong, handing the former colony back to China on the stroke of midnight.

Births

- **1685** John Gay, poet and playwright
- **1917** Lena Horne, singer
- **1919** Susan Hayward, actress
- **1926** Paul Berg, Nobel Prize-winning biochemist
- **1963** Yngwie J. Malmsteen, guitarist
- **1966** Mike Tyson, boxer
- **1975** Ralf Schumacher, race car driver

Deaths

- **1971** Crew of *Soyuz 11*: Viktor Patsayev, Georgi Dobrovolsky, and Vladislav Volkov
- **1984** Lillian Hellman, playwright
- **2001** Chet Atkins, guitarist
- **2003** Buddy Hackett, comic

Gone with the Wind is published

After a childhood spent soaking up stories of the history of Atlanta, Georgia, Margaret Mitchell was a well of information regarding her home town. Four years as a feature writer on the Atlanta journal *Sunday Magazine* filled in the more recent gaps.

After she broke her ankle, Mitchell's husband John Marsh encouraged her to begin writing her own novel. She took up his suggestion, but was desperately insecure about her work. She did a huge amount of research, but did not have a beginning for her Civil War drama featuring her unforgettable heroine – then named Pansy O'Hara – when MacMillan editor Harold Latham came to visit in 1935. Latham had been told of Mitchell's novel by a mutual friend and was struck by Mitchell's ability with words.

Latham knew the manuscript was gold. He and Mitchell decided to change the name of the central character to Scarlett, and the book was finished in January 1936. Before it even hit the shelves it was a huge success, with massive pre-orders and the film rights sold to David O. Selznick for U.S.$50,000.

Mitchell received an Honorary Master of Arts degree from Smith College and in 1937 won the Pulitzer Prize. In 1939 the film adaptation was finally released. Starring Vivien Leigh as Scarlett O'Hara and Clark Gable as Rhett Butler, it won Best Picture at the Academy Awards and made stars out of its cast.

Gone with the Wind became the second best-selling book in the U.S. after the Bible and resulted in a huge amount of Mitchell's time being taken up replying to fan mail. She never wrote another book, and died after being hit by a cab in 1949.

DAYS TO REMEMBER *June*

1
Marilyn Monroe (born Norma Jeane Mortenson, later Norma Jeane Baker), actress was born in 1926

2
Festa della Repubblica (Italy Republic Day) Commemorates the birth of the Repubblica Italiana and the end of the monarchy in 1948

3
Pope John XXIII died in 1963

4
Tonga National Day Celebrates Tonga's independence from the U.K. in 1970

5
World Environment Day Dedicated to improving the environment around the world

8
Frank Lloyd Wright, architect, was born in 1867

9
Feast Day of St. Columba (St. Columcille in Ireland) This saint is honored as one of Ireland's three patron saints

10
Camões Day (Portugal) Commemorates the death in 1580 of revered national poet Luis de Camões

11
Kamehameha Day This official state holiday of Hawaii, U.S., is in honor of King Kamehameha, the unifier and first monarch of Hawaii

12
World Day Against Child Labor Focuses on a different aspect of the illegal child labor trade each year

15
Ella Fitzgerald, singer, died in 1996

16
Youth Day (South Africa) Marks the gunning down of black schoolchildren in the Soweto Uprising, and their fight for decent education

17
M.C. Escher, artist, was born in 1898

18
Thabo Mbeki, President of South Africa, was born in 1942

19
Juneteenth (U.S.) An unofficial holiday that marks the freeing of the last American slaves held after the U.S. Civil War

22
Judy Garland, singer and actress, died in 1969

23
Midsummer's Eve This Christianised Pagan festival is celebrated across much of Europe, most often with bonfires and rites involving water

24
Bannockburn Day (Scotland) Celebrates Robert the Bruce's victory of the English forces of Edward II

25
Fiesta of Santa Orosia The patron saint of bad weather, in the Aragon regions of Spain

26
Willy Messerschmitt, aircraft designer, was born in 1898

29
Feast Day of St. Peter and St. Paul Celebrates the martyred apostles. The day is a local holiday in Rome, where they are patron saints

30
Lillian Hellman, playwright, died in 1984

6

D-Day Anniversary Commemorates the D-Day landings, ceremonies are held in U.K., France, and much of Europe

7

Union Dissolution Day (Norway) Commemorates the 1905 dissolution of the Union between Sweden and Norway

13

William Butler Yeats, writer, Nobel Prize laureate, was born in 1865

14

World Blood Donor Day Celebrates voluntary blood donors, held on the birth date of Karl Landsteiner, who discovered ABO blood groups

20

UNHCR World Refugee Day The plight of refugees from troubled zones around the world is highlighted and governments are called on to provide support

21

The first day of the star sign of Cancer

27

Stonewall Day The date of many Gay Pride celebrations and commemorations for the victims of anti-gay violence in the U.S. and Europe

28

Feast St. Irenaeus of Lyons The first Christian to define the canonical gospels of Matthew, Mark, Luke, and John

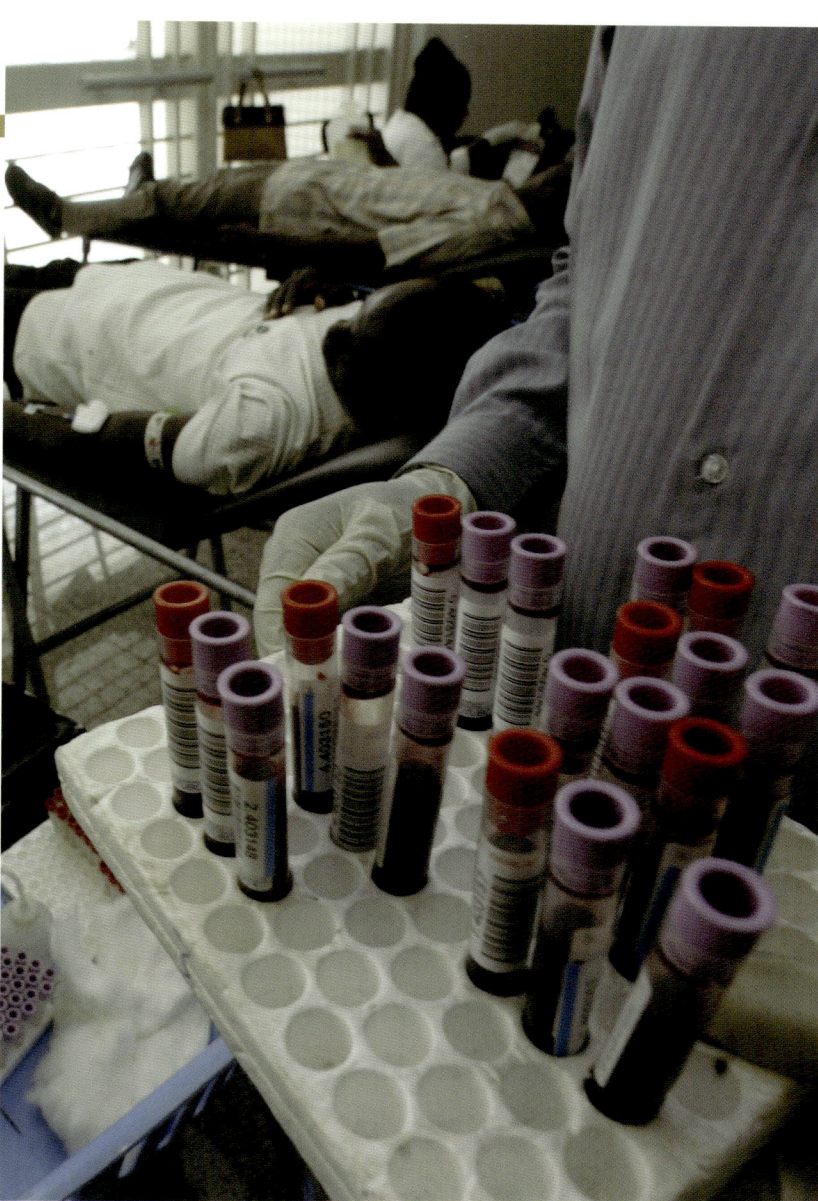

Top Right World Blood Donor Day, June 14
Right World Environment Day, June 5

JULY

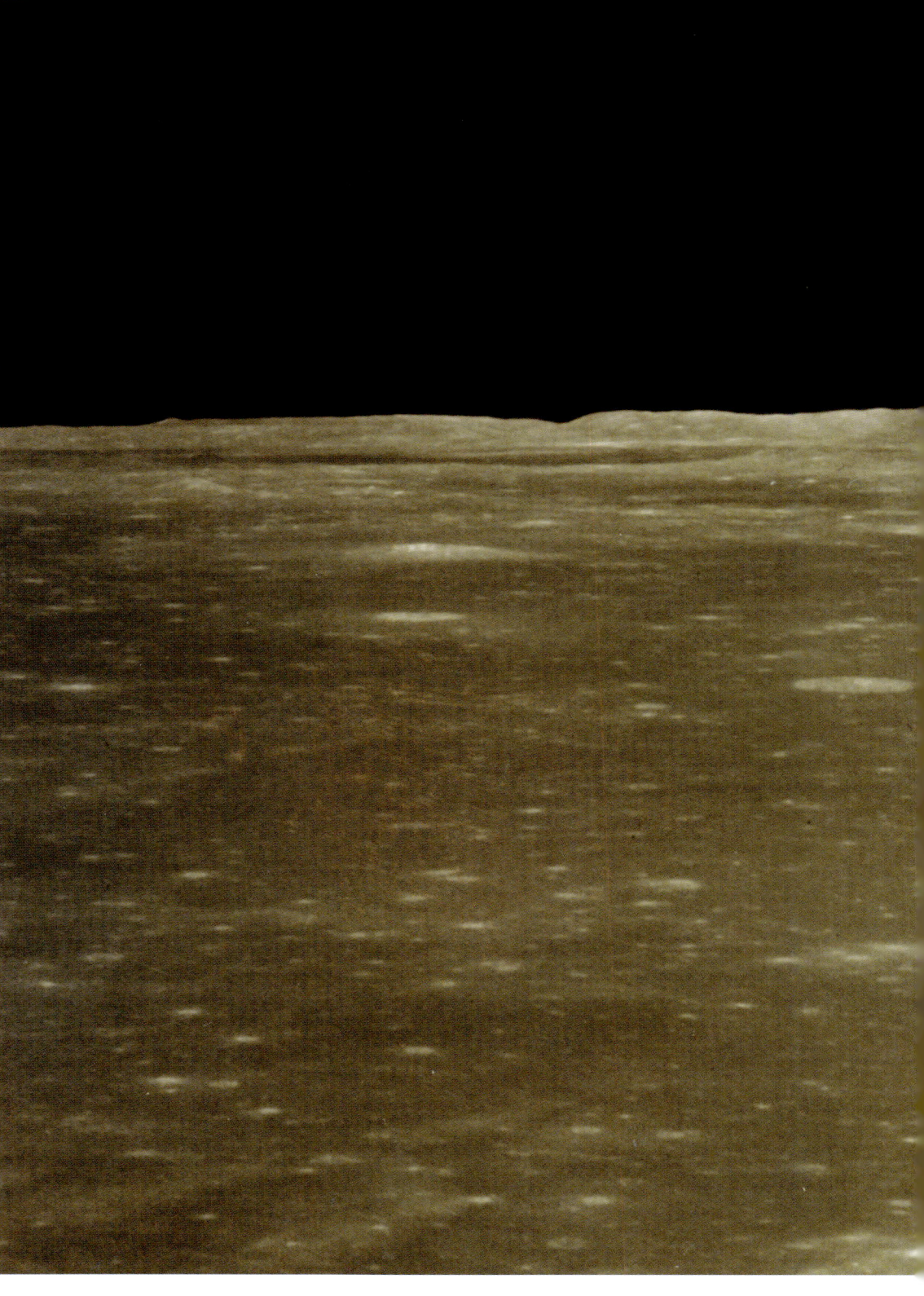

"If the first of July be rainy weather
T'will rain more or less a month together."

ENGLISH SAYING

This photograph of Earthrise over the Moon's horizon was taken from Apollo 11. The first manned mission to Earth's nearest celestial neighbor took place in July, 1969.

July

Leo star sign and man scything wheat from the *Calendar and Book of Hours*, from fifteenth-century France. July begins in the sign of Cancer and ends in the sign of Leo.

SPECIAL DATES

July 1 is the beginning of the new financial year in much of the world, when businesses and governments get their house in order.

Right Marble bust of Gaius Julius Caesar, 100–44 B.C.E., in whose honor July is named, from the Archaeological Museum, Naples.

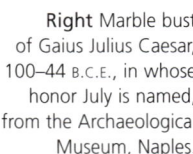

July is the seventh month of the Gregorian calendar. In the Northern Hemisphere, summer is in full swing, and in the south, winter is well entrenched. Although this month does not mark the beginning of a new season, there are plenty of festivals to celebrate. In the north, people have long made use of the good weather, and their entertainments and celebrations have focused on outdoor activities.

THE MONTH OF JULY takes its name from the Roman month *Julius*. Until 44 B.C.E., Julius was called *Quintilis*, which means "fifth," even though it was the seventh month in the Roman calendar. This discrepancy went back to around the seventh century B.C.E. according to the Roman historian Livy, who said that at this time the second king of Rome, Numa Pompilus, changed the original 10-month calendar with 304 days to one of 12 months and 355 days, adding *Januaris* and *Februaris* before March.

Julius Caesar introduced the Julian calendar in 44 B.C.E. in an attempt to bring the calendar back into alignment with the seasons. Caesar had been elected *Pontifex maximus*, the chief priest, or pontiff, of Rome in 63 B.C.E. It had always been the task of the college of pontiffs to regulate the calendar, pronouncing the festivals related to it and adding days where needed. Now the calendar and the festivals it proscribed were three months out: the spring festivals were occurring in winter. When Caesar returned from Egypt in 46 B.C.E. and was appointed dictator he created the new calendar system with the aid of Greek astronomers from Alexandria.

When Julius Caesar was murdered in March 44 B.C.E., Quintilis, the month of his birth, was renamed in his honor. The change did not become official until after a comet appeared late in Quintilis that year, during games paid for by Octavian (later called Augustus), Caesar's adopted son. The appearance of the comet was taken to be a sign that Caesar had attained divinity. Octavian emerged victorious from the ensuing civil wars, and so Caesar's opponents did not have the opportunity to remove Julius Caesar's name from the calendar.

July festivals and customs

July is not so important in the seasonal, or agricultural sense. In the Northern Hemisphere, summer is well underway and work continues in the fields; the rites welcoming spring have concluded and the offerings of thanks for the harvest are yet to come. In the Southern Hemisphere, the harvest is long since over.

However, this does not mean people cannot find reasons to hold celebrations.

In the Roman world, a number of festivals took place in July. The chief of these was the Neptunalia, held in honor of Neptune on July 23. This god was associated with water in its agricultural use and in relation to the sea. Although ancient references are not numerous, the main celebration seems to have consisted of people making small huts called *umbrae* (shades) of laurel branches

July birthflower

The water lily is the birthflower of July. This graceful flower with its peaked petals is said to promote good luck and an open heart, and is the national flower of Bangladesh. Larkspur is also associated with July. Its common name covers a number of species in the buttercup family with spikes of flowers in various colors.

Neptune surrounded by the four seasons, Roman mosaic, second century C.E., at the Bordo Museum Tunis.

in the fields and woods. Here they drank spring water and cooled wine and camped out overnight – a sort of summer cookout. In this hot, dry time of year the festival was thought to ensure Neptune would provide plenty of rain for the rest of the season to allow the crops to grow.

Another water festival, *Tirgan*, is held on July 1. On this day, Persian legend has it that in order to settle a border dispute between Iran and Turan, Arash, the best archer of the Iranians, was chosen to let his arrow fly toward the east from the top of Mt. Damâvand – wherever it landed the border would lie. His arrow flew from dawn till noon. When it fell, the Turan king left with his army, and once he had fulfilled his promise to leave Iran, heavy downpours in both countries brought an eight-year drought to an end.

Traditionally on this day Iranian people tied rainbow-colored bands on their wrists and took them off to throw into streams 10 days later, on the anniversary of the day the news reached Iran that the Turan had reached their own lands. Tirgan is celebrated with special foods, singing, and dancing. Children enjoy the day by playing in streams and throwing water at each other – a sensible way to have fun in the heat of summer.

Swan Upping on the River Thames has been a tradition since the time of Queen Elizabeth I and still provides plenty of opportunity for messing about in boats. In the third week of July, the Vintners and Dyers companies cruise the

The death of Julius Caesar by Vincenzo Camuccini (1771–1884), at the Galleria d'Arte Morderna, Rome. Julius Caesar was murdered on the steps of the Senate by a group of aristocrats who feared he would declare himself king. To their chagrin, the month of his birth was shortly after renamed in his honor.

Swans and cygnets are corralled during the Swan Upping in 2005.

Thames, catching swans, tipping them upside down and using a sharp knife to scratch cygnets' beaks with the same mark as their parents. These special marks denote ownership of the swans; these days participants own every marked swan on the river, and the English monarch owns the rest. The event culminates in a feast that once traditionally included roast swan.

One of the more solemn commemorations held at this time is the Jewish period of mourning known as The Three Weeks. It begins with a fast on the seventeenth day of the Jewish month of *Tammuz* and ends with another on the ninth day of *Av*, a period which falls in the months of July and August on the Gregorian calendar.

Tammuz 17 is important to Jews because a number of calamitous events occurred in their history on this day, including the breaking of the Tablets of the Law by Moses when he found the Israelites worshipping a golden calf; the cessation of sacrifices in the First Temple shortly before its destruction; and the breaching of the walls of Jerusalem by the Romans in 70 b.c.e. On *Av 9*, both the First and Second Temples were destroyed and Bethar fell to the Romans in the *Bar Kochbar* rebellion of 135 C.E. Mourning marks the entire period between these two fasts and no weddings or other celebrations take place. On the last day, Jews read from the Book of Lamentations while seated on the floor.

Summer fun and games

Because this time of year is warm and pleasant in the Northern Hemisphere, not surprisingly many of July's festivals have an outdoor aspect. One of the earliest major sporting festivals, the ancient Olympics, were held during the warmest time

Below, right *Moses Smashes the Tablets of the Law*, by Domenico Beccafumi (1484–1551), kept at Pisa Cathedral. When Moses descended from Mt. Sinai, he found the Israelites worshipping a golden calf they had made in his absence and he smashed the Tablets of the Law in rage.

Below Jewish men read from the Book of Lamentations in an alcove near the Western Wall on the night before *Av 9*.

July birthstone

The birthstone for July is the ruby, the red version of the mineral corundum, and second only in hardness to the diamond. Being red, the ruby is associated with passion and love, which is why it is often given in an engagement ring. It is said to make the heart stronger and to prevent miscarriage.

of the year, usually after the summer solstice had passed, which placed them in the month of July.

In Mongolia, the three-day national festival of *Naadam* begins on July 11, the anniversary of the day the country became independent in 1921. However, the festival goes back many centuries and the modern political event merely served to pin it down to a particular date. Traditionally a nomadic society, Mongols pitch their *yurts* (elaborate portable dwellings) in a camp near Ulaan Baatar, the capital, for a festival where they dress in their finest traditional costumes and enjoy three days of horse racing, archery, and wrestling. The festivities continue at night with drinking, feasting, and dancing.

The Wimbledon tennis championship is one of the more serious sports events that takes place at this time. The first tournament began on July 9, 1877, and has been held annually by the All England Lawn Tennis and Croquet Club around that time ever since.

A more lighthearted event, and one not requiring such a high level of sporting prowess, is the Wife Carrying Championship in Sonkajärvi, Finland. The male contestants must negotiate a 258-yard (235 m)-course that incudes a 6.5-foot (2 m) deep water obstacle with their wife – or any willing female over the age of 17 – remaining on their backs for the duration. The prizes include a wife-carrying statuette and the wife's weight in beer. This sporting event may not be as serious as Wimbledon, but its roots go back just as far: In the region around Sonkajärvi, it was common in the nineteenth century to steal women from neighboring villages, and one bandit would only allow men to join his gang once they had passed a wife-carrying test over a set course.

In the tropics of the Southern Hemisphere, the weather in July is hot but not as stultifying as it is during the wet season. The big event of the season in Darwin, Australia, is the Beer Can Regatta held on Mindil Beach on a Sunday in July or August, depending on the tides. Along with thong-throwing competitions (rubber footwear not underwear), beauty contests, tug-o-wars and good food, there is the main event: A race between boats made out of empty beer cans. Luckily, the race is held in shallow water.

Not to be outdone, perhaps the silliest competition of all is that held in Santa Rosa, California, on one of the most important and serious of U.S. national holidays, July 4. On this day Americans let their hair down in all sorts of ways. Santa Rosa residents hold the World Pillow Fighting Championships: Two contestants at a time face each other sitting astride a slippery wet pole over a pit of mud, each armed with a pillow. The first to fall is the loser, but, as with many summer festivals, the main aim is to have a laugh, so everyone wins in the end.

Women in traditional dress watch the action at the *Naadam* festival in Mongolia.

July 1

> "There is only one happiness in life, to love and be loved."
> — GEORGE SAND

HISTORICAL EVENTS

1796 Dr. Edward Jenner inoculates eight-year-old James Phipps with smallpox. The boy had been previously vaccinated with cowpox and so was immune to the deadly smallpox virus.

1863 The Battle of Gettysburg begins in Pennsylvania. Three days later Union forces win this decisive battle in the American Civil War and the Confederates retreat. Around 51,000 men are killed, wounded, or missing in action.

1916 In World War I, the Battle of the Somme begins in France. At 7:00 A.M. 100,000 British troops leave their trenches and advance towards the German trenches. By the end of the battle in mid-November, 1,265,000 men have been killed, and the Allies have gained 7 miles (11 km).

1969 Prince Charles had become the Prince of Wales on July 26, 1958, when he was nine years old. On this day he was formally invested at Caernarfon Castle in Wales.

1979 The first Sony Walkman, a portable personal cassette player with headphones, goes on sale in Japan.

1997 Hong Kong is officially handed back from Britain to the People's Republic of China (see below).

Births
- **1804** George Sand (b. Amandine Dudevant), writer
- **1872** Louis Blériot, aviator
- **1903** Amy Johnson, aviator
- **1931** Leslie Caron, actress
- **1945** Deborah Harry, singer
- **1952** Dan Aykroyd, actor, comedian and film director
- **1961** Diana, Princess of Wales
- **1961** Carl Lewis, athlete
- **1977** Liv Tyler, actress

Deaths
- **1860** Charles Goodyear, inventor
- **1995** Wolfman Jack, radio personality
- **1996** Margaux Hemingway, actress and model
- **1999** Forrest Mars Sr., candy manufacturer
- **2003** Herbie Mann, flautist
- **2004** Marlon Brando, actor

Hong Kong returns to China

Britain won control over Hong Kong in the 1800s during the Opium Wars. On January 21, 1841, the British flag was raised on Possession Point. Apart from a few years during World War II, Hong Kong remained in British hands.

Negotiations between Britain and the People's Republic of China began in 1982 over the future of the colony. In 1984 it was agreed Hong Kong would again become part of China, but would retain much of its political, judicial, and economic system.

On June 30, 1997, the British held lavish ceremonies to mark the end of their rule. Bands played as the British flag was taken down and presented to the Governor. Ceremonies, including a dragon dance, continued at what was once the British naval base. At 8:00 P.M. Victoria Harbour was illuminated by a fireworks display, before the British gave a banquet for 4,000 VIP guests at Hong Kong's Convention Center.

Chinese President Jiang Zemin was welcomed at around 11:00 P.M. At midnight the Union Jack was lowered and the flag of the People's Republic of China was raised. Meanwhile, the Special Administrative Region government council was sworn in, with Tung Chee-Hwa as leader.

DAYS TO REMEMBER

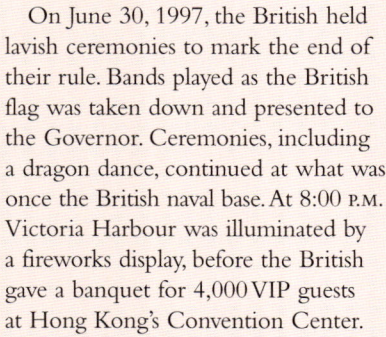

National day Canada Day On this day in 1867, the British Parliament passed the British North America Act, which united the Provinces of Canada, Nova Scotia, and New Brunswick and the Dominion of Canada.

Traditional day Moving day Instead of relaxing on their national holiday, people in the Canadian province of Quebec go into a frenzy of house moving. Old laws protected tenants from being evicted before the winter snows melted, so most leases ran from July 1 to June 30.

Traditional day Keti Koti In Suriname, South America, the festival of *Keti Koti*, or "the breaking of chains," is held to celebrate the day on which Dutch rulers abolished slavery in 1863 after 350 years. The celebrations include feasts, parades, dancing, and music.

DATE*line*

July 2

Middle of the year – 182 days gone, 182 days to go

"I did not have three thousand pairs of shoes, I had one thousand and sixty."

IMELDA MARCOS

HISTORICAL EVENTS

1819 In Britain, the Factory Act is passed, banning children under nine years from working in cotton mills, and limiting children between the ages of nine and 16 to 12 hours work a day.

1881 The twentieth President of the U.S., James Garfield, is shot in the back while waiting for a train. He dies from his wounds on September 19. His assassin, Charles Guiteau, is hanged on June 30, 1882.

1922 Eighteen-year-old Ralph Samuelson uses the first water skis, which he invented, at Lake Pepin, Minnesota.

1937 Amelia Earhart's plane disappears in the Pacific during an attempt to fly around the world (see right).

1964 President Lyndon B. Johnson signs the U.S. Civil Rights Bill, making discrimination on the basis of race, country of origin, or religion illegal.

1990 Some 1,426 pilgrims attending *hajj* in Mecca die when they are crushed in a stampede in a pedestrian tunnel.

2001 In the U.S., the first self-contained, battery-powered, mechanical heart, AbioCor, is implanted in a patient, Robert Tools, who survives for five months.

2005 The Live 8 concerts are held around the world to lobby the meeting of G8 nations to address world poverty. On July 7, the G8 leaders pledge to double the 2004 levels of aid to Africa by 2010.

DAY TO REMEMBER

Religious day Palio di Provenzano In Siena, Italy, this special day takes place in the city square at sunset to honor the Madonna on the feast of the Visitation. There is a colorful medieval-style pageant, followed by a frantic horse race in which 10 of the 17 city wards are represented.

Amelia Earhart, a record-breaking pilot, set out in perfect weather with navigator Fred Noonan in her Lockheed airplane *Electra* from New Guinea on July 2, 1937, on the last leg of their attempt to circumnavigate the globe along the Equator. They were aiming for tiny Howland Island in the Pacific. After two short radio contacts in the early morning, they were never heard from again. Although the U.S. Government spent six weeks searching for the plane, no trace of it was ever found.

Births

1877	Hermann Hesse, writer
1902	Albert Namatjira, painter
1905	Jean Rene Lacoste, tennis player
1929	Imelda Marcos, First Lady of the Philippines
1956	Jerry Hall, model
1971	Evelyn Lau, writer

Deaths

1566	Nostradamus, astrologer
1778	Jean-Jacques Rousseau, philosopher, composer, and writer
1937	Amelia Earhart, aviatrix
1937	Fred Noonan, flight navigator
1961	Ernest Hemingway, writer
1973	Betty Grable, actress
1977	Vladimir Nabokov, writer and lepidopterist
1993	Sir Edward "Weary" Dunlop, surgeon and prisoner of war
1994	Andrés Escobar, footballer

July 3

The first of the Dog Days – the hot sultry days between July 3 and August 15 in the Northern Hemisphere

> "I am interested in anything about revolt, disorder, chaos – especially activity that seems to have no meaning. It seems to me to be the road to freedom." — JIM MORRISON

The Dog Days get their name from the fact that Sirius, the brightest star in the constellation of Canis Major (Big Dog), rises and sets with the Sun at this time. The ancient Romans thought the star added its heat to the Sun's.

Births
- 1567 Samuel de Champlain, explorer
- 1854 Leoš Janácek, composer
- 1883 Franz Kafka, writer
- 1906 George Sanders, actor
- 1927 Ken Russell, director
- 1937 Tom Stoppard, playwright
- 1951 Sir Richard Hadlee, cricketer
- 1957 Laura Branigan, singer
- 1962 Tom Cruise, actor

Deaths
- 1642 Maria de Medici, Queen of France
- 1935 André Gustave Citroën, car manufacturer
- 1969 Brian Jones, musician
- 1971 Jim Morrison, singer and poet
- 1986 Rudy Vallee, singer

HISTORICAL EVENTS

- **1608** The settlement of Quebec is founded by Samuel de Champlain, marking the beginning of European settlement of Canada.
- **1844** Three Icelandic fishermen kill the last pair of great auks. This large flightless relative of the puffin had been hunted to the brink of extinction for feathers and meat. The skins of the last pair, which were nesting, were sold to a specimen collector.
- **1886** In Mannheim, Germany, inventor Karl Benz demonstrates his automobile in public. It travels at 10 miles per hour (16 km/h).
- **1928** Following his demonstration of color television in 1927, inventor John Logie Baird makes the first color television transmission across the Atlantic.
- **1969** Brian Jones, Rolling Stones guitarist, is found drowned in his swimming pool.
- **1971** Jim Morrison, lead singer of The Doors, is found dead in Paris (see below).
- **1988** During the Iran-Iraq war, the U.S.S. *Vincennes* shoots down an Iran Air jet airliner over the Persian Gulf after mistaking it for an Iranian F-14 fighter. The 290 people on board are killed.

DAY TO REMEMBER

Religious day St. Thomas' Day This saint was known as Doubting Thomas, as he wouldn't believe Christ had risen from the dead until he could see Him for himself. It is believed that St. Thomas was later a missionary in India and that a stone cross in Mylapore marks the place where he was buried after being killed by a spear.

Jim Morrison dies at 27

For many, the late 1960s and early 1970s were a time of sex, drugs, and rock and roll. Jim Morrison had been involved in all of these, and along with several performers of his generation, he died young.

While a film student at UCLA in 1965, Morrison had met Ray Manzarek and they formed The Doors with Robbie Krieger and John Densmore. The band took its name from Aldous Huxley's *The Doors of Perception*, a book about the effects of psychedelic drugs. Their music was powerful and often brooding, and Morrison's deep voice half-chanted his poetic, dark lyrics.

The band's performances, especially Morrison's, were fuelled by alcohol and drugs. They were known to turn wild, with equipment destroyed on stage and obscene language hurled at the audience. Morrison was arrested for allegedly exposing himself in a concert in 1969, although his band-mates claimed he only threatened to do so.

Morrison moved to Paris in March 1971. He wanted to concentrate on his writing and hoped to give up music altogether once contractual obligations with his record company were fulfilled.

On July 3, 1971, his girlfriend, Pamela Courson, found his body in the bathtub in his Paris apartment. His death certificate stated that he died of heart failure, probably brought about in part by heavy drinking. His grave lies in the Père Lachaise cemetery in Paris.

July 4

DATEline

"I hold it that a little rebellion now and then is a good thing, and as necessary in the political world as in the physical." — THOMAS JEFFERSON

HISTORICAL EVENTS

1187 Saladin traps the Christian army at the Horns of Hattin without water and defeats them, paving the way for him to take Jerusalem from the Crusaders three months later.

1776 The Declaration of Independence, prepared by U.S. statesman Thomas Jefferson, is signed and approved by John Hancock, the President of the Continental Congress of America. Delegates from the 12 colonies sign on August 2, making the U.S. the world's oldest existing republic, although a treaty with Britain is not signed for a further five years.

1826 On the fiftieth anniversary of the signing of the Declaration of Independence, Thomas Jefferson, its author and signatory, and John Adams, signatory, and second President of the U.S., both die of natural causes.

1865 *Alice's Adventures in Wonderland* is published, three years to the day after Lewis Carroll (Charles Dodgson) began to make up his story for Alice Liddell on a rowing trip.

1946 The Philippines becomes independent for the first time in 400 years. It had been ruled by Spain, declared a republic in 1898 but largely remained in Spanish hands, was then under U.S. sovereignty and briefly occupied by Japan.

1954 Rationing ends in Britain, nine years after the end of World War II and 15 years after the practice had been introduced.

1987 Klaus Barbie, the Butcher of Lyon, a former Gestapo chief, is sentenced in France to life in prison for the torture and murder of thousands of people.

1994 In Rwanda, the Tutsi Rwandan Patriotic Front takes control over the capital, bringing more than three months of genocidal slaughter to an end (see below).

Births

- **1790** Sir George Everest, surveyor
- **1804** Nathaniel Hawthorn, writer
- **1807** Guiseppe Garibaldi, Italian revolutionary and liberator
- **1845** Dr. Thomas Barnardo, humanitarian worker
- **1882** Louis B. Mayer, producer
- **1927** Neil Simon, playwright
- **1927** Gina Lollobrigida, actress

Deaths

- **1826** Thomas Jefferson, third U.S. President
- **1826** John Adams, second U.S President
- **1934** Marie Curie, chemist and physicist
- **1938** Suzanne Lenglen, tennis player
- **1974** Georgette Heyer, writer
- **1991** Victor Chang, heart surgeon
- **2003** Barry White, singer

DAY TO REMEMBER

National day Independence Day (U.S.) This day commemorates the signing of the Declaration of Independence. Many patriotic events have marked the occasion: In 1960 the 50-star U.S. flag was flown for the first time, and in 2004 the cornerstone of the Freedom Tower was laid on the site of the World Trade Center.

Conflict in Rwanda between the majority Hutus and the minority Tutsis had been persistant and long-standing. On April 6, 1994, President Habyariman, a Hutu, was killed when his plane was shot down as it came in to land at the capital, Kigali, sparking a brutal reaction.

Hutu militia groups massacred Tutsis and moderate Hutus. The international community did virtually nothing to stop them. Calm was restored when the Tutsi Rwandan Patriotic Front took over Kigali on July 4. More than 900,000 people had been slaughtered and two million refugees, such as those pictured, had fled to neighboring countries.

July 5

"Without promotion, something terrible happens … nothing."

P. T. BARNUM, FOUNDER OF "THE GREATEST SHOW ON EARTH"

HISTORICAL EVENTS

1865 William Booth holds the first meeting of the East London Christian Mission in a tent in Whitechapel, London. In May 1878, he changes the mission's name to the Salvation Army.

1945 Australia's Prime Minister and wartime leader John Curtin dies in office after a long illness. He is replaced by Ben Chifley on July 13.

1946 The bikini is first shown at a fashion show at a Paris swimming pool (see below).

1950 Israel's Knesset passes the Law of Return, which states that all Jews have the right to settle in Israel.

1956 British Parliament passes the first Clean Air Act to rid the cities of devastating "smog" – fog combined with smoke from industry and coal and wood fires. The Great Smog of December 4–9, 1952, killed 4,000 Londoners outright. The new law phases out coal fires and controls factory fumes. Gradually the smog situation improves.

1977 Zulfika Ali Bhutto, elected Prime Minister of Pakistan in March, is overthrown in a military coup led by General Muhammad Zia ul-Huq. Martial law is then imposed. Bhutto is hanged on April 4, 1979, after being convicted of conspiracy to commit murder.

1980 In a four-hour tennis match, Björn Borg defeats John McEnroe to win Wimbledon for a record fifth consecutive time.

Births
- **1810** P. T. Barnum, circus operator
- **1853** Cecil Rhodes, colonizer of southern Africa, politician
- **1879** Wanda Landowska, harpsichordist
- **1889** Jean Cocteau, poet and artist
- **1911** Georges Pompidou, French President
- **1950** Huey Lewis, singer

Deaths
- **1826** Sir Stamford Raffles, founder of Singapore
- **1894** Sir Austen Henry Layard, archeologist
- **1945** John Curtin, Australian Prime Minister

DAYS TO REMEMBER

National day Tynwald Day (Isle of Man) This day is the midsummer sitting of parliament on the Isle of Man. The Parliament was probably established under the rule of Godred Crovan, which began in 1079, making it the oldest continuous parliament in the world.

National day Independence Day (Venezuela, Algeria) Independence from Spain was declared by Simón Bolívar in Venezuela on this day in 1811, although it did not come into effect for another decade. Algeria also celebrates its independence on this day, which it gained from France in 1962.

On July 5, 1946, a new two-piece swimsuit was revealed to the world. Its creator, Louis Réard, claimed it was the smallest in the world. Stating that it would cause a stir as big as an atomic explosion, he named it the "bikini" after the Pacific atoll where the U.S. detonated an atomic bomb not long before. No model would wear the skimpy bikini in public and Réard hired striptease dancer Micheline Bernardini (pictured) to show it off at a swimming pool in Paris.

July 6

"A legal kiss is never as good as a stolen one." — GUY DE MAUPASSANT

HISTORICAL EVENTS

1535 Sir Thomas More is beheaded in the Tower of London for treason: He had refused to accept Henry VIII as the head of the Church of England or the King's marriage to Anne Boleyn. He was made a saint in 1886.

1885 Louis Pasteur tests his vaccine for rabies on Joseph Meister, a nine-year-old boy who had been bitten by a rabid dog. Joseph is saved and later becomes the director of the Pasteur Institute.

1926 About 100 Aboriginal people are killed in a week in the Eastern Kimberley area by Western Australian police in retaliation for the death of a white boundary rider, speared by an Aboriginal man he was beating with a stockwhip.

1942 Anne Frank and her family go into hiding (see below).

1957 John Lennon (16) is playing with his band the Quarrymen at the Woolton Parish Church Garden Fete, Liverpool, when between sets Paul McCartney (15) introduces himself and demonstrates his guitar-playing abilities. Later Lennon asks McCartney to join the band.

1967 Nigerian forces invade the breakaway state of Biafra, starting the Biafran War. It lasts for two and a half years. Up to one million people die in fighting and of starvation.

Hiding from the Nazis

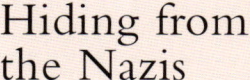

Otto Frank took his family from Germany to live in Amsterdam in the 1930s. In October 1940, the Nazis occupied Holland, and on July 5, 1942, came the event the Franks dreaded: Margot, 16, was "called up." Anne, Margot's 13-year-old sister, wrote in her diary that day, "everyone knows what that means. I picture concentration camps and lonely cells."

But Otto Frank and his friends had planned for such a day. Early next morning the family piled on as many clothes as they could and set out. They were heading for the Secret Annex, a part of the warehouse building Otto's business owned. A hidden flight of stairs led to rooms that Otto had spent months filling with clothes, furnishings, and provisions. Here the Franks and another family hid for the next two years.

A month before her family went into hiding, Anne had been given a diary for her thirteenth birthday. In it she poured out her thoughts and feelings to an imaginary friend named Kitty. Through Anne's eyes we see the daily lives of people living in cramped conditions faced with an uncertain future. Despite all the difficulties, Anne's cheeky, intelligent, critical nature and her hopes for the future shine through.

Anne and her family were given away to the Nazis in August 1944, and all but Otto died in concentration camps in 1945. Miep Gies, one of the friends who had brought them food, found Anne's diary among papers in the Secret Annex. She hid the diary and gave it to Otto when he returned from Auschwitz.

Births

- **1781** Sir Stamford Raffles, founder of Singapore
- **1884** Harold Vanderbilt, railroad heir
- **1907** Frida Kahlo, painter
- **1911** Laverne Andrews, singer
- **1925** Bill Haley, musician and singer
- **1927** Janet Leigh, actress
- **1935** Dalai Lama, exiled leader of Tibet
- **1946** Sylvester Stallone, actor
- **1946** George W. Bush, forty-third U.S. President
- **1951** Geoffrey Rush, actor
- **1958** Jennifer Saunders, comedienne, director and writer

Deaths

- **1535** Sir Thomas More, writer and philosopher
- **1854** George Ohm, physicist
- **1893** Guy de Maupassant, writer
- **1915** Sir Lawrence Hargrave, aeronautical pioneer
- **1932** Kenneth Grahame, children's writer
- **1962** William Faulkner, writer
- **1971** Louis Armstrong, musician and singer
- **1973** Otto Klemperer, conductor and composer
- **1999** Joaquín Rodrigo, composer

DAYS TO REMEMBER

National day Jan Hus Day (Czech Republic) Jan Hus was a church reformer and critic who wanted ceremonies to be performed in Czech and for the sale of indulgences to stop. For refusing to comply with Church orders, he was executed on July 6, 1415.

National day Independence Day (Malawi) On this day, The African republic of Malawi celebrates gaining its independence from Britain in 1964.

July 7

"There were many injured people, and I thought, 'How am I alive when everyone is dying around me?'" — GEORGE PSARADAKIS, DRIVER OF THE BUS BLOWN UP AT TAVISTOCK SQUARE

Rush-hour bombing in London

During London's peak hour on Thursday July 7, 2005, three bombs went off in the Underground at 8:50 A.M. One exploded in a train traveling from King's Cross Station to Russell Square, another on a train approaching Aldgate Station, and a third on a train that had just left Edgware Road Station.

Almost an hour later, at Tavistock Square, a bomb tore the roof off a bus that had been diverted from its normal route due to the earlier blasts. It is thought that the 18-year-old terrorist on board had set off his bomb on the bus because he was unable to reach his Underground target.

With the transport system shut down in case of further blasts, London was thrown into chaos and large areas were cordoned off as rescue workers tried to reach the dead and injured. Fifty-two innocent people are known to have died and 700 sustained serious injuries, including loss of limbs, cuts from flying glass, and major burns.

There are many stories of bravery from that day. On the Aldgate line, passengers in a carriage adjoining the one where the blast took place grabbed fire extinguishers, broke through the carriage door to reach the victims, and tried to put out fires. Rescue workers put themselves in peril working in tunnels that were in danger of collapse.

The four suicide bombers were all young Muslim men and British citizens. Later investigations showed them on CCTV footage calmly undertaking a dummy run nine days before the attack. Al-Qaeda claimed responsibility on September 1.

Births
- 1860 Gustav Mahler, composer
- 1887 Marc Chagall, painter
- 1893 Miroslav Krleža, writer
- 1915 Yul Brynner, actor
- 1919 Jon Pertwee, actor
- 1922 Pierre Cardin, fashion designer
- 1940 Ringo Starr, musician
- 1941 Bill Oddie, comedian and ornithologist
- 1949 Shelley Duval, actress

Deaths
- 1901 Johanna Spyri, writer
- 1930 Sir Arthur Conan Doyle, writer
- 1967 Vivien Leigh, actress
- 1984 Dame Flora Robson, actress

HISTORICAL EVENTS

1898 The U.S. formally annexes Hawaii at the invitation of members of the Republic of Hawaii when U.S. President William McKinley signs the Newlands Resolution.

1969 Canada's House of Commons passes the Official Languages Act, which gives equal weight to the French and English languages in federal government institutions.

1983 After writing a letter to Soviet leader Yuri Andropov, 11-year-old Samantha Smith from Maine, U.S., visits the U.S.S.R. at his invitation, encouraging communication between the two nations.

1984 Prince's single "When Doves Cry" hits the top of the U.S. charts. It becomes the top-selling single of the year.

1990 The three tenors, José Carreras, Placido Domingo and Luciano Pavarotti, perform together for the first time. They hold a charity concert in Rome on the eve of the World Cup Final.

1990 Martina Navratilova wins Wimbledon for the ninth time, the only player to ever have done this.

2005 Terrorists explode four bombs in London (see left).

DAYS TO REMEMBER

Religious day San Fermín This festival held in Pamplona, Spain, celebrates St. Fermín, who according to one story died being dragged through its streets by bulls. The Running of the Bulls is held each morning between July 7 and 14. Young men pray to the saint, then run before the bulls along the cobbled streets.

Religious day Ivan Kupala This midsummer festival is held in Russia. Although it celebrates the birth of St. John the Baptist, it is based on older pagan summer festivals. Late at night, bonfires are lit and parties begin, with dancing and loud celebrations.

July 8

DATE*line*

"Learn to get in touch with the silence within yourself and know that everything in this life has a purpose." — DR. ELISABETH KÜBLER-ROSS, PSYCHIATRIST

On July 8, 1965, Ronald Biggs escaped from England's Wandsworth prison where he was being held for his part in the Great Train Robbery of 1963.

Accomplices threw rope ladders over the prison wall to the exercise yard. While two prisoners distracted guards, Biggs and others climbed over the wall into a removals van (pictured here after the escape had been discovered) that held a getaway car.

Biggs' life on the run took him to Spain, Australia, and Brazil. In May 2001 he returned to England for medical treatment, and to prison.

HISTORICAL EVENTS

1497 Vasco da Gama sets sail from Lisbon, Portugal, to find a sea route to the East Indies.
1889 In New York City, Dow Jones & Company publishes the first issue of the financial newspaper *The Wall Street Journal*. It is four pages long and sells for two cents.
1907 The first of the Ziegfeld Follies is performed at the New York Theater. Promoter Florenz Ziegfeld's revues featured plenty of scantily clad women and were held almost annually on Broadway until 1931.
1943 Jean Moulin, leader of the French Resistance, dies while being held by the Gestapo in Lyon after weeks of torture under the direction of Klaus Barbie.
1965 Ronald Biggs, one of the members of the gang who carried out the Great Train Robbery, escapes from Wandsworth prison (see above).
1986 Kurt Waldheim, former head of the UN, is elected President of Austria despite allegations of his involvement in war crimes in Greece as a German officer.

DAYS TO REMEMBER

Religious day St. Procopius' Day After refusing to make sacrifices to pagan gods, St. Procopius (c. 303) was martyred on this day during the early Domitian persecutions of Christians.

Religious day St. Kilian's Day An Irish priest, St. Kilian was beheaded by Geilana, Duchess of Wurzburg. It is believed Geilana's husband had decided to leave her after Kilian told him the circumstances of their marriage meant that it was forbidden by the Church.

Celtic tree sign

HOLLY

July 8–August 4

In the Celtic tradition, those born under the holly tree sign are honest and trustworthy. They are supportive and loyal, especially to their families. Seldom willing to take risks, they are practical and hardworking, although this does not prevent them from being sensitive.

Births
- 1593 Artemisia Gentileschi, painter
- 1621 Jean de la Fontaine, writer
- 1838 Count Ferdinand Graf von Zeppelin, airship inventor
- 1839 John D. Rockefeller, oil tycoon and philanthropist
- 1851 Sir Arthur Evans, archeologist
- 1882 Percy Grainger, composer
- 1926 Elisabeth Kübler-Ross, psychiatrist
- 1933 Marty Feldman, actor
- 1951 Angelica Huston, actress
- 1958 Kevin Bacon, actor

Deaths
- 1695 Christian Huygens, scientist
- 1822 Percy Bysshe Shelley, poet
- 1855 Sir William Edward Parry, British admiral and explorer
- 1939 Havelock Ellis, doctor and psychologist
- 1943 Jean Moulin, French resistance leader
- 1979 Michael Wilding, actor
- 1994 Kim Il Sung, "Great Leader" of North Korea

July 9

"Do all you can, with what you have, in the time you have, in the place you are."
XOLANI NKOSI JOHNSON, AGED 11

HISTORICAL EVENTS

1893 Dr. Daniel Hale Williams, the only African American surgeon in the American College of Surgeons, performs the world's first successful open-heart surgery in Chicago on a man who had been stabbed.

1900 Queen Victoria gives her consent to the Commonwealth of Australia Constitution Act, already passed by British Parliament, uniting the Australian colonies under a federal government.

1922 At Alamed in California, Johnny Weissmuller is the first person to swim 100 meters in under a minute. In his career, Weissmuller broke 51 world records and won five Olympic gold medals. He also starred in films such as *Tarzan*.

1960 Wearing a lifejacket, Roger Woodward, aged 7, is swept over the Horseshoe Falls at Niagara when the boat he is in capsizes. He is the first person to survive an accidental drop over Niagara Falls.

1982 A man evades security at Buckingham Palace and enters the Queen's bedroom. After talking with him for 10 minutes, the Queen calmly calls for her footman and the man is apprehended.

1984 Lightning strikes the thirteenth-century church in York, York Minster, northern England, causing more than £2 million worth of damage.

2000 Xolani Nkosi Johnson addresses 10,000 delegates at the 13th International AIDS Conference held at Durban in South Africa (see below).

Births
- **1858** Franz Boaz, anthropologist
- **1879** Ottorino Respighi, composer
- **1901** Dame Barbara Cartland, writer
- **1933** Oliver Sacks, neurologist and writer
- **1937** David Hockney, painter
- **1946** Bon Scott, singer (AC/DC)
- **1947** O. J. Simpson, footballer
- **1956** Tom Hanks, actor, director, and producer
- **1964** Courtney Love, musician

Deaths
- **1746** Philip V, King of Spain
- **1747** Giovanni Bononcini, composer
- **1932** King C. Gillette, safety razor manufacturer
- **2002** Rod Steiger, actor

DAY TO REMEMBER

Religious day Martyrdom of the Báb Followers of the Baha'i faith commemorate the martyrdom of the *Báb*, or the Gate, who was executed in Tabriz. One of his followers, Bahá'ulláh, is the founder of the Baha'i faith.

On July 9, 2000, 11-year-old Xolani Nkosi Johnson (pictured with his foster mother) gave an address that he had written himself to the 13th International AIDS Conference. He told his life story: How he was born HIV positive, how he came to be cared for by his foster mother, how his mother died when he was eight, and how he had won the right to attend school. He stressed the need to fight the stigma attached to AIDS and urged the world to care for orphans with AIDS. Nkosi died on June 1, 2001, aged 12.

July 10

"Happiness is beneficial for the body, but it is grief that develops the powers of the mind."
— MARCEL PROUST

The sinking of the *Rainbow Warrior*

In July 1985, the *Rainbow Warrior*, flagship of the conservation organization Greenpeace, was docked at Auckland's Waitemata Harbour. The crew was preparing to lead a fleet to Mururoa Atoll in the Pacific to protest against nuclear tests being conducted by the French Government.

While docked, the ship was opened to the public. French secret agents took the opportunity to reconnoiter the vessel. Two limpet bombs were later placed on the ship's hull. The first bomb blew a large hole in the engine room at 11:38 pm on July 10. As water poured in, everyone left the ship, although Fernando Pereira, a photographer, was still on board when the second bomb exploded. Trapped below deck, Pereira drowned when the ship sank. Others were thrown into the water.

At first the French Government tried to cover up its involvement and joined international condemnation of the bombing. However, it became clear French agents had carried out the attack, acting on orders from the top. Two were arrested and given prison sentences.

The French Minister of Defense, Charles Hernu, resigned, and the head of French intelligence services was fired. The French Government paid Greenpeace compensation.

The *Rainbow Warrior* was unable to be repaired and was sunk offshore, where it serves as a reef habitat for aquatic life.

HISTORICAL EVENTS

1553 Lady Jane Grey, aged 15, is proclaimed Queen of England after the death of Edward VI. Deposed nine days later by Mary Tudor, she is executed for treason on February 12, 1554.

1924 Finnish runner Paavo Nurmi wins the 1,500-meter race and 55 minutes later returns to win the 5,000-meter race at the Paris Olympics. He wins five gold medals at these Olympics.

1929 Charles Kingsford Smith and his aircrew arrive in England in the *Southern Cross* after flying from Australia in the record time of 12 days, 21 hours, and 18 minutes.

1940 The relentless bombing known as the Battle of Britain begins with a daylight attack by the Luftwaffe against shipping convoys off the coast of England.

1962 France sends a live transmission to the U.S. of singer Yves Montand when the U.S. launches the first telecommunications satellite, Telstar, which relays television and telephone signals between the U.S. and Europe.

1985 The *Rainbow Warrior* is blown up in Auckland Harbour, New Zealand, by French secret agents (see above).

DAY TO REMEMBER

Religious day Silence Day The followers of Indian spiritual teacher Meher Baba observe a day of silence to commemorate the day on which he took a vow of silence in 1925. From then until his death in 1969, he communicated only by writing and hand gestures.

Births

- 1509 John Calvin, religious leader
- 1871 Marcel Proust, writer
- 1895 Carl Orff, composer
- 1903 John Wyndham, writer
- 1915 Saul Bellow, writer
- 1931 Alice Munro, writer
- 1943 Arthur Ashe, tennis player
- 1947 Arlo Guthrie, musician
- 1949 Sunil Gavaskar, cricketer

Deaths

- 138 Hadrian, Roman Emperor
- 1099 Rodrigo Díaz, (El Cid), knight
- 1851 Louis-Jacques Daguerre, inventor of daguerreotype photography
- 1941 Ferdinand "Jelly Roll" Morton, musician, composer
- 1989 Mel Blanc, the voice of Bugs Bunny, Daffy Duck, and Porky Pig

July 11

> "Shoot all the bluejays you want, if you can hit 'em, but remember it's a sin to kill a mockingbird." — HARPER LEE

The terracotta army is revealed

In March 1974, villagers in Shaanxi Province, China, were digging a well when they came across unusual pieces of pottery. Archeologists were called in and explorations revealed a huge pit containing life-sized terracotta warriors. A year later, on July 11, 1975, the discovery was announced to the world.

In the first pit uncovered, there were around 6,000 life-sized warriors. They guarded the nearby tomb of Emperor Qin Shihuang (c. 210 B.C.E.), who unified China and ordered the first stage of the Great Wall to be built.

The figures were made in molds with details sculpted on afterwards. They gave great insight into the Chinese army of the time – there were charioteers, cavalry, archers ,and foot soldiers. Their clothing, hairstyles, and facial features were carefully sculpted. They were originally colorfully painted and were equipped with real weapons, some of which have survived. Some of the warriors appear to be modeled on actual individuals.

Excavations continued for some time. The site covers more than 7 acres (2 ha) and an armory has been uncovered, along with figures of acrobats and entertainers. Nearby are burial sites, including a mass grave where convicts who worked on the mausoleum project were disposed of when they died. The site was World Heritage listed in 1987.

Births
- 1274 Robert the Bruce, King of Scotland
- 1767 John Quincy Adams, sixth U.S. President
- 1834 James McNeill Whistler, painter
- 1857 Alfred Binet, psychologist, inventor of IQ test
- 1899 E. B. White, children's writer
- 1916 Gough Whitlam, Australian Prime Minister
- 1934 Giorgio Armani, fashion designer
- 1959 Suzanne Vega, singer and songwriter
- 1975 Lil' Kim Jones, rapper

Deaths
- 1937 George Gershwin, composer
- 1941 Sir Arthur Evans, archeologist
- 1989 Sir Lawrence Olivier, actor
- 2000 Robert Runcie, Archbishop of Canterbury
- 2005 Frances Langford, actress and singer

HISTORICAL EVENTS

- **1893** Kokichi Mikimoto extracts the first cultured pearl at his pearl farm after five years' work. The pearl was imperfect – it took another 10 years to create a perfectly spherical one.
- **1914** Babe Ruth plays in Major League baseball for the first time with the Boston Red Sox.
- **1960** *To Kill a Mockingbird* by Harper Lee is published. The novel about racism in the southern U.S. went on to win the Pulitzer Prize and became one of the best-selling books in history.
- **1975** The discovery of the tomb of the "terracotta warriors" in China is announced (see left).
- **1979** Skylab falls back to Earth after six years in orbit. The debris falls over the southern Indian Ocean and desert regions of Western Australia.
- **1985** Dr. H. Harlan Stone announces that he has devised and used a self-adhesive zipper to be applied instead of stitches on surgical patients who might need to be re-operated on.
- **1991** A dramatic total solar eclipse occurs with the Moon casting a shadow over a 9,000-mile (14,400 km) stretch of the Earth's surface. In some places darkness falls for almost seven minutes.
- **1995** The UN-declared "safe haven" of Srebrenica is captured by Serb troops from Yugoslavia and Bosnia. An estimated 8,000 Muslim men and boys are murdered in the worst atrocity in Europe since World War II.

DAYS TO REMEMBER

Traditional day Eriin Gurvan Naadam In Mongolia this three-day festival begins on July 11. Men participate in Mongolian wrestling, archery, and horse racing. The games are centuries old, but began to be held on this date to commemorate Mongolia's independence in 1921.

International day World Population Day The UN established this observance in 1987 when the world's population reached 5 billion. On this day issues surrounding reproductive health and population control are highlighted.

July 12

"It isn't a matter of black is beautiful as much as it is white is not all that's beautiful."
BILL COSBY, 1969

Protestant William of Orange defeated the Catholic James II at the Battle of the Boyne in Ireland in July 1690. The Orange Order holds parades on July 12 to celebrate the victory. The signing of the Anglo–Irish Agreement in 1985 heightened sectarian tensions in Northern Ireland. On July 12, 1986, violence erupted. It was especially bad in Portadown (pictured right) where marchers were stopped from parading down a street on their traditional route as mainly Catholics resided there. In a week of rioting in Northern Ireland, 300 people were injured and 200 were arrested.

HISTORICAL EVENTS

- **1543** English monarch Henry VIII marries his sixth and last wife, Catherine Parr, who survives him and marries again.
- **1776** Captain James Cook sets sail from Plymouth on the *Resolution*, beginning his third and final voyage of discovery.
- **1794** Horatio Nelson's right eye is badly damaged in a naval attack on the French fortress at Calvi, Corsica.
- **1957** U.S. Surgeon General Leroy E. Burney announces that there is a direct link between lung cancer and smoking.
- **1986** Rioting occurs in Northern Ireland at several of the annual Orange Parades (see above).
- **1990** Soviet President Boris Yeltsin resigns from the Communist Party, splitting it between conservatives and radicals and sparking demonstrations against the party.
- **2005** Prince Albert II becomes ruler of the Principality of Monaco as the three-month period of mourning after his father's death ends, and a week after acknowledging his illegitimate son.

DAY TO REMEMBER

Traditional day Orangeman's Day This day commemorates the Battle of the Boyne and was first held in County Armagh, Northern Ireland, by the Orange Order. Marches are primarily held in Northern Ireland, Scotland, and parts of Canada.

Births

- **100 B.C.E.** Gaius Julius Caesar, Roman politician and general
- **1730** Josiah Wedgwood, pottery manufacturer
- **1817** David Henry Thoreau, writer and philosopher
- **1884** Amedeo Modigliani, artist
- **1895** Oscar Hammerstein II, lyricist
- **1907** Sir Edward "Weary" Dunlop, surgeon and prisoner of war
- **1922** Michael Ventris, linguist
- **1937** Bill Cosby, actor and comedian
- **1943** Christine McVie, musician

Deaths

- **1682** Jean Picard, astronomer
- **1910** Charles Rolls, car manufacturer
- **1926** Gertrude Bell, archeologist, writer and spy
- **1949** Douglas Hyde, Irish President

July 13

> *"Don't go to the pub tonight – please stay in and give us your money."*
> BOB GELDOF, ENCOURAGING TELEVISION VIEWERS OF THE LIVE AID CONCERT TO MAKE DONATIONS

HISTORICAL EVENTS

1793 Noblewoman Charlotte Corday stabs French revolutionary leader Jean Paul Marat in the heart while he is soaking in a bath. She believes in democracy and that Marat is leading France into anarchy. She is executed by guillotine four days later.

1923 The "Hollywood" sign is dedicated in the hills above Hollywood, Los Angeles. It first read "Hollywoodland," but was shortened in 1949.

1947 At a Paris conference, European leaders agree to the Marshall Plan put forward by the U.S. to assist with the rebuilding of Europe after the war.

1977 At around 9:00 P.M. four lightning strikes hit high-voltage power lines in New York, cutting the city's power for 25 hours. There is widespread looting and disorder, causing an estimated U.S. $61 million worth of damage.

1984 Terry Wallis, aged 19, is injured in a car accident in Arkansas, U.S. He comes out of his coma in June 2003 and gradually begins to speak.

1985 The Live Aid concerts, organized by Bob Geldof, raise more than £30 million for Ethiopian famine victims (see right.)

DAYS TO REMEMBER

Religious day Bon Festival The Buddhist *Bon* festival was originally held in Japan in mid-July, but is now held in the East from July 13 to 15, and in August in the West. The festival honors the dead with dancing and music, and families come together to visit their ancestors' graves.

Religious day St. Henry II's Day Although Henry II (973–1024) wished to enter a monastery, he was convinced by an abbot to serve God in his role as Holy Roman Emperor. He restored many dioceses and repaired and built cathedrals and monasteries.

Births
- 1933 David Storey, writer and playwright
- 1940 Patrick Stewart, actor
- 1942 Harrison Ford, actor
- 1944 Erno Rubik, inventor of the Rubik's cube
- 1963 Fatboy Slim, musician

Deaths
- 1793 Jean Paul Marat, French revolutionary
- 1954 Frida Kahlo, painter

Live Aid

In 1984, Bob Geldof, lead singer of British band, the Boomtown Rats, saw a television news report about a feeding center in famine-stricken Ethiopia. There wasn't enough food for everyone, so aid workers had to select those who looked as if they had the greatest chance of survival, dabbing those who would be fed with a marker pen.

This tragic report prompted Geldof and Midge Ure from the band Ultravox to write the song "Do they know it's Christmas?". A group of famous pop artists recorded it and the song quickly raised £8 million.

In 1985, Geldof visited Ethiopia and realized much of the aid wasn't reaching those who needed it. He decided to hold a worldwide telethon to raise money for a fleet of trucks and more food.

On July 13, 1985, two 16-hour concerts were held simultaneously in Wembley Stadium, London, and JFK Stadium, in Philadelphia. Bands in other places joined in via satellite.

The Wembley concert was attended by the Prince and Princess of Wales and began with a royal fanfare. Then the rock concert began, with Status Quo performing "Rocking all over the world."

Seventy-five acts participated, including Elton John, U2, Paul Simon, Paul McCartney, David Bowie, Madonna, The Who, Tina Turner, Wham, the Beach Boys and Bob Geldof. Phil Collins even performed in Wembley then flew to the U.S. to appear at the Philadelphia concert.

The two main concerts were attended by 170,000 people, while 1.5 billion watched on television. The event raised more than £30 million for famine victims, and increased world awareness about African poverty.

LIVE AID

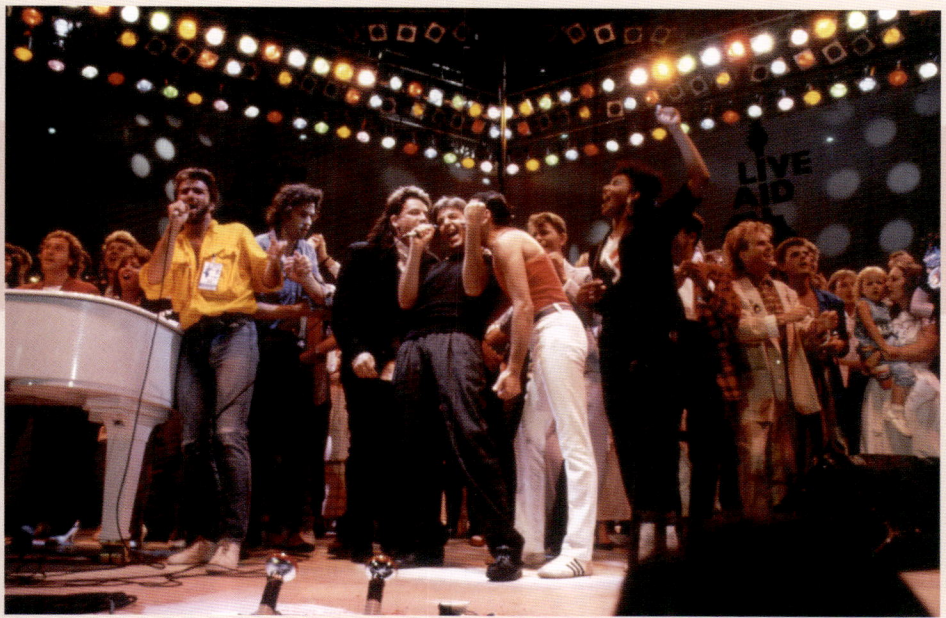

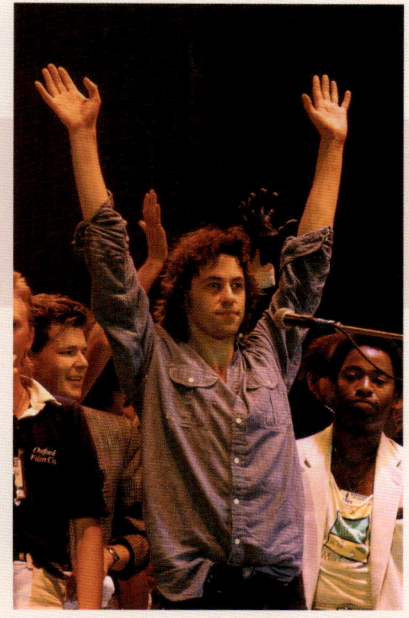

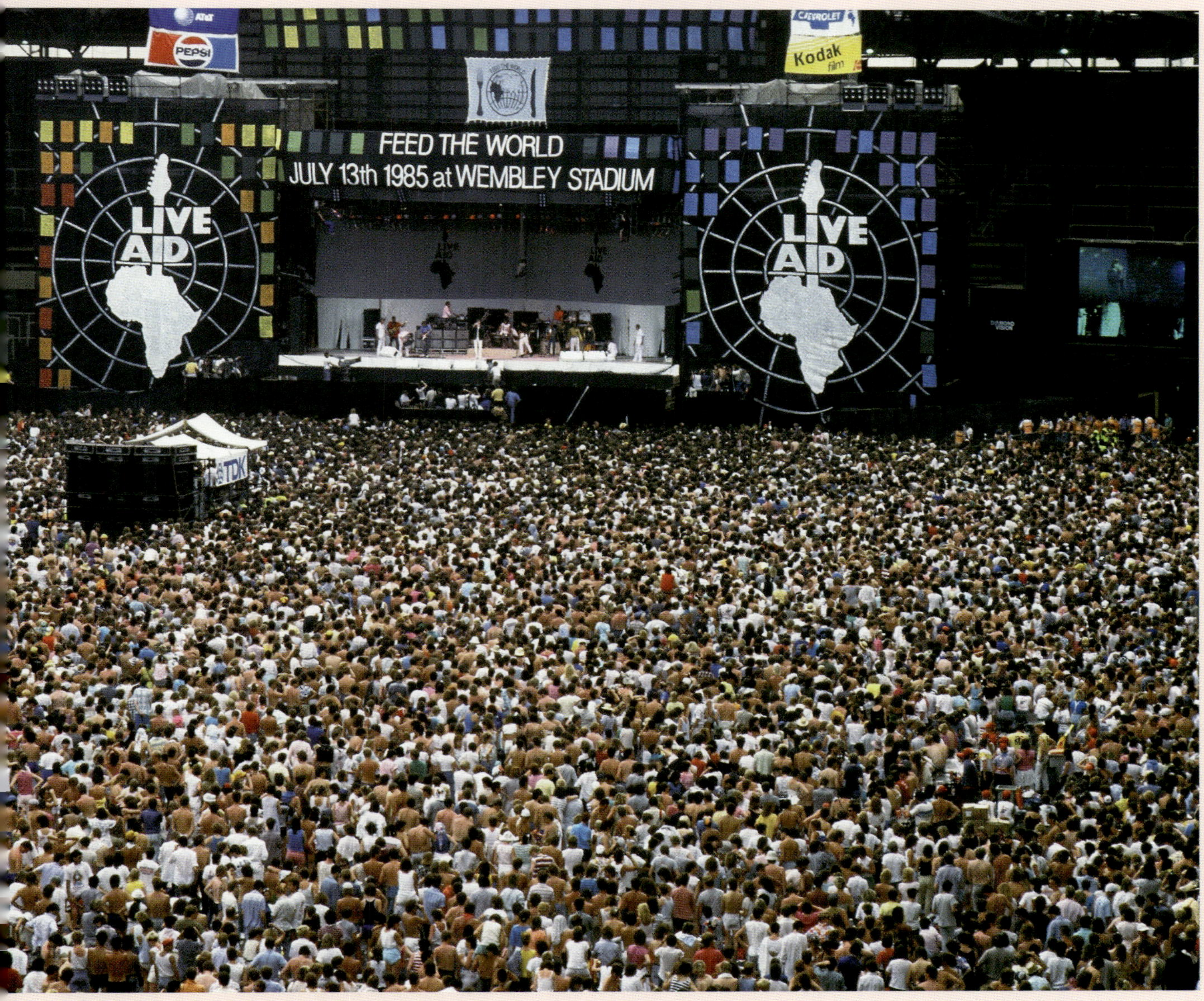
PEPSI
Kodak film
FEED THE WORLD
JULY 13th 1985 at WEMBLEY STADIUM
LIVE AID
LIVE AID
TDK

July 14

"You know more than you think you do." DR. BENJAMIN SPOCK, IN HIS BOOK ON BABY AND CHILD CARE

HISTORICAL EVENTS

1789 Around 800 Parisians armed with muskets and cannons attack the Bastille, a medieval fortress used as a prison. They wipe the garrison out and free the seven prisoners inside. This event triggers the French Revolution.

1791 In Birmingham, England, rioters burn the home and laboratory of Joseph Priestly, the chemist who discovered oxygen, because of his support for the French Revolution. Three years later he leaves for America.

1865 A party led by Edward Whymper reaches the summit of the Matterhorn in the Alps. Three men die on the ascent.

1867 Alfred Nobel demonstrates dynamite in a quarry in Surrey, England. He was an explosives manufacturer whose legacy endows the Nobel Prize.

1946 Dr. Benjamin Spock's *The Common Sense Book of Baby and Child Care* is published and becomes the child-rearing bible of the baby boom.

1958 The monarchy of Iraq is overthrown in a violent military coup and 23-year-old King Faisal is killed. Abdul Karim el Qasim leads the coup and becomes Prime Minister, but is killed when he is overthrown in 1963.

2002 An assassination attempt is made on French President Jacques Chirac during Bastille Day celebrations (see below).

Births
- 1858 Emmeline Pankhurst, suffragist
- 1862 Gustav Klimt, painter
- 1904 Isaac Bashevis Singer, writer
- 1910 William Hanna, animator
- 1912 Woodie Guthrie, musician
- 1918 Ingmar Bergman, film director
- 1921 Leon Garfield, children's writer
- 1926 Harry Dean Stanton, actor

Deaths
- 1881 William H. Bonney (Billy the Kid), outlaw
- 1887 Alfred Krupp, steel and munitions manufacturer
- 1904 Paul Kruger, Boer leader
- 1915 Lawrence Hargrave, aviation pioneer
- 1929 Sir Walter Baldwin Spencer, anthropologist

DAYS TO REMEMBER

Religious day St. Camillus de Lellis' Day After a religious conversion – having once been a soldier who lost his money gambling – St. Camillus (1550–1614) cared for the sick, setting up his own hospital Order, which notably rendered assistance to those with plague and soldiers on the battlefield.

Historical day Bastille Day Held in France and in all French dependencies, this day celebrates the storming of the Bastille in 1789 and represents the beginning of the French Revolution and the forming of the French republic. People celebrate with parades, fireworks, and by holding dances.

In 2002, as French President Jacques Chirac (center) was riding in an open-topped car in the Bastille Day Parade near the Arc de Triomphe, a gunman fired a single shot at him. Neo-Nazi Maxime Brunerie, 25, had smuggled a rifle through the crowd in a guitar case. After he fired the shot, he turned the gun on himself, but members of the public seized it and held him until police arrived. Undeterred by the attack, Chirac continued with the day's celebrations.

July 15

"The thing about inventing is you have to be both stubborn and flexible. The hard part is figuring out when to be which." — JEFF BEZOS, AMAZON.COM

HISTORICAL EVENTS

1099 Jerusalem falls to the First Crusaders after a long siege. Some 15,000 Christian soldiers enter the city and massacre Saracens and Jews.

1799 A soldier in Napoleon's army, Captain Pierre-François Bouchard, finds the Rosetta Stone in the Egyptian village of Rosetta near Alexandria. The stone proves to be the key to deciphering Egyptian hieroglyphics.

1869 Hippolyte Mège Mouriès wins a competition held by Emperor Napoleon III to find a synthetic edible fat by inventing margarine. He names it after the Greek word for pearl, *margaron*, because of its pearly luster.

1927 The acquittal of two right-wing militia men of murder leads to clashes between socialist and right-wing groups in Vienna, which result in the deaths of 85 protesters and four policemen.

1974 The President of Cyprus, Archbishop Makarios, is overthrown in a Greek-backed nationalist coup in Nicosia. On July 20, Turkey invades the island due to fears of a Greek takeover. This leads to the division of Cyprus in August.

1995 Amazon.com opens for business in Seattle, U.S. (see right).

1997 Gianni Versace is murdered outside his home in Miami by Andrew Cunanan, whom he had never met. Cunanan is found dead eight days later, shot with the same gun.

DAY TO REMEMBER

Religious day St. Rosalia's Day When plague struck Palermo, Italy, in the sixteenth century, the hermit Santa Rosalia appeared to a hunter and told him to retrieve her remains from a cave and parade them through the streets. He did so, the plague vanished, and she became Palermo's patron saint.

Births
- **1573** Inigo Jones, architect
- **1606** Rembrandt van Rijn, painter
- **1915** Gavin Maxwell, writer and naturalist
- **1919** Iris Murdoch, writer
- **1926** Leopoldo Galtieri, general and dictator
- **1930** Jacques Derrida, philosopher
- **1933** Julian Bream, guitarist
- **1946** Linda Ronstadt, singer

Deaths
- **1274** Saint Bonaventure, theologian
- **1904** Anton Chekhov, writer
- **1953** John Christie, serial killer
- **1976** Paul Gallico, writer
- **1997** Gianni Versace, fashion designer

Amazon.com is launched

One of the first and largest online retailers, Amazon.com started out selling books. The first book was sold on July 15, 1995. It was *Fluid Concepts & Creative Analogies: Computer Models of the Fundamental Mechanisms of Thought* by Douglas Hofstadter.

Jeff Bezos (pictured), the firm's founder and CEO, graduated from Princeton University with a degree in electrical engineering and computer science. In 1994 he created a company that aimed to use online selling like a catalog. The big advantage of operating the business using online ordering and a warehouse was the number of titles that could be held. The name Amazon.com reflected the volume of titles available: Around 1 million compared to the largest bookstore's maximum of 300,000. Customers could access obscure books they would be hard-pressed to find in an ordinary bookstore.

Other innovative features also made Amazon.com attractive to customers. For instance, they were invited to post reviews on the site of books they had read. Critics told Bezos that broadcasting negative views about his products would be detrimental to sales, whereas he felt that the company would "sell more if we help people make purchasing decisions."

Through word-of-mouth, Amazon.com grew steadily. It branched out into selling other products and services to become the business giant it is today.

July 16

> *"I can't quite imagine life without Harry."*
> J. K. ROWLING, ON WRITING THE FINAL HARRY POTTER BOOK

HISTORICAL EVENTS

- **622** Under threats of murder, the Prophet Mohammed leaves Mecca with his followers and begins his *Hijrah*, or migration, to Medina. This event marks the beginning of the Islamic calendar.
- **1212** King Alphonso VIII of Spain leads soldiers from several Christian nations against a Moorish army and defeats them at the Battle of Las Navas de Tolosa, beginning the retreat of the Moors from Spain.
- **1945** The U.S. detonates the first atomic bomb – nicknamed "The Gadget" – in a test near Alamogordo, New Mexico.
- **1965** The Mont Blanc tunnel is opened. The 7-mile (11.6 km) tunnel links Italy and France. It took six years to build and is the world's deepest tunnel at 8,137 feet (2,480 m).
- **1979** Ailing Hassan al-Bakr resigns as President of Iraq and General Saddam Hussein takes his place. A week later Hussein sends his opponents in his own party to a firing squad.
- **1994** Fragments of the comet Shoemaker-Levy 9 begin to strike Jupiter, causing massive explosions. The Hubble space telescope sends images of the five-day show back to Earth.
- **1999** A small plane that is piloted by John F. Kennedy Jr. crashes off the coast of Martha's Vineyard. Kennedy, his wife, and sister-in-law all die.
- **2005** *Harry Potter and the Half-Blood Prince* is released, breaking all publishing records (see below).

Births
- **1723** Joshua Reynolds, painter
- **1872** Roald Amundsen, explorer
- **1911** Ginger Rogers, dancer and actress
- **1958** Michael Flatley, dancer
- **1967** Will Ferrell, comedian and actor

Deaths
- **1953** Hilaire Belloc, journalist
- **1985** Heinrich Böll, writer
- **1999** John F. Kennedy Jr., lawyer and publisher

DAY TO REMEMBER

Religious day Feast of the Virgin's Appearance Mt. Carmel is the place where the first chapel was built to the Blessed Virgin. The Carmelite order holds a feast commemorating the Virgin's appearance on July 16, 1251, to St. Simon Stock, their leader in Cambridge, when she presented him with the holy garment worn by the order.

Harry Potter and the Half-Blood Prince was released worldwide on July 16. Since the first book about the boy wizard was released in 1997, the series had become a hit with children and adults. In the lead-up to July 16, booksellers were under strict instructions not to sell the sixth Harry Potter book ahead of time. Around 9 million copies were sold in the first 24 hours, breaking all publishing records. A copy signed by the author, Joanne Kathleen Rowling, sold for U.S. $992.40.

July 17

> *"I must rule after my own fashion."*
> — CATHERINE THE GREAT

Walt Disney bought 160 acres (45 ha) of orange groves near Anaheim, south of Los Angeles, and spent U.S. $17 million building an extravagant amusement park, Disneyland.

On July 17, 1955, the opening of Disneyland was televised. Limited numbers of invitations were sent out, but counterfeiters had been busy and thousands of extra people attended. Many attractions weren't yet complete, and food and drink were in short supply. Despite mishaps on the day, Disneyland quickly became a huge success.

Births
- 1899 James Cagney, actor
- 1902 Christina Stead, writer
- 1917 Phyllis Diller, comedienne
- 1920 Juan Antonio Samaranch, chairman of the IOC
- 1935 Donald Sutherland, actor
- 1940 Tim Brooke-Taylor, comedian
- 1947 Camilla, Duchess of Cornwall
- 1952 Phoebe Snow, singer
- 1954 Angela Merkel, German chancellor

Deaths
- 1793 Charlotte Corday, assassin, French aristocrat
- 1903 James McNeill Whistler, painter
- 1912 Henri Poincaré, mathematician
- 1918 Tsar Nicholas II and his family
- 1959 Billie Holiday, singer
- 1967 John Coltrane, musician

DAYS TO REMEMBER

Traditional day Yamaboko Junko (Kyoto, Japan) One of the main events of *Gion Matsuri*, a month-long Japanese festival, is the *Yamaboko Junko*, a parade of traditional wooden floats that are carried through the streets on July 17.

National day Luis Muñoz Rivera's birthday (Puerto Rico) The statesman born on this day in 1859 devoted himself to gaining autonomy for his country, first from Spain and then from the U.S.

HISTORICAL EVENTS

- **1762** Catherine the Great becomes Empress of Russia nine days after her husband, Tsar Peter III, is strangled in his bedroom in a prison fortress. His wife denies any involvement in his death.
- **1918** Tsar Nicholas II of Russia and his wife, Alexandra, their five children, and their remaining servants are executed by Bolsheviks at Ekaterinburg in Siberia.
- **1955** Disneyland, the world's first theme park, has its grand opening at Anaheim, California (see above).
- **1975** The American *Apollo* and Soviet *Soyuz* spacecraft dock in space, a difficult feat as they are different in design. This is the first link between spacecraft of the two nations.
- **1979** Sandinista rebels close in on the Nicaraguan capital of Managua, deposing the ruling U.S.-supported Somoza family. President General Anastasio Somoza Debayle resigns and flees to Miami.
- **1996** Trans World Airlines flight 800 explodes over the ocean shortly after take-off from New York, killing all 230 on board. In 1998, investigators announce that mechanical failure was the cause, not terrorism or an accidental missile strike by the U.S. Navy.
- **1998** Three tsunami waves, the last of which is 46 feet (14 m) high, strike Papua New Guinea. Ten low-lying villages are swept away, killing at least 3,000 people.

July 18

"It is better to die on your feet than to live on your knees."
DOLORES IBARURRI, SPANISH COMMUNIST LEADER, CALLING REPUBLICAN SUPPORTERS TO ARMS, JULY 18, 1936

Births
- 1811 William Makepeace Thackeray, writer
- 1848 William Gilbert Grace, cricketer
- 1918 Nelson Mandela, South African President
- 1921 John Glenn, astronaut
- 1933 Yevgeny Yevtushenko, writer and political activist
- 1937 Hunter S. Thompson, journalist
- 1949 Dennis Lillee, cricketer
- 1950 Sir Richard Branson, entrepreneur
- 1982 Priyanka Chopra, actress

Deaths
- 1610 Michelangelo Merisi da Caravaggio, painter
- 1698 Johann Heinrich Heidegger, theologian
- 1721 Jean Antoine Watteau, painter
- 1817 Jane Austen, writer
- 1892 Thomas Cook, travel agent
- 1937 Julian Bell, poet
- 1988 Nico, model and singer

HISTORICAL EVENTS

- **1814** Matthew Flinders' *A Voyage to Terra Australis* is published, in which he advocates using the name "Australia" for the southern continent. He dies the next day.
- **1898** Marie and Pierre Curie announce they have discovered a new, highly unstable element, which they call polonium after Marie's homeland, Poland. It is the first element discovered by radioactive analysis.
- **1925** The first volume of *Mein Kampf* (*My Struggle*) by Adolf Hitler is published, outlining his life and his political ideas.
- **1936** The Spanish Civil War begins when General Francisco Franco leads an army uprising in Spanish North Africa and in a radio broadcast urges the army in Spain to rise against the republican government. As soldiers arrest government officials, members of left-wing parties fight back.
- **1976** At the Montreal Olympics, Romanian gymnast Nadia Comaneci is awarded the first perfect score in Olympic gymnastics (see below).
- **1995** The oldest-known musical instrument, a 45,000-year-old bear bone with four holes made along it, is found in the Indrijca River valley in Slovenia.
- **2003** The body of a missing weapons expert on Iraq, Dr. David Kelly, is found after he commits suicide. It soon becomes clear that he was the source of reports that the British Government "sexed up" assessments of Iraq's weapons.

DAY TO REMEMBER

National day Constitution Day (Uruguay) This national holiday commemorates the signing of Uruguay's first constitution in 1830.

Nadia Comaneci's Olympic perfection

The star of the Montreal Olympics in 1976 was 14-year-old Romanian Nadia Comaneci. On July 18, her performance on the uneven bars earned her 10 out of 10: The first perfect score in Olympic gymnastics.

Reflecting as an adult, Comaneci said, "I was not one for looking straight at the scoreboard…but I remember this incredible noise." Afterward, she recalled, "I was not sure what was happening because the scoreboard only had three digits and it was showing 1.00."

Comaneci went on to score seven more 10s in the competition, earning three gold medals, two silvers, and one bronze. It was not only Comaneci's routines that won her admiration, but her poise and calmness. Comaneci has stated that she believes her youth and obscurity helped as she felt little of the pressure that many athletes struggle with as they approach a major competition.

She was met on her return to Romania by a crowd of 10,000 people. Although she went back to training, she came under the scrutiny and control of Nicolae Ceausescu's brutal regime.

At the Moscow Olympics in 1980, Comaneci won a further two gold and two silver medals. She attended her last major competition in 1981. After that, she coached Romanian gymnasts.

She defected from Romania to the U.S. in 1989, and after several turbulent years married U.S. gymnast Bart Conner. The couple run a gymnastics academy and work for charity.

July 19

DATE*line*

> *"Hollywood is a place where they'll pay you a thousand dollars for a kiss and fifty cents for your soul."* — MARILYN MONROE

On this day in 1946, Mrs. Norma Jeane Dougherty, former munitions factory worker and model, took a screen test at 20th Century Fox Studios. She passed and signed a contract on August 26. The studio suggested she take the stage name "Marilyn" after the 1920s musical star Marilyn Miller, and she decided on the last name "Monroe", which was her mother's maiden name. For six months after she signed, Marilyn Monroe learned about hair, make-up, and acting. She divorced James Dougherty, a returned U.S. merchant marine, in September.

HISTORICAL EVENTS

64 C.E. The Great Fire of Rome begins and rages for six days, destroying three of the 14 precincts of the city and damaging seven more. Some Romans believe Emperor Nero lit the fire and he is overthrown four years later.

1545 The *Mary Rose* sinks during a military engagement with the French off Portsmouth. About 300 people drown. The ship is raised and put in a British museum in 1982.

1903 Frenchman Maurice Garin wins the first Tour de France. Only 20 of the 60 competitors finish the race.

1935 The world's first parking meters are introduced in the business district of Oklahoma City, U.S., to prevent workers from taking parking places all day, and to gain revenue.

1946 Marilyn Monroe takes her first screen test at 20th Century Fox Studios (see left).

1966 Frank Sinatra (50) marries Mia Farrow (21). They divorce two years later.

2001 Sir Jeffrey Archer, British politician and novelist, is sentenced to four years' prison for perjury and perverting the course of justice during a libel case he brought against the *Daily Star* newspaper in 1987.

DAYS TO REMEMBER

National day Martyrs' Day (Myanmar) On this day in 1947 General Aung San and six of his cabinet ministers were assassinated by U. Saw, a former Prime Minister and rival. It is known as *Azani*, or Martyrs' Day in Myanmar.

National day Liberation Day (Nicaragua) This day celebrates the establishment of the Sandinista takeover in Managua, the Nicaraguan capital, in 1979, two days after the resignation of dictator General Anastasio Somoza Debayle.

Births
- 1814 Samuel Colt, gun manufacturer
- 1834 Edgar Degas, artist
- 1860 Lizzie Borden, alleged murderer
- 1947 Brian May, musician (Queen)

Deaths
- 1374 Francesco Petrarch, poet
- 1814 Matthew Flinders, explorer
- 1947 General Aung San, Burmese nationalist
- 1965 Syngman Rhee, first president of South Korea
- 2004 Zenko Suzuki, Japanese Prime Minister

July 20

Buzz Aldrin stands on the moon.

"The *Eagle* has landed."

The Apollo 11 mission blasted off from the Kennedy Space Center in Florida at 9:32 A.M. on July 16, 1969. On board were Commander Neil Armstrong, Colonel Edwin "Buzz" Aldrin and Lieutenant Colonel Michael Collins.

On July 20, Apollo 11 began to orbit the Moon. Leaving Collins behind, Armstrong and Aldrin went through a crawlway from *Columbia*, the command module, to *Eagle*, the landing module, then undocked and began their descent.

At around 1,300 feet (400 m) above the Moon's surface, they realized the view outside was of large boulders, not the smooth landscape they had expected – they had overshot the designated landing site. Armstrong overrode the computer controls and guided the *Eagle* to a more suitable spot with less than a minute's fuel remaining.

At 10:56:20 P.M. U.S. Eastern Daylight Time, Neil Armstrong, equipped with a television camera, stepped from the bottom rung of the *Eagle's* ladder onto the surface of the Moon, saying the famous words, "That's one small step for man, one giant leap for mankind." Millions of people on Earth watched.

Aldrin followed 19 minutes later and the men spent two hours on the Moon's surface collecting rock samples and taking photos. They also planted the U.S. flag and revealed a plaque on the leg of the landing gear.

After spending nearly 22 hours on the Moon, the *Eagle* blasted off again. Once it had docked, the astronauts re-entered the *Columbia*; the landing module was then jettisoned. *Columbia* returned safely to Earth, splashing down in the Pacific Ocean on July 24.

HISTORICAL EVENTS

1881 Sioux Indian leader Sitting Bull turns himself in to the U.S. Army after being a fugitive since the Battle of the Little Big Horn in 1876. He is imprisoned for two years.

1944 Colonel Claus von Stauffenberg takes a bomb in a briefcase to a meeting in Adolf Hitler's bunker. He excuses himself, and minutes later the bomb goes off. Four die, but Hitler survives this third assassination attempt.

1960 Sirimavo Bandaranaike becomes Prime Minister of Ceylon, the world's first elected female head of government. She entered politics when her husband, Prime Minister Solomon Bandaranaike, was assassinated in 1959, and retired in August 2000, a month before her death at age 84.

1969 Neil Armstrong is the first man to walk on the Moon (see left).

1989 After political unrest in Burma (now Myanmar), military rulers place the opposition leader Daw Aung San Suu Kyi under house arrest.

2003 In Delhi, working elephants begin wearing reflectors on their flanks and ankles to avoid being hit by cars when working at night.

DAYS TO REMEMBER

National Day Independence Day (Colombia) On this day in 1810, Simón Bolívar defied Spain and declared Colombia's independence. Full independence was gained in 1813.

Traditional Day Friendship Day In Argentina and other (mostly Latin American) nations this is a day for celebrating friendship. Dr. Enrique Febbaro, a professor of sociology, thought of holding a day to mark friendship when he observed how the Moon landing brought the world's people together. On this day, many Argentines have get-togethers and catch up with old friends.

Births
- **1304** Francesco Petrarch, poet
- **1797** Sir Pawel Edmund Strzelecki, explorer
- **1919** Sir Edmund Hillary, mountain climber
- **1924** Robert D. Maurer, physicist, inventor of the optical fiber
- **1938** Dame Diana Rigg, actress
- **1938** Natalie Wood, actress
- **1947** Carlos Santana, guitarist
- **1953** Marcia Hines, singer

Deaths
- **1923** Pancho Villa, Mexican revolutionary
- **1937** Guglielmo Marconi, inventor of the radio
- **1973** Bruce Lee, martial artist and actor

July 21

"My comedy is like emotional hang-gliding." — ROBIN WILLIAMS

HISTORICAL EVENTS

1873 English explorer William Gosse announces the discovery in Australia of the world's largest monolith, which he names Ayers Rock, after South Australian Premier, Sir Henry Ayers. In 1985 it is handed back to the Mutitjulu people and regains the name "Uluru."

1873 Jesse James and his gang pull off the first successful train robbery at Adair, Iowa. They take around U.S. $3,000.

1925 John Thomas Scopes is fined U.S. $100 for teaching Darwin's Theory of Evolution at a school in Tennessee, where it was illegal to teach ideas that contradicted the Old Testament. The ruling is later overturned.

1944 U.S. troops land on Guam and reclaim it from Japanese forces by August 10.

1970 Egypt's Aswan High Dam is completed, controlling the floodwaters of the Nile (see below).

1976 The IRA assassinates the British ambassador to the Republic of Ireland, Christopher Ewart-Biggs, in Dublin.

Births
- 1620 Jean Picard, astronomer
- 1899 Ernest Hemingway, writer
- 1907 A. D. Hope, poet
- 1920 Isaac Stern, violinist
- 1924 Don Knotts, actor and comedian
- 1934 Sir Jonathan Miller, surgeon, actor, and director
- 1948 Yusuf Islam (Cat Stevens), songwriter and singer
- 1951 Robin Williams, actor, comedian

Deaths
- 1796 Robert Burns, poet
- 1944 Colonel Claus von Stauffenberg, would-be assassin of Adolf Hitler

DAYS TO REMEMBER

National day Independence Day (Belgium) This day celebrates the crowning of the first Belgian king, Léopold I, in 1831, marking Belgium's independence from the Netherlands.

National day Racial Harmony Day (Singapore) Held on the anniversary of riots that occurred after a Malay gathering to celebrate the Prophet Mohammed's birthday, this day promotes racial harmony. Schoolchildren share their traditional foods.

Aswan High Dam is completed

Egyptians have depended on the annual summer flooding of the Nile River since ancient times for the success of their agriculture. However, Egypt was also at the mercy of the Nile's floods. In some years the water rose too far, causing severe damage, and in others it didn't rise far enough, resulting in terrible famine.

In 1899 the British began to construct the Aswan Dam in an attempt to control flooding. The dam was subsequently raised, but it still overflowed in 1946. In 1952 plans were made to build the Aswan High Dam. Construction of the Russian-designed clay and rock dam began in 1960. The first stage of the dam had been constructed by 1964 and water began to collect in the 296-mile (480 km) reservoir. On July 21, 1970, the Aswan High Dam was finally completed.

Since the dam reached capacity in 1976 it has prevented both flood and famine, and contributed to Egypt's economy through the regulation of agriculture and the generation of electricity. However, the building of the dam has also created major problems. In the first instance, 90,000 people were displaced from their traditional herding lands and many archeological sites were lost, although the major ones were moved to higher ground.

Long-term environmental problems have also become apparent. Silt that once would have enriched Egypt's fields is now trapped behind the dam, and the use of artificial fertilizers has increased as a result. Soil erosion and salinity have become major issues, and the fisheries that depended on the nutrients that floods carried into the Mediterranean Sea have severely diminished.

July 22

"The Lord is a shoving leopard." REVEREND WILLIAM SPOONER, FOR WHOM SPOONERISMS ARE NAMED

HISTORICAL EVENTS

1793 Sir Alexander MacKenzie and his party arrive at the Pacific Ocean on this day, making them the first Europeans to cross Canada. The journey was carried out on foot and by canoe.

1933 Wiley Smith lands his aircraft in Floyd Bennett Field, Brooklyn, U.S., completing the first solo flight around the world.

1962 The *Mariner 1* spacecraft, heading for a fly-by of Venus, malfunctions shortly after launch and is destroyed by remote control before it can crash into a populated area.

1977 Deng Xiaoping returns to power in China (see below).

1983 Dick Smith, Australian entrepreneur, completes the first circumnavigation of the globe in a helicopter.

1991 American serial killer Jeffrey Dahmer is arrested after one of his would-be victims escapes and leads police back to Dahmer's home.

1992 Colombian drug lord Pablo Escobar escapes from his luxurious prison when government forces tried to remove him. He was afraid he would be extradited to the U.S. He is killed in 1993 when attempts are made to recapture him.

2003 U.S. forces kill Saddam Hussein's sons, Uday and Qusay, and his 14-year-old grandson, in a gun battle in the northern Iraqi town of Mosoul.

Births
- **1822** Gregor Mendel, monk and scientist
- **1844** Reverend William Spooner, Dean and Warden of New College, Oxford
- **1932** Oscar de la Renta, fashion designer
- **1946** Danny Glover, actor
- **1955** Willem Dafoe, actor
- **1973** Rufus Wainwright, singer and songwriter

Deaths
- **1461** Charles VII, King of France
- **1870** Josef Strauss, composer
- **1915** Sir Sandford Fleming, inventor and engineer
- **1932** Florenz Ziegfeld, theater promoter
- **1976** Sir Mortimer Wheeler, archeologist
- **2003** Uday and Qusay Hussein, sons of Saddam Hussein
- **2004** Sacha Distel, singer

DAYS TO REMEMBER

Religious day St. Mary Magdalene's day Mary Magdalene was a close follower of Jesus and the first person to meet him after the Resurrection.

Traditional day Pi Approximation Day On this day – written as 22/7, an approximation of Pi – mathematics departments around the world celebrate Pi by eating pies, pizzas, pineapple, and the like, and by discussing its mathematical significance.

During his career, Deng Xiaoping (center) fell out of favor with Mao Zedong (right) several times because of his promotion of reform within the Chinese Communist Party. When Mao died in 1976, a power struggle ensued between the Gang of Four, led by Mao's widow, and more moderate leaders such as Deng. Backed by Premier Hua Guofeng, Deng was reinstated by the Chinese Communist Party to the position of Vice-Premier and made Chief of the People's Liberation Army on July 22, 1977. This position enabled him to become the effective ruler of China by 1978.

July 23

DATEline

"Monsieur le Maréchal, you who had always done such great honor to your arms, who were once my leader and my example, how had you come to this?"

GENERAL CHARLES DE GAULLE, WRITING OF HENRI PHILIPPE PÉTAIN

HISTORICAL EVENTS

1745 Bonnie Prince Charlie (Charles Stewart) lands in Scotland at Eriksay with only eight supporters. He raises an army, which is defeated by English forces at the Battle of Culloden on April 16, 1746. Evading capture, he finally returns to France on September 26.

1903 The Ford Motor Company of Detroit sells its first car, the Ford Model A, designed by Henry Ford.

1927 An exhibition housing estate opens to the public in Weissenhof, near Stuttgart, Germany. The residences are designed by 16 leading Modernist architects and provide a high standard of living, but are relatively cheap because of their use of prefabricated components.

1952 Military leaders overthrow King Farouk of Egypt in a bloodless coup.

1983 In Sri Lanka, Sinhalese Buddhists, the majority population on the island, begin rioting and massacre about 3,000 Tamils. Some 400,000 Tamils flee to the portion of the island called Tamil Nardu. The incident triggers an ongoing civil war on the island.

2004 The rebuilt Stari Most (Old Bridge) in Mostar is opened 11 years after being destroyed (see below).

DAYS TO REMEMBER

Religious day St. Brigit's day After bearing eight children and serving as Lady in Waiting to the Queen of Sweden, St. Brigit (1303–1373) founded the order of Brigittine nuns. She is the patron saint of Sweden and nuns.

Religious day Haile Selassie's birthday Members of the Rastafarian religious movement celebrate the birthday of the Emperor Haile Selassie I on this day in 1892. He is considered God incarnate in the movement.

Births

- **1888** Raymond Chandler, writer
- **1892** Haile Selassie, Emperor of Ethiopia
- **1939** Nicholas Gage, writer
- **1947** David Essex, singer
- **1961** Woody Harrelson, actor
- **1967** Philip Seymour Hoffman, actor
- **1973** Monica Lewinsky, White House intern
- **1989** Daniel Radcliffe, actor

Deaths

- **1757** Domenico Scarlatti, composer
- **1853** Andries Pretorius, Boer leader
- **1885** Ulysses S. Grant, Union general and U.S. President
- **1951** Henri Philippe Pétain, leader of Vichy France
- **1966** Montgomery Clift, actor
- **2002** Leo McKern, actor

The Stari Most was built in 1566 at the height of the Ottoman Empire. It linked the Croat and Muslim sides of the city of Mostar, symbolizing to many the joining of their cultures. On November 9, 1993, it collapsed after being shelled by Bosnian Croat forces during the Bosnia–Herzegovina conflict. After the war, the bridge was rebuilt using stone recovered from the Neretvan River and new stone from the original quarry. On this day it was reopened with great festivities that included the traditional contest of leaping from the bridge into the river.

July 24

> "It's actually a high-speed chess match on bikes."
> — LANCE ARMSTRONG ON THE TOUR DE FRANCE

HISTORICAL EVENTS

1704 Sir George Rooke leads British forces and takes Gibraltar. The Rock of Gibraltar has remained in British hands ever since, often to great strategic advantage.

1797 A musket ball shatters Admiral Horatio Nelson's right arm when his forces attempt to take Tenerife from the Spanish. He apparently climbs back onboard without assistance, has his arm amputated, and is back in his cabin giving orders shortly after.

1911 Hiram Bingham III, a Yale University professor, rediscovers the ruined Inca settlement of Machu Picchu.

1915 In Chicago, the *Eastland* sinks while still moored. The unstable boat is over-filled with picnickers and lists when many rush to one side to have their photos taken. The boat rolls over and sinks, drowning about 850 people.

1943 Operation Gomorrah begins, in which British and Canadian forces bomb Hamburg by night, and Americans bomb by day. The operation continues until November, by which time 30,000 people have been killed.

2001 Simeon Saxe-Coburg-Gotha, last Tsar of Bulgaria as a child, is sworn in as the elected Prime Minister of Bulgaria.

2005 Lance Armstrong wins a record seventh consecutive Tour de France (see right).

Births

- **1783** Simón Bolívar, South American liberator
- **1802** Alexandre Dumas Sr., writer
- **1895** Robert Graves, writer
- **1897** Amelia Earhart, aviatrix
- **1900** Zelda Fitzgerald, writer
- **1920** Arthur Boyd, artist
- **1929** Oriana Fallaci, journalist
- **1951** Lynda Carter, actress
- **1969** Jennifer Lopez, singer

Deaths

- **1980** Peter Sellers, actor and comedian
- **1991** Isaac Bashevis Singer, writer

Star sign

LEO
July 24–August 23

People born under the sign of the lion are proud, confident, and love to be the focus of attention. Leos can be generous and love life's pleasures; however, they can also be stubborn, resistant to change, and sometimes regal and overbearing.

The Tour de Lance

The Tour de France is a grueling 2,275-mile (3,640-km) road race through France. On July 24, 2005, U.S. cyclist Lance Armstrong, 33, won the race for the seventh consecutive time, the highest number of wins by any cyclist – let alone consecutive wins.

His record was all the more remarkable given the battle Armstrong had faced just to compete. In October 1996, he was diagnosed with advanced testicular cancer. The disease had already spread to his brain and lungs, and doctors gave him a less than 40 percent chance of survival. After he underwent surgery, hoping to keep cycling, he chose a form of chemotherapy that was less likely to damage his lungs.

He was declared cancer free by February 1997 and resumed training. His old team had cancelled his contract, but the U.S. Postal Service Pro Cycling Team took him on. He came fourth in his first post-cancer professional race, and still considers this one of his greatest achievements.

In 1999 he won his first Tour de France, and in 2004, when he won by his greatest margin, some suggested the race should be renamed the "Tour de Lance."

Armstrong retired from professional racing after his 2005 victory. He now devotes himself to the Lance Armstrong Foundation, which raises funds for cancer victims.

DAYS TO REMEMBER

Religious day Pioneer Day In the U.S. state of Utah, Pioneer Day commemorates the arrival of around 150 Mormons led by Brigham Young in what was to become Salt Lake City.

National day Children's Day (Vanuatu) This day is marked by parades of schoolchildren and special child-oriented activities. Issues relating to children's health and wellbeing are highlighted throughout the country.

July 25

"The most happy marriage I can picture or imagine to myself would be the union of a deaf man to a blind woman." — SAMUEL TAYLOR COLERIDGE

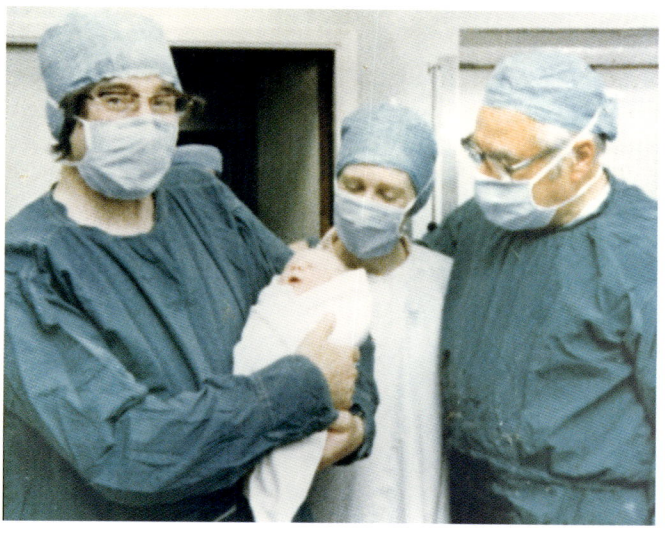
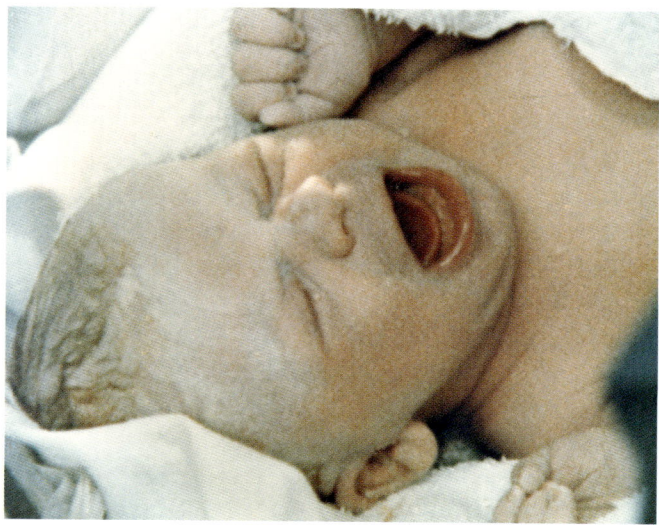

Louise Joy Brown, the world's first IVF baby, was born on July 25, 1978. She was normal, except for the fact that she had been conceived outside her mother's body. Doctors Patrick Steptoe and Robert Edwards took an egg from Louise's mother, Lesley, who had blocked fallopian tubes, and fertilized it with sperm from the baby's father, John, in a laboratory vessel. Two days later, the embryo was implanted in Lesley Brown's womb. By the time Louise was 21, more than 300,000 women had conceived with the help of IVF techniques.

HISTORICAL EVENTS

1943 As poorly equipped Italian forces take heavy losses and the Allies invade Italy in World War II, Benito Mussolini is removed from power by his own party and arrested. Shortly after, he is rescued by German paratroopers.

1946 Dean Martin and Jerry Lewis perform their first stage show together at Club 500 in Atlantic City, New Jersey. They do their last show together there on July 24, 1956.

1959 The hovercraft makes its first journey from England to France, crossing the Channel between Calais and Dover in 2 hours 3 minutes. The inventor, Christopher Cockerell, is a passenger.

1965 Bob Dylan's fans are upset and boo him when he has a sudden change of musical style and performs at the Newport Folk Festival playing an electric guitar, backed by a rock band.

1978 Louise Joy Brown, the first baby conceived through in vitro fertilization, is born in England (see above).

2000 Concorde Flight 4590 crashes just after take-off from Paris airport. All 109 people on board are killed, along with four people in the hotel the plane hits.

DAYS TO REMEMBER

Religious day St. Christopher's Day When a child asked St. Christopher to carry him over a river, he found the child excessively heavy. The child told him this was because he was Christ, and carried the burdens of the world. The saint was later martyred for his faith. He is the patron saint of travelers and motorists.

Religious day St. James' Day St. James the Great was one of the Twelve Apostles. Despite an account of his martyrdom in Jerusalem in 44 C.E., it is also believed that he went to preach in Spain. St. James (Santiago) is the patron saint of Spain. He is said to have appeared to Spanish kings and offered them assistance. He is also the patron saint of laborers and hat makers.

Births
- 1937 Colin Renfrew, archeologist
- 1946 Linda Ronstadt, singer
- 1967 Matt LeBlanc, actor
- 1978 Louise Joy Brown, first IVF baby

Deaths
- 1834 Samuel Taylor Coleridge, poet
- 1934 Engelbert Dolfuss, Austrian Chancellor
- 1963 Ugo Cerletti, neurologist
- 1997 Ben Hogan, golfer

July 26

"A revolution is not a bed of roses. A revolution is a struggle to the death between the future and the past." — FIDEL CASTRO

HISTORICAL EVENTS

1826 Cayetano Ripoli, a teacher of Deist principles, is the last person executed by the Spanish Inquisition, which had been established under Isabella of Castile in 1478 and targeted Moors, Jews, and Protestants.

1895 Pierre Curie and Marie Skłodowska marry in Sceaux, France. In 1896 Marie Curie begins her doctoral thesis on the radioactivity of uranium and Pierre joins her in her work in 1898. Their daughter, Irène, is born in 1897.

1926 The French Government passes a law that permits only the blue sheep's cheese matured in the limestone caves near the village of Roquefort near Toulouse to bear the name Roquefort cheese. This is the first law of its kind.

1945 The Conservative Party loses the British general election and Winston Churchill is no longer Prime Minister.

1953 In Cuba, Fidel Castro leads an unsuccessful attack on the Moncada Barracks, and is imprisoned until 1955.

1956 Egypt's President Nasser nationalizes the Suez Canal (see below).

1963 The world's first geosynchronous satellite, Syncom 2, is launched from Cape Canaveral.

1989 Robert T. Morris Jr. is charged with releasing the Morris Worm computer virus on November 2, 1988, and is the first person to be prosecuted under the 1986 U.S. Computer Fraud and Abuse Act.

2005 Mumbai, India, receives 39 inches (995 mm) of rain in 24 hours, the heaviest monsoon rain on record. The heavy rain continues into August, causing severe flooding and more than 1,000 deaths.

Births
- **1856** George Bernard Shaw, playwright
- **1875** Carl Jung, psychiatrist
- **1894** Aldous Huxley, writer
- **1928** Stanley Kubrick, film director
- **1939** John Howard, Australian Prime Minister
- **1943** Mick Jagger, singer
- **1959** Kevin Spacey, actor
- **1964** Sandra Bullock, actress

Deaths
- **1952** Evita Perón, Argentine First Lady
- **1971** Diane Arbus, photographer

DAYS TO REMEMBER

National day Revolution Day (Cuba) This day commemorates the attack led by Fidel Castro on the Moncada Barracks in 1953 and the birth of the July 26 Movement. Throughout Cuba, the national flag is flown and neighborhood parties take place.

National day Independence Day (The Maldives) After being a British protectorate since 1887, the Maldives became independent in 1965. The country continued to be ruled by a sultan until 1968, when it became a republic.

Egypt takes control of the Suez Canal

On July 26, 1956, Egyptian President Gamal Abdul Nasser announced to the world that he was nationalizing the Suez Canal Company. This company managed the vital shipping lane and although it belonged to Egypt, in 1869 a 99-year lease had been signed giving control, as well as the lion's share of the profits, to British and French concerns. The canal was due to be returned to Egypt in 1968.

President Nasser stated in his announcement that company shareholders would be paid out according to the share price on the Paris Stock Exchange at the end of the day. He said Egypt was taking control of the company so that the profits could go towards financing the Aswan High Dam project. The British, American, and French Governments had recently withdrawn their financial backing from the project in protest when Nasser's government showed signs of forming closer ties with the U.S.S.R. and the People's Republic of China.

The nationalization of the Suez Canal led to a greater crisis. Nasser blocked the Straits of Tiran – Israel's outlet into the Red Sea, and British, French, and Israeli forces invaded the canal zone in late October. The canal was completely closed down in the ensuing conflict, which was resolved in March 1957 with the aid of UN peacekeeping forces and negotiations.

July 27

DATEline

"All generalizations are dangerous, including this one."

ALEXANDRE DUMAS

Births
- 1824 Alexandre Dumas, writer
- 1870 Hilaire Belloc, writer
- 1882 Geoffrey de Havilland, aircraft designer
- 1953 Yahoo Serious, independent filmmaker
- 1972 Maya Rudolph, actress

Deaths
- 1946 Gertrude Stein, writer
- 1980 Muhammad Riza Pahlavi, deposed Shah of Iran
- 1984 James Mason, actor
- 1992 Max Dupain, photographer
- 2003 Bob Hope, comedian, actor

HISTORICAL EVENTS

1586 Sir Walter Raleigh's colonists return to England from Virginia, bringing tobacco and potatoes. Raleigh soon plants the tobacco, so it no longer needs to be imported from Spain, and plants the potatoes on his lands in Ireland.

1866 The laying of the 2,000-mile (3,200 km) long copper Transatlantic Cable between Newfoundland and Ireland is completed; telegraphs can now be sent from Europe to the U.S. Two previous attempts to lay cables had failed.

1921 Frederick Banting and Charles Best of Toronto University announce that they have extracted insulin from dogs and cured other diabetic dogs with it. This is the first step in providing human diabetics with insulin.

1940 Warner Bros. releases *A Wild Hare*, Bugs Bunny's first feature film. In this film, Bugs (Mel Blanc) first utters the line, "Eh, what's up, Doc?"

1953 The Korean War ends after three years when an armistice agreement is signed at Panmunjom, Korea. Both sides claim victory, though neither had made any territorial gains.

1965 In the U.S. it becomes law for health warnings to be printed on cigarette packages.

1996 A bomb made of explosives and nails packed into a pipe goes off at an outdoor concert at the Atlanta Olympics, killing a woman and injuring 100. An anti-abortion activist is later found to be responsible and is caught in May, 2003.

2003 After an investigation using 600 sonar beams, it is announced that there is no monster in Loch Ness (see below).

DAY TO REMEMBER

National day Martyrs' Day (Vietnam) The dead and injured of the Vietnam War are remembered with prayer and the laying of wreaths at war memorials on the anniversary of the day the division of the country took place under the Geneva Accords of 1954.

At Loch Ness in Scotland, sightings had been made of "monsters" since the 1930s. They were as varied in appearance as water serpents and elephant-like water creatures, with the concept of "Nessie" finally settling on a creature much like an ancient plesiosaur. In July 2003, an underwater survey of Loch Ness was conducted using satellite navigation technology, along with 600 separate sonar beams. On July 27, 2003, the BBC announced the findings: Scientists gained a very clear picture of the loch, but no large animals were revealed.

July 28

"I have always had to work hard; anyone who works as hard could do what I do."
JOHANN SEBASTIAN BACH

HISTORICAL EVENTS

1540 Aged 44, Henry VIII marries 19-year-old Catherine Howard, wife number five, after having his marriage of six months to Anne of Cleaves annulled on July 9.

1794 After being arrested the day before, Maximilien Robespierre is guillotined in front of a large crowd in Paris. As head of the Committee for Public Safety he had sent thousands of people to similar deaths during the Reign of Terror.

1903 Mother Jones arrives at the home of President Roosevelt after leading a 100-mile (161 km) march to bring the conditions of child laborers to his attention. At this time, close to 2 million U.S. children under 16 worked in factories and mines.

1914 World War I begins when the Austro-Hungarian Empire declares war on Serbia at 11:00 A.M. when it fails to meet the conditions of an ultimatum set on July 23, which demanded that Serbia find the killer of Archduke Francis Ferdinand.

1945 The pilot of a U.S. bomber, disoriented by foggy conditions, crashes into the Empire State Building. The three men in the plane die, as do 10 in the building.

1976 The most devastating earthquake of the twentieth century strikes the city of Tangshan in China (see below).

2000 Most of the prisoners in Northern Ireland's Maze Prison are released early as part of a peace accord. The prison is closed in September.

DAYS TO REMEMBER

National day Independence Day (Peru) People in Peru celebrate the day José de San Martín declared the nation independent from Spain in 1821.

National day Commemoration of the Great Upheaval (Canada) On July 28, 1755, the British colony of Nova Scotia decided to expel all French colonists unwilling to swear allegiance to Britain, leading to thousands of deaths over the next eight years.

Births
- **1844** Gerard Manley Hopkins, poet
- **1866** Beatrix Potter, children's writer and conservationist
- **1887** Marcel Duchamp, painter
- **1907** Sir Graham Clark, archeologist
- **1922** Jacques Piccard, undersea explorer
- **1929** Jacqueline Kennedy Onassis, First Lady of the U.S.
- **1936** Sir Garfield Sobers, cricketer
- **1938** Robert Hughes, writer and art critic

Deaths
- **1655** Cyrano de Bergerac, poet
- **1741** Antonio Vivaldi, composer
- **1750** Johann Sebastian Bach, composer
- **1794** Maximilien Robespierre, French revolutionary
- **1844** Joseph Bonaparte, King of Naples and Spain
- **1942** Sir Flinders Petrie, Egyptologist
- **1968** Otto Hahn, chemist

Tangshan – a shattered city

In 1976, Tangshan, China, was home to over 1 million people. At 3:42 A.M. on July 28 an earthquake measuring 7.8 on the Richter scale struck the city. Thousands of people were buried by collapsing buildings.

Tangshan was totally isolated. Power and telephone lines were cut, and canals, train lines, and roads were damaged and smothered with debris. Survivors found themselves desperately trying to rescue others in the dark.

At the end of the night shift, 30,000 miners came to the surface. Deep underground, they had not felt the full strength of the earthquake. Horrified by what they found, they began rescue operations with the limited resources available.

Beijing lies only 90 miles (150 km) from Tangshan. The fact that communications from the industrial city had fallen silent went unnoticed in the Chinese capital, which was itself in crisis as Chairman Mao Zedong was gravely ill, and shockwaves had caused 100 deaths. A man managed to drive

out of Tangshan along the one reasonably clear road to Beijing later that day. When he told people of the devastation in Tangshan he was dismissed as insane.

When the truth finally sank in, soldiers and rescue workers were sent to help. Official estimates put the death toll at 255,000, although it is thought as many as 750,000 people died.

July 29

"We have time enough to finish the game and beat the Spaniards, too."
SIR FRANCIS DRAKE, WHEN HIS GAME OF BOWLS IS INTERRUPTED BY THE SIGHTING OF THE SPANISH ARMADA

When Prince Charles, heir to the British throne, married Lady Diana Spencer at St Paul's Cathedral on July 29, 1981, a national holiday was declared in Britain. In London, 600,000 people lined the streets to see Lady Diana arrive at the cathedral in the Glass Coach, and later to watch the newlyweds travel to Buckingham Palace for the reception. Afterwards, the royal couple left for their honeymoon in a landau with a "just married" sign attached by Prince Charles' brothers to the back.

Births
- 1883 Benito Mussolini, Fascist leader
- 1892 William Powell, actor
- 1906 Diana Vreeland, fashion editor
- 1973 Stephen Dorff, actor

Deaths
- 1856 Robert Schumann, composer
- 1890 Vincent van Gogh, painter
- 1974 Erich Kästner, writer
- 1983 David Niven, actor
- 1983 Luis Buñuel, director

HISTORICAL EVENTS

- **1588** The Battle of Gravelines begins off the coast of France. By August 8, the smaller, swifter ships of the English navy, commanded by Sir Francis Drake and Lord Charles Howard, defeats the 130-ship Spanish Armada.
- **1907** Robert Baden-Powell, veteran of the Boer War, takes a group of boys on a camp to England's Brownsea Island, launching the Boy Scouts movement.
- **1954** *The Fellowship of the Ring*, the first part of J. R. R. Tolkien's *Lord of the Rings*, is published in Britain.
- **1976** Donna Lauria is shot and killed in a car outside her parents' home in New York. This is the first of six killings by the "Son of Sam," David Berkowitz.
- **1981** Charles, Prince of Wales, and Lady Diana Spencer marry at St. Paul's Cathedral, London (see above).
- **2005** Astronomers announce the discovery of a tenth planet in the outer solar system that is larger than Pluto. They give it the temporary name 2003 UB313.

DAYS TO REMEMBER

Religious day St. Martha's day The sister of Lazarus, whom Jesus raised from the dead, Martha stated her belief that Jesus was the Son of God. She is the patron saint of homemakers, cooks, and restaurant workers.

National day Ólavsøka (Faroe Islands) *Ólavsøka*, or St. Olaf's Day, is the national holiday of the Faroe Islands. Islanders celebrate with rowing races in Viking-style boats, traditional and modern dances, and an official procession that leads the way to the opening of the *Løgting* (parliament), which is one of the oldest in the world.

July 30

Landslide in Thredbo

Thredbo is a ski resort village in the Snowy Mountains, Australia. At 11:40 P.M. on July 30, 1997, there was a cracking sound and a roar like an airplane taking off. Leaks from an underground water main had destabilized a monutain slope and 4,000 tons (4,000 t) of soil and rock slipped onto Carinya Lodge, which collapsed, slid downhill, and slammed into Bimbadeen Lodge.

Shocked residents in the other ski lodges could hear voices calling from under the rubble, though the voices soon went quiet. Rescue teams began the search for survivors in the freezing conditions.

Under the wreckage, Stuart Diver, a ski instructor who had been asleep in Bimbadeen Lodge, found the roof centimeters from his head. His wife, Sally, was pinned to the bed. Seconds later, cold, muddy water surged over them. Stuart raised himself on his elbows so that his face was in an air pocket, but Sally was unable to move and drowned.

Stuart Diver fought to stay alive, lifting himself clear of repeated deluges, hugging his body and wriggling his toes and fingers to warm himself.

Finally at 5:37 A.M. on August 2, a firefighter heard something, called for silence and shouted, "Rescue party working overhead. Can you hear me?" Diver replied, "Yes, can you hear me?"

Rescuers began tunneling through the unstable wreckage. At first only a small hole could be made, and a tube with fluid was passed through, along with a tube blowing hot air. Diver was freed 66 hours after the landslide, suffering frostbite and exhaustion.

HISTORICAL EVENTS

1836 The Arc de Triomphe, commissioned in 1806 by Napoleon to commemorate the French Army and its victories, is finally completed in 1836 and inaugurated on this day.

1898 William Kellogg invents corn flakes. He and his brother, Dr. John Kellogg, had been experimenting with grain-based health foods to offer patients at their sanitarium. In 1906 William Kellogg founded the Battle Creek Toaster Corn Flake Company to sell his healthy cereals.

1930 Uruguay defeats Argentina 4–2 in the first soccer World Cup in Montevideo.

1945 After delivering components of the bomb to be dropped on Hiroshima, the U.S.S. *Indianapolis* is torpedoed by a Japanese submarine. About 300 of the 1,196 men on board sink with the ship. The survivors are spotted by chance four days later: Only 316 men were rescued from the shark-infested waters.

1967 Seven days of rioting in Detroit finally ends, leaving 43 dead, 467 injured, 7,231 arrested and 412 buildings destroyed or damaged. Racial tensions in Detroit had exploded on July 23 when police officers – mostly white – raided an illegal bar and arrested black patrons.

1973 After an 11-year court case, £20 million is granted in Britain to about 400 victims of the thalidomide drug, which had been given to women suffering morning sickness, causing birth defects in several thousand babies around the world.

1997 A landslide occurs at Thredbo in Australia. Eighteen lives are lost while one man is rescued (see left).

DAYS TO REMEMBER

National day Independence Day (Vanuatu) The archipelago of Vanuatu (formerly the New Hebrides) was ruled jointly by France and Britain from 1887, and celebrates the day it gained independence in 1980.

Religious day St. Julitta's Day Born into a noble family, St. Julitta (c. 303) was a widow with an infant son when the persecution of Christians forced her to flee her home. She was eventually revealed as a Christian and martyred in what is now Turkey.

"If it's hard to remember, it'll be difficult to forget."
ARNOLD SCHWARZENEGGER

Births
- 1818 Emily Brontë, writer
- 1855 Georg Wilhelm von Siemens, industrialist
- 1863 Henry Ford, industrialist
- 1898 Henry Moore, sculptor
- 1939 Peter Bogdanovich, director
- 1947 Arnold Schwarzenegger, bodybuilder, actor, and politician
- 1958 Kate Bush, singer and songwriter
- 1961 Laurence Fishburne, actor
- 1963 Lisa Kudrow, actress
- 1974 Hilary Swank, actress

Deaths
- 1718 William Penn, Quaker leader
- 1898 Prince Otto von Bismarck, Chancellor of Germany
- 1971 Kenneth Slessor, poet
- 1996 Claudette Colbert, actress

July 31

DATEline

"The soul is placed in the body like a rough diamond, and must be polished, or the luster of it will never appear." — DANIEL DEFOE

HISTORICAL EVENTS

1703 Daniel Defoe is put in pillory (stocks) for publishing a satirical political pamphlet, but instead of being pelted with rotten fruit and vegetables, flowers are thrown at him.

1845 The French Army introduces the saxophone to its band, with great success. The saxophone was invented by a Belgian, Adolphe Sax, and was patented by him in 1846.

1902 An explosion at Mt. Kembla colliery in Australia causes a landslide that traps some 250 miners, killing 96.

1910 Dr. Hawley Crippen is arrested en route to Canada aboard the S.S. *Montrose* for the murder of his wife Cora in England. The ship was the first equipped with radio-telegraph, which enabled police in London to verify details and make the arrest.

1945 Pierre Laval, fugitive former leader of Vichy France, gives himself up to Allied soldiers in Austria. He stands trial and is executed on October 15.

1969 Soon after a Russian magazine describes how to do electric conversions on acoustic guitars, a Moscow police chief reports that thousands of public telephones are being destroyed by thieves looking for parts.

1991 Mikhail Gorbachev and President George W. Bush sign the Strategic Arms Reduction Treaty (see below).

2003 The last old-style Volkswagon Beetle is manufactured in Puebla, Mexico. The Beetle first came into production in the 1930s.

Births
- **1912** Milton Friedman, economist
- **1919** Primo Levi, chemist and writer
- **1944** Geraldine Chaplin, actress
- **1951** Evonne Goolagong Cawley, tennis player
- **1952** Alan Autry, footballer, actor, and politician
- **1962** Wesley Snipes, actor
- **1965** J. K. Rowling, children's writer

Deaths
- **1784** Denis Diderot, philospher
- **1886** Franz Liszt, composer
- **1944** Antoine de Saint-Exupéry, pilot and writer

DAY TO REMEMBER

National day Ka Hae Hawai'i (Hawaii) On this day in 1843, King Kamehameha III had his sovereignty restored by Queen Victoria after the British had occupied Honolulu for five months. This day was celebrated during the Hawaiian monarchy's time as *Ka La Ho'iho'i Ea*, or Sovereignty Restoration Day. In 1990, it was proclaimed by Hawaii's governor as *Ka Hae Hawai'i*, or Hawaiian Flag Day.

Gorbachev and Bush sign START I

After World War II, the Cold War between the U.S.S.R. and the U.S. led to a build-up of arsenals of nuclear arms with the potential to annihilate both nations and the rest of the world. Beginning in 1972 with the first Strategic Arms Limitation Talks, attempts were made to limit the nuclear arms race.

In 1987 the President of the U.S.S.R., Mikhail Gorbachev and U.S. President Ronald Reagan signed a treaty in Washington D.C. agreeing to dismantle and destroy short and medium range nuclear weapons in Europe. By 1991 the U.S.S.R. and the whole Eastern Bloc was undergoing dramatic change. Although Gorbachev was able to stay in power, the U.S. became even keener for further nuclear arms reductions as it didn't want Soviet weapons to fall into the hands of unstable enemies.

On July 31, 1991, Presidents Gorbachev and Bush signed the first Strategic Arms Reduction Treaty, which agreed to cut

long-range nuclear warheads by nearly half. This was the most dramatic reduction posed by any treaty between the nations.

The U.S.S.R. collapsed in December 1991, before either government could ratify START. After lengthy negotiations, the Russian Federation and the three other new states that held the old U.S.S.R.'s nuclear weapons agreed to abide by START. The treaty only came into effect in 1994, and its reduction targets were finally met in 2001. Further arms-reduction treaties followed.

DAYS TO REMEMBER *July*

1 Moving Day (Canada) Instead of relaxing on their national holiday, people in the Canadian province of Quebec go into a frenzy of house moving

2 *Palio di Provenzano* (Sienna, Italy) Takes place in the city square at sunset to honor the Madonna on the Feast of the Visitation

3 St. Thomas' Day This saint is known as Doubting Thomas, as he wouldn't believe Christ had risen from the dead until he could see him for himself

4 American Independence Day (U.S.) Celebrates the signing of the Declaration of Independence

5 Tynwald Day On the Isle of Man, Tynwald Day is the midsummer sitting of Parliament

8 St. Procopius' Day This saint was martyred for refusing to sacrifice to Pagan gods in the early Domitian persecutions of Christians

9 Holy Day Followers of the Baha'i faith commemorate the Martyrdom of the Bab, or the Gate, who was executed in Tabriz

10 Silence Day Followers of the Indian spiritual teacher Meher Baba observe a day of silence

11 World Population Day Each year issues surrounding reproductive health and population control are highlighted

12 Orangeman's Day Commemorates the Battle of the Boyne and was first held in County Armagh, Northern Ireland by the Orange Order

15 Feast of Santa Rosalia (Palermo, Italy) Begins on this day and celebrates a twelfth-century hermit

16 Feast Day for Mount Carmel Where the first chapel was built to the Blessed Virgin

17 Gion Matsuri (Kyoto, Japan) Month-long festival. One of the main events is the Yamaboko Junko

18 Constitution Day (Uruguay) Commemorates the signing of Uruguay's first constitution in 1830

19 National Liberation Day (Nicaragua) Celebrates the establishment of the Sandanista takeover in Managua in 1979

22 Pi Approximation Day Mathematians around the world celebrate Pi, expressed as both the fraction and date 22/7

23 Revolution Day (Egypt) Commemorates the overthrow of King Farouk in 1952

24 The first day of the star sign of Leo

25 St. James' Day (Santiago, Spain) Is the highlight of a two-week festival

26 National Day (Maldives) Marks independence in 1965 after being a British protectorate since 1887

29 King Olaf II of Norway's Day (995–1039) The patron saint of woodcarvers

30 National Day (Vanuatu) Celebrates the day Vanuatu gained independence from France and British rule in 1980

31 Ka Hae Hawaii Proclaimed in 1990 by Hawaii's governor as the Ka Hae Hawaii, (the Hawaiian flag) day

6
Jan Hus Day (Czech Republic) Jan Hus was a church reformer and critic

7
San Fermín Held in Pamplona, Spain. The Running of the Bulls is held each morning between July 7 and 14

13
Buddhist Bon Festival Originally held in Japan in mid-July, but now held in the East from July 13

14
Bastille Day (France) Celebrates the storming of the Bastille

20
Friendship Day In Argentina and other mostly Latin American nations, this is a day for celebrating friendship

21
Racial Harmony Day (Singapore) Promotes racial harmony

27
Martyr's Day (Vietnam) The dead and the injured of the Vietnam War are remembered with prayer and the laying of wreaths

28
Independence Day (Peru) Celebrates the day José de San Martín declared the nation independent from Spain in 1821

Top right Bastille Day, France, July 14
Right National Day, Maldives, July 26

AUGUST

"Summer waxes long, then wanes, quietly passing
Her fading green glory on to riotous autumn."

MICHELLE L. THIEME, *AUGUST'S CROWN*

The utterly unique and imposing monolith Uluru – formerly known as Ayer's Rock – proved to be the backdrop for an equally unrepeatable legal saga in Australia when baby Azaria Chamberlain was taken by a dingo in August, 1980.

August

The eighth month of the Gregorian calendar, August was seen by many past agrarian societies in the Northern Hemisphere as the start of autumn and of the harvesting season. As such, rituals were often made to the land and to the gods in thanks for what had been produced. Today, cultures throughout the world view August differently. For the religious, it is the time to remember the Assumption of Mary, and for the hedonistic, a time when some of the world's most colorful festivals take place.

Virgo star sign and scene of baling wheat from *Calendar and Book of Hours*, from fifteenth-century France. August begins in the sign of Leo and ends in the sign of Virgo.

SPECIAL DATES

August 1 is recognized as the first day of the harvest by many European agrarian societies, and as the first day of autumn

The Feast Day of the Assumption of Mary is considered one of the most blessed days in the August calendar, observed as the day the Virgin Mary assumed body and soul into heaven. This page, which depicts the divine event, is from a fifteenth-century Flemish manuscript, *Book of Hours of Philippe de Conrault*.

THE EIGHTH MONTH of the year, August is named after the first Roman Emperor and Julius Caesar's grandnephew Augustus (63 B.C.E.–14 C.E.). Originally the month was called Sextilis as it was the sixth in the Roman calendar. However, the Roman Senate renamed the month after Augustus after he swept to power. The Senate justified the decision by saying this was the month that the most fortunate events occurred in their emperor's life, including his defeat of Marc Antony and the Egyptian queen Cleopatra.

It is said Sextilis had 30 days and that the Senate gave August an extra one so Augustus could claim his month was equal in days and stature as the fifth and Julius Caesar's month, July. But to do this, they had to steal a day from February, leaving it with 28 days and 29 in a leap year. Also, to prevent three months in a row of 31 days, the Senate simply rearranged the number of days in the last four months – so they fell 30, 31, 30, and 31 rather than in the reverse order.

However, this is debated. There are those who claim that Sextilis always had 31 days and was never chosen because of its length but because it was the month in which Augustus had had the most success up to that date. They suggest that the thirteenth-century English scholar, Johannes de Sacrobosco, invented the myth of the extra day given to August. Irrespective of what actually happened, Augustus went on to become arguably Rome's greatest emperor, restoring peace after 100 years of civil war within the empire, extending its reach into Spain and Gaul (now France), improving its infrastructure and strongly supporting the arts. So revered was he by his people because of his significant improvements, and also his own efforts to erect images of himself throughout his kingdom, Augustus was worshipped as a god after his death.

In bygone days

The agrarian societies of medieval Europe often divided their year up into four events. They considered these events to mark the official beginnings of the seasons. Rituals, some still practised today, were often carried out on these event days to placate the gods and ensure the people would prosper throughout the year.

In the Northern Hemisphere, *Lughnasadh* is one of the Pagan festivals of Celtic origin that splits the year into four and is celebrated on or about August 1. Named after the Irish god Lugh, it marks the first day of the Celtic autumn and of the harvesting season, which continues until the Samhain – November 1. According to legend, Lugh dedicated the festival to his foster-mother Tailtiu, who died of exhaustion after clearing a great forest so the land could be cultivated. As she lay dying, Tailtiu told the men of Ireland that as long as they held the festival in her honor, the country would never be without song.

In medieval times, tribes would come from all over Ireland to the site of Tailtiu's death and trade goods, solve intertribal difficulties, sing, and dance. Handfasting or "trial marriages" were arranged on this day as well. Eligible men and women would line up either side of a large wall with holes for them to poke just their hands through. Whoever's hand they grabbed was the person they would live with for a year and a day in a trial marriage. If by the following year the trial hadn't worked out, it could be annulled at the same festival by the couple simply standing back to back and then walking away from each other. However, if the trial had been a success, a marriage ceremony would be performed to make the union official.

In some places, the Celts danced around a woman or an effigy symbolizing Tailtiu who was

In this detail of a fifteenth-century Bohemian fresco from Torre Aquila, Trento – part of the Cycle of Months – August is depicted as the time for harvesting the cornfields and baling wheat to take to the granary. August 1 is recognized as the first day of the harvest by many European agrarian societies, and as the first day of autumn.

August birthflower

The poppy and the gladiolus are both considered the birthflowers for August, representing strength of character, sincerity, generosity, natural grace, imagination, and oblivion. Both flowers also signify remembrance but the red poppy is worn as a mark of respect to those fallen in World War I. The gladiolus also expresses infatuation, telling the receiver they pierce the heart.

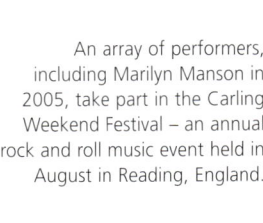

An array of performers, including Marilyn Manson in 2005, take part in the Carling Weekend Festival – an annual rock and roll music event held in August in Reading, England.

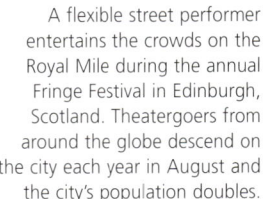

A flexible street performer entertains the crowds on the Royal Mile during the annual Fringe Festival in Edinburgh, Scotland. Theatergoers from around the globe descend on the city each year in August and the city's population doubles.

seated on a throne and had flowers in her hair. Dancers would touch her garlands or take a ribbon from her for good luck.

The Anglo-Saxons of Britain called this time *Lammas*, meaning "loaf Mass." They would bake bread from the first harvested grains and take it as an offering to their local church. The bread would then be used in Communion in a special Mass to thank God for the harvest. Henry VIII put an end to this when he broke from Rome and established the Church of England.

Another Pagan ritual carried out at this time of year was to make a corn dolly out of the last sheaf of corn cut. The dolly was believed to contain the spirit of the grain and was then kept in the house until spring when it would be ploughed back into the fields with the new corn.

Various cultures around the world also recognized August 1 as the start of the harvesting season and autumn. In Finland the month is still known as *elokuu*, which means "month of reaping." In ancient Japan, August was called *hatsuki*, which meant "month of the falling leaves." It was believed that during hatsuki, the leaves on the moon would also turn yellow.

August traditions today

In many Latin American countries, August is considered a cursed month. In Brazil, it is known as *Agosto, mes do desgosto*, or the month of sorrow and grief. Some of the country's worst disasters have apparently occurred during August, including the suicide of President Getulio Vargas in 1954. Brazilians flock to their churches and voodoo healers to avoid disaster. The superstition is not helped by the fact that one of Brazil's most followed religions, Candomble, also allocates August 24 to its god of mischief, Exu. He is considered the most important of the four warrior gods. Exu is said to take pleasure in testing the strengths and weaknesses of men, sitting in judgment and quick to punish those who do wrong. He is also the messenger god, taking followers' prayers to the other gods. In this way, because he is the link between Heaven and Earth, Exu is the most important god, and gifts of toys, lollies, rum, and gin are often offered to him. In some homes an effigy is made of him and placed behind the front door, to ensure a safe and balanced home.

August is also the month when some of the world's largest and most interesting festivals open.

Recognized by *The Guinness Book of Records* as the world's largest arts festival, the Edinburgh Fringe Festival in Scotland usually starts around mid-August and runs for three weeks. Anyone is allowed to perform at the Fringe Festival, as long as they can find a space.

One of the U.K.'s largest rock and roll events – the Carling Weekend – also occurs in August, usually later in the month. The three-day music festival attracts performers from all over the world and more than 100,000 people on any one day.

In Japan, more than a million people visit the city of Tokushima to watch and take part in the *Awa Odori* festival. The Awa Odori is said to be a "fool's dance," but the saying goes: "It's a fool who dances and a fool who watches, so if both are fools, you may as well dance!" And they do. Thousands of people dance the Awa Odori in the streets during this mid-August festival. August is also the month Japan hosts one of the country's three most memorable celebrations – the Fujiyoshida Fire Festival. Held in the city of Fujiyoshida at the base of Japan's highest mountain, Mt. Fuji, the festival begins on August 26 with residents carrying a shrine to the mountain goddess Konohansakuyahime through streets lined with lit lanterns. It is hoped that the sight of the city alight will so impress the goddess that she'll prevent Mt. Fuji from erupting for another year. The procession marks the end of the Japanese summer and the Mt. Fuji climbing season as well.

The second half of the festival begins the next day to mark the start of autumn with a kind of prayer that the season will bring a bountiful harvest and better weather. The residents return to the streets, pick up the shrine where they left it in the city the night before, and return the goddess to her permanent home in the forest.

America hosts one of the most spectacular August festivities in the world, known as Burning Man. Starting late in the month, it is a week of communal artistic madness and expression culminating in the torching of many giant structures in the Black Rock Desert in Nevada. There is nothing quite like it in the world.

Amsterdam hosts its annual Gay Pride march in the first weekend of August, and on the third weekend also hosts the Hartjesdagen festival, where men turn up dressed as women and women dress as men. Some historians believe this festival dates back to the Middle Ages.

Residents of Pokhara in Nepal perform ceremonies in August to safeguard their farms and animals from evil spirits. People with their faces covered in soot, wearing feather headdresses and beating drums parade through the town to drive out negative forces.

Huge burning sculptures light up the night sky at Burning Man, a week-long artistic festival in Black Rock Desert, Nevada, U.S., which culminates in the torching of several large structures.

August birthstone

The birthstone for August is the rare peridot. The Egyptians mined peridot on the island of Zebirget (now St. Johns Island) in the Red Sea as early as the second century B.C.E. It was Cleopatra's favorite gemstone. Peridot is said to bring the wearer good luck, peace, and success, especially if it is set in gold. It has also been used as an amulet to ward off evil.

August 1

"I wish I had invented blue jeans. They have expression, modesty, sex appeal, simplicity – all I hope for in my clothes." — YVES SAINT LAURENT (PICTURED BELOW)

HISTORICAL EVENTS

1834 Slavery is abolished throughout the British Empire, including its colonies in North America.

1914 Germany declares war on Russia, marking the start of World War I.

1944 The Warsaw Uprising begins in an attempt to free the Polish capital from its Nazi occupiers (see right).

1966 Charles Whitman shoots 15 passers-by from a tower at the University of Texas before being killed by police. A day before the massacre the former altar boy also killed his mother and his wife.

1976 Niki Lauda, 26-time F1 champion, is rushed to hospital in a critical condition after crashing his F1 racing car at the German Grand Prix.

1981 MTV begins broadcasting; "Video Killed the Radio Star" by the Buggles is the first video played.

2001 Albanian becomes recognized as one of Macedonia's official languages. Albanians represent 25 percent of the population in the former Yugoslavian republic.

DAYS TO REMEMBER

Traditional day Parent's Day (Democratic Republic of the Congo) Held to mark deceased ancestors, people visit cemeteries on this day to tidy and decorate family graves.

National Day Independence Day (Switzerland) This day marks the day Switzerland gained independence from Austria in 1291.

Warsaw uprising begins

At 5:00 P.M. on this day in 1944, the Polish Home Army rose up in an attempt to regain its capital, Warsaw, and end five years of brutal occupation by the Nazis. Although the end of the war was still distant, the Poles were hopeful.

To the west, the Allies were breaking through German defences at Normandy, France. To the east, the Russian forces were on Warsaw's doorstop, chasing the fleeing Germans from the horrors of Leningrad. The Home Army expected the Soviets to take Warsaw quickly, and that they'd help them sweep out the Germans in less than a week of fighting. But soon after the uprising began, it became apparent they'd receive almost no help from the Allies or the Russians. Joseph Stalin, leader of the U.S.S.R., wanted Poland for Russia and held his troops back to allow the Germans to crush any would-be resistance to his plans. He also prevented the Allies dropping supplies. The Home Army was forced to fight a war of attrition, a war the vastly outnumbered and poorly supplied Poles could not win.

The Germans used various tactics to break the uprising, including using female civilians as human shields in front of tanks attacking Polish positions. They also went from house to house massacring Polish civilians in their homes in an attempt to break the will of the insurgents without having to engage in heavy fighting. After 63 days of fighting, an estimated 200,000 casualties, and no chance of help from the Allies, the Home Army surrendered. On January 17, 1945, the Soviets took Warsaw.

Births		Deaths	
1922	Pat McDonald, actress	1464	Cosimo de' Medici, ruler of Florence
1933	Dom DeLuise, comedian	1589	Jacques Clement, French assassin
1936	Yves Saint Laurent, fashion designer	1714	Queen Anne of Great Britain
1942	Jerry Garcia, musician	2005	King Fahd of Saudi Arabia
1953	Robert Cray, singer		
1960	Chuck D, rapper		
1963	Coolio, rapper		

August 2

"It is well to think well; it is divine to act well." — HORACE MANN

HISTORICAL EVENTS

1492 The last ships carrying Jews expelled by King Ferdinand leaves Spain. The entire community – about 200,000 people – was forced to leave, and tens of thousands died during the expulsion.

1870 The world's first underground tube railway, the Tower Subway, opens in London, England. On its first trip, 12 people travel 450 yards (411 m) in 70 seconds.

1875 "Wild Bill" Hickok is shot dead (see below).

1934 Adolf Hitler becomes Führer of Germany. He held this title until his death more than a decade later; his leadership resulted in the genocide of 11 million people, including 6 million Jews.

1955 Swiss inventor George de Mestral patents Velcro. The design is an adaptation of the burdock seeds which would attach themselves to his clothing while he walked in the Alps.

2004 The computer game "Doom 3" is leaked onto the internet and thousands of people go online to download it for free days before it is to go on sale.

2005 Scientists at Stanford University, U.S., announce that they've used nanotechnology to destroy cancer cells.

Births
- 1925 Jorge Rafael Videla, Argentinean dictator
- 1930 Vali Myers, artist
- 1932 Peter O'Toole, actor
- 1939 Wes Craven, film director
- 1942 Isabel Allende, Chilean author
- 1964 Mary-Louise Parker, actress
- 1977 Edward Furlong, actor

Deaths
- 1859 Horace Mann, U.S. educator
- 1876 James Butler "Wild Bill" Hickok, American gunfighter
- 1922 Alexander Graham Bell, inventor
- 1976 Fritz Lang, film director
- 1997 William S. Burroughs, writer

DAY TO REMEMBER

Religious day Our Lady of the Angels Our Lady, Queen of the Angels, is the patron of Costa Rica. The Catholic faithful make a pilgrimage to a shrine of the Virgin Mary and her baby son Jesus in Cartago, Costa Rica, every year to pay their respects.

On this day in 1875, James Butler "Wild Bill" Hickok entered a saloon in Deadwood, South Dakota, to play a game of poker. The gunfighter sat in a chair with his back to the door – uncustomary for Hickok, who liked to sit in a corner to protect his back. Jack McCall came up behind Bill and shot him in the back of the head. Hickok, 39, held a pair of aces and a pair of eights, with all cards black, which has since become known as a dead man's hand. Jack McCall, in his late 20s, was eventually tried, hanged, and buried with the noose around his neck.

August 3

"Often we have no time for our friends but all the time in the world for our enemies." — LEON URIS

HISTORICAL EVENTS

- **1492** Christopher Columbus sets sail from Palos de la Frontera, Spain. It is his first voyage, and he returns with previously unknown goods such as tobacco, pineapples, the turkey, and the hammock.
- **1783** Mount Asama erupts in Japan, killing 35,000 people. The volcano is still active and most recently erupted on September 1, 2004.
- **1946** The National Basketball Association is founded in America.
- **1960** France grants Niger its independence. Niger had become an autonomous French territory two years earlier.
- **2003** The Anglican Church approves its first gay bishop (see below).
- **2004** The Statue of Liberty is reopened for the first time since the September 11 attacks on America in 2001.
- **2005** King Abdullah becomes the new king of Saudi Arabia. Previously he had been known as Crown Prince Abdullah; he ascends to the throne after the death of his half-brother King Fahd.
- **2005** Adidas buys Reebok for U.S. $3.8 billion.

Births
- 1924 Leon Uris, author
- 1926 Tony Bennett, singer
- 1940 Martin Sheen, actor
- 1941 Martha Stewart, entrepreneur and media personality
- 1946 Jack Straw, British politician
- 1963 James Hetfield, singer
- 1970 Gina G., singer

Deaths
- 1924 Joseph Conrad, author
- 1966 Lenny Bruce, comedian
- 2004 Henri Cartier-Bresson, photographer
- 2005 Steven Vincent, journalist

DAYS TO REMEMBER

Religious day St. Trea's Day After her conversion to Christianity by St. Patrick, Trea lived out the rest of her life as a recluse in Derry, Ireland, during the fifth century.

Religious day St. Peter of Anagni's Day A Benedictine monk who eventually became the bishop of Anagni, Italy, St. Peter (c. 1105) gathered support for the First Crusade to the Holy Land, in which he himself also participated.

The first openly gay man was elected bishop of the U.S. Anglican Church's New Hampshire diocese on this day in 2003. The decision has the potential to divide the church, with bishops from around the world opposed to the appointment and threatening to break away and form their own faction. It comes at a time when many popular religions are in debate over allowing same-sex marriages and gay clergy. Reverend Canon Gene Robinson (pictured) is a divorced father of two who has lived with his male partner for 14 years.

August 4

"Every man's life is a fairytale written by God's fingers." — HANS CHRISTIAN ANDERSEN

HISTORICAL EVENTS

1693 Dom Perignon invents Champagne. The monk's first words upon tasting the beverage were, reportedly, "Come quickly, I am drinking the stars!"

1854 Japan adopts the *Hinomaru* – a red sun on a white background – as its official naval flag. The usage of the red sun symbol in Japan dates back to the twelfth century when it was displayed on fans carried by samurai warriors.

1902 The Greenwich foot tunnel under the Thames River is opened. It replaces a relatively expensive ferry service and facilitates the travel of workers from the south side of the river to the London docks.

1914 Germany invades Belgium. Great Britain declares war on Germany in response.

1944 The Nazi Gestapo captures Anne Frank and her family in an Amsterdam warehouse. Anne dies in the Bergen-Belsen concentration camp just a few weeks before it is liberated by British troops on April 15, 1945.

1991 The Greek luxury liner *Oceanos* sinks off the South African coast. Despite the fact that the crew abandons the passengers, all 571 people who had been aboard are rescued.

1993 A judge sentences Los Angeles police officers Stacey Koon and Laurence Powell to 30 months in prison for the beating of Rodney King.

2002 Ian Huntley murders English schoolgirls Jessica Chapman and Holly Wells, both aged ten (see below).

Births
- 1792 Percy Bysshe Shelley, poet
- 1900 Elizabeth Bowes-Lyon, England's late Queen Mum
- 1901 Louis Armstrong, musician
- 1923 Reg Grundy, media mogul
- 1929 Yasser Arafat, Palestinian leader
- 1955 Billy Bob Thornton, actor

Deaths
- 1875 Hans Christian Andersen, author

DAY TO REMEMBER

National day Constitution Day (Cook Islands) This day marks the day when the islands became a self-governing territory of New Zealand. Celebrations last until August 10 and include traditional activities such as singing, dancing, and inter-island competitions.

English schoolgirls murdered

One of Britain's biggest manhunts began on this day in 2002. Holly Wells and Jessica Chapman, both 10, were last seen wearing red Manchester United supporters' jerseys in their home suburb of Soham. Soccer star and Manchester United striker David Beckham, whose name adorned the girls' tops, made a public appeal for their safe return, but it was too late. Ian Huntley had killed the girls on the day of their disappearance.

Holly and Jessica had left the Wells family home to buy lollies. They'd just been given the jerseys and this photo of them in their outfits, taken on the night of their murders, shows how happy they were. At about 6:00 P.M., they walked past Huntley's home. His girlfriend Maxine Carr was well known to the girls – she was a teaching assistant at their local school.

Huntley invited the girls in, saying Carr was at home and would like to see them. He lied: Carr had gone to visit her family out of town. Huntley, who'd suspected his girlfriend of cheating on him, had just had an argument with her over the phone and slammed down the receiver just as Holly and Jess walked by. Shortly after the girls entered the home, Huntley murdered them. He was caught and tried.

On September 29, 2005, a judge sentenced Huntley to a minimum of 40 years in prison. Carr, who'd provided Huntley with a false alibi, was convicted of perverting the course of justice and served 21 months of a 42-month jail sentence before being released in May 2004.

August 5

"I've been on a calendar, but never on time." — MARILYN MONROE

HISTORICAL EVENTS

1884 The Statue of Liberty's cornerstone is laid on Bedloe's Island, New York.
1914 The first electric traffic light is installed in Cleveland, Ohio. It was designed by James Hoge and had two colors, red and green. The first three-color traffic lights are introduced six years later in New York and Detroit.
1944 At least 545 Japanese soldiers attempt to escape from the POW camp near Cowra, Australia. It is possibly the biggest prison breakout in history. Of the escapees, 234 are killed and 108 wounded. Four Australian soldiers are also killed.
1962 Screen siren Marilyn Monroe is found dead in her home. She is believed to have overdosed on sleeping pills (see below).
1973 Three people are killed and 55 wounded when two Arab gunmen open fire and throw grenades into a crowded passenger terminal at Athens airport.
1981 In the U.S., air traffic controllers had been on strike, seeking a 32-hour work week, better pay, and better working conditions. President Reagan gave them an ultimatum to return to work within 48 hours. Just 1,200 complied; on this day the remaining 11,359 were fired and permanently banned from Federal service.
2003 Terrorists bomb the Australian Embassy in Jakarta, Indonesia.

DAY TO REMEMBER

Religious day St. Afra's Day St. Afra (c. 304 C.E.) was a prostitute in Augsburg, Germany, during the reign of Roman Emperor Diocletanius, who outlawed Christianity. A Spanish bishop, whom she tried to hide from the Emperor, converted her. She was caught and eventually burned to death.

Births
- 1815 Edward John Eyre, explorer
- 1908 Harold Holt, Australian Prime Minister
- 1930 Neil Armstrong, astronaut
- 1946 Loni Anderson, actress
- 1947 Angry Anderson, singer
- 1951 John Jarratt, actor

Deaths
- 1962 Marilyn Monroe, actress
- 1984 Richard Burton, actor
- 2000 Sir Alec Guinness, actor

Celtic tree sign

HAZEL
August 5–September 1

In Celtic tradition, hazel tree people are clever and organised, with an urge to learn. The hazel represents wisdom, poetic knowledge, and intuition, and these people have great intellect and logic. They also enjoy creative energies for work or projects, but they must learn patience to achieve all they are capable of. Their ruling planet is Mercury.

Goodbye, Norma Jeane

There are many conspiracy theories surrounding the death of Norma Jeane Mortensen, better known as screen goddess Marilyn Monroe. One is that Marilyn, who was allegedly having an affair with the then U.S. President, JFK, had in her possession information on the White House that could bring down the administration if released. Theorists point to the alleged theft of Marilyn's diary and a note from her room the night of her death.

There's also a theory that the mafia had Marilyn killed in revenge for U.S. Attorney General Robert Kennedy's harassment of them. (Marilyn was allegedly having an affair with Robert Kennedy as well.) Some say her death from an overdose of barbiturates was a suicide, others say she or someone else accidentally administered the drugs.

What is known is that Marilyn was found dead, lying naked on her bed in the early hours of August 5, 1962, with a bottle of sleeping pills by her side. She was 36. The coroner ruled her death was a possible suicide.

A 1982 investigation found her death "could have been a suicide or a result of an accidental drug overdose." The 29-page report also concluded there was "no credible evidence" to suggest foul play. Before her death she'd started seeing her second husband Joe DiMaggio and the couple had planned to remarry. Joe sent flowers to Marilyn's crypt for 20 years after her death and never married again.

DATE*line*

August 6

"They say that time changes things, but you actually have to change them yourself."
ANDY WARHOL

HISTORICAL EVENTS

1890 At Auburn Prison, New York, murderer William Kemmler becomes the first person to be executed in an electric chair.

1926 American Gertrude Ederle becomes the first woman to swim the English Channel. The crossing takes her 14 hours and 30 minutes to complete.

1945 An atomic bomb is dropped on Hiroshima, Japan (see right).

1960 In response to a U.S. embargo, Cuba nationalizes American and foreign-owned property in the nation.

1984 Pop star Prince releases *Purple Rain*. The album spends 24 consecutive weeks at number one in the Billboard charts and goes on to sell 13 million copies in the U.S. alone.

1990 The UN orders a trade embargo against Iraq in response to the country's invasion of Kuwait.

1991 World Wide Web inventor Tim Berners-Lee puts the first website online.

2001 U.S. President George W. Bush is given a briefing entitled "Bin Laden Determined to Strike in U.S." The document reportedly predicted the September 11 attacks which took place several weeks later.

DAYS TO REMEMBER

Religious day Feast of the Transfiguration This is the day Jesus Christ is said to have been transfigured into all his divine glory before his disciples Peter, James, and John.

National day Independence Day (Bolivia) This is the anniversary of the day Bolivia gained its independence from Spain in 1825.

National day Independence Day (Jamaica) This day commemorates Jamaica's independence from Britain in 1962.

Births		Deaths	
1809	Alfred Lord Tennyson, poet	1623	Anne Hathaway, Shakespeare's wife
1911	Lucille Ball, comedienne	1637	Ben Jonson, writer
1917	Robert Mitchum, actor	1660	Diego Velazquez, artist
1928	Andy Warhol, artist	1973	Fulgencio Batista, Cuban dictator
1951	Daryl Somers, TV presenter	2004	Rick James, musician
1970	M. Night Shyamalan, film director	2005	Robin Cook, politician
1972	Geri Halliwell, singer	2005	Ibrahim Ferrer, musician
1973	Nina Centaine, singer		
1976	Melissa George, actress		

At 8:15 A.M. on August 6, 1945, an American B-29 called the *Enola Gay* flew over Hiroshima, Japan, and dropped an atomic bomb on the city. The bomb was called Little Boy, in reference to U.S. President Harry S. Truman. In a flash, about 70,000 people were killed. Three days later, a further 70,000 were killed instantly when another bomb, called Fat Man after British leader Winston Churchill, was unleashed on Nagasaki. These two events would instigate the end of World War II.

August 7

"People are more violently opposed to fur than leather because it's safer to harass rich women than motorcycle gangs." ALEXEI SAYLE

The man known as the "smiling assassin," Amrozi bin Nurhasyim, is convicted and sentenced to death by firing squad for buying the explosives and van used in the 2002 Bali bombings. In total, 202 people were killed in the blasts, including 88 Australians, 36 Indonesians, 26 Britons, and seven Americans. Many Australians, who'd traveled to the Balinese court just to hear the ruling, received the news with cheers. However, Amrozi just grinned and gave two thumbs up when the verdict was handed down. He said he welcomed a martyr's death. Amrozi is currently on death row in Nusakambangan island prison, dubbed Indonesia's Alcatraz.

HISTORICAL EVENTS

1944 IBM donates the first U.S. automatic digital calculator to Harvard University. It weighs 11,000 pounds (5,000 kg).

1947 After 101 days and a 4,350-mile (7,000 km) journey at sea, Norwegian marine biologist Thor Heyerdahl smashes his balsawood raft, the *Kon-Tiki*, on a reef at Raroia, proving the peoples of South America could have settled the islands of Polynesia.

1955 Tokyo Telecommunications Engineering, the precursor to Sony, begins selling its first transistor radios in Japan.

1958 Playwright Arthur Miller celebrates with his wife Marilyn Monroe the news that Washington's Court of Appeals has quashed his conviction for contempt of Congress for not releasing to it the names of suspected Communist writers.

1972 Ugandan leader Idi Amin orders all Asians who are not Ugandan citizens to leave the country within 90 days.

1987 America's Lynne Cox swims 1.7 miles (2.7 km) from Alaska to Siberia, making her the first person to swim from the U.S. to the Soviet Union.

1998 More than 200 people are killed and 4,500 injured in the U.S. Embassy bombings in Tanzania and Kenya.

2003 Amrozi bin Nurhasyim is sentenced to death for the 2002 Bali bombings, which killed 202 people (see above).

DAYS TO REMEMBER

Religious day St. Cajetan's Day Augustine monk Martin Luther favored splitting from the Church, but St. Cajetan (c. 1547) had faith it could be reformed from within. When he fell sick, doctors tried to move him off the boards he slept on to a softer bed, but he replied: "My savior died on a cross. Let me die on wood at least."

Religious day St. Donatus' Day Before becoming Bishop of Besancon, France, St. Donatus (c. 660) was a monk at Luxeuil. He is honored for founding St. Paul's Abbey.

Births
- **1876** Mata Hari, Dutch spy
- **1948** Greg Chappell, cricket player
- **1952** Alexei Sayle, comedian
- **1958** Bruce Dickinson, singer
- **1960** David Duchovny, actor
- **1975** David Hicks, alleged terrorist
- **1975** Charlize Theron, actress

Deaths
- **1957** Oliver Hardy, comedian
- **2004** Red Adair, U.S. firefighter

August 8

DATEline

"People have got to know whether or not their president is a crook. Well, I'm not a crook. I earned everything I've got." — RICHARD NIXON

HISTORICAL EVENTS

1786 Jacques Balmat and Dr. Michel-Gabriel Paccard are the first people to climb Mont Blanc in Switzerland.

1930 Betty Boop stars in her first animated movie, *Dizzy Dishes*. The character is based on Helen Kane, a famous U.S. singer and contract actress for Paramount Pictures.

1963 In what will become known as the Great Train Robbery, 15 men ambush a mail train in England and steal £2.6 million in banknotes.

1967 The Association of Southeast Asian Nations (ASEAN) is formed by Thailand, Indonesia, Malaysia, Singapore, and the Philippines. It becomes the symbol of solidarity against Communism in Vietnam.

1969 The famous picture for the cover of The Beatles' *Abbey Road* album is taken.

1972 Richard Nixon accepts his nomination as candidate for the U.S. presidency.

1974 Facing a possible impeachment for his role in the Watergate scandal, U.S. President Richard Nixon announces his resignation, effective the next day (see right).

1991 British journalist John McCarthy is freed after being held hostage in Lebanon for more than five years by militant group Islamic Jihad.

DAYS TO REMEMBER

Religious day Blessed Mary MacKillop's Day The first Australian to be beatified, Mary MacKillop (1842–1909) founded the Sisters of St. Joseph of the Sacred Heart, dedicated to education of the poor.

Religious day St. Dominic's Day The patron saint of astronomers, St. Dominic (1170-1221) established the Order of Preachers known as the Dominicans, devoted to the conversion of the Albigensians – the heretics of southern France.

Births
- **1880** Earle Page, former Australian Prime Minister
- **1928** Don Burrows, musician
- **1929** Ronald Biggs, criminal
- **1935** John Laws, radio personality
- **1937** Dustin Hoffman, actor
- **1944** Peter Weir, film director
- **1961** The Edge, musician
- **1981** Vanessa Amorosi, singer
- **1981** Roger Federer, tennis player
- **1988** Princess Beatrice of York

Deaths
- **2004** Fay Wray, actress

A presidency cut short

At 9:00 P.M., Republican Richard Milhous Nixon appeared on national television to announce that he would resign as President of the United States at noon the next day.

Vice-President Gerald R. Ford was to take over and complete Nixon's term. In the broadcast, Nixon told millions of Americans that while it was "abhorrent to every instinct of my body" to leave before his term is over, "as President, I must put the interests of America first." However, had he not resigned, Nixon faced almost certain impeachment and removal from the presidency for his role in the biggest political scandal in U.S. history.

The drama started when, at 2.30 A.M. on June 17, 1972, five men were arrested attempting to break into the Democratic National Committee's offices in the Watergate Hotel to plant listening devices. James McCord, one of the men, was employed as the chief of security for Nixon's re-election committee. It soon came to light that since 1971 the White House had commissioned political spying and sabotage by a unit known as the Plumbers, so called because of its role to plug leaks in the Nixon administration.

It was also revealed that in September 1971, the Plumbers had sought to discredit former defense analyst Daniel Ellsberg, who had leaked the Pentagon Papers – a top-secret document detailing the U.S.'s involvement in the Vietnam War – to newspapers. Two men broke into the office of Ellsberg's psychiatrist, also in the Watergate Hotel, looking for information to use against him.

August 9

"Awards become corroded, friends gather no dust." — JESSE OWENS

HISTORICAL EVENTS

1483 The Sistine Chapel opens in the Vatican, Rome (see below).

1936 Jesse Owens helps America win the 4 x 100-meter men's relay at the Berlin Olympics and becomes the first American to win four gold medals at a single Games.

1945 An atomic bomb is dropped on the city of Nagasaki, Japan, killing between 70,000 and 90,000 people.

1969 Members of "The Family" led by Charles Manson murder five people, including pregnant actress Sharon Tate.

1971 New laws are introduced into Northern Ireland which allow authorities to indefinitely detain suspected terrorists without trial.

1974 U.S. President Richard Nixon resigns from office. His Vice-President, Gerald Ford, replaces him.

1999 Russian President Boris Yeltsin sacks Prime Minister Sergei Stepashin and the entire Cabinet. It is the fourth time in 17 months he has replaced the Government.

2001 U.S. President George W. Bush announces federal funds will be available for limited research into human embryonic stem cells.

DAY TO REMEMBER

International day Day of the World's Indigenous People Started by the UN in 1994, this day honors the contributions made by the world's indigenous peoples.

Births
- **1938** Rod Laver, tennis player
- **1944** Sam Elliott, actor
- **1957** Melanie Griffith, actress
- **1963** Whitney Houston, singer
- **1968** Gillian Anderson, actress
- **1968** Eric Bana, actor
- **1978** Audrey Tautou, actress

Deaths
- **1962** Hermann Hesse, author
- **1969** Sharon Tate, actress
- **1995** Jerry Garcia, musician
- **2002** Peter Neville, peace activist
- **2003** Gregory Hines, dancer

Pope Sixtus IV led the first mass in the new Sistine Chapel on this day in 1483, consecrating and dedicating the chapel to the Assumption of the Virgin Mary. It had taken eight years to build, and, astonishingly, most of the paintings on the walls were completed in about a year. It wasn't until 1534, however, that Michelangelo was commissioned to paint *The Last Judgment* (pictured), which appears on the rear wall of the chapel. He completed the job in 1541. The Sistine Chapel is where cardinals meet to elect a new pope. White smoke is blown out of the chimney when a decision has been made.

DATE*line*

August 10

"Freedom consists not in doing what we like, but in having the right to do what we ought."
POPE JOHN PAUL II

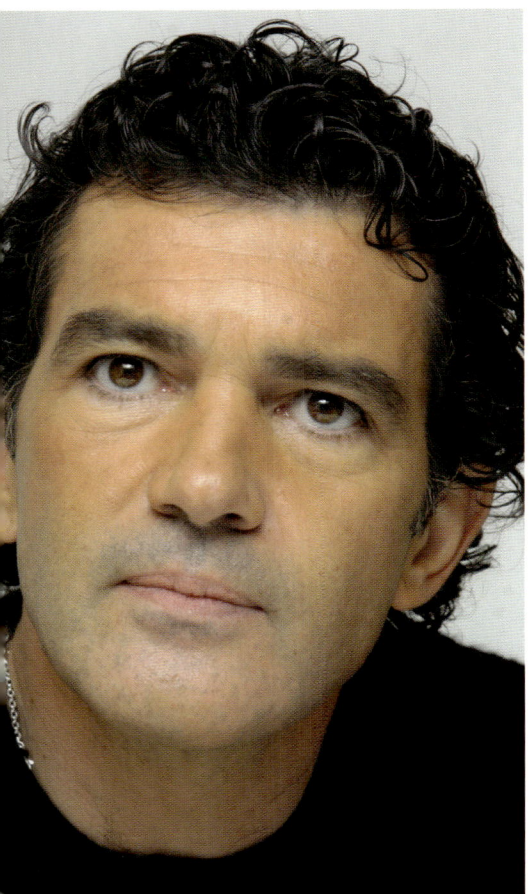

Spanish actor Antonio Banderas celebrates his birthday on August 10.

Births
1872 Bill Johnson, musician
1928 Gus Mercurio, actor
1959 Rosanna Arquette, actress
1960 Antonio Banderas, actor
1961 Jon Farriss, musician
1967 Riddick Bowe, boxer
1971 Roy Keane, soccer player

Deaths
1806 Michael Haydn, composer
1976 Bert Oldfield, cricketer
2003 Carmita Jiménez, singer

HISTORICAL EVENTS

1519 Portuguese explorer Ferdinand Magellan leaves Seville, Spain, on his way to becoming the first person to circumnavigate the globe. Of the 270 men who leave with him, only 18 return.
1792 King Louis XVI of France and his family are arrested on suspicion of treason and taken into custody during what's now known as the French Revolution.
1969 Members of Charles Manson's cult "The Family" kill Leno and Rosemary LaBianca.
1977 Postal worker David Berkowitz (known as the "Son of Sam" by the media) is arrested for killing six people in New York City over the period of one year.
1990 The *Magellan* spacecraft reaches Venus.
1995 Timothy McVeigh and Terry Nichols are indicted on 11 charges for the Oklahoma bombing.
2003 Europe experiences its hottest summer ever, with temperatures in Heathrow soaring to a record 101°F (38°C) and Pope John Paul II calling on the faithful to pray for rain.
2005 South Korean gaming addict Lee Seung-Seop dies from exhaustion after playing on the internet for 50 straight hours (see below).

DAY TO REMEMBER

National day Independence Day (Ecuador) Although the country of Ecuador didn't gain independence until May 1822, its people celebrate on this day because the independence movement began on August 10, 1809, when Quito established the first self-governing junta in the Spanish colonies in America.

Playing a deadly game

A 28-year-old South Korean man collapsed and died of exhaustion after playing a computer game for 50 hours non-stop. Apparently Lee Seung-Seop had not eaten or slept during his marathon session, and most likely died of heart failure. In the preceding weeks, Lee had lost his job due to his gaming obsession and spent most of his time in internet cafes, where the games are played.

He left home on Wednesday but when Lee hadn't returned by Friday, his mother sent friends out to look for him. When they found him, he told them he would finish the game, and then come home. Lee died minutes later.

He was not the first to die at a keyboard. In 2002, another South Korean man died after playing an online game for 86 hours straight.

Gaming is a national phenomenon in South Korea. Internet cafes or PC bangs are hugely popular and often stay open 24 hours a day. Gamers have the opportunity to turn professional and earn a living from the pursuit if they are good enough. To combat the growing problem, the government began sponsoring counseling sessions for gaming addicts, and in 2004, 9,000 sessions were recorded, four times more than in 2003. In the first six months of 2005, 7,600 sessions had been given.

August 11

DATEline

"Part of me suspects that I'm a loser, and the other part of me thinks I'm God Almighty."
JOHN LENNON

HISTORICAL EVENTS

1929 Against the Cleveland Indians, U.S. baseball player Babe Ruth hits his 500th Major League home run, becoming the first man to ever do so.
1934 Alcatraz prison opens in San Francisco Bay. In its 29 years of operation, there was not one single officially logged successful escape from the island.
1956 Jackson Pollock dies in a car crash on Long Island, New York (see below).
1966 John Lennon apologises at a press conference in Chicago for saying The Beatles were more popular than Jesus.
1972 The last U.S. ground combat unit departs South Vietnam. More than 43,000 U.S. airmen and support personnel remain.
1982 East End gangsters Ronnie and Reggie Kray are allowed out of prison for their mother's funeral. During their reign of terror in the 1960s, they were largely kept out of prison by the fact no witnesses were prepared to testify against them.
1984 In the 3,000-meter finals at the Los Angeles Olympic Games, British athlete Zola Budd accidentally trips over American favorite Mary Decker.
2003 The North Atlantic Treaty Organization (NATO) is given command of peacekeeping duties in Afghanistan, the first time in its 54-year history that it has operated outside of Europe.

Births
- 1897 Enid Blyton, author
- 1944 Ian McDiarmid, actor
- 1950 Steve Wozniak, PC inventor
- 1953 Hulk Hogan, professional wrestler
- 1954 Joe Jackson, singer
- 1957 Richie Ramone, musician

Deaths
- 1956 Jackson Pollock, artist
- 1988 Anne Ramsey, actress
- 1994 Peter Cushing, actor

DAYS TO REMEMBER

Religious day St. Clare's Day (1194–1253) St. Clare founded the order of nuns called the Poor Clares. She and her sisters wore no shoes, ate no meat, lived in a poor house, and kept silent most of the time. She is the patron saint of people with sore eyes.

Religious day St. Attracta's Day In the sixth century, Attracta rebelled against her wealthy Irish family's wishes, devoting herself to God and working with St. Patrick.

One of the world's most influential and famous artists of his time, Jackson Pollock (pictured), died when he drove into a tree on Long Island in New York. Pollock, driving drunk, had two passengers with him in his Cadillac – his girlfriend Ruth Kligman, who survived, and her friend, Edith Metzger, who died. *Time* magazine dubbed Pollock "Jack the Dripper" for his technique of painting. In 1973, the National Gallery of Australia bought Pollock's *Blue Poles* for $2 million, which was the highest price paid in Australia for a contemporary piece of art at the time.

August 12

"Creation is a drug I can't do without." — CECIL B. DEMILLE

HISTORICAL EVENTS

- **1851** Isaac Singer of New York patents the sewing machine.
- **1908** The first Model T Ford is built (see below).
- **1952** As ordered by Soviet leader Joseph Stalin, 13 prominent Jewish intellectuals are murdered in Moscow. The event becomes known as "The Night of Murdered Poets."
- **1960** The first communications satellite, Echo 1, is launched. Because of its shiny surface it is clearly discernible from Earth with the naked eye. It is believed to have been the most easily visible artificial satellite ever.
- **1964** Three men break into a high-security prison in England and free one of the Great Train Robbers, Charlie Wilson.
- **2000** The Russian Navy submarine K-141 *Kursk* sinks in the Barents Sea after a massive explosion on board. Despite rescue attempts (which had been belated by Russian politicians) made by Norwegian and British teams, all 118 sailors die.
- **2003** BBC journalist Andrew Gilligan goes before the Hutton Inquiry to defend his report that the British Government had "sexed up" an intelligence dossier on Iraq.

Births
- **1881** Cecil B. DeMille, film director
- **1886** Sir Keith Murdoch, newspaper owner
- **1925** Norris McWhirter, *Guinness Book of Records* co-founder
- **1925** Ross McWhirter, *Guinness Book of Records* co-founder
- **1928** Charles Blackman, artist
- **1949** Mark Knopfler, musician
- **1971** Pete Sampras, tennis player

Deaths
- **30 B.C.E.** Cleopatra
- **1964** Ian Fleming, author
- **1982** Henry Fonda, actor

DAYS TO REMEMBER

International day Youth Day Celebrated annually since 1999, International Youth Day is an opportunity to focus on the needs of people in our community aged between 10 and 24, and to promote intergenerational solidarity.

Religious day St. Euplius' Day A deacon in Sicily during the reign of Roman Emperor Diocletanius, Euplius was beheaded after being found with a copy of the gospels.

Tin Lizzie is born

When Henry Ford and 11 other business associates started the Ford Motor Company on June 16, 1903, he famously proclaimed: "I will build a car for the great multitude." He said his car would be "constructed of the best materials, by the best men to be hired, after the simplest designs that modern engineering can devise. It will be so low in price that no man making a good salary will be unable to own one – and enjoy with his family the blessing of hours of pleasure in God's great open spaces."

And on August 12, 1908, Ford's dream became a reality when the first Model T rolled off the factory floor in Detroit, Michigan. It revolutionized the motor industry by making cars accessible to the common people. Henry sold the first Model T in October that year for $850 (the equivalent of about $16,700 today), rather inexpensive compared to other cars of the time. The price tag of the Model T was determined by its production costs, and in the early days it took about 14 hours to make a single model. So when, in 1913, Ford implemented the automotive industry's first assembly line, a Model T was soon being produced every 93 minutes and the price plummeted to less than $300 – about the average American's annual pay.

By the early 1920s more than half the cars on the road in America were Model Ts, and by 1927 when the last one rolled off the line, more than 15 million had been sold.

August 13

"Men do not shape destiny, destiny produces the man for the hour." — FIDEL CASTRO

East German troops began construction of the Berlin Wall in 1961. This symbol of the Cold War was the brainchild of East German leader Walter Ulbricht and approved by Soviet Union leader Nikita Khrushchev. The 96-mile (155 km) wall was designed to stop the mass exodus of people from the Communist-controlled countries to the Western democratic nations. It worked. Between 1949 and 1961, 2.5 million people fled from East Germany. Between 1962 and 1989, only 5,000 escaped, and another 191 were killed trying. The wall was dismantled on November 9, 1989.

HISTORICAL EVENTS

1913   The circus acrobat Otto Witte is crowned King of Albania. The fraud was based on the resemblance of Witte to Sultan Halim Eddine's nephew, who was meant to be crowned king. Witte's reign lasted 5 days.

1918   Private Opha Mae Johnson becomes the first woman to enlist in the U.S. Marine Corps. She was one of more than 300 women who joined the Marines that day.

1940   The Luftwaffe launches a series of attacks on Britain's Royal Air Force airfields and radar stations in the south of England during the Battle of Britain.

1942   Walt Disney releases *Bambi*, its fifth full-length animated feature film.

1961   Construction of the Berlin Wall begins (see above).

1966   China announces the Cultural Revolution – to purge the country of those suspected of capitalist leanings and opposing Mao Zedong's leadership.

2004   A group of women and children in India stab an alleged criminal as he stands trial in court. Appu Yadav was facing two counts of molestation and rape. The attackers were never caught.

Births
- 1899   Sir Alfred Hitchcock, film director
- 1926   Fidel Castro, Cuban revolutionary
- 1970   Alan Shearer, soccer player
- 1977   Michael Klim, swimmer

Deaths
- 1827   William Blake, poet
- 1910   Florence Nightingale, nurse
- 1946   H. G. Wells, writer
- 1995   Mickey Mantle, baseball player
- 2005   David Lange, New Zealand Prime Minister

DAYS TO REMEMBER

International day   Left-handers Day This designated day increases awareness of the challenges faced by left-handers living among a right-handed majority.

Religious day   St. Hyacinth's Day Also known as the Apostle of Poland, St. Hyacinth (1185–1257) preached in Poland, Denmark, Prussia, Lithuania, Sweden, Norway, Russia, China, and Tibet.

August 14

"There is one thing I would break up over, and that is if she caught me with another woman. I won't stand for that." — STEVE MARTIN (PICTURED LEFT)

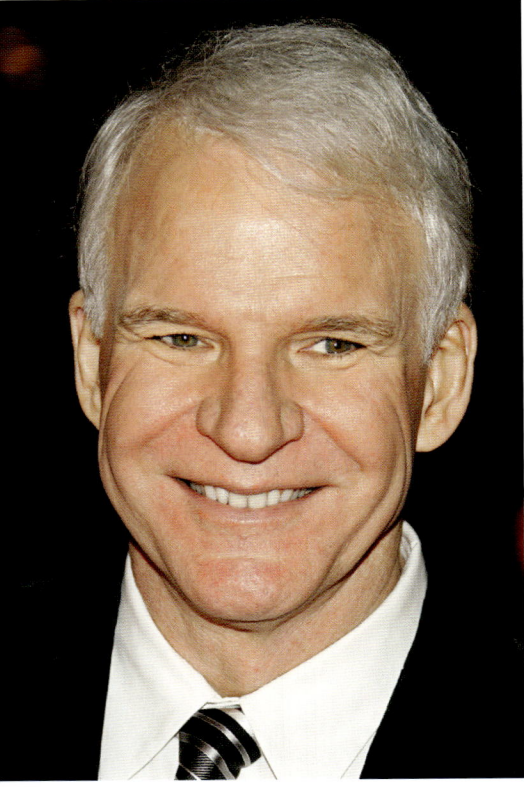

HISTORICAL EVENTS

1880 The Cologne Cathedral in Germany is finally completed. The construction was started in 1248 and was interrupted repeatedly, ultimately dragging on for more than 600 years.

1969 The British Government sends troops into Northern Ireland in response to the IRA's campaign to unify Ireland by force.

1979 Fifteen people die when a freak storm hits crews involved in the Fastnet yacht race in the Irish Sea.

1980 Shipyard workers in Soviet-controlled Gdansk, Poland, go on strike. They are led by electrician Lech Walesa, who was central to the formation of the Solidarity movement and helped put an end to Communism in Poland. Walesa went on to win the Nobel Peace Prize and become President of Poland.

2003 Parts of the U.S. and Canada experience the largest ever blackout in the region (see below).

2004 Hutu men armed with machetes and guns kill 156 people, including women and children, at a Burundi refugee camp for Congolese Tutsi.

2005 A Cypriot airliner crashes into a hill near Athens, killing all 121 on board.

DAYS TO REMEMBER

National day Independence Day (Pakistan) On this day in 1947, Pakistan gained independence from the United Kingdom.

Religious day St. Maximilian's Day When the Nazis invaded Poland, Maximilian (1894-1941) was sent to Auschwitz. He offered his life in place of a young husband and father who had been targeted for a reprisal execution.

Blackout across the American continent

Within three minutes of the first power failure at 4:10 P.M. in 2003, 50 million people were plunged into chaos as the U.S. and Canada experienced a huge blackout. As the blackout swept through about 9,300 square miles (24,000 sq km) of country, people were left stuck in elevators, the subway and traffic, airports were closed, and nuclear power plants shut down.

In New York City, Manhattan was closed down, including Wall Street. Without traffic lights, gridlock occurred across the city, forcing many people to flee their offices on foot. Those unable to make it home slept in their offices, in parks, and on the steps of public buildings, or they just spent the night at bars.

In Detroit, untreated sewage flowed into local rivers. Michigan was in the middle of a heat wave and without air conditioning, some citizens had to be treated for heat stroke. Surprisingly, only a small amount of looting was reported. On the upside, without the light pollution, those in cities could clearly see the Milky Way. Power had been mostly restored by August 18.

It has been estimated that the blackout cost businesses about $6 billion in lost trade. An investigation found the blackout was caused by human error and computer failure at an Ohio power company.

Births
- 1771 Sir Walter Scott, writer
- 1851 Doc Holliday, gunfighter
- 1941 David Crosby, musician
- 1945 Steve Martin, actor
- 1947 Danielle Steel, author
- 1950 Gary Larson, cartoonist
- 1959 Earvin "Magic" Johnson, basketball player
- 1966 Halle Berry, actress
- 1973 Kieren Perkins, swimmer

Deaths
- 1938 Hugh Trumble, cricketer
- 1951 William Randolph Hearst, newspaper owner
- 1988 Enzo Ferrari, car maker

DATE*line*

August 15

"There is one kind of robber whom the law does not strike at, and who steals what is most precious to men: time." — NAPOLEON BONAPARTE

HISTORICAL EVENTS

- **1843** Tivoli Gardens opens in Copenhagen, Denmark. It becomes one of the oldest amusement parks in the world which is still in operation.
- **1877** The first sound recording is made when Thomas Edison says, "Mary had a little lamb" into his phonograph.
- **1914** The Panama Canal opens to seafaring traffic. Its construction represents one of the most ambitious engineering projects in history.
- **1945** Japan surrenders, bringing World War II to an end (see right).
- **1977** An intense radio signal lasting 72 seconds is transmitted from deep space and is picked up by the Big Ear radio telescope in the U.S. It becomes known as the "Wow Signal" due to the note of amazement written by a researcher beside the first printout of the transmission. The signal has never been repeated, nor satisfactorily explained.
- **1998** Twenty-nine people are killed and 220 are injured in Northern Ireland's worst terrorist incident when a 500-pound (230 kg) car bomb explodes in the heart of Omagh.
- **2005** Golfer Phil Mickelson wins the PGA Championship.

DAYS TO REMEMBER

Religious day The Assumption of Mary As a Holy Day of Obligation, this is one of the days other than Sundays on which the Catholic faithful are required to attend Mass. Catholics recognize this as the day the Blessed Virgin Mary was assumed body and soul into heaven.

National day Independence Day (India) On this day in 1947, India gained independence from Britain.

National day Liberation Day (Korea) After being annexed in 1910, Korea was liberated from the Japanese on this day in 1945.

Six days after an atomic bomb was dropped on Nagasaki, nine days after Hiroshima, and three months after Adolf Hitler committed suicide, Emperor Hirohito announced to his people that Japan had surrendered to the Allies. His acceptance of the Potsdam Declaration brought to an end World War II – the deadliest war in history. Up to 62 million people died, mostly civilians, including 18 million Russians, 9 million Chinese, 9 million Germans, 6 million Poles, 2 million Japanese, 500,000 French, 400,000 British, 400,000 Americans, and 30,000 Australians.

Births
- **1769** Napoleon Bonaparte, French Emperor
- **1875** Samuel Coleridge-Taylor, composer
- **1950** Princess Anne, English royal
- **1968** Debra Messing, actress
- **1972** Ben Affleck, actor
- **1974** Natasha Henstridge, actress

Deaths
- **1999** Sir Hugh Casson, artist
- **2005** James Dougherty, Marilyn Monroe's first husband

August 16

"Before Elvis there was nothing."
JOHN LENNON

HISTORICAL EVENTS

1868 A magnitude 8.5 earthquake occurs off the coast of Arica, Peru, creating a tsunami that kills up to 70,000 South Americans.
1954 The first issue of *Sports Illustrated* magazine is published.
1962 The Beatles manager Brian Epstein informs the band's drummer Pete Best that he has been sacked and will be replaced by Ringo Starr.
1974 The Ramones play their first show at New York punk club CBGB's.
1977 Elvis Presley is pronounced dead (see right).
2001 Paul Burrell, a former butler to Princess Diana, is charged with stealing more than 300 items worth $U.S.10 million, from the English royal's household.
2003 Idi Amin, former Ugandan dictator and the man responsible for the death of at least 400,000 people, dies in exile in a hospital in Saudi Arabia.

DAY TO REMEMBER

Religious day St. Stephen's Day The patron saint of Hungary, St. Stephen (977–1038) the Great is recognized as the first Christian king of the country.

Births
1888 T. E. Lawrence, writer
1928 Ann Blyth, actress
1940 Bruce Beresford, film director
1954 James Cameron, film director
1958 Madonna, singer
1960 Timothy Hutton, actor
1980 Robert Hardy, musician

Deaths
1948 Babe Ruth, baseball player
1977 Elvis Presley, singer

The King is dead

On this day in 1997, the man regarded as the King of Rock and Roll, Elvis Presley, was found dead in his Graceland mansion in Memphis, Tennessee, aged 42. His fiancée Ginger Alden woke to find him just after 2:00 P.M. on the floor of their bedroom ensuite. Elvis was rushed to the Baptist Memorial Hospital, where at 3:30 P.M. doctors pronounced him dead. They attributed the cause of death to heart failure, a prevalent killer in his family. His mother Gladys died of a heart attack almost 19 years ago to the day, and his father Vernon died two years after his son with the same problem. Rumors that Elvis died on the toilet have never been substantiated. There is also no hard evidence to verify the conspiracy theory that the King faked his own death and is alive today.

The day after his death, the King was placed in an open coffin at Graceland for thousands of mourners to file past and pay their last respects. He was initially buried next to his mother at Forest Hills Cemetery in Memphis, but after attempts were made to steal his remains, they were both moved to Graceland where they remain today.

Between his first recordings at Sun Studios at the age of 19 and his death 23 years later, Elvis sold more than 300 million albums and starred in 33 films. He has sold more than 1 billion albums in total.

August 17

"One of the things about acting is it allows you to live other people's lives without having to pay the price." ROBERT DE NIRO

HISTORICAL EVENTS

1877 Billy the Kid shoots his first victim, Arizona blacksmith F. P. Cahill, who dies the next day. According to legend, Billy the Kid (Henry McCarty) kills 21 men – one for each year of his life – but the actual number of victims is documented as nine.
1962 Peter Fechter, 18, becomes the first person to be killed trying to cross the Berlin Wall into West Germany. He is shot dead by East German border guards.
1980 A dingo takes Azaria Chamberlain at Ayer's Rock, Australia (see below).
1987 Hitler's former right-hand man, Rudolf Hess, dies in Spandau Prison, West Berlin, aged 93.
1991 Wade Frankum, 33, shoots and kills seven people at Strathfield shopping centre, Australia, before turning the gun on himself.
1998 U.S. President Bill Clinton goes on national television to admit to the public he had an inappropriate relationship with White House intern Monica Lewinsky.
1999 A 7.4-magnitude earthquake hits northwest Turkey, killing more than 18,000.
2005 The Israeli Army begins its first forced evacuation of Jewish settlers.

Births
- 1882 Samuel Goldwyn, producer
- 1893 Mae West, actress
- 1930 Ted Hughes, poet
- 1943 Robert De Niro, actor
- 1952 Nelson Piquet, F1 driver
- 1958 Belinda Carlisle, singer
- 1959 David Koresh, cult leader
- 1960 Sean Penn, actor
- 1966 William E. Dudley, poet
- 1970 Jim Courier, tennis player

Deaths
- 1983 Ira Gershwin, lyricist
- 1987 Rudolf Hess, Nazi deputy

DAY TO REMEMBER

Religious day Caspar and Mary Vaz's Day This Franciscan husband and wife were martyred in Japan. Caspar was burned alive and Mary was beheaded in the city of Nagasaki.

The Azaria Chamberlain saga

The most controversial criminal case in Australian history began when Michael and Lindy Chamberlain took their young family – Aidan, 6, Reagan, 4, and Azaria, 10 weeks – on a holiday to Ayer's Rock (Uluru) in 1980. The Chamberlains were camping near the Rock and had returned to their spot after a day of exploring. It was after sunset and they were sharing a barbecue with another young family, also on a camping holiday in the remote outback destination.

Lindy announced it was time to put Azaria to bed with her brother Reagan. She returned to the barbecue, but soon after, the group noticed a baby's cry coming from the direction of the tent. Returning to the tent to investigate, Lindy screamed, "My God, a dingo's got my baby!"

The first coroner's inquest found a dingo had indeed taken Azaria, but after a further investigation and a new inquiry, Lindy was charged with the murder of her baby. On October 29, 1982, a judge sentenced her to life imprisonment. Michael was found guilty of being an accessory after the fact and given a suspended sentence.

In early 1986, probably the most important discovery in the case was made. Police investigating another incident found Azaria's matinee jacket in a dingo's lair at the foot of Ayer's Rock, and Lindy was released from prison.

August 18

"Good judgment comes from experience. Sometimes, experience comes from bad judgment."
CHRISTIAN SLATER

Jimi Hendrix's performance at the world's most famous music festival, Woodstock, is probably the best remembered of any of the musicians who played there but was also the least attended. Hendrix, who was headlining the gig, was due to come on stage at midnight on August 17, 1969 as the final act. But due to bad weather and other problems, he didn't begin playing until 9:00 A.M. the following day. By that time, many of the 500,000 attendees had partied for three days straight and had left exhausted. Jimi played 16 songs, including the "Star Spangled Banner," finishing with "Hey Joe." Despite high acclaim, he regarded his performance as sub-standard.

Births

- 1904 Max Factor, cosmetics entrepreneur
- 1933 Roman Polanski, film director
- 1935 Sir Howard Morrison, entertainer
- 1936 Robert Redford, actor
- 1952 Patrick Swayze, actor
- 1957 Denis Leary, comedian
- 1969 Edward Norton, actor
- 1969 Christian Slater, actor
- 1992 Frances Bean Cobain, musician Kurt Cobain's daughter

Deaths

- 1227 Genghis Khan, Mongol leader

HISTORICAL EVENTS

- 1958 Vladimir Nabokov's controversial novel *Lolita* is published in the U.S.
- 1963 James Meredith becomes the first African American to graduate from the University of Mississippi.
- 1964 The International Olympic committee bans South Africa from the Tokyo Games because of the country's refusal to condemn apartheid.
- 1966 The Battle of Long Tan begins in the Vietnam War.
- 1969 Jimi Hendrix plays the last day of Woodstock (see left).
- 1971 Australia and New Zealand announce they will withdraw their troops from Vietnam.
- 2005 The Indonesian island of Java experiences a massive power blackout. Some 100 million people are affected.

DAY TO REMEMBER

Religious day St. Jane's Day St. Jane of Frances de Chantal (1572-1641) founded the Visitation Order for the sick and poor women the other orders would turn away.

August 19

"Elegance is not the prerogative of those who have just escaped from adolescence, but of those who have already taken possession of their future." — COCO CHANEL

HISTORICAL EVENTS

1561 Queen Mary Stuart arrives back in Scotland after spending the previous 13 years in France.

1692 Five people are hanged as witches in Salem, Massachusetts. In total, 19 people were executed for witchcraft, of which six were men. The witch hunts become the basis of a play by Arthur Miller which draws parallels to the McCarthyist hysteria of his time.

1960 In the U.S.S.R., a three-man military tribunal sentences downed American U-2 pilot Francis Gary Powers to 10 years imprisonment for spying. He is later released in exchange for the U.S. release of a Soviet prisoner.

1975 A cricket Test match between Australia and England is abandoned after campaigners calling for the release of imprisoned robber George Davis vandalize the cricket pitch at Headingley, England.

1991 Communist hardliners in the U.S.S.R. stage a military coup and place President Mikhail Gorbachev under house arrest (see right).

1999 An estimated 20,000 protestors rally in central Belgrade to demand the resignation of Yugoslav President Slobodan Milosevic.

2003 A massive bomb kills 17 people and destroys the UN headquarters in Baghdad, Iraq.

2005 Russia and China conduct their first joint military exercises.

DAYS TO REMEMBER

National day Independence Day (Afghanistan) In 1919 Afghanistan gained independence from the United Kingdom.

Religious day St. John Eudes' Day Born in France, St. John (1601-1670) was renowned for his work with the victims of the plagues that swept Normandy and for helping "fallen women."

Births
- **1871** Orville Wright, aviation pioneer
- **1883** Coco Chanel, fashion designer
- **1919** Malcolm Forbes, publisher
- **1921** Gene Roddenberry, TV producer
- **1930** Frank McCourt, author
- **1946** Bill Clinton, U.S. President
- **1969** Matthew Perry, actor
- **1983** Tammin Sursok, actress

Deaths
- **14 C.E.** Augustus, Roman Emperor
- **1662** Blaise Pascal, mathematician
- **1980** Otto Frank, father of Anne Frank

Communist coup

U.S.S.R. President Mikhail Gorbachev had grown unpopular with many Communist Party hardliners because of his policies of *perestroika* and *glasnost* ("reconstruction" and "openness") which effectively loosened the state's grip on the economy and media.

So when, in 1991, Gorbachev proposed to grant several republics their independence from the U.S.S.R., major problems ensued.

On August 19, 1991, while Gorbachev was in Crimea, a group of eight men — including the leaders of the KGB, Army, and police — took control of the country. They placed Gorbachev under house arrest and surrounded Russia's parliament house with armed forces.

Known as the Gang of Eight, they told the people they were saving the country from a "national catastrophe," that Gorbachev was ill and had been relieved of state. However, despite the presence of military might, thousands of civilians came out in Leningrad and Moscow to protest against the takeover. At one point Russian Federation president Boris Yeltsin climbed onto a tank outside the parliament and urged the troops not to fire at the people.

This was probably the turning point. Many of the troops began to openly side with the people, and by August 21 the coup was called off. Gorbachev returned to power, but the nation now embraced a new hero in Yeltsin.

On December 25, 1991, Gorbachev resigned and officially dissolved the U.S.S.R. Yeltsin ultimately became Russia's first elected President.

August 20

"Martin Luther King took us to the mountaintop: I want to take us to the bank." — DON KING

Australia's most controversial politician, Pauline Hanson, gasped as the guilty verdict was read out in Queensland's Supreme Court. "Rubbish, I'm not guilty … it's a joke," shouted the former fish and chip shop owner who'd founded the One Nation party on the back of her anti-immigration policies. But it was no joke. She and co-founder David Ettridge (both pictured) were sentenced to three years' imprisonment for fraudulently registering the party and dishonestly obtaining almost $500,000 in electoral funds. But in November that year they were released after an appeal court quashed their convictions amid allegations that their jailing had been politically motivated.

HISTORICAL EVENTS

1940 In Mexico, an assassin fatally wounds exiled Russian revolutionary Leon Trotsky with an ice pick. Soviet leader Joseph Stalin had ordered the murder.

1975 NASA launches the Viking 1 planetary probe toward Mars. It is the first of two space missions that together comprise the most ambitious and expensive exploration of Mars in history.

1989 Lyle and Erik Menendez shoot and kill their parents in their Beverly Hills home. During their first six months as orphans they spend about $1 million of their parents' fortune, but are eventually arrested. Both are sentenced to life in prison, with no possibility of parole.

1992 An English newspaper publishes a photo of Texan businessman John Bryan kissing the foot of the topless Duchess of York, Sarah Ferguson, while they holiday in France.

1993 The Oslo Peace Accords, seeking peace between Israel and Palestine, are finalised. Despite painstaking secret negotiations and high hopes, the conflict is not resolved.

1997 Guerrillas massacre more than 60 people and kidnap 15 women in Souhane, Algeria. The tragedy results in a mass exodus, reducing the town's population from about 4,000 to 103 people.

1998 In retaliation for the August 7 bombings of its embassies in Kenya and Tanzania, the U.S. launches missiles at al-Qaeda camps in Afghanistan and a chemical plant in Sudan.

2003 Former leader of the Australian anti-immigration party One Nation, Pauline Hanson, is sentenced to three years in jail for electoral fraud (see above).

2004 U.S. presidential candidate John Kerry hits back at allegations that he lied about his Vietnam service.

DAY TO REMEMBER

Religious day St. Bernard of Clairvaux's Day The patron saint of farm and agriculture workers, St. Bernard (1090–1153), commissioned by Pope Eugene III, traveled through France and Germany arousing great enthusiasm for the second Crusade. He blamed the eventual failure of the expedition on the sins of the Crusaders.

Births
- 1931 Don King, boxing promoter
- 1941 Slobodan Milosevic, Serbian President
- 1942 Isaac Hayes, singer
- 1948 Robert Plant, singer (Led Zeppelin)
- 1961 Greg Egan, author
- 1966 Dimebag Darrell, musician
- 1970 Fred Durst, singer (Limp Bizkit)

Deaths
- 1912 William Booth, Salvation Army founder
- 1915 Paul Ehrlich, Nobel Prize laureate

August 21

DATEline

"The end may justify the means as long as there is something that justifies the end."

LEON TROTSKY

HISTORICAL EVENTS

1841 John Hampson of New Orleans patents the Venetian blind.
1888 William Seward Burroughs, a bank teller, invents the first successful adding machine in the United States. His grandson, also William S. Burroughs, becomes a writer, well known for novels such as *Naked Lunch*.
1911 A former Louvre employee steals the *Mona Lisa* (see below).
1971 Prison guards at California's San Quentin prison shoot and kill Black Panther George Jackson during an escape attempt.
1973 The coroner presiding over the Bloody Sunday inquest accuses the British Army of "sheer unadulterated murder."
1983 A gunman assassinates Benigno Aquino moments after the exiled Philippines opposition leader returns home.
2005 About 1 million people join Pope Benedict XVI in Cologne, Germany, for a mass to mark the end of World Youth Day.

Births
1923 Shimon Peres, Israel Prime Minister and Nobel Peace Prize recipient
1930 Princess Margaret, English royal
1936 Wilt Chamberlain, basketball player
1938 Kenny Rogers, singer
1944 Peter Weir, film director
1952 Joe Strummer, musician
1956 Kim Cattrall, actress
1967 Carrie-Anne Moss, actress

Deaths
1814 Sir Benjamin Thompson, inventor
1940 Leon Trotsky, Russian revolutionary

The *Mona Lisa* goes missing

In 1911, Vincenzo Peruggio hid out in a small room in the Louvre, France, waiting for people to leave and the museum to close. The Italian stayed there all Sunday night, and on Monday morning crept out, took the *Mona Lisa* off the wall, removed it from its frame and calmly walked outside with the world's most famous painting. He later told police he just wanted to restore the masterpiece to its rightful home – Italy – where Leonardo da Vinci painted it.

Museum staff took a day to even notice the painting was missing. Many thought the museum's photographer had taken it up to his studio to record. When it was noticed missing, police closed the Louvre for a week to investigate. Pablo Picasso, 29 years old at the time, was questioned, but later released. Police also called in Peruggio. He had worked at the Louvre 10 months prior to the theft, placing the museum's masterpieces behind glass. However, police released him, allegedly because he'd appeared too calm to have had anything to do with the crime.

The big break came in 1913, when Peruggio attempted to sell the *Mona Lisa* to a well-known antique dealer in Italy. Peruggio agreed to sell the painting for 500,000 lire under the condition it be hung in the Uffizi gallery in Florence and never given back to France. The meeting was a sting and Peruggio was arrested. The recovered *Mona Lisa* was displayed throughout Italy, including the Uffizi gallery, before being returned to the Louvre, where it remains today.

August 22

"I don't think about time. You're here when you're here. I think about today, staying in tune."
JOHN LEE HOOKER

HISTORICAL EVENTS

1770 Captain James Cook lands in Botany Bay, Australia.
1864 Twelve nations sign the first Geneva Convention protecting vulnerable people in times of conflict.
1910 Japan annexes Korea. Korea's name is changed to *Chōsen*, meaning "ancient."
1922 Commander-in-Chief of the Irish Free State Army Michael Collins is shot dead in an ambush at Beal na mBlath, County Cork.
1962 Opponents of French President Charles de Gaulle's push to grant Algeria its independence attempt to assassinate him.
2004 Two armed men steal Edvard Munch's paintings *The Scream* and *Madonna* from the Munch Museum in Norway.
2005 Held in an English mental hospital where he kept a silent vigil, the man the media dubbed "the Piano Man" reveals his identity and returns home to Germany (see below).
2005 The Atlanta Olympics bomber Eric Rudolph is sentenced to four life terms without parole.

DAY TO REMEMBER

Religious day St. John Kemble's Day One of the 40 Martyrs of England and Wales, St. John (1599–1679) was a Catholic priest living around the time of the English Reformation. At the age of 81, he was falsely accused by Titus Oates as a Catholic conspirator against the king and hanged, drawn, and quartered.

Births
1862 Claude Debussy, composer
1904 Deng Xiaoping, Chinese leader
1917 John Lee Hooker, singer
1934 Norman Schwarzkopf, U.S. general
1958 Vernon Reid, musician
1963 Tori Amos, musician
1964 Mats Wilander, tennis player
1966 GZA, rapper
1967 Layne Staley, singer

Deaths
1485 King Richard III of England
1922 Michael Collins, Irish revolutionary

The enigma of the Piano Man

A four-month-long worldwide campaign to identify the Piano Man, as the media had dubbed him, came to an end when 20-year-old Andreas Grassl was released from a mental hospital in England and sent back to his parents' home in Germany.

Police found Grassl wandering the streets near a beach in Kent, England, wearing a soaking-wet suit. He didn't talk, had no identification on him and the labels had been removed from every item of clothing he was wearing.

The police took him to Medway Maritime Hospital where he was given a pen and paper in the hope he would communicate with staff. Instead, he drew a detailed picture of a grand piano. When taken to a piano in the hospital's chapel, Grassl apparently gave staff a performance of classical music. He was taken to a mental hospital in Kent where he also allegedly wrote music, still without a word.

Outside, the English media conducted a massive search to find out the identity of this supposed mute genius. More than 800 leads were generated. However, on August 22, 2005, an English newspaper reported the man had finally broken his silence and told a nurse he was German. It alleged Andreas was no virtuoso, but in reality he had just kept tapping one key on the piano continuously.

He'd apparently lost his job in Paris, France, and had tried to commit suicide on the beach in England. When police picked him up in Kent, he was too distressed to talk. Andreas flew back to his father's home in Germany the following day.

August 23

"Every man dies. Not every man really lives." — WILLIAM WALLACE

In an attempt to avoid an imminent war, Saddam Hussein appears on Iraqi television with a group of Western hostages in 1990. The Iraqi leader had just invaded Kuwait and was fending off mounting pressure from the international community to withdraw his forces. During the 30-minute broadcast Saddam told his "guests" they had been detained to prevent a war and to ensure their safety. He approached a six-year-old British boy, Stuart Lockwood, ruffled his hair, and asked him if he was getting his milk. Iraq freed the hostages in early September. War broke out in January 1991.

HISTORICAL EVENTS

1939 The Molotov–Ribbentrop Pact, also known as the Hitler–Stalin Pact, is signed. It was described as a non-aggression treaty between the U.S.S.R. and Germany, but in reality, it incorporated an additional secret protocol in which Finland and Poland were shared between the two nations.

1942 The Battle of Stalingrad begins during World War II.

1990 In an effort to stop an impending war, Iraqi leader Saddam Hussein appears on state television talking with a number of Western hostages (see above).

1990 West Germany and East Germany announce plans to reunite on October 3.

1991 Soviet President Mikhail Gorbachev tells his entire Government it should resign for failing to oppose the recent failed coup.

2005 Pat Robertson, a televangelist and former candidate for President of the U.S., calls on America to assassinate Venezuelan President Hugo Chavez. The religious leader is quoted as saying, "It's a whole lot cheaper than starting a war."

2005 Israeli troops remove the last of the Jewish settlers in the Gaza Strip.

Births
- 1754 King Louis XVI of France
- 1912 Gene Kelly, actor
- 1934 Barbara Eden, actress
- 1947 Keith Moon, musician (The Who)
- 1949 Rick Springfield, singer
- 1970 River Phoenix, actor
- 1978 Kobe Bryant, basketball player

Deaths
- 1305 William Wallace, Scottish national hero
- 1926 Rudolph Valentino, actor
- 1960 Oscar Hammerstein II, lyricist

DAY TO REMEMBER

International day Day of Remembrance of the Slave Trade On this day in 1791 African slaves on the island of Santo Domingo (now Haiti and the Dominican Republic) rose up against their captors – a crucial event in the eventual abolition of slavery. The date was chosen to show the slaves were the main agents of their own liberation.

August 24

"You have to take risks. We will only understand the miracle of life fully when we allow the unexpected to happen." — PAULO COELHO

HISTORICAL EVENTS

- **1847** Charlotte Bronte sends her *Jane Eyre* manuscript to publishing house Smith, Elder & Co.
- **1853** George Crum invents the potato chip (see below).
- **1981** A judge in New York sentences Mark David Chapman to at least 20 years in prison for shooting former Beatles member John Lennon.
- **1990** After being held hostage for more than four years, Irishman Brian Keenan is released in Lebanon by his Islamic captors.
- **1991** Soviet President Mikhail Gorbachev suspends the Communist Party and resigns as general secretary.
- **1993** Los Angeles police begin to investigate the first allegations of child abuse against singer Michael Jackson.
- **2004** An independent panel finds responsibility for the abuse of detainees at Iraq's Abu Ghraib prison by American soldiers extends the whole way up the chain of command to include the Pentagon.
- **2005** Torrential rains across Europe cause major flooding – particularly in Romania, Switzerland, and Germany – killing at least 36 people.

Births
- **1890** Duke Kahanamoku, Hawaiian surfer
- **1929** Yasser Arafat, Palestinian leader and Nobel laureate
- **1945** Vince McMahon, professional wrestling entrepreneur
- **1947** Paulo Coelho, author
- **1957** Stephen Fry, comedian
- **1958** Steve Guttenberg, actor
- **1968** Andreas Kisser, musician
- **1973** David Chappelle, comedian
- **1973** Inge de Bruijn, swimmer

Deaths
- **1680** Thomas Blood, Irish-born thief of the British crown jewels

The first potato chips

When chef George Crum attempted to get back at a nuisance customer in 1853 by slicing his potatoes so thin that they couldn't be eaten with a fork, he didn't realise he was starting a billion-dollar industry. But that's exactly how the humble potato chip, or crisps as they are known in some parts of the world, were invented.

Part American Indian, part African American, Crum was working in a very fashionable restaurant known as Moon Lake Lodge in Saratoga Springs, New York, when, according to legend, Cornelius Vanderbilt walked in. Vanderbilt was a very wealthy man who built his empire in shipping and railroads. He ordered fried potatoes but sent them back when they came to him too soggy and thick. However, when Crum send him the new plate of potatoes, he was ecstatic.

Soon afterward, Saratoga chips, as they were named, became a regular menu item at the lodge and eventually started springing up in restaurants all over the country. Crum even set up his own restaurant on the back of their fame. Later, they were sold in sealed bags, and in the 1950s, the technology to add seasoning was invented. "Cheese and onion" and "Salt and vinegar" became the first flavored chips on the market. Prior to that, little bags of salt were included in the chip bags. U.S. sales of potato chips alone turn over more than $6 billion a year.

Star sign

VIRGO
August 24–September 23

The Virgo's motto is "I analyze." People who are born under this star sign are said to be hardworking, reliable, meticulous, and intelligent people, who enjoy helping others but avoid the spotlight. They also tend to be conservative. They are perfectionists and this can make them fussy, overcritical, and harsh.

DAYS TO REMEMBER

Religious day St. Bartholomew's Day This saint was one of the 12 disciples who witnessed Jesus's ascension to heaven after his resurrection. He is said to have brought Christianity to Armenia, but was also flayed alive, then crucified upside down in the same country. He is the patron saint of tanners.

National day Independence Day (Ukraine) On this day in 1991, the Ukraine gained independence from Russia.

August 25

"Woman was God's second mistake." — FRIEDRICH NIETZSCHE

HISTORICAL EVENTS

1609 Galileo Galilei presents his invention, the telescope, to the Venetian Senate.

1718 French explorer Rene-Robert Cavelier founds New Orleans, Louisiana.

1875 Matthew Webb becomes the first person to swim the English Channel (see right).

1932 Amelia Earhart becomes the first woman to fly solo non-stop across the U.S. from Los Angeles, California, to Newark, New Jersey.

1944 The Allies liberate Paris from the Germans during World War II.

1967 John Patler kills the founder of the American Nazi Party, George Lincoln Rockwell. Patler had been a member of the party until his expulsion shortly before the assassination.

1975 Bruce Springsteen releases his highly successful album *Born to Run*.

2003 The most successful men's tennis player ever, Pete Sampras, retires.

2005 Hurricane Katrina hits Florida, killing three people and leaving more than 1 million residents without electricity.

DAYS TO REMEMBER

National day Independence Day (Uruguay) On this day, Uruguay declared its independence from Brazil in 1825.

Religious day St. Louis' Day The patron saint of tertiary orders, Louis (1214–1270), King of France, led two holy Crusades. He was captured, imprisoned, and eventually released during the first Crusade, but was stricken ill and died during the second.

Swimming the Channel

At 10:41 A.M. on August 25, 1875, smeared in porpoise oil, Captain Matthew Webb became the first person to swim the English Channel. It took the Englishman 22 hours to swim almost 39 miles (64 km), taking a zigzag course due to ocean currents, from Dover on the English side to Calais in France. Eight hours into the swim, the 27-year-old was stung by a jellyfish, but continued on after a shot of brandy.

Webb described how he felt after the swim in true English style: "The sensation in my limbs is similar to that after the first day of the cricket season." He became an instant celebrity worldwide. Everywhere he went, crowds turned out to greet him, and legend has it that as a band welcomed Webb back to his birth town of Dawley, a pig even raised itself up on its sty to watch him pass.

Webb continued to earn money from his swimming in England and America, including an amazing £1,000 for floating in a tank of water for 128 hours. He put his name to commemorative merchandise and wrote a book called *The Art of Swimming*. However, buoyed by his success, Webb pushed his luck too far on July 24, 1883. For the chance of winning £12,000, he attempted to swim across rapids on the Niagara River at the foot of Niagara Falls.

Many described the attempt as suicidal, but nevertheless, thousands turned out to watch. At 4:25 P.M., he jumped into the water and began his swim. Within 10 minutes he was dragged under by a whirlpool. The 35-year-old's body was found four days later, and buried at Oakwood Cemetery, Niagara Falls. He was survived by his wife Madeline and their two children, Matthew and Helen. In 1909, Webb's older brother Thomas unveiled a memorial in Dawley, which bore the short inscription: "Nothing great is easy."

Births
- 1918 Leonard Bernstein, composer
- 1930 Sir Sean Connery, actor
- 1938 Frederick Forsyth, author
- 1949 Martin Amis, author
- 1949 Gene Simmons, musician (KISS)
- 1954 Elvis Costello, musician
- 1958 Tim Burton, film director
- 1961 Billy Ray Cyrus, singer
- 1970 Claudia Schiffer, model

Deaths
- 1900 Friedrich Nietzsche, philosopher
- 1984 Truman Capote, author
- 2001 Aaliyah, singer
- 2002 Dorothy Hewett, author

Elvis Costello, still rocking hard, celebrates his birthday on August 25.

August 26

"If people knew how hard I worked to get my mastery, it wouldn't seem so wonderful at all."

MICHELANGELO

On August 26, 1995, the International Rugby Board brought the game's amateur status to an end. The move was an attempt to stem the flow of players going to the game's better-paying cousin, rugby league. There were also rumors media giant Rupert Murdoch was about to start a breakaway professional competition, and the only way for the IRB to maintain control was to get in first.

However, rugby players were being well paid for playing the game long before the official turn to professionalism. In 1991, Australian great David Campese said: "I'm still an amateur, of course, but I became rugby's first millionaire five years ago."

Births
- 1898 Peggy Guggenheim, art critic
- 1921 Benjamin Bradlee, Watergate journalist
- 1940 Don LaFontaine, voice actor
- 1966 Shirley Manson, singer
- 1980 Macaulay Culkin, actor

Deaths
- 1974 Charles Lindbergh, aviator
- 1980 Tex Avery, cartoonist
- 1989 Irving Stone, author
- 2004 Laura Branigan, singer

DAYS TO REMEMBER

National day Women's Equality Day (U.S.) Women were given the right to vote in the U.S. on this day in 1920.

National day Heroes' Day (Namibia) This day recognizes the people who fought for Namibia's independence from South Africa in 1966.

HISTORICAL EVENTS

- 1498 Pope Alexander VI commissions Michelangelo, 23, to carve the Pietà for St. Peter's Basilica, Rome.
- 1883 Mount Krakatoa erupts. Most of Kratatoa Island is destroyed, and the eruption generates the loudest noise reported in history. For five days after the cataclysm, atmospheric shock waves are felt as they reverberate around the Earth seven times.
- 1920 Women are given the right to vote in America thanks to the Nineteenth Amendment to the U.S. Constitution. The two people arguably most committed to the struggle for women's rights were Elizabeth Cady Stanton and Susan B. Anthony, who devoted 50 years of their lives to the cause.
- 1944 Exiled General Charles de Gaulle enters Paris after the Allies reclaim the French capital from the Nazis.
- 1994 Doctors implant the world's first battery-operated heart into a man in Britain, aged 62.
- 1995 The International Rugby Board overturns the game's amateur status (see above).
- 2003 An investigation into the *Columbia* disaster finds that NASA's inaccurate assessment of the risk caused by damage to the space shuttle's heat shielding contributed to the loss of the craft and its seven-member crew.
- 2004 Chile's highest court votes 9 to 8 in favor of lifting the immunity from prosecution granted to the country's former dictator, Augusto Pinochet.

August 27

DATEline

"*I am a little pencil in the hand of a writing God, who is sending a love letter to the world.*"

MOTHER TERESA

HISTORICAL EVENTS

1813 Napoleon Bonaparte, with a force of 100,000 men, beats the 150,000-strong combined Austrian, Prussian, and Russian forces at the Battle of Dresden.
1859 The first oil well in Titusville, Pennsylvania, strikes oil.
1896 The shortest war in history, the Anglo–Zanzibar War between Britain and Zanzibar, lasts about 45 minutes.
1939 The first turbine-powered jet aircraft flight takes place. An experimental jet aircraft using a piston-powered compressor had been unsuccessfully test-flown almost three decades earlier.
1967 Friends find Beatles manager Brian Epstein dead in his London home. He had died of a drug overdose, aged 32.
1979 The IRA kills 22 people, including the Queen's cousin Lord Mountbatten and 18 British soldiers, in three massive bomb blasts that rock Northern Ireland (see right).
2003 Mars and Earth are the closest they've been to each other in 60,000 years. The planets pass within about 35 million miles (56 million km) of each other.

DAY TO REMEMBER

Religious day St. Monica of Hippo's Day The patron saint of wives and abuse victims, St. Monica (333–387) had three children to a violent man, including a wayward son called Augustine. Through her patience and prayer she converted both men to Christianity, and Augustine eventually became a saint.

Births
- **1890** Man Ray, artist
- **1908** Don Bradman, cricketer
- **1908** Lyndon B. Johnson, thirty-sixth U.S. President
- **1910** Mother Teresa, humanitarian and Nobel Peace Prize recipient
- **1976** Carlos Moya, tennis player
- **1976** Mark Webber, Formula 1 driver

Deaths
- **1967** Brian Epstein, manager (The Beatles)
- **1979** Earl Mountbatten, British admiral and statesman
- **1990** Stevie Ray Vaughan, musician

Bombs across Ireland

In 1979, the Queen's cousin Lord Mountbatten and 18 British soldiers were killed in three explosions across Ireland. The IRA took responsibility for the attack. Lord Mountbatten (pictured left) was on board his yacht, *Shadow V,* when the first device, a 50-pound (23 kg) bomb, exploded at 11:30 A.M. Four people died as a result of the blast, including Lord Mountbatten's 14-year-old grandson, and three were wounded. Later that day, and only a few miles away, a 1,100-pound (500 kg) bomb hidden in a truck loaded with hay exploded just as the British Parachute Regiment drove by, killing six men. Twenty minutes later, another bomb exploded nearby, killing 12 soldiers, some of whom had been called in to secure the area.

Apparently, the IRA had studied how the British Army reacted after a bomb blast and had planted and timed the second explosion for maximum impact. The attack is known as the Warrenpoint Massacre. In retaliation, loyalist paramilitaries killed a number of Irish Catholic civilians. The bombers were never caught, but on November 23, 1979, IRA member Thomas McMahon was sentenced to life in prison for his role in the assassination of Lord Mountbatten. He was released in 1998 under the Good Friday Agreement.

August 28

"Rest not. Life is sweeping by; go and dare before you die. Something mighty and sublime, leave behind to conquer time." — GOETHE

HISTORICAL EVENTS

- **1955** In Mississippi, 14-year-old African American Emmett Till is murdered, allegedly for wolf whistling at a white woman.
- **1963** U.S. civil rights leader Martin Luther King Jr. leads the March on Washington where he gives his famous "I have a dream" speech to more than 250,000 people in front of the Lincoln Memorial (see right).
- **1972** U.S. swimmer Mark Spitz wins gold in the 200-meter butterfly at the Munich Olympics – the first of a record-breaking seven he'll win during the Games.
- **1981** The U.S. National Center for Disease Control forms a group to find out why two rare diseases have struck more than 100 gay men in the U.S., killing more than half of them. The diseases will soon be recognised as symptoms of AIDS.
- **1990** Iraq proclaims Kuwait to be its nineteenth province.
- **1994** Tokyo hosts the first Japanese gay pride parade.
- **1996** English royals Prince Charles and Princess Diana announce their agreement to divorce.
- **2005** Mayor Ray Nagin gives the first mandatory order for residents of New Orleans, Louisiana, to evacuate as Hurricane Katrina nears the American coastal city.

DAY TO REMEMBER

Religious day St. Augustine's Day St. Augustine (354–430) is the patron saint of brewers because of his early life of vice. His turnaround and conversion is an inspiration to many who struggle with bad habits.

In 1963, Martin Luther King Jr. delivered his famous "I have a dream" speech to more than 250,000 people gathered in front of the Lincoln Memorial in Washington. The March on Washington for Jobs and Freedom was, at the time, the largest political demonstration in U.S. history. Organizers made several demands on the Government led by John F. Kennedy, including a law prohibiting racial discrimination in employment and an end to racial segregation in schools. Interestingly, Malcolm X called it the Farce on Washington because he did not believe the demands went far enough.

Births
- **1749** Johann Wolfgang von Goethe, author
- **1916** Jack Vance, author
- **1942** Sterling Morrison, musician
- **1947** Des Fitzgerald, golfer
- **1965** Shania Twain, singer
- **1969** Jason Priestley, actor
- **1969** Jack Black, comedian
- **1982** LeAnn Rimes, singer

Deaths
- **1900** Henry Sidgwick, philosopher
- **1987** John Huston, film director
- **1993** William Stafford, writer

DATEline

August 29

"Success is getting what you want; happiness is wanting what you get." — INGRID BERGMAN

HISTORICAL EVENTS

1885 The world's first motorcycle, invented by German Gottlieb Daimler, is patented.
1907 The Quebec Bridge collapses during construction, killing 75 workers. In just 15 seconds, half the bridge – which took almost four years to construct – is destroyed.
1911 A man believed to be the last Native American to make contact with European Americans leaves the wilderness. Ishi, the last of the Yahi tribe, was discovered in northeastern California.
1949 The Soviet Union detonates its first atomic bomb in Kazakhstan. The bomb resembles the "Fat Man" design dropped by the U.S. on Nagasaki, Japan.
1966 The Beatles perform their last public concert in Candlestick Park, San Francisco. The venue's capacity was 42,500, but only 25,000 showed. "Long Tall Sally" is their last song.
1997 Muslim militants trying to overthrow the government massacre more than 300 men, women, and children in the village of Rais, Algeria.
2003 A car bomb kills 126 people and a leading Muslim cleric as they leave the holiest shrine for Shiites in Najaf, Iraq.
2005 Hurricane Katrina smashes into the southeast coast of America, killing more than 1,600 people (see below).

Births
1862 Andrew Fisher, Australian Prime Minister
1898 Preston Sturges, screenwriter
1915 Ingrid Bergman, actress
1938 Eliott Gould, actor
1939 Joel Schumacher, film director
1941 Robin Leach, television host
1958 Michael Jackson, singer
1958 Lenny Henry, comedian
1962 Rebecca De Mornay, actress

Deaths
1982 Ingrid Bergman, actress
1987 Lee Marvin, actor

DAY TO REMEMBER

Religious day St. John the Baptist's Day It is believed that St. John's demise began when he attacked King Herod as incestuous for marrying Herodias, wife of his half-brother. After a performance by Salome, Herodias' daughter, the King was so impressed that he told the girl he would grant any wish she made. At her mother's request, Salome asked for the head of John the Baptist.

Hurricane Katrina strikes

Hurricane Katrina hit the American coastline on August 29, 2005, at 6:10 A.M., bringing winds of up to 155 miles per hour (250 km/h). By the time it had dissipated two days later, the hurricane had killed more than 1,600 people, with 1,840 missing, and caused more than $75 billion worth of damage. It was the costliest and one of the deadliest hurricanes in American history. Worst hit was the state of Louisiana, and in particular the city of New Orleans, where almost 1,300 people died. In comparison, the next-hardest hit was the state of Mississippi, where 238 died.

Faced with the threat of a category-five hurricane – the strongest possible – New Orleans mayor Ray Nagin had ordered a mandatory evacuation of the city on August 28 at 9:30 A.M. He knew the coastal city, of which more than three quarters lays below sea level, faced certain disaster. Those unable to leave, mostly the city's African Americans, were sheltered in refuges of last resort and given food and water. More than 26,000 rode out the storm in the 77,000-seat Louisiana Superdome. When the storm did strike, it caused massive flooding around the city. Around 80 percent of New Orleans was flooded, with some parts under 20 feet (6 m) of water. On August 30, widespread looting was reported in the city – mainly consisting of residents taking food from supermarkets. On August 31, police were ordered to abandon search and rescue operations and focus on stopping the looting.

U.S. President George W. Bush was criticized in the aftermath of the hurricane for taking too long to organize relief efforts after the disaster.

August 30

In 1990, after 23 years of Indonesian occupation, the people of East Timor voted for independence in a UN-supported referendum. In retaliation, anti-independence militia, supported by the Indonesian military, went on a rampage, killing 1,400 people and pushing 300,000 into the Indonesian-controlled West Timor. The carnage didn't end until the arrival of a multi-national peacekeeping force, led by Australia, in September. On May 20, 2002, the international community officially recognised East Timor as an independent state, and independence leader Xanana Gusmao became the country's first elected President.

"Money doesn't talk, it swears." — BOB DYLAN

HISTORICAL EVENTS

1918 Vladimir Lenin survives an attempt on his life by Fanya Kaplan, and in retaliation begins the ideological cleansing known as the Red Terror. Kaplan is captured and sentenced to life at the Katorga prison camp in Siberia.

1945 British troops liberate Hong Kong from Japan. The Japanese occupation had lasted almost four years, during which time many residents of Hong Kong were executed.

1965 Bob Dylan releases his *Highway 61 Revisited* album.

1984 The space shuttle *Discovery* STS-41-D is launched. The craft makes 97 orbits of the Earth, traveling 2.21 million miles (3.6 million km). It takes 6 days and 56 minutes to complete the mission, most of which is recorded with the onboard IMAX camera.

1992 Germany's Michael Schumacher wins his first Formual 1 race at the Belgian Grand Prix.

1995 NATO launches a sustained airstrike campaign, called Operation Deliberate Force, against Bosnian Serb forces.

1999 The people of East Timor vote for independence from Indonesia (see below).

2001 Former Yugoslav President Slobodan Milosevic is informed that he will be charged with genocide at the International War Crimes Tribunal in The Hague.

DAYS TO REMEMBER

Religious day St. Rose of Lima's Day The patron saint of Latin America and the Philippines, St. Rose (1586–1617) was said to be very beautiful. Afraid that her beauty might become a temptation to others, she rubbed her face with pepper until it was red and blistered.

International day Day of the Disappeared This day commemorates and raises awareness of those people who have been taken into custody by state agents in various countries, yet whose whereabouts are denied and concealed by those agents.

Births
- 1797 Mary Wollstonecraft Shelley, author
- 1919 Kitty Wells, singer
- 1922 Lionel Murphy, judge
- 1935 John Phillips, singer
- 1972 Cameron Diaz, actress
- 1982 Andy Roddick, tennis player

Deaths
- 1938 Max Factor, cosmetics entrepreneur
- 1961 Charles Coburn, actor
- 1995 Sterling Morrison, musician
- 2003 Charles Bronson, actor

DATEline

August 31

"The biggest disease this day and age is that of people feeling unloved." — PRINCESS DIANA

HISTORICAL EVENTS

1888 London serial killer Jack the Ripper murders his first victim, Mary Ann "Polly" Nichols.

1994 After 25 years of fighting to force the British out of Northern Ireland, the IRA announces a ceasefire and its willingness to enter into peace talks.

1997 Diana, Princess of Wales, dies in a car crash in Paris (see right).

1999 One person is killed and 40 injured in Moscow in the first of the Russian Apartment Bombings. Over two months, almost 300 people are killed in a series of similar bombings the authorities blame on Chechen terrorists.

2004 Mel Gibson's film *The Passion of the Christ* sells about 4.1 million copies in the U.S. on the first day it is released on DVD and video.

2005 More than 1,000 Shiite Muslims on their way to a holy shrine in Baghdad, Iraq, are killed in a stampede. Rumors that there were suicide bombers among them started the panic.

DAYS TO REMEMBER

National day Independence Day (Kyrgyzstan) On this day in 1991, Kyrgyzstan gained its independence from the U.S.S.R.

National day Independence Day (Trinidad and Tobago) In 1962, Trinidad and Tobago gained independence from Britain on this day.

National day Independence Day (Malaysia) Malaysia also gained independence from the U.K. on this day in 1957.

Death of a princess

On August 31, 1997, people across the world learned that Princess Diana had died as the result of a car crash in Paris, France. Diana and her partner, Harrods heir Dodi Al-Fayed, had dined at the Hotel Ritz that night and attempted to avoid the waiting paparazzi by leaving in a different car to the one in which they'd arrived. However, the ruse was spotted as they fled in the black Mercedes S600.

Shortly after midnight, they entered the underpass below the Place de l'Alma with nine photographers on motorbikes in hot pursuit. Their vehicle struck the right-hand wall of the underpass, bounced across the left-hand lane, hit a pillar supporting the roof, and then spun to a stop. Diana and Dodi hadn't been wearing seatbelts and their driver had been drinking. The paparazzi continued to take photos of the car and its dead and injured occupants after the crash.

The driver, Henri Paul, and Al-Fayed were pronounced dead at the scene. It took emergency crews an hour to free Diana, who was still alive. She was taken to Pitie-Salpetriere Hospital, but was pronounced dead two hours later. Only bodyguard Trevor Rees-Jones survived the crash.

Investigators ruled the accident was the result of an intoxicated driver attempting to evade photographers at high speed. Diana's funeral was held at Westminster Abbey in London, England, on September 6. An estimated three million mourners lined the road from the abbey to her Kensington Palace home, where she was buried.

Births
- **1811** Théophile Gautier, poet
- **1870** Maria Montessori, Italian educator
- **1928** James Coburn, actor
- **1949** Richard Gere, actor
- **1958** Edwin Moses, athlete
- **1972** Chris Tucker, actor
- **1977** Craig Nicholls, singer

Deaths
- **1920** Wilhelm Wundt, psychologist
- **1969** Rocky Marciano, boxer
- **1986** Henry Moore, sculptor
- **1997** Diana, Princess of Wales
- **1997** Dodi Al-Fayed, Egyptian-born film producer

DAYS TO REMEMBER *August*

1 Parent's Day (Democratic Republic of the Congo) Held to mark deceased ancestors, people visit cemeteries on this day to tidy and decorate family graves

2 Our Lady of the Angels Day Our Lady, Queen of the Angels, is the patron of Costa Rica

3 St. Trea's Day After her conversion to Christianity by St. Patrick, Trea lived out the rest of her life as a recluse in Derry, Ireland, during the fifth century

4 Constitution Day (Cook Islands) This day marks the day when the islands became a self-governing territory of New Zealand

5 St. Afra's Day A reformed prostitute in Augsburg, Germany, during the reign of the Roman Emperor Diocletanius, who outlawed Christianity

8 Blessed Mary MacKillop's Day The first Australian to be beatified. Founded the Sisters of St. Joseph of the Sacred Heart, dedicated to education of the poor

9 Day of the World's Indigenous People Honors the contributions made by the world's indigenous peoples

10 Independence Day (Ecuador) Celebrated on this day because the independence movement began on August 10, 1809

11 St. Clare's Day Founded the order of nuns called the Poor Clares. The patron saint of people with sore eyes

12 International Youth Day Celebrated as an opportunity to focus on the needs of people aged between 10 and 24, and to promote intergenerational solidarity

15 The Assumption of Mary Catholics recognize this as the day the Blessed Virgin Mary was assumed body and soul into heaven

16 St. Stephen's Day The patron saint of Hungary, recognized as the first Christian king of the country

17 Caspar and Mary Vaz's Day This Franciscan husband and wife were martyred in Japan. Caspar was burned alive and Mary was beheaded in the city of Nagasaki

18 St. Jane's Day Jane founded the Visitation Order for the sick and poor women the other orders would turn away

19 Independence Day (Afghanistan) In 1919 Afghanistan gained independence from the United Kingdom

22 St. John Kemble's Day One of the 40 Martyrs of England, a Catholic priest living around the time of the English Reformation

23 Day of Remembrance of the Slave Trade In 1791 African slaves on the island of Santo Domingo (now Haiti and the Dominican Republic) rose up against their captors

24 The first day of the star sign Virgo

25 St. Louis' Day The patron saint of tertiary orders

26 Women's Equality Day (U.S.) Women were given the right to vote in the U.S. on this day in 1920

29 St. John the Baptist's Day It is believed that St. John's downfall began when he attacked King Herod as incestuous for marrying Herodias, wife of his half-brother

30 Day of the Disappeared Commemorates and raises awareness of those people who have been taken into custody in various countries, yet whose whereabouts are denied and concealed

31 Independence Day (Kyrgyzstan) On this day in 1991, Kyrgyzstan gained its independence from the U.S.S.R.

6

Scouts Anniversary Day Celebrates the day Baden-Powell began the scouting movement

7

St. Donatus' Day A monk, honored for founding St. Paul's Abbey

13

International Left-handers Day Increases awareness of the challenges faced by left-handers living among a right-handed majority

14

St. Maximilian's Day Maximilian was sent to Auschwitz. He offered his life in place of a young husband and father who had been targeted for a reprisal execution

20

St. Bernard of Clairvaux's Day The patron saint of farm and agriculture workers

21

Leon Trotsky, Russian revolutionary, died in 1940

27

St. Monica of Hippo's Day The patron saint of wives and abuse victims

28

St. Augustine's Day St. Augustine is the patron saint of brewers because of his early life of vice

Top right Women's Equality Day, U.S., August 26
Right Scouts Anniversary Day, August 6

SEPTEMBER

"*September – it was the most beautiful of words, he'd always felt, evoking orange-flowers, swallows, and regret.*" ALEXANDER THEROUX

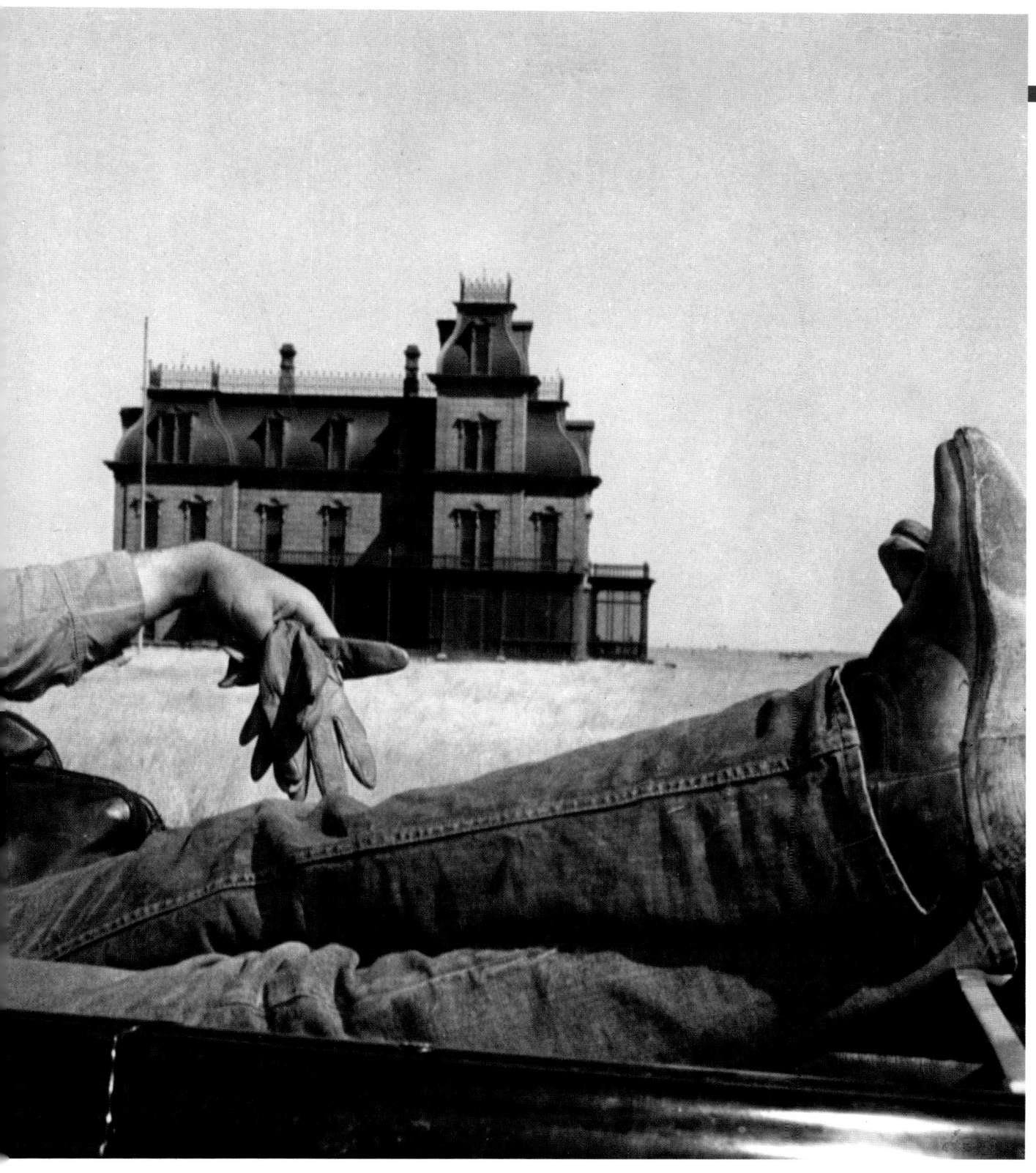

James Dean – the archetypal pop martyr – died on the last day of September in 1955. He is pictured here in the posthumously released *Giant*.

September

Libra star sign and scene of treading grapes from *Calendar and Book of Hours*, from fifteenth-century France. September begins in the sign of Virgo and ends in the sign of Libra.

SPECIAL DATES

In Australia, Father's Day is celebrated on the first Sunday in September.

Labor Day, which has honored working people since the 1800s, falls on the first Monday in September.

Grandparents' Day falls on the first Sunday after Labor Day in the U.S.

Right Niccolo Frangipane's sixteenth-century *Allegory of Autumn* depicts Bacchus surrounded by an abundance of fruits of the season. September is the time of the autumn equinox in the Northern Hemisphere.

September, the ninth month in the Gregorian calendar, marks the beginning of autumn in the Northern Hemisphere. The days begin to grow shorter and the weather cooler, and the leaves turn a myriad of colors as they fall from the trees. In the Southern Hemisphere it is the beginning of spring. September is also the start of the civil year in the Jewish calendar, and marks the first day of the school year in many countries in the Northern Hemisphere.

THE ANCIENT ROMANS named September after the Latin word *septem*, meaning seven, as it was the seventh month of the year until around 45 B.C.E., when the Julian calendar reformed their timekeeping and set January 1 as the first day of the year.

September is one of only four months that consists of 30 days, while seven have 31, and every year it begins on the same day of the week as December does.

Around the world, the most significant event in September is the equinox, which occurs around September 21–23 and marks the turning of the seasons. On this date the Sun is above the equator and casts equal light into both hemispheres, so day and night are of equal length. In the Northern Hemisphere it is the autumnal equinox; from this point forward the days will get shorter and the nights longer as the Earth turns towards winter. The weather becomes cooler and things in nature slow down, turn inward, begin to wither, or to hibernate. The leaves of the trees turn red, gold, and brown and start to fall – hence the American reference to the season as "fall" – and farmers and people of the land commence the harvest.

In the U.K., harvest festivals have taken place around the autumn equinox since ancient times as a way to give thanks for a successful crop and celebrate the abundance of the village. Corn dollies were made from the last sheaf of wheat, corn, or other grain to be harvested, and kept inside throughout the winter to house the spirit of the grain. In spring the dollies would then be

returned to the earth and plowed into the newly prepared fields to begin the cycle of growth and rebirth again. Modern Pagans continue this tradition and still celebrate the autumn equinox, or *Mabon*, as the festival of harvest and thanksgiving. Churches in England have also marked this day since the 1800s, when they started decorating the church with fresh local produce, singing hymns of thanksgiving, and bringing in food to be distributed to the poor.

In the Southern Hemisphere, September 21 marks the spring, or vernal, equinox, and from this day forward the days start to lengthen as the wheel of the year turns toward summer. People celebrate regrowth and renewal, both physically and metaphorically – flowers begin to bloom, leaves grow on the trees, animals are born, and life begins anew. It is time to "spring clean" one's house and one's life, to let go of all that is no longer needed and to move forward toward the future one dreams of.

September around the world

In Japan, the autumn equinox and the three days preceding and following it are called *higan*, or the "other side of the river of death." This is a week-long period of commemorating ancestors, and is marked by visits to the graves of family members, offerings of flowers and food, and the burning of incense.

The Harvest Moon – the full moon closest to the autumn equinox – also usually occurs in September, although it sometimes falls in October. It rises within half an hour of the Sun setting, and is the fullest, brightest, most golden moon of the year. Because of its closeness to the horizon it also appears to be bigger than any other full moon. In ancient times it was vital to farmers who had to work all night to get the harvest in, and were able to do this because of the golden light provided by the Harvest Moon.

In China the Harvest Moon marks the Mid-Autumn or Mooncake Festival, which falls on the fifteenth day of the eighth month of the Chinese calendar, usually around mid or late September in Gregorian terms. It marks the end of the first harvest, and is celebrated with feasting, festivities, fire-dragon dancing, lanterns, gazing at the Moon, and mooncakes. These delicacies consist of a thin pastry layer surrounding a sweeter filling inside. They are often embossed with the Chinese characters for longevity or harmony, or decorated with pictures of the

Moon, flowers, vines, or other harvest images. Stories are also told about the moon fairy who lives in a crystal palace and dances on the surface of the Moon, because in China legend tells of the woman in the Moon, as opposed to the Western version of the man in the Moon.

In Japan, folk tales tell of two rabbits who inhabit the Moon and pound on rice cakes. On the night of the September full moon, people there celebrate *Otsukimi*, or "moon viewing." Tables are set with small rice cakes, fruit, and vegetables in order to give thanks for the harvest of the year.

In Vietnam, *Tet Trung Thu* also occurs on the September full moon. It is an autumn celebration during which children parade through the streets with lanterns, moon cakes are made, and celebrations are held. It honors children and gives parents a chance to take time off and spend it with them after the hard work of bringing in the harvest.

In the Southern Hemisphere September marks the Storm Moon, the full moon nearest the spring

In the north, September has been seen for centuries as a time for gathering the harvest before winter sets in. Guiseppe Arcimboldo's *L'Autunno* from 1753 symbolizes the fruitful activity that autumn encourages. This painting is housed in the Musée du Louvre in Paris.

September birthflower

The aster is September's birthflower. It is a pink, purpley-blue, or white daisy-like flower that is linked to the goddess Venus. Its name comes from the Greek word for "star," and it symbolizes love and elegance. It also represents regret, hence its placement on the graves of soldiers in France. In ancient times, people thought that burning the leaves of the plant would drive away snakes.

equinox, which is also known as Seed Moon, or the Moon of Winds, and the Crow Moon.

The Jewish festival of *Rosh Hashana*, or New Year's Day, also usually falls in September. It is the beginning of the civil year and the start of a new year in the Jewish calendar. It is held on the first day of the month of *Tishri*, which can fall on any Gregorian date from September 5 to October 5. Because of the composition of the Jewish calendar, this will never be a Wednesday, Friday, or Sunday. It is known as the Day of Judgment, the Day of Remembrance, and the Day of the Blowing of the Shofar, named after the tradition of blowing the *shofar*, a trumpet made from a ram's horn. Prayers are also said and special foods are eaten.

In Ethiopia, New Year's Day also falls in September. *Enkutatash* is celebrated on the first day of the month of *Meskerem*, which is September 11 in Gregorian terms, or September 10 in leap years.

In Japan, *Keiro no Hi*, or Respect for the Aged Day, is held on the third Monday of September. It honors the elderly for their long contribution to society. Prayers for their health and longevity are said, people spend time with their elderly relatives or visit senior citizens' homes, and welfare issues are especially considered.

In Venice, Italy, the *Regata Storica*, or Historical Regatta, is held on the first Sunday of September. It is a celebration first begun in the fourteenth century to mark the glory of the republic of Venice, and today consists of a colorful pageant made up of people in traditional costumes floating down the scenic Grand Canal, followed by rowing contests, or regattas.

In the Netherlands, *Prinsjesdag*, or Princes Day, falls on the third Tuesday of September. The queen, or ruling monarch, addresses a joint sitting of the Senate and Lower House of Parliament, outlining policy plans for the year, and the annual budget is presented. Until recently it also marked the opening of Parliament. It is a day rich with ceremony and history, with the queen riding to the Parliament in a horsedrawn gold coach.

Strangely, part of Germany's Oktoberfest takes place during September. Munich's now internationally acclaimed beer festival usually starts on the third Friday of September, and ends 16 days later on the first Sunday in October.

In the South African province of KwaZulu–Natal, which is home to the Zulu monarchy, the hero King Shaka is commemorated on the last Sunday of September. In the early 1800s he transformed the small Zulu tribe into a nation, and was a tireless and powerful leader – until he was murdered on September 22, 1828. Partly due to stories of his exploits being sensationalized in Western cinema and culture, his legend lives on.

> **September birthstone**
>
> The sapphire, a precious gemstone most commonly green or blue, is September's birthstone. It is known as the wisdom stone, and represents truth, calmness, and repentance. It is said to strengthen intuition and encourage deep thought while protecting against negativity. Physically it is believed to calm overactive systems of the body.

Top left In cities such as Beijing in China, chefs band together to make giant mooncakes as part of their Mooncake Festival celebrations, which fall around Harvest Moon time. This creation is embossed with harvest images and Chinese characters.

Far left The first Sunday of September sees boats and barges decked out with costumed competitors, taking to Venice's Grand Canal in *Regata Storica*, a boating contest held in the city since the fourteenth century.

Left On Princes Day in the Netherlands, held on the third Tuesday in September and seen here in 2002, the Dutch royal family give a friendly wave from the balcony of Palace Noordiende in the Hague.

September 1

The first day of autumn in the Northern Hemisphere, and the first day of spring in the Southern Hemisphere

> "Waves of anger and fear circulate over the bright and darkened lands of the earth … The unmentionable odor of death offends the September night."
> FROM W.H. AUDEN'S POEM OF SEPTEMBER 1, 1939, ABOUT THE OUTBREAK OF WAR

HISTORICAL EVENTS

1804 Juno, one of the largest main-belt asteroids, is discovered by German astronomer Karl Ludwig Harding. In his career he also discovers three comets and catalogs 120,000 stars. A crater on the Moon is named after him.

1897 Trolley-car gridlock and street congestion leads to the creation of the first underground metro in the U.S., the Boston Subway in Massachusetts, which is patterned on the Budapest Subway and Paris Metro.

1923 The Great Kanto Earthquake of Japan devastates Tokyo and Yokohama, killing more than 140,000 people. Shocks of 8.4 on the Richter scale hit just before lunchtime, knocking over cooking fires, which led to blazes that raged for three days.

1939 Nazi Germany attacks Poland, beginning World War II (see below).

1951 ANZUS, the Australia, New Zealand, United States Security Treaty, is signed by the three countries. It is a mutual military alliance that binds them to cooperate on defense matters.

1969 A bloodless coup in Libya brings Colonel Muammar Qaddafi to power, ousting King Idris I. Military officers seize power and declare the country a republic. This day is now celebrated as Revolution Day in Libya.

1983 A Korean Airlines Boeing 747 flying from the U.S. to Seoul is shot down and all 269 people on board are killed. The next day, the U.S.S.R. admits to shooting down the aircraft after it entered Soviet airspace.

1991 Uzbekistan, in central Asia north of Afghanistan, declares its independence from the Soviet Union. It is now a republic with authoritarian presidential rule.

2004 More than 1,100 people, mostly children, are taken hostage by Chechen militants at a school in Beslan in southern Russia, the beginning of a three-day siege that ends with the death of 344 people.

Births
- 1653 Johann Pachelbel, composer
- 1875 Edgar Rice Burroughs, U.S. author
- 1923 Rocky Marciano, boxer
- 1939 Lily Tomlin, actress
- 1946 Barry Gibb, singer (Bee Gees)
- 1950 Dr. Phil McGraw, TV host
- 1957 Gloria Estefan, singer
- 1976 Erik Morales, boxer

Deaths
- 1159 Pope Adrian IV
- 1557 Jacques Cartier, explorer
- 1600 Tadéůs Hájek, astronomer
- 1715 King Louis XIV of France
- 1977 Ethel Waters, entertainer
- 2003 Sir Terry Frost, artist

DAY TO REMEMBER

Religious day St. Giles' Day Born in Greece to wealthy parents, St. Giles (640–720) used his money to help the poor, and moved to France to live as a hermit. In medieval art he is depicted with a deer, which was sent to nourish him, and an arrow, which pierced his leg and crippled him. He is the patron saint of cripples and the poor.

On September 1, 1939, Nazi Germany attacked Poland, beginning World War II. The German battleship *Schleswig-Holstein* is pictured, left, bombarding the Polish coast at Westerplatte. German troops also broke down the turnpike at the German–Polish border, beginning their invasion of Poland. Within two days the U.K. and France had declared war on Hitler's Germany. Japan and Italy joined Germany, battling the British Empire, France, and others. In 1941 the U.S., attacked by Japan, joined the Allies. The conflict raged until 1945, spreading throughout the world and changing the course of history.

DATE*line*

September 2

"It needs but one foe to breed a war, and those who have not swords can still die upon them."

J. R. R. TOLKIEN, AUTHOR OF *THE LORD OF THE RINGS*

On September 2, 1995, the Rock and Roll Hall of Fame and Museum opened in Cleveland, Ohio, to document the history of music by acknowledging the talents of influential songwriters, performers, producers, and even journalists. The museum boasts artifacts from the world's top performers, such as instruments, handwritten lyrics, recordings, and stage props. Over the years, stars such as U2 (pictured), Black Sabbath, Elvis Presley, Blondie, Chuck Berry, and *Rolling Stone* magazine publisher Jann Wenner have been inducted.

Celtic tree sign
VINE
September 2–September 29

Vine people are open, forgiving, emotional, and sensual, with a great enthusiasm for life and love. They are great organizers and inspire harmony and stability between friends and family, although they can have a tendency to become dependent on others. People often underestimate their skills.

HISTORICAL EVENTS

- **1666** The Great Fire of London breaks out and burns for three days, destroying 10,000 buildings including St. Paul's Cathedral. Only six deaths are reported, although many more are suspected.
- **1901** Theodore Roosevelt, then Vice-President of the U.S., utters the phrase: "Speak softly and carry a big stick," describing his idea of diplomatic negotiations backed with the threat of military force. This becomes known as "big stick" diplomacy.
- **1945** Japanese officials sign the act of unconditional surrender aboard the battleship USS *Missouri* in Tokyo Bay, bringing the six years of World War II to an end. While Germany surrendered in early May, other countries kept fighting.
- **1945** Vietnamese leader Ho Chi Minh declares Vietnam an independent republic no longer under French rule. Half a million people gather in Hanoi as he reads the Vietnamese Declaration of Independence.
- **1991** The U.S. recognizes the independence of the Baltic states Estonia, Latvia, and Lithuania. Four days later the Soviet Union recognizes their independence too.
- **1995** The Rock and Roll Hall of Fame opens in Cleveland, Ohio, to document the history of music (see above).

Births
- **1838** Queen Liliuokalani, last monarch of Hawaii
- **1853** Wilhelm Ostwald, chemist and Nobel laureate
- **1877** Frederick Soddy, chemist and Nobel laureate
- **1923** René Thom, mathematician
- **1948** Christa McAuliffe, teacher and astronaut
- **1964** Keanu Reeves, actor
- **1966** Salma Hayek, actress

Deaths
- **421** Constantius III, Roman Emperor
- **1910** Henri Rousseau, painter
- **1973** J. R. R. Tolkien, writer

September 3

"Time sometimes flies like a bird, sometimes crawls like a snail; but a man is happiest when he does not even notice whether it passes swiftly or slowly." — IVAN TURGENEV, AUTHOR

Births
- 1568 Adriano Banchieri, composer
- 1695 Pietro Locatelli, composer
- 1875 Ferdinand Porsche, car engineer
- 1899 Frank Macfarlane Burnet, biologist and Nobel laureate
- 1938 Ryoji Noyori, chemist and Nobel laureate
- 1955 Steve Jones, musician (The Sex Pistols)
- 1965 Charlie Sheen, actor

Deaths
- 1658 Oliver Cromwell, ruler of England
- 1883 Ivan Turgenev, author
- 1962 e. e. cummings, poet
- 1969 Ho Chi Minh, Vietnamese President
- 1991 Frank Capra, film director

HISTORICAL EVENTS

- **1609** English explorer Henry Hudson, sailing for the Dutch Kingdom, discovers the island of Manhattan. The Dutch later claim the area and set up the colony of New Amsterdam (now New York).
- **1783** The American War of Independence ends after eight years of fighting with the signing of the Treaty of Paris by the U.S., Spain, France, and Great Britain, and American independence is finally recognized by the British.
- **1895** After a 25-year transformation from English rugby, the first professional American football game is played, in Latrobe, Pennsylvania. John Brallier, the first player to turn pro, accepts $10 and expenses to play for the Latrobe YMCA. His team wins 12–0.
- **1937** A young Orson Welles directs and stars in *Les Miserables*, the first radio play produced by his Mercury Theater group in New York.
- **1984** The worst typhoon in memory sweeps across the southern Philippines, with wind speeds of up to 115 miles per hour (185 km/h). More than 4,300 people die, hundreds more are injured and one million people are left homeless by Typhoon Ike.
- **2004** Shooting breaks out on the third and final day of the Beslan school massacre (see left).

DAY TO REMEMBER

Religious day St. Gregory's Day The Roman-born son of a senator, St. Gregory I (540–604) was well educated and became Prefect of the city for a year. Then in a shock move he sold all his possessions to build monasteries. He was elected Pope on September 3, 590.

Beslan school massacre

On this day in 2004, the Beslan school massacre came to a bloody end. The terrifying siege began two days earlier, when heavily armed Chechen militants took more than 1,100 people hostage at a school in Beslan, Russia. The masked men and women opened fire on the students, who were at an assembly to mark the first day of the school year.

While captured the victims, most of them children, were forced to strip to their underwear and drink their own urine due to a water shortage. Reports claimed that the hostage-takers had demanded the release of Chechen fighters captured in a nearby region.

Soldiers and security forces waited outside the burning school as corpses piled up inside, but on the third day they negotiated to go in and take out the dead. This turned out to be a trap. The attackers opened fire, and naked and screaming children were shot in the back as they tried to flee. Others died inside when a suicide bomber blew herself up in the gym. Special forces ran in, and bombs and mines added to the confusion.

In the end, 344 people were listed as dead, many of them children, and almost 200 more remained missing, with several of the bodies burnt beyond recognition. Most of the attackers were killed – the only one captured was charged with nine charges of murder and terrorism. While it was clearly an act of terrorism, Russian security forces were also criticized for not acting quickly enough or securing the area properly.

DATEline

September 4

"Truth has no special time of its own. Its hour is now — always." — ALBERT SCHWEITZER

HISTORICAL EVENTS

476 The Western Roman Empire falls when Romulus Augustus, the last Emperor, is forced to abdicate by eastern rival Odoacer, who proclaims himself King of Italy. He in turn is later murdered by Theodoric the Great, the real king.

1781 The city of Los Angeles in California is founded as El Pueblo de Nuestra Señora La Reina de los Ángeles de Porciúncula – the City of Our Lady, the Queen of the Angels of the Little Portion – by a group of 44 Spanish settlers.

1886 In the U.S., the wars waged by white settlers against Native Americans almost come to an end with the surrender of Apache leader and shaman Geronimo in Arizona. He dies as a prisoner of war.

1888 George Eastman receives a patent for a camera that uses roll film and registers the trademark Kodak. Before that cameras were the size of a microwave oven and needed chemicals, glass plates, and tanks to take a photo.

1951 The first live transcontinental television broadcast, of President Harry Truman's address, takes place in San Francisco, California, from the Japanese Peace Treaty Conference.

1972 U.S. swimmer Mark Spitz wins his seventh gold medal at the 1972 Olympics in Munich, Germany (see below).

1978 Monsoonal floods devastate northern India, killing more than 1,000 people, destroying the holy city of Benares and making two million people homeless. Some areas are 18 feet (5.5 m) under water.

1985 Three days after a joint American–French expedition locates the wreck of the *Titanic*, 560 miles (900 km) off Newfoundland off the coast of Canada, the first film of the ruined ship is released.

Births
- **1768** François René de Chateaubriand, author
- **1824** Anton Bruckner, composer
- **1892** Darius Milhaud, composer
- **1928** Dick York, actor
- **1937** Dawn Fraser, swimmer
- **1969** Noah Taylor, actor
- **1981** Beyoncé Knowles, singer

Deaths
- **1784** Cesar-François Cassini de Thury, astronomer
- **1907** Edvard Grieg, composer
- **1965** Albert Schweitzer, physician, musician, and Nobel laureate
- **1989** Georges Simenon, author
- **2003** Tibor Varga, violinist

DAY TO REMEMBER

Religious day St. Rose of Viterbo's Day
A virgin saint born in Viterbo, Italy, Rose (1235–1252) is said to have brought her aunt back to life when she was just three, and performed many miracles. She preached penance and had the power of prophecy, and she is the patron saint of exiled peoples.

Californian swimmer Mark Spitz became the golden boy of the pool when he won seven gold medals at the 1972 Olympics in Munich – and broke the world record with each one. No athlete has even come close to equaling his feats in the pool. Having achieved all his goals at the age of 22, he retired after the Games and made forays into television acting, but lacked the charisma to make it in the entertainment world. He attempted a swimming comeback 20 years later, but failed to qualify for the U.S. team going to Barcelona in 1992.

September 5

"Do not wait for leaders; do it alone, person to person." — MOTHER TERESA

HISTORICAL EVENTS

1698 After a trip to western Europe, Tsar Peter I of Russia imposes a tax on beards, in order to move away from Asiatic customs. He cuts the beards off his guests himself.

1901 The National Association of Professional Baseball Leagues (now Minor League Baseball) is formed in Chicago, Illinois, and changes the face of baseball, which has been played in the U.S. since at least 1790.

1960 In the first Olympic Games televised in the U.S., boxer Cassius Clay, 18, wins the gold medal in Rome. He is so proud he wears it for two days. He will later change his name to Muhammad Ali and become one of the most legendary boxers of all time.

1972 A Palestinian terrorist group attacks Israeli athletes at the Munich Olympic Games. Two are shot dead and nine taken hostage, but after a bungled rescue mission the remaining nine are killed, along with a policeman and five of the terrorists.

1984 The space shuttle *Discovery* lands after its maiden voyage. Dr. Judith Resnik, the second American woman in space, is on board. Two years later she dies, along with Christa MacAuliffe, when *Challenger* explodes on take-off.

1984 Western Australia becomes the last Australian state to abolish capital punishment.

1992 Pop star Prince signs a $100 million contract, becoming the highest-paid recording artist in history (see right).

2003 An accident at Disneyland, California, claims the life of Marcelo Torres, aged 22. He is on the Big Thunder Mountain Railroad when the coupler between the engine and the first car snaps and strikes him in the chest. Ten others are injured.

DAY TO REMEMBER

Religious day Mother Teresa's Day Born in Albania, Agnes Gonxhe Bojaxhiu (1910–1997) was the embodiment of a living saint, working in the slums of Calcutta, India, amidst poverty and disease. She won the Nobel Peace Prize in 1979, and six years after her death she was beatified by Pope John Paul II.

Births
- **1187** King Louis VIII of France
- **1638** King Louis XIV of France
- **1735** Johann Christian Bach, composer
- **1847** Jesse James, outlaw
- **1929** Bob Newhart, comedian
- **1940** Raquel Welch, actress
- **1946** Freddie Mercury, pop star (Queen)
- **1951** Michael Keaton, actor
- **1973** Rose McGowan, actress

Deaths
- **1629** Domenico Allegri, composer
- **1803** François Devienne, composer
- **1877** Crazy Horse, Sioux chief
- **1992** Fritz Leiber, author
- **1997** Mother Teresa, missionary

Multi-million-dollar pop star

On September 5, 1992, ground-breaking pop and soul singer Prince, famous for hits including "Purple Rain," "Little Red Corvette," and "1999," became the highest-paid musical artist in the world. He signed a $100 million six-album contract with Warner Bros., making him the highest-paid pop artist in the U.S., and was appointed a Vice-President of A&R for the label.

He had long been breaking records though. Prince was one of the first black performers on MTV. He plays 27 instruments, writes, records, and produces all of his music, as well as writing and producing other artists and running a record label. He starred in a movie, *Purple Rain*, and the soundtrack topped the charts for six months, won two Grammys and sold more than 10 million copies, and its lead song "When Doves Cry" was the highest-selling song of 1984. But although Prince had been with Warner since 1978, less than a year after he signed his multi-million-dollar deal he declared he was restricted by the company and being treated unfairly. In an attempt to get out of the contract, he changed his name to an unpronounceable symbol, known as the love symbol, which led to people referring to him as The Artist Formerly Known As Prince. He also wrote "Slave" on his face whenever he went out in public. When his contract finally expired, he released an album called *Emancipation*; a few years later, when his publishing contract expired, he changed his name back to Prince. Today the man once considered the foremost artist of his generation is still making hit records and touring the world to sell-out crowds.

September 6

"Diana was the very essence of compassion, of duty, of style, of beauty. All over the world she was a symbol of selfless humanity, a standard bearer for the rights of the truly downtrodden."
EARL CHARLES SPENCER, PRINCESS DIANA'S BROTHER, AT HER FUNERAL

The Tasmanian tiger, or *Thylacinus cynocephalus*, was a large carnivorous marsupial native to Australia. But on September 6, 1936, it became extinct when the last surviving animal, Benjamin, died in a zoo in Hobart, Tasmania. While it looked like a tiger, with dark brown stripes down its side and an enormous mouth with canine-sized teeth, it had more in common with kangaroos and koalas, with the female carrying her young in a pouch.

To this day people claim they have seen a Tasmanian tiger in the wild, but no one has ever been able to prove it.

HISTORICAL EVENTS

1620 The Pilgrims, a group of Puritans seeking religious freedom, sail from Plymouth, England, on the *Mayflower* to settle in North America.
1776 A powerful hurricane hits Guadeloupe, in the eastern Caribbean, killing more than 6,000 people. It hit nearby Martinique the day before. This area has a huge hurricane risk.
1870 Louisa Ann Swain of Laramie, Wyoming, is recorded as the first woman in the U.S. to cast a vote.
1936 The last surviving member of the thylacine species, the Tasmanian tiger Benjamin, dies alone in his cage at Hobart Zoo in Australia (see above).
1965 Indian troops invade West Pakistan, claiming Pakistan had launched a covert operation over the ceasefire line agreed to in 1949. After three weeks of fighting both sides agree to a UN-sponsored ceasefire.
1966 Prime Minister Hendrik Verwoerd, the white supremacist who introduced apartheid to South Africa, is stabbed to death by a parliamentary clerk during a Government meeting.
1970 Jimi Hendrix plays what turns out to be his last gig, at the Love and Peace Festival on the Isle of Fehmarn, Germany.
1997 A million people line the route and more than 2.5 billion watch the funeral of Princess Diana at Westminster Abbey. The handwritten note "Mummy" on her coffin reminds everyone that beyond the international celebrity, she was also the mother of two young boys.
2005 The California Legislature is the first in the U.S. to legalize same-sex marriage. Three weeks later Governor Arnold Schwarzenegger vetoes the bill.

Births
1766 John Dalton, chemist and physicist
1892 Sir Edward Appleton, physicist and Nobel laureate
1943 Richard J. Roberts, biochemist and Nobel laureate
1944 Swoosie Kurtz, actress
1964 Rosie Perez, actress
1970 Paul Miller, composer
1973 Greg Rusedski, tennis player
1974 Tim Henman, tennis player

Deaths
972 Pope John XIII
1635 Metius, mathematician and astronomer
1902 Frederick Augustus Abel, chemist
1962 Hanns Eisler, composer
1998 Akira Kurosawa, film director

DAY TO REMEMBER

National day Independence Day (Swaziland) The landlocked country in southern Africa declared its independence from the U.K. on this day in 1968. It is an independent member of the Commonwealth, officially known as the Kingdom of Swaziland.

September 7

"There's nothing on it worthwhile, and we're not going to watch it in this household. I don't want it in your intellectual diet." — PHILO TAYLOR FARNSWORTH, THE INVENTOR OF TV

HISTORICAL EVENTS

1927 The first fully electronic television system is achieved by Utah, U.S., inventor Philo Taylor Farnsworth. He was 21 at the time, but came up with the idea at 14.

1970 An anti-war rally is held at Valley Forge, Pennsylvania, attended by actress Jane Fonda, actor Donald Sutherland, and political aspirant John Kerry (see below).

1979 The Entertainment and Sports Programming Network (ESPN) makes its debut as a 24-hour-a-day cable television sports station that broadcasts everything from football and the Olympics to tractor-pulling contests.

1986 Desmond Tutu becomes the first black South African to lead the Anglican Church in his country when he is appointed Archbishop of Cape Town.

1996 In Las Vegas, Nevada, American rapper Tupac Shakur is shot four times, allegedly by a gang of rival rappers. He dies six days later at just 25 years of age, and his murderers are never found.

1998 The Google search engine is founded by university students Larry Page and Sergey Brin, who develop it as a research project. It becomes the largest on the web, and its name has entered common usage as the verb "to Google," synonymous with searching the internet.

Births
- 1533 Queen Elizabeth I of England
- 1909 Elia Kazan, film director
- 1932 Paul Getty Jr., philanthropist
- 1936 Buddy Holly, singer
- 1950 Julie Kavner, actress (*The Simpsons*)
- 1951 Chrissie Hynde, pop singer
- 1953 Benmont Tench, musician
- 1954 Corbin Bernsen, actor
- 1973 Shannon Elizabeth, actress

Deaths
- 1962 Isak Dinesen, author
- 1978 Keith Moon, drummer
- 1994 James Clavell, author
- 2003 Warren Zevon, musician

DAY TO REMEMBER

National day Independence Day (Brazil) In 1822 the South American country of Brazil declared its independence from Portugal, establishing the independent empire of Brazil. Portuguese remains the official language.

Political activist actors

A Labor Day rally calling for an end to the Vietnam War was held at Valley Forge, Pennsylvania, in the U.S.. The event, on September 7, 1970, was the culmination of a three-day protest hike from Moorestown, New Jersey, and was organized by Vietnam Veterans Against the War (VVAW). It received immense press coverage due to high-profile speakers such as actors Jane Fonda and Donald Sutherland.

Fonda in particular was a passionate campaigner against America's involvement in the Vietnam War, and made allegations against the Nixon administration that proved to be true. She continued to raise finds for VVAW, made a film, *FTA*, which revealed servicemen criticizing the war, and met with political leaders around the world.

In 1972 she visited Hanoi, in Vietnam, and was photographed sitting on an anti-aircraft battery used against U.S. soldiers. Thirty-four years after the Valley Forge rally the image was splashed across front pages all over again because the man sitting with Fonda was political aspirant John Kerry, who also spoke at the rally – and who, in 2004, was running for U.S. President. A navy lieutenant, he had fought in Vietnam and was wounded three times. When he returned home, sickened by what he had seen, he became one of the leaders of the VVAW and later became a U.S. Senator.

"John Kerry served his country bravely," his spokeswoman Stephanie Cutter said. "He was awarded the Silver Star, the Bronze Star, and three Purple Hearts for his service, and he praised the noble service of his fellow servicemen and women. After coming home, he worked to end the war so his fellow soldiers could come home too."

DATE*line*

September 8

"Time is a companion that goes with us on a journey. It reminds us to cherish each moment, because it will never come again." PATRICK STEWART, *STAR TREK: THE NEXT GENERATION*

HISTORICAL EVENTS

1504 Michelangelo's sculpture *David*, which took three years to create, is unveiled in Florence. The 17-foot (5.2 m) marble figure portrays the Biblical King David. Renaissance artist Michelangelo is also famous for painting the ceiling of the Sistine Chapel.

1565 A Spanish expedition establishes the first permanent European settlement in North America, at St. Augustine in Florida, so named because it is founded on the feast day of the saint. The oldest city in the U.S. is today a winter retreat for the rich.

1636 The first college opens in the U.S. near Boston in Massachusetts. Today known as Harvard University, it is one of the most prestigious educational establishments in the world.

1831 William IV is crowned King of Great Britain. The third son of George III, he considered entering politics, but finally inherited the crown and changed policy through his regal office.

1930 The company 3M begins marketing transparent Scotch tape. A young engineer, Richard Drew, who five years earlier invented masking tape for the company, creates the almost invisible sticky tape, and Depression-era America goes crazy for it, using it to fix everything from torn books to toys to window blinds.

1966 The science-fiction television series *Star Trek* premieres on NBC with its first episode "The Man Trap." Captain Kirk and Mr. Spock enchant the world in this groundbreaking series that spawns countless spin-offs and a cult following.

1986 General Augusto Pinochet, the President of Chile, survives an assassination attempt that leaves five of his bodyguards dead and 11 more seriously injured.

1998 The splinter group Real IRA announce a ceasefire in the violent struggles of Northern Ireland. The dissident republican group declares its violence at an end, yet continues to train and meet.

2003 U.S. schoolgirl Brianna LaHara is sued by the RIAA for sharing music illegally in a case that makes international headlines (see right).

Births

- **1474** Ludovico Ariosto, poet
- **1841** Antonin Dvořák, composer
- **1921** Harry Secombe, entertainer
- **1922** Sid Caesar, comedian
- **1925** Peter Sellers, actor
- **1932** Patsy Cline, singer
- **1960** Aimee Mann, musician
- **1979** Pink, singer

Deaths

- **701** Pope Sergius I
- **1721** Michael Brokoff, sculptor
- **1949** Richard Strauss, composer
- **1965** Dorothy Dandridge, actress
- **1981** Roy Wilkins, civil rights activist

DAYS TO REMEMBER

Religious day Blessed Virgin Mary's Day The feast of the nativity of Mary is celebrated in the Orthodox, Anglican, and Roman Catholic churches. Loved as the mother of Jesus Christ, Mary is also celebrated in her own right as a symbol of goodness and love.

National day Fiestas de Santa Fe (New Mexico) This special day has been celebrated in New Mexico since 1712. It commemorates the reconquest of the city of Santa Fe and features a pet parade, dancing, religious observances, ethnic foods, fireworks, and the burning of an effigy of Zozobra, or Old Man Gloom.

New technology, new lawsuits

On this day in 2003, the Recording Industry Association of America (RIAA) filed copyright lawsuits against 261 internet users for trading songs online – which is against the law. After decades of buying songs on vinyl records, cassette tapes, and most recently CDs, the wildly popular new format of music was MP3. Several internet sites allowed people to download songs for free, to play on their computers, burn to disc, or load on their iPod.

Chart-topping bands such as Metallica were already campaigning against the availability of free downloadable music files, because it meant artists do not receive payment for their music, and in the long term, record companies can't afford to develop and promote new artists. The RIAA said the defendants were not occasional users but "egregious" file swappers, people who uploaded and distributed music as well as downloading for their own use.

It seemed an open-and-shut case, but one of the illegal downloaders was a 12-year-old schoolgirl from New York. Brianna LaHara was shocked to learn she was among the hundreds sued in U.S. federal courts. Within 24 hours the RIAA settled with Brianna and her mother for $2,000 and dropped the case.

The RIAA settled most of the lawsuits for a much smaller figure than people were liable for, content in the knowledge that people fully understood that file sharing of music was illegal. Conversely, buying music downloads from official sites such as iTunes is legal.

September 9

"We do not remember days, we remember moments. The richness of life lies in memories we have forgotten." — CESARE PAVESE, ITALIAN POET AND NOVELIST

HISTORICAL EVENTS

1543 Mary Stuart, at nine months old, is officially crowned "Queen of Scots." Her father, James V, died when she was a week old. She grows up to be Queen of Scotland and queen consort of France, but is beheaded at 44.

1839 Astronomer John Herschel takes the first glass-plate photograph. He is instrumental in the development of the craft.

1956 Elvis Presley appears on *The Ed Sullivan Show* for the first time. By his third appearance, the moralistic Ed Sullivan only shows him from the waist up, concerned by the singing legend's hip thrusting.

1971 The Attica Prison riots in Buffalo, New York State, U.S., break out, beginning a four-day siege. Prisoners demand better conditions, showers, and access to education. It ends four days later with 42 deaths.

1993 Former Philippine dictator President Ferdinand Marcos is finally buried in his homeland, four years after his death in exile. His body had been kept in a refrigerated mausoleum in Hawaii.

2004 A car bomb explodes outside the Australian Embassy in Jakarta, Indonesia, killing 10 people and injuring 160. It leaves a crater in the road nine feet (3 m) deep.

DAYS TO REMEMBER

National day Kiku no Sekku (Japan) One of the five sacred festivals of Japan, *Kiku no Sekku*, or Chrysanthemum Day, started in the year 910, when the Imperial Court declared the chrysanthemum the national flower.

National day Republic Day (North Korea) This celebrates the founding of the Democratic People's Republic of Korea in 1948. Japanese rule of Korea ended in 1945 with the conclusion of World War II, and from then, the country was split in two, with the Soviet Union controlling North Korea and the U.S., the south. In 1948 separate governments were established.

Births
- **1754** William Bligh, naval officer
- **1828** Leo Tolstoy, novelist
- **1890** Colonel Harland Sanders, fast-food entrepreneur
- **1908** Cesare Pavese, poet and novelist
- **1939** George Lazenby, actor
- **1941** Otis Redding, singer
- **1960** Hugh Grant, actor
- **1966** Adam Sandler, actor and comedian
- **1969** Rachel Hunter, model

Deaths
- **1000** Olaf I of Norway
- **1513** King James IV of Scotland
- **1901** Henri de Toulouse-Lautrec, painter
- **1976** Chairman Mao Zedong, Chinese leader
- **1978** Jack Warner, film studio founder

English actor Hugh Grant (right), who was born on this day in 1960, became an international star when *Four Weddings And A Funeral*, for which he was paid U.S.$1,000, was a surprise hit. "I quite enjoyed being famous for the first six months," he said. "I call it the honeymoon period. But there is also a downside to fame."

This included being constantly photographed throughout his 13-year relationship with actress Liz Hurley, and having his ensuing relationship with socialite Jemima Khan investigated constantly. He balances his high-profile love life with starring in blockbusters such as *Bridget Jones's Diary*, and is seen here with fellow actors from the film, Renée Zellweger (center) and Colin Firth (left).

September 10

"Strengthen the female mind by enlarging it, and there will be an end to blind obedience."

MARY WOLLSTONECRAFT, AUTHOR AND FEMINIST

HISTORICAL EVENTS

1960 Mickey Mantle of the New York Yankees hits Major League Baseball's longest home run, breaking his own record, when at a game in Detroit, Michigan, he hits the ball 634 feet (193 m).

1963 American Express, one of the biggest banks in the world, introduces its credit card to the U.K., and begins the now-common method of credit.

1977 The last execution by guillotine in France takes place. Hamida Djandoubi, convicted of torture and murder, is executed at Baumettes Prison in Marseille.

1990 The Basilica of Our Lady of Peace, in Yamoussoukro on the Ivory Coast of Africa, is consecrated by Pope John Paul II. It is the largest church in Africa and tallest Christian place of worship on earth.

2002 Switzerland, known for its neutrality, finally joins the UN. In a referendum, citizens vote to join in order to give their country a voice in international issues, after being assured their historic neutrality will be maintained.

2003 Anna Lindh, the Foreign Minister of Sweden, is fatally stabbed while shopping (see right).

DAYS TO REMEMBER

International day World Suicide Prevention Day This day focuses global attention on the one million lives lost each year to suicide. It aims to raise awareness about how to prevent suicide, and to lift the shame associated with suicide so progress can be made.

National day Day of the Child (Honduras) *Dia del Niño* is a day set aside to honor and celebrate children and their lives and contributions to the world.

Births		Deaths	
1487	Pope Julius III	1607	Luzzasco Luzzaschi, composer
1588	Nicholas Lanier, composer	1749	Emilie du Chatelet, physicist
1929	Arnold Palmer, golfer	1797	Mary Wollstonecraft, author and feminist
1938	Karl Lagerfeld, fashion designer	1867	Simon Sechter, composer
1945	José Feliciano, singer	1975	George Paget Thomson, physicist and Nobel laureate
1958	Dan Castellaneta, actor (*The Simpsons*)	1983	Felix Bloch, Swiss physicist and Nobel laureate
1960	Colin Firth, actor		
1968	Guy Ritchie, film director		
1974	Ryan Phillippe, actor		

Assassination in Sweden

On September 10, 2003, Anna Lindh – the popular Foreign Minister, tipped to be the next Prime Minister – was fatally stabbed while shopping in the Nordiska Kompaniet department store in Stockholm. She suffered injuries to the chest, stomach, and arms during the frenzied knife attack. After 10 hours of emergency surgery, she died of her wounds the next morning.

Lindh, who was married with two children, had refused to have bodyguards so she could live a normal life and be accessible to the public. Active in politics since her early twenties, she won her first cabinet post in 1994 as minister for the environment, and had been foreign minister since 1998. She was applauded for her passionate fights for human rights reforms and her outspokenness and honesty. She criticized George W. Bush for deciding to go to war with Iraq against the advice of the UN, and was a strong supporter of the European Union.

"Sweden has lost one of its most important representatives, its face against the world," Swedish Prime Minister Goran Persson said.

"Sweden has lost a successful and a great foreign minister, a great Swede, and a great European. I have also lost a close friend and so has the United Nations," UN Secretary-General Kofi Annan added.

A 25-year-old man, Mijailo Mijailovic, was arrested for the murder. The son of Serbian immigrants, he was initially sentenced to life in prison, but on appeal was sent to a closed psychiatric ward instead. Lindh's murder brought back memories of the assassination of Swedish Prime Minister Olof Palme, who was shot dead while at the movies with his wife and son in 1986.

September 11

"Ethics and equity and the principles of justice do not change with the calendar."
D. H. LAWRENCE

HISTORICAL EVENTS

1792 The diamond now called the Hope Diamond, but then known as Louis XIV of France's French Blue, is stolen along with other crown jewels. It now resides in the Smithsonian Natural History Museum in Washington D.C.

1961 The World Wide Fund For Nature (WWF) is created, which is now one of the world's largest environmental organizations, with offices in 60 countries.

1962 The Beatles record their debut single "Love Me Do" at EMI Studios in London. It is soon followed by their first album. They remain one of the highest-selling bands in the world more than 35 years after their demise.

1987 Reggae star and political activist Peter Tosh is murdered in his own home in Kingston, Jamaica, by an ex-con. Conspiracy theories abound, as the Jamaican Government had been trying to silence him for years.

1989 Communist Hungary opens its borders with Austria, and thousands of East Germans flock to freedom in Austria and West Germany. This opening of the Iron Curtain symbolizes the beginning of the end of the Cold War.

1992 Hurricane Iniki devastates Hawaii, with winds up to 145 miles per hour (235 km/h). It is the third most damaging hurricane in U.S. history, causing two billion U.S. dollars of damage and killing six people.

1997 Scotland votes for home rule and to re-establish its own parliament, after 290 years of union with England. Legislative powers are transferred to Edinburgh from Westminster when Parliament formally opens on July 1, 1999.

2001 The September 11 terrorist attacks take place in New York City, killing almost 3,000 people (see right).

2005 After 38 years of occupation, the State of Israel declares an end to military rule in the Gaza Strip. The next day it completes its withdrawal of all troops and settlers from the area, marking the start of Palestinian self-rule.

DAYS TO REMEMBER

National day Enkutatash (Ethiopia) This day marks the end of the rainy season and the beginning of the sunshine. *Enkutatash* means "gift of jewels" and is celebrated as the start of a new year.

National day Teacher's Day (Latin America) This day commemorates the life and work of Argentinian President, author, and educator Domingo F. Sarmiento, who built several schools and libraries, boosted education policy, and traveled widely to bring revolutionary educational theories to Argentina.

Births
1877 Rosika Schwimmer, feminist
1885 D. H. Lawrence, novelist
1899 Jimmie Davis, composer
1917 Ferdinand Marcos, Philippine President
1933 Dr. William L. Pierce, author
1940 Brian de Palma, film director
1967 Harry Connick Jr., singer

Deaths
1958 Robert W. Service, poet
1971 Nikita Khrushchev, Soviet leader
1994 Jessica Tandy, actress
2003 Anna Lindh, Swedish Foreign Minister
2003 John Ritter, actor

The world stands still

On September 11, 2001, the world was shocked when two planes hijacked by terrorists flew into the World Trade Center buildings in New York City. The second crash was captured live by news cameras trained on the burning north tower, which sent the tragedy live around the world and into people's homes as it happened. An hour after the crash, the 110-story towers collapsed, and people were seen jumping out of the windows to their death as the buildings crumbled.

A third plane flew into the Pentagon in Arlington, Virginia, damaging the building, and a fourth crashed in a field in Pennsylvania. Around 3,000 people died in the four well-planned attacks and thousands more were injured. A state of emergency was declared in Washington D.C. and America's airspace and borders were quickly closed, with the armed forces on high alert.

The attacks were linked to al-Qaeda, the Islamic militant group led by Osama bin Laden. President George W. Bush declared a worldwide war on terror, and on September 19 the Pentagon ordered combat aircraft to the Persian Gulf in response to the attacks. In October the U.S. and Britain hit targets in Afghanistan, where bin Laden was believed to be hiding, and in March 2003 they widened their war to Iraq.

It took almost nine months to clear the rubble at Ground Zero, where the WTC buildings had stood, but today the U.S. is building an even higher structure on the site. Patriot Day is now celebrated on this day each year in America, being signed into law on December 18, 2001, to commemorate the horrific events of 9/11.

DATE*line*

September 12

"Our most basic common link is that we all inhabit this small planet, we all breathe the same air, we all cherish our children's futures, and we are all mortal." JOHN F. KENNEDY

HISTORICAL EVENTS

1846 Elizabeth Barrett, one of the most respected poets of the Victorian era, elopes with English playwright Robert Browning. They live happily in Florence, Italy, where her delicate health improves, until her death in 1861.

1933 Jewish Hungarian physicist Leo Szilard gets the idea for nuclear chain reaction – the concept behind nuclear weapons. He works on the U.S. Manhattan Project in 1945 to develop the first weapons, but is later a vocal critic of these atomic bombs.

1940 Four teenage boys discover ancient cave paintings in Lascaux, in the Dordogne region of France. They include some of the earliest known art, apparently dating as far back as 25,000 B.C.E.

1953 John F. Kennedy marries Jackie Bouvier (see below).

1977 South African anti-apartheid activist Steve Biko is killed in police custody. A post-mortem confirms that he was beaten to death.

1992 NASA launches the space shuttle *Endeavour* on the 50th shuttle mission, STS-47. Surgeon Mae Carol Jemison becomes the first African American woman in space.

2005 The fifth Disneyland theme park, Hong Kong Disneyland, opens on Penny Bay, Lantau Island. Michael Eisner, head of the Walt Disney Company, flies out to open it – and resigns from the company two weeks later.

DAY TO REMEMBER

Religious day St. Ailbhe's Day A bishop of Ireland and a disciple of St. Patrick, St. Ailbhe (c. 541) spent his life preaching throughout the country and become known for his charity.

Births
- 1494 King Francis I of France
- 1570 Henry Hudson, explorer
- 1725 Guillaume Le Gentil, astronomer
- 1892 Alfred A. Knopf, publisher
- 1913 Jesse Owens, athlete
- 1931 Sir Ian Holm, actor
- 1942 Linda Gray, actress
- 1943 Michael Ondaatje, writer
- 1957 Rachel Ward, actress
- 1966 Ben Folds, musician

Deaths
- 1362 Pope Innocent VI
- 1712 Jan van der Heyden, painter
- 1733 François Couperin, composer
- 1764 Jean-Philippe Rameau, composer
- 1919 Leonid Andreyev, writer
- 1992 Anthony Perkins, actor
- 2003 Johnny Cash, singer and songwriter

The autumn wedding of Massachusetts Senator John F. Kennedy to his girlfriend Jacqueline Lee Bouvier, a debutante and budding photographer, took place on September 12, 1953. The Kennedys were the closest America had to a royal family, and the ceremony was suitably lavish. It took place in the picturesque St. Mary's Roman Catholic Church in Newport, Rhode Island, in front of 800 guests. Jackie's millionaire stepfather Hugh D. Auchincloss gave her away, and the reception was held at his oceanfront estate with 1,200 guests. They left the reception in a shower of rose petals and spent the night at the exclusive Waldorf-Astoria in New York, before honeymooning in Acapulco, Mexico.

DATE*line*

September 13

"The peace of the brave is within our reach. We know a difficult road lies ahead. Every peace has its enemies." BILL CLINTON AT THE SIGNING OF THE OSLO ACCORDS

It was the moment that gave hope to peace lovers all over the world. On September 13, 1993, U.S. President Bill Clinton was instrumental in getting Yitzhak Rabin, Prime Minister of Israel, and Yasser Arafat, the leader of the Palestine Liberation Organization, to agree to a Declaration of Principles, as mapped out in the Oslo Accords, for peace between Arabs and Israelis. This declaration related to the autonomy of the Gaza Strip and the West Bank. Their handshake on the lawns of the White House after the historic agreement was signed was the first-ever public handshake between the former enemies.

A year later Arafat, Rabin, and Israel's Foreign Minister Shimon Peres controversially share the Nobel Peace Prize for their efforts to create peace in the Middle East.

HISTORICAL EVENTS

- 122 The construction of Hadrian's Wall begins. The stone and turf wall is built by the Romans from east to west across what is now England, to stop raids from the tribes of Scotland and create a border to their lands.
- 1898 Preacher Hannibal Williston Goodwin gets a patent for his invention of a form of celluloid photographic film which he developed to illustrate his sermons. He lodged it a decade earlier, so his estate later sues Eastman Kodak for infringement and is awarded $5 million.
- 1906 Brazilian inventor Alberto Santos-Dumont, working in France, makes the first flight in Europe when his canvas and bamboo biplane is airborne for 23 feet (7 m) on the outskirts of Paris.
- 1982 The "dingo baby" trial opens in Darwin, Australia. Lindy Chamberlain, who claims her nine-week-old daughter was killed by a wild dog while camping, is charged with her murder and sentenced to life in prison. In 1986 evidence is found that supports her story, and she is released.
- 1993 Yitzhak Rabin and Yasser Arafat shake hands on the White House lawn in Washington, ushering in the Oslo peace process (see above).
- 1994 The unmanned *Ulysses* probe passes the Sun's south pole. It was launched in 1990, and its groundbreaking work teaches scientists much about the nature of the Sun.
- 1999 A bomb explodes in an apartment building in Moscow, Russia; it is the second blast in a week. More than 200 people are killed in the two blasts, and the Government blames Chechen rebels, sending troops into Chechnya for the first time since 1997.
- 2001 Civilian airplane flights in the U.S., grounded by the Federal Aviation Administration following the September 11 attacks, begin again, followed by other sections of the aviation industry.

Births
- 1819 Clara Schumann, composer
- 1857 Milton S. Hershey, chocolate entrepreneur
- 1874 Arnold Schoenberg, composer
- 1916 Roald Dahl, writer
- 1944 Jacqueline Bisset, actress
- 1967 Michael Johnson, athlete
- 1969 Shane Warne, cricketer
- 1971 Goran Ivanisevic, tennis player
- 1971 Stella McCartney, fashion designer

Deaths
- 81 Titus, Roman Emperor
- 1321 Dante Alighieri, poet
- 1928 Italo Svevo, author
- 1996 Tupac Shakur, rapper and actor
- 2004 Luis E. Miramontes, chemist and co-inventor of the Pill

DAY TO REMEMBER

Religious day St. John Chrysostom's Day This saint (347–407) was a Christian bishop and preacher in Syria and Constantinople who continues to have a great influence on Eastern Christianity. He is famous for his eloquence in preaching and is considered a doctor of the church, a rare honor.

September 14

"Remember tonight, for it is the beginning of always." — DANTE ALIGHIERI, AUTHOR OF *THE DIVINE COMEDY*

HISTORICAL EVENTS

1814 American lawyer Francis Scott Key writes the poem "The Star-Spangled Banner," which fits the tune of "To Anacreon in Heaven," an English song from the 1760s by John Stafford Smith.

1901 U.S. President William McKinley, who was shot twice on September 6, dies in Buffalo, New York, after going into shock from his wounds. His assassination gives Vice-President Theodore Roosevelt the top job.

1972 The television drama series *The Waltons* premieres on CBS, and tells the story of a family living in the mountains of Virginia during the Depression and World War II. The show runs until 1981, and is followed by seven television movies.

1975 The first U.S. saint, Elizabeth Ann Seton, is canonized by Pope Paul VI (see right).

1982 Princess Grace of Monaco, formerly American actress Grace Kelly, dies of injuries suffered in a car crash the day before in Monte Carlo. Her youngest daughter Stephanie was also in the car.

1984 American pilot Joe Kittinger becomes the first person to fly a hot air balloon alone across the Atlantic Ocean. He launches from Caribou, Maine, in the U.S., and lands in Montenotte, Italy, 86 hours later, having covered 3,543 miles (5,700 km).

DAY TO REMEMBER

Religious day Triumph of the Cross In the Roman Catholic Church, the Triumph of the Cross (known by Anglicans as Holy Cross Day) is celebrated, while in the Eastern Orthodox Church the Exaltation of the Cross is marked. It commemorates the finding of the original cross on which Jesus was crucified, by St. Helena on a pilgrimage to Jerusalem in 326.

Births
- **1486** Heinrich Cornelius Agrippa, alchemist
- **1737** Michael Haydn, composer
- **1760** Luigi Cherubini, composer
- **1867** Charles Dana Gibson, artist
- **1942** Bernard MacLaverty, writer
- **1947** Sam Neill, actor

Deaths
- **891** Pope Stephen V
- **1321** Dante Alighieri, author
- **1523** Pope Adrian VI
- **1712** Giovanni Domenico Cassini, astronomer
- **1982** Princess Grace of Monaco, actress
- **1982** John Gardner, novelist

America's first saint

On September 14, 1975, America's first saint was canonized by Pope Paul VI. Elizabeth Ann Bayley Seton was born on August 28, 1774, in New York City and raised as an Episcopalian. Her mother died when she was two, leaving her and her two young sisters to grow up with their father, a stepmother, and an uncle.

She married wealthy shipping magnate William Magee Seton on January 25, 1794, and they had five children, Anna Maria, William, Richard, Catherine, and Rebecca. Her husband, who went bankrupt a few years later, died of tuberculosis when she was 29, leaving Elizabeth a poor young widow with five children. A year later she converted to Roman Catholicism and started working for the poor.

She helped create New York's first private charity organization, the Society for the Relief of Poor Widows with Small Children, became a teacher so she could educate her own children, and campaigned for free schooling.

On March 25, 1809, she took vows of poverty, chastity, and obedience, and became known as Mother Seton. She began the Sisters of Charity, a religious organization for women, and established the first Catholic parochial school in the U.S. She died on January 4, 1821, of tuberculosis.

She was not immediately considered for sainthood. The first step was to be declared venerable, which took place on December 18, 1959. She was then beatified by Pope John XXIII on March 17, 1963, and canonized by Pope Paul VI on September 14, 1975. St. Elizabeth is the patron saint of widows, children near death, orphans, and teachers.

September 15

DATE*line*

"If a man can judge success by how many great friends he has, then I have been very successful." — JOHNNY RAMONE

On September 15, 1984, Princess Diana's second son Henry Charles Albert David Mountbatten-Windsor, known as Harry, was born. He is the third in line to the British throne, and his full title is His Royal Highness Prince Henry of Wales. After a tumultuous teenage period during which he was caught drinking underage, smoking cigarettes, going to nightclubs and strip joints, and using marijuana, Harry surprised everyone by graduating ahead of older brother William at the Royal Military Academy of Sandhurst. As of 2006 he was a commissioned officer and will serve in Iraq in 2007. Both he and his brother have insisted that they see active service in the Army and not be protected because of their royal privileges.

HISTORICAL EVENTS

921 The Duchess of Bohemia, later St. Ludmila, is murdered at the command of her daughter-in-law. She and her husband built the first Christian church in Bohemia, and she taught her grandson, later known as Good King Wenceslaus.

1835 Charles Darwin reaches the Galapagos Islands off the South American coast aboard the HMS *Beagle*. There he comes up with his theory of natural selection and evolution, which challenges the church's view of creation and is later supported by scientists internationally.

1965 Reflecting the interest in the space race, the sci-fi television series *Lost in Space* premieres. Set in the far distant future – 1997! – the Robinson family is sent to colonize a distant planet.

1966 The U.S. spaceship *Gemini XI*, with astronauts Charles "Pete" Conrad Jr. and Richard Gordon Jr. on board, returns to Earth after two days, 23 hours, 17 minutes and eight seconds.

1968 The Soviet spaceship *Zond 5* launches, becoming the first spacecraft to fly around the Moon then re-enter the Earth's atmosphere. It is a precursor of manned Moon flights, and has turtles on board to monitor the effects of extended space travel.

1984 Princess Diana, wife of Prince Charles of England, gives birth to her second child Harry at St Mary's Hospital in Paddington, London (see left).

2000 The twenty-seventh Summer Olympics open in Sydney, Australia, in spring. Homegrown hero Ian Thorpe and Dutch swimmer Inge de Bruijn each win four gold medals in the pool, while Australian Aboriginal Cathy Freeman wins her country's 100th gold medal in the 400-meter track event.

2005 Oscar-winning actress Renée Zellweger and country singer Kenny Chesney file for divorce after just four months of matrimony. They had met in January that year, and the marriage was annulled in December.

DAY TO REMEMBER

International day Independence Day The Central American countries of Costa Rica, El Salvador, Guatemala, Honduras, and Nicaragua celebrate this day to mark their declaration of independence from Spain in 1821 after a decade of struggling for autonomy.

Births
- 1254 Marco Polo, explorer
- 1881 Ettore Bugatti, automobile engineer
- 1890 Agatha Christie, writer
- 1894 Jean Renoir, film director
- 1907 Fay Wray, actress
- 1946 Tommy Lee Jones, actor
- 1946 Oliver Stone, film director
- 1979 Sophie Dahl, model

Deaths
- 1750 Charles Pachelbel, composer
- 1945 Anton Webern, composer
- 1989 Robert Penn Warren, writer
- 2004 Johnny Ramone, guitarist

September 16

"Be strong and follow your own convictions. You can't assume there is a lot of time to do what you like. You could die tomorrow." — ENGLISH ROCK STAR MARC BOLAN, WHO DIED IN A CAR CRASH AGED 29

Environmental breakthrough

On September 16, 1987, the Montreal Protocol on Substances that Deplete the Ozone Layer was negotiated and signed by 24 countries. By 2006, more than 180 countries had added their support. Kofi Annan, Secretary-General of the United Nations, described it as "perhaps the single most successful international agreement to date." It was also remarkable for being one of the few issues the world has been able to agree on.

The agreement called for the signatory countries to phase out the use of chlorofluorocarbons (CFCs), halons, and other ozone-depleting chemicals (ODCs). Scientists discovered that once emitted into the atmosphere, these compounds significantly deplete the stratospheric ozone layer that shields the planet from damaging UV-B radiation, thus increasing skin cancer risk and significantly changing world weather patterns.

The original agreement came into force on January 1, 1989, and stipulated that the production and consumption of ODCs was to be phased out by 2000. Further revisions were made as new scientific information became available, speeding up the phase-out. Financial incentives to develop safe alternatives were offered, and member nations were banned from trade with any country which refused to sign. The sanctions were deemed justified because depletion of the ozone layer is seen as a problem most effectively addressed on a global level.

HISTORICAL EVENTS

1812 Rather than surrender to Napoleon's army and be ruled by the French, the Russians set fire to Moscow and leave their city. Within two days 90 percent of houses and 1,000 churches are destroyed.

1908 General Motors is founded in Flint, Michigan, and later becomes the first U.S. corporation to make $1 billion in a year. It is now based in Detroit.

1920 A bomb in a horse-drawn wagon explodes on Wall Street, New York City. Thirty-nine people are killed and 400 more are injured.

1956 Play-Doh is invented by Noah and Joseph McVicker in the U.S. – although they were trying to make wallpaper cleaner! It is similar to modeling clay but easier to use, and becomes one of the most popular toys in the world.

1976 The Episcopal Church in the U.S. approves the ordination of women to the priesthood after 125 years of struggle. In Minneapolis, the church votes to allow both sexes candidacy to be bishops, priests, and deacons.

1977 Pop star Marc Bolan is killed in a car crash in London. His girlfriend Gloria Jones is driving; Bolan never obtained his license because he was terrified he would die in a car accident.

1978 More than 26,000 people die in an earthquake that measures 7.7 on the Richter scale when it hits the town of Tabas in the southeast of Iran.

1987 The Montreal Protocol is signed to protect the ozone layer (see left).

DAY TO REMEMBER

National day Independence Day (New Guinea) On this day, New Guinea celebrates its independence, after declaring itself free from Australia's rule in 1975.

Maria Callas, diva soprano of the 1950s, died on this day in 1977.

Births
- 1875 James C. Penney, department store founder
- 1924 Lauren Bacall, actress
- 1925 Charlie Byrd, musician
- 1925 B.B. King, musician
- 1956 David Copperfield, illusionist
- 1956 Mickey Rourke, actor
- 1958 Jennifer Tilly, actress
- 1969 Marc Anthony, singer

Deaths
- 1087 Pope Victor III
- 1380 King Charles V of France
- 1394 Avignon Pope Clement VII
- 1701 King James II of England and VII of Scotland
- 1736 Gabriel Fahrenheit, physicist
- 1977 Marc Bolan, musician
- 1977 Maria Callas, soprano

September 17

"Like most people, I secretly hope that it's true – that there are witches like Samantha, and that families like hers really do exist." ELIZABETH MONTGOMERY, ON HER CHARACTER IN *BEWITCHED*

Groundbreaking pageant star

On September 17, 1983, Vanessa Williams was crowned Miss America in Atlantic City, New Jersey. She was the first African American woman to win the title. The 20-year-old aspiring entertainer had long been competing in beauty pageants, encouraged by her parents, who wrote: "Here she is, Miss America" in her birth notice.

She spent 10 months performing her Miss America duties, but in the summer of 1984 *Penthouse* magazine announced it would print graphic nude photos of her they had taken long before she entered the competition. As Miss America organizers prided themselves on crowning "not models but role models," she was forced to resign. Williams stood down on July 23, 1984, and runner-up Suzette Charles, the second African American to wear the crown, held the title for 54 days.

The organization didn't appear to hold grudges, stating: "Despite her resignation over questionable photos, she performed her duties as Miss America in an exemplary fashion, and moved into the world of entertainment with ease and grandeur."

The scandal surrounding her resignation didn't hurt her dreams of stardom. Williams has released several platinum albums, and had a number-one hit with the song "Save the Best for Last." She is one of the most popular adult contemporary R&B singers of her time, and has earned 15 Grammy nominations. She has also appeared in several television shows and Hollywood films, including *Eraser*, with Arnold Schwarzenegger, *Soul Food*, and *Shaft*, and starred on Broadway.

On September 17, 1994, Heather Whitestone of Alabama was crowned Miss America, the first deaf woman to win.

HISTORICAL EVENTS

1787 The U.S. Constitution is adopted by the Constitutional Convention in Philadelphia. It creates a federal union of sovereign states and a federal Government to operate that union.

1961 In Trafalgar Square, 15,000 people protest in London's largest ever "ban the bomb" demonstration, which ends with 850 arrests including actress Vanessa Redgrave, jazz musician George Melly, and philosopher Bertrand Russell.

1964 The television show *Bewitched*, starring Elizabeth Montgomery, debuts. In it a beautiful witch marries a mortal man and tries to be a perfect housewife. Her struggles reflect the changing role of women as feminism takes hold.

1976 After more than two years of construction, the first NASA space shuttle, the *Enterprise*, is unveiled. Originally called *Constitution*, a letter campaign has the craft renamed after television show *Star Trek*'s starship *Enterprise*.

1983 Vanessa Williams becomes the first African American Miss America (see above).

2000 British television presenter Paula Yates dies from an accidental drug overdose. She is found by Tiger Lily, her four-year-old daughter.

DAY TO REMEMBER

Religious day St. Lambert's Day Born into nobility, St. Lambert (c. 636–700) became a Catholic bishop in the Netherlands, a position he held for 30 years. He is a martyr saint; after spending seven years in exile, he was later murdered in a family dispute.

Births
- 1550 Pope Paul V
- 1923 Hank Williams, musician
- 1929 Sir Stirling Moss, race-car driver
- 1931 Anne Bancroft, actress
- 1934 Maureen Connolly, tennis star
- 1935 Ken Kesey, author
- 1956 Rita Rudner, comedienne
- 1962 Baz Luhrmann, film director
- 1973 Anastacia, singer

Deaths
- 1762 Francesco Geminiani, composer
- 1991 Zino Francescatti, violinist
- 1997 Red Skelton, comedian
- 2000 Paula Yates, television host
- 2005 Alfred Reed, composer

September 18

"I call upon the scientific community in our country, those who gave us nuclear weapons…to give us the means of rendering these nuclear weapons impotent and obsolete." — RONALD REAGAN

HISTORICAL EVENTS

1809 The Royal Opera House in London opens with a performance of *Macbeth*. The foundation stone was laid by the Prince of Wales, and was incorporated into the present structure after a fire demolished it in 1856.

1895 Daniel David Palmer, who works as a magnetic healer, makes the first chiropractic adjustment in Davenport, Iowa, in the U.S..

1919 The Netherlands gives women the right to vote. The first woman is elected to Parliament in 1946, and to Government 10 years later; however their oldest political party still refuses to allow women to run for parliament.

1965 *I Dream of Jeannie*, a television show about a genie in a bottle who is eager to serve her new master, astronaut Captain Nelson, airs in the U.S. Larry Hagman, who later finds fame in *Dallas*, stars alongside Barbara Eden.

1970 American guitar hero Jimi Hendrix dies of a sleeping pill overdose in London at the age of 27. He had just re-formed his band, the Jimi Hendrix Experience, and was recording a new album.

1978 The leaders of Israel and Egypt agree to a Middle East peace deal at U.S. President Jimmy Carter's Camp David retreat. Egyptian President Anwar al-Sadat and Israeli PM Menachem Begin agree Israeli troops will be withdrawn.

1979 Bolshoi Ballet's star dancers Leonid and Valentina Kozlov defect from Russia while in the U.S. (see right).

1987 In Washington, U.S. President Ronald Reagan and Soviet leader Mikhail Gorbachev agree to the joint disassembly of nuclear warheads by their countries, the first reduction since their invention 50 years earlier.

2004 U.S. pop singer Britney Spears marries backup dancer Kevin Federline in an over-the-top ceremony – her second wedding of the year. Her first, to school friend Jason Alexander, lasted just 55 hours before being annulled.

Following the defection of Russian ballet dancer Mikhail Baryshnikov in Paris five years earlier, three dancers from the celebrated Bolshoi Ballet company of Moscow defected in the U.S. while on a 1979 tour. Alexander Godunov did it in New York at the beginning of the tour, and husband-and-wife team Leonid and Valentina Kozlov defected in Los Angeles at the end.

The graceful couple went on to work as principals with the New York City Ballet, choreographing and performing in some of their most important works. As a result of their bid for freedom, it was almost a decade before the Bolshoi Ballet returned to the U.S., fearing that other high-profile dancers would defect as soon as they touched down in the West.

DAY TO REMEMBER

Religious day St. Joseph of Cupertino's Day An Italian saint, best known for being slow-witted and illiterate, Joseph (1603–1663) lived a life of prayer and poverty, and was reportedly prone to miraculous levitation or "flight" and intense religious esctasies. He was canonized 100 years after his death, and is known as the patron saint of air travelers, aviators, the mentally handicapped, and poor students.

Births
- 1587 Francesca Caccini, composer
- 1905 Greta Garbo, actress
- 1939 Frankie Avalon, film star
- 1961 James Gandolfini, actor
- 1971 Lance Armstrong, cyclist
- 1971 Jada Pinkett Smith, actress

Deaths
- 1180 King Louis VII of France
- 1827 Robert Pollok, poet
- 1961 General Dag Hammarskjold, UN Secretary-General

DATE*line*

September 19

HISTORICAL EVENTS

1893 In New Zealand, the Governor signs the Electoral Act, giving all women the right to vote – the first country in the world to grant that right.

1957 The U.S. Government conducts the first underground nuclear bomb test in the Nevada Desert, one of 29 tests carried out in the area during this year.

1970 *The Mary Tyler Moore Show* debuts on American television. It is about a woman who moves to Minneapolis after a breakup, determined to "make it on her own". It breaks new ground as a sitcom.

1985 An earthquake hits Mexico City and kills more than 4,500 people. Tenor Placido Domingo digs through the rubble in search of relatives – when they are found dead he continues his rescue efforts, drawing international attention and aid to the victims and later playing a benefit concert.

1985 A U.S. Senate committee, pressured by politician's wife Tipper Gore's Parents Music Resource Center, investigates the "pornographic content of rock music," which leads to albums being labeled if they have explicit content.

1991 Otzi the Iceman, a well-preserved mummy of a man from 3,300 B.C.E., is discovered in Italy by German tourists (see below).

1994 The medical drama *ER* airs in the U.S., introducing a new genre of television and providing the big break for George Clooney, who plays Dr. Doug Ross.

Births
- 1901 Joe Pasternak, film producer
- 1911 Sir William Golding, writer
- 1913 Frances Farmer, actress
- 1928 Adam West, actor
- 1934 Brian Epstein, manager of The Beatles
- 1941 "Mama" Cass Elliot, musician
- 1948 Jeremy Irons, actor
- 1949 Twiggy Lawson, model
- 1964 Trisha Yearwood, singer
- 1974 Jimmy Fallon, actor

Deaths
- 1710 Ole Rømer, astronomer
- 1942 Condé Nast, publisher
- 1973 Gram Parsons, musician
- 1985 Italo Calvino, writer
- 2003 Slim Dusty, singer

DAY TO REMEMBER

International day Talk Like a Pirate Day This quirky day is celebrated around the world by anyone who cares to. This parody holiday was proclaimed in 1995, originally as a joke, by two Americans, John Baur and Mark Summers, who decided that everyone should talk like a pirate at least one day a year, such as replacing "hello" with "Ahoy me hearty."

Perfectly preserved prehistoric find

On September 19, 1991, two German tourists, Helmut and Erika Simon, were hiking in the mountains between Italy and Austria when they made an amazing discovery. It was a frozen human body they at first took to be a fellow mountain climber – but which turned out to be the oldest frozen mummy ever found. Otzi the Iceman, named after the Otztal region in which he was discovered, had been frozen inside a glacier for more than 5,000 years, a perfect example of a chalcolithic (Copper-Stone Age) European. His body was incredibly well preserved, and has fascinated the team of international scientists who have been studying his DNA in order to discover more about our evolution.

The initial conclusion was that he had died from exposure, but it was later discovered that there was an arrow lodged in his shoulder and cuts and bruises on his hands, suggesting he had died as a result of a fight. He was still wearing the remains of a grass cape, animal-skin leggings and snowshoes, and had an axe and arrows with him.

Archeologists, forensic scientists, and other researchers have been able to determine his age – between 45 and 50, which is old for that time – and also that he died in the spring, had several tattoos on his body that correspond to modern-day acupuncture points, and even what he ate for his last two meals, including red deer meat, wheat grain, and fruit.

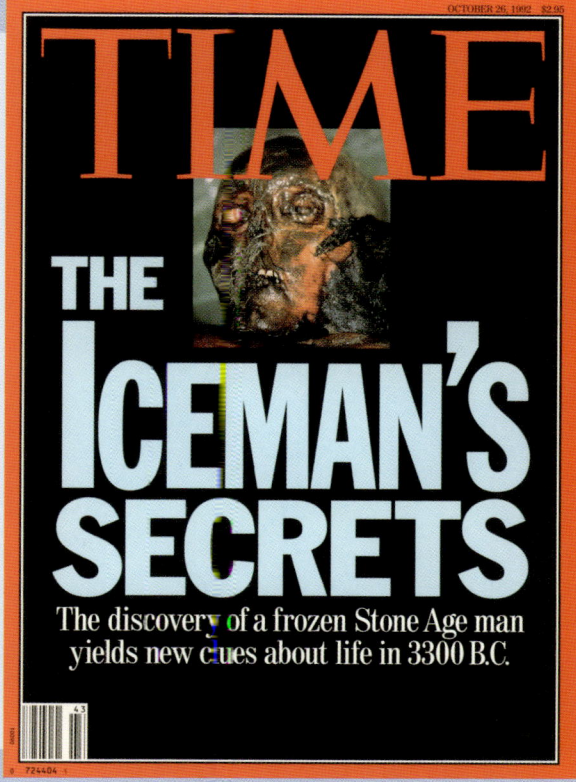

September 20

> "The Festival is…a microcosm of what the world would be like if people could contact each other directly and speak the same language." — JEAN COCTEAU ON THE CANNES FILM FESTIVAL

Billie Jean King was one of the world's best women tennis players. She won 37 Grand Slam titles and was an advocate for equal pay for women. When chauvinistic men's tennis champ Bobby Riggs claimed that women's tennis was so inferior to men's he could beat the top female players of the day, she took him up on the challenge, after he beat champion Margaret Court. Dubbed the "Battle of the Sexes," the Bobby v. Billie Jean match in Houston, Texas, on September 20, 1973, attracted massive publicity. In front of a television audience of 50 million people, she beat him 6–4, 6–3, 6–3, gaining greater recognition and respect for women's tennis. "I thought it would set us back 50 years if I didn't win that match. It would ruin the women's tennis tour and affect all women's self-esteem," a relieved Billie Jean said.

Births

- 1842 Sir James Dewar, inventor
- 1929 Anne Meara, actress
- 1934 Sophia Loren, actress
- 1956 Gary Cole, actor
- 1967 Kristen Johnston, actress
- 1975 Juan Pablo Montoya, race-car driver

Deaths

- 1590 Lodovico Agostini, composer
- 1863 Jakob Grimm, folklorist
- 1908 Pablo de Sarasate, violinist and composer
- 1957 Jean Sibelius, composer
- 1971 Giorgos Seferis, writer and Nobel laureate

DAY TO REMEMBER

Religious day St. Eustace's Day Originally a Roman general, St. Eustace was converted after seeing a vision of Christ between the antlers of a stag he was hunting. After enduring many misfortunes that tested his faith, he was martyred with his wife and children by being roasted in a bronze bull.

HISTORICAL EVENTS

- **1377** Cardinal Robert of Geneva is elected Avignon Pope Clement VII, part of a second line of popes who rival the Roman line as a protest to the incompetence of Pope Urban VI.
- **1519** Portuguese explorer Ferdinand Magellan sets sail. Three years later his ship the *Victoria* returns to Spain, the first to sail around the world, but Magellan does not complete the journey, dying in a skirmish with natives in the Philippines.
- **1893** Charles and Frank Duryea build the first gasoline-powered car in America and take it for a drive in Springfield, Massachusetts.
- **1946** The first Cannes Film Festival is held, after being delayed for seven years due to World War II. It remains the most prestigious film festival in the world.
- **1962** African American student James Meredith is blocked from enroling at the University of Mississippi by the Governor. This sparks riots that lead President Kennedy to send in federal troops. In a milestone for desegregation, four days later the U.S. court of appeals orders the university to admit him.
- **1973** Billie Jean King beats former star Bobby Riggs in a "battle of the sexes" tennis match (see above).
- **1999** A UN peacekeeping force is sent to East Timor to end the military violence that has seen thousands killed since the country voted for independence two weeks earlier.
- **2000** The Whitewater Scandal ends when a third investigation also declares there is insufficient evidence to warrant charges against U.S. president Bill Clinton or his wife Hillary over allegedly improper real estate dealings.

September 21

The autumn equinox in the Northern Hemisphere and the spring or vernal equinox in the Southern Hemisphere. The length of day and night are equal

> "We must not allow the clock and the calendar to blind us to the fact that each moment of life is a miracle and mystery." — H. G. WELLS

HISTORICAL EVENTS

1792 During the French Revolution, the National Convention votes to abolish the monarchy, suspending the rule of King Louis XVI, and establish a republic.

1937 J. R. R. Tolkien's book *The Hobbit* is published. Its first print run is just 1,500 copies, but the acclaimed fantasy novel has now been published in more than 38 languages and sold more than 50 million copies.

1993 U.S. grunge band Nirvana release their third and final album *In Utero*, which tops charts around the world and sells more than six million copies. It is recorded and mixed in less than two weeks.

1996 Magazine publisher and lawyer John F. Kennedy Jr. marries Carolyn Bessette in a secret ceremony on a remote island (see right).

1998 U.S. President Bill Clinton's grand jury testimony about his relationship with intern Monica Lewinsky is aired on American television. In January he insisted: "I did not have sexual relations with that woman," but he now admits he lied.

1998 Olympic gold medal track star Florence Griffith Joyner, known as Flo-Jo, dies in her sleep after suffering an epileptic seizure at the age of 38.

1999 A powerful earthquake strikes Taiwan, killing at least 2,400 people and injuring more than 4,000. The quake, which lasts for just a minute but measures 7.8 on the Richter scale, leaves more than 100,000 homeless.

2001 The UN decides its International Day of Peace will be celebrated on September 21 from now on. It is recognized by the UN as a full day of worldwide ceasefire and nonviolence.

In 1996, John F. Kennedy Jr., one of America's most eligible bachelors, broke the hearts of women all over the world when he married Carolyn Bessette, who he'd been seeing for four years. The elegant blonde fashion publicist was notoriously media shy, and their romantic and top-secret sunset wedding took place on remote Cumberland Island off the coast of the southern state of Georgia in a tiny wooden chapel. Carolyn's long white silk crepe bias-cut gown with silk tulle train was by Narciso Rodriguez of Cerruti and her crystal-beaded satin sandals were from Manolo Blahnik. The couple spent their honeymoon on a yacht to escape prying eyes, then returned to their home in New York City. They died in a plane crash together less than three years later.

Births
- 1866 H.G. Wells, writer
- 1931 Larry Hagman, actor
- 1934 Leonard Cohen, singer and songwriter
- 1945 Jerry Bruckheimer, film and television producer
- 1947 Stephen King, author
- 1950 Bill Murray, actor
- 1957 Ethan Coen, film director
- 1963 Curtly Ambrose, cricketer
- 1967 Faith Hill, singer
- 1968 Ricki Lake, actress and talkshow hostess

Deaths
- 1327 King Edward II of England
- 1719 Johann Heinrich Acker, writer
- 1832 Sir Walter Scott, writer
- 1938 Ivana Brlić-Mažuranić, writer
- 1998 Florence Griffith Joyner, athlete

September 22

"It is our duty to make this world a better place for women."
DAME CHRISTABEL PANKHURST

HISTORICAL EVENTS

1692 Ann Pudeator and Mary Parker are hanged in Salem, Massachusetts, the last to die as a result of the notorious witchcraft trials, which are later found to have been based on lies and false testimony.

1950 The first non-stop jet flight between the U.K. and the U.S. takes place. World War II ace Colonel David Schilling makes the first crossing of the Atlantic in an F-84 Thunderjet fighter; the trip takes 10 hours and 1 minute.

1975 The IRA launches 17 bombings across Northern Ireland, putting the ceasefire declared seven months earlier at risk. They say it is in response to police torture of their people. There are no fatalities.

1980 Iraq invades Iran, bombing several air and military supply bases, and war breaks out between the neighboring countries. The fighting ends only when the UN organizes a ceasefire in August 1988. There are 400,000 casualties.

1981 French President François Mitterrand launches one of the world's fastest trains in Paris. The TGV, or *train à grande vitesse* – French for "high-speed train" – is a passenger train that can travel at up to 200 miles per hour (320 km/h).

1991 The Dead Sea Scrolls, the only surviving Biblical documents from before 100 C.E., are made available for the first time by Huntington Library in California.

1994 The television show *Friends* premieres in the U.S. and becomes one of the longest-running and most popular sitcoms in history (see right).

2004 CBS-owned television stations in America are fined $550,000 for showing pop star Janet Jackson's exposed breast for a second during the Super Bowl halftime show. She blames a wardrobe malfunction.

DAY TO REMEMBER

Traditional Day Hobbit Day
This day is celebrated by fans of author J. R. R. Tolkien. It is the birthday of both Bilbo and Frodo Baggins, characters in the books, and some readers have parties for them, while others spend the day barefoot, as the hobbits never wear shoes.

Births
- **1880** Dame Christabel Pankhurst, suffragist
- **1931** Fay Weldon, author
- **1957** Nick Cave, musician
- **1958** Andrea Bocelli, tenor
- **1976** Ronaldo, footballer
- **1978** Harry Kewell, footballer

Deaths
- **1607** Alessandro Allori, painter
- **1774** Pope Clement XIV
- **1989** Irving Berlin, songwriter

Cute comedy breaks records

On September 22, 1994, the TV show *Friends* premiered, ultimately becoming one of the most successful sitcoms in television history and launching the six previously unknown stars onto the Hollywood A-list. Its clever mix of comedy and drama gained a devout following, influencing language, fashion, and even hairstyles.

In real life the actors became friends too, holidaying together and helping each other through personal dramas. By the end of the series they were receiving $1 million each per episode, thanks to their collective bargaining and their insistence on being considered as an ensemble rather than as individual cast members.

The show came to an end in 2004 after 10 years, largely because the six actors wanted to pursue movie roles. The series finale, considered the biggest TV moment of 2004, attracted more than 52 million viewers in the U.S.

Since then, Jennifer Aniston has become a popular star of Hollywood romantic comedies, and Courteney Cox and Lisa Kudrow have also made a mark in film. The boys, Matt LeBlanc, Matthew Perry, and David Schwimmer, haven't fared quite as well, but still work in the entertainment industry.

DATEline

September 23

"What progress we are making. In the Middle Ages they would have burned me. Now they are content with burning my books." — SIGMUND FREUD

HISTORICAL EVENTS

1846 Neptune, the eighth planet from the sun, is discovered by French astronomer Urbain Le Verrier and British astronomer John Couch Adams. It is named after the Roman god of the sea because of its blue methane clouds.

1848 Chewing gum is invented by John Curtis in Maine, U.S. He boils the resin obtained from spruce trees on a stove at his home, then pours it in a tub of ice water and strains it, selling it as sticks wrapped in tissue paper.

1949 U.S. President Harry Truman announces that the Soviet Union has detonated an atomic bomb, putting an end to the U.S. monopoly on weapons of mass destruction.

1952 Acting legend Charlie Chaplin returns to his native U.K. after 40 years living and working in America, and is refused re-entry to the U.S. due to his "subversive" activities.

1973 Juan Perón, husband of the late Evita, returns to power in Argentina after being exiled for 17 years (see right).

1997 The U.S.–Russian Plutonium Production Reactor Agreement is signed in Moscow, effecting a ban on weapons-grade plutonium. It requires the end of plutonium production and the closure or modification of any plutonium-producing reactors by the end of 2000.

2004 At least 3,000 people in Haiti are killed by Hurricane Jeanne and 300,000 are left without shelter or basic supplies. The terrible storm rages for two weeks.

DAY TO REMEMBER

National day Autumnal Equinox Day (Japan) This seasonal day, usually falling on September 23, is celebrated as a national holiday, *Higan no Chu-Nichi*. Japanese people visit their family tombs to maintain them and commune with their ancestors' spirits.

Births		Deaths	
63 B.C.E.	Augustus Caesar, Roman Emperor	79	Pope Linus
1920	Mickey Rooney, actor	1835	Vincenzo Bellini, composer
1926	John Coltrane, jazz musician	1939	Sigmund Freud, psychiatrist
1930	Ray Charles, singer	1968	Padre Pio, saint
1943	Julio Iglesias, singer	1973	Pablo Neruda, poet and Nobel Prize laureate
1949	Bruce Springsteen, singer and songwriter		
1959	Jason Alexander, actor	1987	Bob Fosse, dancer, choreographer, and actor
1961	Willie McCool, astronaut		

South American political intrigue

He was well-known internationally for his marriage to Eva Perón, A.K.A. Evita, but Juan Perón was also a political force to be reckoned with in Argentina, being elected President of the country three times. On September 23, 1973, the former leader returned to power after almost 20 years in exile.

In 1943, as a colonel, he had helped overthrow Argentina's civilian Government in a military coup. He was secretary of labor and social welfare, and fought for the rights of the workers as well as strengthening the unions. A year later he became Vice-President, and in the next election, in 1946, he won the presidency.

He drew on both left and right policies – he gave benefits to workers, yet restricted civil liberties; gave women the vote, yet limited universities. In 1951, helped by his charismatic actress wife Eva, who acted as de facto minister of health and labor, he was re-elected to the presidency. But economic problems and a withdrawal of support from the Catholic Church, who were angry that he recognized divorce, led to a coup against him in September 1955. He was driven into exile in Spain, where he wed third wife Isabel in 1961, Eva having died of cancer in 1952.

In his absence from Argentina, successive governments failed to revive the economy, suppress escalating terrorism, or stabilize the country. When he returned in 1973, many saw him as the nation's only hope, and he was elected for a third presidential term on September 23. He died less than a year later, on July 1, 1974, in Argentina's capital of Buenos Aires, and Isabel took over the running of the country until she was deposed in a coup two years later.

September 24

"This treaty should reinforce international resolve to achieve a world free of the nuclear arms race, a world free of all nuclear weapons."

UN SECRETARY-GENERAL BOUTROS BOUTROS-GHALI, ON THE AGREEMENT TO STOP NUCLEAR TESTING

Star sign

LIBRA

September 24–October 23

Librans are strong-willed, understanding, diplomatic, easygoing, idealistic, and charming. They seek aesthetic pleasure, admiration, justice, and a harmonious environment, but can be prone to procrastination, indecision, laziness, indulgence, and avoidance of all confrontation. Libra is an air sign and is ruled by Venus, the planet of love.

In Seattle, U.S., on this day in 1991, the band Nirvana released their second album *Nevermind*. Overnight, it propeled them into the realm of global success, becoming one of the highest-selling albums of all time.

The album also changed the face of music, sweeping away the glam rock bands popular at the time and introducing "grunge," a more somber, serious, and altogether dressed-down form of rock music. Alongside bassist Krist Novoselic and drummer Dave Grohl, vocalist/guitarist Kurt Cobain was later considered a spokesman for a generation of alienated teens. Famous for his dirty hair, old cardigans, and self-loathing, Cobain struggled with the burden of fame, and less than three years later it was all over with his suicide.

HISTORICAL EVENTS

1948 The Honda Motor Company is founded in Tokyo, Japan. It doesn't make inroads into the US market until 1972, when its smaller, more economical cars impress a nation suddenly concerned with an energy crisis.

1975 Dougal Haston and Doug Scott climb to the top of Mt. Everest, the first Britons to do so. They set a record for the fastest climb – scaling the 29,028-foot (8,848 m) summit in 33 days.

1976 The Rhodesian Government of southern Africa, now Zimbabwe, reluctantly agrees to introduce black majority rule within two years, forced by the U.K. and U.S. Robert Mugabe becomes the first black Prime Minister in 1980.

1976 Heiress Patty Hearst, who was kidnapped and brainwashed by the Symbionese Liberation Army, is sentenced to seven years for her part in a bank robbery.

1991 Nirvana releases the album *Nevermind*, changing the face of music (see above).

1996 The U.S. and other nuclear powers sign a treaty to end all testing and development of nuclear weapons, including underground blasts. America had conducted 1,030 tests since 1945, creating major health problems both locally and internationally.

DAY TO REMEMBER

Religious day Fiesta de La Mercè (Spain) On this day, Spaniards remember Barcelona's patron saint, La Madonna de la Mercè. In 1637 she is believed to have saved the city from a plague of locusts, gaining her patron saint and protector status.

Births

1717	Horace Walpole, novelist
1724	Sir Arthur Guinness, brewer
1896	F. Scott Fitzgerald, novelist
1899	Sir William Dobell, artist
1936	Jim Henson, puppeteer
1941	Linda McCartney, activist
1942	Gerry Marsden, singer
1949	Pedro Almodóvar, movie director
1962	Nia Vardalos, actress
1966	Michael J. Varhola, author

Deaths

366	Pope Liberius
1143	Pope Innocent II
1541	Paracelsus, alchemist
1605	Manuel Mendes, composer
1991	Dr. Seuss, children's writer
2004	Françoise Sagan, writer

September 25

DATEline

Births
- 1881 Lu Xun, writer
- 1929 Ronnie Barker, comedian and actor
- 1931 Barbara Walters, journalist
- 1944 Michael Douglas, actor
- 1952 Christopher Reeve, actor
- 1961 Heather Locklear, actress
- 1969 Catherine Zeta-Jones, actress
- 1978 Jodie Kidd, model

Deaths
- 1534 Pope Clement VII
- 1849 Johann Strauss Sr., composer
- 1980 John Bonham, drummer (Led Zeppelin)
- 2005 Don Adams, actor and comedian, (Maxwell Smart)

HISTORICAL EVENTS

1066 The Battle of Stamford Bridge in York marks the end of the Viking era when the Saxons, fighting under English King Harold, win a decisive victory over the invading Norwegians, under King Harald Hardrada of Norway.

1929 Jimmy Doolittle, a renowned U.S. aviator, performs the first blind flight, taking off, flying a set course, and landing while under a fabric hood so he can't see outside the plane. This leads to the development of instrument flying.

1957 More than 1,000 paratroopers are ordered by U.S. President Dwight D. Eisenhower to escort nine black children to a high school in Little Rock, Arkansas. The Governor had earlier defied desegregation laws and ordered state troops to stop them attending.

1977 More than 15,000 people attend Steve Biko's funeral in South Africa. The anti-apartheid activist was killed in police custody on September 12 (see below).

1983 Thirty-eight IRA inmates escape from the high-security Maze prison, or H Blocks, in Northern Ireland, killing one guard. Within a few days 19 are recaptured, but many others are never found.

2003 France releases a shocking report that reveals 14,800 people died as a result of the recent summer heatwave when temperatures soared to more than 104°F (40°C).

Murdered and martyred freedom fighter

After his murder in police custody on September 12, 1977, black South African activist Steve Biko's funeral in his hometown of King William's Town was attended by more than 15,000 mourners. Thousands more were barred from attending by security forces, and riot police across the country broke up groups of mourners as they prayed. The service was conducted by Reverend Desmond Tutu, and representatives of governments from around the world flew in, signaling their disapproval of the violent and racist political regime of the country.

Biko's death caused outrage in South Africa and international condemnation. While officials claimed he killed himself, results from a post-mortem revealed that the inspirational activist, who had been in perfect health when he was detained, had died from severe brain damage that was the result of harsh beatings. Five policemen later admitted being involved in his death, although they were never prosecuted.

His grieving widow Nomtsikelelo Biko was left to raise their two children in a country divided by racial hatred and fear, but many credit his death as being the catalyst for serious change in South Africa. The accusations of murder against the Government by white South African newspaper editor Donald Wood, who fled to the U.K. where he campaigned for justice, and the film of Biko's life, *Cry Freedom*, brought his message and his suffering to the world. And the death of the leader of the Black Consciousness Movement helped highlight the plight of the many black political prisoners in the brutal apartheid regime of the nation, who were subjected to particularly gruesome methods of torture, endless detention without trial, and death in custody.

DAY TO REMEMBER

Religious day St. Finbarr's Day The bishop of Cork, in southern Ireland, in the sixth century, St. Finbarr (c. 550–620) became the patron saint for the city. He was known as Lochan, but renamed *Fionnbharr*, or "fairhead" in Irish, for the color of his hair. He died at Cloyne on September 25, 623, after evangelizing several towns and founding schools.

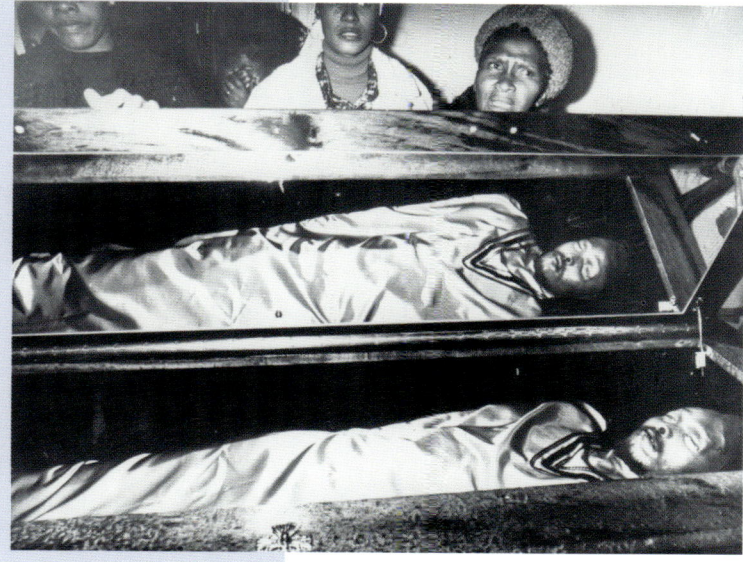

September 26

"Reality is a question of perspective; the further you get from the past, the more concrete and plausible it seems – but as you approach the present, it inevitably seems incredible." SALMAN RUSHDIE

HISTORICAL EVENTS

- **1580** Sir Francis Drake circumnavigates the globe in the *Golden Hind*, commissioned by Queen Elizabeth. He is the first captain to do so, given that Magellan didn't complete his voyage 60 years earlier.
- **1687** The Parthenon in Athens, a temple to the goddess Athena built in the fifth century B.C.E., is partially destroyed when gunpowder stored in the temple by the Turks explodes, damaging the building and many of its ancient sculptures.
- **1960** Around 70 million Americans tune in to watch the first ever televised debate between the presidential candidates. Vice-President Richard Nixon for the Republicans and Democratic hopeful Senator John F. Kennedy debate in a television studio in Chicago, Illinois. JFK wins the debate – and the election.
- **1973** Concorde makes its first non-stop crossing of the Atlantic. Pilots Jean Franchi and Gilbert Defer fly from Washington, U.S., to Orly Airport in Paris in just three hours and 32 minutes, half the previous world record time, flying at an average speed of 954 miles per hour (1,535 km/h).
- **1983** *Australia II*, the first non-American winner in the 132-year history of the race, takes out the America's Cup (see right).
- **1984** After 150 years of British rule, the U.K. agrees to hand over the colony of Hong Kong to China. The handover takes place at midnight on July 1, 1997.
- **1988** Salman Rushdie's book *The Satanic Verses* is published, inspired in part by the life of the prophet Mohammed. Although it is nominated for the Booker Prize, Muslims consider it blasphemous, and it is banned in many countries. At least 20 people are killed because of it, and the Ayatollah Khomeini later issues a *fatwa* calling on Muslims to execute anyone involved in the publication of the book, also placing a U.S. $2.8 million bounty on Rushdie's head.
- **2002** More than 1,000 people die as the Senegalese ferry *Le Joola* capsizes off the coast of Gambia in west Africa. There is outrage when people learn that the boat, licensed to take 531 passengers, had traveled with 1034.

DAY TO REMEMBER

International day The European Day of Languages This day is designated to celebrate linguistic diversity, pluri-lingualism, and lifelong language learning, with about 600 events planned each year to celebrate the beauty and diversity of language.

Births
- 1775 Johnny Appleseed, environmentalist
- 1888 T. S. Eliot, writer and Nobel laureate
- 1897 Pope Paul VI
- 1898 George Gershwin, composer
- 1936 Winnie Mandela, anti-apartheid activist
- 1943 Ian Chappell, cricketer
- 1945 Bryan Ferry, singer
- 1948 Olivia Newton-John, singer
- 1968 James Caviezel, actor
- 1981 Serena Williams, tennis champion

Deaths
- 1820 Daniel Boone, frontiersman
- 1868 August Ferdinand Möbius, astronomer
- 1945 Béla Bartók, composer
- 1965 Clara Bow, actress
- 1998 Betty Carter, singer
- 2003 Robert Palmer, singer

Aussie triumph

On September 26, 1983, an Australian entry won the America's Cup yacht race, the first non-American boat to do so. The defender, the New York Yacht Club, had held the Cup since 1851, the longest winning streak in sport.

The 12-meter yacht *Australia II* was designed by Ben Lexcen, who caused controversy with his innovative winged keel, which many attributed as the winning ingredient in the crew's game plan. The boat represented the Royal Perth Yacht Club of Australia, and was owned and bankrolled by Perth businessman Alan Bond, who was dubbed a national hero for his efforts – and later charged with unrelated criminal activity. The skipper was John Bertrand, a bronze medalist from the 1976 Montreal Olympics. He raced against American Dennis Conner, who sailed *Liberty*, off Newport, Rhode Island.

Australia II came from 3–1 down in the best-of-seven series to win four races to three, successfully beating the Americans for the first time in 132 years and 23 challenges. The next day the America's Cup was presented to Alan Bond, who had spent around $15 million over the years on four challenges.

The response in Australia to the win was ecstatic. Champagne flowed around the country, despite it being the early hours of the morning there, and the Prime Minister, Bob Hawke, famously implied that no one should go to work, saying: "You might as well take the day off. We will all be a team of zombies anyhow. And any boss who sacks anyone for not turning up today is a bum."

As America threatened, they won the Cup back four years later, with beaten skipper Dennis Conner sailing the yacht *Stars & Stripes* to victory for the San Diego Yacht Club.

September 27

"The only real prison is fear, and the only real freedom is freedom from fear." — AUNG SAN SUU KYI

HISTORICAL EVENTS

1822 French linguist Jean-François Champollion deciphers the Rosetta stone, a slab of granite found in Egypt that has a text in three scripts inscribed on it. His work unlocks the secrets of the hieroglyphs and reveals much about ancient Egypt.

1935 Judy Garland, aged 13, signs her first contract with MGM. She becomes a major star four years later when she stars as Dorothy in *The Wizard of Oz*, winning a special Oscar for her performance.

1953 Sri Mata Amritanandamayi Devi, later known as Amma, is born in Parayakadavu in India. She becomes a relentless charity worker and is considered a living saint. Labeled "the hugging saint," she has embraced 24 million people.

1964 After a 10-month investigation, the Warren Commission releases its report into the assassination of President John F. Kennedy, which concludes that killer Lee Harvey Oswald acted alone. Much evidence was suppressed, however, and not everyone accepts the ruling.

1968 The stage musical *Hair* controversially opens in the West End in London after the signing of the Theatres Act the day before abolishes censorship, which had been in force since 1737.

1988 The National League for Democracy, led by Aung San Suu Kyi, is founded in Burma and struggles for freedom from the military-led regime (see below).

DAY TO REMEMBER

Religious day St. Vincent de Paul's Day Born in France to a peasant family, Vincent de Paul (1576–1660) devoted his life to helping the poor. He became a priest, and spent a lot of time convincing the rich that they should contribute to his charities. His work lives on to this day in the welfare organization named after him.

Births
- 1601 King Louis XIII of France
- 1920 William Conrad, actor
- 1927 Romano Scarpa, comic book artist
- 1942 Alvin Stardust, singer
- 1947 Meat Loaf, singer
- 1958 Shaun Cassidy, entertainer
- 1961 Irvine Welsh, writer
- 1984 Avril Lavigne, singer

Deaths
- 1590 Pope Urban VII
- 1660 Vincent de Paul, saint
- 1700 Pope Innocent XII
- 1832 Karl Christian Friedrich Krause, philosopher
- 1917 Edgar Degas, painter
- 1960 Sylvia Pankhurst, suffragette
- 1986 Cliff Burton, musician (Metallica)

Inspirational activist

The National League for Democracy was founded on this day in 1988, a Burmese political party led by general secretary Aung San Suu Kyi. It has become the focus of international interest and a symbol of the fight for democracy and human rights.

In 1990, the military junta of the country called general elections, and the NLD won 406 of the 489 seats. Aung San Suu Kyi should have become Prime Minister – instead the results were overturned and the military retained power by force. She has become an international symbol of heroic and peaceful resistance in the face of oppression, and her nonviolent struggle won her the Nobel Peace Prize in 1991. (She used the $1.3 million prize money to establish a health and education trust for her people.) She has spent nine of the last 15 years in prison or under house arrest, but refused to abandon her country, even in the times she could have escaped.

Irish rock band U2 wrote the hit "Walk On" about Aung San Suu Kyi and have helped bring her plight to the world; other artists have also been publicly supportive of her cause. The devout Buddhist is the daughter of prominent Burmese diplomat Khin Kyi and General Aung San, who negotiated Burma's independence from the U.K. in 1947 before being assassinated. She has sacrificed everything, including her family, in her passionate struggle to see justice and peaceful democratic reform. Inspired by the nonviolent campaigns of U.S. civil rights leader Rev. Martin Luther King, Jr. and India's Mahatma Gandhi, she continues her work in the hopes that her people will one day be free.

September 28

DATE*line*

"Our greatest glory is not in never falling, but in rising every time we fall." — CONFUCIUS

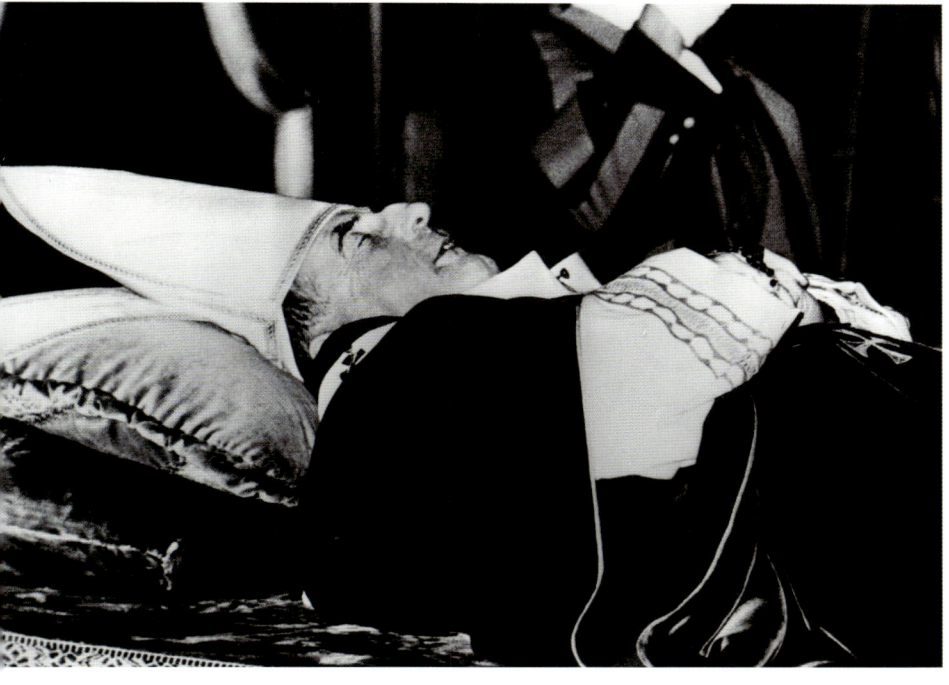

On this day in 1978, Pope John Paul I was found dead only 33 days after being elected to the office, making his pontificate one of the shortest in history. While the Vatican announced the cause of death as "possibly associated to a myocardial infarction," or heart attack, suspicion surrounds his death to this day. The pope's body was embalmed within a day of his death and no autopsy was performed, adding to suspicion of a conspiracy. Some Catholic groups claimed the liberal, working-class pope was poisoned in a plot by traditionalists.

He was known for his friendliness, warmth, and humility, and chose to have a much simpler coronation than usual. He also spoke to the UN about overpopulation in the third world, but died before he could comment on the church's long-held opposition to birth control. Born Albino Luciani on October 17, 1912, in Italy, he was a controversial choice for pope, but took on the role on August 26, 1978. His death created the Summer of Three Popes, as Pope Paul VI ruled until his death in August, John Paul reigned for 33 days, and John Paul II replaced him from October 16.

Births
- 551 B.C.E. Confucius, Chinese philosopher
- 1573 Caravaggio, artist
- 1823 Alexandre Cabanel, painter
- 1901 Ed Sullivan, TV show host
- 1916 Peter Finch, actor
- 1924 Marcello Mastroianni, actor
- 1934 Brigitte Bardot, actress
- 1967 Mira Sorvino, actress
- 1968 Naomi Watts, actress
- 1972 Gwyneth Paltrow, actress
- 1987 Hilary Duff, pop star

Deaths
- 1895 Louis Pasteur, scientist
- 1953 Edwin Hubble, astronomer
- 1964 Harpo Marx, comedian and actor
- 1966 André Breton, poet
- 1991 Miles Davis, jazz trumpeter
- 2003 Elia Kazan, film director

HISTORICAL EVENTS

1066 William the Conqueror, the Duke of Normandy, invades England to fight King Harold, who he believes has stolen the crown from him. He is crowned at Westminster Abbey on Christmas Day.

1871 Brazil passes the Law of the Free Womb, which emancipates the children of slaves. Any children born after this date must serve their mothers' masters without pay from the age of eight to 21, at which point they become fully free.

1973 The ITT Building in New York City is bombed to protest ITT's involvement in the overthrow of democratically elected President Salvador Allende by the Chilean military, led by General Pinochet and supported by the CIA.

1978 Pope John Paul I is found dead only 33 days after being elected (see above).

1985 Riots break out in Brixton, south London, when police shoot an innocent woman, Cherry Groce, in her bed. She spends two years in hospital and is crippled for life, but the officer who shot her is later cleared of any wrongdoing.

1991 American jazz trumpeter Miles Davis dies of pneumonia and other illnesses at the age of 65. He is acclaimed for his innovation in fusing jazz music with rock.

1994 The car ferry MS *Estonia* sinks in the Baltic Sea, killing 852 people, while sailing from Estonia to Sweden. A commission says it sank due to design faults, while the ship builder blames poor maintenance and excessive speed.

DAY TO REMEMBER

National day Teachers' Day (Taiwan) This festival commemorates the birth of the philosopher Confucius, considered a sage and the master educator of ancient China. He emphasised kindness, morality, duty to one's neighbor, and ruling by moral example not force, which developed into a system of philosophy known today as Confucianism.

September 29

"I wanted to hug somebody. This is an experience that you want to turn around and share with someone. Unfortunately when I turned around, there was no one there." — STACY ALLISON

On the top of the world

On September 29, 1988, after 29 days on the mountain, Stacy Allison became the first American woman to reach the summit of Mt. Everest, the world's highest mountain. "We had been trying to get the first American woman to the top for about nine years before I attempted the mountain. It got to the point where I thought: 'Well, why not me?'" she said later.

It was her second attempt at the 29,028-foot (8,848 m) peak. The year before she had been forced to turn back after the worst storm in 40 years trapped her party in a snow cave at 23,500 feet (7163 m) for five days. It was a devastating decision to have to make, given the long planning, huge financial expense, and physical exertion involved in attempting the climb, but she was determined to make it to the top, and soon accomplished her goal.

"Reaching that windswept perch, I decided, would…send me home with a title: The First American Woman to Climb Everest," she said. "When I got to the top I wanted to hug somebody. This is an experience that you want to turn around and share it with someone. But unfortunately when I turned around, there was no one there. There was nowhere else to climb. I was standing on the top of the world."

Nevertheless, Allison has continued to climb, leading expeditions on K2. The world's second highest mountain, K2 is regarded as more difficult to climb than Everest.

The first woman to reach the top of Everest was Junko Tabei of Japan, on May 16, 1975, who famously said: "I can't understand why men make all this fuss about Everest – it's only a mountain."

HISTORICAL EVENTS

1829 In London, the Metropolitan Police becomes the first official police department in the world. Founded by Home Secretary Sir Robert Peel, later the Prime Minister, it significantly reduces crime in London.

1952 At Inverness in Scotland, Londoner John Cobb, who holds the land speed record, dies attempting to set the water speed record at Loch Ness.

1960 Soviet leader Nikita Khrushchev disrupts a UN meeting by pounding his desk and shouting interruptions during a speech by British P.M. Harold Macmillan.

1979 In the first visit by a reigning Pope to the devoutly Catholic country of Ireland, John Paul II calls on the nation to "turn away from the paths of violence and return to the ways of peace." In Dublin he addresses 1.25 million people – nearly a third of Ireland's population.

1988 NASA launches the space shuttle *Discovery*, the first to take off since flights were grounded following the *Challenger* disaster two-and-a-half years earlier.

1995 In Los Angeles, the O. J. Simpson criminal trial is sent to the jury. The former pro footballer is charged with two counts of first-degree murder.

1997 British scientists establish a link between a human brain disease and one found in cows, and conclude that a new version of Creutzfeldt-Jakob disease, which has infected 21 people, was caused by eating meat infected with BSE, or "mad cow disease."

1998 Stacy Allison of Portland, Oregon, becomes the first American woman to conquer Mt. Everest, the tallest mountain in the world (see left).

Births
- 1547 Miguel de Cervantes, author
- 1703 François Boucher, painter
- 1758 Horatio Nelson, admiral
- 1901 Enrico Fermi, physicist
- 1904 Greer Garson, actress
- 1907 Gene Autry, entertainer
- 1931 Anita Ekberg, actress
- 1935 Jerry Lee Lewis, singer
- 1948 Bryant Gumbel, television host
- 1956 Sebastian Coe, athlete
- 1970 Emily Lloyd, actress

Deaths
- 1637 Lorenzo Ruiz, saint
- 1902 Émile Zola, writer
- 1930 Ilya Yefimovich Repin, painter
- 1973 W. H. Auden, poet
- 1988 Charles Addams, cartoonist
- 1997 Roy Lichtenstein, artist

DATE*line*

September 30

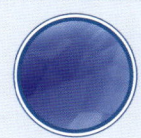

"Out beyond ideas of wrongdoing and rightdoing, there is a field. I will meet you there." RUMI

HISTORICAL EVENTS

1791 Acclaimed Austrian composer Wolfgang Amadeus Mozart premieres his opera *The Magic Flute*, or *Die Zauberflöte*, in Vienna. It is just two months before his death, so he doesn't live to see its immense success.

1846 The use of ether as an anesthetic is recorded for the first time by Boston dentist William Morton, who painlessly removes a tooth.

1927 Baseballer Babe Ruth, most famously of the New York Yankees, becomes the first player to hit 60 home runs in a season, a record that stands for 34 years.

1938 British Prime Minister Neville Chamberlain is applauded for bringing peace to Europe, after signing a non-aggression deal, the Munich Pact, with Adolf Hitler, who promises Germany will never go to war with Britain again. Eleven months later, Hitler invades Poland, and says the agreement was "just a scrap of paper."

1955 Actor James Dean dies in a car crash in California a month before his acclaimed film *Rebel Without a Cause* is released (see below).

1982 The television sitcom *Cheers* premieres in America. It is set in a bar in Boston and lasts 11 years; the hit show *Frasier* is a spin-off.

Births
- **1207** Jalal al-Din Muhammad Rumi, mystic and poet
- **1921** Deborah Kerr, actress
- **1924** Truman Capote, author
- **1931** Angie Dickinson, actress
- **1957** Fran Drescher, actress
- **1961** Eric Stoltz, actor
- **1972** Ari Behn, author
- **1980** Martina Hingis, tennis player
- **1982** Lacey Chabert, actress

Deaths
- **420** St. Jerome, translator of the Vulgate Bible
- **1572** St. Francis Borgia, Jesuit priest
- **1913** Rudolf Diesel, inventor
- **1943** Franz Oppenheimer, sociologist
- **1955** James Dean, actor
- **1990** Patrick White, writer and Nobel laureate

Death of the original "rebel"

On September 30, 1955, rising Hollywood star James Dean died in a car crash at just 24 years of age. He was driving his rare Porsche 550 Spyder to a race meet when the accident occurred near Cholame, California, a small town between Los Angeles and San Francisco. Another driver, student Donald Turnupseed, barreled around a sharp curve on the wrong side of the road and smashed straight into him. Contrary to legend, Dean was not speeding and was not at fault. He suffered a broken neck and several broken bones and was pronounced dead on arrival at a nearby hospital.

His death made him a cult hero, but according to critics he would have become an acting legend anyway. After some small television roles, he beat Paul Newman to play Cal in *East of Eden*. He received an Academy Award nomination for his performance as the alienated son whose problems with his father reflected Dean's own troubled childhood.

A month after his death, his second film *Rebel Without a Cause* was released. His brooding portrayal of youthful angst again garnered high praise, and he was regarded as the voice of a new, rebellious, and misunderstood generation.

Dean remains famous for his quote: "Live fast, die young, and leave a damn good-looking corpse behind." His grave is still visited by thousands of people every year, and his image continues to make millions of dollars annually for his estate.

DAYS TO REMEMBER

International day Translation Day
This day has been celebrated all over the world since 1953. It is organized by the International Federation of Translators and began as a tribute to St. Jerome, the Bible translator and patron saint of translators, writers, librarians, and students, which is why it is held on his feast day. It aims to promote these professions.

Celtic tree sign

IVY
September 30–October 27

Ivy people are unique, independent, and colorful, with their own style and beliefs. They are artistic, talented, and often radical thinkers, but can suffer from being indecisive or manipulative. They are ruthless and shrewd with their finances, yet very generous — a good combination.

DAYS TO REMEMBER *September*

1 — **St. Giles Day** A miracle worker and the patron saint of cripples and the poor

2 — J. R. R. Tolkien, writer, died in 1973

3 — **St. Gregory I's Day** Considered a doctor of the church and the founder of the early medieval papacy

4 — **St. Rose of Viterbo's Day** She is said to have brought her aunt back to life when she was just three, and performed many miracles

5 — **Feast Day of Blessed Mother Teresa** Devoted her life to helping the sick and the poor, working in the slums of Calcutta

8 — **Fiestas de Santa Fe (New Mexico)** Commemorates the reconquest of the city of Santa Fe

9 — **Chrysanthemum Day (Kiku no Sekku) (Japan)** This is one of the five ancient sacred festivals of Japan

10 — **World Suicide Prevention Day** Focuses global attention on the one million lives lost each year to suicide

11 — **Teacher's Day (Latin America)** Commemorates the life and work of Argentinian President, author, and educator Domingo F. Sarmiento

12 — **St. Ailbhe's Day** A bishop of Ireland and a disciple of St. Patrick, who became known for his charity

15 — **Independence Day** Celebrated on this day in the Central American countries of Costa Rica, El Salvador, Guatemala, Honduras and Nicaragua

16 — **Independence Day (New Guinea)** Commemorates New Guinea's independence from Australia in 1975

17 — **Feast Day for St. Lambert** The patron saint of many churches

18 — Jimi Hendrix, musician, died in 1970

19 — **Talk Like a Pirate Day** Celebrated around the world by anyone who cares to talk like a pirate at least one day a year

22 — **Hobbit Day** Celebrated by fans of author J. R. R. Tolkien and his books *The Hobbit* and *The Lord of the Rings*

23 — **Autumnal Equinox Day** Celebrated as a national holiday in Japan on the day of the equinox

24 — The first day of the star sign of Libra

25 — **St. Finbarr's Day** The bishop of Cork, in southern Ireland, in the sixth century. After his death became the patron saint of the city

26 — **The European Day of Languages** Celebrates linguistic diversity, plurilingualism, and lifelong language learning

29 — **Inventors' Day or Dia del Inventor (Argentina)** The birthday of Laszlo Jozsef Biro, the Hungarian-born inventor of the ballpoint pen and later resident of Argentina

30 — **Translation Day** Began as a tribute to St. Jerome, the Bible translator and patron saint of translators, writers, librarians and students

6

Independence Day (Swaziland) Celebrates Swaziland's independence as a member of the Commonwealth, and officially known as the Kingdom of Swaziland

7

Independence Day (Brazil) In 1822 Brazil declared its independence from Portugal

13

St. John Chrysostom's Day Famous for his eloquence in preaching and considered a doctor of the Church

14

Triumph of the Cross Celebrated in the Roman Catholic Church. In the Eastern Orthodox Church the Exaltation of the Cross is marked

20

Blessed Virgin Mary's Day Feast of nativity of Mary is celebrated in the Orthodox, Anglican and Roman Catholic Churches

21

H. G. Wells, writer, was born in 1866

27

St. Vincent de Paul's Day This saint's work lives on today in the welfare organization named after him

28

Teachers' Day (Taiwan) Commemorates the birth of the philosopher Confucius, considered the master educator of ancient China

Right Talk Like a Pirate Day, September 19

Bottom right Chrysanthemum Day, Japan, September 9

OCTOBER

"All things on earth point home in old October: sailors to sea; travelers to walls and fences; hunters to field and hollow and the long voice of the hounds; the lover to the love he has forsaken." — THOMAS WOLFE

In October, 1959, the revolutionary Guggenheim Museum of Art was opened. Designed by architect Frank Lloyd Wright, the museum, on Fifth Avenue, New York, marked a significant change in the way art was presented.

October

Scorpio star sign and scene of sowing seeds from the *Calendar and Book of Hours*, from fifteenth-century France. October begins in the sign of Libra and ends in the sign of Scorpio.

SPECIAL DATES

The first day of the month is International Day for the Elderly.

Columbus Day falls on the second Monday of October, as does Canada's Thanksgiving celebration.

United Nations Day on October 24 commemorates the day the UN Treaty was ratified.

General Napoleon Bonaparte appeared at the Council of 500 at St. Cloud in Paris, as depicted in this painting by François Bouchot, in the French Revolutionary Calendar month of *Brumaire*.

October is the tenth month in the Gregorian calendar and one of seven months with 31 days. The bulk of the year has passed and twilight approaches in the Northern Hemisphere. Autumn leaves have fallen, and living things prepare to hide away for the cold winter months. In the Southern Hemisphere the opposite is true – a crisp winter sleep unfolds into glorious spring as new life permeates the landscape. Libra becomes Scorpio as the astrological scales tip to reveal the sharp wit and bite of the scorpion, and spooks, ghouls, and witches walk the streets on Halloween.

ORIGINALLY THE EIGHTH MONTH of the year, October gets its name from the Latin and Greek *octo*, meaning "eight." The Roman calendar – a lunar calendar with only 10 months said to have been developed by Romulus, the founder of Rome – fell by the wayside in 46 B.C.E. after Julius Caesar consulted Alexandrian astronomer Sosigenes to develop a more user-friendly system to measure time. Two extra months were added, January and February; the new solar calendar (the Julian calendar) came into effect and October became the tenth month. In 1582, the Gregorian calendar further refined time measuring in relation to the movement of the planets when it was proposed by Calabrian doctor Aloysius Lilius and decreed by Pope Gregory XIII.

Various Roman emperors tried to rename the month of October to *Germanicus*, *Antoninus*, and *Faustina*; the French adopted the French Revolutionary Calendar for 12 years starting 1793, in which October was divided into *Vendémiaire* and *Brumaire*. In Anglo-Saxon times the month was known as *Winterfylleth*, and it marked the beginning of winter with the full moon, or fylleth, of that month. October's other names include *říjen* in Czech, *Wijnmaand* or wine month in Dutch, *lokakuu* or month of dirt in Finnish, *Damhar* or rutting time in Gaelic, *Deireadh Fómhair* in Irish, meaning end of harvest time, *Ekim* in Turkish, meaning the sowing of wheat, and *Kan'na dzuki* or absence of god in Japanese.

In Old German, the month was known as Wine Month. The Slavic races called October Yellow Month, after the fiery, rich colors of the leaves of the fall. They had two festivals in October: *Pasdernik*, or Day of the Ancients, on

October 26, a day of remembrance for the Ancient Ones and for the warriors who were killed in 1380 on Kulikovskoe Field in modern-day Russia; and Makoshe's Holiday, from *Pasdernic*, October 25, to *Gruden*, November 1, in which they honor Mother Earth and enjoy a vegetarian feast.

Native Americans and some Western Europeans celebrated the first full moon after the September Harvest Moon – the Hunter's Moon. The October full moon has an eerie yellow glow and travels in a low arc in the sky, therefore emitting more light than full moons in the other months. Hunters could see more clearly, and could easily spot their prey. The Feast of the Hunter's Moon, although still celebrated in some areas of the world (mainly the U.S.) with a festival of dancing, drumming, storytelling, and a festive meal, had died out in Europe by the start of the eighteenth century.

In the Northern Hemisphere, October is the middle month of fall, or autumn, and is a time for taking stock, settling in, and preparing for a cold winter ahead. In the Southern Hemisphere, October marks the middle of glorious spring, and many festivals throughout the world celebrate the mid-seasonal month as a time to give thanks or as a time for spiritual contemplation. Clocks are changed forward an hour for the beginning of daylight saving in the Southern Hemisphere, and backward in the Northern Hemisphere – hence the mnemonic "spring forward, fall back."

Celebrations today

Many festivals and feasts mark the significance of autumn in the Northern Hemisphere – the end of a cycle of life in death – and in the Southern Hemisphere, growth and a new cycle of life in the midst of spring. Hindus and Sikhs in India celebrate *Diwali* by lighting lamps to ward off evil and darkness; joyous religious feasts signify reward for spiritual observance, such as the Arabic *Eid ul-Fitr* following a month of fasting for Ramadan, and the Jewish *Sukkoth*, which falls five days after Yom Kippur. The date of Ramadan relies on the lunar Muslim calendar whereas Yom Kippur uses the Jewish calendar, so their exact dates are not set but usually fall in October.

Diwali, or the Festival of Lights, which is the biggest annual festival in India, brings its cities to life for five days and nights with magical displays of lights and lamps, and the crackles and pops of fireworks fill the air with excitement. The holiday is held in the Hindu month of

During the Hindu festival of *Diwali*, which falls in October, candles and sparklers are lit in celebration of the Hindu god, Lord Rama, leading the people from darkness into light.

October birthflower

Marigold, or calendula, is the birthflower for October. Its Latin meaning is "throughout the months." It signifies grief and jealousy, and has many medicinal uses due to its anti-inflammatory and antifungal properties. Called Mary's Gold by early Christians, the flower was associated with the Virgin Mary and put around her statue as offerings.

> ### October birthstone
> Pink tourmaline and beryl are associated with the month, and the modern October birthstone is opal. Beryl is unremarkable except in its green form – emerald – and its blue form – aquamarine. The name *opal* comes from the Latin *opalus* for precious stone. Its chemical makeup is similar to quartz, but with added pockets or spheres filled with water. This creates the beautiful, multi-colored, light-refractive properties of opals.

Ashwayuja, which is usually in October. Families and friends celebrate together, giving gifts of decoratively boxed sweets, and there's dancing and singing in the streets.

Lighting up the darkness and creating a magical wonderland of lights is significant in Hinduism to ward off evil spirits. The enchanting illuminations signify light banishing the dark, finding hope and joy despite hardship, achieving knowledge from ignorance, and spreading love among hatred. Oil lamps, clay lamps, and candles are lit in lavish displays throughout homes, and doorways are decorated with *torans*, garlands made of mango leaves and marigolds. *Rangolis*, beautiful symbolic designs, are drawn on floors with colored powder.

During this time, business dealings are friendly and fair, and gifts are swapped between clients and business owners. The business community starts its new year during the Diwali festival, and the general mood is one of happiness, celebration, and the exhilaration of a new start. The goddess of wealth is called upon, and Hindu gods Rama and Sita are welcomed with prayers. There is much reflection on the previous year and setting up positive energy for the year ahead. Diwali has the significance of a new year's celebration.

The end of the Islamic observance of Ramadan, a month of fasting, is the first day of the tenth month of the lunar calendar and is marked by Eid ul-Fitr. This usually falls in October. Early on the morning of Eid ul-Fitr, there are prayer ceremonies at mosques, where everyone wears their newest clothes. Families visit each other and gifts are given to children, and the feast of breaking the fast, Eid ul-Fitr, is enjoyed by all.

The Jewish harvest festival called *Sukkoth*, or Feast of the Tabernacles, is one of the oldest Jewish observances. It starts the fifteenth day of *Tishri*, the seventh month in the Jewish calendar, usually around mid-October. Meals are eaten in a temporary shelter, a *sukkah*, to commemorate the booths that sheltered the Israelites as they wandered in the wilderness for 40 years.

The largest fair in the world, Oktoberfest in Germany, now begins in September, to take advantage of the summer weather, and runs to October 3, which is a national holiday to mark the country's reunification in 1990. Each year, six million visitors flock to Munich in the German republic of Bavaria to partake in the celebrations, which center mainly on the consumption of beer. At the Munich celebration, the Mayor of Munich declares the event open with *"O'zapft is,"* which means "It's tapped," and the *bier* stars to flow.

Events shaping history

The Russian Revolution, or October Revolution, marks a violent chapter in history. The tsarist Government was overthrown by the Bolsheviks, led by Vladimir Lenin, in what would become the beginnings of the communist Soviet Union. There had been a long period of repression and unrest in the years after Peter the Great modernized Russia in the eighteenth century, turning it into an empire to rival European powers such as Germany. In 1905, strikes and anti-Government violence broke out against Tsar Nicholas II. This led to his abdication in February 1917. Then, in October of that year, Lenin led a coup d'état, and the Bolsheviks took power in 1922 after the Russian Civil War. Their mottos were: *End the war*, *All land to the peasants*, and *All power to the Soviets*.

The Brits will never forget the Great Storm of 1987. The worst weather in southeast England since 1703 hit on October 15 and 16, 1987, and

The Feast of the Tabernacles is a Jewish celebration which falls in mid- to late October. This eighteenth-century engraving by Bernard Picart depicts the tradition, where, even today, families eat in temporary shelters.

caused major damage to electricity supplies, roads, houses, and trees as winds ravaged the landscape at 58 miles per hour (94 km/h). Trucks were turned over and ancient forests leveled as the winds made their way across the countryside. Fifteen million trees were felled and ships were driven to shore. Sixteen people died, and the damage bill ran into millions. Another unexpected severe storm swept across England in 1990.

October finishes with Halloween. Many people have childhood memories of makeshift Halloween costumes and shy door-knocking while a parent stood by to supervise, finally being rewarded with bags of sweets. Now mainly observed in the U.S., Canada, and the U.K., after sundown on October 31 children dress as witches, ghosts, and ghouls, and go trick or treating. "Trick or treat?" usually garners the answer "Treat" as bags fill up with sweets. Jack-o'-lanterns peep out from windows, and apple-bobbing and other Halloween games provide fun and laughter.

Beer is the order of the day during Oktoberfest, which takes place in Munich, Germany, and runs from mid-September into October.

Although celebrated on a huge scale in the U.S., the origins of Halloween date back to Celtic Ireland. The postcard below, from the early 1900s, depicts the magical world of the Witch's Dance, complete with dancing pumpkins.

October 1

"We will not learn how to live together in peace by killing each other's children."

FORMER U.S. PRESIDENT JIMMY CARTER

HISTORICAL EVENTS

1869 Austrian economics professor Dr. Emanuel Herrmann sends the world's first postcard. It is "no larger than an envelope, sent open via the mails."

1903 The first official World Series Baseball game is played between Boston Americans (later Red Sox) and the Pittsburgh Pirates.

1962 In a significant civil rights move, James Meredith is admitted to the University of Mississippi after refusal to admit him sparked vicious riots.

1964 The Free Speech Movement begins at the University of California, Berkeley, leading to other major student protests of the time.

1964 Bullet Trains, or *Shinkansen*, begin service in Japan (see below).

1971 The Walt Disney World Resort opens in Orlando, Florida, in the U.S., the second Disney theme park after Disneyland, which opened in 1955 in California.

1975 Muhammad Ali wins his third fight against Joe Frazier in the "Thrilla in Manila" to retain the world heavyweight boxing title.

Births
- 1881 William Boeing, engineer
- 1887 Violet Jessop, *Titanic* survivor
- 1910 Bonnie Parker, outlaw
- 1920 Walter Matthau, actor
- 1924 Jimmy Carter, U.S. President
- 1930 Sir Richard Harris, actor
- 1932 Albert Collins, musician
- 1935 Julie Andrews, actress

Deaths
- 1310 Beatrice of Burgundy, heiress
- 1404 Pope Boniface IX, religious leader
- 1708 John Blow, composer
- 1864 Rose Greenhow, spy
- 1985 E. B. White, author

DAYS TO REMEMBER

Religious day St. Thérèse de Lisieux's Day Known as the "Little Flower of Jesus," St. Thérèse (1873–1897) is patron saint of the missions, and best known for her spiritual autobiography, *The Story of a Soul*.

National day People's Republic Day (China) The people of China celebrate the anniversary of the founding of the People's Republic of China in 1949 with parades, celebrations, and fireworks. The festivities last from a few days to a week.

In a race for faster public transport, Japanese *Shinkansen* first went into service on this day in 1964, in time for the Summer Olympics in Tokyo. The high-speed passenger train carried excited commuters from Tokyo to Osaka in a record time of four hours, and traveled at a speed of 200 miles per hour (321 km/h). The line was extended to Fukuoka on the island of Kyushu in 1975, and now the network links most of Japan's major cities. A decade later, the trains reached speeds of 186 miles per hour (300 km/h). The Japanese have now developed an even faster train – the *Maglev*. The train levitates above the track, and without the friction of a track to slow it down, reaches speed of up to 361 miles per hour (581 km/h).

DATE*line*

October 2

"Each morning when I open my eyes I say to myself: I, not historical events, have the power to make me happy or unhappy today." — GROUCHO MARX

HISTORICAL EVENTS

1836 British naturalist Charles Darwin completes his journey of four years, nine months and five days on H.M.S. *Beagle* to South America, where he collects data and specimens for research into his theory of evolution.

1889 Nicholas C. Creede discovers silver at Willow Creek, Colorado, in the last silver boom in the U.S. Old West.

1950 Syndicated daily comic strip *Peanuts*, by cartoonist Charles M. Schulz, is first printed in seven U.S. newspapers. It continues until the year 2000.

1958 Science-fiction TV series *The Twilight Zone* premieres on CBS in the U.S., hosted and created by Rod Serling.

1962 Johnny Carson becomes host of NBC's long-running *Tonight Show*, a role he would continue for 30 years, until 1992, when Jay Leno takes over.

1968 Demonstrations held 10 days before the Olympic Games in Mexico City end in the Tlatelolco Massacre, in which 300 civilians are killed by army and police personnel.

1974 U.S. scientists announce that cannabis causes brain damage, after testing monkeys' reactions to the drug (see right).

1993 Violent riots erupt in Moscow as pro-communist demonstrators clash with President Boris Yeltzen's security forces.

DAYS TO REMEMBER

Religious day Memorial Day for Guardian Angels This day is set aside in honor of the protective spirits, or guardian angels, who are said to be assigned to each person to protect them from danger throughout their lives.

National day Gandhi Jayanti (India) On this national holiday every year, the birthday of spiritual leader Mohandas Karamchand (Mahatma) Gandhi is celebrated as people pay homage to the man who was instrumental in helping the country achieve independence from Britain.

Births
- 1869 Mahatma Gandhi, political leader
- 1890 Groucho Marx, comedian and actor
- 1895 Bud Abbott, comedian and actor
- 1945 Don McLean, songwriter
- 1948 Donna Karan, fashion designer
- 1951 Sting, musician

Deaths
- 1803 Samuel Adams, revolutionary leader
- 1968 Marcel Duchamp, Dada artist
- 1985 Rock Hudson, actor
- 1998 Gene Autry, singer

Monkey magic

The plant *Cannabis sativa* is believed to have originated in the mountainous regions of India, near the Himalayas, but has been used for thousands of years in various cultures for spiritual and medicinal purposes, and woven as fabric. Although made illegal in the U.S. in 1937, use of the plant as a recreational drug flourished and by the 1960s the drug was synonymous with the music scene, hippies, and peace.

The Establishment went to great lengths to discourage users and to ascertain the damage caused by the drug. In 1974, it was thought medical science reached a breakthrough when New Orleans doctor Robert Heath experimented with 21 rhesus monkeys, assessing the temporary and lasting brain effects of cannabis use.

The creatures were given two marijuana cigarettes a day for a year, while electrodes measured their brain activity. Dr. Heath's findings stated that major damage *was* incurred. The brain patterns were tested again after six months, and showed the damage still existed and may have been permanent. His conclusion: Cannabis causes brain damage. Dr. Heath's findings are now considered inconclusive due to the low number of monkeys tested.

October 3

"The four sweetest words in the American lexicon are: I told you so."

GORE VIDAL, FROM *IMPERIAL AMERICA*

HISTORICAL EVENTS

1789 U.S. President George Washington proclaims the first Thanksgiving Day, setting aside November 26 as a day of public thanksgiving and prayer, originally for a good harvest.

1942 Germany takes a leap in the "space race" by launching the first artificial object to reach space – the A4 Rocket – from Peenemünde test site.

1960 *The Andy Griffith Show*, a comedy starring Andy Griffith and Ron Howard, debuts on U.S. TV network CBS.

1962 Spacecraft *Sigma* 7, manned by astronaut Walter "Wally" Schirra, completes six Earth orbits as part of NASA's Mercury 8 project.

1988 Cable network Turner Network Television (TNT) is launched by U.S. media mogul Ted Turner.

1990 East Germany and West Germany reunite to become the Federal Republic of Germany (see below).

1995 U.S. football star O. J. Simpson is found "not guilty" of murdering his ex-wife Nicole and her friend Ronald Goldman in a controversial nine-month trial.

2004 *Desperate Housewives* premieres in the U.S., starring Teri Hatcher, Eva Longoria, Nicollette Sheridan, and Marcia Cross, and gains phenomenal success.

Births
- **1790** John Ross, Cherokee chief
- **1900** Thomas Wolfe, author
- **1925** Gore Vidal, author
- **1941** Chubby Checker, musician
- **1962** Tommy Lee, musician (Mötley Crüe)
- **1969** Gwen Stefani, singer
- **1973** Neve Campbell, actress
- **1984** Ashlee Simpson, singer

Deaths
- **1226** St. Francis of Assisi, friar
- **1965** Zachary Scott, actor
- **1967** Woody Guthrie, musician
- **1998** Roddy McDowall, actor
- **2004** Janet Leigh, actress

DAY TO REMEMBER

National day Foundation Day (South Korea) Also called the Festival of the Opening of Heaven, celebrations on this day mark the founding of Gojoseon, the original kingdom of Korea, in 2333 B.C.E. by mythological grandson of the god of heaven, Dangun Wanggeom.

Reunification of Germany

The German Democratic Republic (East Germany) was incorporated into the Federal Republic of Germany (FRG) on this day in 1990. The FRG offered a higher standard of living than the GDR, and the imbalance caused countless problems.

At the end of World War II, Berlin was divided into four sectors: American, British, French, and Soviet. Travel between the sectors was difficult. In 1949 the FRG and GDR were founded. The borders between East and West were closed in 1952, and by 1961 all crossings between East and West Berlin were blocked by the Berlin Wall.

Families and friends were separated, causing suffering and heartbreak. Communist East Berlin was drab in contrast to the wealthy West, but tourists flocked there – partly out of curiosity and partly because of its historical treasures.

Many entered through Checkpoint Charlie, where guards meticulously checked tour buses for illegal imports and, on their return, for illegal aliens. Then U.S. President Ronald

Reagan visited Berlin in 1987, imploring Soviet General Secretary Mikhail Gorbachev to tear down the wall to improve living standards and wealth in the East.

It wasn't until 1989 that the city was opened up and citizens of both East and West could cross the borders freely. The Fall of the Berlin Wall on November 9, 1989, marked the end of the Cold War. The division of East and West was abolished and there was much jubilation. Berliners and visitors hammered off chunks of the wall, a symbol of division that had caused so much sorrow.

October 4

DATEline

"We don't deliberately set out to offend, unless we feel it's justified."
GRAHAM CHAPMAN, MEMBER OF COMEDY TEAM MONTY PYTHON

On this day in 1999, the iconic "Welcome to Fabulous Las Vegas" sign went dark when new owners overlooked an electricity bill. The sign was created by Western Neon in 1959, and soon became synonymous with the gambling capital. Once the paltry amount owing – U.S.$60 – had been paid, the sign returned to its former glory, welcoming visitors at the south end of the strip. Although the sign is instantly recognizable, it's small in size and pales in comparison to the larger-than-life structures and bright lights of modern-day Vegas.

HISTORICAL EVENTS

1537 The Matthew Bible is printed under the pseudonym Thomas Matthew. It is the first complete English Bible, translated from the original languages.
1582 The Gregorian calendar is decreed by Pope Gregory XIII, and October 4 of this year is followed by October 15 in Italy, Spain, Portugal, and Poland.
1824 The Mexican Constitution of 1824 is adopted and Mexico becomes a republic.
1895 The U.S. Golf Association hosts the first U.S. Open Men's Golf Championship on a nine-hole course in Newport, Rhode Island.
1931 Cartoonist Chester Gould's hard-hitting detective comic strip *Dick Tracy* first appears, in the *Detroit Mirror*.
1957 Russian satellite *Sputnik I* is launched, becoming the first artificial object to leave Earth's atmosphere.
1983 Richard Noble, in his vehicle *Thrust 2*, sets a land speed record of 633.468 miles per hour (1019.44 km/h) at Black Rock Desert in Nevada in the U.S.
1999 The gambling capital's iconic "Welcome to Fabulous Las Vegas" sign goes black when the owners neglect to pay their electricity bill (see above).

Births
1625 Richard Cromwell, Lord Protector of England
1814 Jean-François Millet, painter
1895 Buster Keaton, comedian and actor
1924 Charlton Heston, actor
1937 Jackie Collins, author
1941 Anne Rice, writer
1946 Susan Sarandon, actress
1960 Afrika Bambaataa, musician
1967 Liev Schreiber, actor
1976 Alicia Silverstone, actress

Deaths
1669 Rembrandt, painter
1821 John Rennie, engineer
1970 Janis Joplin, singer
1989 Graham Chapman, comedian

DAYS TO REMEMBER

Religious day St. Francis of Assisi's Day Nature-lover and patron of animals, Francis (1181–1226) founded the Franciscan Order, which stood for the virtues of humility and poverty, in 1209. Many would follow his teachings – he called them *fraticelli*, or "little brothers."

International day World Animal Day Humans' relationship with animal life is celebrated the world over with special events on this day. The various roles of animals – as companions, helpers, and as food – are honored. The day was started in 1931 in Italy as a way of raising awareness of the plight of endangered species.

October 5

> *"Everything that rock and roll is meant to be is happening now."*
> SIR BOB GELDOF

HISTORICAL EVENTS

1905 Pioneer of flight Wilbur Wright sets a world record in *Flyer III* with 39 minutes in the air for a flight of 24½ miles (39 km).
1921 World Series Baseball games receive radio coverage for the first time, reaching many more fans and increasing the popularity of the game.
1945 Warner Bros workers riot at the studio gates after a six-month strike in what is known as Hollywood Black Friday.
1947 U.S. President Harry S. Truman gives the very first televised White House address, in which he asks citizens to refrain from eating meat on Tuesdays and poultry on Thursdays to help stockpile grain for starving Europeans.
1962 The Beatles release their first hit, "Love Me Do."
1994 Forty-eight members of religious cult Order of the Solar Temple die in apparent mass suicides in Cheiry and Granges-Sur-Salvan in Switzerland.
2001 A Boca Raton, Florida, man dies of anthrax poisoning when he receives contaminated mail (see right).

DAYS TO REMEMBER

National day Republic Day (Portugal) On this day of national celebration, the Portuguese commemorate the day the country was proclaimed an independent republic in 1910, after the monarchy was overthrown.

International day World Teachers' Day Each year on this day, inspirational teachers are honored for their hard work and wisdom. The observance was launched in 1994 by UNESCO.

Births
- 1829 Chester A. Arthur, twenty-first U.S. President
- 1902 Ray Kroc, fast food entrepreneur
- 1919 Donald Pleasence, actor
- 1933 Diane Cilento, actress
- 1947 Brian Johnson, musician
- 1951 Bob Geldof, musician
- 1967 Guy Pearce, actor
- 1975 Kate Winslet, actress
- 1983 Nicky Hilton, hotel heiress

Deaths
- 877 Charles the Bald, King of France
- 1565 Lodovico Ferrari, mathematician
- 1837 Hortense de Beauharnais, Queen of Holland
- 1983 Earl Tupper, inventor
- 2004 Rodney Dangerfield, comedian

Anthrax attacks

Five people died and 22 developed severe anthrax infections as a result of bio-terrorism attacks when anthrax spores were sent through the U.S. postal system. The attacks occurred over the course of a few weeks in 2001 in the aftermath of the World Trade Center terrorist attacks on New York, and the crimes were never solved.

Anthrax, an infectious disease of cattle and sheep characterized by skin ulcers, usually ends in death for humans who have not been vaccinated against it. Weaponised strains of the disease have been used in biological warfare programs by the U.S. and other countries.

The affected letters were mailed to various news media offices – ABC News, CBS News, NBC News, the *New York Post*, and American Media Inc (AMI) – and to U.S. Senators Tom Daschle of South Dakota and Patrick Leahy of Vermont. The first casualty was Robert Stevens, who worked as picture editor for AMI newspaper *The Sun*. He died from the disease on this day, soon after being infected.

Thomas Morris Jr. and Joseph Curseen from the Brentwood mail facility in Washington D.C. were the next victims, and New York resident Kathy Nguyen and Ottilie Lundgren, a Connecticut widow, also died, possibly from cross-contamination of mail.

In the days after the attacks, many hoaxes were reported. The FBI issued a warning that any perpetrators of such hoaxes would be fined, arrested, and jailed.

October 6

"The best time I ever had with Joan Crawford was when I pushed her down the stairs."

BETTE DAVIS

HISTORICAL EVENTS

1889 Inventor Thomas Edison shows his first motion picture on a predecessor to the modern film projector.
1927 The first feature-length talking movie, *The Jazz Singer*, starring Al Jolson, opens on Broadway.
1945 Greek immigrant Vasili Sianis and his pet billy goat are ejected from the field at a World Series Baseball game in Wrigley Field, Chicago, as their presence is believed to be bad luck.
1966 The psychedelic drug LSD is made illegal in the U.S. Prior to this, psychiatrists would use the drug to gain an understanding of schizophrenia.
1995 The planet Bellerophon is found orbiting 51 Pegasi (see below).
2000 Slobodan Milosevic, President of the Federal Republic of Yugoslavia, is forced to resign after public rebellion.
2001 A record 74,554 attend a Michigan University hockey game. The record is broken three years later at a game in Edmonton, Canada.
2004 A U.S. arms inspector in Iraq, Charles Duelfer, admits to finding no stockpiles of weapons of mass destruction in Saddam Hussein's Iraq.

DAYS TO REMEMBER

International day Mad Hatter Day This is a second nonsense day to complement April Fools' Day, at the opposite end of the year. On this day, people are encouraged to act like the Mad Hatter from *Alice in Wonderland*. It is celebrated in the U.K. in June.

National day Ivy Day (Ireland) On this day every year, the Irish wear sprigs of ivy to commemorate the death of Irish patriot Charles Stuart Parnell in 1891. This leading political figure was known as the "Uncrowned King of Ireland."

Births
1289 King Wenceslaus III, Bohemian King
1846 George Westinghouse, engineer
1887 Le Corbusier, architect
1905 Helen Wills Moody, tennis player
1908 Carole Lombard, actress
1931 Riccardo Giacconi, physicist
1935 Bruno Sammartino, strongman
1942 Britt Ekland, actress
1943 Gerry Adams, politician
1963 Elisabeth Shue, actress

Deaths
1536 William Tyndale, Bible translator
1873 Sir Paul Edmund Strzelecki, explorer
1892 Alfred Lord Tennyson, poet
1946 Johnny O'Keefe, singer
1980 Hattie Jacques, actress
1989 Bette Davis, actress
1992 Denholm Elliott, actor

Planet discovered around 51 Pegasi

Prior to the discovery of a Jupiter-like planet orbiting the star 51 Pegasi in 1995, the Sun was thought to be the only major star with orbiting planets, and therefore perhaps the only solar system able to support life forms. The new discovery had the astronomy world speculating about possibilities of life in the newly discovered solar system.

A yellow-orange dwarf star approximately 7.5 billion years old, 51 Pegasi is 50.1 light years away from Earth. It is visible from Earth with binoculars, or even with the naked eye in good weather conditions if there is no light pollution present. Its planet, nicknamed Bellerophon after the Greek hero who tamed Pegasus, was discovered using radial velocity measuring techniques by astronomers Michel Mayor and Didier Queloz at the Observatoire de Haute-Provence in the southeast of France. They used the Elodie spectrograph, which measures the properties of light over the electromagnetic spectrum using the Doppler effect. With this process, they could ascertain the speed at which stars, galaxies, and other celestial beings move away from or toward us — their radial velocity — to give an indication of their nature and rotation speed.

Although we may never be able to see Bellerophon due to its great distance from Earth, research indicates it has a dark gray or brown appearance due to the presence of sodium gases, with clouds of silicates creating a white shroud around it. The planet, said to experience an eternal sunset due to its tidally locked rotation, is not conducive to living creatures as its surface temperature reaches 2,000°F (1,093°C), and extremely hot winds batter its rocky surface.

October 7

"A gentleman with a pug nose is a contradiction in terms." — EDGAR ALLAN POE

HISTORICAL EVENTS

1769 Captain James Cook discovers and maps New Zealand. Abel Tasman had charted the west coast in 1642, unaware of the extent of the land.
1919 Airline KLM is founded by pilot Albert Plesman in the Netherlands. It is the oldest airline still using its original name, although it is now owned by Air France–KLM.
1931 The first infrared photograph is taken in Rochester, New York. The process allows pictures to be taken in total darkness.
1957 Television show *American Bandstand* debuts in Philadelphia as *Bob Horn's Bandstand*, later to be hosted by Dick Clark.
1959 The U.S.S.R.'s *Luna 3* spacecraft takes the first photographs of the Moon's far side.
1963 Hurricane Flora kills 7,190 people in Haiti and the Dominican Republic.
1982 The Andrew Lloyd Webber musical *CATS* opens on Broadway. It runs for 18 years and 7,485 performances (see below).
2001 The U.S. and British Armies launch air strikes against the Taliban in Afghanistan.
2003 Action movie star Arnold Schwarzenegger is elected Governor of California.

Births
1697 Canaletto, artist
1900 Heinrich Himmler, Nazi leader
1931 Desmond Tutu, archbishop
1935 Thomas Keneally, author
1951 John Cougar Mellencamp, singer
1952 Vladimir Putin, Russian President
1955 Yo-Yo Ma, cellist
1959 Simon Cowell, record executive

Deaths
1849 Edgar Allan Poe, writer
1959 Mario Lanza, opera tenor
1994 Niels Kaj Jerne, immunologist

DAY TO REMEMBER

Religious day Feast day for Our Lady of the Rosary Pope St. Pius V established this feast day in 1573 to commemorate the role of the rosary in the victory of the Christians over the Turks in the Battle of Lepanto.

Based on T. S. Eliot's book of children's poems, *Old Possum's Book of Practical Cats*, published in 1939, composer Andrew Lloyd Webber's musical opened at the Winter Garden Theater and went on to be seen by more than 10 million people during its incredible 18-year Broadway run. After 7,485 performances, *CATS* had its final curtain call on Broadway on September 10, 2000. The winner of seven Tony Awards, it still holds top honors, followed by *Phantom of the Opera* and *Les Miserables*, as Broadway's longest-running show.

October 8

DATEline

"I'm Chevy Chase, and you're not." CHEVY CHASE ON *SATURDAY NIGHT LIVE*

Martha Stewart goes to jail

Educated at Barnard College, New York, Martha Stewart's early career began with modeling and television commercials, and included a stint as a stockbroker between 1967 and 1973.

Following the huge success of her catering business, started in 1976, and run from her home in Westport, Connecticut, Stewart went on to coauthor the book *Entertaining*, and continued to build a lucrative empire in television and publishing – aimed at home-care advice ranging from cooking to gardening and crafts – until her indictment on June 4, 2003.

The original indictment – including charges of making false statements, obstruction of justice, and insider trading – arose from an investigation by the U.S. Securities and Exchange Commission into Stewart's sale of 4,000 shares of biopharmaceutical company ImClone on the day before the price of the shares fell dramatically on the stock exchange. Stewart was ultimately indicted for her part in the cover-up rather than the more serious charge of insider trading. She maintained her innocence and pleaded not guilty on all charges.

After five weeks of evidence, and three days of deliberation by the jury, Stewart was found guilty and sentenced to five months in a minimum-security prison, five months house arrest, and two years probation.

Following her release from prison on March 4, 2005, Martha Stewart began rebuilding her TV and publishing interests. She made a TV comeback with the show *Martha*, garnering six nominations at the Daytime Emmy Awards in 2006.

HISTORICAL EVENTS

1871 The Great Chicago Fire starts. The blaze kills 300 and leaves 100,000 homeless.
1944 Family sitcom *The Adventures of Ozzie and Harriet* debuts on CBS Radio.
1956 New York Yankees player Don Larsen pitches the first and only perfect game in Game 5 of the World Series Baseball, to beat the Brooklyn Dodgers. The following year the Dodgers move to LA.
1978 Motorboat racer Ken Warby sets a world water speed record of 317.6 miles per hour (511.11 km/h) at Blowering Dam, NSW, Australia.
1998 Oslo's modern, larger Gardermoen Airport opens, taking over from Fornebu as Norway's gateway to the world.
2004 Lifestyle guru Martha Stewart goes to jail for "obstructing justice and lying to investigators about a well-timed stock sale" (see above).
2005 A 7.6 magnitude earthquake hits mountainous Northern Pakistan and India, with its epicenter in Kashmir, and kills 87,350 people.

DAY TO REMEMBER

Religious day St. Keyne's Day This pious virgin traveled widely throughout Wales, Cornwall, and Somerset in the U.K. in about 409, spreading the message of peace on Earth. She was also an early campaigner for the equality of women. There is a church named in her honor in Cornwall, and newlyweds rush to drink from its well with the promise of gaining the upper hand in their marriage.

Births
1895 Juan Perón, Argentinian President
1936 Rona Barrett, gossip columnist
1936 David Carradine, actor
1939 Paul Hogan, actor
1941 Jesse Jackson, civil rights activist
1943 Chevy Chase, actor
1948 Johnny Ramone, musician
1949 Sigourney Weaver, actress
1956 Stephanie Zimbalist, actress
1970 Matt Damon, actor

Deaths
1869 Franklin Pierce, U.S. President
1978 Jacques Brel, singer
1983 Joan Hackett, actress
2004 Jacques Derrida, philosopher

October 9

"Many will call me an adventurer – and that I am, only one of a different sort: one of those who risks his skin to prove his platitudes." — "CHE" GUEVARA

HISTORICAL EVENTS

- **1776** Father Francisco Palou founds Mission San Francisco de Asis, which later becomes the U.S. city of San Francisco.
- **1919** In the most famous scandal in baseball history, the Chicago White Sox "throw in" the series against the Cincinnati Reds. Eight players are banned from baseball for life.
- **1930** Pioneer aviatrix Laura Ingalls is the first woman to fly across the U.S., from New York to California with nine stops. The same year, she performs 344 loops, setting a women's record, then beats her own record with 930. She also breaks both the women's and men's record for barrel rolls with 714.
- **1936** The first generator at Boulder Dam (later renamed Hoover Dam) began commercial operation, transmitting electricity from the Colorado River to LA.
- **1967** Ernesto "Che" Guevara is executed by Bolivian soldiers (see below).
- **1989** A Soviet Union news agency reports that scientists confirm the landing of a UFO in Voronezh, southern Russia, and the alien spaceship carries giant "humanoids."
- **1992** A 3-pound (1.4 kg) meteorite lands in the Knapp family's driveway in Peekskill, New York, destroying Michelle Knapp's Chevy Malibu.
- **2005** China's Bureau of Surveying and Mapping officially announces the height of Mt. Everest as 29,017.16 feet (8,844.43 m) – 12.14 feet (3.7 m) lower than previously thought.

Births
- **1201** Robert de Sorbon, Sorbonne founder
- **1873** Charles Walgreen, entrepreneur
- **1908** Jacques Tati, filmmaker
- **1940** John Lennon, musician and Beatle
- **1944** John Entwistle, musician
- **1944** Peter Tosh, musician
- **1948** Jackson Browne, musician
- **1952** Sharon Osbourne, music manager
- **1953** Tony Shalhoub, actor
- **1969** P. J. Harvey, musician
- **1975** Sean Lennon, musician

Deaths
- **1729** Richard Blackmore, physician and writer
- **1934** Alexander I, Yugoslav King
- **1958** Pope Pius XII, 260th pope
- **1974** Oskar Schindler, businessman
- **1978** Jacques Brel, musician

DAYS TO REMEMBER

National day Hangul Day (South Korea) The proclamation of the Korean phonetic alphabet by King Sejong the Great in 1446 is celebrated on this day in South Korea.

National day Leif Erikson Day (Scandinavia and U.S.) This day honors Nordic explorers and Viking pioneers. Leif Erikson was the first European to set foot in North America.

National day Guayaquil Independence Day (Ecuador) Citizens of Ecuador celebrate their independence from Spain on this day in 1820.

It was while working for Cuban newspaper *Revolution* that Albert Korda (born Alberto Diaz Gutierrez) took his most famous photograph: That of "Che" Guevara, Cuban guerilla leader and left-wing revolutionary. The photograph was taken in 1960 at a memorial service attended by Guevara and Cuban leader Fidel Castro. The picture, called *Guerrillero Heroico*, was not published, however, until 1967 – in Italy, on a poster after Guevara's death in Bolivia on October 9. Korda continued his work as a photographer until his death in Paris in 2001, aged 72. He received no royalties for the famous image. The image of Guevara in this mosaic is modeled on Korda's photograph.

October 10

"I am a very committed wife. And I should be committed too – for being married so many times." — ELIZABETH TAYLOR

Births
- 1731 Henry Cavendish, scientist
- 1813 Giuseppe Verdi, composer
- 1917 Thelonious Monk, jazz pianist
- 1924 Ed Wood, filmmaker
- 1930 Harold Pinter, playwright
- 1954 David Lee Roth, singer

Deaths
- 1659 Abel Tasman, explorer
- 1875 Aleksey Konstantinovich Tolstoy, novelist and poet
- 1985 Orson Welles, actor and director
- 2004 Christopher Reeve, actor

HISTORICAL EVENTS

- **1933** In the first proven case of sabotage of a commercial airline flight, a United Airlines Boeing 247 explodes en route from Cleveland to Chicago, killing seven.
- **1966** The album *Parsley, Sage, Rosemary, and Thyme* by Simon and Garfunkel is released. it will become number 201 in *Rolling Stone* magazine's list of greatest albums of all time.
- **1967** The Outer Space Treaty comes into force, detailing guidelines for exploration of space and banning the stationing of weapons of mass destruction in outer space.
- **1971** The rebuilding of London Bridge in Lake Havasu City, Arizona, is completed (see right).
- **1975** Richard Burton and Elizabeth Taylor secretly remarry in Africa, 16 months after their divorce.
- **1979** Pac-Man is released to the Japanese market by Namco, soon to become a worldwide craze.
- **1980** Three thousand die and 8,000 are injured after a 7.3-magnitude earthquake in El Asnam, Algeria.

DAYS TO REMEMBER

International day World Mental Health Day Founded by the World Federation for Mental Health, this day has been observed since 1992. Each year a different theme is chosen, relating to common mental health issues. The Foundation hopes to raise awareness of mental health issues and encourage treatment.

National Day Independence Day (Fiji) On this day in 1970, Fiji gained independence from Britain. Fijians celebrate for an entire week leading up to October 10 with religious ceremonies, dance, and music based around a different theme each year.

London Bridge dedication in Lake Havasu City

When it was discovered, in 1962, that London Bridge was sinking into the Thames River, a buyer was sought. It was purchased in 1968, by American Robert P. McCulloch, for just under $2.5 million. McCulloch's plan was to disassemble and rebuild the bridge in Lake Havasu City, Arizona, the city founded by him in 1963.

The construction of the London Bridge purchased by McCulloch – designed by engineer John Rennie – began in 1824 and was completed in 1831. This bridge replaced the previous London Bridge, which had been completed in 1209 and had stood for more than 600 years, during which time it had displayed on pikes the heads of men like William Wallace and Thomas More.

The dismantled granite bridge was taken by sea to Long Beach, California, before being transported to its final destination in Arizona. At a cost of $7 million, and taking three years to complete the dismantling, removal, and rebuilding process, London Bridge, now spanning an artificial canal in Lake Havasu City, was completed in 1971. The cornerstone was laid, at the dedication ceremony on October 10, by the Lord Mayor of London. The bridge became a drawcard for tourists and is second only to the Grand Canyon as Arizona's most popular tourist destination.

When London Bridge was moved to Arizona, a new London Bridge was built across the Thames in the same place where the old bridge had stood. Construction was completed in March 1973.

October 11

"To get an Oscar would be an incredible moment in my career, there is no doubt about that. But the Lord of the Rings films are not made for Oscars, they are made for the audience."

PETER JACKSON, BEFORE *RETURN OF THE KING* WON 11 OSCARS

HISTORICAL EVENTS

1811 The first steam-powered ferry begins service between New York and Hoboken, New Jersey.

1910 Theodore Roosevelt is the first U.S. President to fly in a plane. He almost falls out while waving to supporters.

1958 NASA lunar probe *Pioneer 1* is launched, but fails to reach the Moon. It returns two days after take-off. The previous attempt to reach the Moon also failed, with *Pioneer 0* burning up 77 seconds after launch.

1968 *Apollo 7*, the first successful manned Apollo mission, is launched, manned by Walter "Wally" Schirra, Donn F. Eisele, and Walter Cunningham.

1976 Communist radicals, dubbed The Gang of Four, are arrested just a month after the death of Chairman Mao Zedong.

1982 The *Mary Rose* is raised from a waterway near Portsmouth in the south of England, after 437 years.

1984 Kathryn D. Sullivan becomes the first U.S. woman to walk in space, onboard the space shuttle *Challenger*.

1999 Principal photography begins on the phenomenally successful *Lord of the Rings* movie trilogy (see right).

DAYS TO REMEMBER

Historic day Meditrinalia In Ancient Rome, this day held great significance as a celebration of wine and the cultivation of vineyards. Meditrinalia was the goddess of health, longevity, and wine, which was thought to have medicinal properties.

National day Coming Out Day (U.S.) Different themes, such as Talk About It, Come Out, and It's a Family Affair, are chosen each year for this celebration of gay, lesbian, bisexual, and transgender sexuality.

Births
- **1815** Pierre Napoleon Bonaparte, politician
- **1884** Eleanor Roosevelt, U.S. First Lady
- **1919** Art Blakey, jazz drummer
- **1937** Bobby Charlton, footballer
- **1949** Daryl Hall, musician
- **1957** Dawn French, comedienne
- **1962** Joan Cusack, actress and comedienne
- **1966** Luke Perry, actor

Deaths
- **1889** James Prescott Joule, physicist
- **1961** Chico Marx, comedian
- **1963** Jean Cocteau, writer
- **1963** Édith Piaf, singer and actress
- **1991** Redd Foxx, comedian and actor

Lord of the Rings movie success

British writer J. R. R. Tolkien created a complex fantasy in which hobbits, wizards, elves, and dwarfs roamed, had wars, performed magic, and made dangerous journeys. His world was so detailed, so sophisticated, that the *Lord of the Rings* books were touted as literary masterpieces. Tolkien sets the scene in his previous book, published in 1937, *The Hobbit*. Here we meet hobbit Bilbo Baggins, who journeys through Middle Earth with his friend, Gandalf the wizard. Bilbo stumbles across a ring – not realizing its significance.

Small-time New Zealand filmmaker Peter Jackson, a fan of Tolkien's, set out to recreate his world on the big screen. With the help of his wife Fran Walsh and Philippa Boyens, a screenplay was written, and after roping in New Line Cinema, who bravely put forward $200 million for all three films, filming was begun near Jackson's home in Wellington in October 1999. It would continue for 14 months. Jackson preferred not to go to Hollywood, instead putting New Zealand on the movie map, choosing picturesque locations throughout the country, such as Milford Sound, Otago, Taupo, Wairarapa, and Waikato.

With stars Elijah Wood, Orlando Bloom, Liv Tyler, Cate Blanchett, Viggo Mortensen, Ian Holm, and others – and the three movies earning $47,211,490, $62,007,528, and $72,629,713 respectively at the box office, on their first weekend – Peter Jackson and his *Lord of the Rings* trilogy have been a phenomenal success.

DATEline

October 12

"Now, there are some who would like to rewrite history – revisionist historians is what I like to call them." — U.S. PRESIDENT GEORGE W. BUSH

HISTORICAL EVENTS

1931 Olympic swimmer Johnny Weissmuller is offered the role of Tarzan by MGM after being spotted at a hotel swimming pool. He makes 12 Tarzan movies throughout the 1930s and 1940s (see below).

1933 The U.S. Department of Justice acquires the Army Disciplinary Barracks on Alcatraz Island in San Francisco Bay for use as a federal prison.

1968 The Summer Olympic Games open in Mexico City, Mexico, amid controversy about the city's high altitude and one-third less oxygen in the air.

1978 Sex Pistols bass player Sid Vicious is arrested on suspicion of murdering his girlfriend, Nancy Spungen, in their room at the Chelsea Hotel in New York.

1986 Superpower leaders Presidents Reagan and Gorbachev fail to agree on the future of nuclear weapons, particularly Reagan's Star Wars proposal, at a summit in Reykjavik, Iceland.

1994 NASA's Magellan mission to Venus ends when radio contact is lost and the spacecraft burns up in the atmosphere of the planet.

2001 U.S. President George W. Bush requests a special screening of *America's Most Wanted*, showing 22 of the world's most dangerous terrorists.

2002 Terrorists detonate bombs at the Sari Club and Paddy's Bar in Bali, Indonesia, killing 202 people and wounding hundreds.

Births

- **1537** Jane Grey, Queen of England
- **1725** Etienne Louis Geoffroy, entomologist
- **1865** Arthur Harden, chemist
- **1866** Ramsay MacDonald, UK Prime Minister
- **1872** Ralph Vaughan Williams, composer
- **1875** Aleister Crowley, occultist
- **1935** Luciano Pavarotti, tenor
- **1944** Angela Rippon, TV personality
- **1968** Hugh Jackman, actor and singer

Deaths

- **1870** Robert E. Lee, Confederate general
- **1924** Anatole France, author
- **1965** Paul Hermann Müller, chemist
- **1971** Gene Vincent, musician
- **1997** John Denver, singer
- **2003** Jim Cairns, politician

DAYS TO REMEMBER

National day Hispanic Day (Spain) This major national holiday in Spain commemorates the reunification of Spain and the voyage of Christopher Columbus to America in 1492. The Spanish mark the occasion with festivities and food, and most businesses are closed for the fiesta.

Religious day St. Seraphinus' Day Known for his services to the poor and for healing the sick, St. Seraphinus (1540–1604) lived in the Ascoli-Piceno friary in Italy, where he acted as spiritual adviser to church and state dignitaries.

Born on June 2, 1904, Johnny Weissmuller was a heart throb of the 1930s, 1940s, and beyond, both for his role as jungle hero Tarzan and for his success in swimming. After taking up the sport when he was a child to combat ill health, he became a top-class athlete and went on to win gold in the 1924 and 1928 Olympic Games (three gold medals in 1924 and two in 1928). Born in Romania, the swimmer swapped identities with his American-born brother Pete Weissmuller in order to compete in the U.S. team. He was dubbed "the best swimmer of all time," and never lost an official competition. He also established 67 world records and won 52 national championships in the U.S. On this day in 1931, Weissmuller was offered the role of Tarzan by MGM Studios.

October 13

"I never make stupid mistakes. Only very, very clever ones."
JOHN PEEL, RADIO DJ AND PROMOTER OF NEW TALENT

HISTORICAL EVENTS

1775 The Continental Navy is officially established in Philadelphia. It would later become the U.S. Navy.

1792 The cornerstone of the White House is laid in Washington D.C. The building was known as the U.S. Executive Mansion until 1818.

1917 The Miracle of the Sun, an apparition of the Virgin Mary, is witnessed by 70,000 people in Fatima, Portugal.

1923 Ankara is declared the new capital of Turkey. The former capital was Constantinople, which is now called Istanbul.

1960 Pittsburgh Pirates baseball player Bill Mazeroski finishes the World Series with a dramatic home run. The Pirates win 10-9.

1962 The Edward Albee play *Who's Afraid of Virginia Woolf?* opens on Broadway. In 1966, it is made into a movie starring Elizabeth Taylor and Richard Burton.

1972 The deaths of 176 people occur when an Aeroflot Ilyushin-62 plane crashes into a pond near Moscow. Heavy rain mars visibility and eye-witnesses report seeing four landing attempts before the tragic incident.

1972 A Fairchild plane carrying a rugby union team from Uruguay to Chile crashes into a mountain in the Andes (see below).

DAYS TO REMEMBER

National day John Peel Day (U.K.) Much-loved BBC radio announcer John Peel is remembered on this day. The music guru brought cutting-edge bands into the public arena on his popular radio show and recorded many bands over four decades in *The Peel Sessions*.

Religious day Edward the Confessor's Day King of England from 1041 to 1066, when he was succeeded by Harold, Earl of Wessex, Edward (c. 1002–1066) founded Westminster Abbey in 1065 and was canonized in 1161.

Births
- 1909 Art Tatum, pianist
- 1921 Yves Montand, singer and actor
- 1925 Lenny Bruce, comedian
- 1925 Margaret Thatcher, U.K. Prime Minister
- 1934 Nana Mouskouri, singer
- 1941 Paul Simon, songwriter
- 1959 Marie Osmond, singer
- 1962 Kelly Preston, actress
- 1969 Nancy Kerrigan, ice skater
- 1971 Sacha Baron Cohen, comedian
- 1982 Ian Thorpe, swimmer

Deaths
- 1815 Joachim Murat, King of Naples
- 1974 Ed Sullivan, TV host
- 1990 Le Duc Tho, general
- 1998 Gunpei Yokoi, Game Boy creator
- 2003 Bertram Brockhouse, physicist

Andes flight disaster

Of the 40 passengers and five crew aboard Uruguayan Air Force Flight 471, only 16 survived the crash in the Andes Mountains on this day in 1972. The passengers mainly comprised a rugby union team and their families and friends, who had chartered the air force plane as a cheaper alternative to a commercial flight.

The aircraft crashed while descending through the mountains between Chile and Argentina, the pilot mistakenly believing that the plane was over Curicó. Only 12 people were killed outright, but in the following days, with no proper medical equipment or appropriate clothing, more lives were lost as passengers succumbed to their injuries. On the seventeenth day another eight died when an avalanche engulfed the plane's fuselage, where the survivors had taken shelter. With their meager supplies dwindling, the remaining passengers of Flight 471 were forced to resort to cannibalism in order to survive.

After 62 days, two men, Fernando Parrado and Robert Canessa, trekked for 10 days before finally finding help, and on December 22 and 23, helicopters airlifted the other 14 survivors to Santiago. The dead were buried on the mountain.

October 14

"Of course I do not regret the Bond days, I regret that sadly heroes in general are depicted with guns in their hands." — ROGER MOORE, JAMES BOND ACTOR

More than 100,000 men and women attended the National March on Washington for Lesbian and Gay Rights, calling for an end to the "oppression of lesbian and gay people." The march followed in the wake of the assassination of Harvey Milk, a gay rights activist and openly gay politician. In 1978, while working as a supervisor for the city of San Francisco, Milk was shot and killed by Dan White. The gay community was outraged when White was sentenced on a lesser charge of voluntary manslaughter, and the sentencing became the catalyst for the demonstrations that followed, culminating in the march on Washington.

HISTORICAL EVENTS

- 1066 Duke William of Normandy deafeats Harold II of England in the Battle of Hastings and becomes William the Conqueror.
- 1926 The first *Winnie-the-Pooh* book by A. A. Milne is published, becoming one of the most successful children's books of all time. It was inspired by his son Christopher Robin's love for a bear in the London Zoo called Winnipeg.
- 1947 The *Bell X-1*, piloted by Captain Charles E. "Chuck" Yeager, becomes the first aircraft to travel faster than the speed of sound in level flight.
- 1949 Eleven Communist Party leaders in the U.S. are convicted of conspiring to incite an overthrow of the U.S. Government.
- 1962 The Cuban Missile Crisis begins when U.S. U-2 spy planes flying over Cuba take photos of Soviet nuclear weapons being installed.
- 1968 U.S. runner James Hines breaks the 10-second barrier in the 100-meter final in the Mexico City Olympics. His record would stand until 1983.
- 1979 The First National March on Washington D.C. for Lesbian and Gay Rights draws more than 100,000 people (see above).

DAYS TO REMEMBER

International day World Day for Organ Donation and Transplantation (WDODT) On this day, patients, medical professionals, donor families, and health organizations worldwide meet and discuss issues regarding organ transplants.

International day World Standards Day The International Organization for Standardization, the International Electrotechnical Commission, and the International Telecommunication Union developed this day of awareness and planning for a safer world.

Births

- 1574 Queen Anne of Denmark
- 1644 William Penn, founder of Pennsylvania
- 1801 Joseph Plateau, physicist
- 1890 Dwight D. Eisenhower, thirty-fourth U.S. President
- 1893 Lillian Gish, actress
- 1894 e. e. Cummings, poet
- 1911 Le Duc Tho, general and politican
- 1927 Roger Moore, actor
- 1939 Ralph Lauren, fashion designer
- 1940 Cliff Richard, singer

Deaths

- 1256 Kujo Yoritsugu, Japanese shogun
- 1318 Edward Bruce, King of Ireland
- 1959 Errol Flynn, actor
- 1977 Bing Crosby, singer and actor
- 1990 Leonard Bernstein, composer and conductor
- 2003 Patrick Dalzel-Job, James Bond inspiration

October 15

"All truth is simple...is that not doubly a lie?" — FRIEDRICH NIETZSCHE

HISTORICAL EVENTS

- **1815** Napoleon I of France begins his exile on St. Helena in the Atlantic Ocean. He would die there six years later.
- **1878** The U.S. Edison Electric Company and American Electric and Illumination in Canada begin operation.
- **1917** Dutch dancer Mata Hari is executed by firing squad at Vinciennes, near Paris, for spying for Germany in World War I.
- **1951** Sitcom *I Love Lucy* starring Lucille Ball premieres on the U.S. TV network CBS (see below).
- **1969** Thousands take part in National Moratorium peace demonstrations across the U.S., protesting against the Vietnam War.
- **1990** USSR President Mikhail Gorbachev is awarded the Nobel Peace Prize for "his leading role in the peace process."
- **1997** *Cassini-Huygens* launches from the Kennedy Space Center at Cape Canaveral, Florida, on its way to Saturn. It would be a journey of seven years.
- **2001** The *Galileo* spacecraft gets within 112 miles (180 km) of Jupiter's moon, Io.

DAY TO REMEMBER

National day White Cane Safety Day (U.S.) The symbol of the growing spirit of the blind to achieve independence is observed on this day each year. The day was inaugurated in 1964 by the National Federation of the Blind and President Lyndon B. Johnson.

Births
- **70 B.C.E.** Virgil, poet
- **1844** Friedrich Nietzsche, philosopher
- **1940** Peter Doherty, immunologist
- **1942** Penny Marshall, actress
- **1946** Richard Carpenter, composer
- **1953** Tito Jackson, musician
- **1959** Sarah Ferguson, Duchess of York
- **1959** Todd Solondz, film director
- **2005** Prince Christian, Danish royal

Deaths
- **1880** Victorio, Apache leader
- **1945** Pierre Laval, politician
- **1946** Hermann Göring, military leader
- **1964** Cole Porter, composer
- **1976** Carlo Gambino, gangster

Premiering on CBS in 1951, *I Love Lucy* clocked up 180 episodes until its finale in 1957. Based on the radio program *My Favorite Husband*, featuring Lucille Ball and Richard Denning, *I Love Lucy* saw Ball starring with real-life husband, Cuban-born musician, Desi Arnaz. Ball and Arnaz (front) played married couple Lucy and Ricky Ricardo, and they were joined by regulars William Frawley and Vivian Vance (behind) as close friends and neighbors, Fred and Ethel Mertz. Rerun episodes of *I Love Lucy* continue to be seen by a worldwide audience.

October 16

DATE*line*

"Most modern calendars mar the sweet simplicity of our lives by reminding us that each day that passes is the anniversary of some perfectly uninteresting event." — OSCAR WILDE

HISTORICAL EVENTS

1793 Marie Antoinette, wife of King Louis XVI of France, is executed by guillotine, without proof of her crimes.

1975 Five TV reporters from Australia, covering the Indonesian invasion of East Timor, are killed in the town of Balibo. Circumstances around the deaths of the Balibo Five are shrouded in mystery.

1978 Polish cardinal Karol Wojtyla is appointed Pope John Paul II, the first non-Italian pope since Pope Adrian VI in 1523.

1984 Archbishop Desmond Tutu is awarded the Nobel Peace Prize for his efforts in promoting civil rights and equality.

1991 In the worst mass shooting in U.S. history, George Hennard, an unemployed 35-year-old from Texas, kills 23 people and wounds 20 in Luby's Cafeteria.

1992 Sarah Ferguson, Duchess of York, files a lawsuit against French tabloids for printing photos of her topless with Texas millionaire John Bryan on the French Riviera.

1995 More than 250,000 African Americans gather in Washington D.C. for the Million Man March (see right).

1996 More than 80 people are crushed to death and 180 injured when 47,000 soccer fans squeeze into the 36,000-seat Mateo Flores Stadium in Guatemala City.

DAYS TO REMEMBER

International day World Food Day Each year on this day, the UN holds events to bring awareness to the plight of an estimated 850 million starving people around the world.

National day Boss's Day (U.S.) This day, honoring bosses, was registered with the U.S. Chamber of Commerce by Patricia Bays Haroski in 1958, on her father's birthday. (He was also her boss.)

Births		1941	Tim McCarver, baseball player
1483	Gasparo Contarini, cardinal	1958	Tim Robbins, actor
1535	Niwa Nagahide, warlord	**Deaths**	
1758	Noah Webster, lexicographer	1865	Andrés Bello, philosopher
1854	Oscar Wilde, writer	1937	Jean de Brunhoff, writer
1890	Michael Collins, patriot	1959	George Marshall, U.S. Secretary of State
1903	Cecile de Brunhoff, storyteller	1990	Art Blakey, jazz drummer
1931	Charles Colson, Watergate conspirator	1992	Shirley Booth, actress

The Million Man March

On this day in 1995, Washington D.C.'s National Mall was the scene for one of the largest marches ever seen in the U.S. – the Million Man March. More than 250,000 African Americans gathered for a peaceful day of praying, singing, and speeches, in a successful awareness-raising campaign for race relations.

Organized by Nation of Islam leader Rev. Louis Farrakhan, there were participants from most religions, and school and community groups. Among the messages brought to the masses at the foot of the Capitol Building were "clean up your lives and rebuild your neighborhoods," and "take responsibility for your lives and families."

As a result of the march and related media attention, thought-provoking race issues were brought to the fore. It is believed the atmosphere of brotherhood and community experienced that day has contributed to building a stronger community among African Americans, and a greater awareness of racial injustices in the wider community.

The day was not without controversy, however. Rev. Farrakhan had in the past been accused of being homophobic, anti-Semitic, and sexist. This created some confusion over his morals in relation to the message of the gathering, and it is said perhaps the effect on the public may have been stronger were it not for his reputation. In fact, the President at the time, Bill Clinton, remarked: "One million men are right to be standing up for personal responsibility, but one million men do not make right one man's message of malice and division."

October 17

"Some people stay in the academic world just to avoid becoming self-aware. You can quote me on that." — MICHAEL MCKEAN, ACTOR AND COMEDIAN

The world's tallest building

Before the pinnacle was placed on Taipei 101 on October 17, 2003, the Petronas Twin Towers in Kuala Lumpur held the record, at a height of 1,483 feet (452 m). But the majestic Taipei 101 in Taiwan (pictured) outshone its rival by 165 feet (50 m), reaching a dizzying height of 1,671 feet (509 m) – at a dizzying cost of $1.7 billion.

The most technologically advanced ever built, the building has a traditional Chinese-inspired pagoda shape and bamboo-like tower. There are 101 floors above ground, and five underground. The observatory is the highest in the world, on the eighty-ninth floor, and there's an outdoor observation deck on the ninety-first floor.

The Council on Tall Buildings and Urban Habitat ranks the world's 100 tallest buildings, and certifies Taipei 101 as holding the record for ground to structural top, after the Kuala Lumpa buildings. The Sears Tower retains the record for ground to pinnacle at 1,703 feet (529 m). Taipei 101 boasts the fastest elevators in the world – a Guinness record – you can reach the top in 30 seconds, at a speed of 37.5 miles per hour (60.6 km/h). Developers say the building is also designed to withstand earthquakes of up to 7.0 on the Richter scale, and it's typhoon-proof.

Buildings planning to upstage Taipei 101 in the near future include the Shanghai World Financial Centre, Union Square Phase 7 in Hong Kong, Fordham Spire in Chicago, Freedom Tower in New York City, and Burj Dubai in the UAE.

HISTORICAL EVENTS

1604 German astronomer Johannes Kepler discovers the last supernova in the Milky Way in the constellation Ophiuchuc and calls it Kepler's Star.
1961 French police kill 200 Algerian protesters in Paris. The immigrants were protesting peacefully for the independence of their country from French rule.
1967 The "tribal love-rock musical," *Hair*, created by James Rado and Gerome Ragni, opens on Broadway.
1968 Athletes Tommie Smith and John Carlos protest silently against discrimination at the Mexico Olympics by giving "black power" salutes from the medal podium.
1979 Mother Teresa is awarded the Nobel Peace Prize for her services to humanity as leader of the Order of the Missionaries of Charity.
1989 In San Francisco, an earthquake measuring 6.7 on the Richter scale kills nine people and injures hundreds.
2003 Taipei 101 becomes the world's tallest building, taking over from Kuala Lumpur's Petronas Twin Towers (see above).

DAYS TO REMEMBER

National day Black Poetry Day (U.S.) This day honors the African American poets who have documented their lives, social changes, and artistic expression. The first published African American poet was Long Island Jupiter Hammon, born on this day in 1711.

International day Eradication of Poverty Day A day for raising public awareness of the need to eradicate poverty was officially recognized by the UN in 1992, but the French started the event in 1987 with mass rallies to honor the world's impoverished.

Births
- 1912 Pope John Paul I
- 1915 Arthur Miller, playwright
- 1918 Rita Hayworth, actress
- 1920 Montgomery Clift, actor
- 1938 Evel Knievel, daredevil
- 1942 Gary Puckett, musician
- 1947 Michael McKean, actor and comedian
- 1948 Margot Kidder, actress
- 1968 Ziggy Marley, musician

Deaths
- 1586 Philip Sidney, courtier, soldier, and writer
- 1849 Frédéric Chopin, composer
- 1934 Santiago Ramón y Cajal, neuroscientist
- 1970 Pierre Laporte, politician
- 1991 Tennessee Ernie Ford, singer and TV host
- 1992 Herman Johannes, professor, scientist, and politician

DATEline

October 18

"Whatever you do, don't do it halfway." — BOB BEAMON, OLYMPIC GOLD MEDAL WINNER

Historical events

1851 Herman Melville's *Moby Dick* is published by Richard Bentley of London. It is one of the greatest literary works in the English language.

1912 Balkan Allies declare war on Germany 10 days after Montenegro's lead, starting the First Balkan War.

1954 The manufacture of the first transistor radio, the Regency TR-1, is announced. It goes on sale for $49.95 – a lot in 1954 – and 150,000 units are sold.

1968 John Lennon and Yoko Ono are arrested and charged with possession of cannabis. The police raid of their flat in London uncovered 6 ounces (168 g) of marijuana. They were later fined £150.

1968 Bob Beamon sets a world record of 29.2 feet (8.9 m) in the long jump at the Mexico City Olympics. The achievement is later named by *Sports Illustrated* magazine as one of the five greatest sporting moments of the twentieth century (see below).

1974 *The Texas Chainsaw Massacre*, a schlock horror flick starring chainsaw-wielding killer Leatherface, opens in cinemas.

1985 Nintendo releases the Nintendo Entertainment System (NES) in the U.S. The eight-bit video game console becomes the most successful game system of its era with the game "Super Mario Bros."

DAYS TO REMEMBER

Religious day St. Luke the Evangelist's Day St. Luke is believed to be author of the New Testament book Gospel of Luke and Acts of the Apostles. He is the patron saint of painters, doctors, and healers.

National day Alaska Day (U.S.) Celebrated in the U.S., this marks the raising of the U.S. flag at Sitka, Alaska, after the territory was purchased from Imperial Russia in 1867.

Births
- 1595 Edward Winslow, Plymouth Colony leader
- 1679 Ann Putnam Jr., Salem witch trials witness
- 1919 Pierre Elliott Trudeau, Canadian Prime Minister
- 1926 Chuck Berry, musician
- 1926 Klaus Kinski, actor
- 1927 George C. Scott, actor
- 1939 Lee Harvey Oswald, JFK's assassin
- 1946 Howard Shore, composer
- 1960 Jean-Claude Van Damme, actor
- 1961 Wynton Marsalis, musician

Deaths
- 1545 John Taverner, English composer
- 1931 Thomas Edison, inventor
- 1982 Bess Truman, U.S. First Lady
- 2000 Julie London, singer and actress
- 2004 Veerappan, bandit

Although the favorite in the men's long jump event, no one could have guessed that 22-year-old Bob Beamon, representing the U.S., would set a new world record which surpassed the existing record by an astounding 21 inches (53 cm). The jump, measuring 29 feet 2½ inches (8.9 m), was so extraordinary that the judges were forced to use a metal tape measure when the optical measuring device, used to measure at the point of impact, was unable to cope with the length of the jump. The record stood for 23 years, until 1991, when Mike Powell jumped 29 feet 4½ inches (8.95 m) at the World Championships in Tokyo.

415

October 19

"We cannot do great things on this Earth, only small things with great love." — MOTHER TERESA

Black Monday on Wall Street

Worse even than the Wall Street crash of 1929, the Black Monday crash in 1987 saw the Dow Jones Industrial Average fall by 22.6 percent – in dollar terms, a loss of $500 billion on the value of the Dow – in just one day. Beginning in Hong Kong, the crash spread through Europe before hitting the U.S.

Although there had been some erratic trading leading up to the crash, causing uneasiness among traders, no conclusion has been reached regarding the causes.

Many theories abound. Some saw program trading – essentially, trading done by computers – as the culprit. Another theory is that road closures in London, arising from the Great Storm of 1987 which hit England on Friday, 16 October, prevented traders from reaching their offices in time to deal with open positions; This, in turn, created the worldwide panic selling of the following Monday.

The Black Monday crash resulted in the deaths of several stockbrokers, when a disgruntled client entered the offices of his broker and opened fire. Unlike the 1929 crash, no

depression followed the 1987 crash. In 1988, in the hope of preventing a recurrence of Black Monday, the circuit breaker system – an electronic system designed to prevent trading continuing when markets become dangerously unstable – was put in place.

HISTORICAL EVENTS

- **1781** The American Revolutionary War ends as Major General Lord Charles Cornwallis surrenders to George Washington at Yorktown, Virginia.
- **1943** Streptomycin is isolated by Selman A. Waksman at Rutgers University in New Jersey It is used as an antibiotic for tuberculosis.
- **1954** An inquiry into two separate Comet airline crashes concludes that "metal fatigue" is the likely cause. The findings lead to an improvement in air travel safety.
- **1987** The Dow Jones Industrial Average falls by 22.6 percent in the second highest one-day percentage decline in stock market history. It is dubbed Black Monday (see above).
- **1989** The Guildford Four are released when their convictions are quashed by the U.K. Court of Appeal. Gerry Conlon, Patrick Armstrong, Carole Richardson, and Paul Hill had been jailed for the Guildford pub bombings that killed four people and injured 44.
- **2005** Saddam Hussein's trial commences in Baghdad for crimes against humanity comitted in the city of Dujail, where 143 were killed.
- **2005** Hurricane Wilma becomes the most intense Atlantic hurricane on record, and sets a record for the most storms of hurricane strength in one season.

DAYS TO REMEMBER

National day Mother Teresa Day (Albania) On this national holiday, Albanians honor humanitarian and Nobel Peace Prize laureate Mother Teresa (1910–1997), who was born Agnes Gonxha Bojaxhiu in the city of Skopje in Macedonia, of Albanian descent.

Births
- **1562** George Abbot, Archbishop of Canterbury
- **1784** John McLoughlin, fur trader
- **1907** Roger Wolfe Kahn, bandleader
- **1910** Subrahmanyan Chandrasekhar, physicist
- **1916** Jean Dausset, immunologist
- **1931** John le Carré, novelist
- **1932** Robert Reed, actor
- **1945** Divine, actor
- **1969** Trey Parker, cartoonist and comedian

Deaths
- **1813** Józef Antoni Poniatowski, Polish prince
- **1897** George Pullman, inventor and industrialist
- **1988** Son House, musician
- **2003** Faith Fancher, TV journalist and activist
- **2004** Kenneth E. Iverson, computer scientist

DATEline

October 20

"The first time you marry for love, the second for money, and the third for companionship."

JACQUELINE KENNEDY ONASSIS

Births
- 1469 Guru Nanak Dev, Sikh leader
- 1616 Thomas Bartholin, physician, theologian, and mathematician
- 1632 Sir Christopher Wren, architect
- 1882 Bela Lugosi, actor
- 1890 Jelly Roll Morton, composer
- 1905 Ellery Queen, writer (pseudonym)
- 1950 Tom Petty, musician
- 1958 Viggo Mortensen, actor
- 1971 Snoop Dogg, rapper
- 1971 Dannii Minogue, singer

Deaths
- 1977 Cassie Gaines, Steve Gaines, and Ronnie Van Zant, musicians (Lynyrd Skynyrd)
- 1984 Carl Ferdinand Cori, biochemist
- 1989 Anthony Quayle, actor
- 1994 Burt Lancaster, actor

HISTORICAL EVENTS

- 1803 The U.S. Senate ratifies the Louisiana Purchase with a vote of 24 to 7. The following day President Jefferson takes possession of the territory.
- 1827 The Battle of Navarino ends the Greek Liberation War, marking the beginning of modern Greece.
- 1944 Liquid natural gas leaks from storage tanks in Cleveland and explodes, leveling 30 blocks and killing 130 people.
- 1955 *Lord of the Rings: The Return of the King*, written by J. R. R. Tolkien, is published.
- 1967 Roger Patterson and Robert Gimlin film Bigfoot in northern California on a wilderness expedition in search of the creature.
- 1968 Former First Lady Jacqueline Kennedy marries Greek shipping tycoon Aristotle Onassis in Greece (see below).
- 1973 Iconic landmark the Sydney Opera House, designed by Danish architect Jørn Utzon, is opened by Queen Elizabeth II.
- 1973 The drama series about bionic man *The Six Million Dollar Man*, starring Lee Majors, premieres on ABC in the U.S.

DAYS TO REMEMBER

Religious day Birth of the Báb One of the 11 holy days in the Baha'i calendar, the Birth of the Báb is celebrated around the world by those of the Baha'i religion. The Báb was born on October 20, 1819, in Persia.

Religious day St. Bertilla Boscardin of Vicenza's Day Also known as Anna Francesca Boscardin (1888–1922), the Italian girl was a simple, uneducated soul. She worked first as a servant, then as a nurse in a children's ward. She was well loved by her patients, and continued nursing into World War I. She was canonized on June 8, 1952, by Pope Pius XII.

When the widow of assassinated President John F. Kennedy married the Greek shipping magnate Aristotle Onassis, she earned herself the nickname Jackie O. Admired for her stoicism in the wake of her previous husband's tragic death, Jacqueline Kennedy's marriage to Onassis, 23 years her senior, was not popular with the American people, but the couple remained married until Aristotle Onassis' death in 1975. Both Jackie O and Aristotle Onassis lost their only sons in an untimely way – tragically, both in plane crashes – with the deaths of Alexander Onassis in 1973, and JFK Jr. in 1999, his five years after the death of his mother.

October 21

"Formula for success: Rise early, work hard, strike oil." — J. PAUL GETTY, INDUSTRIALIST

Births
- 1650 Jean Bart, admiral
- 1833 Alfred Nobel, Nobel Prize founder
- 1917 Dizzy Gillespie, musician
- 1956 Carrie Fisher, actress and writer
- 1957 Wolfgang Ketterle, physicist
- 1959 Ken Watanabe, actor

Deaths
- 1266 Birger Jarl, Stockholm founder
- 1805 Horatio Nelson, admiral
- 1969 Jack Kerouac, novelist
- 1984 François Truffaut, film director
- 2003 Elliott Smith, musician

HISTORICAL EVENTS

1805 Admiral Lord Nelson leads the British Royal Navy to defeat the French and Spanish fleets in the Battle of Trafalgar.

1945 Argentine leader Juan Perón marries his mistress, actress Eva Duarte, nicknamed Evita, who would help him lead the country.

1957 Elvis Presley's third movie, *Jailhouse Rock*, opens in the U.S.

1959 New York's Solomon R. Guggenheim Museum, designed by Frank Lloyd Wright, opens to the public (see below).

1967 Close to 100,000 people gather in Washington D.C. to protest against the Vietnam War. The peaceful rally turns violent, with 100 people injured and 681 arrested.

1973 John Paul Getty III, grandson of the oil billionaire, has his ear cut off by kidnappers and sent to a newspaper. It takes 18 days to arrive.

1978 Australian pilot Frederick Valentich vanishes over Bass Strait, south of Melbourne, after reporting seeing a UFO.

DAYS TO REMEMBER

Historical day Trafalgar Day Admiral Horatio Nelson led the British fleet to victory on this day in 1805, and throughout the British Empire, Trafalgar Day was celebrated with parades and dinners until the mid-twentieth century, when views of celebrating war changed. Armistice Day on November 11 became a new, more sombre war observance.

National day Day of the Nacho (U.S. and Mexico) The US and Mexico honor the popular dish, rumored to have been invented by Ignacio "Nacho" Anaya in 1943 as *nachos especiales*. Feasts consist mainly of nachos.

National day Overseas Chinese Day On this day each year, Chinese expats and all people of Chinese heritage gather to celebrate both their culture of origin and their contribution to their new cultures, with colorful parades and feasts.

Designed by architect Frank Lloyd Wright at the request of philanthropist and art collector Solomon R. Guggenheim, the Guggenheim Museum was unique – and controversial – not only for its unusual spiral exterior design but also for the distinctive slanted ramps which visitors use to make their way through the main displays inside the museum. Located on Fifth Avenue, New York, the Guggenheim stood out from the more traditional buildings surrounding it. The museum's opening marked a historical change in the way art is housed, and in the way it is presented to the public.

October 22

"Love is suffering. One side always loves more." — CATHERINE DENEUVE, ACTRESS

HISTORICAL EVENTS

1797 Andre-Jacques Garnerin makes the first recorded jump with a silk parachute, 3,200 feet (1,000 m) above Paris.

1836 Sam Houston becomes the President of Texas. The state became a breakaway republic for nearly a decade after the Texas Revolution, also incorporaing parts of what is now New Mexico, Oklahoma, Kansas, Colorado, and Wyoming.

1883 The Metropolitan Opera House in New York opens with a performance of Gounod's opera *Faust*.

1934 Bank robber Charles Arthur "Pretty Boy" Floyd is shot and killed by FBI agents in an open field near East Liverpool, Ohio, U.S.

1957 The Vietnam War claims the first of 58,226 U.S. casualties.

1960 Ed Yost flies the first modern, manned hot air balloon at an air base in Nebraska.

1964 Existentialist Jean-Paul Sartre famously turns down the Nobel Prize for Literature.

1966 *The Supremes A' Go-Go* is the first album by an all-female group to reach number-one album status (see right).

1968 *Apollo 7* orbits the earth 163 times, and safely lands in the Atlantic Ocean.

1975 Technical Sergeant Leonard Matlovich of the U.S. Air Force is discharged after appearing on the cover of *Time* magazine stating, "I am a homosexual."

DAY TO REMEMBER

Religious day St. Mary Salome's Day Her name means "health and peace," and she was said to have witnessed Christ's death on the cross, and anointed him the morning of the resurrection. She moved to Veroli, Italy, spreading the word of God.

Births
- 1811 Franz Liszt, composer
- 1844 Sarah Bernhardt, actress
- 1887 John Reed, journalist
- 1920 Timothy Leary, writer
- 1925 Robert Rauschenberg, painter and sculptor
- 1938 Christopher Lloyd, actor
- 1942 Annette Funicello, actress
- 1943 Catherine Deneuve, actress
- 1949 Stiv Bators, musician
- 1952 Jeff Goldblum, actor

Deaths
- 1906 Paul Cezanne, painter
- 1934 Charles Arthur "Pretty Boy" Floyd, gangster
- 1978 John Riley, poet
- 1986 Albert Szent-Györgyi, physiologist
- 1995 Sir Kingsley Amis, writer

The Supremes rise to number one

With the release of their fifth album, *The Supremes A' Go-Go*, The Supremes became the first female group to reach number one on the American Billboard album charts, and "You Can't Hurry Love," taken from the album, became their seventh number-one hit single, following on from previous hits which included "Baby Love" (1964) and "Stop! In the Name of Love" (1965).

They started in 1959 in the Detroit Brewster housing projects under the name The Primettes. The group, originally a quartet, comprised Florence Ballard, Mary Wilson, Diana Ross, and Betty McGlown, who was later replaced by Barbara Martin. The Primettes recorded only one single, and following the departure of Martin in 1961, they were signed to Motown Records as a trio and became The Supremes.

Following a string of flops through the early 1960s, The Supremes finally hit the number one spot with the release of "Where Did Our Love Go?" in 1964. This was the first of 12 number-one hits for the group between 1964 and 1969.

Original member Florence Ballard left the group – now know as Diana Ross and The Supremes – in 1967, and was replaced by Cindy Birdsong. As Diana Ross and The Supremes, the group went on to release another five number-one singles before performing their final show with Ross in January 1970 at Las Vegas' Frontier Hotel. Despite the loss of Ross, the group continued to record and perform in various line-ups, before finally disbanding in 1977.

October 23

HISTORICAL EVENTS

- **425** Valentinian III becomes Emperor of Rome at the age of six.
- **1915** Around 30,000 women march along Fifth Avenue in New York, demanding the right to vote. The right was granted in 1920.
- **1958** Belgian cartoonist Peyo introduces *The Smurfs*. They are translated into 25 languages, including Dutch, German, French, English, Spanish, Afrikaans, and Hebrew.
- **1973** U.S. President Richard Nixon agrees to turn over audiotapes of his Oval Office conversations about the Watergate Scandal.
- **1998** Dr. Barnett Slepian is shot dead in his New York home by anti-abortion activist James Charles Kopp.
- **2001** The iPod, a hard drive that "puts 1,000 songs in your pocket" is released in the U.S. (see below).
- **2002** Chechen rebels seize the House of Culture theater in Moscow and take 900 people hostage. After two days, Russian special forces raid the building with knockout gas, and the 42 rebels – and 130 hostages – are killed.
- **2004** An earthquake, 6.8 on the Richter scale, hits Niigata in Japan, killing 35 people, injuring 2,857, and leaving thousands homeless.

DAYS TO REMEMBER

National Day Hungary Hungarians celebrate the 1956 uprising for freedom against Soviet rule, and the Proclamation of the Republic of Hungary in 1989 on the thirty-third anniversary of the uprising.

International day Mole Day Celebrated annually around the world from 6:02 A.M. to 6:02 P.M. on this day, Mole Day aims to increase interest in chemistry by remembering Amedo Avogadro (1776–1858), who discovered what is now called Avogadro's number, 6.023×10^{23}, a fundamental unit of measurement in chemistry.

Births
- 1844 Sarah Bernhardt, actress
- 1892 Gummo Marx, actor and comedian
- 1905 Felix Bloch, physicist and Nobel Prize laureate
- 1925 Johnny Carson, TV host
- 1940 Pelé, footballer
- 1954 Ang Lee, director and producer
- 1956 Dwight Yoakam, singer, songwriter, and actor
- 1959 "Weird Al" Yankovic, comedian

Deaths
- 1910 Chulalongkorn, Thai King
- 1944 Charles Glover Barkla, physicist
- 1950 Al Jolson, singer and actor
- 1986 Edward Adelbert Doisy, biochemist

Launched by Apple Computer with the slogan "Say Hello to iPod," the iPod stood out from other MP3 players in the marketplace due to its size – a quarter that of its competitors – and storage capacity (more than 1,000 songs could be stored on its hard disk). Designed by hardware expert Tony Fadell, the idea for the iPod had been turned down by several companies before finding interest at Apple Computer. Its popularity came as a surprise to its critics, who predicted that the iPod's hefty price tag would deter consumers, and to the company itself.

DATE*line*

"Every kid around the world who plays soccer wants to be Pelé. I have a great responsibility to show them not just how to be like a soccer player, but how to be like a man."

PELÉ, THE WORLD'S GREATEST FOOTBALLER

October 24

"Each person must live their life as a model for others." — ROSA PARKS, CIVIL RIGHTS ACTIVIST

HISTORICAL EVENTS

1260 Chartres Cathedral in France, now a UNESCO World Heritage Site, is dedicated in the presence of King Louis IX of France.
1861 The first transcontinental telegraph line across the U.S., between St. Joseph, Missouri, and Sacramento, California, is completed by the Western Union Company.
1929 "Black Thursday" at the New York Stock Exchange is one of the worst days of the stock market. It leads to the Great Crash of 1929.
1945 The five founding United Nations members ratify the UN Charter in Washington D.C. (see right).
1957 The U.S. Air Force starts the X-20 Dyna-Soar program – a single-manned space plane.
1973 The Yom Kippur War, between Israel and a coalition of Arab nations, ends.
1989 TV evangelist Jim Bakker is sentenced to 45 years in prison and fined $500,000 for fraud and conspiracy.
1998 *Deep Space 1* is launched from Cape Canaveral, Florida, on a mission to study comets and asteroids.
2003 Supersonic air travel comes to an end as Concorde makes its last commercial flight, from New York to London.
2004 A Hendrick Motorsports plane carrying 10 NASCAR drivers and their relatives crashes en route to Martinsville Speedway, Virginia, killing all on board.

DAY TO REMEMBER

Religious day St. Antonio Maria Claret's Day A missionary in Catalonia and the Canary Islands, St. Antonio (1807–1870) established the Congregation of the Missionary Sons of the Immaculate Heart of Mary, founded a religious library at Barcelona, and contributed to the revival of the Catalan language.

Births
1632 Anton van Leeuwenhoek, microbiologist
1932 Pierre-Gilles de Gennes, physicist
1936 Bill Wyman, musician
1947 Kevin Kline, actor
1960 Jaime Garzón, journalist and comedian

Deaths
1537 Jane Seymour, wife of Henry VIII
1944 Louis Renault, car manufacturer
1957 Christian Dior, fashion designer
2005 Rosa Parks, civil rights activist

Star sign

SCORPIO
October 24–November 22

Those people born under Scorpio, the sign of the Scorpion, are said to be the most intense of the 12 zodiac signs. They are passionate about those they love, and their determination allows them to achieve greatness. Stay on a Scorpio's good side and they'll be a loyal friend; invoke their wrath and they will seek revenge.

The UN ratifies charter

The United Nation's predecessor, the League of Nations, was formed in 1919 as a means of establishing and maintaining global peace and security following the loss of millions of lives in World War I. With the outbreak of World War II, the League of Nations was tested, and found lacking. It was eventually dissolved in 1946. But it had sown the seed for what was to be the United Nations, which began with the Allied countries' signing of the Inter-Allied Declaration on June 12, 1941, in London.

The signing of the Atlantic Charter by President Woodrow Wilson of the U.S. and the U.K. Prime Minister, Winston Churchill, on August 14, 1941, was a further move toward the establishment of an organization whose aim was peace and security for the world, and the defense of human rights.

The United Nations Charter – the constitution of the United Nations – was signed by the original member countries, 50 in total, on June 26, 1945, in San Francisco, and ratified later that year, on October 24, by the five founding members: the Republic of China, France, the U.S.S.R., Great Britain, and the United States of America.

Three years later, in 1948, the first meeting of the Security Council was convened. The Council can be called into a meeting to respond to international crises, and fulfils the mission for world peace by negotiating solutions and mediating between the parties involved in each situation.

DATEline

October 25

"I formed a new group called Alcoholics Unanimous. If you don't feel like a drink, you ring another member and he comes over to persuade you." RICHARD HARRIS, ACTOR

California's largest fire, the Cedar Fire, resulted in the deaths of 15 people – including one fire fighter – the loss of 2,232 homes, and the destruction of over 270,000 acres (109,000 ha) of land. Driven by dry Santa Ana desert winds, the fire moved through the towns of San Diego County at a frightening speed and raged for 10 days before finally being contained. The fire was started by deer hunter Sergio Martinez, who became lost in the Cleveland National Park and set a fire to signal for help. Martinez was later indicted and subsequently sentenced to five years' probation.

HISTORICAL EVENTS

- **1415** Henry V of England defeats the French at the Battle of Agincourt in northern France.
- **1854** The British Light Brigade is overcome by Russian fire in the Battle of Balaclave in the Crimean War.
- **1936** The Rome–Berlin Axis is signed by Adolf Hitler and Benito Mussolini.
- **1983** U.S. forces invade Caribbean island Grenada, restoring democratic rule after four years of Marxist Government.
- **1986** Boston Red Sox baseball player Bill Buckner's famous fielding error gives the New York Mets the World Series.
- **1991** The last Yugoslav soldier leaves Slovenian territory, three months after the Ten-Day War. Despite the war's short duration, it has major consequences, especially for Slovenia. The country is able to attain and uphold its independence from Yugoslavia, becoming a prosperous and successful member of the European Union and the United Nations.
- **2003** The Cedar Fire becomes the largest wildfire in Californian history (see above).
- **2003** Australia beats Namibia by a record 142 to nil in the 2003 Rugby World Cup.
- **2004** Cuban President Fidel Castro announces the ban of the U.S. dollar, which comes into effect on November 8.

DAYS TO REMEMBER

National day Thanksgiving Day (Virgin Islands) These Caribbean islanders celebrate the end of the hurricane season on this day.

Religious day St. Crispin's Day St. Crispin was the patron saint of shoemakers, tanners, and leatherworkers. Roman Crispin and his twin brother Christian made shoes and spread the word of Christianity, and were ultimately tortured and beheaded.

Births
- 1825 Johann Strauss II, composer
- 1838 Georges Bizet, composer
- 1881 Pablo Picasso, painter
- 1892 Leo E. Carroll, actor
- 1912 Minnie Pearl, comedienne and singer
- 1913 Klaus Barbie, Nazi war criminal
- 1928 Marion Ross, actress
- 1942 Helen Reddy, singer
- 1959 Nancy Cartwright, voice actress
- 1976 Joshua P. Warren, author

Deaths
- 1400 Geoffrey Chaucer, poet
- 1920 Alexander I, King of Greece
- 1974 Nick Drake, songwriter
- 1992 Roger Miller, composer
- 1993 Vincent Price, actor
- 2002 Richard Harris, actor
- 2004 John Peel, radio presenter

October 26

"The challenge now is to practice politics as the art of making what appears to be impossible, possible." — HILLARY CLINTON

Baby Fae receives baboon's heart

Born in Barstow Community Hospital, California, on October 12, 1984, the infant known as Baby Fae suffered from hypoplastic left heart syndrome. In lay terms, this meant that only half her heart was functioning. In the majority of cases the condition is fatal.

The surgeon who performed the operation to save Baby Fae's life, Dr. Leonard Lee Bailey, of Loma Linda University Medical Center, had spent seven years researching cross-species transplants, known as xenotransplantation. In all cases there had been a survival rate of less than six months. Nevertheless, the hope that a baboon's heart could be successfully transplanted into the body of Baby Fae was offered to the infant's parents.

Bailey was not the first surgeon to attempt an animal-to-human heart transplant, the first having been performed in 1964, when Dr. James D. Hardy transplanted a chimpanzee's heart into the body of a 68-year-old man. The recipient survived for 90 minutes.

Following the four-hour operation on this day in 1984 to replace Baby Fae's defective heart with that of a young female baboon, the procedure appeared to have been a success, as the infant's condition improved over a number of days. However, as increasing amounts of an immunosuppressive drug – designed to prevent the body rejecting the transplanted organ – were administered, the infant's kidneys failed, and 20 days after the operation to save her, Baby Fae's new heart stopped beating.

Births
- 1854 C. W. Post, entrepreneur
- 1865 Benjamin Guggenheim, businessman
- 1914 Jackie Coogan, actor
- 1916 François Mitterrand, French President
- 1942 Bob Hoskins, actor
- 1947 Hillary Rodham Clinton, U.S. First Lady and Senator
- 1951 Bootsy Collins, musician
- 1961 Dylan McDermott, actor
- 1962 Cary Elwes, actor
- 1967 Keith Urban, singer

Deaths
- 899 Alfred the Great, King of England
- 1440 Gilles de Rais, serial killer
- 1633 Horio Tadaharu, warlord
- 1957 Gerty Cori, biochemist
- 2002 Movsar Barayev, terrorist

HISTORICAL EVENTS

- **1881** The legendary Gunfight at the OK Corral, between two opposing families, the Earps and the Clantons, takes place in Tombstone, Arizona.
- **1958** Pan American Airways (PAA) flies the first direct commercial flight, a Boeing 707, from New York to Paris.
- **1977** The last case of smallpox is diagnosed in Somalia. After this case, the World Health Organization and Center for Disease Control and Prevention (CDC) declare that smallpox is officially eradicated, due to the success of vaccination.
- **1979** Park Chung Hee, the President of South Korea, is assassinated by the country's Chief of Intelligence, Kim Jea Kyu.
- **1984** Baby Fae, born on October 12, receives a heart transplant from a baboon, and lives for another 20 days (see left).
- **1984** Nineteen-year-old John D. McCollum shoots himself with a .22 caliber handgun after listening to *Suicide Solution* by Ozzy Osbourne. His parents file a lawsuit, but the case is later dismissed.
- **1994** Jordan and Israel sign a peace treaty in a symbolic ceremony on the Israeli–Jordanian border, ending 46 years of war. U.S. President Clinton attends.
- **2000** A report into "mad cow disease" in the U.K. reveals that Government ministers misled the public by waiting six months before revealing incidences of the disease.
- **2000** Video game console PlayStation 2 (PS2) is released in the U.S.

DAYS TO REMEMBER

National day Treaty Day (Austria) On this day each year, Austrians celebrate the day foreign troops left their soil after the Austrian State Treaty came into force and the country gained independence in 1955. Events are held throughout the country and in Vienna new members of the armed forces are sworn in.

National day Angam Day (Nauru) "Day of Fulfilment," or Angam Day, commemorates the anniversary of the day when the population of this small western Pacific island reached 1,500 again after being decimated by an influenza epidemic in the 1920s. Before that, the small country faced an outbreak of dysentery, so citizens were thrilled to get their dwindling population back up.

October 27

DATEline

"A war can perhaps be won single-handedly. But peace – lasting peace – cannot be secured without the support of all." LUIS INACIO "LULA" DA SILVA, PRESIDENT OF BRAZIL

Births
- 1728 James Cook, explorer
- 1782 Niccolò Paganini, violinist
- 1858 Theodore Roosevelt, twenty-sixth U.S President
- 1914 Dylan Thomas, poet
- 1923 Roy Lichtenstein, artist
- 1932 Sylvia Plath, poet
- 1939 John Cleese, actor
- 1940 John Gotti, gangster
- 1945 Luis Inácio "Lula" da Silva, Brazilian President

Deaths
- 1674 Hallgrímur Pétursson, poet
- 1990 Xavier Cugat, musician
- 1990 Elliott Roosevelt, war hero and author
- 1992 David Bohm, physicist, philosopher, and neuropsychologist

HISTORICAL EVENTS

- 1904 One of the biggest subway lines in the world, and the biggest in the U.S., opens in New York.
- 1946 *Geographically Speaking*, a TV program featuring the travels of Mrs. Wells is sponsored by Bristol-Myers. It is the first commercially sponsored TV program.
- 1949 Forty-eight people are killed when an Air France plane from Paris to New York flies into a mountain after two failed landing attempts. Two of the dead are boxing champion Marcel Cerdan and violinist Ginette Neveu.
- 1954 Benjamin O. Davis Jr. becomes the first African American general in the U.S. Air Force.
- 1961 *SA-1* is launched in Cape Canaveral, Florida, as part of NASA's Mission Saturn–Apollo 1.
- 1973 The Canon City meteorite, a 3-pound (1.4 kg) chondrite meteorite, strikes in Fremont County, Colorado, in the U.S.
- 1997 Stock markets around the world experience a "mini-crash." The Dow Jones Industrial Average plummets 554.26 points to 7,161.15. The New York Stock Exchange halts trading.
- 2005 Iran launches its first satellite, *Sina 1*, on Russia's *Kosmos-3M* rocket. The satellite is intended for telecommunications and research purposes.
- 2005 Riots begin in Paris after the deaths of two Muslim teenagers in the poor Clichy-sous-Bois district. Cars are burnt, 2,900 arrests are made, and there is at least one fatality.

DAYS TO REMEMBER

National day Independence Day (Saint Vincent and the Grenadines) This Windward Islands nation celebrates gaining full independence in 1979 after a referendum. The country, which neighbors Grenada, Barbados, and St. Lucia, had been self-governing since 1969.

National day Independence Day (Turkmenistan) When Turkmenistan declared itself independent after the collapse of the Soviet Union in 1991, there was revelry in the streets in the capital Ashgabat. Now the event is marked with a military parade, with thousands of civilians watching and cheering.

Affectionately known as "Lula," Workers' Party leader Luis Inácio da Silva was born on this day in 1948. He was elected President of Brazil on October 6, 2002. In a shift from the ideals of former President Fernando Henrique Cardoso, who privatized many large companies during his leadership, Lula promised to focus on major social change – ending hunger and providing basic health care and education for the millions of poor in Brazil. He acquired a large following in his days as a trade union leader in the 1960s and 1970s, co-founded the Workers' Party in 1980, and successfully campaigned for a direct popular presidential vote in the years of Brazil's military dictatorship.

October 28

"Your most unhappy customers are your greatest source of learning." — BILL GATES, SOFTWARE PIONEER

HISTORICAL EVENTS

- **1868** Thomas Edison applied for his first patent for the electric vote recorder.
- **1914** The Dow Jones Industrial Average records the single largest one-day decline, in terms of percentage, in recorded stock market history.
- **1943** A destroyer is reportedly made invisible and teleported from Philadelphia, Pennsylvania, to Norfolk, Virginia, in a secret U.S. Navy experiment, the Philadelphia Experiment.
- **1948** Swiss chemist Paul Müller is awarded the Nobel Prize in Chemistry for his discovery of the insecticidal properties of DDT.
- **1962** The Cuban Missile Crisis ends as the U.S.S.R. promises to dismantle its bases in Cuba.
- **1981** The band Metallica is formed in San Francisco. It becomes the most successful metal band in history, selling more than 100 million albums.
- **1986** New York celebrates the centennial of the Statue of Liberty's dedication (see below).
- **2005** U.S. Assistant for National Security Lewis Libby Jr. is indicted in the Valerie Plume case, which investigates the leaking of Plume's identity as an undercover agent.

Celtic tree day
REED
October 28–November 24

In the Celtic tradition, the reed tree evokes passion and achievement. Reed people are vibrant, decisive, and forceful. They can seem impatient at times, but simply want to achieve quickly. They can sometimes be perceived as arrogant, as they dislike weakness and are forceful catalysts for change. They are well respected and have a powerful presence.

DAY TO REMEMBER

National day Oxi (No) Day (Greece)
This day commemorates Greek dictator Ioannis Metaxas' answer to Mussolini's request to use Greece for military operations at the beginning of World War II. Metaxas simply said: "No." Greeks celebrate with parades in the main streets of most cities, with major military parades in Athens and Thessoloniki.

Births
- 1793 Eliphalet Remington, firearms manufacturer
- 1903 Evelyn Waugh, writer
- 1907 Edith Head, costume designer
- 1909 Francis Bacon, painter
- 1955 Bill Gates, software pioneer
- 1963 Lauren Holly, actress
- 1967 Julia Roberts, actress
- 1968 Ben Harper, musician
- 1974 Joaquin Phoenix, actor

Deaths
- 1818 Abigail Adams, U.S. First Lady
- 1998 Ted Hughes, poet
- 2002 Margaret Booth, film editor
- 2005 Eugene K. Bird, Spandau prison director

Liberty lights up New York

Designed by French sculptor Frederic Auguste Bartholdi, "Liberty Enlightening the World," or the Statue of Liberty, is synonymous with New York. Given to the U.S. by France in 1886 as a gesture of friendship between the two nations and as a centennial gift, the massive structure celebrated its hundredth birthday on this day in 1986.

Bartholdi, who excelled in creating patriotic monuments, had personally chosen the location for his commission on a trip to the U.S. He considered Liberty Island in New York Harbor, the gateway to New York, to be the perfect place for his creation. Constructed of copper in the neo-classical style, she stands tall, at 305 feet (93 m), with an iron frame engineered by Gustave Eiffel. The face of the statue is said to be modeled on Bartholdi's mother.

Liberty holds a torch in her right hand, and a tablet in her left with the inscription JULY IV MDCCLXXVI (the day the Declaration of Independence was ratified). She stands on chains, symbolizing freedom, and the spikes on her crown represent the world's seven seas and continents.

The official dedication of the statue was October 28, 1886, by President Grover Cleveland, who said: "We will not forget that liberty here made her home; nor shall her chosen altar be neglected." One hundred years later, after a facelift and a new torch in 1984, Liberty still stands tall as a welcoming figure to New York and a symbol of independence.

October 29

"There is still no cure for the common birthday." — JOHN GLENN

Births
- 1656 Edmond Halley, astronomer
- 1891 Fanny Brice, singer
- 1897 Joseph Goebbels, Nazi Propaganda Minister
- 1920 Baruj Benacerraf, immunologist
- 1947 Richard Dreyfuss, actor
- 1948 Kate Jackson, actress
- 1964 Yasmin Le Bon, model
- 1967 Joely Fisher, actress
- 1971 Winona Ryder, actress

Deaths
- 1618 Sir Walter Raleigh, explorer
- 1666 James Shirley, dramatist
- 1911 Joseph Pulitzer, publisher
- 1987 Woody Herman, musician
- 1997 Anton LaVey, Church of Satan founder

HISTORICAL EVENTS
- **1863** An international conference in Geneva ends in an agreement to form the International Red Cross.
- **1929** The New York Stock Exchange crashes, causing mass panic and the loss of millions of dollars, and leads to The Great Depression.
- **1969** The U.S. Defence Advanced Research Project Agency (DARPA) creates ARPAnet, precursor to the Internet.
- **1991** The *Galileo* spacecraft becomes the first probe to reach an asteroid, photographing Gaspra.
- **1992** The U.S. Food and Drug Administration approves the injectable contraceptive Depo-Provera for use.
- **1998** John Glenn becomes the oldest person to go into space, in space shuttle *Discovery* (see right).
- **1998** South Africa's Truth and Reconciliation Commission accuses leading figures from across the political spectrum of human rights violations, in its Apartheid Report.
- **1999** A cyclone hits Orissa in northeastern India, killing an estimated 9,615 and leaving thousands more homeless.
- **2004** Arabic Al Jazeera TV network broadcasts a video of Osama bin Laden in which he admits direct responsibility for the September 11, 2001, attacks on New York.

DAYS TO REMEMBER

Religious day St. Narcissus' Day The bishop of Jerusalem, St. Narcissus (c. 100–222) performed miracles, his most famous being turning water into oil for use in church lamps.

Religious day James Hannington's Day Remembered by the Anglican Church, James Hannington (1847–1885) was a missionary who met a violent death in Uganda at the hands of King Mwanga's men. Hannington's last words were: "Go tell your master that I have purchased the road to Uganda with my blood."

The oldest person in space

Astronaut John Herschel Glenn Jr. was the first American to orbit Earth on February 20, 1962, and he made another first in 1998 when, at 77, he became the oldest person to venture into space. Glenn and his crewmates returned to a ticker-tape parade in their honor, making him one of the few people outside the sporting world to receive two parades in a lifetime.

Glenn started his flying career as a pilot in the U.S. Air Force, receiving many accolades. He then became a flight instructor, and in 1959, after being assigned to NASA's Project Mercury, he prepared for his first space mission. In February 1962, he piloted the Mercury-Atlas 6 spacecraft, *Friendship 7*, on a solo voyage, launching from Kennedy Space Center in Florida, and successfully orbiting Earth three times. His mission took 4 hours 55 minutes at 17,500 miles per hour (28,163 km/h) at 162 miles (261 km) altitude. He landed 800 miles (1,287 km) southeast of the Florida Space Center in the Atlantic Ocean.

Thirty-five years later, Glenn and seven other crew members took a mission in STS-95 *Discovery* for various research projects, including monitoring the effects of space flight on the aging. This voyage lasted nine days, orbiting Earth 134 times. Duties also included deployment of the *Spartan* solar-observing spacecraft and the Hubble Space Telescope Orbital Systems Test Platform.

The mission brought back vital information on weightlessness and other comparative studies of the effects of space travel on the same person at different ages. In later life, Glenn went into politics and was elected as senator for Ohio.

October 30

"I did it with the hand of reason." FOOTBALLER DIEGO MARADONA, AFTER SMASHING A PHOTOGRAPHER'S CAR

Births
- 1735 John Adams, U.S. President
- 1885 Ezra Pound, poet
- 1896 Ruth Gordon, actress
- 1928 Daniel Nathans, microbiologist
- 1930 Clifford Brown, jazz trumpeter
- 1939 Grace Slick, singer
- 1945 Henry Winkler, actor
- 1960 Diego Maradona, footballer

Deaths
- 1910 Henry Dunant, Red Cross founder
- 1968 Rose Wilder Lane, journalist
- 1975 Gustav Ludwig Hertz, physicist
- 1978 Edgar Bergen, ventriloquist
- 2002 Jam Master Jay, rapper

HISTORICAL EVENTS

- **1918** The Ottoman Empire signs an armistice with the Allies, ending World War I in the Middle East.
- **1938** Orson Welles recites H. G. Wells' *The War of the Worlds* on radio, causing a nationwide panic as people mistake the fiction for a news report.
- **1961** The Soviet Union detonates the hydrogen bomb "Tsar Bomba" over Novaya Zemlya in the northwest of the country. It is the largest nuclear device ever detonated.
- **1970** The worst monsoon to hit Vietnam in six years causes flooding, kills 293 people, and leaves 200,000 homeless.
- **1974** Muhammad Ali knocks out George Foreman in "The Rumble in the Jungle" in Zaire to regain the World Heavyweight Boxing Championship.
- **1975** Prince Juan Carlos officially becomes Spain's acting head of state after taking over from General Francisco Franco.
- **1991** U.S. President George Bush opens a Middle East peace conference in Spain with a speech encouraging Arabs and Israelis to "lay down the past."
- **2001** George W. Bush throws out the first pitch of Game 3 of the baseball World Series, in an intended defiant gesture, weeks after the September 11 attacks (see right).

DAY TO REMEMBER

National day Devil's Night (U.S.) Also known as Mischief Night in some areas of the U.S., on the night before Halloween, teenagers – and some adults – perform harmless practical jokes, such as egging houses and "borrowing" garden fixtures. The long-standing Detroit tradition started innocently in the 1930s, but by the 1970s and 1980s, the mischief became more serious, and sadly, many acts of vandalism and arson occurred.

In front of a crowd of more than 57,000 people, President George W. Bush threw the ceremonial first pitch at Game 3 of the World Series, at Yankee Stadium. It was the first time in 45 years that a sitting President had thrown the first pitch at a World Series. The game, between the Arizona Diamondbacks and the New York Yankees, followed closely on the tragic events of the September 11 terrorist attacks in New York. Bush wore a FDNY windcheater, a tribute to the many lives lost by the city's Fire Department.

October 31

DATE*line*

"It is only when I am doing my work that I feel truly alive." — FEDERICO FELLINI

HISTORICAL EVENTS

1876 A tidal wave ravages the Megna River Delta in India, resulting in 100,000 deaths. The ensuing spread of disease kills an additional 100,000.

1923 The first day of a heatwave at Marble Bar in Western Australia, which lasts 160 days, sees temperatures climb above 100°F (37.8°C).

1941 After 14 years of work, drilling is finally completed on Mt. Rushmore. It is the largest work of art on Earth.

1941 American photographer Ansel Adams photographs a moonrise over the town of Hernandez, New Mexico. It later becomes one of the most famous images in the history of photography (see below).

1956 The U.K. join with France and Israel in a military intervention to prevent Egypt from nationalizing the Suez Canal.

1998 Iraq announces it will no longer cooperate with UN weapons inspectors.

1999 EgyptAir flight 990 from New York to Cairo crashed into the Atlantic Ocean 60 miles (97 km) south of Nantucket Island, Massachusetts, in the U.S., killing all 217 aboard.

Births

- 1795 John Keats, poet
- 1860 Juliette Low, Girl Scouts founder
- 1920 Dick Francis, novelist
- 1920 Helmut Newton, photographer
- 1922 Barbara Bel Geddes, actress
- 1930 Michael Collins, astronaut
- 1936 Michael Landon, actor
- 1950 John Candy, comedian and actor
- 1950 Jane Pauley, news anchor
- 1961 Peter Jackson, director
- 1963 Rob Schneider, actor

Deaths

- 1926 Harry Houdini, magician
- 1984 Indira Gandhi, Indian Prime Minister
- 1993 Federico Fellini, filmmaker
- 1993 River Phoenix, actor

DAYS TO REMEMBER

Traditional day Halloween Originating from Celtic folklore, Halloween is traditionally celebrated on the night of October 31, and was brought to the U.S. in the nineteenth century. "Trick or treat?" is the catchcry for children on this night as they traverse their neighborhoods for sweets, dressed up as spooks and witches.

National day Allantide (U.K.) Traditionally, large, polished Allantide apples went on display in the shops at Penzance, in Cornwall, U.K., with one to be given to each family member for good luck. Young girls put them under their pillow to bring dreams of the man they would one day marry, and games were played with them, such as trying to bite apples hanging from a cross with candles dripping wax on the players.

Ansel Adams' famous black and white photograph *Moonrise over Hernandez* was taken as he was returning to Santa Fe, New Mexico, after an unsuccessful day spent on a commercial assignment. Stopping on Highway 84, he managed to take only one shot of the scene before the light changed. In this portrait of Adams, taken in 1974, he stands in front of the famous photograph in his home in Carmel, California. Born in San Francisco in 1902, Adams, a classically trained pianist, started taking photographs after visiting Yosemite National Park with his parents when he was 14. Adams was also a keen environmentalist. A mountain in Yosemite was named after him, following his death in 1984.

DAYS TO REMEMBER *October*

1
China National Day The people of China celebrate the anniversary of the founding of the People's Republic of China in 1949

2
Memorial Day for Guardian Angels In honor of the protective spirits, or guardian angels, who are said to be assigned to each person to protect them

3
Foundation Day (South Korea) Celebrations mark the founding of Gojoseon, the original kingdom of Korea, in 2,333 B.C.

4
World Animal Day Humans' relationship with animal life is celebrated the world over with special events

5
World Teachers' Day Each year the teachers who shape our future are honored for their hard work and wisdom

8
St. Keyne's Day (Wales and Cornwall) An early campaigner for the equality of women

9
Leif Erikson Day (Scandinavia, U.S.) This day honors Nordic explorers and Viking pioneers

10
World Mental Health Day Raises awareness of mental health issues and encourages treatment

11
Coming Out Day (U.S.) A celebration of gay, lesbian, bisexual, and transgender sexuality

12
Hispanic Day (Spain) Commemorates the reunification of Spain and the voyage of Christopher Columbus to America in 1492

15
White Cane Safety Day (U.S.) The symbol of the growing spirit of the blind to achieve independence is observed

16
World Food Day Brings awareness to the plight of an estimated 850 million starving people around the world

17
Black Poetry Day (U.S.) Honors the many African-American poets who have documented their lives, social changes, and artistic expression in poetry

18
Feast Day for St. Luke the Evangelist The patron saint of painters, doctors, and healers

19
Mother Teresa Day (Albania) Albanians honor humanitarian Mother Teresa, who was of Albanian descent

22
Feast Day for St. Mary Salome Said to have witnessed Christ's death on the cross, and anointed him the morning of the resurrection

23
International Mole Day Celebrated from 6:02 A.M. to 6:02 P.M. Aims to increase interest in chemistry

24
The first day of the star sign of Scorpio

25
Thanksgiving Day (Virgin Islands) The residents of this small Caribbean island group celebrate the end of the hurricane season

26
National Day Austria Celebrates the day foreign troops left Austrian soil after the Austrian State Treaty came into force

29
Feast Day for St. Narcissus Performed miracles, his most famous being turning water into oil for use in church lamps

30
Devil's Night (Detroit, U.S.) On the night before Halloween, teenagers – and some adults – perform harmless practical jokes

31
Halloween "Trick or treat?" is the catchcry for children on this night, dressed up as spooks and witches

6
Mad Hatter Day People are encouraged to act like the Mad Hatter from *Alice's Adventures in Wonderland*

7
Feast Day for Our Lady of the Rosary Pope Commemorate the role of the rosary in the victory of the Christians over the Turks in the Battle of Lepanto

13
John Peel Day (U.K.) Much-loved BBC radio announcer John Peel is remembered

14
World Day for Organ Donation and Transplantation A day of meetings worldwide to discuss issues regarding organ transplants

20
Birth of the Báb One of the 11 holy days in the Bahá'í calendar

21
Overseas Chinese Day Chinese expats and all people of Chinese heritage gather to celebrate both their culture of origin and contribution to new cultures

27
Independence Day (St. Vincent and the Grenadines) This Windward Islands nation gained full independence in 1979 after a referendum

28
Oxi (No) Day (Greece) Commemorates Ioannis Metaxas' answer to Mussolini's request to use Greece for military operations in World War II

Top right Mad Hatter Day, October 6
Right Halloween, October 31

NOVEMBER

"No warmth, no cheerfulness, no healthful ease,
No comfortable feel in any member –
No shade, no shine, no butterflies, no bees,
No fruits, no flowers, no leaves, no birds, November!"

THOMAS HOOD, "NO!"

In November, 1918, the final hostilities of World War 1 ended. Pictured are American troops rejoicing at the war's conclusion; the event is commemorated internationally at the eleventh hour on the eleventh day of the eleventh month.

November

November is the eleventh month of the Gregorian calendar. In the Northern Hemisphere it is the last month of autumn and celebrations connected to the harvest season take place. In the Southern Hemisphere, the last of the mild spring weather is enjoyed before the summer heat begins, but many traditional festivals transferred from the North are celebrated there as well. Not all of November's major events are connected to the seasons — Remembrance Day's origins grew out of the history of the twentieth century.

The star sign Sagittarius and a scene showing a man beating nuts from a tree, from *Calendar and Book of Hours*, from fifteenth-century France. November begins in the sign of Scorpio and ends in the sign of Sagittarius.

SPECIAL DAYS

Melbourne Cup Day in Australia is held annually on the first Tuesday of November. Cup Day is a holiday in Melbourne, and the rest of the nation stops for three minutes when the horse race is run.

U.S. Election Day is the first Tuesday after the first Monday in November. Many public officials are elected on this day and they take up their posts in the following January.

Ambrogio Figino (c. 1550–1595), *Jupiter and Juno,* held in the Civiche Racc d'Arte Pavia. During the *Epulum Jovis* banquet of the Plebian Games, which were held in November in ancient Roman times, Jupiter and Juno were guests of honor.

NOVEMBER TAKES ITS NAME from the Latin word for "nine," *novem*, as it was the ninth month in the ancient Roman calendar. In the seventh century B.C.E. Januaris and Febuaris were added during the winter and November became the eleventh month.

For Romans, the major event of this month was the Plebian Games, which took place from November 4 to 17. The festival was held chiefly in honor of Jupiter and was the responsibility of the plebian *aediles*, the public officers drawn from the general population. Festivities began with a procession of those who were to compete in the sporting, dramatic, and musical events. The statues of the gods were taken from their temples and placed on stretchers, then were carried in the parade to the Circus where they were set to rest on couches to watch the proceedings.

The high point of the games was the *Epulum Jovis*, a lavish banquet held in honor of Jupiter on November 13 at the Capitol. The statues of Jupiter, Juno, and Minerva were anointed with perfumes and set up at the banquet tables as guests of honor. Food was set before the gods and the officers in charge of the feast performed the duties of eating it for them.

Giving thanks

No doubt the Epulum Jovis was in part such a lavish feast because the hard work of the harvest was now over. There was time for celebration and plenty of food to enjoy. Throughout the

November birthflower

The chrysanthemum is one of the few flowers that still bloom in autumn, so not surprisingly it is November's birthflower. Chrysanthemums were first cultivated in China and were brought to Europe in the seventeenth century. They are usually associated with compassion, friendship, and cheerfulness.

St. Martin and the Beggar by El Greco (1540–1614), kept at the National Gallery of Art, Washington D.C. St. Martin's Day is celebrated in November throughout western Europe. When St. Martin was still a Roman soldier, he cut his cloak in half to give to a naked, starving beggar. Soon afterward he became a monk.

Northern Hemisphere many similar festivals associated with the harvest occur in November.

Throughout western Europe, St. Martin's Eve on November 10 and St. Martin's Day on November 11 are marked with great festivities. St. Martin is known as a friend of the poor and of children, and his festival is one of sharing, feasting, and fun. In much of Italy the new wine is tasted and St. Martin's statue is carried through the streets. In Belgium and the Netherlands, children go from house to house singing and are given presents. In Düsseldorf, children carrying lanterns are led in a parade by an adult dressed as St. Martin. In many countries his day marks the beginning of harvest festivals, and people sample the new wine and eat roast goose.

In Switzerland, the Onion Market is one of the biggest market days of the year. It is held on the fourth Monday in November in the square in front of the Swiss Parliament building in Bern. As its name suggests, onions are the main fare on display, but they aren't just ordinary onions. These ones, usually harvested in early August, have been dried with their long leaves left on and are braided into wreaths and long ropes. Dried flowers are woven in among the yellow, white, brown, and purple onions. Around 70 tons of onions are sold each year at the market.

Thanksgiving Day in the U.S. is one of the world's most famous celebrations of the harvest. There were many Thanksgiving celebrations held at various times by European settlers in the New World, grateful for their survival after perilous journeys and tenuous starts in their new land, but the event to which Americans trace Thanksgiving Day took place in Plymouth, Massachusetts. According to tradition, this Thanksgiving was held sometime in the fall of 1621 by a group of Puritan settlers and the local Wampanoag people. The Pilgrims had been heading for Virginia when their ship, the *Mayflower*, was blown off course. Instead they landed at Plymouth Rock in November 1620. During the following winter the settlers had few supplies and many died. Without the food and assistance given by the local people they all would have perished. After the Pilgrims harvested their first crop of

Crowds in New York watch the annual Macy's Parade on Thanksgiving Day. Giant balloons in the shape of cartoon characters are always part of the event. Here Chicken Little floats above the 2005 crowds.

pumpkins and corn they invited the Wampanoag people to a three-day Thanksgiving celebration.

Over the next 150 years Thanksgiving feasts were held sporadically in relation to specific events. In 1789 George Washington declared a national day of thanks in honor of the new constitution. He connected this celebration to the day on which the Pilgrims' day of thanks was thought to have been held. Even then, Thanksgiving Day didn't become a regular tradition until 1863, when Abraham Lincoln declared the last Thursday in November a national holiday. In 1939 Franklin Roosevelt moved the holiday forward to the fourth Thursday in the month, where it has stayed. As Christmas shopping traditionally started on the day after Thanksgiving, this gave busy people an extra week to prepare.

Today Thanksgiving Day is celebrated all over the U.S. with family get-togethers and a large meal including roast turkey, candied yams, and pumpkin dishes. In New York, Macy's department store has held a Thanksgiving Day parade since 1924. Many football matches have come to be held on this day, so an afternoon of watching games on the television has become the norm in many households.

New beginnings

In Celtic tradition, November marked the end of one year and the beginning of the next. In Irish it is called *Samhain*, meaning "summer's end," and similar words exist in other Celtic languages. As the world began to die off for winter, many Celts held a three-day festival in honor of the dead and darkness. All home fires were extinguished and a large fire was lit outdoors. The English word "bonfire" originates from the fact that bones of dead cattle were cast into the flames. Other more personal tokens were also burnt in offering and thanks for a bountiful harvest.

On the night of summer's end the world was thought to be in a state of flux. The spirits of the dead and of those who were yet to be born roamed the Earth. Dancing and feasting took place to entertain the spirits. The world was thought to be topsy-turvy, and people were allowed to flout convention. In some regions boys and girls swapped clothes and played tricks on their elders, often pretending to be the spirits of the dead.

As the Pagan beliefs faded, these customs were absorbed into the Christian religion. In the Western church the first of November became

November birthstone

Topaz is the birthstone of November. The ancient Egyptians believed its yellow color came from the glow cast by the sun god Ra. This precious stone is seen as a gift of friendship.

All Saints Day or Hallowmas, which was probably first held in the fourth century C.E. in recognition of martyrs, and grew to be a day on which all saints were honored. The night before this, All Hallows Eve, or Halloween, retained the riotous celebrations associated with Samhain. The second of November became All Souls Day, when people prayed for the souls of their departed loved ones and for all those who might be in purgatory doing penance before they could rise to heaven. These days remain important in many denominations of the church, with special services held on All Saints Day, and families visiting the graves of their loved ones on All Souls Day to leave flowers or light candles. The Eastern Orthodox churches celebrate All Saints Day as a moveable feast on the first Sunday after Pentecost.

Remembering the dead

All Souls Day isn't the only day on which the dead are remembered in November. On the eleventh hour of the eleventh day of the eleventh month in 1918 all fighting in World War I ceased. An estimated 9 million soldiers and 6 million civilians had died during the four-year war. One year later, the first Armistice Day was held to commemorate those who died and suffered in the war.

World War I did not prove to be the war to end all wars, and Armistice Day has come to commemorate all war dead. In France and Belgium, November 11 is still known as Armistice Day, but since World War II it has been known as Remembrance Day in Commonwealth nations and as Veterans Day in the U.S.

Flanders poppies are associated with Armistice Day, but because they don't bloom in November, paper and plastic versions have to be made to wear at memorial services. In northern France and Belgium these brilliant red flowers bloomed in spring in the churned-up mud of the battlefields and over the recently dug graves of soldiers. On May 3, 1915, Canadian doctor Lt. Col. John McCrae wrote the poem "In Flanders Fields" in memory of his friend and former student Lt. Alexis Helmer, who had recently died in the Second Battle of Ypres and had been laid to rest in European soil. McCrae was not to survive the war either. He caught pneumonia and meningitis in the field hospital where he worked and died on January 28, 1918.

In Flanders Fields
In Flanders Fields the poppies blow
Between the crosses, row on row,
That mark our place; and in the sky
The larks, still bravely singing, fly
Scarce heard amid the guns below.

We are the Dead.
Short days ago
We lived, felt dawn, saw sunset glow,
Loved, and were loved, and now we lie
In Flanders fields.

Take up our quarrel with the foe:
To you from failing hands we throw
The torch; be yours to hold it high.
If ye break faith with us who die
We shall not sleep, though poppies grow
In Flanders fields.

Lieutenant Colonel John McCrae

In Mexico, All Saints Day and All Souls Day are celebrated in a lively, two-day festival called the Day of the Dead. Families go to cemeteries to spend time with their departed loved ones, taking food and having picnics and lighting candles for them.

Special treats are made for children, such as the skull-shaped candies above.

November 1

"The harder you work, the luckier you get." — GARY PLAYER, GOLFER

HISTORICAL EVENTS

1512 Michelangelo begins to paint the 5,000 square foot (1,520 sq m) ceiling of the Sistine Chapel of the Vatican in July 1508. On October 31, 1512, he is finished, and the scaffolding is removed so that on this day, the completed ceiling is visible to the public for the first time.

1755 An earthquake estimated to be over 9 on the Richter scale strikes Lisbon, Portugal. The quake, fires that break out in the ruins and three subsequent tsunamis kill an estimated 100,000 people and devastate the city.

1884 Greenwich Mean Time is adopted as the universal 0-degree longitude line, or International Date Line, at a meeting of the International Meridian Conference in Washington D.C.

1959 Jacques Plante, goalie for Montreal Canadiens, wears the first ice hockey face mask in a match in Montreal. He had made the fiberglass mask soon after a match in which he received a cut to his face that required seven stitches.

1986 A fire at a chemical factory near Basel, Switzerland, causes tons of toxic waste to spill into the Rhine River (see below).

1987 In Los Angeles on the Joshua Tree Tour, the band U2 pretends to be a country-rock group called The Dalton Brothers and opens for itself. The Daltons appear twice more on the tour and accept a Grammy Award on behalf of U2 in 1989.

1993 On this day, the Maastricht Treaty comes into effect, creating the European Union. The aim of the union is to engender greater cooperation, especially in the fields of security and economics.

DAYS TO REMEMBER

Historical day Samhain The Celtic word *Samhain* means "summer's end," and this day also marks the beginning of winter and the new year. Festivities took place at night and involved offerings of harvest foods, lighting bonfires, and cooking meals for ancestors. The modern customs of Halloween are thought to derive from these festivities.

Religious day All Saints or All Hallows Day This day celebrates those who came to reflect Christ most closely on Earth during their lives. The Greek and Russian Orthodox churches celebrate All Saints on the first Sunday after Pentecost.

Births
- **1935** Gary Player, golfer
- **1942** Larry Flynt, magazine publisher
- **1957** Lyle Lovett, singer
- **1958** Charlie Kaufman, writer
- **1962** Anthony Kiedis, singer (Red Hot Chili Peppers)
- **1972** Toni Colette, actress

Deaths
- **1588** Jean Daurat, poet
- **1700** Charles II, King of Spain
- **1894** Alexander III, Tsar of Russia
- **1972** Ezra Pound, editor, writer, and critic
- **1999** Walter Payton, gridiron player

The Rhine turns red

In the 1880s salmon and no less than 50 other species of fish could be found in the Rhine River, flowing across four countries in Europe. As pollution from agriculture, industry, and sewage grew, the fish disappeared and the river became too toxic to swim in. In the 1970s huge efforts went into cleaning the river up, but in one night its road to recovery was undone.

During the early hours of November 1, 1986, a fire broke out in a chemical factory in Basel, Switzerland, near the river's head. Firemen poured water on the blaze and captured the run-off behind a containment wall. This wall gave way and 30 tons of agricultural chemicals and heavy metals poured out. A deadly red soup swept downriver, killing aquatic life and land animals that drank the water. In 10 days it had traveled the length of the Rhine and entered the North Sea.

The outcry in the nations through which the Rhine flows – one of which is Germany, where the Rheinstein castle (pictured right) stands – led to redoubled efforts to clean it, and keep it clean. Some of the improved standards included water basins to trap firefighting water, should it be needed again. By 1997, salmon returned to the river to breed – a real achievement, as these fish are highly sensitive to pollution. It is hoped that by 2020 the river will be clean enough for people to swim in it safely.

November 2

DATE*line*

"Old men are dangerous; it doesn't matter to them what is going to happen to the world."
GEORGE BERNARD SHAW, *HEARTBREAK HOUSE*, 1919

HISTORICAL EVENTS

1899 The Boers begin their siege of British-occupied Ladysmith in South Africa. The siege lasts 118 days before the Gordon Highlanders arrive and the Boers are driven off.

1942 After more than three months of fighting, heavily outnumbered and poorly equipped Australian troops recapture the important strategic village of Kokoda in New Guinea from the Japanese army, so preventing the capture of Port Moresby.

1960 A court in London finds that Penguin hasn't broken obscenity laws by publishing *Lady Chatterley's Lover* in its unexpurgated version (see right).

1963 South Vietnamese President Ngô Đìen Diêm is assassinated after a military coup, further destabilizing the nation. After this, U.S. involvement in the Vietnam War increases.

1964 After a decade of financial mismanagement, King Saud of Saudi Arabia is deposed in a family coup with the backing of the *ulema* (council of Muslim scholars) and is replaced by his half-brother, King Faisal.

2000 The first crew – two Russians and an American – arrives in a Russian spacecraft to live for four months in the International Space Station.

DAYS TO REMEMBER

Religious day All Souls Day On this day, prayers are offered for the dead to ask for their deliverance from purgatory into heaven. It is a day on which many families visit the graves of their loved ones.

Religious day Coronation of Haile Selassie I Rastafarians celebrate the crowning of the founder of their movement, Emperor Haile Selassie of Ethiopia, on this day in 1930.

Lady Chatterley's Lover published at last

When D. H. Lawrence wrote *Lady Chatterley's Lover* in 1928 he was unable to find a publisher willing to print the work – the book told the story of a love affair between an upper-class woman and a working-class man, and contained swear words and explicit sex scenes. He printed the book privately and soon sold all his copies. Lawrence died of tuberculosis in 1930, possibly earlier than he might have, due to strain caused by controversy over the book.

"Clean" versions of *Lady Chatterley's Lover* were printed but the unexpurgated novel continued to be banned until 1959 when Grove Press in the U.S. decided to print it. However, the Post Master General and President Eisenhower found it offensive and banned it from entering the postal system. Deliveries couldn't be made until the courts overturned the ban.

In 1960, Penguin tested the recent Obscene Publications Act in the U.K. and published the book in its original form. The case made headlines, with many testifying as to its literary merit, and its opponents being accused of being out of touch with society.

On this day in 1960, the courts decided that Penguin had not breached the obscenity law by publishing the book and the public could read Lawrence's novel in the form he intended. The 30,000 copies of the book that had been printed were delivered to bookstores and sold out by November 10. It has never been out of print since.

Births
- **1734** Daniel Boone, U.S. frontiersman
- **1755** Marie Antoinette, Queen of France
- **1877** Victor Trumper, cricketer
- **1877** Aga Khan III, spiritual leader
- **1885** Harlow Shapley, astronomer
- **1906** Luchino Visconti, film director
- **1913** Burt Lancaster, actor
- **1920** Ann Rutherford, actress
- **1942** Shere Hite, writer
- **1950** Graeme Murphy, choreographer and ballet dancer
- **1961** k. d. lang, singer

Deaths
- **1950** George Bernard Shaw, writer
- **1961** James Thurber, humorist writer
- **1963** Ngô Đinh Diêm, South Vietnamese president

November 3

"The quickest way to a man's heart is through his chest." — ROSEANNE BARR

HISTORICAL EVENTS

1503 According to some sources, Leonardo da Vinci is commissioned to paint a portrait of Lisa Gherardini by her husband, merchant Francesco del Giocondo. The painting, now known as the *Mona Lisa*, is completed four years later.

1871 After six months of trekking in Africa searching for missionary Dr. David Livingstone, Henry Stanley finds him living on the shores of Lake Tanganyika. Dr. Livingstone hadn't seen another white man for six-and-a-half years. He refused to return to England and died two years later.

1954 The first *Godzilla* movie is released in Japan. The classic monster film is the story of a giant beast awoken from a million-year slumber by the nuclear weapons being tested in the South Pacific.

1957 The U.S.S.R. launches *Sputnik II* carrying Laika, the first living animal to be sent into space. Although provided with food, water and air, the dog can't return to Earth and dies when her oxygen runs out.

1966 The Arno River breaks its banks, flooding Florence for three days. The floodwaters rise to levels not reached since 1333, destroying and damaging untold art treasures and drowning an estimated 150 people (see below).

1979 Communist Workers' Party members clash with Ku Klux Klan members and neo-Nazis at a "Death to the Klan" rally in Greensboro, North Carolina. Fighting breaks out and shots are fired, killing five Communist Party members.

1986 Lebanese magazine *Ash Shiraa* reveals that the U.S. administration has sold arms to Iran in attempts to have hostages held by pro-Iranian kidnappers in Lebanon released. It later becomes clear that funds from the sales were channeled to Contra forces in Nicaragua and President Reagan was possibly involved.

Births
- **1801** Karl Baedeker, travel writer and publisher
- **1801** Vincenzo Bellini, composer
- **1920** Oodgeroo Noonuccal, writer
- **1921** Charles Bronson, actor
- **1933** John Barry, composer
- **1948** Lulu (Marie Lawrie), singer and actress
- **1952** Rosanne Barr, comedienne and actress

Deaths
- **1793** Olympe de Gouges, feminist and revolutionary
- **1926** Annie Oakley, sharpshooter
- **1954** Henri Matisse, painter
- **1967** Alexander Aitken, mathematician
- **1990** Mary Martin, actress
- **1998** Bob Kane, cartoonist, creator of Batman
- **2002** Lonnie Donegan, skiffle musician

DAYS TO REMEMBER

National day Culture Day Held in Japan to commemorate the constitution that was signed on this day in 1946, the first Culture Day was held in 1948 to promote peace and freedom. Celebrations include cultural events and awards ceremonies for cultural achievement.

National day Emperor Day On this day each year prior to 1946, the anniversary of Emperor Meiji's birth in 1852 was celebrated in Japan.

After weeks of wet weather in Northern Italy, heavy rain began to fall on November 3, 1966. Water from two dams on the Arno River was released for fear they would collapse. In the early hours of November 4, the Arno burst its banks in Florence. The floodwater reached 22 feet (6.7 m) in some narrow streets. Florence's treasures – paintings, statues, books, and buildings – were damaged by water and the dirt, fuel oil, and debris it carried. It took conservators decades to repair them. Throughout the north, close to 150 people drowned.

November 4

DATE*line*

> "What passing-bells for these who die as cattle?
> Only the monstrous anger of the guns."
> WILFRED OWEN, FROM *ANTHEM FOR DOOMED YOUTH*, WRITTEN DURING WORLD WAR I

Births
- 1916 Walter Cronkite, news broadcaster
- 1916 Ruth Handler, inventor of Barbie©
- 1923 Alfred Heineken, businessman and brewer
- 1937 Loretta Swit, actress
- 1946 Robert Mapplethorpe, photographer
- 1947 Rodney Marsh, cricketer

Deaths
- 1781 Johann Nikolaus Götz, poet
- 1847 Felix Mendelssohn, composer
- 1918 Wilfred Owen, soldier and poet
- 1995 Yitzhak Rabin, Israeli Prime Minister

HISTORICAL EVENTS

1899 Sigmund Freud's *The Interpretation of Dreams* is published in Switzerland. Only 600 copies of the book are initially printed, and it takes eight years to sell them all.

1942 During World War II, the Second Battle of El Alamein ends after 12 days when Field Marshal Erwin Rommel orders German and Italian forces to retreat, turning the tide against the Axis powers in Northern Africa.

1956 Soviet forces enter Hungary to end the uprising that had begun on October 23 (see right).

1979 Iranian students storm the U.S. Embassy in Tehran, taking 90 hostages and demanding the deposed Shah (who had been allowed into the U.S. for medical treatment) be returned to stand trial. The last 52 hostages are released 14 months later, after the Shah has died of cancer and when the U.S. agrees to return $8 billion of assets to Iran.

1993 A firestorm in the Santa Monica Mountains in Los Angeles that had begun on November 2 is finally declared under control. It had killed three and destroyed at least 400 homes. Arsonists had lit many of the fires.

1995 Yitzhak Rabin, Prime Minister of Israel, attends a peace rally in Tel Aviv. Returning to his car, he is shot by Yigal Amir, a right-wing Israeli, and dies in hospital soon after.

DAYS TO REMEMBER

Religious day St. Charles Borromeo's Day An archbishop of Milan who carried out important church reforms, Charles Borromeo (1538–1584) was born a noble. Even so, he devoted his life to helping the poor and sick. He died on this day aged 46.

National day Unity Day (Russia) President Putin announced this new Russian national holiday in 2005. It commemorates a popular uprising on November 4, 1612.

The Hungarian uprising is crushed

The Hungarian uprising against the control of the U.S.S.R. began on October 23, 1956, with peaceful demonstrations in Budapest. Protesters were calling for the reinstatement of Prime Minister Imre Nagy, who had been dismissed the year before for his liberal policies, and the withdrawal of Soviet troops from the country. Clashes between armed police and demonstrators became more violent and Soviet tanks were called into action.

That night the Hungarian Communist Party reinstated Nagy but fighting continued. On October 25, Soviet tanks fired at demonstrators in Parliament Square and hundreds of protesters were killed. The tanks withdrew from the city on October 30. Nagy announced that his Government was dedicated to gaining freedom from the U.S.S.R. and Hungary was withdrawing from the Warsaw Pact.

Nikita Khrushchev, leader of the U.S.S.R., ordered a crackdown on November 4. The Soviet Air Force bombed Budapest, and tanks and soldiers invaded the city at dawn. By November 12 the uprising had been crushed. An estimated 30,000 people had been killed in Budapest alone and more than 200,000 fled to the West.

Nagy had called for help from the UN and the West, but they did not respond beyond expressing their disapproval of Soviet actions. He took refuge in the Yugoslav Embassy but was captured by Soviet agents and on June 16, 1958, was executed for treason. In 1989 his body was exhumed from an unmarked grave and he was buried with full honors on the anniversary of his death. Soviet troops finally withdrew from Hungary in 1991.

November 5

"A desperate disease requires a dangerous remedy."
GUY FAWKES, GIVING HIS REASON FOR CARRYING OUT THE GUNPOWDER PLOT

NASA launched *Voyager 1* in September 1977. On this day in 2003, scientists at Johns Hopkins University announced that readings being sent back by *Voyager* indicated it had entered the termination shock zone where hot solar winds blow, suggesting it was at the edge of our solar system. Others didn't believe this point had been reached, but it was beyond dispute that *Voyager 1* had traveled more than 8 billion miles (13 billion km), further than any other artificial object.

Births
- 1913 Vivien Leigh, actress
- 1935 Lester Piggott, jockey
- 1940 Elke Somer, actress
- 1941 Art Garfunkel, musician and singer
- 1943 Sam Shepard, actor and playwright
- 1963 Tatum O'Neal, actor

Deaths
- 1879 James Clerk Maxwell, scientist
- 1977 Guy Lombardo, band-leader
- 1977 René Goscinny, comic book writer
- 1979 Al Capp, cartoonist
- 1982 Jacques Tati, comedian and director
- 1989 Vladimir Horowitz, pianist
- 1991 Fred MacMurray, actor
- 1991 Robert Maxwell, media magnate

HISTORICAL EVENTS

1605 The Gunpowder Plot is foiled when Guy Fawkes is discovered in a cellar below the English Houses of Parliament lighting a long fuse, set to explode as King James I opens Parliament. Fawkes is later executed.

1872 Susan B. Anthony and 14 other women vote in the U.S. presidential elections. In 1873 Anthony is tried for "unlawful voting" and is fined $100. She refuses to pay the fine but isn't jailed.

1914 Britain had leased Cyprus from the Ottoman Empire in 1878. Days after the Ottoman Empire allies itself with Germany in World War I, Britain annexes Cyprus and declares war on the Ottoman Empire.

1935 In early 1935 Parker Brothers buys the game Monopoly from Charles B. Darrow. They later learn the game is played with homemade sets all over the eastern U.S. and derives from the Landlord's Game, patented in 1904 by a Quaker named Elizabeth Magie. On this day they buy her patent for $500, leaving the way open to expand the production of their board game.

1955 The rebuilt Vienna State Opera opens with a performance of Beethoven's *Fidelio*. A bomb had destroyed it during an Allied air raid on March 12, 1945.

1987 Govan Mbeki is released in South Africa after serving 24 years in Robben Island prison. In 1964 he had been given a life sentence for treason against the South African Government. He went on to serve in the post-apartheid Government.

2003 NASA announces that the *Voyager 1* spacecraft has reached the edge of the solar system (see above).

DAYS TO REMEMBER

Religious day Zechariah and Elizabeth's Day John the Baptist's parents were childless until the angel Gabriel appeared to Zechariah and said Elizabeth would have a son, whom they must call John. Zechariah was disbelieving, so the angel struck him dumb until the child was born and circumcized.

Traditional day Guy Fawkes' Night This celebration is held in Britain and New Zealand with fireworks and bonfires to celebrate the failure of the Gunpowder Plot.

November 6

"Actually, we're not into music, we're into chaos." — STEVE JONES, GUITARIST FOR THE SEX PISTOLS

HISTORICAL EVENTS

1860 Abraham Lincoln is elected the sixteenth President of the U.S. He is the first Republican President, and his party's anti-slavery stance leads to the secession of the southern states soon after.

1889 Fusajiro Yamauchi forms the Nintendo company to make and distribute the card game "Hanafuda." His grandson Hiroshi Yamauchi later runs the company and diversifies into arcade and electronic games.

1973 After singer Gram Parsons dies of a drug overdose on September 23, 1973, Phil Kaufman, his manager, steals his body and takes it to the Joshua Tree Desert where he pours petrol over it and sets it alight. On this day, Kaufman, who claims he was fulfilling Parsons' wishes, is fined for stealing and burning a coffin – it was not a crime to steal a body.

1975 In London, the Sex Pistols make their debut performance (see below).

1975 As part of the Green March organized by King Hassan II, 160,000 unarmed Moroccans cross into Spanish-ruled Western Sahara. Spain soon agrees to hand the territory over instead of allowing the Saharawi people the right to self-determination, as had been planned.

1991 In Kuwait, the last of more than 600 oil wells set alight in January by invading Iraqi forces is extinguished. The smoke had created pollution problems on a global scale and the fires had left the Kuwaiti oil industry in ruins.

1999 A referendum to make Australia a republic and replace the British monarch with a president as head of state is defeated, 55 percent against, 45 percent for.

Births
- **1494** Suliman the Magnificent, Ottoman Sultan
- **1661** Charles II, King of Spain
- **1814** Adolph Sax, inventor of the saxophone
- **1860** Ignacy Jan Paderewski, composer, pianist, and Polish Prime Minister
- **1860** James Naismith, inventor of basketball
- **1946** Sally Field, actress
- **1949** Nigel Havers, actor
- **1955** Maria Shriver, journalist
- **1970** Ethan Hawke, actor

Deaths
- **1796** Catherine the Great, Empress of Russia
- **1893** Peter Ilyich Tchaikovsky, composer

The Sex Pistols' first performance

The Sex Pistols played for the first time on November 6, 1975, at Central Saint Martins College of Art and Design in London. The gig was characteristically loud, harsh, and aggressive, and after 20 minutes they were told to get off.

Original band members Paul Cook and Steve Jones had joined together in 1972 as The Strand. Jones often went to a shop called "Let it Rock," and knew one of the shop's managers, Malcolm McLaren, had connections in the music business. In 1975 Jones convinced him to be their manager. In August, after a number of name and personnel changes, John Lydon (Johnny Rotten) auditioned in the shop, singing along with the jukebox. McLaren helped the band work out a new name and the Sex Pistols debuted soon after.

Their first gig might not have been a success, but the Sex Pistols went on to play at pubs, clubs, and other art schools. They came to national attention in December 1976 when they swore on live-to-air television. Over the next two chaotic years the British public continued to be shocked by the band's seminal punk look, and even more by the lyrics of such songs as "God Save the Queen" and "Anarchy in the U.K."

Although the Sex Pistols weren't around for long, they had a huge impact on British culture and music. Their ripped clothes, spiked hair, chains and safety pins, and direct, abrasive criticism of the establishment became trademarks of the punk ethos. Fan Paul Davis was a teenager when he saw their first concert. On its 30th anniversary he said, "I'd never seen anything like it. It was working-class people doing something for themselves. After that, I couldn't listen to anything else."

November 7

"History is the endless repetition of the wrong way of living." — LAWRENCE DURRELL, *LISTENER*

HISTORICAL EVENTS

1861 One of the world's most famous horse races, the Melbourne Cup, is run for the first time and is won by Archer, ridden by J. Cutts – they win again in 1862.

1895 Canada's first transcontinental railway is completed six years ahead of schedule. The track is 2,875 miles (4,600 km) long.

1917 Bolshevik revolutionaries led by Vladimir Lenin seize power with almost no bloodshed in Petrograd (St. Petersburg) from the provisional Government that came to power after Nicholas II was deposed in March. This is known as the October Revolution, as it falls in October according to the Julian calendar, which was used in Russia at the time.

1929 The Museum of Modern Art opens in New York City in a rented space on Fifth Avenue in Manhattan. The opening is well attended, despite the recent stock market crash on Wall Street.

1991 "Magic" Johnson announces he is HIV positive (see below).

1997 Chinese engineers complete the cofferdam across the Yangtze River, diverting it to begin the construction of the world's biggest dam, the Three Gorges Dam.

2000 In a cliff-hanger U.S. presidential election, it is unclear whether the winner will be Republican George W. Bush or Democrat Al Gore. A controversy erupts over the counting of votes in Florida, with a recount finally declared unconstitutional on December 12. Gore concedes defeat the next day.

Births
- **1867** Marie Curie, physicist and chemist
- **1900** Heinrich Himmler, head of the Nazi SS
- **1903** Konrad Lorenz, zoologist
- **1913** Albert Camus, writer and philosopher
- **1918** Billy Graham, evangelist
- **1926** Dame Joan Sutherland, opera singer
- **1943** Joni Mitchell, singer and songwriter

Deaths
- **1913** Alfred Russel Wallace, biologist
- **1980** Steve McQueen, actor
- **1990** Lawrence Durrell, writer

DAY TO REMEMBER

Historical day Catalan Day On this day in 1659 France and Spain signed the Treaty of the Pyrenees and North Catalonia became part of France. On the anniversary of this event Catalanists often hold protest demonstrations as French became the official language and Catalan has had no place in public life.

In 1991, the Los Angeles Lakers' star point guard Earvin "Magic" Johnson announced his retirement from basketball at a press conference the day after he learned he was HIV positive. Doctors had advised that his demanding training could compromise his health. He immediately became a spokesperson for AIDS awareness: "I'm here saying it can happen to anybody, even Magic Johnson." However, he couldn't stay away from basketball altogether and returned to play in an All Stars match, the Olympics, and some games for his old team, the Lakers.

DATEline

November 8

"Poets who sing about the beauty of the stars, without understanding what makes them shine and how they were created, are missing more than half of the real splendor of the heavens."

BEN BOVA, SCIENCE FICTION WRITER

HISTORICAL EVENTS

1519 Spanish conquistador Hernando Cortés enters Tenochtitlan, welcomed as the god Quetzalcoatl by Aztec King Montezuma II. Soon afterward Montezuma is taken prisoner and Cortés controls the Aztec empire.

1793 The Louvre is opened as a museum to the public. King Francis I, a collector of art, established the building as the royal residence in 1546. The royal collections were added to as the French army made conquests under Napoleon.

1895 Wilhelm Röntgen discovers radiation emitted by cathode-ray tubes while he is conducting electrical experiments. He names them x-rays, with the "x" standing for "unknown." He is awarded the Nobel Prize for Physics in 1901.

1958 The blue, 45-carat Hope Diamond, once owned by kings, is sent to the Smithsonian in Washington D.C. by its last owner, Harry Winston. He wasn't donating the diamond because of its alleged curse, but because he believed it should be part of a national gem collection.

1965 *Days of Our Lives* debuts (see right).

1993 Thieves cut through the roof of the Museum of Modern Art in Stockholm, Sweden, and steal artworks including paintings by Pablo Picasso and Georges Braque. The uninsured paintings were valued at around U.S. $60 million.

DAY TO REMEMBER

Religious day Archangelovden (Archangel's Day) As winter approached in the Northern Hemisphere, Archangel Michael was traditionally honored on this day with a ceremonial blessed meal of bread, red wine, and a freshly killed male animal.

Births		1976	Brett Lee, cricketer
1656	Edmond Halley, astronomer	**Deaths**	
1710	Sarah Fielding, writer	1674	John Milton, poet
1847	Bram Stoker, writer	1887	John Henry "Doc" Holliday, dentist and gunfighter
1900	Margaret Mitchell, writer		
1922	Christiaan Barnard, surgeon	1935	Sir Charles Kingsford Smith, aviator (missing presumed dead)
1932	Ben Bova, writer		
1949	Bonnie Raitt, singer	1978	Norman Rockwell, painter and illustrator
1954	Rickie Lee Jones, singer and songwriter	1990	Anya Seton, writer
		2004	Eddie Charlton, snooker player

"Like sands through the hourglass…so are the days of our lives."

The U.S. soap opera *Days of Our Lives* has started with these words for more than 40 years. They are spoken by Macdonald Carey who played Dr. Tom Horton from the first episode until his death in 1994. The other main element of the opening – the hourglass – has also remained.

The show, set in the fictional town of Salem, premiered on NBC TV on November 8, 1965. In the first episode, teenager Julie Olson (then played by Charla Doherty) is caught stealing. Meanwhile, her grandmother, Alice Horton, is fretting because her daughter is about to marry and she feels all her children are leaving.

Francis Reid (pictured front row, center) played Alice Horton in that first episode, and she still played her, more than 40 years later when she was over 90 years old. When approached to play Alice, Reid was hesitant – she was an accomplished actress who had played Shakespearean and movie roles. However, roles for 40-year-old actresses were hard to come by in the 1960s so she took the part. By 2005 Alice was a widowed great-grandmother and *Days of Our Lives* focused on the turbulent lives of several families.

Days of Our Lives is by no means the longest-running U.S. soap opera. That honor goes to *Guiding Light* which started out as a radio drama in January 1937. This was the era in which soap operas gained their name: They were daytime radio melodramas, and cleaning products were often advertised during their time slot. *Guiding Light* transferred to CBC TV in June 1952, where it has been running ever since.

445

November 9

"To make an apple pie from scratch, first you must invent the universe." — CARL SAGAN, *COSMOS*, 1980

HISTORICAL EVENTS

1799 Napoleon Bonaparte, just returned from Egypt, takes over France in a coup. He is declared First Consul on November 11 and holds absolute power until his abdication in 1814.

1825 After watching a demonstration of light created by burning lime, Thomas Drummond sets up a limelight in front of a reflector on a hill near Belfast, Ireland. The light can be seen 66 miles (106 km) away, and limelights come to be used in lighthouses and theaters.

1888 Jack the Ripper kills Mary Jane Kelly, his last known victim. The brutal murders of at least five prostitutes had taken place in London over a 9-week period.

1921 Albert Einstein is awarded the Nobel Prize for Physics (see below).

1938 In Germany, *Kristallnacht*, the Night of Broken Glass, takes place on the nights of November 9–10, when Nazi troops and sympathizers destroy and loot 7,500 Jewish businesses, burn 267 synagogues, kill 91 Jews, and round up 25,000 Jewish men to be sent to concentration camps.

1967 The first issue of *Rolling Stone* magazine goes on sale.

1985 Russian Garry Kasparov becomes the youngest World Chess Champion at 22 years of age when he defeats Anatoly Karpov, who had held the title for 10 years.

DAYS TO REMEMBER

National day Independence Day (Cambodia) On this day, Cambodia celebrates gaining independence from France in 1953 after 90 years of colonial rule. Independence was gained in large part through the efforts of King Norodom Sihanouk.

National day Schicksalstag (Germany) This day – whose name translates to "day of fate" – is remembered because a number of momentous events occurred on it: Revolutionary Robert Blum was executed in 1848, Germany became a republic in 1918, Hitler's Beer Hall Putsch spread to the streets of Munich in 1923, *Kristallnacht* took place in 1938, and in 1989 the Berlin Wall fell.

Births

- 1877 Allama Muhammad Iqbal, poet and philosopher
- 1889 Claude Rains, actor
- 1913 Hedy Lamarr, actor
- 1928 Anne Sexton, poet
- 1929 Imre Kertész, writer
- 1934 Carl Sagan, astronomer
- 1941 Tom Fogerty, musician
- 1965 Bryn Terfel, opera singer
- 1982 Jana Pittman, hurdler
- 1984 Delta Goodrem, singer and songwriter

Deaths

- 1848 Robert Blum, German revolutionary
- 1940 Neville Chamberlain, British Prime Minister
- 1952 Chaim Weizmann, Israel's first President
- 1953 Dylan Thomas, poet and playwright
- 1970 General Charles de Gaulle, French President
- 1991 Yves Montand, actor and singer
- 2003 Gordon Onslow Ford, painter

Einstein wins the Nobel Prize

In 1921 Albert Einstein was awarded the Nobel Prize for Physics "for his services to Theoretical Physics." To say that he had made a contribution to science was a vast understatement.

In 1905, when he was a clerk in the Swiss Patents Office, he submitted three papers to the *Annalen der Physik*, all of which were accepted for publication. In what has become known as his *annus mirabilis*, or "year of miracles," he published two more papers. His papers dealt with Brownian motion, the electromagnetic effect, and the special theory of relativity, which claimed light had a mass and space, and time was relative. His elegant ideas explained phenomena that Newtonian physics could not cope with. Science would never be the same afterward.

In 1915 Einstein, now director of the Kaiser Wilhelm Institute and professor at the University of Berlin, presented a series paper that explained his General Theory of Relativity. In 1921 when he was awarded the Nobel Prize, this theory was still being debated, although it had gained considerable acceptance when Arthur Eddington observed a solar eclipse in 1919 and measured the gravitational effect of the light from a star as it passed close to the Sun. Einstein was awarded the prize "especially for his discovery of the law of the photoelectric effect."

The award confirmed his fame in the eyes of the world, helping to make his name synonymous with genius. Although many of us may not fully understand the Theory of Relativity, we take for granted the technology it led to, such as nuclear energy and global positioning systems.

November 10

"Wealth is the smallest thing on Earth, the least gift that God has bestowed on mankind."

MARTIN LUTHER

HISTORICAL EVENTS

1775 The Continental Marines (later renamed the U.S. Marine Corps) is founded early in the War of American Independence to serve with the new Continental Navy.

1928 Michinomiya Hirohito is crowned the 124th Emperor of Japan. He was Emperor until his death in 1989, although after World War II he had to renounce his claims to divinity.

1969 *Sesame Street* debuts on television in the U.S. It aims to teach children the fundamentals of numbers and letters and introduces other educational topics.

1970 The Great Wall of China is opened to foreign tourists for the first time (see below).

1991 The South African cricket team plays its first international match in 21 years after the International Cricket Council's bans against it due to apartheid are lifted.

1995 The Nigerian Government hangs environmental activist, journalist, and playwright Ken Saro-Wiwa and eight others. Saro-Wiwa had publicized the environmental destruction of his homeland, Ogoni, which had been drilled for oil for 50 years.

1995 Massive avalanches in the Everest region of the Himalayas caused by heavy snowfalls trap close to 600 people; 32 Nepalese and 24 tourists are found dead.

1997 Louise Woodward, a 19-year-old English au pair in the U.S., has her charge of murdering baby Mathew Eapen by shaking him reduced to manslaughter. The 279 days she has already served in prison is pronounced as her sentence.

Births
- **1483** Martin Luther, church reformer
- **1697** William Hogarth, painter
- **1728** Oliver Goldsmith, poet
- **1759** Friedrich von Schiller, writer
- **1925** Richard Burton, actor
- **1932** Roy Scheider, actor
- **1939** Russell Means, activist and actor
- **1940** Screaming Lord Sutch, musician and politician
- **1944** Sir Tim Rice, lyricist

Deaths
- **1852** Gideon Mantell, physician and paleontologist
- **1891** Arthur Rimbaud, poet
- **1938** Mustafa Kemal Atatürk, Turkish President
- **1982** Leonid Brezhnev, Russian leader
- **1995** Ken Saro-Wiwa, playwright and journalist
- **2001** Ken Kesey, writer

DAYS TO REMEMBER

National day Remembrance day (Turkey) People in Turkey commemorate the life of their first President and founder of the modern nation of Turkey, Mustafa Kemal Atatürk, who died on this day in 1938, largely as a result of overwork.

National day The Marine Corps' Birthday (U.S.) Since 1921 U.S. Marine Corps units around the world have held birthday dinners to celebrate the founding of the Corps on this day.

Construction of the first section of the Great Wall of China began under orders from the first Emperor of the Qin Dynasty, Qin Shi Huang Di, in around 220 B.C.E. and the last was built in the seventeenth century. Throughout the 1950s and 60s, the Chinese Government restored and rebuilt sections of the crumbling walls. On this day in 1970, some of these sections were opened to foreign tourists. Billed as the only artificial structure visible from space, around 10,000 people now visit the Great Wall each day.

November 11

"Ah well, I suppose it has come to this. Such is life."
NED KELLY, AS THE HANGMAN'S NOOSE WAS PUT AROUND HIS NECK

HISTORICAL EVENTS

1831 Slave Nat Turner is executed on this day for leading a rebellion in Virginia on August 22, in which 55 white adults and children were killed. In the aftermath, whites killed 200 African Americans, many of whom had nothing to do with the uprising.

1880 The notorious Australian bushranger, Ned Kelly, is hanged at Melbourne jail, aged 25, despite a petition signed by 32,000 people protesting his death sentence.

1918 Germany signs a treaty with the Allies in a railway carriage outside Compiègne in France, bringing World War I to a close on the Western Front. Hostilities officially cease at the eleventh hour of the eleventh day of the eleventh month.

1965 The white minority Rhodesian Government, led by Ian Smith, declares Rhodesia's independence from Britain to avoid a move towards black majority rule. The declaration leads to the imposition of international sanctions.

1975 The elected Federal Government in Australia is dismissed by the Governor-General (see right).

1977 Greek archeologists announce that the recently discovered unplundered tomb in Vergina holds Macedonian King Philip II, father of Alexander the Great.

2000 At Kaprun in the Austrian Alps, a funicular train catches on fire in a tunnel leading to ski fields, and 155 people die in the fierce blaze.

DAYS TO REMEMBER

Religious day Bishop Martin of Tours' Day This bishop (c. 316–97) was initially a soldier and died on or around this day. In winter in Amiens, France, he cut his soldier's cloak in half to give to a starving, naked beggar. Martin became a hermit and disciples joined him to form the first monastery north of the Alps.

International day Armistice Day Many of the nations involved in World War I lay wreaths at memorials and stop for a minute's silence at 11:00 A.M. to commemorate those who died in the conflict, and in wars since.

Births
- **1821** Fyodor Dostoyevsky, writer
- **1858** Alessandro Moreschi, last castrato singer
- **1869** Victor Emmanuel III, Italy's last monarch
- **1922** Kurt Vonnegut Jr., science fiction writer
- **1945** Daniel Ortega Saavedra, Nicaraguan President
- **1962** Demi Moore, actress
- **1962** James Morrison, trumpeter
- **1974** Leonardo DiCaprio, actor

Deaths
- **397** Martin of Tours, saint
- **1831** Nat Turner, American slave rebel
- **1855** Søren Kierkegaard, philosopher
- **1880** Ned Kelly, bushranger
- **1917** Liliuokalani, last Queen of Hawaii
- **1938** Mary Mallon, "Typhoid Mary"
- **1939** Jan Opletal, student activist
- **2004** Yasser Arafat, Palestinian leader
- **2005** Lord Lichfield, photographer

A Government is dismissed

The role of Governor-General, the Queen's representative in Australia, was thought of as largely ceremonial until November 11, 1975. The Australian Labor Government, led by Gough Whitlam, had introduced many dramatic reforms since it came to power in 1972. On October 15, the Opposition, led by Malcolm Fraser, refused to pass the Government's budget through the Senate. The business of governing the nation ground to a halt and the way to break the stalemate was unclear.

At 1:00 P.M. the Governor-General, Sir John Kerr, called the Prime Minister to Government House and handed him a letter of dismissal. The Government did not accept this decision and spent the afternoon in Parliament attempting to circumvent the Governor-General's actions. However, at 4:40 P.M. a proclamation from the Governor-General was read on the steps of Parliament House: The Government was dismissed, Gough Whitlam was replaced as Prime Minister with Malcolm Fraser as caretaker, and an election was called for December 13.

As the proclamation was read, the tall and imposing ex-Prime Minister emerged from the House and gave a speech in which he uttered the famous line: "Well may we say 'God Save the Queen' because nothing will save the Governor-General." He went on to describe the new prime minister as "Kerr's cur."

The Labor Party lost the ensuing election and Malcolm Fraser served as Prime Minister for seven years. Debate about the role of the Governor-General in the affairs of the Australian Parliament continues, unresolved, into the twenty-first century.

DATE*line*

November 12

> "It was pitch black, but in the distance I could see a glow. The glow got nearer and bigger and then I realized it was the crest of a huge wave."
>
> KAMALUDDIN CHODURY, 1970 EAST PAKISTAN CYCLONE SURVIVOR

HISTORICAL EVENTS

1859 Jules Leotard performs the first flying trapeze act at the *Cirque Napoleon* in Paris on equipment he invented. He is also the designer of the leotard, which gave performers freedom of movement.

1927 After Leon Trotsky is expelled from the Communist Party, Joseph Stalin becomes ruler of the U.S.S.R.

1942 In World War II, the Naval Battle of Guadalcanal begins between Japanese and U.S. forces. Despite heavy losses, the U.S. Navy prevents the Japanese from landing reinforcements. It is a decisive victory for the U.S. in the six-month battle for the Solomon Islands.

1948 At the conclusion of a two-and-a-half year trial conducted by the International Military Tribunal of the Far East, former Prime Minister and military commander Hideki Tojo and six other Japanese wartime leaders are sentenced to hang. The sentence is carried out on December 23.

1954 The Ellis Island immigration station and detention center in New York Harbor closes. Since opening in 1892, more than 12 million immigrants to the U.S. had been processed there.

1970 A cyclone strikes East Pakistan (Bangladesh). In terms of loss of life, it is the worst disaster of the twentieth century (see below).

1990 Emperor Akihito, who became emperor on the death of his father on January 7, 1987, is formally enthroned, becoming the 125th Emperor of Japan.

DAY TO REMEMBER

National day Dr. Sun Yat-Sen's Birthday The leader of the rebellion against the Qing Dynasty, Dr. Sun Yat-Sen was born on this day in 1866. His birthday is commemorated in mainland China, Taiwan, and Chinese communities throughout the world.

Births

- **1729** Louis-Antoine de Bougainville, explorer
- **1817** Bahá'u'lláh, founder of the Baha'i faith
- **1833** Alexander Borodin, composer
- **1840** Auguste Rodin, sculptor
- **1866** Sun Yat-Sen, revolutionary and first President of the Republic of China
- **1929** Michael Ende, writer
- **1929** Grace Kelly, actress and Princess of Monaco
- **1945** Neil Young, singer and songwriter
- **1961** Nadia Comaneci, gymnast
- **1966** David Schwimmer, actor
- **1970** Tonya Harding, figure skater

Deaths

- **1035** King Canute, King of England, Denmark, and Norway
- **1865** Elizabeth Gaskell, writer
- **1947** Baroness Emmuska Orczy, writer
- **1990** Eve Arden, actress

During the night of November 12, 1970, a cyclone swept over the Bay of Bengal and East Pakistan. Winds reached at least 138 miles per hour (222 km/h) and a tidal surge swept over low-lying land. As many as 1 million people are thought to have drowned in the storm or died from starvation and disease in the following weeks. The feeble response of the Government in West Pakistan prompted the civil war that led to the formation of Bangladesh by the end of 1971.

November 13

DATEline

"Being a star has made it possible for me to get insulted in places where the average Negro could never hope to go and get insulted." — SAMMY DAVIS JR.

HISTORICAL EVENTS

1907 Paul Cornu, French inventor and cyclist, is the first person to "fly" a helicopter when he lifts off the ground for 20 seconds in a prototype model he built himself.

1916 During World War I, the conscription issue divides Australians and the Labor Party: Prime Minister William Hughes is expelled from the Labor Party due to his support for conscription and forms a minority Government with his supporters.

1942 Five brothers – George, Francis, Joseph, Madison, and Albert Sullivan – die when the ship they are serving on, the USS *Juneau*, is torpedoed. They had insisted on serving together.

1960 African American entertainer and actor Sammy Davis Jr. marries Swedish actress May Britt. At this time, interracial marriage is illegal in 31 U.S. states and the couple become the target of racist jokes and death threats.

1974 U.S. union activist Karen Silkwood dies in a suspicious one-car crash when she is traveling to an interview with a *New York Times* investigative reporter. The files she is meant to be carrying with her relating to safety in the nuclear power plant where she works are never found.

1982 The U.S. Vietnam Veterans Memorial in Washington D.C. is dedicated (see right).

1985 After a year of minor eruptions, Nevado del Ruiz in Colombia erupts violently, sending a *lahar* (volcanic mud slide) over the town of Armero. About 23,000 people are killed.

U.S. Vietnam veterans recognized

When the Vietnam War ended in 1975, there was no great ceremony when U.S. servicemen and women returned home. It was as if the nation wanted to put the war behind them. In April 1979 a group of veterans established the Vietnam Veterans Memorial Fund Inc. to raise money for a national monument that would give veterans tangible acknowledgment of the service they had given on behalf of their country.

In 1980 Congress set aside three acres (about one hectare) in Washington D.C. for the building of a monument and a competition for its design was announced. Entrants were instructed not to make any political statement about the war as the monument was to be a symbol of healing.

Controversy broke out when the unanimously chosen design was revealed. It contained few of the elements normally associated with monuments to war dead: The memorial was to be a simple V-shaped black marble wall cut into the ground, chronologically listing all those who lost their lives or were missing in action. The designer was 21-year-old Yale University architecture student Maya Ying Lin. She felt the monument would be a place of quiet contemplation and "The names would become the memorial."

Despite the controversy, the monument was finished in October 1982. On November 13, 1982, thousands of Vietnam veterans attended the dedication of the memorial. Ceremonies included a reading of the more than 58,000 names inscribed on the wall. Since then, it has become one of the most visited monuments in the U.S. and each day, flowers, beer, and other personal tokens are left in front of the names of loved ones and comrades.

DAY TO REMEMBER

Historical day Epulum Jovis In ancient Rome this lavish feast held in honor of Jupiter was the central point of the Plebian games and divided the theatrical events from the sporting events.

Births
- 1312 Edward I, King of England
- 1850 Robert Louis Stevenson, writer
- 1955 Whoopi Goldberg, actress and comedienne

Deaths
- 1460 Prince Henry the Navigator, patron of exploration
- 1868 Gioacchino Rossini, composer
- 1903 Camille Pissarro, painter
- 1974 Karen Silkwood, activist

November 14

"Dr. Croone says, may, if it [blood transfusion] takes, be of mighty use to man's health, for the amending of bad blood by borrowing from a better body." SAMUEL PEPYS' DIARY, 1666

Norodom Sihanouk played a key role in the turbulent history of his nation from when he became King of Cambodia in 1941. He claimed independence from France in 1953, was briefly head of state under the Khmer Rouge in 1975, was then exiled and headed the resistance against Vietnamese invaders between 1982 and 1989. When a peace agreement between the Vietnamese-backed Cambodian Government was finally negotiated in 1991, Prince Sihanouk was welcomed home on November 14 by jubilant crowds.

HISTORICAL EVENTS

1666 English diarist Samuel Pepys writes about the first (partially) successful blood transfusion – a blood transfusion between two dogs conducted at a meeting of the Royal Society. The dog that received the blood survived, the donor didn't.
1914 The Sultan of the Ottoman Empire, recently allied with Germany, declares *jihad* (holy war) on Britain, Russia, and France and enters World War I.
1922 The British Broadcasting Corporation (BBC) officially begins domestic radio broadcasts when Arthur Burrows reads the 6 P.M. news in London.
1925 Surrealists open their first joint show at the *Galerie Pierre* in Paris. Included are works by Hans Arp, Giorgio de Chirico, Pierre Roy, André Masson, Paul Klee, Max Ernst, Joan Miró, Pablo Picasso, and Man Ray.
1940 Most of the English town of Coventry is destroyed in a German bombing raid and 1,000 people die. In response, the RAF bombs Hamburg two days later.
1963 The Greek Government announces it will release hundreds of people who had been imprisoned during the Civil War between 1944 and 1949.
1991 Prince Norodom Sihanouk returns to Cambodia after 13 years in exile (see above).

DAYS TO REMEMBER

International day World Diabetes Day At the time of printing, more than 200 million people worldwide have diabetes. The International Diabetes Federation and the World Health Organization established this day in 1991 to raise awareness of issues surrounding the illness.

National day Children's day (India) Since Jawaharlal Nehru's death in 1963, his birthday has been celebrated as Children's Day in India in memory of his love of children and his commitment to them. Children are given sweets and schools organize special cultural and entertainment activities.

Births
- **1650** William of Orange, King of England
- **1797** Charles Lyell, geologist
- **1840** Claude Monet, painter
- **1889** Jawaharlal Nehru, first Indian Prime Minister
- **1891** Frederick Banting, physiologist
- **1907** Astrid Lindgren, children's writer
- **1908** Joseph McCarthy, U.S. Senator
- **1922** Boutros Boutros-Ghali, UN Secretary-General
- **1947** P. J. O'Rouke, writer
- **1948** Prince Charles, heir to the British throne
- **1959** Paul McGann, actor

Deaths
- **565** Justinian, Byzantine Emperor
- **1687** Nell Gwynne, mistress of Charles II of England
- **1716** Gottfried Leibniz, mathematician and philosopher
- **1831** Georg Hegel, philosopher and inventor
- **1882** Billy the Kid, outlaw

November 15

"I've been absolutely terrified every moment of my life – and I've never let it keep me from doing a single thing I wanted to do." — GEORGIA O'KEEFFE

HISTORICAL EVENTS

1492 Two of Christopher Columbus' men return from exploring Cuba and inform him they have seen Indians smoking tobacco wrapped in maize leaves. This is the first European record of smoking.

1684 King Louis XIV of France opens the *Galerie des Glaces* (Hall of Mirrors) in the Palace of Versailles. In this room the German empire was proclaimed on January 18, 1871, and the Treaty of Versailles was signed on June 28, 1919.

1920 The first assembly of the League of Nations is held in Geneva, which is chosen due to Switzerland's neutrality.

1923 The German currency collapses and after 15 months of runaway inflation, the German Reichsbank introduces the Rentenmark. The new currency isn't overissued and the economy begins to stabilize.

1941 Nazi leader Heinrich Himmler officially orders the arrest and deportation to concentration camps of all homosexuals in Germany, except for a few Nazi leaders. Two years later on the same day, he orders that Gypsies be rounded up and interred. Both groups had been persecuted in Nazi Germany before these official orders were given.

1985 The Anglo–Irish Agreement is signed by Margaret Thatcher and Irish leader Garret Fitzgerald. This allows the Irish Republic to be involved in peace negotiations in Northern Ireland.

1990 Milli Vanilli's producer announces the duo has never sung on their albums (see below).

2004 Bhutan in the Himalayas is the first nation to ban the sale of cigarettes and tobacco. Any foreigner caught selling tobacco products to Bhutanese citizens can be charged with smuggling.

Births

- 1511 Johannes Secundus, poet
- 1731 William Cowper, poet
- 1738 Sir William Herschel, astronomer
- 1887 Georgia O'Keeffe, painter
- 1891 Erwin Rommel, German military leader
- 1930 J. G. Ballard, writer
- 1932 Petula Clark, singer
- 1936 Wolf Biermann, writer and singer
- 1942 Daniel Barenboim, conductor and pianist

Deaths

- 1630 Johannes Kepler, mathematician and astronomer
- 1787 Christoph Willibald Gluck, composer
- 1954 Lionel Barrymore, actor
- 1958 Tyrone Power, actor
- 1978 Margaret Mead, anthropologist
- 1983 John Le Mesurier, actor

DAY TO REMEMBER

National day Palestinian Independence Day On this day in 1988, the Palestinian National Council in Algiers declared Palestine's independence, in effect accepting the UN resolution that divided Palestine into an Arab and a Jewish state. Palestinians celebrate this day unofficially, as there is no Palestinian state as such.

Pop duo Milli Vanilli was awarded the Grammy for Best New Artist of 1989. However, there were rumors that Rob Pilatus and Fab Morvan lip-synched to their songs. These rumors proved true when the recording of "Girl You Know It's True" skipped during a live performance at an MTV concert in 1990. Their producer, Frank Farian, revealed on this day that studio performers had recorded the Milli Vanilli songs, and Pilatus and Morvan (pictured) had never sung a note on their records. Their Grammy Award was withdrawn.

November 16

"Video games are bad for you? That's what they said about rock and roll." — SHIGERU MIYAMOTO

HISTORICAL EVENTS

1539 Francisco Pizarro and his men defeat the Inca army at Cajamarca and capture the Inca Emperor Atahualpa, who is strangled in August the following year.

1938 George "Willie" Hall scores football's fastest-ever hat-trick when he scores three goals in four minutes for England in a match against Northern Ireland. He goes on to score two more goals, and England wins 7–0.

1940 In occupied Poland, the Warsaw Ghetto is closed off from the outside world. The original population was officially 410,000. Before it was liquidated in May 1943, the population had dropped to around 70,000 due to deaths from starvation, disease, and deportation to death camps.

1959 *The Sound of Music*, starring Mary Martin and Theodore Bikel, opens at New York's Lunt Fontaine Theater.

1972 UNESCO's World Heritage Convention is adopted. This convention aims to protect sites of high natural or cultural significance around the world.

2000 President Bill Clinton arrives in Hanoi, the first serving U.S. President to visit the unified communist nation of Vietnam.

2002 The virus that comes to be known as SARS breaks out in Guangdong Province, China (see below).

Births
- 42 B.C.E. Tiberius, Roman Emperor
- 1807 Jónas Hallgrimsson, poet
- 1836 David Kalakaua, last King of Hawaii
- 1880 Alexander Blok, poet
- 1896 Oswald Mosley, British fascist
- 1873 William Christopher Handy, band-leader, "father" of Blues
- 1907 Burgess Meredith, actor
- 1952 Shigeru Miyamoto, electronic games designer
- 1971 Alexander Popov, swimmer

Deaths
- 1272 Henry III, King of England
- 1960 Clark Gable, actor
- 1981 William Holden, actor
- 1982 Arthur Askey, comedian

DAY TO REMEMBER

National day Dagur Islenskrar Tungu (Iceland) This celebration, whose name translates to Icelandic Language Day, is held on the birthday of Jónas Hallgrimsson, Iceland's most famous poet. Cultural events are held to promote and celebrate the living language that has changed little in the 11 centuries since the island was settled.

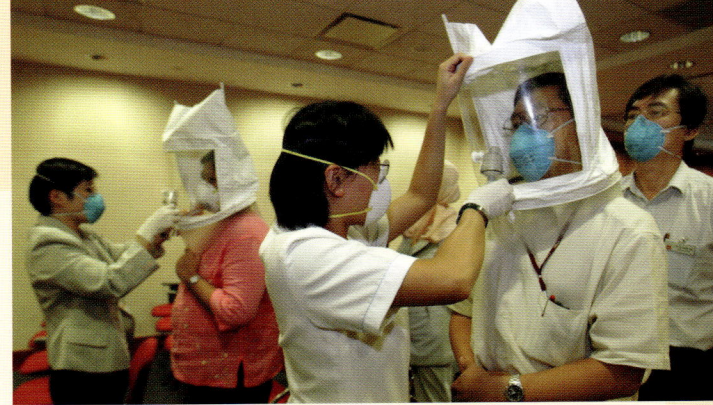

First case of SARS

On this day in 2002, a farmer admitted to hospital in the city of Foshan in Guangdong Province, China, was diagnosed with severe atypical pneumonia. This illness is now known as severe acute respiratory syndrome (SARS), a previously unknown strain of coronavirus. More cases appeared and deaths occurred as the virus proved difficult to treat. Although the outbreak of this new illness was reported to Government authorities by late December, efforts to contain it weren't effective and it spread across China.

Chinese health authorities only allowed limited press coverage of the epidemic, apparently in an effort to prevent panic in the community, and didn't report it to the World Health Organization (WHO). The epidemic was exposed when an American businessman who had visited Guangdong Province became ill on a return flight from China and was transferred to a hospital in Hanoi, Vietnam, where he died. Several doctors and nurses who treated him came down with the same illness and also died. At around the same time a doctor from Guangdong Province staying in a hotel in Hong Kong fell ill and died. Chinese officials finally notified the WHO of the epidemic.

The WHO and other health agencies cooperated to identify and isolate infected people and investigate the mysterious disease. Travel warnings were issued for Guangdong Province and Hong Kong, the two worst-affected areas.

By July 2003 the epidemic was declared over. The WHO reported that more than 8,000 people in 27 countries had been infected and 774 had died. Important lessons had been learned, and the responses to outbreaks of the H5N1 avian flu virus that first occurred in January 2004 were swifter and more effective.

November 17

"It's the most difficult decision I've made in my entire life, except the one I made in 1978 when I decided to get a bikini wax."

ARNOLD SCHWARZENEGGER, ANNOUNCING HIS INTENTION TO RUN FOR GOVERNOR OF CALIFORNIA

HISTORICAL EVENTS

1558 Queen Mary I, known as Bloody Mary for her persecution of Protestants, dies of influenza at the age of 42 and Elizabeth I becomes Queen of England.

1922 Under British protection, the last Sultan leaves Turkey. The Grand National Assembly had, on November 1, accepted Kemal Atatürk's proposal to abolish the sultanate.

1950 Tenzin Gyatso, the fourteenth Dalai Lama, is enthroned as the Tibetan head of state at age 15.

1970 Electrical engineer Douglas Engelbart receives the U.S. patent for the "X-Y position indicator for a display system" which he nicknames the computer "mouse" because its cord looks like a tail.

1989 In Prague, Czechoslovakia, the Velvet Revolution begins with mass protests demanding the resignation of the communist Government. The Government ultimately resigns and is replaced on December 29.

1997 Islamic militants open fire on tourists outside the Temple of Hatshepsut in Luxor, southern Egypt and are killed in a gun battle with police; 68 people are left dead.

2003 Arnold Schwarzenegger is inaugurated as the Governor of California (see right).

DAYS TO REMEMBER

International day Students' Day Student activist groups around the world commemorate the day in 1939 when Nazi troops stormed the University of Prague to break up demonstrations against the killing of student Jan Opletal, who had died from injuries sustained in an earlier demonstration against the Nazis.

National day Polytechneíon Day (Greece) In 1973 at Athens Polytechnic, soldiers killed 34 students after a commemoration of the death of Jan Opletal sparked three days of demonstrations. Students across Greece mark this event with street marches.

Births		
9 C.E.	Vespasian, Roman Emperor	
1887	Sir Bernard Montgomery, military commander	
1906	Soichiro Honda, car manufacturer	
1925	Rock Hudson, actor	
1937	Peter Cook, comedian	
1942	Martin Scorsese, director	
1944	Danny DeVito, actor and director	
1966	Jeff Buckley, musician	
Deaths		
1558	Queen Mary I of England	
1917	Auguste Rodin, sculptor	

Schwarzenegger wins the recall

When economic recession hit the U.S. in 2000, it hit California hard. Democrat Californian Governor Gray Davis was criticized for his handling of the crisis. Republicans seized the opportunity to begin proceedings for a recall election for his office. In July 2003, the first recall for Governor in California's history was set for October 7.

There had been speculation as to whether actor and former bodybuilder Arnold Schwarzenegger would stand for governor. He had long supported the Republican Party and had shown interest in entering politics. On August 6, he announced his intention to run.

Backed by Republicans and several of his Democrat Hollywood colleagues, Schwarzenegger promised to get California back on the road to economic stability without cutting back on vital services. He was instantly recognizable because of his movie roles, but his campaign for governor was not all smooth sailing. He was accused of sexual misconduct and taking drugs in his earlier days, allegations he dealt with by admitting that although he hadn't always behaved well, many stories circulating were untrue.

On October 7, Schwarzenegger defeated his opponents by around 1.3 million votes. He was sworn in as Governor on November 17, saying in a speech afterwards, "I learned something from all those years of lifting and training hard: When I thought I couldn't lift another ounce of weight, what I learned is that we are always stronger than we know – California is like that, too."

November 18

"They simply came into the room and said, 'You're going to be released,' and threw in some clothes, which were all far too small – I looked ridiculous."

TERRY WAITE, SPEAKING ABOUT HIS RELEASE BY SHI'ITE KIDNAPPERS

HISTORICAL EVENTS

1095 Pope Urban II convenes the Council of Clermont in Auvergne, France. As part of this church council, he later launches the First Crusade when he addresses a crowd on November 28. In his speech he offers remission of penance for those who go to the aid of Christians in Jerusalem, who he says are suffering under Islamic rulers.

1307 According to legend, William Tell refuses to bow to the tyrant Gessler's hat and is forced to shoot an apple from his own son's head.

1477 William Caxton prints the first book in England, entitled *Dictes or Syengis of the Philosophres*.

1820 Nathaniel Palmer, captain of a U.S. sealing ship, the *Hero*, sails south in the hope of finding more hunting grounds and discovers Antarctica.

1978 In Jonestown, Guyana, members of the Peoples Temple cult commit mass suicide (see right).

1991 Terry Waite returns to Britain after nearly five years as a captive. He had gone to Lebanon in 1987 as the Archbishop of Canterbury's Special Envoy to negotiate for the release of several hostages held by Shi'ite Muslim terrorists and had been taken hostage himself.

DAY TO REMEMBER

National Day Independence day (Latvia) People in Latvia celebrate the day this nation was declared an independent republic in the wake of World War I. Soviet forces occupied the nation in 1940, and the Republic of Latvia was restored on August 21, 1991.

Births		Deaths	
1787	Louis-Jacques-Mandé Daguerre, inventor	1922	Marcel Proust, writer
1836	Sir William S. Gilbert, librettist	1962	Niels Bohr, physicist
1870	Dorothy Dix, columnist	1976	Man Ray, photographer and painter
1906	Klaus Mann, writer		
1939	Margaret Atwood, writer	1994	Cab Calloway, band-leader
1946	Alan Dean Foster, writer		
1960	Kim Wilde, singer		

Suicide in the jungle

Jim Jones founded the Peoples Temple church in the 1950s in the U.S. Some respected the church because it preached racial equality and social justice. However, it later developed the traits of a cult, with Jones claiming he was God incarnate and members being cut off from their families and often abused.

In 1977 the Peoples Temple began to be investigated for tax evasion. Jones and around 1,000 of his followers went to Guyana to set up a utopian community, Jonestown, where they could be free from persecution.

On November 14, 1978, Congressman Leo J. Ryan arrived in Jonestown with other U.S. Government officials and reporters to investigate allegations of abuse and even murder. During the visit, an attempt was made to kill Ryan. His delegation and several cult members decided to leave. As they boarded a plane on November 18, a truck drove onto the airstrip and Jones' armed guards started shooting. Ryan and four others were killed.

Back at Jonestown, Jones told his followers that enemies who wished to shut the Peoples Temple down for good were going to attack and brutally slay them all. He said the time had come for them to commit the "revolutionary suicide" they had been prepared for. Children were given cyanide-laced drinks, which the adults also then drank. Others who refused were shot, or injected with poison. Some managed to escape into the surrounding jungle.

When police arrived at Jonestown they found the bodies of 914 people, including 276 under 18 years of age. Jones himself had been shot in the head, though it wasn't clear whether the gunshot was self-inflicted.

DATE*line*

November 19

"…this nation, under God, shall have a new birth of freedom – and that Government of the people, by the people, for the people, shall not perish from the earth."

CLOSING WORDS OF THE GETTYSBURG ADDRESS, DELIVERED BY PRESIDENT ABRAHAM LINCOLN

HISTORICAL EVENTS

1850 English poet Alfred Tennyson becomes Poet Laureate, an office he holds until his death in 1892. He becomes a lord in 1884.

1863 U.S. President Lincoln delivers the Gettysburg Address when dedicating a national cemetery at the Gettysburg battlefield in Pennsylvania. Notable orator Edward Everett spoke before the president for two hours. Lincoln spoke for two minutes.

1897 In London, Charles Wilson admits that he is a woman when asked to take a shower at a charity lodging house. Catherine Coombes had begun to dress as a man to escape from her husband and had worked as a painter for 40 years.

1941 In a battle off the coast of Western Australia, HMAS *Sydney* and HSK *Kormoran* sink each other – 77 Germans and all 645 Australians are lost.

1942 In the Battle of Stalingrad, one of the most bitter of World War II, the Soviet forces under General Georgi Zhukov launch a counterattack and in three days surround the German troops, who surrender on January 31, 1943.

1969 Pelé scores his 1000th goal in a professional football match (see below).

1994 The UN Security Council authorizes NATO to bomb rebel Serb forces that are striking UN-declared safe areas in Bosnia–Herzegovina from neighboring Croatia.

2004 At an NBA game in Detroit, Indiana Pacer's guard Ron Artest and Ben Wallace of the Detroit Pistons clash, setting off a massive brawl between players and fans.

Births
- 1600 Charles I, king of England
- 1917 Indira Gandhi, Indian Prime Minister
- 1942 Calvin Klein, fashion designer
- 1961 Meg Ryan, actress
- 1962 Jodie Foster, actress

Deaths
- 1823 Franz Schubert, composer
- 1883 Sir William Siemens, engineer

DAYS TO REMEMBER

International day World Toilet Day
This designated day is promoted each year by the World Toilet Organization to encourage hygienic toilet practices and the provision of hygienic, healthy public toilet facilities for public health.

National day Discovery Day (Puerto Rico)
This national holiday commemorates the day Christopher Columbus landed on the island, which he originally named San Juan Bautista in honor of St. John the Baptist.

"How do you spell Pelé? G-O-D."

Edson Arantes do Nascimento, better known as Pelé, was discovered at age 11 when Waldemar de Brito, former Brazil World Cup team member, invited him to play for his new team. In 1956, de Brito took his star player to São Paulo to try out for Santos Futebol Clube. Pelé was accepted and before he turned 16 he had scored his first goal in a professional match. He amazed everyone with his speed and skill, especially his ability to head the ball.

Pelé went on to play for Brazil in the FIFA World Cup in 1958, 1962, 1966, and 1970, winning each time except for 1966. On this day in 1969, he scored his 1,000th goal in a professional match. It was after he scored Brazil's 100th World Cup goal during the final in Mexico that the *Times* ran the famous headline that spelled his name G-O-D. After retiring from Santos in 1974, Pelé went on to play for New York Cosmos. When he played his last match in 1977 he had scored 1,281 goals in 1,363 professional games, a world record.

Since then Pelé has been a Goodwill Ambassador for UNICEF, a position he takes very seriously, once stating that: "Every kid in the world who plays football wants to be Pelé – which means I have the responsibility of showing them how to be a footballer but also how to be a man." In December 1999, the International Olympic Committee named him the top athlete of the century.

457

November 20

"I'd like to be a queen of people's hearts, in people's hearts, but I don't see myself being Queen of this country." — PRINCESS DIANA

HISTORICAL EVENTS

1945 The Nuremberg Trails begin, with 24 top Nazis put on trial for war crimes and crimes against humanity. On October 1, 1946, 12 are sentenced to death.

1947 Princess Elizabeth, 21, marries Philip Mountbatten, Duke of Edinburgh, 26, at Westminster Abbey in London.

1948 New Zealand's flightless takahe bird had only been seen four times between 1800 and 1900 and was presumed extinct. On this day, scientist Dr. Geoffrey Orbell located the first of what turned out to be a colony of 250 birds in the Murchison Mountains on the South Island.

1962 Satisfied that the U.S.S.R. had made good on its agreement to remove its missiles after the Cuban crisis, the U.S. lifts its quarantine of Cuba.

1995 In a frank interview on the BBC, Princess Diana, who is separated from Prince Charles, reveals she has had an affair.

1996 The Tamagotchi toy is released in Japan (see below).

Births
- **1889** Edwin Hubble, astronomer
- **1908** Alistair Cooke, journalist
- **1923** Nadine Gordimer, writer
- **1925** Robert F. Kennedy, U.S. Senator
- **1956** Bo Derek, actress

Deaths
- **1910** Leo Tolstoy, Russian revolutionary
- **1975** General Francisco Franco, dictator
- **1995** Sergei Grinko, figure skater

DAYS TO REMEMBER

International day Universal Children's Day Across the world, 120 nations celebrate Universal Children's Day, the day on which the UN adopted the Declaration of the Rights of the Child in 1959 and the Convention of the Rights of the Child in 1989.

International day Transgender Day of Remembrance Transgender groups in the U.S., Canada, and other nations hold a day of remembrance for transgender victims of violence. It was first held in San Francisco in 1999 in memory of Rita Hester, a transsexual who was murdered in her apartment in 1998.

On this day in 1996, Japanese toy company Bandai released the Tamagotchi, a toy that became a worldwide craze. Bandai employee Aki Maita invented the Tamagotchi because she wanted a pet she could take anywhere. The virtual pet is a liquid crystal display screen set in a plastic egg-shaped toy attached to a key ring or bracelet. It sleeps, wakes, plays, and beeps when it needs to be fed or cleaned. The owner presses the right buttons to satisfy the "pet's" needs. If it isn't cared for, the Tamagotchi can "die" prematurely.

November 21

"One of the most important prehistoric finds of our time has been made in Sussex."
THE GUARDIAN NEWSPAPER ANNOUNCING THE FINDING OF THE PILTDOWN MAN SKULL, NOVEMBER 21, 1912

Peace negotiations for the bitter conflict in Bosnia–Herzegovina began on November 1, 1995, on neutral ground at an air force base near Dayton, Ohio. There on November 21 (left to right) Serbian President Slobodan Milosevic, Bosnian President Alija Izetbegovic, and Croatian President Franjo Tudjman initialed the first of the Dayton Peace Accords. The agreement fixed the borders of the states involved and outlined the arrangements to be made for the resettlement of displaced people and the prosecution of those involved in war crimes and crimes against humanity.

HISTORICAL EVENTS

1783 The first successful free flight takes place when François Pilâtre de Rozier and François Laurent, Marquis d'Arlandes, fly for 25 minutes over Paris in a balloon.
1877 Thomas Edison announces the invention of the phonograph.
1920 In an event known as Bloody Sunday, British troops fire on a Dublin–Tipperary friendly Gaelic Football match at Croke Park, Dublin, in retaliation for the shooting of several British Intelligence agents in their homes in Dublin that morning. Full-back Michael Hogan is shot dead, along with 13 spectators, and 65 are wounded.
1953 The British Museum announces that the famous Piltdown Man skull, said to be the "missing link" between humans and apes, is a hoax.
1968 On this day Sheri Schroeder is born with several birth defects. Her family lived at Love Canal, a residential area of Niagara Falls, New York, built on land previously used as a dump for chemical waste. Her birth spurs on campaigners who uncover one of the worst pollution scandals in U.S. history.
1977 World Series cricket is launched in Melbourne. Media tycoon Kerry Packer had not been able to secure broadcasting rights with the Australian Cricket Board, so he signed 60 players to start their own series.
1995 The signing of the first Dayton Peace Accord brings three-and-a-half years of fighting in Bosnia–Herzegovina to an end (see above).

Births
1694 François-Marie Arouet (Voltaire), writer and philosopher
1818 Lewis Henry Morgan, anthropologist
1898 René Magritte, painter
1912 Eleanor Powell, dancer and actress
1929 Marilyn French, writer
1941 Juliet Mills, actress
1945 Goldie Hawn, actress
1965 Björk Gudmundsdottir, singer

Deaths
1695 Henry Purcell, composer
1916 Franz Joseph I, Austrian Emperor
1969 Norman Lindsay, artist and writer
1993 Bill Bixby, actor and director
1999 Quentin Crisp, actor and writer

DAY TO REMEMBER

National day Armed Forces Day (Bangladesh) The formation of the armed forces during the war of liberation from Pakistan is commemorated on this day. Wreaths are laid and special prayers are offered for those who fought and died in the war.

November 22

"Freedom has many flaws and our democracy is imperfect, but we have never had to put up a wall to keep our people in." JOHN F. KENNEDY, SPEECH DELIVERED IN WEST BERLIN, JUNE 26, 1963

Births
- 1808 Thomas Cook, travel businessman
- 1819 George Eliot (Mary Ann Evans), writer
- 1890 Charles de Gaulle, general and French President
- 1901 Joaquin Rodrigo, composer
- 1913 Lord Benjamin Britten, composer
- 1940 Terry Gilliam, comedian and film director
- 1943 Billie Jean King, tennis player
- 1967 Boris Becker, tennis player
- 1967 Mark Ruffalo, actor
- 1984 Scarlett Johansson, actress

Deaths
- 1718 Blackbeard (Edward Teach), pirate
- 1916 Jack London, writer
- 1954 Roy Rene (Mo), comedian
- 1963 John F. Kennedy, U.S. President
- 1963 C. S. Lewis, writer
- 1963 Aldous Huxley, writer
- 1980 Mae West, actress
- 1997 Michael Hutchence, singer (INXS)
- 2000 Emil Zátopek, long-distance runner

DAYS TO REMEMBER

National Day Lebanon celebrates its independence from France on the anniversary of the day in 1943 when French authorities relinquished their mandate over the country and released Lebanese politicians who were being held prisoner.

Religious day St. Cecilia's Day A Roman noble, St. Cecilia refused to consummate her arranged marriage because of her vow of chastity. When she later refused to worship pagan gods, soldiers attempted to suffocate her, then boil her in a bath, then behead her. She survived three blows to her neck for three days, singing sacred songs for comfort.

HISTORICAL EVENTS

- 1906 "SOS," meaning "Save Our Souls," is adopted as the international distress call, by the International Radio Telegraphic Convention in Berlin.
- 1956 The sixteenth Olympic Games open in Melbourne. This is the first time they are held in the Southern Hemisphere.
- 1963 U.S. President John F. Kennedy is assassinated in Dallas, Texas (see below).
- 1975 Two days after the death of dictator General Francisco Franco, Juan Carlos I is proclaimed King of Spain. Although Franco appointed Juan Carlos as his heir, the King institutes reforms to make Spain a democratic constitutional monarchy.
- 1979 Prompted by false reports that the U.S. was behind the takeover of the Great Mosque in Saudi Arabia on the previous day, Pakistani students mob the American Embassy in Islamabad. Seven members of staff are killed. Fundamentalists who wanted Saudi Arabia to return to strict Islamic rule were behind the hostage-taking in Mecca.
- 1995 Britain's worst female serial killer, Rosemary West, is found guilty of murdering 10 young women and girls, including her daughter and stepdaughter, and is given 10 life sentences. She committed the crimes with her husband, who killed himself in his cell in January 1995.
- 1995 Pixar Films releases *Toy Story*, the first computer-animated feature-length film.

The assassination of a President

After arriving in Texas earlier that morning, the U.S. presidential party departed for a 10-mile (16 km) motorcade through downtown Dallas to the Trade Mart where President John F. Kennedy was to deliver a speech. It was a clear day, so the President and Mrs. Kennedy were traveling in an open-topped limousine.

At 12:30 P.M. the motorcade turned the corner from Houston Street into Elm Street. As the President's car passed in front of the seven-story Texas School Book Depository, a series of rifle shots was fired from the building. President Kennedy grabbed his throat as he was struck in the neck, then Texas Governor John Connolly, sitting in front of him, turned around and was shot in the chest, then another shot hit the President in the back of the head.

In the confusion that followed, security officer Clint Hill clambered into the car and, pushing Mrs. Kennedy down, shielded her and her husband. In five minutes the President's speeding limousine reached the Parkland Memorial Hospital where President Kennedy was pronounced dead at 1:00 P.M.

The President's body was taken aboard *Air Force One*. Vice-President Lyndon B. Johnson was sworn in aboard the plane at 2:39 P.M., watched by about 30 people, including Mrs. Kennedy, still wearing clothes stained by her husband's blood. Seven minutes later *Air Force One* took off for Washington.

DATE*line*

November 23

"Those who don't believe in magic will never find it." — ROALD DAHL

The first episode of the BBC television science fiction series *Dr. Who* aired at 5:16 P.M. on this day. In this episode, two schoolteachers go to the home of one of their pupils, Susan Foreman, and meet her grandfather, the Doctor. They soon find out that Susan and the Doctor are aliens who travel through time and space in the TARDIS, which from the outside looks like an ordinary telephone box. Here the first Doctor, played by William Hartnell, jokes with two cast members in 1965, with a Dalek – one of the series' most memorable and recurring exponents – in the background.

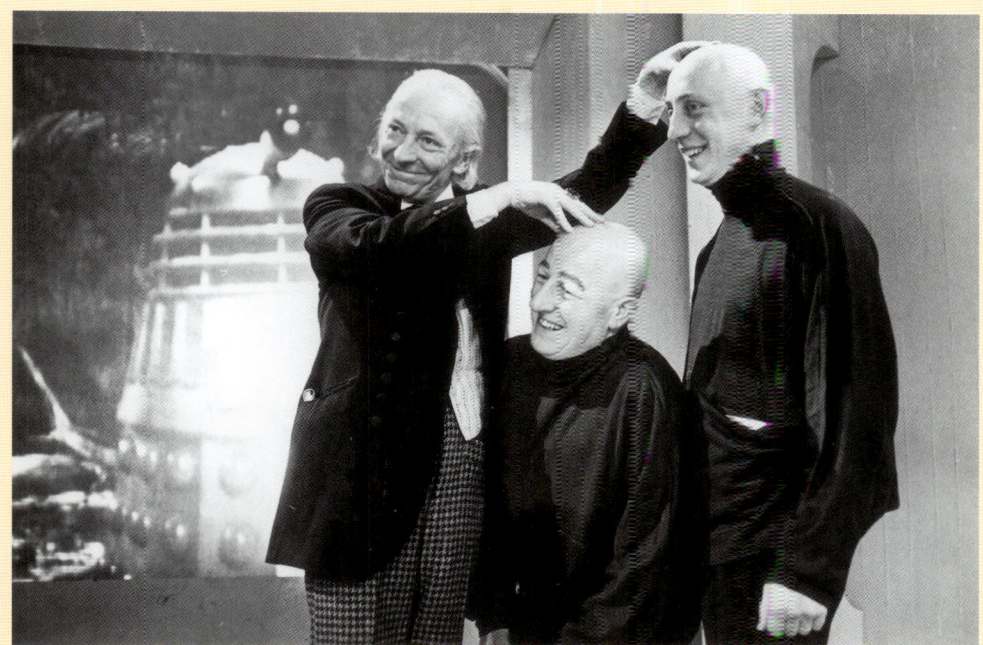

HISTORICAL EVENTS

1815 Canada's first street lights are lit in Montreal. They are fueled by whale oil, which burns cleanly.
1889 In San Francisco, the first jukebox is installed at the Palais Royale Saloon.
1963 In the U.K., the BBC airs *Dr. Who* for the first time (see above).
1971 The United Nations recognizes The Peoples Republic of China as the sole representative of China, ousting the Republic of China (Taiwan) from the UN Security Council.
1979 IRA member Thomas McMahon is sentenced to life in prison for the murder of Lord Mountbatten, who was killed by a bomb on August 27, 1979, while holidaying in the Republic of Ireland. McMahon was released in 1998 as part of the Good Friday Agreement.
1996 Ethiopian Airlines Flight 961 is hijacked on its way from Addis Ababa to Nairobi, Kenya, by three Ethiopian men, and ordered to fly to Australia. The jet runs out of fuel and crashes into the Indian Ocean off the coast of Comoros – 123 of the 175 people on board perish.
2003 Miss World contestants leave Nigeria after 215 people are killed when offended citizens riot.

DAY TO REMEMBER

Religious day St. Clement's Day The third Pope, St. Clement (c. 101 C.E.) wrote a letter to rebels in the church in Corinth who had overthrown their leaders. It is the first Christian document outside the New Testament. According to legend, he was banished to Crimea and thrown into the Black Sea weighed down by an anchor.

Births
1859 Billy the Kid, outlaw
1887 Boris Karloff, actor
1888 Harpo Marx, comedian
1956 Shane Gould, swimmer

Deaths
1979 Merle Oberon, actress
1990 Roald Dahl, children's writer
1991 Klaus Kinski, actor

Star sign
SAGITTARIUS
November 23–December 21

Sagittarius the Archer is a centaur – half-man, half-horse. People born under this sign love travel, are restless, and enjoy physical activities, though they are also often intellectual and seek the truth through law, religion, or study.

November 24

"I have called this principle, by which each slight variation, if useful, is preserved, by the term of Natural Selection." — CHARLES DARWIN, *ON THE ORIGIN OF SPECIES*

HISTORICAL EVENTS

1642 Abel Tasman sights Tasmania from his ship, the first European to do so. On November 25 he names the island "Anthony van Diemen's Land, in honor of the Hon. Governor General our high Superior, who has sent us out to make this discovery."

1859 Charles Darwin's *On the Origin of Species by Means of Natural Selection* is published. It is an immediate if controversial best-seller, which puts forward the theory of evolution, challenging the idea of Biblical creation. It has never been out of print since.

1963 Lee Harvey Oswald, charged with killing U.S. President Kennedy, is being moved between jails when nightclub owner Jack Ruby leaps from the crowd of reporters and shoots him in the abdomen. Oswald is rushed to hospital but is pronounced dead soon after.

1974 The hominid fossil "Lucy" is found in Ethiopia (see right).

1995 Voters in the Republic of Ireland pass a referendum by one percent, legalizing civil divorce.

1998 Queen Elizabeth II delivers a speech in which the Labour Party's plans for peers to lose their hereditary right to sit in the House of Lords are outlined. In 1999 the reforms begin, with more than half the peers losing their positions.

DAY TO REMEMBER

Religious day St. Andrew Dung-Lac's Day One of 117 Vietnamese martyrs who were killed over a 50-year period, mostly by beheading, St. Andrew Dung-Lac (c. 1839) was killed for following the Catholic religion.

Lucy is unearthed

On the morning of November 24, 1974, anthropologist Donald Johanson and student Tom Gray were walking in the Afar Depression in Ethiopia when they came across fossilized fragments of an arm bone from a hominid. They checked the surrounding ground and found ribs, a jaw, leg bones, and vertebrae. Eventually a remarkable 40 percent of the skeleton was to be located.

That evening the team celebrated their promising find in base camp with champagne. The Beatles song "Lucy in the Sky with Diamonds" was playing on a small cassette tape deck, and it was agreed that the fossil would be named Lucy.

When the fossilized bones were excavated, reconstructed, and studied, they were found to have belonged to a female hominid approximately 20 years old, 3 feet 8 inches (1.1 m) tall who probably weighed around 65 pounds (29 kg). The bones were dated to around 3.2 million years old, at the time making her the oldest known fossil of a species in the hominid line. The alluvial deposit she lay in suggested she may have drowned.

Lucy was given the scientific name *Australopithecus afarensis*, a group in which all individuals had a relatively small brain capacity, but had teeth like a human and were bipedal. The structure of Lucy's knees made it clear that she walked on two feet, though probably with the side-to-side gait of an ape.

Although older fossils and ones that have been shown to be more closely linked to humans have been discovered since Lucy, she remains a landmark find that changed anthropologists' thinking about the way hominids evolved.

Births
- 1632 Benedictus de Spinoza, philosopher
- 1713 Laurence Sterne, writer
- 1849 Frances Hodgson Burnett, writer
- 1864 Henri de Toulouse-Lautrec, painter
- 1868 Scott Joplin, musician
- 1876 Walter Burley Griffin, architect
- 1942 Billy Connolly, comedian
- 1946 Ted Bundy, serial killer
- 1955 Ian Botham, cricketer

Deaths
- 1572 John Knox, church reformer
- 1963 Lee Harvey Oswald, alleged assassin
- 1991 Freddie Mercury, rock singer
- 2004 Arthur Hailey, writer

DATE*line*

November 25

"He'd been mistaken in thinking that if he killed himself the sordid bourgeois world would perish with him." YUKIO MISHIMA, ACTS OF MEMORIES, 1948

HISTORICAL EVENTS

1703 The worst recorded gale in the British Isles strikes the south of England. As many as 30,000 sailors drown when 300 ships sink; on land, 9,000 people are killed.
1947 The Hollywood Ten are blacklisted from movie studios for Communist leanings.
1952 *The Mousetrap*, a play by Agatha Christie, opens in The Ambassadors Theatre in London. It moved to the St. Martin's Theatre on March 25, 1974, and was still playing in 2006.
1970 Author Yukio Mishima, considered Japan's greatest living writer, commits *seppuku* (ritual suicide) after kidnapping a Japanese general and urging the Japanese people to overthrow the constitution.
1990 Poland holds its first free presidential election (see below).
2000 The Spanish Paralympic Committee sets up an investigation into allegations that some members of the Spanish team who competed in the 2000 Games did not suffer from any mental handicaps. It is discovered that 15 athletes suffer no disability, and the Spanish basketball team members have to hand their gold medal back.

DAYS TO REMEMBER

Religious day St. Catherine's Day After being sentenced to death by Emperor Maximinus, Catherine (c. 310) was tied to a spiked wheel, which miraculously broke, and she was beheaded. She is the patron saint of philosophers, and the Catherine wheel firework is named after her.

National day Independence Day (Suriname) On this day in 1975, Suriname gained its independence from the Netherlands.

Births
1844 Karl Benz, inventor of the car
1914 Joe DiMaggio, baseball player
1915 Augusto Pinochet, Chilean President
1952 Imran Khan, cricketer and politician
1960 John F. Kennedy Jr., publisher

Deaths
1968 Upton Sinclair, writer
1970 Yukio Mishima, writer and coup leader
1993 Anthony Burgess, writer

Celtic tree sign

ELDER
November 25–December 23

People born between November 25 and December 22 are under the sign of the elder tree and are said to hunger for knowledge and the truth, making them curious and often restless. They are also thoughtful and open to change.

The first free election in Poland

During the years of the Second Polish Republic after World War I, the Polish president was elected by parliament. In the years after World War II, Poland was ruled by Soviet-backed Communist Governments that instituted policies approved by the U.S.S.R. Any dissent was stamped out.

However, Poles continued to speak up against the Government through the 1970s and 1980s. The labor union Solidarity emerged as one of the Government's chief opponents. As the U.S.S.R. began to lose its grip on Eastern bloc countries in the late 1980s, the Polish Government struggled with a collapsing economy. In January 1990, the Government called a series of Round Table talks with key figures in the country, including representatives of Solidarity. It was agreed that free elections should be held, and the U.S.S.R.-directed Communist leader General Jaruzelski was to abide by the outcome of these elections.

The first free presidential election in Poland took place on this day in 1990. There were six candidates, and Solidarity leader Lech Walesa and Stanisław Tymiński, a Canadian businessman of Polish origin, emerged as the leaders. On December 9, a second election between these two candidates took place. Walesa was the clear winner with 74.6 percent of the vote. He was sworn in as President on December 22.

Walesa's victory was not a great surprise. He was a high-profile leader who had long spoken out against communist rule. In 1970 he had been one of the organizers of strikes at the Gdansk shipyards and, despite losing his job and being arrested several times, he continued to organize protests over the next two decades. In 1980 he was a founding member of the Solidarity Trade Union and in 1983 he received the Nobel Peace Prize.

November 26

"When Lord Carnarvon said to me, 'Can you see anything?'
I replied to him, 'Yes, it is wonderful'." HOWARD CARTER, JOURNAL ENTRY, 1922

HISTORICAL EVENTS

1857 The Legislative Assembly in the Colony of Victoria proclaims universal manhood suffrage for the first time in Australia.
1917 The National Hockey League is formed in Canada with four teams. Seven years later the first American team is admitted and by 1999 there are six teams in the NHL.
1922 Howard Carter and Lord Carnarvon open the tomb of Tutankhamen (see below).
1966 President Charles de Gaulle opens the world's first tidal electricity-generating plant at the Rance River estuary in Brittany.
1983 Robbers dressed as armed guards make off with 6,800 gold bars worth nearly £25 million from a warehouse near London's Heathrow Airport. Most of the gold is never recovered, and only three of the men are convicted.
1992 Queen Elizabeth II volunteers to begin paying taxes and takes most of her family off the public payroll.

DAY TO REMEMBER

National day Republic Day (Mongolia) This national holiday marks the proclamation of the Republic of Mongolia in 1925, which brought feudalism and the rule of the monarchy to an end.

Births
1607 John Harvard, founder of Harvard University
1908 Vernon "Lefty" Gomez, baseball player
1910 Cyril Cusack, actor
1922 Charles M. Schulz, cartoonist
1939 Tina Turner, singer
1951 Ilona Staller (A.K.A. Cicciolina), porn star and politician

Deaths
1504 Isabella I, Queen of Castile and Aragon
1886 Sojourner Truth, abolitionist and evangelist
1956 Tommy Dorsey, band-leader

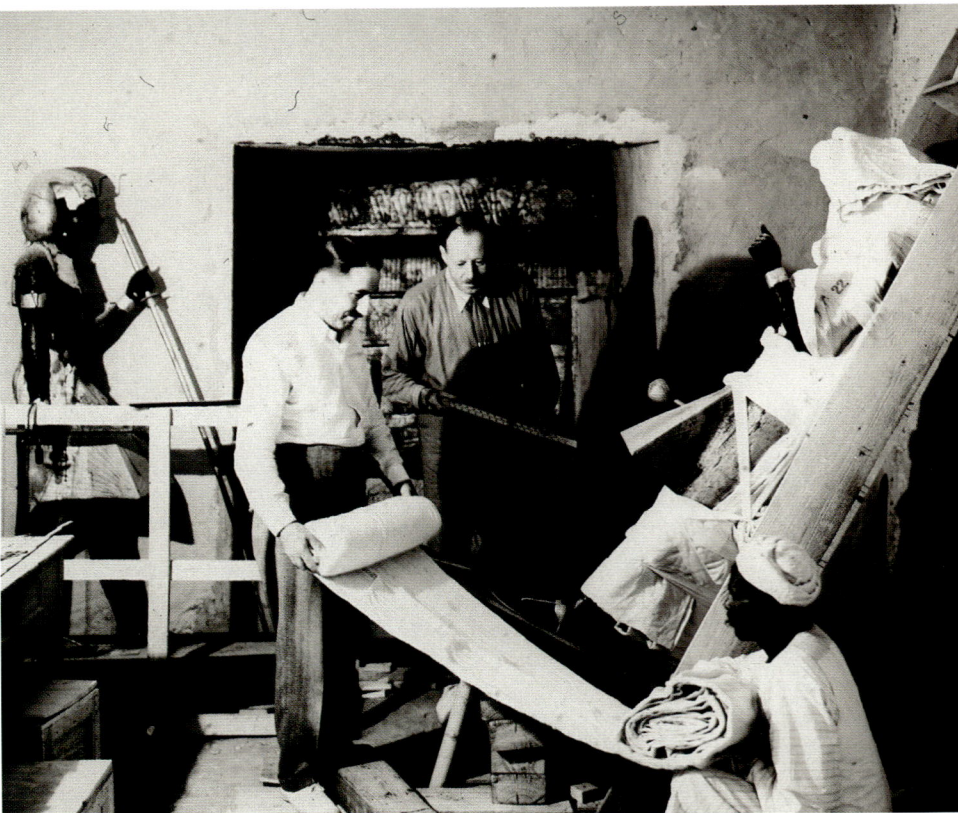

On November 4, 1922, archeologist Howard Carter uncovered a stairway near the tomb of Ramses VI. Excavation of the tomb halted until Lord Carnarvon, Carter's financial backer, arrived on November 23. The first doorway encountered was inscribed with the cartouches of Tutankhamen. A second door was reached on November 26. Making a small hole, Carter peered through and had his first glimpse of the treasures of Tutankhamen. Carter is pictured on the left, removing objects from the first two rooms, a process which took 10 weeks. On February 17, 1923, the pharaoh's burial chamber was finally entered.

November 27

"My arrows are made of desire…from far away as Jupiter's sulphur mines." — JIMI HENDRIX

HISTORICAL EVENTS

1770 Horatio Nelson joins the Royal Navy as a 12-year-old midshipman on the HMS *Raisonnable*.
1893 Women vote for the first time in a national election in New Zealand – the first nation to grant all women the right to vote and to hold a general election.
1924 The first Macy's Thanksgiving Day Parade is held in New York City.
1942 In Brisbane, Australia, tensions between Australian and American servicemen become clear when they brawl in riots for the second night running. One soldier is killed.
1975 Ross McWhirter, television presenter and co-founder of *The Guinness Book of Records*, is shot dead outside his home by the IRA after he offers a reward for information leading to the capture of IRA bombers.
2005 Isabelle Dinoire in Amiens, France, becomes the first person to receive a partial face transplant (see below).

Births
- **1880** Sir Ralph Freeman, engineer
- **1925** Ernie Wise, comedian
- **1940** Bruce Lee, martial arts expert and actor
- **1942** Jimi Hendrix, guitarist

Deaths
- **8 C.E.** Horace, Roman poet
- **511** Clovis, Frankish king, founder of France
- **1934** George "Baby Face" Nelson, gangster
- **1953** Eugene O'Neill, playwright
- **1978** Harvey Milk, politician
- **1988** John Carradine, actor

DAY TO REMEMBER

Religious day First day of Advent Advent is the holy time of preparation for the birth of Christ. Originally it was a period of fasting during which no marriages took place. In the Western Christian church, Advent begins on the Sunday closest to St. Andrew's Day (November 30) and ends after the last Sunday before Christmas. The earliest that the first day of Advent can begin is November 27, and the latest is December 3.

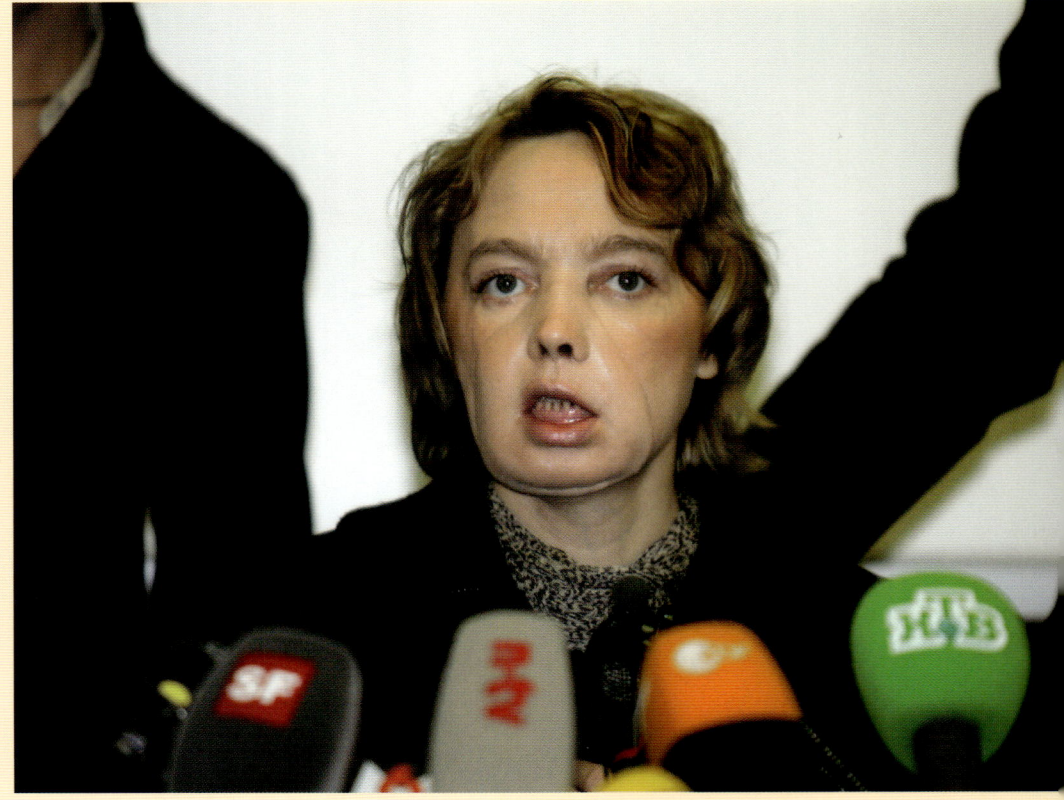

After Isabelle Dinoire of France was mauled by her dog in May 2005, she was left without her nose, lips, and chin. She had great difficulty speaking and eating as a result. On this day in 2005, Professors Bernard Devauchelle and Jean-Michel Dubernard led a medical team in Amiens that transplanted a section of a brain-dead female donor's face onto the patient's face. Dinoire's appearance wasn't the same as it had been before her accident and she had to be placed on a permanent course of immunosuppressant drugs, but after the transplant she was able to eat and speak.

November 28

DATEline

*"A dog starv'd at his Master's Gate
Predicts the ruin of the State."* — WILLIAM BLAKE

Tourist flight hits Mount Erebus

Early on November 28, 1979, Air New Zealand Flight 901 departed from Auckland Airport for a sightseeing fly-over of Antarctica. The strong magnetic fields around the South Pole mean that magnetic compasses are of little use there. Instead, pilots have to rely on grid coordinates programmed into a computer navigation system to guide the plane, as well as checking on visible landmarks. Unbeknown to pilot Captain Jim Collins, the computer on Flight 901 had been programmed with incorrect coordinates.

Due to low-lying clouds, the crew could only catch glimpses of the landscape below – they thought they were viewing the coastline of mainland Antarctica, but they were actually looking at Ross Island. Captain Collins radioed the U.S. base at McMurdo Station at 12:32 P.M. and was granted permission to drop below the cloud so his passengers would have a better view. The plane flew lower, and at just after 12:49 P.M. slammed into Mount Erebus at 300 miles per hour (480 km/h). It was impossible to visually distinguish the mountain from its surroundings – cloud cloaked the top of the snow-covered mountain and fog covered its lower slopes.

Personnel at McMurdo Station raised the alarm when they couldn't contact Flight 901. After the time elapsed when the airplane would have run out of fuel, an announcement was made in New Zealand that the plane must have crashed. U.S. Navy aircraft began a search and located the crash site: all on board had perished.

The flight recorders indicated that the crew had no inkling of the impending disaster until the altimeter broadcast a warning just moments before the crash.

HISTORICAL EVENTS

- **1520** Ferdinand Magellan rounds the tip of South America, completing his navigation of the Straits of Magellan, and reaches the Pacific Ocean from the Atlantic.
- **1582** William Shakespeare and Anne Hathaway marry at Stratford-upon-Avon.
- **1660** The Royal Society is founded at Gresham College by 12 men, including Christopher Wren, Robert Boyle, John Wilkins, and Sir Robert Moray.
- **1905** The nationalist Irish political party, Sinn Fein, is founded in Dublin.
- **1979** Air New Zealand Flight 901 crashes into Mount Erebus (see above).
- **1989** Gymnast Nadia Comaneci flees Romania and is granted political asylum in the U.S.
- **1990** Margaret Thatcher formally hands in her resignation as Prime Minister of Britain to the Queen after 11 years and three terms as leader. She had announced her intention to resign on November 21 after realizing that she had little possibility of winning a party ballot to remain leader.

DAY TO REMEMBER

National day Independence day (Albania) People in Abania celebrate the day they gained independence from the Ottoman Empire in 1912, and the day on which they gained a new constitution in 1998.

Births
- **1628** John Bunyan, religious minister and writer
- **1757** William Blake, painter and poet
- **1820** Friedrich Engels, philosopher
- **1904** Nancy Mitford, writer
- **1908** Claude Lévi-Strauss, anthropologist
- **1943** Randy Newman, composer and musician
- **1961** Martin Clunes, actor
- **1967** Anna Nicole Smith, model

Deaths
- **1859** Washington Irving, writer
- **1939** James Naismith, inventor of basketball
- **1954** Enrico Fermi, physicist
- **1968** Enid Blyton, children's writer
- **1976** Rosalind Russell, actress

November 29

"Women have been called queens for a long time, but the kingdom given them isn't worth ruling." — LOUISA MAY ALCOTT

The partitioning of Palestine

After World War I, Britain was given a mandate over the area of the Ottoman Empire known as Palestine. After the end of World War II, Jewish refugees from Europe began to pour into the area. Jewish and Arab people had lived side by side in the region for centuries. Arab concerns over this sudden influx grew and armed conflict erupted.

Britain was having difficulty controlling the numbers of immigrants arriving illegally on overcrowded boats, as well as the outbreaks of violence on both sides. At a time when Britain was trying to rebuild after the devastation of World War II, the British Government was also feeling the strain of dealing with the economic cost of the crisis in Palestine. It turned to the newly formed UN to help find a solution in February, 1947.

In May the UN appointed an 11-member committee to discuss possible solutions. Three months of deliberation then followed, after which two proposals were put forward. One was to divide the British mandate of Palestine into two nations, one for the Arab population and one for the Jewish, and the other was to create one combined nation.

After further intense debate, Resolution 181 – the proposal for the creation of two states in Palestine, with Jerusalem under international control – was put to a vote in the UN's General Assembly on November 29, 1947. When the vote was announced Jewish people throughout the world were jubilant, but Arab nations reacted angrily at the displacement of Arabs that would occur. Violence in Palestine quickly escalated and by early 1948 all-out war had begun.

Births
- **1797** Gaetano Donizetti, composer
- **1799** Amos Alcott, writer and educator
- **1803** Christian Doppler, physicist
- **1832** Louisa May Alcott, writer
- **1895** Busby Berkeley, director
- **1898** C. S. Lewis, writer
- **1932** Jacques Chirac, French President
- **1947** Petra Kelly, activist and politician

Deaths
- **1530** Cardinal Thomas Wolsey, adviser to Henry VIII
- **1924** Giacomo Puccini, composer
- **1981** Natalie Wood, actress
- **1986** Cary Grant, actor
- **2001** George Harrison, musician, Beatle

HISTORICAL EVENTS

- **1781** The commander of the slave ship *Zong*, Luke Collingwood, begins to dump 133 ill members of his living cargo into the sea to claim the insurance. If the slaves had died on board, he could not claim, but he could if he threw them overboard while still alive for the safety of the ship.
- **1864** The Sand Creek Massacre takes place in Colorado when Colonel John Chivington leads troops to kill an estimated 400 unarmed Cheyenne and Arapaho Indians who had been given permission to make camp.
- **1907** Florence Nightingale, aged 87, is awarded the Order of Merit for her services during the Crimean War more than 50 years earlier and for setting up the first school of nursing after the war.
- **1929** U.S. Navy Commander Richard Byrd leads a party that flies over the South Pole and drops an American flag as they do so.
- **1947** The UN General Assembly passes a resolution to divide Palestine between Arab and Jewish people (see left).
- **2004** The French Government announces plans to build the Louvre II in Lens in northern France to exhibit close to 600 works of art currently in the Louvre's storage.

DAY TO REMEMBER

National day Unity Day (Vanuatu) This is a day of commemoration of the civil unrest that caused upheaval in the then New Hebrides. The day is a national holiday, marked with prayer and traditional dancing.

November 30

DATE*line*

"Either that wallpaper goes, or I do." LAST WORDS OF OSCAR WILDE

The World Trade Organization's international trade talks were scheduled to begin in Seattle, Washington, on November 30, 1999. While police expected some disruptions by people concerned about the possible ill effects of the globalization of trade, they weren't prepared for the scale of the protests. In the morning at least 40,000 people took to the streets and delegates were unable to reach talk venues. Clashes between police and protesters became more violent and a state of emergency was declared, the National Guard was called in, and opening events for the trade negotiations were cancelled.

HISTORICAL EVENTS

1609 In Padua, Italy, Galileo Galilei looks through his telescope at the Moon and makes several drawings. He notes that the Moon is not smooth, but pitted, changing forever people's notions of objects in the sky.

1886 The Folies Bergère in Paris stages its first revue show featuring young women wearing elaborate but revealing costumes.

1936 Fire breaks out in London's Crystal Palace, the glass and steel hall built in 1851 for the International Exhibition. The building is evacuated, but 350 firefighters can't save it. Crowds gathered on highpoints throughout the city to watch the blaze, and the display that occurred when a fireworks storeroom exploded.

1982 An extremist animal activist group sends a letter bomb to British Prime Minister Margaret Thatcher at Number 10 Downing Street; one staff member is injured.

1991 In the inaugural football Women's World Cup, held in Guangzhou, China, the U.S. defeats Norway, 2–1.

1999 In Seattle, Washington, major protests by the anti-globalization movement catch organizers of the World Trade Organization meeting unawares (see above).

DAYS TO REMEMBER

Religious day St. Andrew's Day A fisherman and a follower of John the Baptist, St. Andrew, along with his brother Simon (later Peter), was the first disciple to follow Jesus. After the Resurrection, Andrew became a missionary, and was crucified on an X-shaped cross in Patras, Greece (c. 70 C.E.). He is the patron saint of fishermen.

International day Cities For Life Day Around 300 cities worldwide bring the issue of the death penalty to public attention by commemorating the day when Peter Leopold Joseph, Duke of Tuscany, abolished the death penalty, making his state the first in Europe to do so. Participating cities illuminate a symbolic monument, such as the Colosseum in Rome.

Births
- 1667 Jonathan Swift, author
- 1835 Mark Twain (Samuel Clemens), author
- 1874 Winston Churchill, British Prime Minister
- 1937 Ridley Scott, director
- 1955 Billy Idol, singer
- 1965 Ben Stiller, actor and writer

Deaths
- 1900 Oscar Wilde, writer
- 1901 Edward Eyre, explorer
- 1930 Mary Harris Jones (Mother Jones), labor activist
- 1979 Joyce Grenfell, actress
- 1987 James Baldwin, author
- 1996 Tiny Tim, entertainer

DAYS TO REMEMBER *November*

1
Samhain Means "summer's end", and marks the beginning of winter in the Northern Hemisphere

2
Rastafarians celebrate the crowning of the founder of their movement, Emperor Haile Selassie of Ethiopia

3
Culture Day (Japan) Commemorates the constitution that was signed in 1946

4
National Unity Day (Russia) Commemorates a popular uprising against Polish forces occupying Moscow on November 4, 1612

5
Guy Fawkes Night (Britain and New Zealand) Celebrates the failure of the Gunpowder Plot with fireworks and bonfires

8
Archangelovden (Archangel's Day) Archangel Michael lead the dead away to determine whether their souls went to Heaven or Hell

9
Schicksalstag (Germany) "The day of fate," so-called as a number of momentous events occurred on this day

10
The U.S. Marine Corps' Birthday Since 1921 Marine Corps units around the world have held birthday dinners to celebrate the founding of the corps

11
Armistice Day Many nations stop for a minute's silence to commemorate those who died in wars

12
Dr. Sun Yat-Sen's birth is commemorated in mainland China, Taiwan, and Chinese communities throughout the world

15
Palestinian Independence Day In 1988 a meeting of the Palestinian National Council in Algiers declared Palestine's Independence

16
Icelandic Language Day Held on the birthday of Jónas Hallgrimsson, Iceland's most famous poet

17
International Students Day Commemorates the day in 1939 when Nazi troops stormed the University of Prague to break up demonstrations

18
Latvia National Day Celebrates the day Latvia was declared an independent republic in the wake of World War I

19
World Toilet Day Promotes hygienic toilet practices and the provision of hygienic, healthy public toilet facilities

22
Lebanon National Day Celebrates Lebanon's independence from France

23
The first day of the star sign of Sagittarius

24
Andrew Dung-Lac's Day Andrew and 116 other Vietnamese martyrs were killed over a fifty-year period, mostly by beheading

25
Independence Day (Suriname) Celebrates the day Suriname gained independence from the Netherlands in 1975

26
Proclamation Day (Mongolia) Marks the proclamation of the Republic of Mongolia in 1925, which brought feudalism and the rule of the monarchy to an end

29
Unity Day (Vanuatu) Commemorates the civil unrest that caused upheaval in the then New Hebrides

30
Cities For Life Day Around 300 cities the world over bring the issue of the death penalty to public attention

7
Peter Tchaikovsky, composer died in 1893

7
In 1659, France and Spain signed the Treaty of the Pyrenees, and North Catalonia became part of France

Right Armistice Day, November 11
Below Guy Fawkes Night, November 5

13
Epulum Jovis This lavish feast in ancient Rome was the central point of the Plebian games

14
World Diabetes Day Established in 1991 to raise awareness of issues surrounding diabetes

20
Universal Children's Day Marks the day the UN adopted the Declaration of the Rights of the Child and the Convention of the Rights of the Child

21
World Television Day Promotes television as a means of communication around the world

27
First day of Advent Advent is the holy time of preparation for the birth of Christ. The earliest that Advent can begin is November 27, and the latest is December 3

28
Independence Day (Albania) Celebrates the day Albania gained independence from the Ottoman Empire in 1912

DECEMBER

"The sun that brief December day
Rose cheerless over hills of gray,
And, darkly circled, gave at noon
A sadder light than waning moon."

JOHN GREENLEAF WHITTIER

In all but a few countries of the Western world, boisterous celebrations have been associated with the year's end on December 31, according to the Gregorian calendar since its inception in the sixteenth century. The New Year's celebrations in Dresden, Germany, are a fine example of such revelry.

December

December is the twelfth and final month in the Gregorian calendar. According to some classifications, it is the first month of the Northern Hemisphere winter, with the solstice on or around December 21 marking the official change of season. Other cultures and calendars regard this date as midwinter. In the Southern Hemisphere, the longer, hotter days of summer are rolling in. December is a month marked by abundant feast days and holidays, from the Pagan "festivals of light" associated with the winter solstice, to the religious and secular celebrations of Christmas, Hanukkah, and New Year's Eve.

Capricorn star sign and scene of killing a goat from *Calendar and Book of Hours*, from fifteenth-century France. December begins in the sign of Sagittarius and ends in the sign of Capricorn.

SPECIAL DATES

The season of Advent occupies the first half of December, beginning on the fourth Sunday before Christmas Day and ending on Christmas Eve. It celebrates the coming of Jesus. Children are often given Advent calendars to mark the countdown to Christmas Day.

THE MONTH'S NAME is derived from the Latin word *decem*, meaning ten, as December was the tenth month in the earliest Roman calendar. With the introduction of the Julian calendar, December became the twelfth month, and two days were added to its complement of 29 to make it a month of 31 days. According to Pagan lore, it is the time of the "cold moon."

A traditional Irish name for December is *Mí na Nollaig*, or "month of winter," while in other parts of Europe it is sometimes called the "frosty month." Highlighting a different aspect of December is the Old German name of *Heilagmanoth* or "holy month," acknowledging its many sacred festivals. Similarly, in the old Japanese calendar, December was known as *Shiwasu*, or "month of running priests."

A time for festivals and holidays

The latter half of December has been a holiday season since ancient times, with many festivities associated with the solstice, around December 21. This is the time when the Sun reaches its southernmost distance from the celestial equator and its lowest point in the midday sky, causing the Northern Hemisphere to experience its shortest day and longest night, and the reverse of this in the Southern Hemisphere. Each day thereafter the Sun rises a little further north, providing great cause for celebration and thanks among the ancient tribes and races of the northern latitudes, as they looked forward to extended hours of sunlight. The symbolic importance of the solstice in prehistory is

This page from the sixteenth-century *Book of Hours* depicts the Nativity. The birthday of Jesus Christ, known as Christmas, is celebrated in December in most Christian countries.

evident in the design of the Stone Age tomb of Newgrange in Ireland, where the first shafts of light from the winter solstice sunrise illuminate the passage and inner chamber through a precisely aligned vent in the structure's roof.

Countless different cultures over the ages held festivals to celebrate the symbolic victory of light over darkness and the renewal of the Sun. In northern Europe, the festival of Yule was celebrated around the time of the solstice, with feasting and the sacrificing of pigs to honor the fertility god Freyr. This has translated into the Nordic tradition of serving ham over the Christmas period.

The ancient Roman festival of *Saturnalia*, which commenced on December 17 and continued over the winter solstice, was a period of feasting and merrymaking in honor of Saturn, the god of agriculture. Homes would be decorated with greenery, candles and lanterns lit, and the usual order of the year suspended in favor of the playing of pranks and role reversals, and the crowning of a mock king, the Lord of Misrule. *Yalda*, an even older Persian festival (also called *Shab e Cheleh*) was celebrated in similar fashion, and has carried over into modern-day Iranian culture with family gatherings on the day of the solstice, and the eating of dried and fresh winter fruits, symbolic of the ancient feasts once held in hopeful anticipation of good harvests to come.

In China, the day of the solstice is called *Dong-zhi*, or "winter's extreme," a time when families prepare *tong yuen*, balls of brightly colored glutinous rice, which symbolize reunion. The Korean solstice festival, *Dongji*, traditionally marked the start of the new year. It is customary to eat a red bean soup on this day to drive away evil spirits, which were thought to be most active on the longest night of the year. Ancient Egyptians filled their homes with green palm rushes to celebrate the solstice, which represented the Sun god Ra's triumph over ill health and weakness.

Rituals associated with the solstice involved the burning of bonfires and the lighting of candles and lanterns to fill the darkness with light, lift the spirits and hasten the return of the Sun. During Yule, a large log would be brought into the home, and families would feast and make merry for as long as it burned. The word "Yule" came from the Norse word, *hweol*, or wheel, as it was believed the Sun was a great wheel of light that rolled toward the Earth then away again.

The Jewish faith has its own festival of light, called *Hanukkah* (or *Chanukah*), which usually commences during the month of December. This eight-day holiday commemorates the success of a Jewish rebellion against Syrian oppression in 165 B.C.E. At the re-dedication of the temple in Jerusalem that followed the victory, only enough oil to fuel the eternal flame for a single day could be found. Miraculously, the oil lasted for eight days, allowing enough time to prepare a

During Hanukkah, a candlestick called a *menorah* is burned. The menorah in this thirteenth-century Hebrew manuscript, illuminated by Joseph Assarfati in Spain, has seven branches.

December birthflower

December is associated with several birthflowers. Holly, with its spiky, evergreen leaves and festive red berries, is a plant for celebration, said to promote success, wealth, and reassurance. The white narcissus is also symbolic of December. While much of the garden is dormant in northern latitudes, the narcissus is one of the few flowers to brave the winter snow. Named after a beautiful youth from Greek mythology, who was turned into a flower after becoming transfixed by his reflection in a pool, it represents vanity and egotism, but also sweetness and purity. Poinsettia is also associated with December.

This Christmas card from the early twentieth century, part of the John Johnson collection, is titled "Bringing Home the Yule-Log." Burning the Yule log is a northern European Christmas tradition which has its roots in the Pagan midwinter Yule festival.

Christmas celebrations

Acknowledging the importance of the religious aspects of Christmas, many cultures observe midnight mass on Christmas Eve. In countries of southern Europe and Latin America, a creche or manger scene made with carved and painted figurines is an important feature of Christmas, as well as colorful pageants enacting the life of Jesus. The English tradition of carol-singing from house to house has its origins in the ancient practice of wassailing. The word is derived from the Anglo-Saxon *wes hale*, meaning "be thou hale," a toast traditionally offered with a drink of hot ale, roasted apples, sugar, and spices, which was passed round in a special wassail bowl. A similar custom from the Middle Ages involved the Christmas mummers, bands of colorfully attired actors and musicians who visited homes performing plays in return for money or a hot meal.

new batch. This miracle is celebrated in Jewish households by the lighting of the menorah, a many-branched candlestick, after sundown on each day of the festival. Blessings are then made and traditional songs sung, and families play the dreidel game, with a special spinning top and foil-wrapped chocolate coins, known as *gelt*. During Hanukkah (meaning "dedication"), it is traditional to eat *latkes* (potato pancakes), sweet doughnuts, and other foods cooked in oil, to honor the miracle.

Often overlapping with Hanukkah, the celebrations associated with Christmas consume much of the latter part of the month of December in Christian countries of the world. In fact, the Finnish name for December is *joulukuu*, meaning "Christmas month." This celebration of the birth of Jesus is the most important holiday in the Christian calendar, aside from Easter. In most countries, Christmas Day is recognized as December 25, although in some parts of eastern Europe which continue to use the Julian calendar, it is celebrated on January 7.

Many Christmas rituals have their origins in pre-Christian religious and secular practices. In northern Europe, the burning of the Yule log, decorating the house with evergreens, and kissing under the mistletoe were appropriated from the Pagan midwinter festival of Yule. In Mexico, piñatas and poinsettia plants have become closely associated with Christmas celebrations.

The origins of the Christmas tree are thought to go back to Germany in the 1500s, when Martin Luther was said to have attached candles to a small evergreen tree to simulate the twinkling stars of heavens. But it was Queen Victoria and her German-born husband Prince Albert who made it fashionable throughout the English-speaking world, after an 1848 etching published in *The Illustrated London News* showed the royals gathered around a tree decorated with candles and glass ornaments at Windsor Castle.

Secular aspects of Christmas are largely associated with the figure of Santa Claus (or Father Christmas) and the exchanging of gifts. The name "Santa Claus" is a derivation of the Dutch name for St. Nicholas – Sinter Klaas – a third-century bishop known for his acts of kindness to the poor and needy. The tradition of leaving stockings or shoes by the fireplace to be filled with presents goes back to legends about St. Nicholas. Depending on the country, children receive gifts on the eve of St. Nicholas' feast day on December 6, on Christmas Eve or Christmas Day, or 12 days after Christmas, on Twelfth Night

The Adoration of the Magi is depicted in this sixteenth-century relief work featuring gold enameling. The visit to the baby Jesus on his birthday by the three Magi from the East is celebrated on Twelfth Night, falling twelve days after Christmas.

or Three Kings Day, in recognition of the gifts of gold, frankincense, and myrrh offered to the baby Jesus by the three Magi from the East.

The popular images of Santa as a portly, bearded, red-clad gentleman riding his reindeer sleigh across the sky on Christmas Eve were shaped by a poem written by Clement Clarke Moore in 1822, and later illustrated by cartoonist Thomas Nast. Even in non-Christian countries, such as Japan and India, Christmas has been adopted as a secular celebration largely centered around Santa and the Christmas tree.

Feasting is an important focus of Christmas celebrations around the world. In English-speaking countries, the traditional Christmas Day lunch or dinner consists of a roast turkey or goose "with all the trimmings", and a rich plum pudding with good-luck coins hidden within. The Southern Hemisphere's countries have adapted such typically cold-weather fare to better suit their climate. In Australia, for instance, the beach picnic and backyard barbecue have become popular Christmas Day customs.

For German families, gingerbread figures and houses, and cinnamon star cookies are traditional Christmas treats. After midnight mass on Christmas Eve, French households often serve a dessert called *bûche de Noël*, a chocolate cake shaped in the form of a Yule log. On this night, Scandinavian countries celebrate with a large dinner or smorgasbord, and a rice dessert containing a single almond. The person who finds the nut is said to be the next to marry in the coming year.

Immediately following Christmas are the religious feasts of St. Stephen on December 26, St. John the Evangelist on December 27, and Holy Innocents' Day on December 28.

December birthstone

Turquoise is the birthstone for December. Prized by ancient Egyptians and Native Americans, it was thought to have predictive powers associated with its subtle changes in tone. Persians believed it protected from the evil eye and improved sight. A popular love charm, it is often featured in Russian wedding rings. Zircon, a diamond-like gem with many variations in colour, is an alternative December birthstone. The flashing brilliance of the cut stone is said to cheer the heart.

In Commonwealth countries, December 26 is a secular holiday known as Boxing Day, while *Kwanzaa*, the African-American week-long holiday, commences on this day.

For a month of so many festivals, it is fitting that December should end with a bang. On December 31, the final day of the Gregorian year, many cultures celebrate the transition to a new year with partying, firework displays, and massive public gatherings in the major cities of the world.

Many nationalities prepare special New Year's Eve feasts, and the Scottish celebrate over a three-day holiday period called *Hogmanay*. The countdown to midnight is an integral part of these festivities. In New York, the dropping of a 6-foot (180 cm) ball from high above Times Square to mark the stroke of midnight is a 100-year-old tradition. In Spain, it is customary to eat a grape on each chime of the clock in Madrid's Puerta del Sol square. Aside from the partying, this is a time for nostalgia and reflection on the year just passed, while looking to new beginnings and resolutions in the year about to begin.

Left The popular image of Santa Claus was shaped by a poem written in 1822 and later illustrated by a cartoonist. The Santa depicted in this wooden block puzzle, manufactured in New York in c. 1900, is from the same era.

African Americans celebrate Kwanzaa during the week after Christmas by lighting a special candle for each of the seven guiding principles of Kwanzaa culture – one for each day of the observance.

December 1

The first day of winter in the Northern Hemisphere, and the first day of summer in the Southern Hemisphere

"The world knows of Rosa Parks because of a single, simple act of dignity and courage that struck a lethal blow to the foundations of legal bigotry." — U.S. PRESIDENT BILL CLINTON

HISTORICAL EVENTS

- **1804** Napoleon Bonaparte marries Joséphine of Martinique.
- **1913** The Ford Motor Company revolutionizes car manufacturing by introducing the moving assembly line at its Highland Park plant in Michigan, U.S.
- **1919** Lady Nancy Astor becomes the first female member of Parliament in Britain, less than a year after women in England were given the vote.
- **1952** The "sex change" of former GI George Jorgensen, who is now known as Christine, makes front-page news.
- **1955** In Montgomery, Alabama, Rosa Parks refuses to relinquish her bus seat to a white man, sparking a bus boycott and the beginnings of the U.S. civil rights movement.
- **1959** A treaty in Washington sets aside Antarctica for scientific purposes. Signed by 12 countries, including the U.S. and the Soviet Union, during the Cold War, the treaty bans military activity of any kind on the continent.
- **1976** Punk group The Sex Pistols cause a public outcry in Britain by swearing on live prime-time television.
- **1990** Channel Tunnel workers break through the final wall of rock to create the first ground link between Britain and France since the ice age (see below).

Births
- **1913** Mary Martin, actress
- **1935** Woody Allen, actor, filmmaker
- **1935** Lou Rawls, soul singer
- **1939** Lee Trevino, golfer
- **1945** Bette Midler, actress, singer, and entertainer
- **1959** Wally Lewis, rugby league player

Deaths
- **1973** David Ben-Gurion, Israeli statesman
- **1987** James Baldwin, writer
- **1990** Lloyd Rees, artist
- **1997** Stephane Grappelli, violinist

The Channel Tunnel breakthrough

Cheers and handshakes, followed by the popping of champagne corks, marked the breakthrough on this day in 1990 when the two ends of the Channel Tunnel, excavated simultaneously from French and British shores, were united beneath the seabed. British construction worker Graham Fagg and his French counterpart, Philippe Cozette, shook hands through the opening after drilling through the remaining chalk wall, establishing the first walkable connection between Britain and mainland Europe since the last ice age, more than 8,000 years ago. Construction began in 1986, using massive boring machines and guided by laser surveying techniques. Spanning 31 miles (50 km), it is the world's second-longest rail tunnel, with 23 miles (37 km) of it running beneath the sea floor.

The idea of linking Britain with continental Europe has preoccupied the minds of engineers and politicians since Napoleon's time. A project in the 1970s had progressed as far as the building of an 820-foot (250 m) test tunnel before it was abandoned due to financing problems. The vision was revived in 1984 when the British and French Governments invited firms to submit designs for a fixed link. The successful tender, by Eurotunnel, comprised twin rail tunnels with a service/access tunnel sandwiched in between.

The Channel Tunnel was officially opened by Queen Elizabeth II and French President François Mitterand on May 6, 1994, having cost $15 billion, more than double the original 1987 estimate. Despite continuing financial woes, it is considered a masterpiece of engineering and has been declared one of the Seven Wonders of the Modern World.

DAYS TO REMEMBER

Religious day St. Eligius' Day
A goldsmith and later, master of the Paris mint, Eligius (c. 590–660) used his wealth to build churches, and help the poor.

International day World AIDS Day
Marking the day in 1981 when the first case of AIDS was diagnosed, this annual event is dedicated to raising awareness of the global AIDS epidemic.

DATEline

December 2

"I knew I had lost millions of pounds, but I didn't know how much. I was too frightened to find out – the numbers scared me to death." — NICK LEESON

Births
- 1859 George Seurat, painter
- 1923 Maria Callas, soprano
- 1946 Gianni Versace, fashion designer
- 1968 Lucy Liu, actress
- 1973 Monica Seles, tennis player
- 1978 Nelly Furtado, pop singer
- 1981 Britney Spears, pop singer

Deaths
- 1814 Marquis de Sade, writer
- 1859 John Brown, slave abolitionist
- 1982 Marty Feldman, comedian and actor
- 1990 Aaron Copland, composer
- 1985 Philip Larkin, poet
- 1993 Pablo Escobar, drug baron
- 2004 Alicia Markova, ballerina

HISTORICAL EVENTS

1804 Napoleon Bonaparte is crowned Emperor Napoleon I of France, by himself. He places the crown on his head with his own hands.

1942 Italian scientist Enrico Fermi achieves the first controlled nuclear chain reaction in a squash court at the University of Chicago. The basic principles behind his design are used in reactors to this day.

1954 The U.S. Senate condemns Joseph McCarthy for "conduct that tends to bring the Senate into dishonor and disrepute," following his anti-Communist reign of terror.

1972 Gough Whitlam leads the Australian Labor Party to election victory after more than two decades in opposition. Three years later, he becomes the only Prime Minister to be dismissed, along with his parliament, by the Governor-General.

1988 Benazir Bhutto becomes Prime Minister of Pakistan, making her the first female to head a modern-day Muslim country (see right).

1990 Helmut Kohl's coalition wins the first federal election since German unification.

1995 Rogue trader Nick Leeson, who lost £850 million for Barings, Britain's oldest merchant bank, is sentenced to six-and-a-half years jail. The bank is later sold for £1.

2005 Australian Van Tuong Nguyen, 25, is executed in Singapore after being convicted of drug trafficking.

Benazir Bhutto assumed leadership of Pakistan's People's Party (PPP) during her exile in England, after the assassination of her father, the former Pakistan Prime Minister Zulfikar Ali Bhutto, in April 1979. She returned to her homeland in April 1986 and commenced her campaign to lead the country when open elections, Pakistan's first in more than a decade, were announced for November 16, 1988. Bhutto, 35, who had given birth only a month before launching her leadership campaign in mid-October, won the largest block of seats in the National Assembly, and was sworn in as Pakistan's Prime Minister on this day in 1988. "I felt a tremendous sense that Pakistan had paved the way for other Muslim countries – that a woman could be elected as chief executive," she said of her election victory, during a BBC World Service interview years later.

December 3

> "The cruellest lies are often told in silence." — ROBERT LOUIS STEVENSON

In the early hours of the morning on December 3, 1984, a cloud of toxic methyl isocyanate gas escaped from an underground holding tank at the Union Carbide pesticide plant on the outskirts of Bhopal, in central India. As the deadly plume enveloped the city, it caused death and blindness on a massive scale. The Indian Government declared Bhopal a disaster zone and called for volunteers to assist in the clearing of corpses from the streets and people's homes. The immediate death toll is thought to have been around 2,500, while thousands needed hospital treatment for breathing difficulties, swollen eyes, and the symptoms of poisoning. Five years later, the Indian Government sued the American-owned Union Carbide on behalf of 500,000 victims, settling for $140 million in damages. Most survivors, however, were never compensated, and may face the long-term prospects of failing sight, kidney and liver complications, or chronic lung disease as a bitter legacy of the tragedy.

HISTORICAL EVENTS

- **1854** Protests by gold miners over the imposition of licence fees in Ballarat, Australia, culminate in the Eureka Stockade uprising, the most celebrated rebellion in the country's history.
- **1920** Visitors to the Paris Motor Show are introduced to the neon lamp, invented by physicist Georges Claude.
- **1937** The launch issue of *Dandy*, the world's longest running comic, goes on sale.
- **1967** Dr. Christiaan Barnard and his team perform the first successful human heart transplant, in Cape Town, South Africa. The recipient, Louis Washkansky, has his immune system weakened by anti-rejection drugs and dies from pneumonia after 18 days.
- **1973** The *Pioneer 10* spacecraft, the first artificial object to travel through the asteroid belt, captures the first close-up images of Jupiter. It had been launched in March of the previous year.
- **1984** A poisonous gas leak from the Union Carbide pesticides plant at Bhopal, India, becomes the world's worst industrial accident (see above).
- **1997** Britain places a ban on the sale of unboned beef in a precautionary move to prevent human contraction of BSE (mad cow disease).
- **1999** The *Mars Polar Lander* mission fails as NASA loses contact with the space probe as it attempted to touch down on the Red Planet's south pole.

Births
- 1857 Joseph Conrad, writer
- 1895 Anna Freud, psychoanalyst
- 1906 Frank Packer, businessman
- 1927 Andy Williams, singer
- 1930 Jean-Luc Godard, film director
- 1948 Ozzy Osbourne, singer
- 1953 Franz Klammer, skier
- 1960 Julianne Moore, actress
- 1960 Daryl Hannah, actress
- 1968 Brendan Fraser, actor

Deaths
- 1894 Robert Louis Stevenson, writer
- 1919 Pierre-Auguste Renoir, painter
- 1980 Oswald Mosley, politician
- 1994 Elizabeth Glaser, AIDS activist

DAYS TO REMEMBER

Religious day St. Francis Xavier's Day Born in Spain, this great missionary (1506–1552) was one of the early Jesuits. He traveled to many countries, living simply and converting thousands. St. Francis Xavier is the patron saint of Australia, Borneo, China, India, Japan, and New Zealand, and of missionaries.

International day Day of Disabled Persons Adopted by the UN General Assembly in 1982, this annual event aims to increase public awareness of disability issues and improve the wellbeing of people with disabilities.

December 4

DATE*line*

"If we went into the funeral business, people would stop dying."
PAN AM VICE-CHAIRMAN MARTIN SHUGRUE, ON THE AIRLINE'S DECLINE

Births
- 1866 Wassily Kandinsky, painter
- 1892 Francisco Franco, dictator
- 1940 John Cale, musician
- 1949 Jeff Bridges, actor
- 1964 Marisa Tomei, actress
- 1973 Tyra Banks, actress and model

Deaths
- 1976 Benjamin Britten, composer
- 1993 Frank Zappa, musician

HISTORICAL EVENTS

- **1154** Cardinal Nicholas Breakspear is elected Pope Adrian IV, the first and only Englishman to have headed the Roman Catholic Church.
- **1791** The world's first Sunday paper, *The Observer*, is published in the U.K.
- **1872** After leaving New York for Genoa, Italy, the brigantine *Mary Celeste* is found drifting west of Gibraltar, undamaged but with no one on board. The fate of her crew has remained a mystery.
- **1961** Henri Matisse's painting *Le Bateau* had hung upside down at New York's Museum of Modern Art for more than six weeks before someone noticed and corrected the faux pas.
- **1969** On the North Shore of Oahu, Hawaii, Californian surfer Greg Noll rides a 65-foot (20 m) wave, regarded as the largest paddled-in wave ever surfed.
- **1980** British rock group Led Zeppelin officially announces its break-up, following the death of drummer John Bonham.
- **1991** The last American hostage in Lebanon, journalist Terry Anderson, is set free after six years and nine months in captivity (see below).
- **1991** Pan Am, the 64-year-old American airline, ceases operation with massive debts.

DAY TO REMEMBER

Religious day St. Barbara's Day
The patron saint of the military, firemen, miners, architects, builders, and stonemasons, St. Barbara (c. 306) was a virgin locked away by her pagan father in a tower that had two windows. When she added a third to symbolize the Holy Trinity, her father struck off her head in a fit of rage, and at that moment was struck dead himself by a bolt of lightning.

Journalist released

As news filtered through of Terry Anderson's release, there was an agonising wait for his arrival in Syria. Snow hampered his passage from Lebanon, causing further anguish for his family who feared another false alarm. Anderson, who was chief Middle East correspondent for Associated Press at the time of his capture and had served as a combat correspondent in the U.S. Marines during the Vietnam War, finally emerged at a packed news conference in Damascus looking reassuringly well.

"I have thought about this moment for a long time," he said. "Now it is here and I am scared to death. I do not know what to say." He went on to thank the authorities who had secured his release, and paid tribute to his family and friends, and the many well-wishers who had campaigned on the hostages' behalf. In particular, Anderson's sister, Peggy Say (shown here with Anderson, a month after his release), had been a dedicated activist for his release.

The journalist was kidnapped by Hezbollah Shi'ite Muslims in Beirut after finishing a game of tennis on March 16, 1985. His freedom saw him united with his fiancée and their six-year-old daughter Sulome, whom he had never met. Anderson would later join the two other U.S. hostages, Joseph Cicippio and Alann Steen, who had been released earlier in the month, at the American military hospital in Wiesbaden, Germany. Meanwhile two Western hostages, Thomas Kemptner and Heinrich Struebig, both from Germany, remained captive in Lebanon. On his return to America, Anderson went on recount his experience as a hostage in his best-selling memoir, *Den of Lions*.

December 5

"She cannot see an institution without hitting it with her handbag."

CONSERVATIVE MP, JULIAN CRITCHLEY, ON BRITISH PRIME MINISTER MARGARET THATCHER

Births
- 1839 George Armstrong Custer, American general
- 1890 Fritz Lang, film director
- 1901 Walt Disney, animator
- 1932 Little Richard, musician
- 1938 J. J. Cale, musician

Deaths
- 1791 Wolfgang Amadeus Mozart, composer
- 1870 Alexandre Dumas, writer
- 1926 Claude Monet, artist
- 1973 Robert Watson-Watt, physicist
- 2005 Kevin "Big Kev" McQuay, businessman

HISTORICAL EVENTS

1757 At the Battle of Leuthen, Frederick the Great of Prussia wins his greatest victory of the Seven Years' War, with an army of some 35,000 troops against Austria's estimated 60,000-strong force.

1766 London auctioneers Christie's conducts its first sale.

1924 Percy Christmas opens Australia's first Woolworths store in Sydney's Imperial Arcade. From this first bargain basement, the store grows into a nationwide chain of supermarkets.

1933 America officially repeals National Prohibition, which had rendered illegal the manufacture, sale, and transportation of alcohol for 13 years.

1952 A killer fog shrouds London for five days, causing an estimated 12,000 deaths from respiratory illnesses, and throwing transport into chaos, with visibility close to zero (see below).

1974 In the U.K., the final episode of *Monty Python's Flying Circus* goes to air.

1989 British Prime Minister Margaret Thatcher survives her first leadership challenge, as disquiet among members of the Conservative Party over her anti-European stance increases.

1991 Sons of the late Robert Maxwell, publishing tycoon, call in the administrators in a bid to salvage the Maxwell business empire, which is facing debts of more than $1 billion.

DAY TO REMEMBER

National day King's Birthday (Thailand) This holiday celebrates the birthday of Thailand's King Bhumibol Adulyadej, who was born in Cambridge, Massachusetts, in 1927.

London was cold and bright on the morning of December 5, 1952, but by nightfall the city had become cloaked in a fog that would linger for five long days. Smoke belching from factories and homes in the metropolitan area added thousands of tons of soot, tar, and sulphur dioxide to the steadily thickening fog, creating a toxic smog, or "pea-souper," that would cause or contribute to the deaths of an estimated 12,000 people. The elderly, the very young, and those with respiratory or heart problems were most at risk, with many victims dying in their beds from asphyxiation. With visibility down to nil in some areas, transport services were severely disrupted, and crime reached a peak as thieves made use of the cover the fog provided. The Great Smog of 1952, as it became known, precipitated the introduction of the nation's first Clean Air Acts, which established smokeless zones in urban areas.

December 6

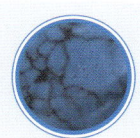

DATEline

"You get to know more of the character of a man in a round of golf than in six months of political experience." — U.K. PRIME MINISTER DAVID LLOYD GEORGE

HISTORICAL EVENTS

1768 The first volume of the *Encyclopaedia Britannica* is published in Edinburgh, Scotland.

1907 An explosion at the Monongah coal mine in West Virginia kills 362, making it the worst mining disaster in U.S. history.

1916 Welshman David Lloyd George becomes Prime Minister of Britain.

1917 French munitions ship the *Mont Blanc* explodes in Halifax Harbor, Canada, after colliding with another vessel, decimating an entire city suburb and costing 2,000 lives.

1921 The Anglo–Irish Treaty is signed, creating an independent Irish Free State, with the six northeastern counties remaining part of the U.K.

1989 After screaming about how much he hates feminists, Canadian Marc Lépine fatally shoots 14 women at the École Polytechnique in Montreal, before turning the gun on himself.

1992 Hindu activists destroy an ancient Muslim shrine in Ayodhya, India, sparking off violent clashes between Muslims and Hindus across the country.

2001 Celebrated New Zealand yachtsman and environmentalist Sir Peter Blake is murdered by pirates on the Amazon River in Brazil (see right).

2002 American actress Winona Ryder is sentenced to three years' probation and 480 hours community service for stealing merchandise worth more than $5,500 from a Beverly Hills department store.

DAYS TO REMEMBER

Religious day St. Nicholas' Day The bishop of Myra (Bari) in Asia Minor, St. Nicholas (c. 270–350) was known for his acts of kindness, miracle working, and gift giving. In northwest Europe and North America, he is more closely identified with Santa Claus.

National day Independence Day (Finland) On this day, Finland celebrates the anniversary of gaining its independence from Russia in 1918.

Births		Deaths	
1896	Ira Gerschwin, lyricist	1882	Anthony Trollope, novelist
1900	Agnes Moorehead, actress	1988	Roy Orbison, musician
1920	Dave Brubeck, jazz musician	1997	Billy Bremner, soccer player
1945	James Naughton, actor		

Mourning an ocean hero

Mourners from around the world paid tribute to Sir Peter Blake, one of the most successful sailors in yachting history, at his funeral in Hampshire, England, on this day in 2001. The 6 foot, 8 inch (2.03 m) New Zealander, who was knighted in 1995 for his services to yachting, twice led his home country to victory in the America's Cup, was two-times winner of the Sydney to Hobart yacht race, and took out the 1990 Whitebread round-the-world race.

In 2001, Sir Peter announced he was retiring from competitive yachting, to devote himself to environmental causes. In the same year, he was appointed goodwill ambassador for the United Nations Environmental Programme. It was while carrying out his UN duties that he joined a five-year round-the-world expedition to monitor global warming and pollution. During the South American leg of the trip, he had moored his ship, *Seamaster*, off Macapa, at the mouth of the Amazon River. As the crew awaited customs clearance to leave Brazilian waters, looting pirates boarded the vessel. Sir Peter attempted to fight them off, but was killed by two shots in the back. The bandits injured two more crew members before taking off with an outboard motor and several wristwatches.

During the funeral, New Zealand Prime Minister Helen Clark paid a special tribute to one of her country's favorite sons. "He was the Hillary of the waters, our greatest sailor," she said in reference to fellow New Zealander and conqueror of Mt. Everest, Sir Edmund Hillary. "Peter Blake was a living legend – for his courage, for the causes he espoused, and for being a decent human being." He was posthumously bestowed the Olympic Order, one of the International Olympic Committee's highest honors, in recognition of his sporting achievements.

December 7

"Men and women are like right and left hands: It doesn't make sense not to use both."
JEANNETTE RANKIN

The Soviet leader Mikhail Gorbachev and U.S. President Ronald Reagan were all smiles at the White House after signing the historic Intermediate Range Nuclear Forces (INF) treaty to scrap nuclear arms. The friendly exchange surprised many observers, given the bleak outcome from last year's Iceland summit, when disarmament talks collapsed. Since arriving in America on December 7, 1987, Gorbachev and his wife Raisa had received the kind of welcome usually reserved for movie stars. Images of the Soviet leader even appeared on mugs, T-shirts, and badges. While many found Gorbachev's easy talk of *glasnost* and *perestroika* seductive, not everyone was caught up in the hysteria. Protests over the Soviet Union's human rights abuses also shadowed the Soviet leader's moves during his time in Washington.

Births

- 1598 Gian Lorenzo Bernini, sculptor and architect
- 1761 Marie Tussaud, wax sculptor
- 1860 Sir Joseph Cook, Australian Prime Minister
- 1915 Eli Wallach, actor
- 1932 Ellen Burstyn, actress
- 1942 Harry Chapin, singer and songwriter
- 1949 Tom Waits, singer and songwriter
- 1957 Geoff Lawson, cricketer

Deaths

- 43 C.E. Cicero, Roman statesman and writer
- 1985 Robert Graves, writer and poet
- 1990 Joan Bennett, actress

HISTORICAL EVENTS

- **1916** Jeannette Rankin becomes the first woman to be elected to the U.S. Congress.
- **1941** Japanese bombers launch a surprise attack on the U.S. naval base at Pearl Harbor, Hawaii, on what President Roosevelt proclaims "a date which will live in infamy." More than 2,400 American lives are lost and the Pacific Fleet is left in tatters.
- **1975** Indonesian troops invade East Timor following Portugal's withdrawal from the territory. It is not until 1999 that East Timor becomes independent of Indonesian control after a UN-supervised referendum.
- **1987** Mikhail Gorbachev arrives in Washington for a summit with President Ronald Reagan, causing a wave of "Gorbymania" as the Soviet leader and his wife, Raisa, captivate the American public (see above).
- **1988** A massive earthquake rocks the Soviet republic of Armenia, destroying several towns and villages, and killing an estimated 55,000 people.
- **1995** After a six-year journey, U.S. space probe *Galileo* reaches Jupiter and is the first craft to go into orbit around the planet.
- **2002** Iraq delivers a 12,000-page report to the UN in which it denies having weapons of mass destruction.
- **2005** The European Union establishes its own TLD (top-level domain) – ".eu" – for the world wide web.

DAY TO REMEMBER

Religious day St. Ambrose's Day As Bishop of Milan, St. Ambrose (c. 339–397) surrendered his personal wealth, and that of the Church, to ransom hostages and aid the unfortunate. St. Ambrose is the patron saint of teachers, orators, and bee-keepers.

December 8

DATE*line*

"A leader who doesn't hesitate before he sends his nation into battle is not fit to be a leader."

GOLDA MEIR

HISTORICAL EVENTS

- **1941** The U.S. declares war on Japan, the day after the Japanese bombing of the American Pacific Fleet at Pearl Harbor.
- **1963** Frank Sinatra, Jr. is kidnapped then released two days later after his famous father foots the $240,000 ransom demand (see below).
- **1980** John Lennon is shot dead by a crazed fan outside his New York apartment. After committing the crime, 25-year-old Mark David Chapman drops his revolver and awaits his arrest.
- **1987** Soviet leader Mikhail Gorbachev and U.S. President Ronald Reagan sign a treaty in Washington to eliminate all short- and medium-range nuclear weapons in Europe. It is the first agreement between the two superpowers to reduce arms.
- **1987** Frank Vitkovic, 22, fatally shoots eight people at the Australia Post offices in Melbourne's Queen Street before leaping to his death from the eleventh floor.
- **1993** U.S. President Bill Clinton signs the North American Free Trade Agreement (NAFTA) between the U.S., Canada, and Mexico.
- **1995** Cult rock band the Grateful Dead calls it a day, four months after the death of lead guitarist Jerry Garcia and 30 years after forming.

Births
- **1542** Mary Queen of Scots
- **1865** Jean Sibelius, composer
- **1886** Diego Rivera, artist
- **1922** Lucien Freud, artist
- **1925** Sammy Davis Jr., singer, dancer, actor, and entertainer
- **1936** David Carradine, actor
- **1939** Sir James Galway, flautist
- **1953** Kim Basinger, actress
- **1966** Sinead O'Connor, singer
- **1964** Teri Hatcher, actress

Deaths
- **1978** Golda Meir, Israeli Prime Minister

DAYS TO REMEMBER

Religious day The Immaculate Conception Adopted in the seventh century, this feast day celebrates St. Anne's conception of Mary, mother of Jesus. The Immaculate Conception is the doctrine that states that Mary was born without the stain of original sin. St. Anne is the patron saint of pregnant women.

Religious day Bodhi Day This is a Buddhist celebration of the day that Siddhartha Gautama attained enlightenment and became Buddha, in 596 B.C.E.

Two days after being kidnapped from a hotel room in Lake Tahoe, Nevada, on December 8, 1963, the 19-year-old Frank Sinatra, Jr., was safely reunited with his famous father, who negotiated payment of a $240,000 ransom bill. During the ordeal, Sinatra Sr. was forced to communicate with the hostage-takers via pay phones. During one call, he ran out of coins and feared the lost connection may have cost his son. He vowed, thereafter, never to be caught without small change and supposedly always carried a roll of dimes with him until his death. In 2003, the kidnapping became the subject of a made-for-television film *Stealing Sinatra*, which was based on the account of one of the convicted kidnappers, Barry Keenan.

December 9

"He has not a single redeeming defect." — BENJAMIN DISRAELI OF U.K. PRIME MINISTER WILLIAM GLADSTONE

Births
- 1608 John Milton, poet, historian, and writer
- 1886 Clarence Birdseye, frozen foods pioneer
- 1909 Douglas Fairbanks Jr., actor
- 1915 Elizabeth Schwarzkopf, singer
- 1916 Kirk Douglas, actor
- 1929 Bob Hawke, Australian Prime Minister
- 1934 Dame Judi Dench, actress
- 1950 Joan Armatrading, singer
- 1953 John Malkovich, actor
- 1957 Donny Osmond, singer
- 1962 Felicity Huffman, actress

Deaths
- 1641 Anthony Van Dyck, painter
- 1964 Dame Edith Sitwell, poet and critic
- 1972 Louella Parsons, gossip columnist

HISTORICAL EVENTS
- 1758 Matthew Flinders and naval surgeon George Bass confirm that a channel exists between Australia's mainland and Van Diemen's Land (Tasmania).
- 1868 William Gladstone becomes Britain's Prime Minister, an office he held four times before his retirement in 1892, aged 85.
- 1960 Episode one of *Coronation Street*, Britain's longest-running soap opera, is aired on U.K. television.
- 1987 The first riots of the Palestinian *intifada* break out in the Israeli-occupied Gaza Strip (see below).
- 1992 Prince Charles and Princess Diana announce their plans to separate.
- 1992 U.S. Marines land in Mogadishu, Somalia, in an effort to bring relief to a country ravaged by civil war and famine.
- 2002 America's second-largest air carrier, United Airlines, files for "Chapter 11 bankruptcy" after losing $4 billion over the previous two years.

On this day in 1987, an Israeli truck crashed into a passenger vehicle in Gaza, killing four Palestinians. With Arab tensions already at breaking point over Israel's 20 years of occupation and continued appropriation of Palestinian land, the incident was seen as a deliberate act of revenge for the fatal stabbing of an Israeli a few days earlier. Rioting broke out the next day in the Jabalya refugee camp, the home of the four dead Palestinians, and quickly spread throughout the rest of the occupied territory of Gaza and the West Bank. This was the start of the *intifada*, or uprising. It was a rebellion waged with stones and gasoline bombs rather than firearms, as well as by non-violent means of resistance, such as strikes and the boycotting of Israeli goods. The intifada continued, despite sometimes brutal Israeli opposition, until the signing of the Declaration of Principles in September 1993, after which land was handed back to the Palestinians.

December 10

"We stand today at the threshold of a great event in the life of the United Nations and in the life of mankind." — ELEANOR ROOSEVELT, ON SUBMITTING THE DECLARATION OF HUMAN RIGHTS

HISTORICAL EVENTS

1868 The first traffic lights, comprising red and green gas lamps and semaphore arms, are installed near London's Houses of Parliament.

1898 Spain and the U.S. sign a peace treaty in Paris to end the Spanish–American War.

1901 The inaugural Nobel prizes are awarded, marking the fifth anniversary of the death of their Swedish instigator, Alfred Nobel (see right).

1902 In Egypt, the Aswan Dam is declared complete. Built to control the flow of the River Nile, it measures 130 feet (40 m) high and 1¼ miles (2 km) long, and took four years to construct.

1919 Brothers Ross and Keith Smith fly a Vickers Vimy from England to Australia in just under 28 days – the first aviators to cover the distance within 30 days.

1941 The British World War II battleship *Prince of Wales* and battle cruiser *Repulse* sink off Singapore, destroyed by Japanese torpedo bombers.

1948 In Paris, the UN General Assembly adopts and proclaims the Universal Declaration of Human Rights. The anniversary of the event is marked annually, as International Human Rights Day.

1963 A six-year-old Donny Osmond launches his singing career on the *Andy Williams Show* in America.

1996 President Nelson Mandela signs South Africa's new democratic constitution.

DAYS TO REMEMBER

Historical day Lux Mundi This Roman festival, meaning "light of the world," is still celebrated in Europe, especially France, where the day commemorates Liberty, the goddess of light.

National day Constitution Day (Thailand) This is a holiday commemorating the advent of the constitutional monarchy in Thailand in 1932. Previously, the country's government was an absolute monarchy.

Births		1952	Susan Dey, actress
1830	Emily Dickinson, poet	1960	Kenneth Branagh, actor
1870	Adolf Loos, architect	**Deaths**	
1914	Dorothy Lamour, actress and pin-up girl	1896	Alfred Nobel, chemist and philanthropist
1938	Billy Dunk, golfer	1967	Otis Redding, singer
		2005	Richard Pryor, comedian

The first Nobel prizes

The Nobel prizes, which award outstanding contributions in chemistry, physics, literature, medicine, and peace, were presented for the first time on this day in 1901. The prizes are funded by a legacy from Alfred Nobel, a brilliant Swedish chemist who made his fortune by inventing dynamite.

According to the terms of Nobel's will, the bulk of his fortune was to be placed in a fund, the interest from which would be "annually distributed in the form of prizes to those who, during the preceding year, shall have conferred the greatest benefit on mankind" in the various fields. Although never officially stated, it is thought that the pacifist Nobel created the prizes out of moral misgivings over the impact of his invention.

Jean Henri Dunant (pictured), the Swiss founder of the Red Cross, was among the first Nobel laureates, receiving the peace prize, while Wilhelm Röntgen was awarded the physics prize for his discovery of X-rays. Subsequent presentations have always taken place on December 10, marking the anniversary of Nobel's death in 1886, and are considered the world's most prestigious prizes in each field. The absence of a prize for mathematics is popularly attributed to the rumor that Nobel's love interest rejected him in favor of a famous mathematician of the time.

Among the many to have been honored over the years are Albert Einstein, Marie Curie, Winston Churchill, Martin Luther King, Jr., the Dalai Lama, Ernest Hemingway, and Nelson Mandela. In addition to a cash prize, the laureates receive a gold medal.

December 11

"I have found it impossible to … discharge my duties as King, as I would wish to do, without the help and support of the woman I love." — KING EDWARD VIII

HISTORICAL EVENTS

- **1894** The world's first auto show opens in Paris, showcasing four makes of vehicle.
- **1936** King Edward VIII abdicates after the British Government and Church of England condemn his decision to marry American divorcee Wallis Simpson.
- **1941** Germany and Italy declare war on the U.S. following President Franklin Roosevelt's announcement that America is at war with Japan after the Pearl Harbor attack.
- **1946** The United Nations International Children's Emergency Fund (UNICEF) is established (see below).
- **1994** Russian President Boris Yeltsin launches a massive military offensive against the breakaway Russian republic of Chechnya. The Chechen guerilla forces prove impossible to defeat, despite vast Russian superiority in terms of military force, and a peace agreement is signed by Yeltsin in 1996.
- **1997** At the Kyoto conference on global warming in Japan, 38 industrialized nations agree to set limits on greenhouse gas emissions.
- **1999** The Sistine Chapel reopens after 20 years of restoration work, which included the cleaning of Michelangelo's ceiling frescoes and his *Last Judgement* altar panel.
- **2005** Explosions at an oil storage terminal near Hemel Hempstead in Hertfordshire, England, cause a massive fire and a plume of smoke visible from space.
- **2005** Mob violence directed at people of Middle Eastern appearance erupts at Cronulla Beach in Sydney, Australia, in retaliation for the bashing of two local lifeguards a week earlier.

DAY TO REMEMBER

Historical day Day of Bruma The ancient Roman goddess of the winter season, Bruma, was honored in this annual festival.

Births
- **1803** Hector Berlioz, composer
- **1918** Aleksandr Solzhenitsyn, writer
- **1929** Sir Kenneth MacMillan, choreographer
- **1938** Reg Livermore, entertainer
- **1944** Brenda Lee, singer
- **1949** Teri Garr, actress
- **1950** Christina Onassis, heiress
- **1954** Jermaine Jackson, singer

Deaths
- **1964** Sam Cooke, soul singer
- **1996** William Rushton, actor, author, and cartoonist

UNICEF is formed

Following the end of World War II, the UN voted to establish the United Nations International Children's Emergency Fund (UNICEF) on this day in 1946, as a means to provide food, clothing and health care to children in countries devastated by war. It soon became apparent that a global focus was needed, to address the millions of children who were dying of sickness and starvation in Africa, Asia, Latin America and the Middle East. As a response, the UN decided in 1953 to extend UNICEF's mandate indefinitely.

It subsequently launched a global campaign against yaws, a disfiguring disease suffered by millions of children, but which is treatable with penicillin. In 1954, it took the pioneering step of using celebrities to further its cause, employing actor Danny Kaye as the first in a long line of UNICEF ambassadors. Audrey Hepburn, Harry Belafonte, Whoopi Goldberg, and Susan Sarandon are members of the list, past and present. In 1965, UNICEF was awarded the Nobel peace prize "for the promotion of brotherhood among nations."

The organization continued to develop as a powerful advocate of children's rights and, during the 1980s, helped the UN Commission on

Human Rights draft the Declaration of the Rights of the Child. This was to become the most widely ratified human rights treaty in history, with only Somalia and the U.S. voting in opposition. UNICEF would go on to serve a key role in enforcing the Declaration, which defines a child's rights to protection, education, health care, shelter, and sound nutrition.

December 12

"[She has] the smile of a woman who has just dined off her husband."
LAWRENCE DURRELL, ENGLISH NOVELIST, ON THE *MONA LISA*

Protests were a way of life at the women's peace camp that grew up around the military air base at Greenham Common in Berkshire, England. Established in 1981 in response to plans to store American cruise missiles on the site, it became the scene of numerous headline-making demonstrations, from the blockade of bomb-carrying vehicles, to the forming of a human chain around the site's perimeter fence on December 12, 1982. For some women, the camp was their permanent place of residence, which they listed as such on the electoral roll. "We provided a role model for non-violent direct action," said one regular visitor, during an interview with the BBC. "We also succeeded in fostering a women-only environment, where women learned that they didn't need to speak or act on men's terms."

HISTORICAL EVENTS

- **1800** Washington D.C. becomes the capital of the United States, replacing the interim capital Philadelphia.
- **1901** Guglielmo Marconi receives the first transatlantic radio signal in Newfoundland, using a 400-foot (120 m) antenna. Later studies show that the signal, sent from an incredibly powerful transmitter in Cornwall, England, must have bounced off the ionosphere twice to traverse that distance.
- **1913** Two years after it was stolen from the Louvre museum in Paris, Leonardo da Vinci's masterpiece *Mona Lisa* is located in a former Louvre employee's hotel room in Florence.
- **1939** Nylon, a new synthetic fiber invented by Wallace Carothers of DuPont, goes into commercial production at the company's new Seaford plant in Delaware, U.S.
- **1963** Kenya (formerly British East Africa) gains its independence from the U.K.
- **1980** American copyright law is amended to address computer software.
- **1982** In England, 30,000 female peace protesters form a human chain around the perimeter fence at Greenham Common military base (see above).

DAY TO REMEMBER

Religious day Our Lady of Guadalupe's Day The Virgin Mary appeared to Juan Diego in Mexico on this day c. 1531. She instructed him to pick roses and take them to the bishop. When he did so, an image of the Virgin Mary appeared on his cloak, which has been preserved at the Basilica of Our Lady of Guadalupe, in Mexico City.

Births
- 1821 Gustave Flaubert, novelist
- 1863 Edvard Munch, artist
- 1915 Frank Sinatra, singer and actor
- 1927 Honor Blackman, actress
- 1938 Connie Francis, singer
- 1949 Dionne Warwick, singer
- 1962 Tracy Austin, tennis ace

Deaths
- 1889 Robert Browning, poet
- 1939 Douglas Fairbanks, actor
- 1968 Tallulah Bankhead, actress
- 1995 Andrew Olle, journalist
- 1999 Joseph Heller, author
- 2003 Keiko, the killer whale from the *Free Willy* movies

December 13

"Dream as if you'll live forever. Live as if you'll die today." — JAMES DEAN

HISTORICAL EVENTS

1577 Francis Drake sets sail from Plymouth, England, on a round-the-world voyage that would last almost three years.

1642 Dutch explorer Abel Tasman becomes the first European to sight the group of islands now known as New Zealand.

1918 Woodrow Wilson, the first American President to visit Europe while in office, arrives in France to attend peace talks at Versailles.

1937 Nanking, then capital of China, falls to the Japanese, who embark on a six-week rampage, killing 300,000 people and leaving the city in smouldering ruins.

1951 James Dean launches his career by dancing around a jukebox in a Pepsi television commercial.

1955 Dame Edna Everage (Barry Humphries) makes her stage debut, at the Union Theatre in Melbourne, Australia (see right).

1995 The death of a black man in police custody leads to rioting in Brixton, south London. It is the area's third riot in 15 years which is triggered by racial tensions.

2003 After an eight-month hunt, American troops capture former Iraqi leader Saddam Hussein. He is found in a dishevelled state, hiding in an underground bunker near his home town of Tikrit, Iraq.

Births
- **1906** Sir Laurence van de Post, author
- **1925** Dick Van Dyke, actor
- **1927** Christopher Plummer, actor
- **1941** Anouska Hempel, actress
- **1948** Ted Nugent, rock musician
- **1967** Jamie Foxx, actor

Deaths
- **1784** Dr. Samuel Johnson, literary figure
- **1944** Wassily Kandinsky, painter
- **1961** Grandma Moses, painter

DAYS TO REMEMBER

Religious day St. Lucy's Day
This virgin martyr (c. 304) is said to have plucked out her eyes and given them to an unwelcome suitor, because he had obsessed about them. Her eyes were then miraculously restored, due to her great piety. St. Lucy (or St. Lucia) is the patron saint of writers and weavers.

National day Republic Day (Malta)
This former British colony celebrates becoming a republic within the Commonwealth of Nations on this day in 1974.

DATE*line*

Dame Edna Everage (pictured right), a satirical character created by Australian actor Barry Humphries, made her stage debut at the Union Theatre, Melbourne, on this day in 1955. The self-proclaimed "housewife megastar," with her trademark lilac-colored hair, winged spectacles, and outrageous frocks, has since taken on a life of her own to become an internationally celebrated stage and television personality. Demonstrating a passion for gladioli and invariably greeting audiences with the line "Hello possums," Dame Edna's searing wit often challenges as much as entertains. Among Humphries' other creations are the grotesque Australian cultural attaché Sir Les Patterson (pictured above) and trade union con-man Lance Boyle. Humphries (pictured left), who was born in Melbourne in 1934, is also an acclaimed landscape artist and author. He was awarded the Order of Australia in 1982.

December 14

"This is the equivalent of finding a small dinosaur alive on Earth."
PROFESSOR CARRICK CHAMBERS, ON THE DISCOVERY OF THE WOLLEMI PINE

HISTORICAL EVENTS

1900 Max Planck presents a paper to the German Physical Society, proposing that energy exists in discrete packets, which he called "quanta." It is an event that marks the birth of quantum physics.

1911 The race to the South Pole is won by Norwegian explorer Roald Amundsen and his team, who beat the British party led by Captain Robert Scott by 35 days.

1918 In Britain, women exercise their right to vote for the first time in a general election.

1959 In Detroit, Michigan, the Motown record label is formed by record producer Berry Gordy, Jr.

1986 Dick Rutan and Jeana Yeager embark on the first non-stop, un-refuelled flight in the pioneering *Voyager* aircraft. The plane is designed by the two pilots and Rutan's brother Burt, who goes on to conduct the first successful private space launch with *SpaceShip One*.

1994 The discovery of the Wollemi pine, a relic species from the dinosaur age found growing in the Blue Mountains, in Australia, makes news headlines (see below).

1995 Serb, Croat, and Muslim leaders sign a treaty in Paris, offering hopes for peace in Bosnia.

1999 Charles M. Schultz, creator of the *Peanuts* comic strip, announces he will be retiring after producing the cartoon for almost 50 years.

DAYS TO REMEMBER

Traditional day Agnostica This secular event commemorates the birth of quantum physics in 1900. Traditionally, Agnostica continues for an indeterminate time, from a few minutes to several weeks, as dictated by Heisenberg's Uncertainty Principle.

Historical day Halcyon Days In the Roman calendar, the Halcyon Days are the seven days preceding and following the winter solstice, when the waters of the Mediterranean remain unusually calm. The Greek festival honoring the Kingfisher goddess goes by the same name.

Births
- 1503 Nostradamus, astrologer, prophet, and physician
- 1895 George VI, King of England
- 1918 B. K. S. Iyengar, yoga advocate
- 1935 Lee Remick, actress
- 1946 Stan Smith, tennis ace
- 1946 Jane Birkin, actress
- 1948 Kim Beazley, Australian politician
- 1979 Sophie Monk, pop singer and actress

Deaths
- 1799 George Washington, first U.S. President
- 1964 William Bendix, actor
- 1989 Andrei Sakharov, dissident

Living "dinosaur" discovered

When news broke on this day that a tree from the Jurassic age, 200 million years ago, was growing in a wilderness area less than 100 miles (160 km) northwest of Sydney, Australia, it was heralded as the botanical find of the century. A grove of the native Australian conifer, the Wollemi pine, was discovered by a parks and wildlife officer, David Noble, growing in a deep canyon in the Wollemi National Park. The tree was given the botanical name *Wollemia nobilis* in recognition of both the park in which it was found and its discoverer. Among its closest living relatives are trees from the Araucariaceae family, which includes the Chilean monkey puzzle, the Norfolk Island pine and the New Zealand kauri.

The Wollemi pine has unusual frond-like foliage which changes color and becomes more spine-like as it matures. Male and female cones are produced on the same tree, and the bark has an unusual bubbly appearance. Multiple stems lend a bushy appearance to the tree, which grows to more than 110 feet (33 m) in height. Its buds develop a protective waxy coating during the colder months, which is possibly an adaptation that helped it survive the many ice ages it endured. In order to protect the species, of which only 100 adults have been found growing in the wild, the location of the gorge remains a secret. Seeds and cuttings were collected to establish a population outside the park and safeguard the tree's future.

December 15

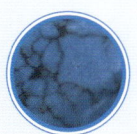

"I love you still, but in politics there is no heart, only head."

NAPOLEON, ON DIVORCING JOSÉPHINE

Hopes of bringing together Iraq's ethnic and religious groups were buoyed by the large numbers who turned out to vote in the nation's election on December 15, 2005, to choose the first full-term Government since the ousting of Saddam Hussein in April 2003. Officials estimate that about 10 million of the 15 million registered voters participated. Among those who streamed to polls were Sunni Arabs, who had stayed away in previous elections. "It's been a good day for Iraq," said Laith Kubba, a top aide to the transitional Prime Minister, Ibrahim al-Jaafari. Only scattered pockets of violence were reported, and UN observers declared the election valid, despite protests from Sunni Arabs that voting was rigged in favor of the main religious Shi'ite coalition.

HISTORICAL EVENTS

1791 The Bill of Rights becomes part of the U.S. Constitution.

1809 Emperor Napoleon divorces Joséphine for her failure to produce an heir. The divorce reportedly causes great anguish for both of them; Napoleon marries Marie Louise of Austria in 1811 and has a son with her soon after.

1978 President Jimmy Carter announces that the U.S. will recognize Communist China and sever ties with Taiwan, reversing the stance it had held since Mao Zedong's revolution in 1949.

1988 "Godfather of Soul" James Brown is imprisoned for aggravated assault and a string of other charges.

1993 In signing the Downing Street Declaration, the U.K. commits itself to searching for a solution to the problems of Northern Ireland.

1999 Two weeks of unrelenting rain in coastal Venezuela result in catastrophic floods and mud slides, which cause an estimated 30,000 deaths and leave 100,000 people homeless.

2005 Ten million Iraqis take part in the first democratic elections since the toppling of Saddam Hussein (see above).

Births
- 37 C.E. Nero, fifth Roman Emperor
- 1832 Gustave Eiffel, engineer
- 1892 J. Paul Getty, oil tycoon
- 1932 Edna O'Brien, writer
- 1942 Dave Clark, drummer
- 1949 Don Johnson, actor
- 1959 Greg Matthews, cricketer

Deaths
- 1675 Jan Vermeer, painter
- 1890 Sitting Bull, Sioux chief
- 1962 Charles Laughton, actor
- 1966 Walt Disney, animator

DAY TO REMEMBER

Traditional day Zamenhof Day This day commemorates the birthday of Ludwig Zamenhof, creator of the international language Esperanto. Zamenhof Day is observed as a holiday reunion for Esperantists.

December 16

"Always remember you are absolutely unique. Just like everyone else." — MARGARET MEAD

HISTORICAL EVENTS

1653 Oliver Cromwell is declared Lord Protector of England, following the execution of Charles I.

1773 In an act popularly known as the Boston Tea Party, colonists disguised as Mohawk Indians fling a cargo of tea into the harbor in protest of British taxes and trade restrictions.

1944 The Battle of the Bulge commences in Belgium, with Hitler's surprise offensive resulting in heavy losses on both German and Allied sides.

1944 American jazz composer and band-leader Glenn Miller's plane disappears over the English Channel on a flight to Paris.

1997 An episode of *Pokémon* on Japanese television causes epileptic seizures in an estimated 685 children (see right).

1998 U.S. President Bill Clinton calls for American and British airstrikes on Iraq in response to Saddam Hussein's non-compliance with UN weapons inspections.

DAYS TO REMEMBER

Religious day Posadas A nine-day festival to commemorate the journey of Joseph and Mary to Bethlehem begins on this day. *Posadas* is celebrated in Latin American countries, especially Mexico.

Religious day Cock Crow Mass During this feast, houses in the Philippines are strewn with star-shaped lanterns, symbolic of the star of Bethlehem. Just before dawn a band marches through streets to call people to church.

National day Victory Day (Bangladesh) This day marks the end of a nine-month war in 1971, following the Pakistani army's surrender in Dhaka and subsequent independence for its former province of Bangladesh.

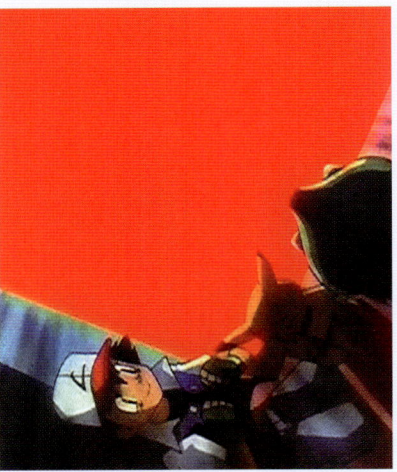

Cartoon episode causes seizures

About 20 minutes into an episode of the popular children's cartoon *Pokémon*, which screened on this day in 1997, the cartoon's main character Pikachu (shown above) caused an explosion with red and blue lights flashing in rapid succession. At this point some children began to experience feelings of nausea, blurred vision, headaches, and dizziness, while others suffered convulsions, seizures, and loss of consciousness. A reported 685 children were taken to hospital by ambulance. Although the majority recovered en route, more than 150 were admitted to hospital.

By way of explaining the high numbers of individuals affected, most of whom were children, a *Pokémon* website stated, "Photo-induced epileptic attacks can be caused by exhaustion, stress, and sitting too close to the television. Experts have speculated that the children were intensely focused and involved with the show when the scene went off like a bomb in their faces."

After the episode, entitled "Electric Soldier Porygon," went to air, further episodes of *Pokémon* were suspended while Japanese broadcasters and medical officials established guidelines for future animated programs that would prevent such an event from happening again. "Electric Soldier Porygon" is no longer broadcast anywhere in the world.

Births
- **1770** Ludwig van Beethoven, composer
- **1775** Jane Austen, novelist
- **1899** Sir Noel Coward, playwright
- **1901** Margaret Mead, anthropologist
- **1917** Arthur C. Clarke, sci-fi author
- **1938** Liv Ullmann, actress
- **1946** Benny Andersson, musician and songwriter (ABBA)
- **1963** Benjamin Bratt, actor
- **1967** Miranda Otto, actress

Deaths
- **1859** Wilhelm Grimm, fairytale collector
- **1965** William Somerset Maugham, writer
- **1985** Rock Hudson, actor
- **1989** Lee Van Cleef, actor
- **1994** Mary Durack, poet

December 17

"No one is useless in this world who lightens the burdens of another." — CHARLES DICKINS

HISTORICAL EVENTS

- **1538** King Henry VIII is excommunicated by Pope Paul III after declaring himself head of the Church of England.
- **1843** *A Christmas Carol*, by Charles Dickens, is published, to critical acclaim.
- **1903** Brothers Orville and Wilbur Wright make aviation history by managing the first successful flight in a heavier-than-air, mechanically propelled airplane, at Kitty Hawk, North Carolina.
- **1967** Australian Prime Minister Harold Holt disappears while swimming at Cheviot Beach, Victoria. His body is never recovered, spawning much speculation about whether he had in fact drowned as a result of strong currents (as is generally believed), or faked his own death.
- **1969** Singer Tiny Tim gets married to Victoria Budinger on live American television.
- **1983** Six people are killed and about 90 injured when an IRA car bomb explodes outside Harrods department store in London (see right).
- **1986** Davina Thompson becomes the first patient to receive a heart, lung and liver transplant, at Papworth Hospital in Cambridge, England.
- **1989** *The Simpsons*, a spin-off from *The Tracey Ullman Show*, premieres on U.S. television.

DAY TO REMEMBER

Historical day Saturnalia December 17 was the first day of this week-long ancient midwinter festival honoring the Roman god Saturn. During this time of feasting, wild merrymaking, and candle-lighting, no wars were fought or business conducted, and slaves and masters were treated as equals.

Births
- 1924 Clifton Pugh, artist
- 1936 Tommy Steele, singer and actor
- 1937 Kerry Packer, media magnate
- 1945 Christopher Cazenove, actor
- 1975 Milla Jovovich, actress

Deaths
- 1830 Simon Bolivar, revolutionary
- 1957 Dorothy L. Sayers, novelist and playwright

Kerry Packer, one of Australia's most successful business people, was born on this day in 1937.

The Harrods bombing

On this day in 1983, at the height of the Christmas shopping rush, a car bomb exploded outside the exclusive Harrods department store in Knightsbridge, London. The blast ripped through the crowded streets, billowing black smoke and scattering glass and debris in the path of unsuspecting shoppers. Three police officers and three members of the public were killed, and around 90 people injured.

Ambulances sped to the scene, ferrying those with serious injuries to hospital and treating the many walking wounded on the spot. Staff at Harrods reported seeing shattered shopfront windows blown into the store, and colleagues and shoppers who were badly wounded. The chaos continued as police attempted to clear the area, after what turned out to be a prank call caused them to suspect that more bombs might go off. They found their efforts thwarted by the crowds of panicking pedestrians.

The following day, the IRA admitted responsibility for planting the bomb and claimed to have given a clear warning about the explosion. A coded warning had been received at 2:45 p.m. local time on the day, but the bomb had detonated just 45 minutes later. The catastrophe came only days after the IRA issued a series of threats that it was planning to wage a pre-Christmas bombing campaign in London. As security in the capital was stepped up, the store reopened three days after the explosion. In a statement, Harrods' owners said the store refused to be defeated by acts of terrorism.

December 18

"I think greed is healthy. You can be greedy and still feel good about yourself."

IVAN BOESKY, MAY 18, 1986

HISTORICAL EVENTS

1915 ANZAC forces complete their retreat from Gallipoli, Turkey, without a casualty. The rest of the campaign had cost more than 10,000 Australian and New Zealand lives.

1916 The Battle of Verdun, the longest engagement of World War I, ends with close to half a million French and German troops killed and a similar number wounded.

1938 German chemist Otto Hahn and his team bombard uranium with neutrons, resulting in nuclear fission. The first person to split the atom, Hahn is unable to accept his Nobel prize in person, due to his imprisonment by the Allies, who incorrectly fear his involvement in a German atomic bomb project.

1972 Following the collapse of peace talks, the U.S. launches a massive bombing campaign in North Vietnam in an attempt to break the stalemate.

1987 New York financier Ivan Boesky is handed a three-year jail sentence and fined $100 million for insider dealing (see below).

1994 Australian fugitive Christopher Skase is a free man after a Spanish appeal court overturns an earlier extradition order on medical grounds. He had fled to Majorca in 1991 after the collapse of his business empire in Australia.

Births

1707 Charles Wesley, co-founder of Methodist movement
1879 Paul Klee, painter
1913 Willy Brandt, German Chancellor
1915 Betty Grable, actress and pin-up girl
1943 Keith Richards, musician
1946 Steve Biko, anti-apartheid activist
1946 Steven Spielberg, film director
1950 Gillian Armstrong, film director
1963 Brad Pitt, actor
1966 Kiefer Sutherland, actor
1978 Katie Holmes, actress
1980 Christina Aguilera, pop singer

Deaths

1737 Antonio Stradivari, violin maker
1993 Sam Wanamaker, actor

To many people, Ivan Boesky symbolized the excesses of the 1980s. The financier's speciality was trading stock in companies that were targeted for takeover, and by the mid-80s he had amassed a fortune estimated to be worth $200 million. On November 14, 1986, Boesky was charged by Wall Street's Securities and Exchange Commission (SEC) with insider dealing, following a tip-off arising from the prosecution in May of fellow Wall Street trader Denis Levine. Boesky pleaded guilty and on December 18, 1987, was sentenced to three years jail and fined $100 million. By agreeing to cooperate with the SEC in a Wall Street insider-trading investigation, Boesky helped to bring about the fall of junk bond king Michael Milken, and the "Guinness Four" in the U.K.

December 19

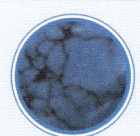

"I will never abandon the fight for human freedom. Peace depends on the freedom of each and every man." — ANDREI SAKHAROV, AFTER HIS RELEASE FROM EXILE

Panama City quickly became a battleground after President George H. W. Bush ordered 9,500 troops into the Central American country, on December 18, 1989. Only hours after the invasion, codenamed Operation Just Cause, General Manuel Noriega was ousted and Guillermo Endara sworn in as Prime Minister. Noriega, who the President wanted extradited to the U.S to face charges of drug trafficking, remained at large. A reward of $1 million was offered for information leading to his arrest. Tracking him down to the Vatican diplomatic mission in Panama City, the U.S. military resorted to playing loud rock music day and night to drive him out of hiding. The U.S. Government justified the invasion, which was condemned by the UN, because of earlier attacks by Noriega's paramilitary that had killed an American soldier and posed "an imminent danger to the 35,000 Americans in Panama." An estimated 19 American soldiers, 59 Panamanian troops, and 200 civilians were killed during Operation Just Cause.

HISTORICAL EVENTS

1932 The BBC begins shortwave transmission overseas with its Empire Service, the forerunner of its World Service.

1984 Harvard Professor Christoph Wolff announces his find of a collection of 33 unknown organ preludes, attributed to J. S. Bach, discovered in a Yale University library.

1986 Soviet leader Mikhail Gorbachev releases dissident Andrei Sakharov and his activist wife Yelena Bonner from internal exile. Sakharov, a prominent physicist, had been interned since January 1980 after criticizing Soviet intervention in Afghanistan.

1989 U.S. President George H. W. Bush orders U.S. troops into Panama to overthrow General Manuel Noriega's regime (see above).

1998 U.S. President Bill Clinton is impeached for perjury and obstruction of justice over the Monica Lewinsky affair, popularly called "Monicagate."

2003 Colonel Gaddafi's Libya makes a surprise pledge to destroy its arsenal of weapons of mass destruction.

Births
- 1902 Sir Ralph Richardson, actor
- 1906 Leonid Brezhnev, Soviet leader
- 1910 Jean Genet, novelist
- 1915 Edith Piaf, singer
- 1964 Beatrice Dalle, actress
- 1974 Ricky Ponting, cricketer
- 1980 Jake Gyllenhaal, actor

Deaths
- 1848 Emily Brontë, novelist
- 1851 William Turner, artist

December 20

"Being spokesman for a generation is the worst job I ever had." — BILLY BRAGG

HISTORICAL EVENTS

1860 South Carolina secedes from the United States, setting the course for the American Civil War.

1892 The pneumatic car tyre is patented in Syracuse, New York, by Alexander Brown and George Stillman.

1957 At the height of his fame, Elvis Presley receives his draft notice ordering him to join the U.S. Army for two years.

1979 The U.S. Congress intervenes to save car manufacturer Chrysler from bankruptcy by approving a $1.2 billion loan deal (see right).

1987 In the Philippines, the *Doña Paz* ferry sinks after colliding with an oil tanker, causing the deaths of more than 4,300 passengers and crew.

1991 Paul Keating is sworn in as Prime Minister of Australia, after defeating Bob Hawke in a party-room ballot.

1994 A sudden devaluation of the Mexican peso causes a currency crisis that ripples throughout the region in what becomes known as the "tequila effect." The U.S. Government responds with a $50 billion bail-out package to help restore stability.

DAY TO REMEMBER

Religious day St. Dominic of Silos' Day A Spanish-born Benedictine abbot, Dominic (c. 1073) rebeled against King Garcia III's demands that he turn over part of the land belonging to his monastery. He was exiled as a result.

Chrysler is rescued

In the mid-1970s, the Arab oil embargo, rising fuel prices, and falling sales both at home and abroad were taking a heavy toll. By 1979, Chrysler, the weakest of America's Big Three car manufacturers, was losing 6–8 million dollars a day and was teetering on the verge of bankruptcy.

The corporation appealed to the U.S. Government to organise a federal bail-out, as it had done earlier in the decade to save aviation company Lockheed. Initially, President Jimmy Carter was reticent, seeing such intervention as violating the principles of the free market. Conversely, allowing the American giant to crash would result in massive job losses at the Detroit car maker and hundreds of thousands more in related industries.

On December 20, 1979, a reluctant Congress passed the Chrysler Corporation Loan Guarantee Act, later signed into law on January 7, 1980. The rescue deal included $1.5 billion in federal loan guarantees and a package of concessions worth several billion dollars more from other parties, such as Chrysler's bankers, its dealers, and the union, with interests in the corporation's survival.

At a news conference in 1980, President Carter justified the Government's involvement as necessary "to avoid the loss of hundreds of thousands of American jobs." Aided by the rescue package and the introduction of some innovative car and mini-van models, Chrysler avoided bankruptcy and slowly fought its way back from the brink.

Births

1894 Sir Robert Menzies, Australian Prime Minister
1905 "Tiger" Bill O'Reilly, Australian cricketer
1944 Ray Martin, reporter and television host
1946 Uri Geller, psychic
1952 Jenny Agutter, actress
1957 Billy Bragg, singer and songwriter

Deaths

1968 John Steinbeck, author
1973 Bobby Darin, singer
1983 Bill Brandt, photographer
1996 Carl Sagan, astronomer

December 21

The winter solstice in the Northern Hemisphere marks the shortest day and longest night. In the Southern Hemisphere, the summer solstice marks the longest day and shortest night.

"There are three kinds of lies: Lies, damned lies, and statistics." — BENJAMIN DISRAELI

Police and emergency services pick through the wreckage of Pan Am Flight 103, which exploded over the Scottish town of Lockerbie on the evening of December 21, 1988. A bomb in the cargo hold detonated an hour after the jumbo departed London for New York, killing all 259 passengers and crew on board as well as 11 people on the ground, as flaming plane parts rained down on the town and surrounding countryside. Witnesses of the tragedy, Britain's worst air disaster, described a "fireball" falling from the sky. In early 2001, a Libyan agent was convicted of masterminding the bombing and sentenced to life in prison.

HISTORICAL EVENTS

- **1620** Pilgrims on *The Mayflower* land at Plymouth, Massachusetts, where they establish one of America's earliest successful colonies.
- **1913** The world's first crossword puzzle, devised by Arthur Wynne, is published in the *New York World* newspaper. It becomes a weekly feature, and by the time a crossword puzzle book is released in 1924, the idea has become a global craze.
- **1948** With the signing of the Republic of Ireland Act, enforced on April 18, 1949, the state of Eire becomes a republic and leaves the British Commonwealth.
- **1958** General Charles de Gaulle wins a landslide election victory to become the first President of France's Fifth Republic.
- **1962** The U.S. agrees to supply Polaris missiles to the U.K. as part of a multilateral NATO nuclear deterrent.
- **1975** Pro-Palestinian militants led by Venezuelan terrorist Carlos the Jackal raid an Organization of Petroleum Exporting Countries (OPEC) meeting in Vienna, Austria, killing three people and taking 70 others hostage.
- **1988** Pan Am Flight 103 to New York explodes over Lockerbie, Scotland (see above).

DAYS TO REMEMBER

Religious day Karachun This Pagan festival is a Slavic version of Halloween, when the Black God and other evil spirits are most potent. On this night, Hors, the old sun, is defeated by the dark powers of the Black God. On December 23, Hors is resurrected and becomes the new sun, Koleda.

Religious day St. Thomas Becket's Day Thomas Becket (1118–1170) was Henry II's Lord Chancellor and close friend. When made Archbishop of Canterbury, Thomas' loyalty to the Church regularly put him in opposition to the king, who in a fit of exasperation ordered him to be murdered.

Births

- **1118** Thomas Becket, Archbishop of Canterbury
- **1804** Benjamin Disraeli, British statesman
- **1879** Josef Stalin, Russian dictator
- **1937** Jane Fonda, actress
- **1940** Frank Zappa, musician
- **1948** Samuel L. Jackson, actor
- **1953** Tina Brown, journalist and editor
- **1954** Chris Evert, tennis ace
- **1966** Kiefer Sutherland, actor
- **1969** Julie Delpy, actress

Deaths

- **1940** F. Scott Fitzgerald, author
- **1945** General George Patton, Commander of the U.S. 3rd Army

December 22

"There is no feeling, except the extremes of fear and grief, that does not find relief in music."
— GEORGE ELIOT

HISTORICAL EVENTS

- **1938** The coelacanth, a fish considered to be extinct for 70 million years, is discovered in the Indian Ocean.
- **1964** The first flight of an SR-71 reconnaissance aircraft takes place. The planes, capable of speeds in excess of Mach 3, flew 3,551 missions before being retired in 1989, without the loss of a single aircraft for any reason.
- **1974** A bomb, thought to be planted by the IRA, explodes at the London home of the Conservative leader and former Prime Minister Edward Heath. Heath was absent and there were no casualties, despite extensive damage to the property.
- **1984** Bernhard Hugo Goetz achieves notoriety as a New York subway vigilante when he shoots four African American youths who allegedly tried to rob him.
- **1988** Chico Mendes, Brazilian rubber tapper and environmental campaigner, is shot dead by the son of a cattle rancher.
- **1993** In Australia, the Federal Government's Native Title Bill is passed (see below).
- **2000** Pop singer Madonna marries British film director Guy Ritchie in Scotland.

Star sign

CAPRICORN
December 22–January 20

People born under the sign of the goat are said to be practical, ambitious, and persevering. Blessed with intelligence and great organizational skills, these high achievers need to balance work and play. Their off-beat sense of humor, adventurous spirit, and loyalty make them good companions. In love, they look for a lasting relationship with someone who will lavish them with affection.

DAYS TO REMEMBER

Religious day Tohji-Taisai This Shinto festival honors the Japanese sun goddess Amaterasu, who, having withdrawn into a cave, needs to be enticed out with music and dance.

Religious day Festival of Wang-Mu This is a Taoist holy day honoring the Empress Mother and celebrating the pinnacle of the feminine 'yin' half of the year.

Births
- **1890** Charles de Gaulle, leader of France
- **1907** Dame Peggy Ashcroft, actress
- **1913** Benjamin Britten, composer
- **1943** Billie Jean King, tennis ace
- **1949** Robin and Maurice Gibb, musicians
- **1961** Yuri Ivanovich Malenchenko, cosmonaut
- **1962** Ralph Fiennes, actor
- **1972** Vanessa Paradis, model and actress

Deaths
- **1440** Giles de Laval, the original "Bluebeard"
- **1880** George Eliot, novelist
- **1943** Beatrix Potter, author and illustrator
- **1989** Samuel Beckett, playwright
- **2002** Joe Strummer, musician

Native Title legislation is passed

After a long battle by the indigenous people of Australia for recognition of land rights in their country, the federal Labor Government under Prime Minister Paul Keating introduced Native Title legislation on December 22, 1993. The Act, which came into effect on January 1, 1994, defined native title as the traditional rights and interests held by Aboriginal and Torres Strait Islander people in relation to land.

The legislation followed the landmark Mabo decision of June 3, 1992, in which the High Court of Australia ruled that Eddie Mabo and the Meriam people had the traditional right to possess and inhabit the lands under dispute. The Mabo decision also acknowledged that Australia was not *terra nullius* (land belonging to no one), as had been claimed since European settlement, but belonged to Aboriginal and Torres Strait Islander people. The Act never properly clarified whether the same applied to land subject to pastoral leases. This was later put to the test in the Wik case, regarding land in Queensland's Western Cape York. On December 23, 1996, the High Court made the controversial ruling that the rights of native title and those of pastoralists could coexist, although those of the latter would prevail in the event of a conflict.

December 23

"When I have a terrible need of – shall I say the word – religion… I go out and paint the stars." — VINCENT VAN GOGH

Births
- **1805** Joseph Smith, founder of the Mormon Church
- **1853** Giacomo Puccini, composer
- **1918** Helmut Schmidt, German Chancellor
- **1965** Slash, guitarist
- **1965** Eddie Vedder, rock singer (Pearl Jam)

Deaths
- **1834** Robert Malthus, economist and demographer
- **1996** Ronnie Scott, jazz musician

HISTORICAL EVENTS

1888 Dutch painter Vincent Van Gogh slices off the lower part of his left ear with a razor following an argument with fellow artist Paul Gauguin.

1947 The transistor is introduced by John Bardeen, Walter Brattain, and William Shockley of Bell Labs, heralding a new era in electronics.

1948 Japanese general Hideki Tojo and six other military leaders are hanged for crimes against humanity.

1956 British and French forces pull out of Egypt, ending their armed occupation that followed President Abdel Nasser's nationalisation of the Suez Canal.

1972 An earthquake rocks the Nicaraguan capital, Managua, sparking huge fires and flattening large areas of the city center. More than 10,000 people are thought to have perished in the disaster.

1986 The *Voyager* aircraft, piloted by Americans Dick Rutan and Jeana Yeager, completes the first non-stop flight around the globe on one load of fuel.

1992 The Queen's Christmas speech is leaked and published in a national newspaper (see right).

1997 Woody Allen, 62, causes controversy by marrying Soon-Yi Previn, 27, the adopted daughter of his ex-wife Mia Farrow.

DAYS TO REMEMBER

National day Emperor's Birthday (Japan) The birthday of the current Emperor is always observed as a national holiday in Japan. Presently it is December 23.

Traditional day Festivus This is a fictional holiday invented as a plot device in an episode of the sitcom *Seinfeld*. Created as a reaction to the commercialism of Christmas, Festivus quickly caught on and is now celebrated by fans of the show.

National day Night of the Radishes (Mexico) Celebrated in Oaxaca, Mexico, by artists carving nativity scenes out of giant Mexican radishes.

The monarchy's year of woe

The Queen's *annus horribilis* of 1992, the year she celebrated her fortieth anniversary as the reigning British monarch, came to a fitting close when the *Sun* tabloid newspaper published a leaked copy of her Christmas Day speech in its December 23 edition. Certainly, little had gone right for the Windsors that year. On March 9, the Duke and Duchess of York had announced their separation, which was followed by the news on April 13 that the Princess Royal had begun divorce proceedings to end her 18-year marriage to Captain Mark Phillips.

Then came revelations that rocked the monarchy, with the publishing of Andrew Morton's biography, *Diana: Her True Story*, on June 7. In it, the royal reporter claimed that the Princess had made five attempts at suicide and that her marriage to the "uncaring" Prince Charles was clearly a sham. More royal scandal hit the headlines on August 20 when a topless Fergie was photographed having her toes sucked by her Texan "financial adviser" John Bryan.

The year drew to a close with a devastating fire at the royals' home of Windsor Castle on November 20, then the news that the Prince and Princess of Wales were to separate. Among the rare royal highlights of 1992 was the marriage of the Princess Royal to Commander Tim Laurence, during a modest ceremony in Scotland, on December 12.

December 24

"The Moon is essentially gray. No color. Looks like plaster of Paris. Sort of a grayish beach sand." APOLLO 8 ASTRONAUT, JAMES LOVELL

Births
- 1167 John, King of England
- 1881 Juan Ramón Jiménez, poet
- 1888 Michael Curtiz, film director
- 1905 Howard Hughes, politician and aviator
- 1922 Ava Gardner, actress

Deaths
- 1524 Vasco da Gama, navigator
- 1863 William Makepeace Thackeray, writer
- 1994 John Osborne, dramatist

After disappearing a month earlier, leaving behind a pile of his clothes on a Miami beach, British politician John Stonehouse, 49, re-emerged in Melbourne, Australia, on December 24, 1974, carrying a false passport and accompanied by his former secretary, Sheila Buckley, 28. The Labour MP, who claimed to be in Australia "to establish a new life," was later extradited to the U.K., where he faced charges of fraud relating to a series of failed businesses he had set up before faking his death. On August 6, 1976, the man once seen as a likely future prime minister of Britain was sentenced to seven years in jail after a marathon 68-day trial. Stonehouse was released after three years, and died in 1988 of a heart attack, aged 62.

HISTORICAL EVENTS

- 1851 Fire rips through the Library of Congress in Washington D.C., destroying 35,000 volumes, including most of Thomas Jefferson's personal collection, acquired in 1815.
- 1865 Six Confederate veterans of the American Civil War establish the Ku Klux Klan, in Pulaski, Tennessee.
- 1968 The *Apollo 8* astronauts are the first humans to orbit the Moon, flying 69 miles (110 km) away from its surface.
- 1974 Former British Cabinet Minister John Stonehouse is arrested in Melbourne, Australia, after faking his own death (see above).
- 1994 In Algiers, an Air France plane bound for Paris is hijacked by four Islamic terrorists and flown to Marseilles before being stormed by French commandos. The hijackers kill three hostages but don't survive the rescue mission.
- 1997 Venezuelan terrorist "Carlos the Jackal" (real name Ilich Ramirez Sanchez) is handed a life prison sentence for three murders committed in Paris in 1975.
- 2003 America's first suspected outbreak of BSE (mad cow disease), in Washington State, prompts several countries to ban imports of U.S. beef.

DAYS TO REMEMBER

Religious day Christmas Eve In the Roman Catholic Church, the Christmas season liturgically begins on Christmas Eve. In some European countries, Christmas presents are opened on Christmas Eve.

National day Sowans Nicht A traditional Scottish name for Christmas Eve, when a dish made from oak husks and fine meal (called *sowan*) would be eaten, and rowan branches burnt to symbolize the putting aside of any bad feelings for yuletide.

Celtic tree sign

BIRCH
December 24–January 20

The birch tree symbolizes rebirth, and so people born under this sign possess the energy to foster new beginnings. They are ambitious, imaginative, and patient. In the same way as the tree, they can appear fragile and delicate but have an inner strength that allows them to triumph over adversity. Vivacious, loyal, and friendly, they have an integrity that shines like the white bark of the tree.

December 25

DATE*line*

"Nothing is permanent in this wicked world — not even our troubles." — CHARLIE CHAPLIN

HISTORICAL EVENTS

1914 During World War I, an unofficial Christmas truce takes place between British and German troops on the Western Front.

1926 Prince Hirohito becomes the 124th Emperor of Japan. He reigned until his death in 1989, the longest-serving Emperor in Japanese history.

1938 After auditioning hundreds of actresses for the role of Scarlett O'Hara in *Gone With the Wind*, producer David O. Selznick offers the coveted part to Vivien Leigh.

1974 Cyclone Tracy hits Darwin, Australia, killing some 63 people, injuring hundreds, and destroying 90 percent of the city's buildings.

1989 Former Romanian president Nicolae Ceausescu and his wife, Elena, are shot by a firing squad after being found guilty of genocide and crimes against the state.

1991 Mikhail Gorbechev resigns as President of the Soviet Union, signaling the end of the USSR (see below).

2003 Shortly before its scheduled landing on Mars, the British-built *Beagle 2* space probe mysteriously vanishes, never to be heard from again.

Births
- **1642** Isaac Newton, physicist and mathematician
- **1887** Conrad Hilton, hotel mogul
- **1870** Helena Rubinstein, cosmetician
- **1899** Humphrey Bogart, actor
- **1907** Cab Calloway, band-leader
- **1946** Jimmy Buffett, singer and songwriter
- **1949** Sissy Spacek, actress
- **1954** Annie Lennox, singer
- **1968** Helena Christensen, model and actress
- **1971** Dido, singer

Deaths
- **1946** W. C. Fields, actor
- **1977** Charlie Chaplin, actor
- **1983** Joan Miro, artist
- **1995** Dean Martin, singer and actor

DAYS TO REMEMBER

Religious day Christmas Day Literally the "mass of Christ," Christmas is a Christian holiday celebrating the birth of Jesus in Bethlehem, Judea. In modern times, the secular aspects of Christmas have tended to overshadow the religious significance of the day.

Historical day Newtonmas This annual celebration of science marks the birthday of Isaac Newton. Observed since 1984 or earlier, the event is also known as Gravmas, a play on "gravitational mass." Practices associated with the day include decorating a Christmas tree with apples and the exchange of educational gifts.

Last days of the Soviet Union

With the announcement of his resignation, President Mikhail Gorbachev brought the final chapter of the Soviet Union's existence to a close on December 25, 1991. He had served as leader of the U.S.S.R. for almost seven years, and as its executive president for nearly two. Only a year earlier, he had won the Nobel Peace Prize for his role in ending the Cold War, and *Time* magazine had named him both "Man of the Year" and "Man of the Decade" in 1989.

While celebrated in the West, in the Soviet Union his support and popularity had gradually diminished as economic conditions worsened following the reforms he had implemented. The fatal blows were dealt when the republics of Russia, Belarus, and the Ukraine met in secret and subsequently declared the formation of a new union, the Commonwealth of Independent States (CIS), on December 8. Four days later, they were joined by eight more republics.

In his 10-minute resignation speech, which was broadcast live on television, the 60-year-old Gorbachev said, "In light

of recent events and the formation of the Commonwealth of Independent States, I hereby resign the office of president of the Union of Soviet Socialist Republics." Control of the former Soviet Union's nuclear force was handed over to Boris Yeltsin, the first Prime Minister of the new Russia. As Gorbachev delivered his short speech, the red Soviet flag was being lowered over the Kremlin and replaced with the white–blue–red tricolor of the Russian state.

December 26

"A scientist in his laboratory is not only a technician: He is also a child placed before natural phenomena which impress him like a fairy tale." — MARIE CURIE

The coastal communities of 11 nations bordering the Indian Ocean had little or no warning of the catastrophe that was about to unfold on December 26, 2004. An earthquake of 9.0 magnitude, thought to be the second-largest ever recorded, struck off the coast of Indonesia at 8:00 A.M. local time. This triggered a massive tsunami that spawned waves up to 100 feet (30 m) high, which wreaked havoc on coastlines as far away as Somalia, in Africa. The exact number of victims remains unknown, although more than 200,000 people are confirmed to have perished. The Indonesian Province of Aceh (its capital, Banda Aceh, is pictured), closest to the earthquake's epicenter, suffered the most from the tsunami's deadly passage, with an estimated 170,000 lives lost. More than a million people were left homeless, with their livelihoods destroyed from the damage left in the tsunami's wake.

HISTORICAL EVENTS

1492 Christopher Columbus founds his first settlement, La Navidad, in South America, with crew members from the *Santa Maria*, which ran aground on Christmas Eve.

1898 Scientists Pierre and Marie Curie announce their discovery of the radioactive element radium.

1908 In Sydney, Australia, Texan Jack Johnson becomes the first African American boxer to win the world heavyweight title, knocking out Canadian Tommy Burns in the fourteenth round.

1939 A massive earthquake, measuring 8 on the Richter Scale, rocks Erzincan, Turkey, with the loss of over 30,000 lives.

1943 British warships sink the German battleship *Scharnhorst* in the Barents Sea. Only 36 members of its crew of almost 2,000 survived.

1982 *Time* magazine deviates from its annual tradition of naming a "Man of the Year" by choosing a "Machine of the Year," the computer.

2003 Close to 26,000 people perish in a massive earthquake that rocks the ancient city of Bam in southeastern Iran.

2004 A tsunami devestates 11 nations bordering the Indian Ocean, with a loss of more than 250,000 lives (see above).

DAYS TO REMEMBER

Religious day St. Stephen's Day St. Stephen (c. 35 C.E.) was a Jew who became one of the first church deacons of Jerusalem. He was accused of blasphemy and stoned to death, making him the first Christian martyr.

Traditional day Boxing Day The day after Christmas, called Boxing Day in countries of the British Commonwealth, is a public holiday in most Christian nations, with the notable exception of the U.S. The name comes from the small boxes traditionally used to collect donations, typically holiday cash for tradesmen, on this day.

Births
- **1855** Arnold Ludwig Mendelssohn, composer
- **1891** Henry Miller, author
- **1893** Mao Zedong, founding father of the People's Republic of China
- **1901** Georgy Mikhaylovich Rimsky-Korsakov, composer
- **1939** Fred Schepisi, film director
- **1949** Phil Spector, record producer
- **1971** Jared Leto, actor

Deaths
- **1970** Lillian Board, Olympic athlete
- **1972** Harry Truman, twenty-third U.S. President
- **1999** Curtis Mayfield, soul singer and songwriter
- **2001** Nigel Hawthorne, actor

December 27

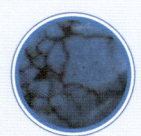

"The highest possible stage in moral culture is when we recognize that we ought to control our thoughts." — CHARLES DARWIN

Births
- 1571 Johannes Kepler, astronomer
- 1822 Louis Pasteur, bacteriologist
- 1879 Sydney Greenstreet, actor
- 1879 Robert Greig, actor
- 1901 Marlene Dietrich, actress
- 1944 Bob Brown, Australian Senator
- 1948 Gérard Depardieu, actor
- 1952 David Knopfler, musician
- 1953 Kevin Wright, cricketer

Deaths
- 1943 Curtis Veeder, inventor
- 2003 Alan Bates, actor

HISTORICAL EVENTS

1831 Naturalist Charles Darwin sets sail from Plymouth, England, in HMS *Beagle*, bound for South America on what would be a five-year voyage.

1934 In Tehran, the Government declares that Persia will be renamed Iran.

1945 The World Bank and International Monetary Fund come into formal existence.

1949 After heavy international lobbying, as well as warfare for independence, Queen Juliana of the Netherlands signs a treaty ending Dutch colonial rule of Indonesia.

1979 Soviet troops invade Afghanistan to support the country's embattled Marxist Government.

1985 American naturalist Dian Fossey is found murdered at a gorilla research station in Rwanda (see right).

1997 Protestant paramilitary leader Billy Wright is murdered by a rival faction of inmates at the maximum-security Maze prison in Northern Ireland.

2004 Opposition leader Viktor Yushchenko gains victory in the re-run of Ukraine's presidential election, after the country's Supreme Court declared the first election a fraud.

DAYS TO REMEMBER

Religious day St. John's Day St. John the Apostle and Evangelist was a Galilean fisherman until called by Jesus, with his brother St. James, to be a disciple. He later went to Ephesus, where he wrote the Gospel of St. John. He is said to have drunk poison to prove the power of God, and was left unharmed.

Historical day Birthday of Freya In Norse culture, the birthday of Freya, the goddess of fertility, love, and beauty, was celebrated on this day. She is associated with the plant mistletoe, said to bestow health, fertility, and peace, a symbolism that has translated into the secular tradition of kissing under the mistletoe.

Death of a naturalist

The blood-stained body of Dian Fossey was found on December 27, 1985. An American scientist who had spent the previous 18 years protecting rare mountain gorillas in a remote part of Central Africa, she had been murdered in her jungle cabin at Karisoke, the research camp she founded in 1967 in Rwanda. Certainly, Fossey's was dangerous work, based in an isolated area, rife with armed poachers, and in a country plagued by tribal wars and political instability.

While the gorillas themselves also posed a potential danger, Fossey worked hard to gain their trust and built extraordinary bonds with the creatures. In 1970, a young adult male, named Peanuts, touched her hand, the first recorded human contact with the species.

As well as producing numerous scientific publications based on her research, Fossey penned a single book, *Gorillas in the Mist*, which brought her posthumous fame when, in 1988, it was made into a Hollywood film of the same name, starring Sigourney Weaver. Public exposure to her work, through articles in *National Geographic*, and the donations that followed, allowed Fossey to dedicate her life to her work.

In 1977, when a gorilla named Digit, with whom she had built a special rapport, was killed by poachers, Fossey embarked on a personal war against poaching. As well as her controversial "active conservation" methods, which included carrying a pistol to ward off poachers, she established the first ranger patrols in Rwanda.

Fossey was 53 when she died, which was four years before a new census revealed that the mountain gorilla population had finally reversed its previously downward trend. The words inscribed on her gravestone are a fitting epitaph: "No one loved gorillas more."

December 28

"I belong to the Russian convict world no less than I do to Russian literature. I got my education there, and it will last forever." — ALEKSANDR SOLZHENITSYN

Seas were calm and skies were blue when the 115 yachts competing in the 630-nautical-mile (1,167 km) Sydney to Hobart yacht race set sail on December 26, 1998. But by the time the boats hit a stretch of ocean popularly known as "hell on high water," south of Eden, New South Wales, it was an entirely different story. A severe storm, with waves up to 32 feet (11 m) high and winds of comparable strength to a low-category hurricane, unleashed its fury. As December 28 drew to a close, six sailors had been reported lost, later confirmed drowned. The U.S. maxi yacht *Sonara* (pictured) was first to reach the Tasmanian capital, one of only 44 boats to cross the finishing line. A coroner's inquest deemed that the race organizers had "abdicated...responsibility to manage the race," and was critical of the Bureau of Meteorology in not keeping officials properly informed of the storm's upgrading.

HISTORICAL EVENTS

1065 London's Westminster Abbey is consecrated, shortly before the funeral of King Edward the Confessor, who ordered its building.

1895 French brothers Louis and Auguste Lumière screen the first true motion picture on their new invention, the *cinématographe*, which gave birth to the word *cinema*.

1908 Europe's most destructive earthquake and tsunami devastate cities and towns around the Straits of Messina, between Sicily and mainland Italy, killing an estimated 100,000 people.

1973 In Paris, Aleksandr Solzhenitsyn publishes *The Gulag Archipelago*, his powerful literary account of the Soviet Union's prison camp system.

1973 U.S. President Richard Nixon signs the Endangered Species Act, providing broad protection for wildlife, fish, and plant species listed as threatened or endangered in the U.S. or elsewhere.

1989 Australia suffers its first fatalities from an earthquake, at Newcastle, New South Wales, which causes the loss of 11 lives.

1998 The search continues for sailors lost at sea as violent storms lash competing yachts in the annual Sydney to Hobart race (see above).

DAY TO REMEMBER

Religious day Feast Day for The Holy Innocents A feast day commemorating King Herod's massacre of children in Bethlehem, this is traditionally considered the unluckiest day of the year. In Spain and Latin American countries it is a day for pranks, similar to April Fool's Day.

Births

- **1856** Woodrow Wilson, twenty-eighth U.S. President
- **1922** Stan Lee, comics artist and creator of Spiderman and the Incredible Hulk
- **1932** Roy Hattersley, British politician
- **1934** Maggie Smith, actress
- **1947** Andrew Ollie, journalist
- **1953** Richard Clayderman, pianist
- **1954** Denzel Washington, actor
- **1956** Nigel Kennedy, violinist
- **1960** John Fitzgerald, tennis player
- **1972** Patrick Rafter, tennis player

Deaths

- **1734** Rob Roy (Robert MacGregor), outlaw
- **1932** John Blackham, cricketer
- **1937** Maurice Ravel, composer
- **1983** Dennis Wilson, musician
- **2004** Susan Sontag, writer and activist

December 29

"I have never found, in a long experience of politics, that criticism is ever inhibited by ignorance." — HAROLD MACMILLAN

HISTORICAL EVENTS

1890 In the last major act of resistance by Native Americans, 150 Sioux are shot by U.S. troops at Wounded Knee, South Dakota.

1895 Dr. Leander Starr Jameson commences his disastrous raid on Johannesburg, in a bid to overthrow the Transvaal's anti-British Boer Government. The raid is believed to have been central in triggering the Second Boer War.

1916 *A Portrait of the Artist as a Young Man* by James Joyce is published in New York. The semi-autobiographical book becomes one of his best-known works, despite being initially rejected for publication.

1940 At the height of the Blitz bombing campaign in London, German incendiary bombs create a firestorm in the historic heart of the city. Miraculously, St. Paul's Cathedral survives.

1972 After their rescue, survivors of a Uruguayan plane crash in the Andes admit to eating the bodies of fellow passengers to stay alive.

1997 Hong Kong begins a massive cull of all chickens within its territory to prevent the spread of avian flu to humans (see below).

1998 Khmer Rouge leaders publicly apologize for the deaths of an estimated 1.7 million Cambodians during the "killing fields" atrocities of the 1970s.

Births

- **1721** Jeanne-Antoinette Pompadour, Louis XV's mistress
- **1809** William Ewart Gladstone, British statesman
- **1825** Jacques Louis David, artist
- **1936** Mary Tyler Moore, actress
- **1938** Jon Voight, actor
- **1947** Marianne Faithfull, singer
- **1947** Ted Danson, actor
- **1960** David Boon, cricketer
- **1972** Jude Law, actor
- **1974** Brad Hodge, cricketer

Deaths

- **1170** Thomas Becket, Archbishop of Canterbury
- **1890** Big Foot, Sioux Indian chief
- **1967** Paul Whiteman, jazz band-leader
- **1986** Harold Macmillan, British statesman
- **2003** Bob Monkhouse, comedian and television host

The bird flu cull

In Hong Kong, hundreds of poultry markets and farms were the scenes of mass slaughter on this day in 1997, after the Government ordered the culling of the territory's entire chicken population. The drastic measure was a precautionary move to prevent an outbreak of bird flu at a local poultry farm and wholesale market from infecting humans. Earlier in the year, the first documented cases of the transfer of the virus to humans had been recorded in Hong Kong. The virus caused severe respiratory illness in 18 people, six of whom died.

Government teams wearing gloves and face masks executed the cull, collecting the carcasses in plastic garbage bags, and scrubbing down premises with disinfectant. The bags were then transported to Government landfill sites across the territory for disposal. Within three days, an estimated 1.2 million chickens had been slaughtered, as well as unspecified numbers of ducks, geese, quail, and other poultry. Authorities believe at least some of the infected chickens came from mainland China, which supplies around 80 percent of Hong Kong's poultry. Emergency legislation was passed to compensate farmers and vendors for their losses.

December 30

"If history is taught in the form of stories, it would never be forgotten." RUDYARD KIPLING

Births
- 1865 Rudyard Kipling, author
- 1879 Sri Rámana Maharshi, Hindu yogi and philosopher
- 1945 Davy Jones, musician
- 1945 Mike Nesmith, musician
- 1946 Patti Smith, musician
- 1959 Tracey Ullman, comedienne and entertainer
- 1961 Ben Johnson, athlete
- 1965 Heidi Fleiss, Hollywood madam
- 1969 Jay Kay, singer (Jamiroquai)
- 1975 Tiger Woods, golfer

Deaths
- 1916 Grigori Rasputin, monk
- 1944 Erwin Rommel, Field Marshall
- 1979 Richard Rogers, composer
- 2003 Nora Heysen, artist
- 2004 Artie Shaw, musician

HISTORICAL EVENTS

1903 Some 600 people perish when Chicago's newly opened Iroquois Theater goes up in flames, despite being advertised as "absolutely fireproof."

1913 An explosion at a colliery in South Wales kills 439 miners, becoming the worst mining disaster in British history.

1922 The Union of Soviet Socialist Republics (U.S.S.R.), or Soviet Union, is formally established.

1924 American astronomer Edwin Hubble reveals that there are galaxies beyond the Milky Way. He is one of the first to postulate that the red shift he observes in the light spectrum from these distant galaxies is caused by the continuing expansion of the universe.

1986 The use of canaries to indicate the presence of harmful gases is discontinued in favor of hand-held gas detectors in Britain's coal mines (see below).

1999 Former *Beatles* member George Harrison is stabbed several times in the chest by an intruder who broke into his home in Oxfordshire, England. He recovers from the attack and lives another two years before dying from lung cancer.

DAYS TO REMEMBER

National day Rizal Day (Philippines) This commemorates the execution of the country's proclaimed national hero, José Rizal, who died for his motherland on December 30, 1896. He was condemned for a rebellion against the Spanish.

National day Kwanzaa Created in California in 1966, this week-long celebration of African American heritage offers an alternative holiday to Christmas and is observed mostly in the U.S. Activities center around candle-lighting, feasting, and gift-giving, and homes are decorated with colorful African cloth and fresh fruit.

A British mining tradition of using canaries to detect the presence of dangerous gases underground came to a close on December 30, 1986, when the Government announced that the yellow-feathered birds were being superseded by electronic detectors. Canaries had been the miners' constant companions since 1911, with two birds employed in each pit. The birds are highly sensitive to toxic gases, such as carbon monoxide, which is colorless, odorless, and tasteless, and the explosive gas methane. In the presence of these gases, they would stop singing or show other signs of stress, signaling to the miner that it was time to evacuate the pit. The new hand-held devices, which provide a digital reading, are considered more effective and cheaper to run in the long term. More than 200 canaries are replaced over the following year. Miners expressed sadness at the news, although they did not attempt to contest the Government's decision.

DATEline

December 31

"Russia must enter the new millennium with new politicians, with new faces, with new, smart, strong, energetic people." — BORIS YELTSIN, IN HIS RESIGNATION SPEECH

Technically, the last century and millennium ended on December 31, 2000. However, most of the world chose to ignore the fact and opted to focus their millennial celebrations on the transition from 1999 to 2000 instead. In Bombay, fireworks erupted over the famous Gateway of India (pictured), while Brazilians partied on the sand at Rio de Janeiro's Copacabana Beach, and a giant ferris wheel lit up the London sky in Britain. From Cambodia's Angkor Wat to Machu Picchu in Peru, and from Iceland to South Africa, the world partied and paraded into the small hours of the nascent "noughties," as the new decade was unofficially called. New York's Time Square captured the global dimension of the event by installing giant television screens that broadcast millennium events from each of the world's 24 time zones.

Births

1720	Bonnie Prince Charlie
1869	Henri Matisse, artist
1908	Simon Wiesenthal, Nazi hunter
1937	Anthony Hopkins, actor
1941	Alex Ferguson, soccer coach
1943	John Denver, singer and songwriter
1943	Sir Ben Kingsley, actor
1948	Donna Summer, singer
1959	Val Kilmer, actor

Deaths

1948	Malcolm Campbell, race-car driver
1985	Sam Spiegel, film producer
1985	Ricky Nelson, musician
1994	Leigh Bowery, designer
1997	Michael Kennedy, son of Robert F. Kennedy

HISTORICAL EVENTS

1933 Charles Darrow patents the board game "Monopoly" in the U.S. A London version of the game was launched the following year.

1964 Donald Campbell sets a world water speed record of 276.33 miles per hour (444.71 km/h) in his speedboat, *Bluebird*, in Perth, Western Australia. The British pioneer is the first to hold world land and water speed records in the same year.

1984 Rock band Def Leppard's drummer, Rick Allen, loses his left arm in a car crash. The band stands by him during his recovery; an electronic drum kit largely triggered by his feet is developed for him, and the subsequent record *Hysteria* is regarded as the most successful of the band's career.

1999 Boris Yeltsin takes the world by surprise by resigning as Russian President, handing over power to Vladimir Putin, as Acting President.

1999 Nations around the world launch celebrations to usher in the new millennium, a year before it actually begins (see above).

2000 President Clinton signs the UN treaty to establish a permanent International Criminal Court, which will try cases of genocide, war crimes, and crimes against humanity.

DAYS TO REMEMBER

Traditional day New Year's Eve An occasion of partying and general merrymaking on the last day of the Gregorian year. The main focus is the countdown to midnight when revelers welcome in the New Year.

National day Hogmanay The Scottish name for New Year's Eve, which is celebrated with more gusto and importance than Christmas, with up to three days of festivities. The origin of the name *Hogmanay* is uncertain, although some like to think it is derived from "hug many."

DAYS TO REMEMBER *December*

1
World Aids Day Dedicated to raising awareness of the global Aids epidemic, which has claimed more than 25 million lives

2
Maria Callas, soprano, was born in 1923

3
International Day of Disabled Persons Aims to increase awareness of disability issues

4
St. Barbara's Day Patron saint of the military, firemen, miners, architects, builders, and stonemasons

5
National Day (Thailand) Celebrates the birthday of Thailand's King Bhumibol Adulyadej

8
Bodhi Day A Buddhist celebration of the day that Siddhartha Gautama attained enlightenment and became Buddha, in 596 B.E.

9
John Malkovich, actor, was born in 1953

10
Lux Mundi This Roman festival, meaning "light of the world," commemorates Liberty, the goddess of light

11
Day of Bruma The ancient Roman goddess of the winter season, Bruma, was honored in this annual festival

12
Our Lady of Guadalupe (Mexico) Commemorates the day when the Virgin Mary appeared to Juan Diego in c. 1531

15
Zamenhof Day Commemorates the birthday of Ludwig Zamenhof, creator of the international langauge called Esperanto

16
Posadas The first day of a nine-day festival to commemorate the journey of Joseph and Mary to Bethlehem

17
Saturnalia First day of this week-long ancient midwinter festival honoring the Roman god Saturn

18
Steve Biko, anti-apartheid activist, was born in 1946

19
Leonid Brezhnev, Soviet leader, was born in 1906

22
The first day of the star sign of Capricorn

23
Emperor's Birthday (Japan) The birthday of the current Emperor is always observed as a national holiday

24
Sowans Nicht A traditional Scottish name for Christmas Eve

25
Christmas Day A Christian holiday celebrating the birth of Jesus

26
Boxing Day The name comes from the small boxes used to collect donations on this day

29
Thomas Becket, Archbishop of Canterbury, died in 1170

30
Kwanzaa (U.S.) A week-long celebration of African-American heritage

31
New Year's Eve An occasion of partying and general merrymaking on the last day of the Gregorian year

6
National Day (Finland) Celebrates Finland's independence from Russia in 1918

7
St. Ambrose's Day Patron saint of teachers, orators, and bee-keepers

13
Republic Day (Malta) This former British colony celebrates becoming a republic within the Commonwealth in 1974

14
Agnostica A secular event commemorating the birth of quantum physics in 1900

20
On this night in old England, young girls would stick nine pins into a large peeled onion and sing a special rhyme

21
Karachun This Pagan festival is a Slavic version of Halloween

27
Birthday of Freya In Norse culture, the birthday of Freya, the goddess of fertility, love and beauty, was celebrated

28
Feast Day for The Holy Innocents Commemorates King Herod's massacre of children in Bethlehem

Top right World Aids Day, December 1
Right Christmas Day, December 25

Index

A

A4 Rocket 400, 519
ABBA 163, 530
Abbey Road 325, 528
Abel, Rudolf 89, 525
Abelard, Peter 240
abortion 68, 69, 212, 517, 528, 529
Abu Ghraib prison 126, 178, 342, 544, 545
Academy Awards 98, 109, 145, 159, 171, 214, 516, 526, 529, 544, 546
accordion 52
Adams, Ansel 429, 519
Adams, Bryan 55
Adams, Eddie 80
Adams, Gerry 131, 207, 533
Adams, John 281
Adidas buying Reebok 320, 545
Advent 466, 474
The Adventures of Huckleberry Finn 98
The Adventures of Ozzie and Harriet 405
Aeroflot Ilyushin-62 crash 410
aerosol spray ban 63, 531
Afghanistan
　air strikes against Taliban 404
　Buddhas of Bamiyan 127, 542
　Independence Day 337, 515
　Iranian calendar 30
　NATO peacekeeping mission 329, 544
　Soviet invasion 505, 532
　Soviet withdrawal 94, 172, 213, 535
　U.S. attacks 338, 368, 541
　U.S. invasion 119
　war casualties 552
African National Congress 81, 186, 248, 536
Ağca, Mehmet Ali 51, 211, 545
Agincourt, Battle of 423
Agnostica 492
AIDS *see* HIV/AIDS
Air France
　crash 425
　hijacking 502
Air India crash 40, 553
Air New Zealand crash 467, 532, 553
Airbus A380 186
aircraft safety 416
aircraft used in warfare 122, 513
airmail 98, 223, 514
airplane, first flight 495, 512
Al-Fayed, Dodi 349
al-Qaeda 284, 338, 368, 541
al-Sadat, Anwar 144, 376
Alamo siege 123
Alaska 166
Alaska Day 415
Alaska to Siberia swim 324, 535
Albania
　fraudulent king 331, 514
　Hoxha statue 100, 537
　Independence Day 467, 513
　Warsaw Pact 212
Albee, Edward 410, 525
Alcatraz 139, 201, 249, 329, 409, 517, 525
Alcock, John 252
Alcohol Awareness Month 157
Alcoholics Anonymous 248, 517
Aldrin, Edwin "Buzz" 298, 517
Algeria
　earthquake 407, 532
　French peace treaty 136
　independence 47, 340, 524, 525
　Independence Day 282
　Rais massacre 347, 540
　Souhane massacre 338, 540
Ali, Muhammad 105, 125, 188, 205, 258, 265, 362, 398, 428, 519, 524, 527, 529, 530, 532
Alice's Adventures in Wonderland 281
All Saints Day 437, 438
All Souls Day 437, 439
Allantide (U.K.) 429
Allen, Rick 509, 534
Allen, Woody 501, 541
Allende, Salvador 387, 530
Alliluyeva, Svetlana 126, 527
Allison, Stacy 388
Alpert, Richard 227, 525
Amazon.com 293, 539
America Online/Time Warner merger 49, 542
American Bandstand 404, 523
American Civil War 130, 166, 170, 177, 178, 239, 278
American Electric and Illumination 412
American Express 136, 367, 525
American football 360
American War of Independence 157, 176, 177, 360, 416, 447
America's Cup yacht race 385, 533
America's Most Wanted 409
Ames, Aldrich 187
Amin, Idi 65, 81, 169, 324, 334, 529, 532

Amnesty International 226, 525
Amristar Massacre 171, 515
Amrozi bin Nurhasyim 324
Amundsen, Roald 254, 256, 294, 492, 513
anaesthetic 148, 389
ancient Greek calendar 32
Anderson, Terry 481, 537
Andes plane crash 410, 507, 529
Andress, Ursula 205
Andrews Sisters 41, 519
Andropov, Yuri 183, 284, 533
The Andy Griffith Show 400
Angam Day (Nauru) 424
Anglican Church 329, 539, 544
Anglo-Irish Agreement 289, 453, 483, 515, 534
Anglo-Zanzibar War 345
animated cartoon, first 163
Annan, Kofi 367, 374, 550
Anschluss 171, 518
Antarctica
　discovery 456
　Mt Erebus plane crash 467, 532, 553
　solo crossing 57, 540
　South Pole 43, 135, 468, 492, 513, 516, 523
　treaty banning military activity 478, 524
Anthony, Susan B. 344, 442
anthrax attacks 402, 543
anthrax vaccine 548
antibiotics 260, 416, 513
ANZUS Treaty 358, 524
apartheid 109, 136, 186, 336, 363, 427, 522, 538
Apgar score 245, 513
Apgar, Virginia 245, 513
Apollo 1 67, 527
Apollo 7 408, 419, 528
Apollo 8 502, 528
Apollo 13 169, 175, 528
Apollo 16 173, 178, 529
Apollo-Soyuz link 295, 530
Apple Computers 58, 158, 187, 420, 530
Appleseed, Johnny 128, 384
April Fool's Day 158
Aquinino, Benigno 339, 533
Aquinino, Corazon 105, 534
Arafat, Yasser 201, 262, 321, 342, 371, 448, 539, 550
Arbor Day (China) 129
Arc de Triomphe 308
Archangelovden 445
Archbishop of Canterbury 139, 181, 499
Archduke Franz Ferdinand 267, 306, 514
Archer, Jeffrey 297, 543
Argentina
　Día de la Revolución de Mayo 223
　Falklands War 137, 159, 252, 533
　first female President 268
　Peron as President 104, 381
Arias, Roberto 180
Aristotle 90, 124, 531
Armenian earthquake 484, 535
Armistice Day 418, 437, 448
Armstrong, Lance 302, 376, 545
Armstrong, Neil 298, 322, 517, 528
around world flight 45
ARPAnet 427
Ascension Day 235
ASEAN 325, 527
Ash Wednesday 78
Ash Wednesday bushfires 95, 533
ASPCA 168
aspirin 123
Assumption of Mary 314, 326, 333
asteroids 41, 244, 358, 427
Astley's circus 48
Astor, Lady Nancy 478, 515
astrology 23, 24, 200, 535
　zodiac signs *see* zodiac signs
Aswan Dam, Egypt 299, 304, 487, 512, 528
Atatürk, Mustafa Kemal 447, 455, 518
Athenagoras I 44, 526
Athens
　airport bombing 322, 529
　invasion in WWII 186, 519
　Olympics 163
　Parthenon 384
　Polytechnic, demonstration at 530
Atkins, Susan 65
Atlanta Olympics bombing 305, 340, 540
Atlantis space shuttle 268
ATM 266, 527
atomic bomb 106, 294, 323, 326, 347, 370, 520, 521, 522, 524
atomic structure 128, 513
Attica Prison riots 366, 529
Aum Shinrikyo 138, 539
Aung San, General 297, 386, 521
Aung San Suu Kyi 257, 298, 386, 535, 536, 550, 550
Auschwitz 64, 67, 244, 252, 519, 520, 534
Australia
　brawls with American soldiers 466, 519
　bushfires 50, 57, 90, 533, 545
　conscription in WWI 451
　convicts transported to 57
　Cook landing in 188, 340
　Declaration of Reconciliation 225, 542
　dismissal of government 448, 479

Eastern Kimberley massacre 283, 516
first Aboriginal parliamentarian 222, 529
first federal elections 147, 512
first freed convict 108
flag 207, 512
formation of Commonwealth of 286, 512
homosexuality decriminalised 246, 534
indigenous land rights 240, 500, 538
indigenous people in census 225, 527
National Sorry Day 224
Native Title Act 500, 538
republic referendum 443, 542
royal assent to Constitution 286
sugar growers subsidy 54, 512
voluntary euthanasia law 142, 540
Australia 66
Australia Post shooting 485
Australia II 384, 533
Austria
　French declaration of war on 178
　funicular train fire 448, 542
　Galtür avalanche 103, 541
　OPEC meeting raid 499, 530
　Treaty Day 424
　Vienna riots 293, 516
　Vienna State Opera 442, 523
automatic digital calculator 324, 520
automobile 69, 280, 378
automobile show, Paris 488
autumn equinox 11, 355
Autumnal Equinox Day (Japan) 355, 381
avian flu 507, 541, 552
Avignon Pope Clement VII 378
Avogadro's number 420
Awa Odori (Japan) 317
Axis of Evil 69
Ayres Rock 299, 335
Ayyám-i-Há (Bahai) 106
Azerbaijan 187, 515
Azores Islands 87

B

Baba Marta (Bulgaria) 118
Babbage, Charles 252
baboon heart transplant 424, 534
Baby Fae 424, 534
Babylonian calendar 32
Bacardi 83
Bacchanalia (Ancient Rome) 134
Bach, Johann Sebastian 306, 497, 534
Baden Powell, Sir Robert 64, 102, 307, 513
Baedeker Raids 181
Baekeland, Leo 548
Baha'i calendar 33
Baha'i faith 179, 221, 417
Bailey, Dr Leonard 424
Baird, John Logie 66, 280, 516
Baisakhi 171
Bakker, Jim 422, 536
Balaclave, Battle of 423
Bali bombing 320, 324, 409, 543, 544
Balibo Five 413, 530
Balinese calendar 31
Balkan War 415, 513
Ball, Lucile 412
Ballard, Dr Robert 173
Balmat, Jacques 325
Bam earthquake 504, 544
Bambi 331, 519
Banana, Dr Canaan 176
Bandaranaike, Sirimavo 298, 524
Bandaranaike, Solomon 298
Banderas, Antonio 328
Baneshwar Fair 78
Bangladesh
　Armed Forces Day 459
　cyclone 450, 528
　independence 494, 529
　Victory Day 494
Banja Luka massacre 86, 519
bank robbery, biggest 102, 545
Bannister, Roger 141, 203, 522
Bannockburn, Battle of 262
Bannockburn Day 262
Banting, Frederick 50, 305, 452, 515
Bar Kochbar rebellion 276
The Barber of Seville 100
Barbie, Ken 91, 126, 524
Barbie, Klaus 281, 285, 423, 519, 535
barcode scanner 265, 530
Bardeen, John 269, 501
Barings Bank collapse 106, 479, 539
Barnard, Dr Christian 41, 445, 480, 527
Baroness de Laroche 125, 513
Barrett, Elizabeth 370
Bartholdi, Frederic 426
Barton, Edmund 147, 512
Baryshnikov, Mikhail 376
baseball 257, 405
　Minor League 362, 512
　White Sox "throw in" 406, 515
　World Series 398, 402, 410, 423, 512, 543
Bashir, Abu Bakar 120
BASIC computer program 198, 526
Basilica of Our Lady of Guadalupe 489
Basilica of Our Lady of Peace, Yamoussoukro 367

basketball
　brawl in Detroit 457, 544
　National League 320, 521
　televising 108, 518
Bass Strait 486
Bastille Day 292
Bataan Death March 168, 519
battery-powered watch 42, 523
Bauby, Jean-Dominique 127
Bay of Pigs invasion 175, 215, 525
Bayley, William 261, 517
Beach Party 383
Beaconsfield mine collapse 206, 545
Beagle 2 space probe 544
Bealtaine 198
Beamon, Bob 415
The Beatles 70, 82, 86, 121, 125, 147, 168, 238, 325, 329, 334, 345, 347, 368, 402, 525, 526, 527, 528, 534
Bede the Venerable's Day 225
Bedford, James 51, 527
Beer Hall Putsch 446, 515, 516
Beethoven, Ludwig van 164, 442, 494
Begin, Manachim 144, 376
Beirut, U.S. embassy bombing 176
Belafonte, Harry 488
Belgium
　Battle of the Bulge 494, 520
　collapse of government 136, 522
　dikes bursting 71, 522
　German invasion 321, 514
　Heysel Stadium riot 227, 534
　Independence Day 299
　Sabena air crash 94
　St Martin's Day 435
　same sex marriage 70, 543
Bell, Alexander Graham 46, 93, 127, 319, 515
Bell X-1 411
Bell X-2 247
Bellerophon 403, 359
Beltane 11, 194, 195
Ben-Gurion, David 65, 478, 521
Benenson, Peter 226, 550
Bennett, Elizabeth Hog 53
Benny, Jack 161, 518
Bentley, John 501
Benz, Karl 69, 280, 463
Bergen-Belson concentration camp 173, 321, 520
Bergh, Henry 168
Berkowitz, David "Son of Sam" 307, 328, 531
Berlin
　Airlift 262, 521
　Battle of 199, 520
　Blockade 262
　bombing in WWII 60, 123, 520
　German capital 258, 537
　JFK's visit 265, 525
　La Belle disco bombing 162, 172, 534
　Trades Exposition 229
　Wall 250, 331, 335, 400, 446, 525, 535, 536
Bernard, Claude 178
Berners-Lee, Tim 106, 323, 537, 548
Beslan school massacre 358, 360, 544
Bessette, Carolyn 294, 379, 540
Best, Charles 50, 305, 515
Betty Boop 325, 517
Bewitched 375, 526
Bezos, Jeff 293
Bhopal gas leak 480, 534
Bhutan
　television 239, 542
　tobacco ban 453, 544
Bhutto, Benazir 259, 479, 535
Bhutto, Zulfikar Ali 124, 161, 282, 479, 531, 532
Biafran War 283, 524
Bible, printing of 103, 140, 401
bicycle 219
Biertag (Germany) 181
bifocals 221
The Big Bopper 82, 524
Big Ear telescope 333, 531
Bigfoot 417, 527
Biggs, Ronald 285, 325, 526
bikini 282, 521
Bikini Atoll 118, 282
Biko, Steve 370, 383, 496, 531
Bill of Rights (U.S.) 493
Billy the Kid 335, 452, 461
Bin Laden, Osama 127, 323, 368, 427, 523, 544
Bingham, Hiram III 302, 513
biplane flight 371
bird flu 507, 541, 552
Birmingham Six 131, 537
birth control 90, 206, 212, 514
Birth of the Báb 206
Bishop Martin of Tours' Day 448
Black Consciousness Movement 383
Black Day (Sth Korea) 172
Black History Month (U.S.) 79
Black Hold of Calcutta 258
Black May (Thailand) 215
Black Monday on Wall Street 416
Black Poetry Day (U.S.) 414
Black Thursday, NYSE 512, 516
Black Tuesday bushfires 50, 545
Blackweel, Elizabeth 63
Blaine Act (U.S.) 96
Blair, Tony 104, 198, 203, 540

Blake, Sir Peter 483, 543
Blamey, Sir Thomas 522
Blanc, Mel 287, 305
Blessed Mary MacKillop's Day 325
Blessed Virgin Mary's Day 365
Bligh, Capt William 187, 252, 366
blood transfusion 253, 452
Bloody Sunday
    Ireland 70, 81, 339, 459, 515, 529
    Russia 62
blue jeans 218
Blum, Robert 446
Blyton, Enid 41, 329, 467, 535
Bob Marley Day 85
Bobbitt, Lorena and John 61, 538
Bodhi Day 485
Boeing 747 88
Boer War 127, 229, 439, 507, 512
Boesky, Ivan 496, 535
Bolan, Marc 374, 531
Boleyn, Anne 257, 283
Bolimov, Battle of 71
Bolívar, Simón 282, 298, 302, 495
Bolivia Independence Day 323
Bolshoi Ballet 376, 532
Bombay Docks Explosion 172, 519
Bon Festival 290
Bonaparte, Napoleon 126, 138, 149, 169, 200,
    215, 216, 256, 307, 333, 345, 394, 408,
    412, 446, 478, 479, 493
Bondar, Roberta 62
Bonham, John 481
Bonhoeffer, Dietrich 165, 520
Bonner, Neville 222, 529
Bonner, Yelena 497
Bonnie and Clyde 221
Bonnie Prince Charlie 301, 509
Bontade, Stefano 181, 532
"Boogie Woogie Bugle Boy" 41, 519
Booker Prize winners 546
Booth, John Wilkes 172, 184
Booth, William 282, 338
Borg, Björn 282
Born to Run 343, 530
Bosnia Herzegovina
    Dayton Peace Accord 459, 539
    Ikari diving competition 274, 301
    joining UN 220, 538
    NATO bombing 348, 457, 538, 359
    Operation Deliberate Force 348
    peace treaty 492
    Srebrenica massacre 288, 539
    Stari Most 274, 301, 544
Boss's Day (U.S.) 413
Boston
    British evacuation 135
    Marathon 157
    molasses disaster 54, 515
    Subway 358
    Tea Party 494
Botham, Ian 257, 462, 531
Bouchard, Pierre-François 293
Boulder (Hoover) Dam 406, 518
Bounty mutiny 187, 252
Bouvier, Jacqueline see Kennedy, Jackie
Bowie, David 244, 290
Boxer rebellion 245, 512
Boxing Day 477, 504
Boxing Day Tsunami 504, 544
Boy Scouts 64, 102, 217, 307, 513
Boyle, Robert 467
Braille, Louis 43, 45, 549
Brailler, John 360
Branch Davidians 108, 177, 538
Brandeis, Louis D. 68
Brando, Marlon 145, 160, 278, 529
Brandt, Willy 137, 496
Brattain, Walter 269, 501
Braun, Eva 189
Brazil
    Brasilia as capital 179, 524
    da Silva as president 425
    Independence Day 364
    Law of the Free Womb 387
    pirates on Amazon River 483, 543
    Rolling Stones concert 99, 545
Breakspear, Nicholas 481
breast implants 45, 538
Brezhnev, Leonid 256, 447, 497, 531, 532
Bridge Over Troubled Water 134
Brin, Sergey 364
Britain
    Anglo-Irish Agreement 289, 453, 483, 515
    Armed Services 158
    bombings in WWI 58
    bombings in WWII 331
    Clean Air Act 282, 523
    declaring war on France 216
    Downing Street Declaration 493
    Factory Act 279
    first female judge 43
    first female MP 478, 515
    first "parliament" 125
    flag 170
    foot-and-mouth disease 53, 543
    formation of Great Britain 198
    gale 463
    Great Storm of 1987 396
    hereditary peerage abolished 462, 541

Labour Party 107, 512
Peasants' Revolt 253
rationing 281, 523
Royal Air Force 158, 514
Royal Society 467
South Wales mine explosion 508
Tea Act 186
tidal electricity plant 464
travel to Britain suspended 130, 520
women's vote 203, 478, 492, 515
Britain, Battle of 287, 331, 519
British Airways 50
British Broadcasting Corporation (BBC) 268,
    452, 497, 515, 517, 524
Britt, Mary 451, 524
Brixton bombing 175, 541
Brixton riots 169, 387, 490, 532, 534, 540
Bronte, Charlotte 342
Brown, Alexander 498
Brown, Arthur Whitten 252
Brown, James 493
Brown, Louise Joy 303, 531
Brown Simpson, Nicole 83, 250, 255, 400,
    539, 540
Browning, Robert 204, 370, 489
Bru na Boinne 14
Bruno, Bishop of Würzburg's Day 215
Bryan, John 338, 413, 501
Bryant, Martin 187, 540
BSE see mad cow disease
Bucharest earthquake 121, 531
Buchenwald 54
Buckingham Palace 188, 286, 538
Buckner, Bill 423
Budd, Zola 329, 534
Buddha 199, 485
Buddhas of Bamiyan 127, 542
Budinger, Victoria 495
Bugs Bunny 189, 305, 519
Bulgaria
    Independence Day 120
    last Tsar 302, 543
    Warsaw Pact 212
Bulge, Battle of the 494, 520
Bulger, James 47, 542
bullet train 398, 526
Bun Bang Fai 196
Bundy, Ted 64
Burma (Myanmar)
    assassination of ministers 297, 521
    Martyr's Day 297
    National League for Democracy 386, 535
Burning Man festival (U.S.) 317
Burning of the Clavie (Scotland) 50
Burns Day (Scotland) 65
Burns, Tommy 504
Burrell, Paul 334, 543
Burrows, William S. 339
Burrows, William Seward 339
Burton, Richard 132, 250, 322, 407, 410, 447,
    526, 530
Burundi President killed 163, 539
Bush, George H. W. 42, 47, 107, 221, 250, 265,
    309, 428, 497, 536, 537, 538
Bush, George W. 69, 94, 146, 283, 323, 326, 347,
    367, 368, 409, 428, 444, 542, 543
Bush, Neil 221
Butcher of Lyon 281
Bwana Devil 98
Byng, Admiral John 131
Byrd, Richard 468, 516

C

Caesarian section 53
Californian gold rush 64
Callanish Stone Circle 15
Callas, Maria 374, 479
Calment, Jeanne 101
Cambodia
    Independence Day 446, 522
    Khmer Rouge 170, 175, 199, 452, 507, 530,
        541, 551
    New Year 21, 171
    Prince Norodom Sihanouk 446, 452, 537
    refugees in Thailand 199
    Songkran 21
camera 361
Camões Day 248
Camp David 376, 531
Campbell, Donald 509
Campbell, Kim 264, 538
Campese, David 344
Canada
    abortion and contraception legalised 212,
        528
    blackout 332
    Canada Day 278
    ceded to Britain 89
    cholera epidemic 245
    Commemoration of the Great Upheaval 306
    female Governor-General 212, 533
    female Prime Minister 264, 538
    first Canadians to cross 300
    first meeting of Parliament 246
    flag 94, 526
    formation of nation 256
    Halifax Harbor explosion 483, 514

National Hockey League 464, 514
North American Free Trade Agreement 485
Official Languages Act 184, 528
Ottawa Parliament buildings fire 82, 514
Royal Canadian Mounted Police 80, 515
same sex marriage 218, 541
street lights 461
transcontinental railway 444
Vancouver Island shelling 258, 519
canaries used in mines 508, 535
Canberra 81
    bushfires 57
cancer
    cellular phones 206
    nanotechnology to treat 319, 545
    smoking 289
Candlemas 81, 94
Candomble 316
cannabis 399, 415, 530
Cannabis Celebration 178
Cannes Film Festival 378, 521
Canon City meteorite 425
Canterbury Tales 175
Canton Uprising 147, 513
Cantona, Eric 67
Canute IV's Day 58
Cape Matapan 146
capital punishment see death penalty
Capone, Al 93, 139, 201, 517, 521
Capote, Truman 172, 343, 389
Capriati, Jennifer 122, 536
Cardoso, Fernando 425
Carling Weekend Festival 316
Carlos, John 414, 528
Carlos the Jackal 499, 502, 530
Carmen 120
Carnarvon, Lord 464
Carnegie Hall NY 202
Carothers, Wallace H. 95, 489, 518
Carr, Maxine 321
Carreras, José 284, 536
Carroll, Lewis 281
Carson, Johnny 220, 399, 420, 525, 538, 545
Carter, Howard 42, 95, 119, 464, 516
Carter, Jimmy 61, 164, 182, 256, 376, 398, 492,
    498, 531, 532, 550
Cartier, Jacques 207
cartoons 163, 206
Caruso, Enrico 136, 512
Caspar and Mary Vaz's Day 335
Cassini-Huygens spacecraft 249, 412
Castro, Fidel 95, 159, 173, 175, 180, 215, 228,
    304, 331, 406, 423, 516, 522, 524, 525, 536
Catalan Day 444
Catherine del Ricci's Day 81
Catherine the Great 199, 215, 295, 443
Catholic Church see Roman Catholic Church
CATS 208, 404, 532
Cavelier, Rene-Robert 343
Caxton, William 456
Ceausescu, Nicolae and Elena 503, 536
Cedar Fire, California 423, 544
Cedar Revolution 93
celluloid photograph film 199, 371
Celtic tree signs 553
    Alder 136
    Ash 98
    Birch 502
    Elder 463
    Hawthorn 211
    Hazel 322
    Holly 285
    Ivy 378
    Oak 248
    Reed 426
    Rowan 61
    Vine 359
    Willow 173
Cenepa War 96, 539
Cerdan, Marcel 425
Ceylon see Sri Lanka
Challenger space shuttle 68, 161, 362, 388, 408,
    533, 534
Chamberlain, Azaria 335, 371, 532
Chamberlain, Lindy 335, 371, 532
Chamberlain, Michael 335
Chamberlain, Neville 211, 389, 446, 518
Champollion, Jean-François 386
Channel Tunnel 203, 478, 537, 539
Chanukah 475
Chaplin, Charlie 84, 159, 174, 381, 503, 518,
    522, 531, 529
Chapman, Graham 208, 401
Chapman, Jessica 321, 543
Chapman, Mark David 260, 342, 485, 533
Charles de Gaulle Airport collapse 221, 544
Chartres Cathedral 422
"Chattanooga Choo Choo" 204, 519
Chaucer, Geoffrey 175, 194, 423
Chavez, Hugo 341, 545
Chechan rebels 85, 349, 371, 420, 543, 544
Chechnya 488, 539
Cheddar Caves skeleton 124
Cheers 218, 389
Chelmno death camp 238
chemical warfare 180, 526
Chernobyl nuclear disaster 184, 534
Chesney, Kenny 373
chess 47, 96, 201, 540

chewing gum 75, 381
Chicago
    Eastland sinking 302, 514
    Fordham Spire 414
    Great Fire 413
    Iroquois Theatre fire 508, 512
    St Valentine's Day massacre 93, 516
    Sears Tower 190, 414, 529
    "White ox show in" 406, 515
Chicora Lake 67
Chief Sitting Bull 298, 493
Chifley, Ben 212, 282
Child Abuse Prevention Month 157
Children's Day
    India 472
    Universal 412
    Vanuatu 302
Chile
    Concepcion earthquake 100
    founding of Santiago 91
    joining UN 6
China
    Aristotle/Shakespeare/Dickens ban lifted 90,
        531
    Boxer rebellion 245, 512
    Canton Uprising 147, 513
    China Airlines crash 95
    civil war casualties 552
    Cultural Revolution 331, 527
    earthquakes 239, 306, 531, 552
    Gang of Four 408, 531
    "Great Leap Forward" 221, 523
    Great Wall 41, 528
    Gregorian calendar 91, 513
    Hong Kong handed back 269, 278, 384, 540
    Japanese bombing 240, 516
    joint military exercises with Russia 337, 545
    Mid-Autumn Festival 23, 355
    New Year 20
    People's Republic Day 398, 521
    Rape of Nanking 490, 518, 550
    recognition of People's Republic 45, 461,
        493, 531
    relations with U.S.S.R. 214
    Rolling Stones concert 129
    Shaanxi earthquake 63, 552
    Tangshan earthquake 306, 531, 552
    terracotta warriors 288, 530
    Three Gorges Dam 444, 540
    Tiananmen Square protests 173, 179, 214,
        215, 242, 493, 536
    UN Security Council 461, 529
    Yangtze River cofferdam 444, 540
China Airlines crash 95, 541, 553
Chinese astrology 23
Chinese calendar 22
Chinese New Year 20
Ch'ing Ming (China) 162
Chirac, Jacques 204, 292, 468, 539, 540, 543
chiropractic 376
chlorofluorocarbon ban 119, 374, 535
Christie, Agatha 174, 463, 522, 530
Christie, James 295, 531
Christies auctioneers 482
Christmas 12, 13, 15, 46, 474, 476, 503
A Christmas Carol 495
Christmas Eve 501
Christmas Jeers 92
Christmas truce WWI 503, 514
Chrysanthemum Day (Japan) 366
Chrysler Corporation 204, 244, 498, 516, 532
Church of England 124, 129
Church of the Nativity, Bethlehem 159, 543
Churchill, Winston 106, 122, 129, 162, 182, 204,
    211, 223, 231, 256, 304, 323, 422, 469,
    487, 499, 521, 522, 523, 526, 550
Cicippio, Joseph 341
cigar-rolling machine 107
cinematograph 59
circumnavigation of globe
    helicopter 308, 533
    ship 161, 323, 378, 384, 490
    solo boat 268
    solo flight 304
Cisterna, Battle of 59
Cities for Life Day 469
Citizen Kane 192, 519
Claude, Georges
Clay, Cassius see Ali, Muhammad
Cleopatra 12, 250
Cleveland gas explosion 417, 520
Clinton, Bill 46, 52, 66, 91, 104, 146, 224, 265,
    335, 367, 375, 378, 379, 413, 424, 454,
    478, 485, 493, 497, 509, 538, 541, 542
Clinton, Hillary 324, 378, 424, 538, 542
cloning 51, 302, 410, 541, 549
Clooney, George 177
clowns' church service 79
Cobain, Kurt 156, 165, 336, 382, 539
Cobb, John 88, 522
Coca-Cola 129
Cock Crow Mass 494
coelacanth 500, 518
Colby, William E. 192, 540
Cold War 122, 311, 368, 503
Colefax Massacre 71
Coligny calendar 15
Collingwood, Luke 468
Collins, Eileen 308, 539

513

Collins, Jim 467
Collins, Michael (astronaut) 298, 429
Collins, Michael (patriot) 340, 413, 515, 550
Cologne Cathedral 332
Colt revolver 105, 549
Columbia
   Independence Day 298
   Nevado del Ruiz eruption 451
Columbia space shuttle 55, 80, 170, 298, 344, 532, 543
Columbine High School Massacre 178, 541
Columbus, Christopher 109, 218, 320, 453, 457, 504
Columbus Day 394
Comaneci, Nadia 296, 450, 467, 531, 536, 547
Comic Relief 84, 535
Coming of Age Day (Japan) 38
Coming Out Day (U.S.) 408
The Common Sense Book of Baby and Child Care 292, 521
The Communist Manifesto 101
computer
   copyright in software 489, 532
   Deep Blue 96, 201, 540
   laptop 160, 534
   mouse 455, 528
   Pentium processor 140, 538
   personal 182, 520
   Time Machine of the Year 504
Computing-Tabulating-Recording Company (later IBM) 93, 513, 516
Concepción earthquake 100
Concorde 110, 119, 222, 384, 422, 528, 530, 531
   crash 303, 542
   last flight 422, 544
Confederate States of America 257
Confucius 387
Congo possessed by King Léopold II 84
Congo, Democratic Republic of
   Mt Nyiragongo eruption 56, 543
   Parent's Day 318
Connery, Sean 205, 343
Conrad, Charles "Pete" 373
Constantinople 146, 227, 410
contraception 206, 212, 245, 427, 524, 526, 528, 538
Cook, Captain James 56, 93, 188, 218, 289, 340, 404, 425
Cook Islands
   Constitution Day 321
   New Zealand annexing 249, 512
Coombs, Catherine 457
Copeland, David 175, 541
Cornu, Paul 451
Corday, Charlotte 290, 295
Cornwallis, Lord Charles 416
Coronation of Haile Selassie 439
Coronation Street 486, 524
Cortés, Hernando 445
Costa Rica Independence Day 373
Costello, Elvis 343
Cottin, Angélique 54
Couch Adams, John 381
Council of Clermont 456
Courrieres coalmine explosion 127, 512
Coventry bombing 452, 519
cow, first to fly 98
Cowra breakout 322, 520
Cox, Lynne 324, 535
Cozette, Philippe 478
Crab Pulsar 60, 528
Cramner, Thomas 139
Crane, Alanson 89
Creede, Nicholas C. 399
cremation 57
Creutzfeldt-Jakob disease 143, 388, 540
Crick, Francis 101, 183, 522, 548, 549
cricket
   first hat-trick 41
   first Test 132
   South Africa ban 58, 447, 537
   vandalism at Headingley 337
   World Series 459, 531
Crimean War 146, 148, 259, 265, 423, 468
Crippen, Hawley 309, 513
Cromwell, Oliver 360, 494
Cronulla Beach riots 488, 545
Croatia
   independence 168, 519
   joining UN 220, 538
crossword puzzle 499, 514
Crown Prince Dipendra of Nepal 238, 543
Cruise, Tom 84, 542
Crum, George 342
Crusades 61, 245, 281, 293, 338, 343, 456
Cry Freedom 383
cryonic preservation 51, 527
Crystal Palace fire 469, 518
Cuba
   Bay of Pigs invasion 175, 215, 525
   Castro see Castro, Fidel
   independence 218, 512
   nationalisation of foreign-owned property 323, 524
   Revolution Day 304
   U.S. dollar ban 423
Cuban Missile Crisis 258, 411, 426, 458, 525
Cullinan diamond 66, 512
Culloden, Battle of 301

Cultural Revolution (China) 331, 527
Culture Day (Japan) 440
Cunanan, Andrew 293
Curie, Marie 63, 178, 264, 281, 296, 304, 444, 487, 504, 512, 513, 517
Curie, Pierre 178, 264, 296, 304, 504, 512
Curtin, John 282, 520
Curtis, Charles 63
Curtis, John 381
Curtiss, Glenn H. 66
Custer, General George 264, 482
Cyclone Tracy 503, 530
Cypriot airliner crash 332, 545
Cyprus 293, 442, 530
Czechoslovakia
   Nazi invasion 132, 518
   Soviet invasion 55, 528
   Velvet Revolution 455, 536
   Warsaw Pact 212

D

D-Day 213, 244, 520
da Gama, Vasco 285, 502
da Silva, Luiz Inácio "Lula" 425
da Vinci, Leonardo 173, 199, 226, 339, 440, 489
Dachau concentration camp 188, 520
daguerreotype photography process 48
Dagur Islenskrar Tungu 454
Daimler, Gottlieb 160, 347
Daimler-Benz-Chrysler merger 204, 541
Daladier, Edouard 168, 518
Dalai Lama 102, 149, 283, 455, 487, 517, 518, 522, 530
Dali, Salvador 63, 208
Dallas 139, 159, 376, 531, 532
dam buster bombs 131, 520
Dame Edna Everage 490, 491, 523
dance marathon 54, 517
Dandy comic 480, 518
D'Aquino, Iva Toguri (Tokyo Rose) 58, 531
Darrow, Charles 442, 509
Darwin
   Beer Can Regatta 277
   bombing 99, 519
   Cyclone Tracy 503, 530
Darwin, Charles 177, 256, 373, 399, 462, 505
   theory of evolution 256, 299, 373, 462, 516, 518, 549
Davenport, Thomas 105
David 365
Davis, Benjamin 425, 523
Davis, Bette 403, 513
Davis Cup 88, 512
Davis, Jacob 218
Davis, Miles 387
Davis, Sammy Jr 451, 485, 524
"Davy Crockett" bomb 223
Day of Bruma 488
Day of Disabled Persons 480
Day of Judgement (Jewish) 356
Day of Remembrance (Jewish) 356
Day of Remembrance of the Slave Trade 341
Day of the Blowing of the Shofar 21, 356
Day of the Child (Honduras) 367
Day of the Dead (Mexico) 437
Day of the Disappeared 348
Day of the Nacho 418
Day of the World's Indigenous People 326
Days of Our Lives 445, 526
Dayton Peace Accord 459, 539
DDT 426
de Bruijn, Inge 373
de Champlain, Samuel 280
De Forest, Lee 129
de Gaulle, Charles 187, 301, 340, 344, 446, 460, 464, 499, 500, 524, 525, 528
de Klerk, F.W. 81, 136, 186, 199, 536, 550
De La Beckwith, Byron 250, 525
De Leon, Jerrick 85, 545
De Leon, Juan Ponce 159
de Mestral, George 319, 523
de Montfort, Simon 125
de Sacrobosco, Johannes 314
de San Martín, José 306
de Valdivia, Pedro 91
De Valera, Eamon 126, 517
Dead Sea Scrolls 92, 380, 537
Dean, James 389, 490, 522, 523
Death of a Salesman 199, 521
death penalty 44, 56, 64, 65, 82, 87, 323, 362, 469, 479, 527, 534, 538, 545
"Death to the Klan" rally 440
decimal currency 181, 527
Decker, Mary 329, 534
Declaration of Independence (U.S.) 248, 281
Declaration of Reconciliation (Aust.) 225, 542
Declaration of Rights of the Child 458, 488, 524
Declaration of the Báb 221
Deep Blue computer 96, 201, 540
Deep Space 1 422, 541
Def Leopard 509, 534
Defer, Gilbert 384
Defoe, Daniel 309
Demjanjuk, John 95, 176
Deng Xiaoping 214, 221, 242, 300, 340, 531
Denis, Jean Baptiste 253

Denmark
   Battle of Carnival Bands 197
   Constitution Day 243
   same sex marriage 224, 536
   Tivoli Gardens, Copenhagen 333
   Virgin Islands sold by 64, 512
Depo-Provera 427, 538
Desai, Moraji 140
Desperate Housewives 400, 544
Detroit
   blackout 332
   race riots 308, 527
Devil's Footprints 87
Devil's Night (U.S.) 428
Dia dos Namorados (Brazil) 250
Dick Tracy 401, 517
Dickens, Charles 86, 90, 247, 495, 531
Dickson, William 46
Dictes or Syengis of the Philosophres 456
Diesel, Rudolf 103
difference engine 252
Dilberovic, Suada 162, 538
DiMaggio, Joe 53, 125, 213, 322, 463, 519, 522
Dinoire, Isabelle 466, 545
Dinsdale, Peter 261, 529
Discovery space shuttle 82, 182, 348, 362, 388, 427, 534
Disneyland
   Anaheim, California 295, 362, 523
   Hong Kong 370
   Orlando, Florida 398, 529
   Tokyo 173, 533
Disraeli, Benjamin 177, 486, 499
Diver, Stuart 308, 540
divorce 107, 124, 462, 540
Diwali (India) 395
DNA 101, 172, 183, 522
Dr Sun Yat-Sen's Birthday 450
Dr Who 461, 526
Dodd, Westley Allan 44, 538
Dog Days 280
dogs in space 62, 440
Dolly the sheep 51, 102, 540, 543, 549
Dom Perignon 321
Domingo, Placido 284, 377, 536
Dominican Alas Nacionales air crash 85
Doña Paz sinking 498, 535
Donald Duck 247, 517
Dongji (Korea) 475
Dong-zhi (China) 475
Doolittle, Jimmy 383, 516
Doom 3 computer game 319, 544
The Doors 280
Douglas, Bob 84
Douglass, Frederick 79
Dow Jones Industrial Average 224, 416, 425, 426, 535
Downing Street Declaration 493
Dracula 216
Dragobete (Romania) 104
Drake, Sir Francis 161, 307, 384, 490
Dresden, Battle of 345
Dreser, Herman 123
Drew, Richard 365
drinking straws 42
Drummond, Thomas 446
Drury Lane Theatre 104, 204
Duchess of Bohemia 373
Duelfer, Charles 403, 544
Duke of Edinburgh 458, 521
Duke of Wellington 256
Duluth lynching 253, 515
Dunant, Jean Henri 487
Dunblane Primary School massacre 130, 540
Dunkirk, Battle of 242, 518
Duryea, Charles and Frank 378
dusky seaside sparrow 255, 535
Duvalier, François "Papa Doc" 180, 529
Dwyer, R. Budd 62, 535
Dyer, Mary 284
Dylan, Bob 303, 348, 526

E

Eapen, Matthew 447
Earhart, Amelia 50, 218, 256, 279, 302, 343, 517, 518
earthquakes 552
   Aleppo, Syria 552
   Algeria 407, 532
   Armenia 484, 535
   Avezzano, Italy 52, 514
   Bam, Iran 504, 544
   Bucharest 121, 531
   Chungar Peru 137
   Colombia 65
   Concepcion, Chile 100
   El Salvador 52, 92
   Erzincan, Turkey 504
   Greek Islands 47
   Guatemala and Honduras 83
   Gujarat, India 66
   India 66, 161, 405, 512, 552
   Indian Ocean 504, 552
   Iran 168, 374, 504, 531, 552
   Italy 52, 506, 513, 552
   Kanto, Japan 358, 515, 552
   Kingston, Jamaica 53

Kobe, Japan 56, 539
   Lisbon, Portugal 66, 438, 552
   Los Angeles 56, 538
   Managua, Nicaragua 501, 529
   Mexico City 377, 534
   Morocco 109, 524
   Napier NZ 82, 516
   Newcastle, Australia 506, 536
   Niigata, Japan 420
   Pakistan 405, 545, 552
   Peru 334, 552
   San Francisco 176, 414, 512
   Shaanxi, China 63, 552
   Straits of Messina 506, 513
   Taiwan 379
   Tangshan, China 306, 531, 552
   Tokyo 139
   Turkey 335, 504, 518, 542
East Timor
   Balibo Five 413, 530
   independence 348
   Indonesian invasion 484, 530
   UN peacekeeping force 378, 542
EastEnders 99, 534
Easter 19, 78, 115, 155, 177
Easter Rebellion 182, 188, 514
Eastland sinking 302, 514
Eastman, George 361
Eastwood, Clint 165, 534
Echo 1 satellite 330, 524
Ecuador
   Cenepa War 96, 539
   Guayaquil Independence Day 406
   Independence Day 328
   joining UN 93
Ecuadorian Airlines crash 68
Ed Sullivan Show 366
Ederle, Gertrude 323, 516
Edict of Worms 224
Edinburgh Fringe Festival 316, 317
Edison Electric Company 412
Edison, Thomas 43, 58, 80, 99, 172, 222, 333, 403, 415, 426, 459, 514, 517
Edward the Confessor's Day 410
Egypt
   Aswan Dam 299, 304, 487, 512, 528
   Great Pyramid 14
   Luxor shootings 455, 541
   military coup 301
   obelisk returned to 545
   peace treaty with Israel 140, 144, 376, 531, 532
   Reqa Al-Gharbiya train fire 100, 543
   Suez Canal 96, 125, 183, 304, 429, 501, 523
   United Arab Republic 102, 523
EgyptAir crash 429, 542
Egyptian calendar 32
Egyptian ferry sinking 81, 545
Ehime-Maru sinking 88, 543
Ehrlich, Paul 260, 338, 513
Eichmann, Adolf 90, 169, 524
Eid al-Adha 49
Eid ul-Fitr 28, 395, 396
Eiffel Tower 149, 203
eight-hour work day 257, 513
Einstein, Albert 88, 138, 176, 269, 446, 487, 494, 515, 523, 548
   Theory of Relativity 138, 269, 446, 514, 549
Eisenhower, Dwight 173, 205, 213, 244, 265, 383, 411, 439, 523
El Alamein, Battle of 441, 519
El Cinco de Mayo 202
el Qasim, Abdul Karim 292, 524
El Salvador
   earthquake 52, 92
   Independence Day 373
   Romero murdered 142, 532
electric lighting system 58
electric printing press 105
electric railway 229
electric shock therapy 146, 518
electric tabulating machine 47
electric telegraph 222
electric traffic light 322, 514
electric vote recorder 426
elephants wearing reflectors 298, 544
ELISA AIDS test 124
Ellen 198
Ellington, Duke 188
Ellis Island 40, 450
Ellsberg, Daniel 325
Elm Farm Ollie 98
Elson, Andy 107
Emancipation Proclamation 257
embryo transplant 82, 533
embryonic stem cell research 326
Emperor Akihito 450, 536
Emperor Atahualpa 454
Emperor Augustus 337, 361, 381
Emperor Day (Japan) 440
Emperor Hirohito 333, 337, 503, 516, 535
Emperor Huang Di 22
Emperor Jimmu 90
Emperor Napoleon see Bonaparte, Napoleon
Emperor Nero 247, 297, 493
Emperor Valentinian I 108
Emperor Valentinian III 420
Emperor's Birthday (Japan) 188, 501
Empire State Building 198, 306, 517, 520

Encyclopaedia Brittanica 483
Endangered Species Act (U.S.) 506, 530
Endara, Guillermo 497
Endeavour space shuttle 370
Engelbart, Douglas 455, 528
Engels, Friedrich 131, 467
English Channel
    hovercraft 303, 524
    swimming 323, 343, 516
    Tunnel 203, 478, 537, 539
English Peasants' Revolt 253
Enkutatash (Ethiopia) 21, 356, 368
Ennen no Mai (Japan) 60
Enron fraud 48, 543
Enterprise space shuttle 375, 531
Entertainment and Sports Programming
    Network (ESPN) 364
envelope-folding machine 61
Epiphany 45
Episcopal Church 374
Epstein, Brian 334, 345, 377, 527
Epulum Jovis 451
equinox 10, 11, 115, 354
ER 377
Eradication of Poverty Day 414
Erikson, Leif 406
Eritrea National Day 222
Errin Gurvan Naadam (Mongolia) 277, 288
Escobar, Pablo 300, 538
Esperanto 493
Estonia
    independence 359, 514, 537
    Independence Day 104
    Liberation War 261, 515
    Victory Day 261
Estonia car ferry 387, 539
Estrada, Joseph 60, 542
Ethiopia 159
    Christmas 46
    Enkutatash 21, 356, 368
    Jews airlifted from 222, 537
    National Day 226
    New Year 21, 356, 368
Ethiopian Airlines hijack 461, 540
Eton College 262
Ettridge, David 338
Eureka Stockade 480
Euro 40, 208, 541
Europe Day 206
European Day of Languages 384
European Economic Community 143, 523
European Union 86, 206, 438, 484, 538
Eurovision song contest 163, 530
Evans, Sir Arthur 137, 288, 512
Evatt, Herbert Vere 550
Eve of St John the Baptist 261
Evel Knievel 119, 228, 414, 527, 529
Everett, Edward 457
Evers, Medgar 250, 525
evolution, theory of 256, 299, 373, 462, 516,
    518, 549
Ewart-Biggs, Christopher 299
exhibition housing estate 301
extra-solar planetary system 179, 539
Exxon-Mobil merger 225, 541
Exxon Valdez oil spill 107, 142, 258, 535, 536
Eye of the Needle, Seattle 220

F

FA Cup 134
face transplant 466, 545
Fagg, Graham 478
Fahlberg, Constantine 107
Fairbanks, Douglas 262, 489
Falkland Islands Liberation Day 252
Falklands War 137, 159, 252, 533
The Family 65, 177, 326, 328, 528, 529
The Fantasticks 200, 524
Fargo, William 136
Farnsworth, Philo Taylor 364, 548
Farrakhan, Louis 413
Farrow, Mia 297, 501, 527
Fasci Italiani di Combattimento 141
Fascist Party, Italy 103, 515
Fastnet yacht race 332, 532
Father's Day 137, 354
Fatima, apparition of Virgin Mary 410, 514
Fawkes, Guy 67, 171, 442
Feast of Glory (Jalal) 166
Feast of Our Lady of Lourdes 90
Feast of Our Lady of the Rosary 404
Feast of St Paul's Shipwreck (Malta) 89
Feast of the Annunciation of Mary 143
Feast of the Assumption of Mary 314, 333
Feast of the Black Nazarene 48
Feast of the Chair of St Peter 102
Feast of the Hunters Moon 395
Feast of the Tabernacles 396
Feast of the Three Hierarchs 70
Feast of the Transfiguration of Christ 314, 323
Feast of the Virgin's Appearance 294
Febbaro, Enrique 298
February Revolution 125, 134, 514
Fechter, Peter 335, 525
Ferguson, Sarah 137, 338, 412, 413, 501, 538
Fermi, Enrico 479, 519, 548
Ferrari, Enrico 255, 515

Festa della Repubblica (Italy) 239
Festival of Jaisalmer 78
Festival of St Basil 38
Festival of Wang-Mu 500
Festival of Weeks 234
Festivus 501
Fête de la Musique 259
Fiesta de La Mercè (Spain) 382
Fiestas de Santa Fe (New Mexico) 365
51 Pegasi 403, 359
Fiji Independence Day 407
film
    cinematographe 92
    computer animation 460, 540
    first color newsreel 44
    first motion picture 403, 506
    first studio 80
    first talkie 403, 516
    first with soundtrack 129, 515
    last silent movie 84
    Oscars *see* Academy Awards
    patent 46
    Phonofilm 129
    showing of first 140
    3D movies 98, 168
    top grossing films 546
fingerprint evidence 145, 512
Finland
    Independence Day 483, 515
    Wife Carrying Championship 277
fire extinguisher 89
First Council of Nicaea 19
First Martyrs of the Franciscan Order 55
Firth, Colin 366, 367
Fischer, Bobby 47, 126
Fitzgerald, Garret 453, 534
Flaubert, Gustave 264, 489
Fleiss, Heidi 222, 519
Fleming, Alexander 548
Fleming, Ian 205, 226, 330
Flinders, Matthew 296, 297, 486
Flipper, Henry Ossian 253
Flora's Day 221
Florence floods 440, 527
Flores de Mayo 196
Florida 159
    election controversy 444
    Hurricane Katrina 343, 545
    St Augustine 365
    Sunshine Skyway Bridge collapse 206, 532
Florida to Cuba swim 210, 540
Florifertum 187
Floyd, Charles "Pretty Boy" 419, 517
flushing toilet patent 210
Flyer III 402, 512
flying blind 383, 516
flying trapeze 450
Focke-Wulf Fw 61 265, 517
Folies Bergère 469
Fonda, Jane 364, 528
Fonteyn, Margot 180, 216, 255, 524
foot-and-mouth disease 53, 543
Ford, Gerald 58, 181, 325, 326, 530, 531
Ford, Henry 301, 308, 330
Ford Motor Company 330
    assembly line 53, 478, 514
    buying Volvo 68
    Falcon 218, 524
    minimum wage 44
    Model A Ford 301
    Model T Ford 229, 330, 513, 516
    Mustang 175
    Soybean Car 52
Foreman, George 428
forensics 261, 517
45-rpm singles 107
Fossey, Dian 505, 534
Founder's Day/Thinking Day 102
France *see also* Paris
    annexure of Papal States 215
    Britain declaring war on 216
    Courrieres coalmine explosion 127, 512
    declaration of war on Austria 178
    first female pilot 125, 513
    guillotine 138, 183, 239, 367, 413, 531
    heatwave 544
    Hundred Days Rule 138
    Jews transported to Germany 107, 519
    metric system 164
    miners strike for eight hour-day 122, 512
    National Convention 379
    nuclear testing 69, 92, 540
    Reign of Terror 239, 306
    religious wars 118, 552
    TGV train 216, 380, 533, 536
    treaty to form Indochina 125
    women's vote 179, 520
    Woodrow Wilson visit 490
Franchi, Jean 384
Franco, General Francisco 146, 184, 296, 428,
    458, 460, 481, 518, 530
Frank, Anne 212, 250, 283, 321, 519, 520, 534
Frank, Otto 283, 337
Frankenstein 40, 43
Franklin, Aretha 42
Franklin, Benjamin 9, 175, 221, 253
Frankum, Wade 335, 537
Fraser, Dawn 109, 119, 361, 526
Fraser, Malcolm 448

Frazier, Joe 125, 398, 529
Frederick the Great of Prussia 482
Free Speech Movement 398, 526
Freedom 7 202
freedom of religion 55, 171, 177
Freeman, Cathy 373
French Alps avalanche 89
French Foreign Legion 127
French Revolution 292, 328, 379
French Revolutionary calendar 33
Freud, Sigmund 203, 381, 441, 518, 548
Freya's Birthday 505
Freya's Day 68
Friends 380, 539
Friendship Day 298
Friendship 7 100, 427, 525
Frisbee 52, 523
Fu Mingxia 43
Fujiyoshida Fire Festival (Japan) 317
Fulton, Robert 90
Funicello, Annette 383
Funny Girl 144, 526
Furse, Clara 144

G

Gable, Clark 80, 269, 512
Gaddafi, Col Muammar 358, 497, 528
"The Gadget" 294
Gagarin, Yuri 170, 517, 524, 551
Gaius Caesar (Caligula) 64
Galapagos Islands 55, 373, 542
Galilei, Galileo 46, 47, 92, 170, 260, 349, 469,
    549
Galileo spacecraft 412, 427, 484, 540
Gallipoli, Battle of 99, 183, 496, 514
Galtür avalanche 103, 541
Galveston Bay fire 174, 521
Galveston, Texas 239, 257
Gandhi, Indira 46, 58, 140, 176, 219, 243, 429,
    457, 526, 532, 534
Gandhi Jayanti (India) 399
Gandhi, Mohandas (Mahatma) 50, 70, 129, 386,
    399, 513, 517, 521, 550
Gandhi, Rajiv 219, 537
Gang of Eight 337
Gang of Four 408, 531
Garcia, Jerry 485
Garfield, James 279
Garfunkel, Art 134, 407, 442, 529
Garibaldi, Giuseppe 208, 239, 281
Garin, Maurice 297, 512
Garland, Judy 386
Garnerin, Andre-Jacques 419
gasoline-driven car 69, 378
Gates, Bill 200, 426, 523, 541
Gay and Lesbian Mardi Gras (Aust.) 262, 531
Gay Pride parade
    Amsterdam 317
    Tokyo 346
Gaza Strip *see* Palestine
Gdansk shipyard strike 207, 332, 463, 533, 535
Gehrig, Lou 259, 518
Geldof, Bob 290, 402
Gemini XI spaceship 373, 527
General Motors 374, 513
genetic engineering 217, 539
Geneva Conference 184
Geneva Convention 340
Geographically Speaking 425
geosynchronous satellite 304
Germany
    capital moved back to Berlin 258
    Cologne Cathedral 332
    currency collapse 453, 515
    Federal Republic of 221, 521
    flooding 342
    meeting of leaders of East and West 137, 523
    Nazis *see* Nazis
    reunification 92, 137, 341, 400, 536
    Schicksalstag 446
    space race 400
    Warsaw Pact 212
    witch trials 169
Geronimo 254, 361
Gestapo 184, 517, 520
Getty, Pope John Paul III 418, 530
Gettysburg Address 457
Gettysburg, Battle of 278
Ghana Independence Day 123, 523
Gibraltar 136, 302, 543
Gibson, Mel 349
Gibson, Violet 164
Giles Mary-of-Saint-Joseph's Day 86
Gilliam, Terry 208, 460
Gilligan, Andrew 330
gladiator competition 40
Gladiator insects 176
Gladstone, William 486, 507
glam rock 244
glasnost 337, 484
Glenn, John 100, 427, 525, 541, 551
Global Positioning System 93, 535
Globe Theatre, London 268
"Goal of the Century" 260, 534
Goddard, Robert H. 247, 517, 548
Godra train fire 107
Godse, Nathuram 70

Godunov, Alexander 376
Godzilla 440
Goebbels, Joseph 98, 189, 198, 427
Goetz, Bernard 500, 534
Goldberg, Whoopi 488
Golden Gate Bridge 225, 518
Golden Temple attack 243, 534
Goldman, Emma 90, 514
Goldman, Ronald 183, 250, 255, 400, 540
Goldstein, Baruch Kapel 105
Gone with the Wind 200, 269, 503, 518, 546
Gonzalez, Elian 80
Good Friday Agreement 168, 345, 461, 541
Goodwin, Harold W. 199, 371
Google search engine 364, 541
Gorbachev, Mikhail 119, 128, 159, 214, 225,
    242, 250, 259, 337, 341, 342, 376, 400,
    409, 412, 484, 485, 497, 503, 517,
    534, 535, 536, 547, 550
Gordon, Richard 373
Gordy, Berry 192
Gore, Al 444, 541
Gore, Tipper 377
gorilla reserve creation, Rwanda 505
Gosse, William 279
Gotti, John 261, 538
Gould, Chester 441
Grand Slam bowls 131
Grandparents' Day (U.S.) 354
Grant, Hugh 365
Grant, Ulysses S. 66, 261, 301
Granville rail disaster 57, 531
Grassl, Andrea 100
Grateful Dead 485
Gravelines, Battle of 307
Gravmas 503
Gray, Elisha 95
great auk 240
Great Council Exhibition 198
Great Crash (NYSE) 422
Great Depression 427, 516
Great Fire of London 359
Great Fire of Rome 297
Great Kanto Earthquake 358, 515
"Great Leap Forward" 221, 523
Great Ormond Street Hospital 94
Great Pyramid 27
Great Smog of 1952 482, 522
"Great Society" 220, 526
Great Storm of 1987 396
Great Train Robbery 174, 285, 325, 525, 526
Great Wall of China 447, 528
Great White Hurricane 128
Greece *see also* Athens
    ancient Greek calendar 32
    Commemoration of Pontian Greeks'
        Genocide 217
    coup d'état 168
    earthquake 347
    freeing of Civil War prisoners 452, 526
    Independence Day 143
    Oxi (No) Day 426
    Polytechneio Day 455
    War of Independence 143, 417
Green Granite Bomb 213
Green March 530
Greenham Common military base protests
    489, 533
Greenough, John 101
Greensboro rally 440, 532
Greenwich Foot Tunnel 321, 512
Greenwich Mean Time 438
Gregorian calendar 16, 18, 19, 38, 40, 76, 91, 93,
    401, 513, 547
Grenada 422, 533
Gretzky, Wayne 26, 539
Grey, Lady Jane 287, 409
Grimaldi, Joseph 121
Groce, Cherry 399
Grohl, Dave 162, 532
Grounation Day (Jamaica) 179
Gruelle, John B. 491
Guadalcanal, Battle of 450, 519
Guadeloupe hurricane 363
Guam
    Japanese on 520
    reclaimed from Japanese 299
    WWII soldier found on 64, 529
Guatemala
    earthquake 51
    Independence Day 373
    Mateo Flores stadium disaster 413, 540
    Pilgrimage of Cristo Negro de Esquipulas 54
Guernica bombing 184, 518
Guevara, Ernesto "Che" 212, 252, 406, 527, 550
Guggenheim Museum 418, 524
Guildford Four 536
guillotine 138, 183, 239, 367, 413, 531
Guiteau, Charles 279
Guinness Four 417
The Gulag Archipelago 506, 530
Gulf War 51, 54, 95, 103, 105, 107, 127, 537
Gunfight at the O.K. Corral 424
Gunpowder Plot 442
Guru Gobind Singh, Birthday of 44
Gusmao, Xanana 38, 550
Gutenberg Bible 140
Guy Fawkes Night 442

515

H

Gyatso, Tenzin 102, 455, 518
Gypsies in concentration camps 453, 519

Hadrian's Wall 371
Hagman, Larry 376, 379
Hahn, Otto 496, 518
Haile Selassie's birthday 301
Hair 386, 414, 527, 528
Haiti
    Hurricane Flora 404, 525
    Hurricane Jeanne 381, 544
    rebellion 84, 544
Hale-Bopp comet 158, 540
Haley, Bill 207, 283, 522
Hall, George "Willie" 454, 518
Hallgrímsson, Jónas 454
Halloween 397, 429
Ham the Chimp 71, 524
Hamburg bombing 452, 519
Hamilton, Thomas 130
Hana-matsuri (Japan) 165
Hand-in-Hand Rally, Taiwan 108, 544
Handler, Ruth 126, 441
Hands Across America rally 223, 534
Handsel Monday 38
Hangul Day (Sth Korea) 406
Hannington, James 427
Hanson, Pauline 338, 544
Hanukkah 26, 475
Hanuman Jayanti 156
Happy Days 54, 530
Harding, Karl Ludwig 358
Harding, Tonya 45, 450, 538
Hardy, Dr James 63, 424
Hariri, Rafik 93, 545
Harris, Paul 103
Harrison, Benjamin 180
Harrison, George 168, 468, 478, 508, 542
Harrods bombing 495, 533
Harry Potter and the Half-Blood Prince 294, 545
Harry Potter and the Philosopher's Stone 265, 540
Hartjesdagen (Nederlands) 317
Hartley, Catherine 43
Harvard University 365, 520
Hastings, Battle of 411
Haston, Dougal 382
Hathaway, Anne 467
Havel, Vaclav 550
Hawaii 56
    biggest wave ever surfed 481, 528
    first Japanese in 88
    Hurricane Iniki 368
    Ka Hae Hawai'i 309
    Kamehameha Day 249
    Pearl Harbor bombing 484, 519
    United Airlines Flight 811 104
    U.S. annexure 284
Hawke, Bob 385, 486, 498
Hayes, Rutherford B. 94
Hays, Anna Mae 249, 528
Hearst, Patty 83, 138, 382, 530
heart, lung, and liver transplant 495, 535
heart transplant 41, 99, 279, 344, 480, 527, 534
    animal to human 63, 424, 534
    artificial heart 99, 279, 344
Heath, Edward 500, 530
heatwave in Europe 544
Heaven's Gate sect 144, 540
Hebrew calendar 26
Heilborn, Rose 43
helicopter 451
    circumnavigation of globe 300, 533
Hemel Hempstead explosions 488
Henderson, Florence 93
Hendrick Motorsports plane crash 422
Hendrix, Jimi 149, 256, 336, 363, 376, 466, 527, 528
Henley Royal Regatta 252
Hennard, George 413
Hepburn, Audrey 201, 488
Hepburn, Katharine 268, 543
Herald of Free Enterprise sinking 123, 535
Herrmann, Emanuel 398
Herschel, John 366
Herschel, William 130, 453
Hess, Rudolf 335, 535
Hester, Rita 458
Heyerdahl, Thor 187, 324, 521
Heysel Stadium riot 227, 534
Hickok, "Wild Bill" 339
Higan no Chu-Nichi (Japan) 355, 381
Highway 61 Revisited 348
Hill, Clint 460
Hillary, Sir Edmund 43, 227, 298, 483, 522, 523
Hillsborough Stadium disaster 173, 536
Himalayan avalanches 447, 539
Himalayan Broad Peak 247
Himmler, Heinrich 453, 519, 520
Hina Matsuri (Japan) 120
Hinckley, John Jr 148, 259, 533
Hindenburg airship crash 203, 518
Hindenburg, Paul von 69, 129, 517
Hindu calendar 31
Hines, James 411, 528
Hippocratic Oath 548
Hiroshima bombing 308, 323, 333, 520

Hispanic Day 409
Hitchcock, Alfred 254, 524
Hitchhiker's Guide to the Galaxy 125, 531
Hitler, Adolf 55, 67, 69, 81, 94, 105, 124, 129, 132, 158, 189, 211, 220, 251, 269, 296, 298, 319, 333, 389, 423, 446, 515, 516, 517, 518, 520
Hitler-Stalin Pact 341
HIV/AIDS 124, 181, 200, 243, 286, 346, 444, 478, 532, 533, 534, 537, 541, 542
HMAS *Melbourne* 89, 241, 526, 528
HMAS *Sydney* 457, 519
HMAS *Voyager* 89, 526
HMS *Beagle* 373, 399, 505
Ho Chi Minh 119, 217, 359, 360, 520, 521, 550
The Hobbit 379, 408, 518
Hobbit Day 380
Hodgkin's disease 49
Hoffman, Albert 164, 174, 519
Hoffmann, Felix 123
Hogan, Michael 459
Hoge, James 322
Hogmanay (Scotland) 477, 509
Hoisington, Elizabeth P. 249, 528
Holi 116
Holly, Buddy 82, 524
Hollywood Black Friday 402
Hollywood sign 290, 515
Hollywood Ten 463, 524
Hollywood Walk of Fame 88, 524
Holocaust aid fund 84, 540
Holocaust Memorial Day 67
Holt, Harold 322, 495, 527
Holy Innocents' Day 477, 506
homosexuality
    decriminalisation in NSW 246, 534
    gay Anglican bishop 320, 544
    Nazi concentration camps 453, 519
    same sex marriage 70, 215, 218, 224, 536, 541, 543
    U.S. Air Force 419, 530
Honda Motor Company 382, 521
Honduras
    earthquake 83
    Independence Day 373
Hong Koh disaster 136
Hong Kong
    avian flu 507, 541
    Disneyland 370
    handed back to China 269, 278, 384, 540
    liberation in WWII 348
Honkeiko Colliery disaster 184
Honshu-Shikoku suspension bridge 162
Hoover Dam 406, 518
Hoover, J. Edgar 199, 207, 516
Hope Diamond 368, 445, 524
Hornby, Frank 48, 512
hot air ballooning 107, 242, 372, 419, 459, 534
"hot-line" between U.S.S.R. and U.S. 258, 525
House Un-American Activities Committee 205, 521
Houston, Sam 419
hovercraft 183, 524
Howard, Charles 307
Howard, John 225, 304, 542
Howard, Leslie 238, 519
Hoxha, Enver 100, 537
HSK *Kormoran* 457, 519
Hu Yaobang 173, 536
Hubble, Edwin 182, 458, 508, 516, 548, 549
Hubble telescope 182, 294
Hudson, Henry 360, 370
Hughes, Langston 79
Hughes, Ted 254, 426, 523
Hughes, William 451, 514
Human Genome Project 172
Humphries, Barry 490, 523
Hundred Years War 228, 256
Hungary
    Independence Day 132, 536
    National Day 420
    1956 uprising 420, 441, 523
    opening border with Austria 368, 536
    rally for independence 132
    Warsaw Pact 212
Huntley, Ian 321, 543
Hurricane Flora 404, 525
Hurricane, Great White 128
Hurricane Iniki 368
Hurricane Jeanne 381, 544
Hurricane Katrina 343, 346, 347, 545
Hurricane Wilma 416
hurricane names 210, 531
Hus, Jan 283
Hussein, Saddam 106, 138, 166, 187, 294, 341, 403, 416, 490, 493, 494, 518, 532, 536, 537, 541, 543, 544, 545
Hussein, Uday and Qusay 300, 544
Hyde, Douglas 264, 518
hydrogen bomb 46, 84, 118, 428, 522, 523

I

I Dream of Jeanie 376
I Love Lucy 412, 522
I LOVE YOU email virus 201, 542
IBM 93, 160, 182, 253, 324, 513, 516, 520, 532, 534

Ibrox football stadium disaster 41
ice hockey 87, 403, 438, 464, 514, 524, 541
ice rink, artificial 91
Iceland
    abortion legalised 68, 517
    Dagur Islenskrar Tungu 454
    Laki volcano 246
Ides of March 132
Ikari diving competition 274
Iliescu, Adriana 55, 545
Imbolc 12, 80
The Immaculate Conception 485
In Old Arizona 60
In Utero 379
Inauguration Day (U.S.) 60, 121
Independent Air crash 87
India
    Air India crash 40, 553
    Amristar Massacre 171, 515
    Bhopal gas leak 480, 534
    Bombay Docks Explosion 172, 519
    Children's Day 452
    earthquakes 405, 512, 552
    elephants wearing reflectors 298, 544
    flooding 304, 361, 531, 545
    Godra train fire 117, 543
    Golden Temple attack 243, 534
    Gujarat earthquake 66
    Hindu calendar 31
    Independence Day 333, 521
    killing of missionaries 63, 541
    killing of Muslims in Assam 102, 533
    Mega River Delta tidal waves 429
    New Dehli as capital 89, 517
    Orissa cyclone 427, 542
    Punjabi new year 21
    stabbing of alleged criminal 331
    stampede during pilgrimage 65
    Vaisakhi 21
Indonesia
    Australian embassy bombing 322, 366, 544
    Bali bombing 120, 324, 409, 543, 544
    blackout 336
    Dutch surrender to Japanese 125, 519
    end of Dutch rule 505, 521
    invasion of East Timor 484
    student protest re Wahid 69
    Suharto as President 128, 527
    tsunami 504
infrared photography 404
Ingalls, Laura 406, 517
Inghean Bhuidhe's Day 203
instant camera 48, 101
insulin 50, 305, 515
integrated circuit 85, 524
Intel Pentium processor 140, 538
internal combustion engine 158
International Children's Book Day 159
International Criminal Court 509
International Date Line 438
International Day for the Elderly 394
International Day of Peace 379
International Human Rights Day 487
International Military Tribunal of the Far East 450, 521
International Monetary Fund 505, 520
International Mother Language Day 101
International Red Cross 427, 487
International Space Station 439, 542
International Youth Day 330, 339
Internet adoption scandal 58, 542
interracial marriage 250, 451, 527
Inventors' Day (U.S.) 97
iPod 420, 543
IRA 50, 86, 87, 88, 98, 140, 182, 240, 248, 253, 299, 332, 345, 380, 461, 466, 495, 500, 528, 533, 536, 539, 540
Iran
    earthquakes 168, 374, 504, 531, 544, 552
    hostage crisis 58, 60, 182, 532
    Iranian calendar 30
    Iraqi invasion of 380, 532
    Islamic Republic 158, 532
    Norooz (New Year) 21, 30, 115, 139
    Persia renamed 505, 517
    Sina 1 satellite 425, 545
    Tirgan 275
    U.S. embassy hostages 441, 532
    U.S. selling weapons to 202, 264, 440
Iran Air jet shot down 280, 535, 553
Iran-Contra affair 202, 264, 440, 534, 535
Iran-Iraq War 134, 280, 535
Iranian embassy siege, London 202
Iraq
    Abu Ghraib prison 126, 178, 342, 544, 545
    bombing raids on 52, 138
    elections 70, 493, 545
    Gulf War *see* Gulf War
    Interim Government 267
    invasion of Iran 380, 532
    Kuwait *see* Kuwait
    military coup 292
    missile attacks 265, 538, 543
    Najaf bombing 347, 544
    National Assembly 70, 134, 545
    Oil for Food Program 218

poison gas attack on Halabja 535
protests against war in 543
"sexing up" intelligence on 296, 330
stampede in Baghdad 349, 545
trade embargo 323
UN Headquarters bombing 337, 544
U.S. control of 166, 543, 544
U.S. helicopter crash 66
weapons inspections 296, 330, 403, 429, 484, 494, 541, 544
Western hostages 341, 536
Iraq War protests 94
Ireland *see also* Northern Ireland
    Anglo-Irish Agreement 289, 453, 483, 515, 534
    Battle of the Boyne 289
    Bloody Sunday 70, 81, 339, 459, 515, 529
    British embassy destroyed 81, 529
    divorce legalised 107, 462, 540
    Easter Rebellion 182, 188, 514
    Good Friday Agreement 168, 345, 461, 541
    Irish Free State 126, 340
    Ivy Day 403
    Republic of Ireland Act 499, 521
    smoking ban 147, 544
    travel to Britain suspended 130, 520
    uprising against English rule 122
Irish Republican Army *see* IRA
iron ships, battle between 126
Iroquois Theatre fire 508, 512
Irving, John 108
Islamic calendar 27
Islamic New Year 21
Isle of Man 282
Israel
    admitted to UN 208, 521
    forced evacuation of Gaza Strip 335, 545
    invasion of Lebanon 231, 531
    Jordan-Israel peace deal 424, 539
    Law of Return 282, 522
    Lod Airport shootings 227, 529
    Oslo Peace Accords 338, 371, 538
    peace treaty with Egypt 140, 144, 376, 531, 532
    Pope John Paul II visit 144, 542
    release of Arab prisoners 118, 539
    reunification of Jerusalem 268
    Six Day War 243, 248, 267, 527
    Weizman as President 96
    withdrawal from Gaza Strip 368
    withdrawal from Lebanon 222, 542
    Yom Kippur War 422, 530
Istanbul 146
Italy
    aircraft used in warfare 122, 513
    Battle of Cisterna 69
    earthquakes 52, 506, 513, 514, 552
    Fascist Party, Italy 103
    Florence floods 440, 527
    Great Fire of Rome 297
    Gregorian calendar 401
    invasion in WWII 303, 519
    Kingdom of Italy proclaimed 135
    La Fenice opera house fire 69, 540
    Republic Day 239
    republic referendum 239, 521
    Rome Olympics 1960 362, 524
    women's vote 240, 515
iTunes 187, 365, 543
Ivan Kupala 284
Ivanov, Yevgeny 140
IVF baby 303, 531
Ivy Day 403
Izetbegovic, Alija 459

J

Jack the Ripper 349, 446
Jackson, Andrew 70
Jackson, George 339, 529
Jackson, Janet 380, 544
Jackson, Michael 67, 71, 120, 342, 347, 533, 534, 538, 545
Jailhouse Rock 418
Jaime Hilario Barbal's Day 57
Jalaali calendar 30
Jamaica
    earthquake 53
    independence 89, 525
    Independence Day 323
James Bond 205, 226, 411, 525
James Hannington's Day 427
James, Henry 108, 514
James, Jesse 299
Jane Eyre 361
Jameson, Leander Starr 507
Jan Hus Day 283
Japan *see also* Tokyo
    apology for "comfort women" 52, 538
    cherry blossom season 197
    Culture Day 440
    Emperor Day 440
    Emperor's Birthday 188, 501
    flag 321
    founding 90
    Great Kanto Earthquake 358, 515, 552
    Honshu-Hokkaido tunnel 67, 203, 533
    Honshu-Shikoku suspension bridge 162

Japan Airlines crash 553
Kobe earthquake 56, 539
Korea annexed by 340, 513
May sickness 197
Mt. Asama eruption 320
new constitution 440, 521
New Year celebrations 41
Niigata earthquake 420
Nippon Airways crash 83
Okinawa returned to 213, 529
Russian-Japanese War 85, 512
Shogunate abolished 169
surrender, WWII 333, 359, 520
Treaty of Mutual Co-operation with U.S. 261, 524
WWII bombing 126, 520
Jaruzelski, General 463
Jarvis, Anna 197
The Jazz Singer 403, 516
Jefferson Memorial 171, 519
Jefferson, Thomas 177, 281, 417, 502
Jemison, Mae Carol 370
Jenner, Edward 205, 212, 278, 548
Jerusalem
  East Jerusalem annexed by Israel 527
  reunification 268
  Siege of 245, 293
Jesus Christ 16, 19, 115, 155, 160, 162, 323, 474, 503, 527
Jewish people
  art stolen from 67, 540
  Chelmno death camp 238
  Ethiopia, airlifted from 222, 537
  evacuation from Gaza Strip 335, 545
  expulsion from Spain 131, 319
  freedom of religion 177
  French Jews transported to Germany 107, 519
  genocide 319
  Hebrew calendar 26
  Holocaust Memorial Day 67
  killing of, Switzerland 48
  Kristallnacht 446, 518
  Law of Return 282, 522
  Nazi concentration camps 453, 519
  New Year 21, 26, 356
  partitioning of Palestine 468
  SS *St Louis* 242, 518
  uprising against Nazis, Poland 57
Joan of Arc 48, 101, 123, 188, 228, 256
Jolson, Al 403, 420
Jon Frum Day (Vanuatu) 94
John, Elton 104, 143, 290, 541
John Peel Day 410
Johnny Appleseed Day 128
Johnson, Andrew 130, 173
Johnson, Ben 122, 508, 538
Johnson, Earvin "Magic" 444, 537
Johnson, Jack 504
Johnson, Lyndon B. 47, 123, 220, 279, 345, 412, 460, 526, 527
Johnson, Opha Mae 331
Johnson, Samuel 173, 490
Johnson, Xolani Nkosi 286, 542
Johnson's *Dictionary of the English Language* 173
Jones, Brian 280, 528
Jones, Jim 456
Jones, Mary Harris 306, 469
Jones, Paula 91
Jonestown mass suicide 456, 531
Jordan-Israel peace deal 424, 539
Jordan, Michael 214, 534
Jorgensen, George 478, 522
Joseph, Peter Leopold 469
Joséphine of Martinique 478, 493
Joyce, James 254, 507, 514, 519
Joyner, Florence Griffith 379
juke box 461
Julian calendar 16, 18, 38, 40, 76, 274
Julian the Hospitaller's Day 91
Julius Caesar 17, 18, 38, 109, 127, 132, 274
Juneteenth 257
Juno asteroid 358
Jupiter 484, 530, 532, 539, 540

K

Ka Hae Hawai'i 309
Kaczynski, Theodore 62, 160, 540, 541
Kakizome 41
Kalgoorlie–Boulder 80
Kamehameha Day (Hawaii) 249
Kane, Helen 325
Kang, David 66
Kaplan, Fanya 348, 515
Karachun 499
Karpov, Anatoli 221, 446
Kashmir Day 84
Kasparov, Garry 96, 171, 201, 446, 534, 540
Kaufman, Phil 443, 530
Kaye, Danny 246, 488
Kazakhstan, atomic bomb detonation 347, 521
Keating, Paul 498, 500
Keeler, Christine 140, 525
Keenan, Barry 485
Keenan, Brian 342, 536
Keir no Hi (Japan) 357
Keller, Helen 238, 246, 266, 528
Kellog, John and William 99, 308, 512

Kelly, Dr. David 296, 544
Kelly, Grace 177, 372, 450, 523, 532
Kelly, Mary Jane 446
Kelly, Ned 267, 448
Kelly, Oakley 200
Kemmler, William 323
Kemptner, Thomas 481
Kennedy, Jackie 217, 262, 306, 370, 417, 460, 522, 528
Kennedy, John F. 131, 208, 217, 220, 223, 252, 262, 265, 322, 346, 370, 378, 384, 386, 460, 462, 522, 525, 526
Kennedy, John F. Jr 294, 379, 417, 463, 540, 542
Kennedy, Robert F. 175, 228, 243, 244, 322, 458, 528
Kenya
  independence 489, 526
  Mau Mau movement 165, 522
  U.S. embassy bombing 324, 338, 541
Kenyatta, Jomo 165, 522
Kepler, Johannes 414, 453, 505, 549
Kerr, Sir John 448
Kerrigan, Nancy 45, 410, 538
Kerry, John 338, 364
Keti Koti 278
Key, Francis Scott 372
Keynes, John Maynard 548
Khamoro 197
Khayyam, Omar 30
Khmer Rouge 170, 175, 199, 452, 507, 530, 541, 551
Khomeini, Ayatollah 80, 90, 93, 215, 240, 384, 532, 535
Khrushchev, Nikita 145, 175, 331, 368, 388, 441, 523
Kidman, Nicole 84, 258, 542
kidney transplant 121, 255, 522
Kiku no Sekku (Japan) 366
Kilby, Jack 85, 524
Kim Jea Kyu 424, 532
kinetoscope 172
King Abdullah of Saudi Arabia 320, 545
King Alphonso VIII of Spain 294
King Bhumibol Adulyadej of Thailand 482
King, Billie Jean 378, 460, 500, 530
King Birendra of Nepal 238
King Brian of Ireland 181
King Charles I 127, 145, 457, 494
King Christian I 100
King Edward the Confessor 410, 506
King Edward III 66, 451
King Edward IV 121, 219
King Edward VIII 488, 518
King Fahd of Saudi Arabia 318, 320
King Faisal of Iraq 292, 524
King Faisal of Saudi Arabia 143, 439, 526, 530
King Farouk of Egypt 301
King Ferdinand of Spain 319
King Francis I 445
King George III 242, 365
King George VI 204, 213, 239, 492, 522
King Harold 383, 387, 410
King Hassan II of Morocco 443, 530
King Henry II 499
King Henry V 423
King Henry VI 121, 219, 262
King Henry VIII 63, 68, 107, 124, 180, 181, 249, 257, 262, 267, 283, 289, 306, 316, 495
King Herod 347, 506
King James I 142, 145, 442
King John 253, 502
King Juan Carlos I 428, 460, 530
King Kamehameha of Hawaii 249, 309
King Kong 119, 517
King Léopold I of Belgium 299
King Léopold II 84
King Léopold III 136, 522
King Louis XIV 203, 212, 358, 362, 368, 413
King Louis XVI 214, 328, 341, 379, 413
King, Martin Luther Jr 140, 160, 161, 163, 220, 246, 249, 346, 386, 487, 516, 523, 525, 527, 528, 550
King Montezuma II 445
King Odoacer of Italy 361
King of Hejaz 47
King Philip II of Macedonia 448
King Pompilius of Rome 17
King Richard II 254
King Robert I 145, 245, 262
King, Rodney 120, 188, 321, 537, 538
King Saud (of Saudi Arabia) 439, 526
King Shaka of the Zulus 357
King, Stephen 257, 379, 542
King Umberto II 239
King Victor Emmanuel 135
King Wenceslas of Bohemia 373
King William III 103, 125
King William IV 365
Kingsford Smith, Charles 287, 445, 516
Kittinger, Joe 372, 534
KLM airline 404, 515
  Tenerife crash 145, 531, 553
K-Mart 62
Knossos palace 137, 512
Koch, Ilse 54
Koch, Robert 142
Kodak 48, 361, 371
Kohl, Helmut 479, 537
Kolff, Dr Willem 499

Komarov, Vladimir 182, 551
Kon-Tiki 187, 324, 521
Koon, Stacey 120, 321, 538
Kopp, James 420
Korda, Albert 406
Korea
  annexation by Japan 340, 513
  calendar 23
  Liberation Day 333
  mass wedding 105, 527
  peace talks 122, 540
  Sampoong Department Store collapse 268, 539
Korean Airlines jet shot down 358, 532
Korean War 169, 264, 269, 305, 522, 552
Koresh, David 108, 177, 335
Kosmolets submarine 164, 536
Kosmos 110 62
Kosovo War 141, 247, 248, 541, 542
Kozlov, Leonid and Valentina 376, 532
Kray, Ronnie and Reggie 329, 532
Kremlin Accords 53, 538
Kristallnacht 446, 518
Ku Klux Klan 250, 259, 440, 502, 525, 526, 532
Kubba, Laith 493
Kursk submarine 330, 542
Kuwait
  Gulf War 51, 54, 56, 95, 103, 105, 107, 127, 537
  Iraqi invasion 323, 536
  Iraqi withdrawal 106, 537
  oil wells set alight 443, 537
  Operation Desert Storm 54, 56, 107, 537
  proclaimed province of Iraq 346, 537
  Western hostages 341, 536
  women's vote 214, 541
Kuwait Airlines hijack 162
Kwanzaa 477, 508
Kyoto conference on global warming 488, 541
Kyoto Protocol 95, 146, 543, 545
Kyrgyzstan Independence Day 349, 532

L

La Belle disco bombing 162, 172, 534
La Boheme 80
La Fenice opera house fire 69, 540
La Navidad 504
LaBianca, Leno and Rosemary 328, 528
Labor Day 354
Lady Chatterley's Lover 439, 524
Ladysmith siege 439
LaHara, Brianna 365
Lammas 11, 316
Land Day 148
Land, Edwin 101, 521
land speed record 401, 509, 533
Landy, John 203
Lang, Fritz 49, 516
Langside, Battle of 211
Laos Independence Day 440
laptop computer 160, 534
Larsen, Don 405
Las Navas de Tolosa, Battle of 294
Las Vegas sign 401
Lascaux cave paintings 370, 519
"The Last Supper" 226, 541
Latvia
  independence 359, 515, 537
  Independence Day 456
  summer solstice 237
Lauda, Niki 318, 531
Lauria, Donna 307
Laval, Pierre 309, 520
Lawler, Richard 255, 522
Lawrence, D. H. 368, 439
Lawrence, Richard 70
Le Bateau hung upside down 481, 525
Le Joola ferry disaster 384, 543
Le Mans Grand Prix 249, 265, 513, 523
Le Verrier, Urbain 381
League of Nations 422, 453, 515
Leaning Tower of Pisa 46, 536
leap year 19, 76, 109
Learn from Lei Feng Day 122
Leary, Timothy 227, 229, 419, 525
Lebanon
  Cedar Revolution 93
  hostages 325, 342, 440, 456, 481, 535, 536, 537
  Independence Day 460, 520
  Israeli invasion 132, 531, 533
  Israeli withdrawal 222, 542
  Syrian withdrawal from 184, 545
Lebanon War 244
Led Zeppelin 51, 481, 532
Lee, Harper 288, 524
Lee, Robert E. 166, 178, 409
Lee Seung-Seop 328, 545
Leeson, Nick 106, 479, 539
Left-handers Day 331
legionnaire's disease 57, 531
Leif Erikson Day 406
Leigh, Vivien 269, 284, 503, 518
Lenin, Vladimir 134, 160, 174, 180, 348, 396, 444, 514, 515, 516
Leningrad 64, 225, 506, 519
Lennon, John 121, 143, 168, 260, 283, 329, 334, 342, 406, 415, 485, 519, 523, 527, 528, 532, 533

Lent 78
Leonov, Alexei 96, 526, 551
Leotard, Jules 404
Lepanto, Battle of 404
Lépine, Marc 536
Lerner, Alan Jr 94, 252
Les Misérables 518
Leuthen, Battle of 482
Levi Strauss & Co. 218
Levine, Denis 46
Lewinsky, Monica 46, 66, 91, 301, 335, 379, 497, 541
Lewis, Jerry 349, 521
Libby, I. Lewis 335, 545
Libya
  bombing 172
  Lockerbie air disaster 189, 200, 499, 542, 543
  military coup 358
  pledge to destroy weapons 497, 544
  Revolution Day 358
Libyan Airlines jet shot down 101, 529
Liebknecht, Karl 44, 515
limelight 44-6
Limelight Department 249
Lin, Maya Ying 23, 451, 532
Lincoln, Abraham 79, 172, 173, 175, 184, 436, 443, 457
Lindbergh, Charles III 118, 210, 344, 512, 517
Lindh, Anna 353, 544
Lisbon earthquake 66, 438, 552
Liston, Sonny 12
Lithuania independence 359, 537
Little Big Horn, Battle of 264, 298
Little, Malcolm, see Malcolm X
Little Rock Nine 205, 523
Littlefeather, Sacheen 145
Live Aid 290, 534
Live 8 concerts 279, 545
Livingstone, Dr David 440
Lloyd Webber, Andrew 208, 404, 532
Lloyd Wright, Frank 227, 246, 418
Locarno Pact 484
Loch Ness
  monster 305, 514
  water speed record 388, 522
Lockerbie air disaster 189, 200, 499, 535, 542, 543
Lockwood, Stuart 341
Lodge, Henry Cabot 224, 524
Loewe, Frederick 94, 252
Lohri 52
Lolita 336
London
  ban the bomb demonstration 375, 525
  Bishopsgate bombing 182, 536
  Blitz 307, 519
  Brixton bombing 175, 541
  Brixton riots 199, 387, 490, 532, 534, 540
  Crystal Palace fire 469, 518
  Drury Lane Theatre 104, 204
  gold theft 46, 533
  Great Fire 355
  Great Ormond Street Hospital 94
  Great Smog 452, 522
  Harrods bombing 495, 533
  IRA bombings 56, 88, 98, 182, 495, 500, 533, 536, 540
  Iranian embassy siege 202, 532
  Metropolitan Police 388
  Moorgate station crash 108
  Royal Albert Hall 147
  Royal Opera House 376
  St Paul's Cathedral 259, 359, 507
  Selfridges 132, 513
  Stock Exchange admitting women 144, 529
  suffragette demonstrations 118, 513
  taxi cabs 102, 513
  10 Downing Street attack 86, 537
  terrorist bombings 284, 545
  traffic lights 484
  Underground railway 49, 284, 319
  venereal disease clinic 71
  Westminster Abbey 506
  Westminster Bridge 222
  WWII bombing 69, 119, 251, 507, 519
London Bridge, Arizona 407, 529
Long, Dr Crawford 148
Long Tan, Battle of 336, 527
Lord of the Rings 17, 408, 417, 523, 542, 544, 546
Lord Snowdon 15, 530
Loren, Sophia 237, 378, 533
Los Angeles
  earthquake 56, 538
  firestorm 441
  founding 361
  Olympics 189, 205, 329, 533
  radioactive cloud 526
  riots 120, 188, 538
  St Francis Dam burst 130, 516
Lost in Space 373, 526
Louisiana Purchase 189, 417
The Louvre 445, 459, 513
The Louvre II 544
Love Canal pollution scandal 459, 528
"Love Me Do" 5, 402, 525
LSD 164, 174, 462, 519, 527
Luby's Cafeteria shooting 413
Lucas, Charles 259

Lucas, George 219
"Lucy" fossil 462, 530
Luddite riots 128
Lughnasadh 11, 315
Luis Muñoz Rivera's birthday (Puerto Rico) 295
Lumière, Auguste and Louis 92, 140, 506
Luna 1 41, 43
Luna 3 404, 524
Luna 5 211
lunar calendars 15
Lupercalia (Ancient Rome) 94
Lusitania sinking 204, 514
Luther, Martin 224, 324, 447, 476
Luxemburg, Rosa 54, 515
Lynch, David 165, 536

M

Maastricht Treaty 438, 538
Mabo case 240, 500, 538
Mabon 354
Macapagal-Arroyo, Gloria 60
MacArthur, General Douglas 128, 169, 177, 519, 522
McAuliffe, Christa 68, 362
McCandless, Bruce 86
McCarthy, John 325, 537
McCarthy, Joseph 88, 180, 199, 247, 452, 522, 523
McCartney, Linda 129, 175, 528
McCartney, Paul 65, 128, 129, 168, 256, 283, 290, 519, 523, 528, 540
McCollum, John 424
McCord, James 325
McCrae, John 437
McCready, John 200
McCullough, Robert 407
McDonalds 71, 222, 257, 537, 540
McEnroe, John 282
McFarlane, Robert 202
Machu Picchu 12, 302, 509, 513
MacKenzie, Sir Alexander 300
MacKillop, Mary 325
McKinley, William 284, 382, 512
McMahon, Thomas 345, 461
Macmillan, Harold 388, 507
McVeigh, Timothy 177, 249, 328, 539
McVicker, Noah and Joseph 374
McWhirter, Ross 466
Macy's Thanksgiving Day Parade 436, 466, 516
Mad Bomber 62, 523
mad cow disease 106, 143, 388, 424, 480, 502, 540, 541, 542
Mad Hatter Day 403
Madame Bovary 264
Madame Tussauds 120, 534
Madonna 334, 500, 542
Madonna (by Munch) 340
Madrid bombing 128, 544
Maestà Altarpiece 247
Magellan, Ferdinand 134, 328, 378, 384, 467
Magellan spacecraft 328, 409, 536, 539
The Magic Flute 389
Magna Carter 253
Mainassar, Ibrahim Bare 166, 541
Makarios, Archbishop 293, 530
Malawi Independence Day 283, 526
Malaysia
  Independence Day 349, 523
  Petronas Twin Towers, Kuala Lumpur 414
Malcolm X 79, 101, 217, 346, 526
Maldives Independence Day 304
Malta
  Feast Day of St Paul's Shipwreck 89
  Freedom Day 149
  Republic Day 490
  riots against British rule 245, 515
  self-government 245
  Sette Giugno 245
Manchester IRA bombing 253, 540
Manchuria colliery explosion 184, 519
Mandela, Nelson 81, 90, 186, 199, 248, 250, 254, 296, 487, 515, 526, 536, 539, 540, 550
Mandela, Winnie 211, 384, 537
Manhattan Island 201, 360
Manhattan Project 370
Manson, Charles 65, 177, 177, 326, 328, 528, 529
Mantle, Mickey 55, 367, 524
Mao Zedong 122, 221, 300, 306, 331, 366, 408, 493, 504, 523, 530
Maradona, Diego 260, 428, 534
Marat, Jean Paul 239, 290
Marble Bar heatwave 429, 515
Marconi, Guglielmo 239, 298, 489, 512
Marcos, Ferdinand 105, 366, 368, 534, 538
margarine 293
Maria Dolores Rodriguez Sponeña's Day 49
Marie Antoinette 214, 413, 439
Marie Louise of Austria 493
Marine Corps' Birthday (U.S.) 447
Mariner 1 300, 525
Mariner 10 147, 530
Marino, Dan 130
Marley, Bob 85, 176, 240
Maroney, Susie 210, 540
The Marriage of Figaro 198

Mars 99, 164, 248, 338, 345, 480, 543
Mars Odyssey space probe 99, 164
Mars Polar Lander 480, 541
Mars Radiation Environment Experiment 164
Mars Spirit Rover 248, 543
Marshall Plan 160, 243, 290, 521
Marshall, Thurgood 251
Martin, Dean 303, 503, 521
Martin, Steve 332
Martyr Antipas' Day 169
Martyrdom Day of Guru Arjan Dev 254
Martyrdom of the Báb 286
Marx, Karl 101, 131, 202
Mary Celeste 481
Mary, Mother of Jesus 485
Mary, Queen of Scots 87, 123, 211, 366, 485
Mary Rose 297, 408, 533
The Mary Tyler Moore Show 377
MASH 108, 533
mass wedding, Korea 105
Mata Hari 412, 514
Matisse, Henri 481, 509, 525
Matlovich, Leonard 419, 530
Matterhorn 292
Matthew Bible 401
Mau Mau movement, Kenya 165, 522
Maxwell, Robert 482
May Day 194, 198
Mayan calendar 33
Mayflower 363, 435, 499
Mayon Volcano eruption 80
maypole 195
Maze Prison 306, 383, 505, 533, 541, 542
Mazerowski, Bill 410
Mbeki, Thabo 254, 535, 542
Mecca pilgrims killed 51, 279, 536
Meccano 48, 512
medical milestones 548
Meditrinalia 11
Mega River Delta tidal waves 429
Mein Kampf 158, 251, 296, 516
Meir, Golda 135, 200, 485, 528
Meister, Joseph 283
Melbourne Cup 444
Melbourne Cup Day 434
Melbourne Olympics 1956 460, 523
Melissa computer virus 144, 541
Melly, George 375
Melville, Herman 415
Memorial Day for Guardian Angels 399
Mendeleev, Dmitri 123, 549
Mendes, Chico 500, 535
Menendez, Lyle and Erik 338, 536
Mengele, Josef 244, 534
Menorca, British loss of 131
Mercedes 149, 512
Mercury 147, 530
Mercury 8 project 400
Mercury Redstone 2 71, 524
Meredith, James 336, 378, 398, 525
Metallica 365, 426, 533
Metaxas, Ioannis 426, 519
Meteski, George P. 62, 523
metric system 164
Metropolis 49, 516
Metropolitan Opera House 57, 419, 520
Mexico
  Constitution 401
  currency crisis 498, 539
  Dia de la Constitucion 77
  El Cinco de Mayo 202
  Flag Day 104
  meteorite shower 87, 528
  Night of the Radishes 501
  North American Free Trade Agreement 485
Mexico City
  Basilica of Our Lady of Guadalupe 489
  earthquake 377, 534
  Olympics 399, 409, 411, 414, 415, 528
  World Cup 1986 534
MGM Studios 175, 516
Michael Kozal's Day 66
Michelangelo 123, 326, 344, 365, 438, 488
Michelangelo computer virus 123, 538
Michrom, Morris and Rose 94, 512
Mickey Mouse comic strip 52, 517
Mid-Autumn Festival (China) 23, 355
Midsummer's Eve 236, 261
Midway, Battle of 245, 284, 519
Mijailovic, Mijailo 367
Mikimoto, Kokichi 288
Milk, Harvey 411, 466, 532
Milken, Michael 496
millennium bug 10
millennium celebrations 509
Miller, Arthur 199, 324, 337, 414, 521, 524, 545
Miller, Glen 204, 494, 519, 520
Milli Vanilli 453, 536
Million Man March 413, 359
Million Mom March 212, 542
Milne, A.A. 411, 516
Milosevic, Slobodan 91, 128, 141, 158, 200, 337, 338, 428, 403, 459, 541, 543, 545
Milton, John 186
Minor League Baseball 362, 512

Minuit, Peter 201
Mir space station 47, 99, 141, 187, 264, 268, 534, 543
Miracle of the Sun 410
Mishima, Yukio 463, 528
Miss America 375, 533
Miss World pageant riot 461, 544
missionaries, killing of 63, 541
"Mississippi Burning" murders 259
Mr Ed 44, 524
Mitchell, Margaret 200, 269, 445, 518
Mitterand, François 203, 207, 380, 424, 478, 532, 533
Miura, Yuchiro 528
Miyazawa, Kiichi 47, 52
Mizoram 78
mobile phones 160, 206, 529
Moby Dick 415
Model A Ford 301
Model T Ford 229, 330, 513, 516
Modern Times 84, 518
Mohammed *see* Muhammad
Mole Day 420
Molotov-Ribbentrop Pact 341, 518
Mona Lisa 339, 440, 489, 513, 514
Mongolia
  Naadam festival 277, 288
  Republic Day 464, 516
Monongah mine disaster 482, 513
Monopoly 442, 509, 517
Monroe, Marilyn 53, 217, 238, 297, 322, 324, 521, 522, 525
Mont Blanc 325
  tunnel 294, 526
Mont Blanc explosion 483, 514
Monte Carlo car rally 61, 513
Montessori, Maria 45, 349, 513
Montgomery, Elizabeth 375
Montreal
  École Polytechnique shooting 483, 536
  Olympics 1976 296, 531
Montreal Protocol 374, 535
Monty Python 208, 482, 528, 530
Moon 41, 43
  Apollo 11 mission 298
  festivals 355
  Galileo's observations 469
  landing on 174, 178, 184, 211, 223, 239, 298, 529
  lunar calendars 15
  photographing 404
  ruby laser beam 206
  solar eclipse 163, 288
Moon, Sun Myung 216, 533
Mooncake Festival (China) 355, 356
Moorgate station crash 108
More, Sir Thomas 283, 407
Mormon Church 213, 247
Moro, Aldo 134, 206, 531
Morocco
  earthquake 109, 524
  Green March 443, 526
Morris Worm computer virus 304, 536
Morrison, Jim 280, 448, 529
Morse, Samuel 45, 222, 549
Moscow
  alleged bugging of U.S. embassy 224, 524
  Apartment Bombings 349, 371, 542
  burning of 374
  German pilot landing in 226, 535
  McDonalds 71, 537
  murder of Jewish intellectuals 522
  riots 399, 538
  suicide bomb on metro 85, 544
  telephones vandalised to make electric guitars 309, 528
  theatre hostages 420, 543
Mother Jones' march 306, 512
mother, oldest 55, 545
Mother Teresa 345, 362, 414, 415, 532, 540
Mother Teresa's Day 362, 415
Mother's Day/Mothering Sunday 114, 196, 207, 513
motorcycle 347
Motown record label 492, 524
Moulin, Jean 285, 519
Mt. Asama eruption 320
Mt. Bezymianny eruption 148
Mt. Erebus plane crash 467, 532, 553
Mt. Everest 227, 382, 388, 406, 522, 528, 530, 545
Mt. Fuji 317
Mt. Kanchenjunga 223, 523
Mt. Kembla colliery explosion 309, 512
Mt. Krakatoa eruption 344
Mt. Nyiragongo eruption 56, 543
Mt. Rushmore 429, 519
Mt. St Helens eruption 216, 532
Mt. Tarawera eruption 248
Mt. Unzen eruption 240, 537
Mt. Vesuvius eruption 164
Mountbatten, Lord 345, 461, 532
The Mousetrap 463, 522
Moving Day (Canada) 278
Mozambique Independence Day 264, 530
Mozart, Wolfgang Amadeus 198, 388, 482
MTV 318, 533
Mugabe, Robert 121, 135, 382, 532, 543

Muhammad, the Prophet 21, 29, 178, 246, 294, 384
Müller, Paul 426, 521
Munch, Edvard 340, 489, 520, 544
Munich Olympics 1972 346, 361, 362, 529
Murdoch, Rupert 41, 128, 344
Museum of Modern Art
  New York 444, 481, 516, 525
  Stockholm 445, 538
Musharraf, Pervez 258, 543
musical instruments 296, 539, 549
Mussolini, Benito 103, 141, 164, 187, 220, 240, 251, 303, 307, 423, 426, 515, 516, 518, 519, 520
Muzorewa, Bishop 238
My Lai massacre 134, 527
Myanmar *see* Burma

N

Nabokov, Vladimir 336
Nagasaki bombing 323, 326, 333, 520
Nagasaki Martyrs 85
Nagin, Ray 346, 347
Nagy, Imre 441
Namibia, Heroes' Day 344
Nanking, Rape of 490, 518, 550
Nanterre University riots 140, 527
Napoleon I *see* Bonaparte, Napoleon
Nasser, Gamal Abdel 261, 304, 501, 523
National Association for the Advancement of Colored People 91, 513
National League for Democracy 386
National March on Washington for Lesbian and Gay Rights 411, 532
National Poetry Month (U.S.) 157
National Popcorn Day (U.S.) 58
National Sorry Day (Aust.) 224
National Veterans' Day (U.K.) 266
Native Americans
  citizenship 239, 516
  first U.S. senator 63
  Ishi, last of Yahi tribe 347
  last to make contact with Europeans 347, 513
  reservations 71
  Sand Creek Massacre 468
  Sauk war on U.S. 163
  white men scalping 100
  Wounded Knee massacre 507
Native Title Act (Aust.) 500, 538
NATO 141, 161, 258, 329, 348, 457, 521, 538, 539, 541, 544
Navarino, Battle of 417
Navratilova, Martina 284, 536
Nazis
  American Nazi Party 343
  Anschluss 129, 518
  art stolen by 67, 540
  "degenerate art" 240, 518
  "final solution" 60
  French Jews transported to Germany 107
  Gestapo 184, 517, 520
  invasion of U.S.S.R. 260
  Kristallnacht 446, 518
  legislation for sterilisation 40
  Nazi Party 44
  Night of Broken Glass 446, 518
  Night of the Long Knives 269, 517
  Nuremberg Trials 458, 518
  persecution of Catholic Church 66
  Soviet offensive against 51, 174
  Sportpalast speech 98
  surrender to Soviets 81
  war crimes trials 90, 95, 169
NEAR *Shoemaker* 91
Nehru, Jawaharlal 225, 452, 550
Neighbours 130, 534
Neilson, Donald (Black Panther) 53
Nelson, Horatio 289, 302, 388, 418, 466
neon lighting 58, 480, 515
Nepal
  August ceremonies 317
  murder of royal family 238, 543
  Nepalese People's War 92, 540
  Unity Day 50
Neptunalia 274
Neptune 381
Netherlands
  death sentence for heresy 95
  dikes bursting 71, 522
  Gay Pride parade 317
  Princes Day 357
  St. Martin's Day 435
  women's vote 376, 515
neutron bomb 164, 531
Nevado del Ruiz eruption 451
Nevermind 382, 537
Neveu, Ginette 425
New Dehli 89
New Mexico, breakaway state 419
New Orleans 343
  Hurricane Katrina 346, 347, 545
New Year's Day 20, 37, 40, 53, 118, 171, 172, 356
New Year's Eve 477, 509
New York City
  blackout 332, 531

Central Park anti-nuclear rally 250, 533
crew-less train 43, 525
Ellis Island 40, 450
Empire State Building 198, 306, 517, 520
factory fire 143, 513
first car accident 228
Freedom Tower 281
Guggenheim Museum 418, 524
ice rink 91
ITT Building bombing 387, 530
lightning strikes 290
Mad Bomber 62, 523
Metropolitan Opera House 57, 419, 520
Museum of Modern Art 444, 481, 516, 525
September 11 attacks 323, 368, 371, 427, 428, 543, 544
Shephardic refugees 67
Statue of Liberty 320, 322, 426
subway 142, 425, 512
taxi cabs 229, 513
Wall St. *see* Wall Street
Windsor Hotel fire 135
women's vote 377
World Trade Center *see* World Trade Center
World's Fair 179
Yankee Stadium 176, 515
New York Stock Exchange 202, 422, 425, 516
New Zealand
 annexing Cook Islands 249, 512
 Cook's discovery of 404
 first British colonists 62
 Mt. Tarawera eruption 248
 Napier earthquake 82, 516
 rugby union 212
 takahe bird 458, 521
 Tasman's sighting of 490
 Tauranga Campaign 259
 Treaty of Waitangi 219
 women's vote 377, 466
Newcastle earthquake 506
Newfoundland 207
Newsweek 96, 517
Newton, Sir Isaac 138, 162, 503, 549
Newtonmas 503
Ngô Đình Diệm 439, 525
Nguyen, Van Tuong 479, 545
Niagara Falls 286, 343
Nicaragua
 Contra affair 202, 264, 440, 534, 535
 Independence Day 373
 Liberation Day 297
 Managua earthquake 501, 529
 Sandinista takeover 295, 297, 532
Nichols, Terry 328, 359
Niger, independence 320, 524
Nigeria
 Biafran War 283, 527
 explosion in military dump 67
 hanging of activists 447, 539
 military junta 166
 Miss World riot 461, 544
Night of Broken Glass 446, 518
Night of Murdered Poets 330
Night of the Long Knives 269, 517
Night of the Radishes 501
Nightingale, Florence 331, 468, 513
Nineteen Eighty-Four 246, 521
Nintendo 415, 443
Nippon Airways crash 83
Nirvana 162, 379, 382, 537
Nirvana Day 87
Nixon, Richard 44, 63, 180, 189, 226, 254, 256, 260, 325, 326, 384, 420, 506, 529, 530
Nobel, Alfred 292, 418, 487, 512
Nobel Prize 292, 487, 512, 550
 Annan, Kofi 550
 Arafat, Yasser 371, 550
 Aung San Suu Kyi 257, 298, 386, 550
 Bardeen, John 269
 Begin, Manachim 144
 Brandt, Willy 137
 Brattain, Walter 269
 Carter, Jimmy 550
 Churchill, Winston 487
 Curie, Marie and Pierre 63, 178, 487, 513
 Dalai Lama 149, 487, 550
 Dunant, Jean Henri 487
 Einstein, Albert 446, 487, 515
 Gorbachev, Mikhail 412, 503, 536, 550
 Hahn, Otto 496
 Hemingway, Ernest 487
 Kilby, Jack 85
 King, Martin Luther Jr. 161, 487
 Koch, Robert 142
 laureates 487, 550
 Mandela, Nelson 487, 550
 Mother Teresa 345, 362, 414, 415, 532
 Müller, Paul 426, 521
 Peres, Shimon 371, 550
 Rabin, Yitzhak 371, 550
 Röntgen, Wilhelm 445, 487
 Sadat, Anwar 144
 Sartre turning down 419, 526
 Shockley, William 269
 Solzhenitsyn, Aleksandr 92, 225
 Tutu, Desmond 109, 413, 534
 UNICEF 488
 Walesa, Lech 332, 463
Noble, David 492

Noble, Richard 401, 533
Noddy books 41, 535
Nolan, Christopher 58
Noll, Greg 481, 528
Norgay, Tensing 206, 227, 522
Noriega, Manuel 497, 536
Normandy, Battle of 244
Norooz 21, 115, 139
North American Free Trade Agreement 485
North Korea
 defection from 221, 540
 nuclear weapons 89, 545
 peace talks with South Korea 122, 540
 Republic Day 366, 521
North Magnetic Pole 238
North, Oliver 202
North Sea oil rig collapse 145, 532
Northern Ireland
 Bloody Sunday 70, 81, 339, 459, 529
 British troops in 332
 detention of terrorists 326
 Downing Street Declaration 493
 Good Friday Agreement 168, 345, 461, 541
 IRA *see* IRA
 IRA bombing 345, 380, 532
 IRA ceasefire 349, 380
 Maze Prison 306, 383, 505, 533, 541, 542
 Omagh bombing 333, 541
 Orange Parade riots 289, 534
 Orangeman's Day 289
 peace talks 248, 539, 540
 Sinn Fein *see* Sinn Fein
 The Troubles 178, 493, 530
Norway
 Gardermoen Airport 405
 invasion in WWII 166, 518
 National Day 215
 separation from Sweden 245, 512
 Union Dissolution Day 245
Novoselic, Krist 162, 382
nuclear chain reaction 479, 519
nuclear fission 496
nuclear weapons 370
 atomic bomb 106, 294, 323, 326, 370, 520, 521, 522, 524
 British testing 523
 French testing 69, 92, 287, 524, 540
 hydrogen bomb 46, 84, 118, 428, 522, 523
 Intermediate Range Nuclear Forces treaty 484, 535
 North Korea 89, 545
 Outer Space Treaty 67, 407, 527
 rally against 250, 533
 Russia not targeting U.S. 66
 SALT II pact 256, 532
 Seabed Treaty 90, 529
 Star Wars proposal 409
 thermonuclear bomb 213
 treaty to end testing 382, 540
 "Tsar Bomba" 428, 525
 U.S.-Soviet agreements 42, 309, 376, 381, 484, 535, 540
 U.S. testing 51, 223, 377, 522, 523
 U.S.S.R. detonating 347, 381
Nuremberg Trials 458, 520
Nureyev, Rudolf 180, 255, 525
Nurmi, Paavo 287, 516
nylon 95, 489, 518
nylon stockings 213, 518

O

Oak Apple Day (U.K.) 227
Oates, Captain Lawrence 135
Obelisk of Axum 183
Obninsk nuclear power station 266, 522
The Observer 481
Oceanos sinking 321, 537
October Revolution 396, 444
oil discovery in Texas 49, 512
Oil for Food Program 218
Okinawa
 Battle of 259, 520
 returned to Japan 213, 529
Oklahoma
 breakaway state 419
 land rush 500
Oklahoma City
 bombing 177, 328, 539
 parking meters 297, 517
Oktoberfest 357, 396
Ólavsóka (Faroe Islands) 307
oleomargarine 42
Olympic Games 547
 ancient 163
 Athens 1896 163
 Atlanta 1996 305, 340, 540
 Berlin 1936 326
 Los Angeles 1984 205, 329, 533
 medal tallies 547
 Melbourne 1956 460, 523
 Mexico City 1968 399, 409, 411, 414, 415, 528
 modern Olympiad 163
 Montreal 1976 296, 531
 Munich 1972 346, 361, 362, 529
 Paris 1924 287, 516
 Rome 1960 362, 524

South Africa banned 336, 526
Soviet boycott 205
Sydney 2000 373
Tokyo 1964 119, 336, 526
top medalists 547
Omagh bombing 333, 541
On the Origin of the Species 462
Onassis, Aristotle 417, 528
Onassis, Jackie *see* Kennedy, Jackie
Ono, Yoko 143, 415, 528
OPEC meeting raid 499, 530
open heart surgery 85, 286, 545
Operation Anaconda 119
Operation Barbarossa 260
Operation Deliberate Force 348
Operation Desert Storm 54, 56, 107, 537
Operation Gomorrah 302, 519
Operation Just Cause 497
Opletal, Jan 455
Orange Free State invasion 93, 512
Orangeman's Day 289
Order of the Solar Temple 402
ordination of women 374, 531, 539
Oregon wagon trains 220
Orgreave, Battle of 256, 534
Orion lunar module 178
Orissa cyclone, India 427
Orwell, George 246, 264, 521, 522
Osbourne, Ozzy 424, 480
Oslo Peace Accords 338, 371, 538
Osmond, Donny 487, 526
Oswald, Lee Harvey 131, 386, 415, 462, 526
Otis, William 104
Otsukimi (Japan) 355
Ottawa Parliament buildings fire 82, 514
Otzi the Iceman 377, 537
Our Lady of Guadalupe's Day 489
Our Lady of the Angels 319
Ousland, Boerge 57, 540
Outer Space Treaty 67, 407, 527
Overseas Chinese Day 418
Ovid 195
Owen, Wilfred 441
Owens, Jesse 326, 370
Oxford University 258
ozone layer 374, 531

P

Pac-Man 407, 532
Paccard, Michel-Gabriel 325
Packer, Kerry 459, 495
Pact of Steel 220, 518
Page, Larry 364
Pakistan
 Bangladesh cyclone 450
 coup d'état 258
 cyclone 450, 528
 earthquake 405, 545, 552
 election rigging 124
 female Prime Minister 479
 Independence Day 332, 521
 Indian invasion 363, 526
 Islamic Republic 141, 523
 National Day 141
 train disaster 43
 U.S. embassy attack, Islamabad 460
Pakistani Airways hostages 132
Palach, Jan 55, 528
Palestine
 British Mandate over 213, 468
 evacuation of Jewish settlers from Gaza 335, 545
 Independence Day 453, 535
 Intifada riots 486, 535
 Oslo Peace Accords 338, 371, 538
 partitioning 468, 521
 PLO 262, 526, 533
 riots in Gaza Strip 486, 535
 self-rule in Gaza Strip 201, 368, 371, 529, 545
Palio di Provenzano 279
Palme, Olof 108, 367, 534
Palmer, A. Mitchell 41
Palmer, Daniel David 376
Palmer, Nathaniel 456
Pan Am Airways 424
 ceasing operations 481, 537
 Lockerbie disaster 189, 200, 499, 535, 542, 543
 Tenerife crash 145, 531, 553
Panama
 conflict over flag 48, 526
 Martyrs' Day 48
 U.S. troops invading 497, 536
Panama Canal 333, 514
Pancake Day 79
Pankhurst, Emmeline 550
Papadopoulos, Col George 179, 527
paper currency 82, 516
Papon, Maurice 159, 541
Papua New Guinea
 Independence Day 374, 530
 Japanese troops in 124, 519
 recapture of Kokoda, WWII 439, 519
 tsunami 295, 541
parachute jump, first 419
Paraguay joining UN 93

Paralympics, Spanish team 463, 542
Paris
 airport collapse 221, 544
 Algerian protesters killed 414, 525
 Arc de Triomphe 308
 art stolen by Nazis 67, 540
 auto show 48
 Commune 136
 Eiffel Tower 149, 203
 first public art exhibition 166
 Folies Bergère 469
 liberation WWII 343, 344, 520
 Louvre 445, 489, 513
 riots 425, 544
 surrender to Russia 149
 Tomb of the Unknown Solider 68, 515
Paris Treaty 208
Park Chung Hee 424, 532
Parker, Mary 50
Parker Bowles, Camilla 166, 295, 545
parking meter 297
Parks, Rosa 161, 422, 478
Parnell, Caarl Stuart 403
Parsley, Sage, Rosemary and Thyme 407
Parsons, Gram 443, 530
Parthenon 38
Pascha 15
The Passion of the Christ 349
Passover 116
Pasteur, Louis 78, 283, 387, 505, 548, 549
Patay, Battle of 356
Patler, John 34
Patriot Day (U.S.) 368
Patriot's Day (U.S.) 157, 176
Paulinerkirche Leipzig 228, 527
Pavarotti, Luciano 284, 409, 536
Payola scandal 55
Peanuts comic 42, 399, 522, 542
Pearl, Daniel
pearl, first cultured 288
Pearl Harbor bombing 484, 485, 488, 519
Peel, John 410, 423
Peel, Sir Robert 388
Pelé 420, 457, 528
Pemberton, Dr. John 129
penicillin 248
The Pentagon 368, 543
Pentecost 235
Pentium processor 140, 538
Peoples Temple 456, 531
Pepys, Samuel 52
Pequet, Henri
Peres, Shimon 371, 550
perestroika 137, 534
periodic table of elements 123
Perlman, Louis Henry 83, 514
Perón, Eva "Evita" 204, 304, 381, 418, 520
Perón, Isabel 227, 381, 530
Perón, Juan D. 268, 381, 405, 418, 520, 521, 530
Perry, Stephen 35
Persian calendar 30
personal computer 182, 532
Peru
 Cenepa War 46, 539
 Chungar avalanche 137, 529
 earthquake 234, 552
 Independence Day 306
 Japanese embassy siege 180, 540
 joining UN 93
 landslide 541
Peruggia, Vincenzo 339
Pesach 116
Peterson, Lori 54
Petronas Twin Towers, Kuala Lumpur 414
The Philadelphia Experiment 426, 520
Philadelphia Spelling Book 247
Philippines
 Aquino as President 105
 Cock Crow Mass 494
 Doña Paz sinking 498, 535
 Feast of the Black Nazarene 48
 ferry bombing 107, 544
 Independence 281, 521
 liberation of Manila 104, 520
 Magellan reaching 134
 Mayon volcano eruption 80
 ousting of President Estrada 60, 542
 Rizal Day 503
 school hostages 68, 541
 Typhoon Ike 460, 534
Phonofilm 129
phonograph 95, 459
photography
 camera 261
 daguerreotype process 48
 first glass plate photo 366
 infrared 404
 instant camera 48, 101, 521
 snowflake 52
Pi Approximation Day 300
"The Piano Man" 340
Picasso, Pablo 15, 262, 339, 423, 445, 452, 512, 529
Pickford, Mary 152, 514
Pilgrimage of Cristo Negro de Esquipúlas 54
Pilgrims on the *Mayflower* 363, 435, 499
Piltdown Man skull 459, 522
Pinochet, Augusto 344, 365, 463, 535, 544

519

Pioneer Day (U.S.) 302
Pioneer 0 408
Pioneer 1 408
Pioneer 10 251, 480, 530, 533
Pizarro, Francisco 454
plagues 552
Plame, Valerie 426, 545
Planck, Max 492, 512
plant naming 40, 524
Plante, Jacques 438, 524
plastic bubble, boy in 102
Plath, Sylvia 254, 425, 523
Play-Doh 374, 523
PlayStation 2 424, 542
Plough Sunday 38
Plowing Festival 196
Pluto 86, 98, 130, 189, 260, 517
pneumatic car tyre 498
Pocahontas 162
Poindexter, John 202
Poitier, Sidney 171, 526
Pokémon 494, 541
Pol Pot 173, 217, 541
Poland
   anti-communist revolutions 242
   free elections 242, 463, 536
   Gdansk shipyard strike 207, 332, 463, 533, 535
   Gregorian calendar 401
   Jewish uprising against Nazis 57
   Koniuchy massacre 69
   liberation of Auschwitz 64, 520
   liberation of Warsaw 56, 520
   massacres by U.S.S.R. 122
   Nazi invasion 358, 389, 518
   Pope John Paul II visit 239, 261, 532
   Solidarity movement 242, 332, 463, 536
   Warsaw Ghetto 454, 519
   Warsaw Pact 212
   Warsaw Uprising 318, 520
Polar Bear Day 107
Polaris missiles 499
polio vaccination 103, 144, 522, 548
Pollock, Jackson 329
Polyakov, Valeri 47
Pongal (India) 53
Pope Adrian IV 481
Pope Alexander VI 344
Pope Benedict XVI 177, 182, 235, 339, 545
Pope Clement I 461
Pope Clement VII 124
Pope Gregory I 95, 360
Pope Gregory VII 126
Pope Gregory XII 17
Pope Gregory XIII 19, 401
Pope John Paul I 387, 414, 531
Pope John Paul II 51, 66, 144, 159, 165, 170, 203, 211, 216, 239, 261, 328, 367, 387, 388, 413, 531, 532, 533, 540, 542, 543, 544, 545
Pope Paul III 495
Pope Paul VI 44, 144, 372, 384, 526, 530
Pope Pius V 105, 404
Pope Pius VII 215
Pope Sixtus IV 19, 326
Pope Urban II 456
Pope Urban VI 378
Popeye the Sailor Man 56, 516
pop-up toaster 227, 515
Port Arthur massacre 187, 540
A Portrait of the Artist as a Young Man 507, 514
Portugal
   Fatima, apparition of Virgin Mary 410, 514
   Freedom Day 183
   Gregorian calendar 401
   Lisbon earthquake 66, 438, 552
   recognition as nation 92
   Republic Day 402, 513
Posadas 494
postage stamps 104
postcard 398
posting children 251, 515
potato chip 342
Potemkin revolt 252, 512
Potsdam Declaration 333
Pound, Ezra 176, 438, 523
Powell, Laurence 120, 321, 538
The Power of Sympathy 61
Powers, Francis Gary 89, 337, 524, 525
Prattis, Percival 82, 521
Pravda 180, 514
Prescot, Colin 107
Presley, Elvis 60, 102, 142, 160, 198, 265, 334, 359, 366, 418, 517, 523, 527, 531
Presley, Pricilla 198, 527
Pretoria, renaming 124
Previn, Soon-Yi 501, 541
Priestly, Joseph 292
Primrose Day (U.K.) 177
Prince 323, 362, 534, 538
Prince Albert of England 476
Prince Albert of Monaco 289, 545
Prince Andrew 137, 501, 538
Prince Charles 66, 104, 166, 176, 278, 307, 346, 452, 458, 486, 501, 521, 528, 532, 533, 534, 538, 539, 540, 545
Prince Henry (Harry) 373, 534
Prince Juan Carlos of Spain 428, 460, 530
Prince Norodom Sihanouk 446, 452, 537

Prince of Wales sinking 487
Prince Rainier of Monaco 177, 523
Prince William 259, 373, 533
Princess Anne 130, 333, 501
Princess Diana 104, 278, 307, 334, 346, 349, 363, 373, 458, 486, 501, 532, 533, 534, 538, 539, 540, 543
Princess Grace of Monaco 177, 372, 450, 523, 532
Princess Margaret 137, 339, 530
Princip, Gavrilo 267, 514
Profumo, John 140, 243, 525, 526
Progress spacecraft 264
Prohibition, end of 96, 482, 517
Psycho 254, 524
Pudeator, Ann 380
Puerto Rico
   Discovery Day 457
   Luis Muñoz Rivera's birthday 295
Pulitzer Prize
   Lee, Harper 288
   Miller, Arthur 199, 521
   Mitchell, Margaret 200, 269, 518
   winners 546
pulsar 60, 528
Punch magazine 142
Purple Rain 323, 362, 534
Putin, Vladimir 144, 404, 441, 509, 542

Q

"Quake" computer game 260, 540
quantum physics 492, 512
Quarter Day 143
Quebec 280
   bridge collapse 347, 513
Queen Aishwarya of Nepal 238
Queen Anne 125, 318
Queen Elizabeth I 87, 105, 142, 364, 455
Queen Elizabeth II 85, 121, 128, 130, 182, 188, 203, 204, 239, 251, 265, 286, 417, 458, 462, 464, 478, 501, 516, 521, 522, 533, 538
Queen Elizabeth II 199, 528
Queen Isabella of Castile 131, 304, 464
Queen Jane 287
Queen Juliana of the Netherlands 505
Queen Liliuokalani of Hawaii 56, 359, 448
Queen Mary I 139, 287, 321, 337, 455
Queen Mother 148, 166
Queen Victoria 147, 222, 258, 265, 286, 476, 512
Quigley, John 200

R

Rabe, John 550
rabies vaccine 283, 548
Rabin, Yitzhak 201, 371, 441, 539, 550
Racial Harmony Day (Singapore) 299
radiation 445
radio 239, 512
radioactivity 178, 296
radium 178, 264, 504, 512
Raek Na (Thailand) 196
Raffles, Sir Thomas Stamford 85, 282, 283
Raggedy Ann doll 226, 514
Rainbow Warrior 287, 534
Raleigh, Sir Walter 305, 427
Rama Navami 156
Ramadan 27, 29, 395, 396
The Ramones 334, 530
Rankin, Jeanette 159, 216, 484, 514
Rastafarians 159, 179, 301, 439
Ratzinger, Joseph 177, 182, 545
Ray, James Earl 161, 246, 528
Ray, Man 452, 456
Reagan, Nancy 200
Reagan, Ronald 60, 148, 172, 200, 202, 223, 243, 250, 256, 259, 309, 322, 376, 400, 409, 440, 484, 485, 532, 533, 534, 535
Real IRA 365
Réard, Louis 282
Rebel Without a Cause 389
Red Baron 179
Red Cross 427, 487
Red Nose Day 84, 535
Red Terror 348
Redgrave, Vanessa 385
Reeve, Christopher 225, 383, 407, 539
The Reformation 219
refrigerator car 55
Regata Storica (Italy) 356
Regency TR-1 415
Reign of Terror 239, 306
Religious Freedom Day (U.S.) 55
Remembrance Day 437
Repulse sinking 487
Resnik, Judith 68, 362
Respect for the Aged Day (Japan) 357
Revere, Paul 157, 176, 207
Revolutionary Artibonite Resistance Front 84, 544
Rhine River chemical spill 438, 535
Rhode Island 251
Rhodesia *see* Zimbabwe

Riccio, David 123
Rice, Condoleezza 66, 545
Richelieu, Cardinal 211
Riggs, Bobby 378
right-to-die debate 149
Rights of the Terminally Ill Act (NT) 142
Ripoli, Cayetano 304
The Rise and Fall of Ziggy Stardust and the Spiders from Mars 244
Ritchie, Guy 500, 542
Rizal Day (Philippines) 508
Robert the Bruce 145, 245, 262, 288
Robertson, Pat 341, 545
Robespierre, Maximilien 306
Robinson, Bill "Bojangles" 223
Rock and Roll Hall of Fame 359, 359
"Rock Around the Clock" 207, 522
Rock of Gibraltar 302
Rocket Festival (Thailand) 196
rocket-fuelled aircraft 247, 517
Rockwell, George 343, 527
Roddenberry, Gene 216, 240
Roe v. Wade 62, 529
Roentgen, Wilhelm 44
Rolfe, John 162
Rolland, Kayla 109
roller coaster 60
Rolling Stone magazine 446, 527
The Rolling Stones 99, 129, 528, 545
Rolls-Royce Company 132, 512
Roma National Day 165
Roman Catholic Church
   divorce 107
   freedom of religion 171
   married priest excommunicated 126
   Nazi persecution 66
   Netherlands sentenced to death for heresy 95
   outlawed 55
   reform 65, 524
Roman New Year 118
Romania
   Bucharest earthquake 121, 531
   Dragobete 104
   execution of Ceausescu 503, 536
   flooding 342
   Warsaw Pact 212
Rome
   Birthday 179
   Great Fire 297
   Olympics 1960 362
Rome-Berlin Axis 423, 518
Romero, Archbishop Oscar 142, 532
Röntgen, Wilhelm 445, 487
Roosevelt, Eleanor 408, 487
Roosevelt, Franklin D. 53, 60, 170, 204, 436, 484, 488, 520, 550
Roosevelt, Theodore 306, 359, 382, 408, 425, 512
Roquefort cheese 304
Rosenberg, Julius and Ethel 147, 162, 257, 522
Rosenkowitz sextuplets 50
Rosetta Stone 293, 386
Rosh Hashana 21, 26, 356
Ross, James Clark 238
Rossini, Gioachino 100
Rotary Club 103, 512
Rowan & Martin's Laugh-In 62
Rowling, J.K. 265, 294, 309
Royal Canadian Mounted Police 80, 515
Royal Society 467
rubber band 135, 215
Ruby, Jack 131, 462, 526
Rudolph, Eric 340, 545
rugby union 66, 344, 423, 359
"Rumble in the Jungle" 428
RuneScape 43, 542
Running of the Bulls, Pamplona 284
Rushdie, Salman 93, 257, 384, 535
Russel, Bertrand 385
Russell, Todd 206
Russia *see also* Moscow; Soviet Union
   Alaska bought from 148, 166
   Beatles records on sale 147, 534
   Beslan school massacre 358, 360, 544
   Bloody Sunday 62
   Bolshevik revolution 444, 514
   Commonwealth of Independent States 503
   elections 145, 536
   February Revolution 125, 134, 514
   Gregorian calendar 93, 514
   Independence Day 250
   joint military exercises with China 337, 545
   ownership of private property law 123, 536
   relations with China 214
   sovereignty 250
   Ufa train crash 242, 536
   Unity Day 441
Russian Revolution 62, 396, 444, 512
Russian-Japanese War 85, 512
Rutan, Dick 492, 501
Ruth, Babe 288, 329, 334, 389, 514, 516
Rutherford, Ernest 128, 513
Rwanda
   genocide 164, 281, 539
   gorilla research station 505
   President killed 163, 281, 539
   Republic of 68, 524
   Tutsi Rwandan Patriotic Front 281
Ryan, Leo J. 456

Ryan, Ronald 82, 527
Ryder, Winona 483, 543

S

SA-1 425
Sabatini, Gabriela 122
Sabena Flight 548 crash 94
saccharin 107
Sadat, Anwar 144, 376
St. Abban's Day 211
St. Acacius' Day 166
St. Adela's Day 105
St. Afra's Day 322
St. Agatha's Day 84
St. Agnes' Day 61
St. Ailbhe's Day 370
St. Alexandra 138
St. Ambrose's Day 484
St. Andrew Dung-Lac's Day 462
St. Andrew's Day 469
St. Anicetus' Day 175
St. Anne 485
St. Anthony of Padua's Day 251
St. Antonio Maria Claret's Day 422
St. Apollonia's Day 88
St. Aquilinus' Day 69
St. Attracta's Day 329
St. Auguste's Day 107
St. Augustin Schoeffer's Day 199
St. Augustine, Florida 365
St. Barbara's Day 481
St. Bartholomew's Day 342
St. Basil's Day 38, 41
St. Bathild's Day 70
St. Benedict of Nursia 89
St. Benedict's Day 139
St. Bernadette 90
St. Bernadette's Day 174
St. Bernard of Clairvaux's Day 338
St. Bertilla Boscardin 417
St. Boniface's Day 243
St. Brigit's Day 301
St. Cajetan's Day 324
St. Camillus de Lellis' Day 292
St. Casimir's Day 121
St. Catherine's Day 463
St. Cecilia's Day 460
St. Charles Borromeo's Day 441
St. Christopher's Day 303
St. Clare's Day 329
St. Clement's Day 461
St. Columba's Day 247
St. Comgall's Day 207
St. Crispin's Day 423
St. Daniel's Day 95
St. David's Day 121
St. Dominic of Silos' Day 498
St. Dominic's Day 325
St. Donatus' Day 324
St. Dwynwen's Day 65
St. Dymphna's Day 213
St. Eleanora's Day 101
St. Elena's Day 219
St. Eligius 236
St. Eligius' Day 478
St. Elizabeth 372, 530
St. Euplius' Day 330
St. Felix of Cantalica's Day 216
St. Felix of Nola's Day 53
St. Fermín 284
St. Finbarr's Day 383
St. Fintan's Day 96
St. Florian's Day 201
St. Francis Caracciolo's Day 242
St. Francis Dam burst 130, 516
St. Francis de Sales' Day 64
St. Francis of Assisi Day 400
St. Francis of Rome's Day 126
St. Francis Xavier's Day 480
St. Fulcran's Day 92
St. Fulk's Day 227
St. Genevieve's Day 42
St. George of Antioch's Day 177
St. George's Day 181
St. Giles' Day 358
St. Godfrey of Cappenberg's Day 50
St. Gregory's Day 360
St. Hedwig's Day 108
St. Helena 372
St. Henry II's Day 290
St. Hugh's Day 158
St. Hyacinth's Day 331
St. Ildephonsus' Day 63
St. Irenaeus of Lyon's Day 267
St. Isaac of Dalmatia's Day 228
St. Ita of Killeedy's Day 54
St. Ita's Day 79
St. James' Day 198, 303
St. Janero's Day 336
St. Jenaro's Day 56
St. Jerome's Day 389
St. Joan of Arc's Day 228
St. John Bosco's Day 71
St. John Chrysostom's Day 371
St. John de Brito's Day 83
St. John Eudes' Day 337
St. John Kemble's Day 340

St. John Neumann's Day 44
St. John of Matha's Day 87
St. John Ogilvie 127
St. John the Baptist's Day 237, 262, 347
St. John's Day 477, 505
St. Joseph of Cupertino's Day 376
St. Joseph's Day 137
St. Julitta's Day 308
St. Jutta's Day 202
St. Keyne's Day 405
St. Kilian's Day 285
St. Knut's Day 52
St. Lambert's Day 375
St. Lawrence Seaway 265, 524
St. Louis' Day 343
St. Lucy's Day 490
St. Ludmila 373
St. Luke the Evangelist's Day 415
St. Mamertus' Day 208
St. Martha's Day 307
St. Martin's Day 435
St. Martin's Eve 435
St. Mary Magdalene's Day 300
St. Mary Salome's Day 419
St. Mary's Day 160
St. Maximilian's Day 332
St. Michael de Sanctis' Day 168
St. Mocius' Day 208
St. Monica of Hippo's Day 345
St. Narcissus' Day 427
St. Nestor's Day 106
St. Nicephorus' Day 239
St. Nicholas 476, 483
St. Nicholas' Day 483
St. Nil Sorsky's Day 204
St. Odran's Day 99
St. Olaf's Day 307
St. Orosia's Day 264
St. Oswald's Day 108
St. Pancras' Day 210
St. Paternus' Day 173
St. Patrick's Day 135
St. Paul's Cathedral, London 259, 359, 507
St. Perfecto's Day 176
St. Perpetua and Felicity's Day 124
St. Peter of Anagni's Day 320
St. Peter's and St Paul's Day 235, 268
St. Petersburg renamed Leningrad 64, 516
St. Philip Neri's Day 224
St. Philip's Day 198
St. Piran's Day 122
St. Polycarp's Day 103
St. Procopius' Day 285
St. Pudentiana's Day 217
St. Raymond of Peñafort's Day 46
St. Rosalia's Day 293
St. Rose of Lima's Day 348
St. Rose of Viterbo's Day 361
St. Sarah's Day 222
St. Sava's Day 51
St. Scholastica's Day 89
St. Scholastica's Day riot 89
St. Sebastian's Day 60
St. Seraphinus' Day 409
St. Sixtus I's Day 163
St. Stephen of Piperi's Day 218
St. Stephen's Day 82, 334, 477, 504
St. Teresa of Avila 19
St. Theodore's Day 178
St. Theodosius of Kiev's Day 200
St. Theophan's Day 48
St. Thérèse de Lisieux's Day 398
St. Thomas Aquinas' Day 68
St. Thomas Becket's Day 499
St. Thomas' Day 280
St. Trea's Day 320
St. Trifon's Day 93
St. Trudpert's Day 184
St. Valentine 76
St. Valentine's Day 93
St. Valentine's Day massacre 93, 516
St. Veronica's Day 83
St. Vincent and the Grenadines, Independence Day 425
St. Vitus' Day 253, 267
St. William's Day 98
St. Wulfric's Day 100
Sakharov, Andrei 497, 535
Salem witch trials 118, 337, 380
Salk, Jonas 144, 261, 522, 548
SALT II pact 256, 532
Salt Lake City, Utah 247, 302
Salvation Army 282
same sex marriage 70, 215, 218, 224, 363, 536, 541, 543, 545
Samhain 11, 436, 437, 438
Sampras, Pete 330, 343, 544
Samuelson, Ralph 279
San Fermín 284
San Francisco 70
  earthquake 176, 414, 512
  founding 406
  Golden Gate Bridge 225, 518
Sand Creek Massacre 468
Sandinista rebels 295, 297, 532
Santa Claus 476, 483
Santa Maria 504
Santacruzan 196
Santiago, Chile 91

Santos-Dumont, Alberto 371
Sapporo snow festival 77
Sapporo Winter Olympics 82, 529
Sarajevo
  siege of 162, 538
  terrorist attack 170
Sarandon, Susan 488
Sarmiento, Domingo F. 368
Saro-Wiwa, Ken 447
SARS 132, 181, 454, 543
Sartre, Jean-Paul 259, 419, 526
The Satanic Verses 93, 384, 535
Saturday Evening Post 49
Saturn 249, 425
Saturnalia 475, 495
Saudi Arabia 47
  family coup 439
  Mecca pilgrims killed 51, 279, 536
Sauk Indians 163
Sauvé, Jeanne 212, 533
Sax, Adolphe 215, 309, 443, 549
Saxe-Coburg-Gotha, Simeon 302, 543
saxophone 215, 309, 549
Say, Peggy 481
Scharnhorst sinking 504, 520
Schiavo, Terri 149, 545
Schicksalstag 446
Schilling, Col David 380
Schirra, Wally 400, 408, 551
Schroeder, Sheri 459, 528
Schroeder, William 99, 534
Schultz, Charles M. 42, 399, 464, 492, 542
Schumacher, Michael 348, 538
Schuman Declaration 206
Schwarzenegger, Arnold 308, 363, 375, 404, 455, 544, 545
Schweitzer, Albert 361, 550
Scopes, John Thomas 299, 516
Scorpion submarine 219, 527
scotch tape 365, 517
scotch whisky 238
Scotland
  Dunblane Primary School massacre 130, 540
  formation of Great Britain 198
  Glen Coe killings 92
  home rule 368, 540
  independence 145
  re-establishment of parliament 368, 540
  women proposing in leap year 109
Scott, Captain Robert 43, 135, 147, 244, 492, 513
The Scream 340, 544
Seabed Treaty 90, 529
seaplane 66
Sears Tower, Chicago 200, 414, 529
Seattle anti-globalization protests 469, 542
Sechselauten (Switzerland) 157
seduction as crime 180
Seijinshiki (Japan) 38
Seikan submarine tunnel 67, 203, 533
Seinfeld 229, 536
Selassie, Haile 159, 179, 301, 439, 517
Seles, Monica 189, 479, 538
Selfridges, London 132, 513
Selznick, David 269, 503
Senna, Ayrton 179, 198, 534
September 11 attacks 323, 368, 371, 427, 428, 543, 544
Serbia and Montenegro 83, 186, 415, 538, 543
Serling, Rod 399
Sesame Street 447, 528
Seton, Elizabeth Ann 372, 530
Setsubun (Japan) 82
Sette Giugno (Malta) 245
Seven Years War 89, 482, 552
Seward, William H. 148
sewing machine 101, 330
sex change 478, 522
The Sex Pistols 443, 478, 531, 532
Seychelles Independence Day 268, 531
Sgrena, Giuliana 121, 545
Sgt Pepper's Lonely Hearts Club Band 238, 527
Shakespeare 51, 70, 90, 181, 237, 268, 467, 531
Shakur, Tupac 364, 371
Sharman, Helen 537
Sharon, Ariel 244
Sharpeville massacre 139, 524
Shavu'ot 234
Shephard, Alan 202, 525, 551
Shergar 87, 533
Sheridan, Richard 104
Shetland Islands
  oil tanker disaster 44
  pawned by Christian I 100
  Viking fire festival 39
Shinkansen 398, 526
Shockley, William 269, 501, 548
Shoemaker-Levy 9 comet 294, 539
Shostakovitch, Dmitri 210, 516
Shrove Tuesday 78
Sianis, Vasili 403
Sierra Leone, independence 186, 525
Sigma 7 spacecraft 400
Silence Day 287
Silkwood, Karen 451, 530
Simon, Paul 50, 134, 290, 407, 410, 529, 538
Simpson, O.J. 83, 250, 255, 286, 388, 400, 539, 540
Simpson, Wallis 257, 488, 518
The Simpsons 53, 495, 536

Sina 1 satellite 425
Sinatra, Frank 212, 297, 485, 489, 526, 527
Sinatra, Frank Jr 485, 526
Singapore 85, 158, 169
  British ships bombed off 487, 519
  Racial Harmony Day 299
Sinn Fein 50, 61, 131, 207, 248, 512, 533, 539, 540
Sino-Japanese War 490, 552
Sirhan Sirhan 175, 243, 528
Sistine Chapel 326, 365, 438, 488, 542
Six Day War 243, 248, 267, 527
Six Million Dollar Man 417
Sizdah be-dar (Iran) 154, 159
Skase, Christopher 496, 539
Skylab 288, 532
Skylab 2 260, 529
slavery 40, 119, 143, 243, 245, 251, 257, 260, 318, 341, 387
Slepian, Barnett 420, 541
Slocum, Joshua 266
Slovenia
  European Union 423
  joining UN 220, 423, 538
  oldest musical instrument found 296, 549
  Ten Day War 423
  Yugoslav Wars 266, 537
smallpox vaccination 205, 212, 424, 278, 548
Smith, Dick 300, 533
Smith, Edmund Kirby 239
Smith, Ian 119, 238, 448, 528
Smith, John Stafford 372
Smith, Joseph 213, 266, 501
Smith, Perry 172
Smith, Dr Robert 248, 517
Smith, Ross and Keith 487, 515
Smith, Samantha 284, 533
Smith, Tommie 414, 528
Smith, Wiley 300
Smithsonian Museum 266, 368, 445, 524
smoking
  ban in Ireland 147, 544
  Bhutan tobacco ban 453, 544
  health risks 50, 214, 289, 526
  warnings on cigarette packets 305, 526
The Smurfs 420, 524
Socrates 94, 242
solar calendars 15
solar eclipse 163, 288
Solomon Islands 450
solstice 11, 12, 236, 259, 474
Solzhenitsyn, Aleksandr 92, 225, 506, 529, 530, 539
Somalia
  tsunami 504
  U.S. troops in 486, 538
Somerset, James 260
Somme, Battle of 139, 161, 278, 514
Somoza Debayle, Anastasio 295
"Son of Sam" murders 307, 328, 531
"Sonic the Hedgehog" video game 261, 537
Sony
  transistor radio 324, 523
  Walkman 278, 532
Sorenstam, Annika 220, 543
SOS signal 46, 248, 460, 513
The Sound of Music 454, 524
sound recording, first 333
South Africa
  apartheid 109, 136, 186, 336, 363, 522, 538
  Apartheid Report 427, 541
  ban on weapons exports 223
  cricket ban 58, 447, 537
  Cullinan diamond 66, 512
  democratic elections 186, 199, 539
  Gandhi jailed in 50, 513
  independence 229, 525
  Ladysmith siege 439
  National Constitution 205, 540
  Orange Free State invasion 93, 512
  Paul Simon recording in 50, 538
  Population Registration Act repeal 255, 537
  raid on Johannesburg 507
  Rosenkowitz sextuplets 50
  Sharpeville massacre 139, 524
  Soweto uprising 254, 531
  Tokyo Olympics, banned from 336, 526
  Tshwane 124
  UN embargo lifted 539
  Youth Day 254
South Carolina seceding from U.S. 498
South Korea *see* Korea
South Pole 43, 135, 468, 492, 513, 516, 522
Southern Cross 287
Soviet Communist Party 86, 180
Soviet Union *see also* Russia
  Afghanistan, in 94, 172, 213, 505, 532, 535
  atomic bomb detonation 347, 521
  Azerbaijan joining 187, 515
  China, relations with 214
  Cold War 122, 331, 368, 503
  Communist Party suspended 342, 537
  Czechoslovakia invasion 55
  end of 503, 537
  establishment 508, 515
  German invasion in WWII 260, 519
  Los Angeles Olympics boycott 205, 533
  military coup 337, 537
  nuclear weapons *see* nuclear weapons

Obninsk nuclear power station 266, 522
offensive against Nazis 51, 174
purge of army 245, 518
space program *see* space travel
The Voice of America radio broadcasts 96, 521
Young Pioneer movement 217, 515
Sowans Night 42
Soweto uprising 254, 531
Soybean Car 5
Soyuz 1 152, 172, 527
Soyuz 11 259, 529
space travel *see also* names of space craft
  dogs 52, 440, 523
  first African American woman 370
  first British person 216, 537
  first female astronaut 82, 539
  first manned mission 170
  first meal 55
  first U.S. astronauts 166
  first woman space walk 408, 534
  first women 254, 534, 551
  Ham the Chimp 71, 524
  moon landings *see* Moon
  oldest person 27, 541
  space tourists 37, 543
  space walk 85, 164
  successes 55
  untethered spacewalk 86, 533
  U.S. space shuttle program 44, 529
  U.S.S.R. winning space race 170
Spain
  Gregorian calendar 401
  Hispanic Day 409
  Jews expelled from 131, 319
  Madrid bombing 128, 544
  Moors, war on 294
  Paralympics in 463, 542
  U.S. declares war on 183
Spanish Armada 307
Spanish Civil War 146, 184, 296, 518
Spanish Communist Workers' Party 171
Spanish Inquisition 304
Spears, Britney 56, 479
spectrometer 47
speed of light 227, 542
speed of sound 1, 521
Spencer, Lady Diana *see* Princess Diana
Spiritual Baptists (Trinidad and Tobago) 148
Spitz, Mark 340, 61, 529, 547
splitting the atom 496, 518
Spock, Dr Benjamin 292, 521
Spofforth, Fred 1
Sports Illustrated 54
spring equinox 10, 19, 115
Springsteen, Bruce 343, 381, 530
Spungen, Nancy 409
Sputnik I 401, 1, 551
Sputnik II 440, 523, 551
Sputnik III 213
SR-71 reconnaissance aircraft 500
Srebrenica massacre 238, 539
Sri Lanka (formerly Ceylon)
  civil war 301, 533
  first female elected head of government 298, 524
  independence 53, 521
  massacre of Tamils 301
  New Year's Day 172
Sri Mata Amritanandamayi Devi (Amma) 386
SS *Montrose* 305
SS *St Louis* 242, 518
SS *Slavonia* 248, 513
Stains, Graham Stewart 63
Stalin, Joseph 3, 22, 126, 160, 246, 249, 318, 330, 338, 510, 515, 516, 518, 522
Stalingrad, Battle of 81, 341, 457, 519
Stamford Bridge, Battle of 383
Stanley, Henry 49
Stanton, Elizabeth Cady 344
star signs *see* zodiac signs
The Star-Spangled Banner 120, 336, 372, 517
Star Trek 215, 239, 365, 375, 526, 527, 528
Star Wars 279, 534, 549
Star Wars program 409
Stari Most, Mostar 274, 301, 544
Starr, Ringo 165, 284, 334, 525
Statue of Liberty 320, 322, 426
steamboat 40, 5
steam locomotive 101
steam-powered ferry 408
steam shovel 10
Steen, Alann 482
Steinbeck, John 77, 498, 512
Steward, Robert L. 86
Stewart, George 73, 541
Stewart, Martha 205, 544
Stillman, George 93
Stoke Field, Battle of 254
Stoker, Bram 175, 216, 445
Stone, H. Harlan 288
Stonehenge 14, 236
Stonehouse, John 502, 530
Stonewall Day 45
Stonewall riots 45, 528
Stoph, Willi 131
Story, Musgrave 54
Stowe, Harriet Beecher 243, 252
Straits of Tiran 225, 512
Strategic Arms Reduction Treaty 309

521

Strathfield shopping centre shootings 335, 537
Strauss, Levi 218
Streisand, Barbra 144, 182, 526
Streptomycin 416, 520
Strite, Charles 227, 515
Struebig, Heinrich 481
Stubblefield, Nathan B. 210
Students' Day 455
Sudan
  ceasefire 543
  Darfur Conflict 165
  Humanitarian Ceasefire Agreement 165
  Islamic law 60, 537
  U.S. missile attack 338, 541
Suez Canal 96, 125, 183, 304, 429, 501, 523
Sugamo Togenuki Jizosan (Japan) 64
sugar growers subsidy 54, 512
Suharto 128, 527
Suicide Solution 424
Sukkoth 395, 396
Sullivan, George, Francis, Joseph, Madison and Albert 451
Sullivan, Kathryn 408, 534
Sultana steamboat explosion 186
Sumardagurinn Fyrsti (Iceland) 157
summer solstice 11, 236
Sunshine Skyway Bridge collapse 206, 532
Supernova 1987A 103, 535
The Supremes A' Go-Go 419, 527
surfing, biggest wave 481, 528
surgical zipper 288
Suriname Independence Day 463, 530
Surrat, Mary 175
Surrealists 452, 516
Surveyor 1 239
Sutherland, Donald 364, 528
Swan Lake 96, 121
Swan Upping 275
Swatch watches 118, 533
Swaziland Independence Day 363
Sweden
  aerosol spray ban 63, 531
  leap year 76
  National Day 244
  separation from Norway 245, 512
Switzerland
  flooding 342
  Independence Day 318
  joining UN 367, 543
  killing of Jews 48
  neutrality 138
  Onion Market 435
  Rhine River chemical spill 438, 535
  women's vote 86, 529
Sydney
  Cronulla Beach riots 488
  Gay and Lesbian Mardi Gras 262, 531
  Harbour Bridge 137, 517
  Japanese submarine attack 229, 246, 519
  Olympics 2000 373
  Opera House 417, 530
Sydney to Hobart yacht race 506, 541
Sykes, Sir Richard 140
Symbionese Liberation Army 83, 382, 530
Syncom 2 304
syphilis cure 260, 513
Syria
  Aleppo earthquake 552
  Pope John Paul II visit 203, 543
  United Arab Republic 102, 523
  withdrawal from Lebanon 184, 545
Szilard, Leo 370

T

Tabas earthquake 374, 531
Tabei, Junko 388, 530
table knife 211
Tailtiu 315
Taiwan
  civilian massacre 108, 521
  earthquake 379
  Hand-in-Hand Rally 108, 544
  ousted from UN Security Council 461, 529
  Taipei 101 414, 544
  Teacher's Day 387
  U.S. severing ties with 493, 531
  whale exploding 69, 544
Taj Mahal 255
takahe bird 458, 521
Talk Like a Pirate Day 377
Tamagotchi 458, 540
Tammuz 17 276
Tangshan earthquake 306, 531, 552
Tanzania 51
  U.S. embassy bombing 324, 338, 541
Tap Dance Day (U.S.) 223
Tasman, Abel 404, 462, 490
Tasmanian Electoral Act 1856 86
Tasmanian tiger 363, 518
Tate, Sharon 65, 177, 326, 528, 529
Tatiana Day (Russia) 65
Tauranga Campaign 259
taxi cabs
  London 102, 513
  New York 229, 513
Taylor, Elizabeth 107, 132, 250, 407, 410, 517, 526, 530

Tchaikowsky, Peter Ilyich 96, 121, 202, 443
Teacher's Day 146, 368, 387, 402
teddy bear 94, 512
telephone 127
  battery operated switchboard 48
  first transatlantic call 46
  mobile 160, 206, 529
  patent 93
telescribe 222, 514
television 364
  basketball televised 108, 518
  Bhutan 239, 542
  color 96, 266, 280, 518
  Elvis singing live 160, 523
  first commercially sponsored program 425
  first demonstration 66, 516
  first live transcontinental broadcast 361, 522
  political debate 384, 524
  White House address 402, 521
Tell, William 456
Telstar telecommunications satellite 287, 525
Tenerife aircraft disaster 145, 531, 553
tennis
  Bobby v. Billie Jean 378, 530
  Capriati youngest finalist 122, 536
  Davis Cup 88, 512
  lawn tennis patent 103
  Wimbledon 269, 277, 282, 284, 536
Tennyson, Alfred 457
tenth planet 545
Tereshkova, Valentina 254, 525, 551
terracotta warriors 288, 530
Terry, Luther 50, 526
test tube baby 68
Tet Offensive 70, 527
Tet Trung Thu (Vietnam) 355
The Texas Chainsaw Massacre 415
Texas Revolution 419
TGV train 216, 380, 533, 536
Thailand 208
  Constitution Day 487, 517
  King's Birthday 482
  pro-democracy protests 215, 538
  Siam renamed 208, 521
  Songkran (New Year) 21
thalidomide drug case 308, 529
Thanksgiving Day 400, 423, 435
Thatcher, Margaret 42, 201, 240, 265, 410, 453, 467, 469, 482, 532, 533, 534, 535, 537
Theo J. Buell Elementary School 109
Theophan Zatvornick 48
thermonuclear bomb 213
Thingyan (Myanmar) 157
Thinking Day 102
Thompson, Davina 495, 535
Thorpe, Ian 373, 410
Thredbo landslide 308, 540
3-D movies 98, 168
3M 365, 517
Three Gorges Dam, China 444
Three Kings Day 45, 477
Three Mile Island nuclear accident 146, 532
Three Tenors 284, 536
The Three Weeks 276
Tiananmen Square protests 173, 179, 214, 215, 242, 243, 536
tidal electricity plant 464, 527
Till, Emmett 346, 523
Tintin 49, 516
Tiny Tim 495
Tipsa Diena (Latvia) 173
Titanic 168, 172, 173, 361, 513, 534
tire-carrying rim 83, 514
Tirgan 275
Titus Andronicus 51
Titusville oil well 345
Tivoli Gardens, Copenhagen 333
Tlatelolco Massacre 399
To Kill A Mockingbird 288, 524
Tohji-Taisai (Japan) 500
Tojo, Hikedi 450, 501, 521
Tokyo
  Disneyland 173, 533
  earthquake 139
  gay pride parade 346
  Olympics 1964 119, 336
  subway gas attack 138, 539
Tokyo Rose 58, 531
Tolkien, J.R.R. 307, 359, 379, 380, 408, 518, 523
Tomb of Abraham massacre 105, 539
Tomb of the Unknown Solider 68, 515
Tombaugh, Clyde 98, 130
Tommy 221, 528
Tonbridge bank robbery 102, 545
Tonight Show 220, 399, 525, 538
toothbrush, nylon bristle 104, 518
top hat 54
Torrey Canyon oil spill 137
Tosh, Peter 368, 535
Tour de France 297, 302, 512
Towton, Battle of 147
Toy Story 460, 540
Trafalgar, Battle of 418
Trafalgar Day 418
Trans-Alaska Pipeline System 258, 531
Transatlantic Cable 305

trans-Atlantic flight 252, 256, 380, 515, 517, 522, 531
Transgender Day of Remembrance 458
transistor 501, 521
transistor radio 415, 523
Translation Day 389
Treaty of Mutual Co-operation 261, 524
Treaty of Paris 89, 360
Treaty of Rome 143
Treaty of Versailles 124, 267, 515
Treaty of Waitangi 219
Tri State Tornado 136, 516
Trinidad and Tobago Independence Day 349, 525
Triumph of the Cross 372
Trotsky, Leon 71, 338, 339, 450, 516, 519
Troy, storming of 182
Truman, Harry S. 46, 160, 169, 170, 204, 207, 264, 269, 323, 361, 381, 402, 504, 521, 522
Tsar Alexander II 120, 130
"Tsar Bomba" 428, 524
Tsar Nicholas II 134, 138, 174, 295, 396, 444, 514
Tsar Peter I (Peter the Great) 225, 362, 396
Tsar Peter III 295
Tsarina Alexandra 138, 295
tsunami
  Indian Ocean 504, 544
  Papua New Guinea 295
  Straits of Messina 506, 513
Tu B'Shevat 78
tuberculosis 142, 416, 520, 548
Tudjman, Franjo 459
Tunguska explosion, Siberia 269, 513
turbine-powered jet aircraft 345, 518
Turing, Alan 548
Turkey
  Ankara as capital 410, 515
  Constantinople changed to Istanbul 146, 410
  earthquake 335, 504, 518, 542
  Erzincan earthquake 504
  fall of Constantinople 227
  last Sultan 455, 515
  Remembrance Day 447
Turkish Airlines crash 120, 530, 553
Turkmenistan
  earthquake 552
  Independence Day 425, 537
Turner, Nat 448
Turner Netword Television (TNT) 400, 535
Tutankhamen's tomb 42, 95, 464, 515, 516
Tutu, Archbishop Desmond 109, 364, 383, 404, 413, 534, 535
TWA flight 800 explosion 295, 540, 553
TWA flight 847 hijacking 252, 534
Twain, Mark 98, 469
Twelfth Night 476
The Twilight Zone 399, 524
Twin Peaks 165, 536
2003 UB313 307
Tybee bomb 84
Tyler, Wat 253
Tyminski, Stanislaw 463
Tynwald Day (Isle of Man) 282
Typhoon Ike 360

U

Ufa train crash 242
Uffizi bombing 225, 538
UFO landing 406
Uganda
  Asians ordered to leave 324, 529
  doomsday cult mass suicide 135, 542
  Idi Amin 65, 81, 169, 324, 529
Ukraine
  Chernobyl nuclear disaster 184, 534
  Commonwealth of Independent States 503
  Independence Day 342, 537
  Kiev McDonalds 222
  re-run of presidential elections 505, 544
Ulbricht, Walter 228, 331, 527
Uluru 299, 335
Ulysses 254
Ulysses space probe 371, 539
umbrella, folding 201
Unabomber 62, 100, 160, 535, 540, 541
Uncle Tom's Cabin 243
UNESCO World Heritage Convention 454, 529
UNHCR World Refugee Day 258
UNICEF 488, 521
Union Jack flag 170
United Airlines
  accidents 104, 407, 535
  bankruptcy 486, 543
  sabotage 517
United Arab Republic 102, 523
United Nations
  Bosnia, Croatia and Slovenia joining 220
  Charter 265, 422, 520, 521, 550
  Chile, Ecuador, Paraguay and Peru joining 93
  Commission for Human Rights 188
  first General Assembly 49, 521
  Israel admitted 208, 521
  Oil for Food Program 218
  Switzerland joining 367, 543
United Nations Day 394

United States *see also* New York City
  Air Force 419, 425, 530
  air traffic controllers strike 322
  anti-discrimination 246
  anti-globalization protests 469
  Asian immigration ban 84, 514
  attack on demonstrators 124
  Bill of Rights 493
  blackout 332
  Civil Rights Bill 279, 526
  civil rights movement 478
  Cold War 122, 331, 368
  Communism 88, 180, 246, 411, 463, 515, 521, 522
  Constitution 121, 148, 375, 493
  daylight saving early 45, 530
  Declaration of Independence 248, 281
  declaring war on Britain 256
  declaring war on Japan 485, 519
  declaring war on Spain 183
  Election Day 434
  Emancipation Proclamation 257
  Endangered Species Act 506, 530
  female attorneys 94
  first African American general 425, 523
  first African American Military Academy graduate 253
  first African American Supreme Court justice 251
  first female Congress member 159, 484, 514
  first female doctor 63
  first female generals 249, 528
  first female marines 331, 515
  first Jewish judge 67
  first Native American senator 63
  flag 161, 252, 281
  flag burning 259
  flight across 200, 343, 406, 515
  Great White Hurricane 128
  Independence Day 281
  interracial marriage 250, 451, 527
  Marine Corps 447
  Monongah mine disaster 482, 513
  Native American reservations 71
  Navy 410
  North American Free Trade Agreement 485
  nuclear weapons *see* nuclear weapons
  oil discovery in Texas 49, 512
  Prohibition, end of 96, 482, 517
  race riots 163, 308, 378, 527
  racial segregation 205, 210, 216, 229, 249, 383, 522, 523
  raids on radicals 41
  Reserve Officers Training Corps 240
  same sex marriage 363, 545
  segregation in schools, ban 122
  South Carolina seceding from 498
  Southern States readmitted 257
  space program *see* space travel
  transcontinental telegraph line 422
  Tri State Tornado 136, 516
  voting age 260
  war on poverty 47
  Washington D.C. as capital 489
  women's military rights 212, 529
  women's vote 51, 242, 344, 363, 420, 442, 515
Unity Day (Russia) 441
Universal Children's Day 458
Universal Declaration of Human Rights 487, 521
universal suffrage 464
University of Mississippi 336, 378, 398, 525
University of Texas shooting 318, 527
Up-helly-aa 39
Uranus 130
Ure, Midge 290
Uruguay
  Constitution Day 296
  Independence Day 343
  World Cup victory 308, 517
Uruguayan Air Force crash 410, 507
U.S. Open Golf Championship 401
USS *Frank E. Evans* disaster 240, 528
USS *Greeneville* 88, 520
USS *Indianapolis* 308, 520
USS *Juneau* 451, 519
USS *Missouri* 359
USS *Vincennes* 280, 535
U.S.S.R. *see* Soviet Union
Utopia sinking 135
Utzen, Jørn 417
Uxmal Mayan ruins 15
Uzbekistan, independence 358, 537

V

vaccine discoveries 548
Vaisakhi (India) 21
Valens, Richie 82, 524
Valentich, Frederick 418
Valley Forge anti-war rally 364, 528
Vallon-Pont-d'Arc cave paintings 57, 539
Van Gogh, Vincent 148, 307, 501, 535
Vanguard 2 weather satellite 96, 524
Vanuatu
  Children's Day 302

Independence Day 308, 532
Jon Frum Day 94
Unity Day 468
Vargas, Getulio 316
Vasant Panchami 78
Vaseline 212
Vatican City 245, 516
vaudeville theatre 108
VE Day 204
Velcro 319, 523
Velvet Revolution 455, 536
Venera 3 118, 527
Venera 5 214, 528
Venetian blind 339
Venezuela
  Flag Day 129
  floods 493, 542
  Independence Day 282
Venice, Regata Storica 356
Venus 118, 214, 328, 409, 527, 528, 536
Vénus de Milo 165
Verdun, Battle of 496, 514
Versace, Gianni 293, 479, 540
Versailles 203, 453
Verwoerd, Hendrik 363
Vestalia festival 234
Vetter, David 102
Vicious, Sid 409, 531, 532
Victoria Cross 259, 265
"Video Killed the Radio Star" 318
Vienna State Opera 442, 523
Vietnam
  Bryan Adams performing 55
  calendar 23
  Clinton visit 454, 542
  Declaration of Independence 359, 520
  First Indochina War 204, 522
  flooding 428
  French fleet arriving 125, 521
  Ho Chi Minh 119, 359
  Martyr's Day 305
  Second Indochina War *see* Vietnam War
  treaty to form Indochina 125, 522
Vietnam War
  American POWs 91, 147
  assassination of Ngô Diên Diêm 439, 525
  attack on U.S. embassy 71
  Australian troops 239, 336, 526, 529
  Battle of Long Tan 336, 527
  casualties 552
  chemical warfare 140, 514
  draft lottery 123
  end of 181, 189, 530
  first casualty 419, 523
  Muhammad Ali evading draft 258
  My Lai massacre 134, 527
  New York Times Pentagon Papers 251
  pardoning of draft evaders 61, 531
  peace accord 63, 529
  peace talks collapse 496, 529
  protests against 201, 224, 364, 412, 418, 527, 528
  start of 204, 208
  Tet Offensive 70, 527
  U.S. troops 88, 125, 147, 329, 525, 526, 529
  Veteran's Memorial 203, 451, 490, 532, 533
  videotaped execution 80
Viking 1 probe 338, 530
Viking fire festival 39
Virgin Atlantic 50
Virgin Islands 64, 512
Vitkovic, Frank 485
The Voice of America 96, 521
Volkswagen 94, 518
  Beetle 309
volleyball 88
voluntary euthanasia 142, 540
Volvo 68, 172, 516
von Richthofen, Manfred 179, 199
von Stauffenberg, Claus 298, 299, 550
Voskhod 2 136, 551
A Voyage to Terra Australis 296
Voyager 1 202, 442, 492, 501, 532, 535, 544
Vulcan 41

W

Waco, Texas siege 108, 177, 538
Wade, Virginia 269
Wahid, Abdurrahman 69
Waite, Terry 456, 537
Wake, Nancy 550
Waksman, Selman 416
Waldheim, Kurt 285, 534
Walesa, Lech 261, 332, 463, 533, 537, 550
The Wall of D.C. 203
Wall Street
  Black Monday 416
  Black Thursday 422, 516
  bombing 374, 515
  crash 496, 535
  insider trading 496, 535
The Wall Street Journal 285
Wallace, Alfred Russel 256
Wallace, George 249
Wallis, Terry 290
Walpurgis Night 189

The Waltons 372, 529
Wanke, Daouda 166
War of the Roses 121, 147, 254
War of the Worlds 428, 518
war on terror 368
Warby, Ken 405, 531
Warhol, Andy 102, 323, 516, 535
Warner Brothers 44, 305, 402, 520
Warren Commission 386, 526
Warsaw Ghetto 454, 519
Warsaw Pact 149, 212, 523, 537
Warsaw Uprising 318, 520
Washington D.C. 489
  lesbian and gay rights march on 411, 532
  Library of Congress fire 502
  Million Man March 413, 359
  Million Mom March 212, 542
  Vietnam Veteran's Memorial 203, 451, 490, 532, 533
Washington, George 83, 400, 436, 492
Washkansky, Louis 41, 480
water-cooled engine 160
water skis 279, 515
water speed record 388, 405, 509, 522, 531
Watergate scandal 189, 226, 254, 325, 420, 529, 530
Waterloo, Battle of 256
Watson, James D. 101, 183, 522, 548, 549
Watson, Thomas J. 253
"We Are the World" 146, 534
Webb, Brant 206
Webb, Matthew 343
Webster, Noah 172, 226, 413
Webster's Dictionary of the English Language 172
"The Wedding March" 65
Wei Jingheng 50
Weissenhof exhibition housing estate 301
Weissmuller, Johnny 286, 409, 515, 517, 533
Weizman, Chaim 96, 446, 521
Welch, Joseph 247
Welles, Orson 198, 203, 360, 407, 428, 518, 519
Wells, H.G. 331, 379, 428, 518
Wells, Henry 136
Wells, Holly 321, 543
West, Mae 177, 335, 460, 516
West, Rosemary 460, 540
West Side Story 202, 525, 546
Westminster Abbey 506
Westminster Bridge 222
whale exploding, Taiwan 69
wheat flakes 99, 512
Wheel of the Year 10
Whit Sunday 235
White Cane Safety Day (U.S.) 412
White Day 131
White House 410
Whitewater scandal 378, 542
Whitlam, Gough 288, 448, 479, 529
Whitman, Charles 318, 527
Whittle, Lesley 53
The Who 221, 290, 528
Who's Afraid of Virginia Woolf? 410, 525
Whymper, Edward 292
Wiesenthal, Simon 99, 544
Wife Carrying Championship (Finland) 277
Wikipedia 54, 542
Wilde, Oscar 163, 223, 413, 469
Wilhelm Gustloff sinking 70, 520
Wilkins, John 467
William of Orange 92, 137, 289, 452
William the Conqueror 387, 411
Williams, Daniel Hale 286
Williams, Vanessa 375, 533
Willow Creek silver boom 399
Wilson, Bill 248, 517
Wilson, Charlie 330, 526
Wilson, Harold 134, 222, 530
Wilson, Woodrow 84, 197, 422, 490, 506, 515
Wimbledon 269, 277, 282, 284, 536
Windsor Castle fire 501
Windward Islands, independence 425, 532
Winfield, Walter 103
Winfrey, Oprah 106
Winnie-the-Pooh 411, 516
Winston, Harry 445
Winter Olympics 82, 87, 529, 541
winter solstice 12, 474, 475
wireless radio broadcasting 210, 513
The Wise Little Hen 247
witch trials 118, 169, 337, 380
Witte, Otto 331, 514
The Wizard of Oz 386
Wojtyla, Karol *see* Pope John Paul II
Wolff, Christoph 497, 534
Wollemi Pine 492, 539
Wolszczan, Aleksander 179
Women's Day 125
Women's Equality Day (U.S.) 344
women's military rights 212, 529
women's suffrage 51, 86, 179, 203, 240, 242, 344, 363, 376, 377, 420, 442, 466, 492, 514, 515, 520, 529
Women's World Cup (football) 469, 537
Woods, Tiger 171, 508, 540
Woodstock 336, 528
Woodward, Joanne 88, 107, 524
Woodward, Louise 447
Woodward, Roger 286
Woolworths stores 102, 482

World AIDS Day 478
World Animal Day 401
World Bank 505, 520
World Blood Donor Day 252
World Braille Day 43
World Cup (football) 138, 260, 284, 363, 457, 517, 527, 534
  Women's 469, 537
World Cup (rugby) 423, 544
World Day Against Child Labor 250
World Day for Organ Donation and Transplantation 411
World Day of Design 186
World Diabetes Day 452
World Environment Day 243
World Food Day 413
World Health Day 164
World Health Organisation 164, 521
World Heritage Convention 454
World Mental Health Day 407
World No Tobacco Day 229
World Pillow Fighting Championship 277
world population 105, 545
World Population Day 288
World Roma Festival 197
World Standards Day 411
World Suicide Prevention Day 367
World Teachers' Day 402
World Toilet Day 457
World Trade Center 281
  bombing 106, 222, 538, 539
  September 11 attack 323, 368, 427, 428, 543, 544
World Tuberculosis Day 142
World War I
  Armistice Day 418, 437, 448
  Battle of Bolimov 71
  Battle of Gallipoli 99, 183, 496, 514
  Battle of the Somme 139, 161, 278, 514
  Battle of Verdun 496, 514
  Battle of Ypres 180
  beginning 306, 318, 514
  bombing civilian targets in U.K. 58
  Britain entering 321
  casualties 552
  Christmas truce 503, 514
  conscription 451
  end of 267, 428, 448, 515
  invasion of Belgium 321, 514
  Ottoman Empire entering 452, 514
  poison gas 71, 180, 514
  Tomb of the Unknown Soldier 68, 515
  U.S. entering 163, 514
World War II
  Athens invasion 186, 519
  Baedeker Raids 181
  Banja Luka massacre 86, 519
  Bataan Death March 168, 519
  Battle of Berlin 199, 520
  Battle of Britain 287, 331, 519
  Battle of Cisterna 69
  Battle of Dunkirk 242, 518
  Battle of El Alamein 441, 519
  Battle of Guadalcanal 450, 519
  Battle of Midway 245, 284, 519
  Battle of Normandy 244
  Battle of Okinawa 259, 520
  Battle of Stalingrad 81, 341, 457, 519
  Battle of the Bulge 494, 520
  beginning 358, 389
  Berlin bombing 60, 123, 520
  "Big Week" 100, 520
  Cape Matapan 146
  casualties 552
  Churchill's "Finest Hour" speech 256, 519
  Coventry bombing 452, 519
  D-Day 213, 244, 520
  dam buster bombs 131, 520
  Darwin bombing 99, 519
  Dutch surrender in Java 125, 519
  end 333, 359
  German surrender 81, 204, 520
  Guam, Japanese on 64, 520
  Hamburg bombing 452, 519
  Hiroshima 323, 333, 520
  invasion of Czechoslovakia 132, 518
  invasion of Italy 303, 519
  invasion of Poland 358, 389, 518
  invasion of U.S.S.R. 260, 519
  Italian surrender 242, 520
  Italy joining Germany 248, 518
  Japan bombing 126, 520
  Japanese "comfort women" 52, 538
  Japanese surrender 333, 359, 520
  Kokoda 439, 519
  Koniuchy massacre 69
  liberation of Auschwitz 64, 67, 520
  liberation of Bergen-Belson 173, 520
  liberation of Dachau 188, 520
  liberation of Hong Kong 348
  liberation of Lod 58
  liberation of Manila 104, 520
  liberation of Paris 343, 344, 520
  liberation of Warsaw 56, 520
  London bombing 69, 119, 251, 507, 519
  Nagasaki 323, 326, 333, 520
  New Guinea 124, 439, 519
  Norway invasion 166, 518
  Operation Gomorrah 302, 519

Pearl Harbor bombing 484, 485, 488, 519
Polish massacre by U.S.S.R. 122
POWs killed, Gardlegen 171
Remembrance Day 437
Solomon Islands 450
Sydney submarine attack 229, 519
U.S. air effort 30
U.S. declares war on Japan 485, 488, 519
Vancouver Island shelling 258, 519
Warsaw Uprising 318, 520
Yugoslavia invasion 160, 519
World War III 40
World Wide Fund for Nature 368, 525
World Wide Web 106, 189, 323, 484, 537, 538, 548
World's Fair 123, 558
"Wow Signal"
Wren, Christopher 259, 417, 467
Wright, Billy 541
Wright, Orville 495, 512, 548
Wright, Wilbur 2, 495, 512, 548
Wynne, Arthur 9

X

X-rays 44, 544
X-20 Dyna-Soar program 422

Y

Y2K bug 9, 541
Yalda festival 13
Yamaboko Junko (Japan) 295
Yamauchi Fujiko and Hiroshi 443
Yangtze River, Verdam 444, 540
Yankee Doodle Dandy 227, 519
Yankee Stadium 176, 515
Yashoda's Day 99
Yates, Paula 373
Yeager, Charles 411, 521
Yeager, Jeana 521
Year of the Monkey 61
Yellowstone National Park 118
Yeltsin, Boris 36, 144, 211, 225, 227, 250, 289, 320, 399, 488, 503, 509, 517, 526, 535, 534, 539, 542
YMCA 244
Yokoi, Shoichi 529
Yom Kippur
Yom Kippur War 22, 530
York Minster 334, 534
Yosemite Valley 39
Yost, Ed 39
Young Pioneers movement 217, 515
Youth Day
  China 147
  International 20, 339
  South Africa 174
Yugoslavia 83
  Federal Republic of 186, 538, 543
  invasion in WWII 160, 519
  NATO bombing campaign 258
  peace treaty with NATO 542
  protest against Milosevic 337
  Tito as President for life 164, 525
  Yugoslav War 66, 537
Yuki Matsuri (Japan) 77
Yule 12, 15
Yuri's Night
Yushchenko, Viktor 505, 544
YWCA 9

Z

Zamenhof, Ludwig 3
Zanzibar 9
  Anglo-Zanzibar War 345
Zapata, Emiliano 68
Zechariah and Elizabeth's Day 442
Zellweger, Renée 86, 373
Zhukov, Georgi 57, 550
Ziegfield Follies 335, 513
Zimbabwe (formerly Rhodesia)
  black majority rule 382, 532
  independence 19, 176, 238, 448, 526, 528, 532
  Mugabe as President 121, 135, 382, 532, 543
  Rhodesia named 238, 532
  suspension from Commonwealth 543
zodiac signs
  Aquarius
  Aries 19
  Cancer 25
  Capricorn
  Chinese zodiac 24
  Gemini 22
  Leo 30
  Libra 32
  Pisces 20
  Sagittarius
  Scorpio 42
  Taurus 7
  Virgo
Zond 5 spacecraft 373, 528
Zong slave ship
Zuolin, Zhang 516

Picture credits

The Publisher would like to thank the following image libraries and copyright holders for permission to use their images and for their assistance in sourcing images. Every endeavor has been made to obtain permission from copyright holders to use all images, however the Publisher would be pleased to hear about any omission or errors.

Key: (t) top of page; (b) bottom of page; (l) left side of page; (r) right side of page; (c) center of page.

The Art Archive, London
20, 272-3, Art Archive; 8-9(b), 15(b), National Anthropological Museum Mexico/Dagli Orti; 9(t), 36(t), 76(t), 114(t), 154(t), 194(t), 234(t), 274(t), 314(t), 314(b), 354(t), 394(t), 434(t), 474(t), 476(t), Bodleian Library Oxford; 10(b), 11, 15(t), 19(b), Dagli Orti; 12, 237(b), Bibliothèque des Arts Dècoratifs Paris/Dagli Orti; 13, Osterreichisches National Bibliothek Vienna/Harper Collins Publishers; 16, Musèe de la Civilisation Gallo'Romaine Lyons/Dagli Orti; 17, Archivio di Stato di Sienna/Dagli Orti; 21, Marc Charmet; 23, British Library; 26, Israel Museum Jerusalem/Dagli Orti; 8(c), 27, Archeological Museum Istanbul/Dagli Orti; 31. Mirielle Vautier; 32, Ragab Papyrus Institue Cairo/Dagli Orti; 33, Musée Carnavalet Paris/Dagli Orti; 36(b), British Museum; 37, 194(b), Torre Aquila Trento/Dagli Orti; 76(b), Marc Charmet; 114(b), Museo del Prado Madrid; 115(b), Academia BB AA S Fernando Madrid/Dagli Orti (A); 117(b), Palatine Library Parma/Dagli Orti; 154(b), National Gallery London/Eileen Tweedy; 155, Museo del Prado Madrid; 195(b) National Archives Washington D.C.; 234(b), Museo della Civilta Romana Rome/Dagli Orti; 274(b), Archaeological Museum Naples/Dagli Orti; 275(t), Bardo Museum Tunis/Dagli Orti; 275(b), Galleria d'Arte Moderna Rome/Dagli Orti (A); 276(br), Cathedral Pisa/Dagli Orti (A); 315(t), Torre Aquila Trento/Dagli Orti (A); 354(b), Museo Civico Udine/Dagli Orti (A); 355(t), Musée du Louvre Paris/Dagli Orti (A); 394(b), Musée du Château de Versailles/Dagli Orti; 396(b), Galerie Saphir Paris/Dagli Orti; 397(b), 432-3, Culver Pictures; 434(b), Civiche Racc d'Arte Pavia/Dagli Orti; 435®, National Gallery of Art Washington; 474(b), Douce 40 folio 60v/Bodieian Library Oxford; 475(t), Biblioteca Nacional Lisbon/Dagli Orti; 476(b), Victoria and Albert Museum London/Eileen Tweedy; 477(tl), Museum of the City of New York/MCNY09.

Kobal Collection
54, Henderson/Miller, Milkis/Paramount; 140, Kobal; 208-9, Universal/Celandine/Monty Python; 269, Selznick/MGM; 322, 30th Century Fox; 352-3, Warner Bros; 366, Universal/Studio Cana/Miramax/ Bell, Jason; x409, MGM; 412, CBS-TV.

Getty Images
1-7, 8(t), 14, 18, 19(t), 24-25, 28-29, 34-35, 37(t), 38-42, 44-53, 55-56, 58,73, 74-75, 77-113, 115(t), 116, 117(t), 119-139, 142-153, 155(t), 156-193, 195(tl), 196-207, 210-233, 235-236, 237(t), 238-244, 246-254, 256-268, 270-271, 275(t), 276(t), 276(bl), 277-313, 315(b), 316-321, 323-351, 355(b), 356-365, 367-378, 380-393, 395, 396(t), 397(t), 398-408, 410-411, 413-431, 435(l), 436-473, 475(b), 477(tr), 477(b), 478-511. All cover images except "Bravo" explosion (tc).

Other image sources
10(t), Monte Boyd; 57, Herbert Thiess; 118, U.S. National Archives; 245, Patrycja Arvidssen; 255, U.S. Fish and Wildlife Service; 379, *New Idea* magazine.

Publisher's Note

Dateline has been designed in order to convey an extensive and eclectic array of information. Due to layout limitations specific to text, some duplication of specific wording and phrasing from source material may have unintentionally occurred. Every effort has been made to clear copyright on original material. The Publisher would be pleased to hear from anyone who feels their copyright may have been infringed.

Dateline contributors sourced data and images from a broad range of sources, including websites, printed matieral, and a variety of published visual media. While the authors, publishers, and other representatives of *Dateline* have made every effort to provide accurate information and to verify sources, the Publisher specifically disclaims that the material represents research from first sources in every case.